GERHARD FIESELER

The man behind the Storch

Nigel Holden

Helion & Company

Helion & Company Limited
26 Willow Road
Solihull
West Midlands
B91 1UE
England
Tel. 0121 705 3393
Fax 0121 711 4075
Email: info@helion.co.uk
Website: www.helion.co.uk
Twitter: @helionbooks
Visit our blog at http://blog.helion.co.uk/

Published by Helion & Company 2017
Designed and typeset by Mary Woolley, Battlefield Design (www.battlefield-design.co.uk)
Cover designed by Paul Hewitt, Battlefield Design (www.battlefield-design.co.uk)
Printed by Gutenberg Press Limited, Tarxien, Malta

Text © Nigel Holden 2017
Illustrations © as individually credited

Every reasonable effort has been made to trace copyright holders and to obtain their permission for the use of copyright material. The author and publisher apologize for any errors or omissions in this work, and would be grateful if notified of any corrections that should be incorporated in future reprints or editions of this book.

Front cover: Taken in 1927, this photograph shows a resolute-looking Fieseler at the beginning of his illustrious career as an aerobatics pilot (Getty Images). Rear cover: The iconic and still much-admired Fi 156, the Fieseler Storch. Britain's greatest test pilot, Eric 'Winkle' Brown, described it as 'a virtuoso of slow flight' and ranked it in his top twenty outstanding planes of the 487 he flew during and after the Second World War. (Bundesarchiv, Bild 146-1977-110-05)

ISBN 978-1-911512-74-5

British Library Cataloguing-in-Publication Data. A catalogue record for this book is available from the British Library. All rights reserved. No part of this publication may be reproduced, stored in a retrieval system, or transmitted, in any form, or by any means, electronic, mechanical, photocopying, recording or otherwise, without the express written consent of Helion & Company Limited.

For details of other military history titles published by Helion & Company Limited, contact the above address, or visit our website: http://www.helion.co.uk We always welcome receiving book proposals from prospective authors.

Contents

List of Illustrations	iv
Preface	vii
Introduction	11

Part One: Aerial Gladiator — 15
1. Unpromising beginnings — 17
2. Some damn silly thing in the Balkans — 35
3. An airman the equivalent of three infantry divisions — 54
4. Tiger of Macedonia — 75

Part Two: Hardship and Triumph — 93
5. Weimar, Versailles and Atlantis — 95
6. The alpha and omega of flying — 113
7. 1933: new spirit, new hope — 133

Part Three: Companion to Catastrophe — 157
8. Industrialist of consequence — 159
9. If we lose this war — 183
10. The redesigning of aerial terror — 213

Part Four: After the Storm — 239
11. Time of reckoning — 241
12. What was granted to him — 264

Appendix A: Fieseler Storch Thematic Chart	291
Appendix B: Gerhard Fieseler's aerial victories in Macedonia from August 1917 to September 1918	294
Bibliography	295
Index	302

List of Illustrations

Fieseler's boyhood hero, Otto Lilienthal, perhaps the greatest aeronaut of the 19th century. Fieseler had a photograph of Lilienthal on display at home until he died. (Otto-Lilienthal-Museum) — i

An outstanding fighter pilot in the First World War, Fieseler was awarded the Golden Military Merit Cross, Prussia's highest award for bravery for non-commissioned officers and the Iron Cross First and Second Class. He also received awards from Austria and Bulgaria. (Oscar Azevedo) — i

Manfred von Richthofen, the most celebrated fighter pilot of the First World War, who had 81 aerial victories to his credit. But was Fieseler with his 19 confirmed victories a better pilot? (Bundesarchiv, Bild 183-S54131) — ii

The battle cruiser *Goeben*, named after a Prussian general who was Fieseler's mysterious grandfather. It was transferred to the Ottoman Navy in 1914 and finished its days as the flagship of the Turkish Navy until decommissioning in 1950. (Bundesarchiv, Bild 134-B0030) — ii

Fieseler in plus-fours, at the Berlin Air Show in September 1927, aside his Raab-Katzenstein RK-26 Schwalbe with his name on the fuselage. (Bundesarchiv, Bild 102-04780, photographer: Georg Pahl) — iii

Fieseler arm-in-arm with his French rival Marcel Doret in October 1927 at an unidentified venue. At his first international competitive event Fieseler had outpointed Doret at the Zürich Air Show in August 1927, but he was cheated out of first place on account of being German. (Oscar Azevedo) — iii

The F3 was an early form of delta-wing aircraft, which Fieseler's company built in cooperation with Alexander Lippisch in 1932-33. Commissioned by the HB cigarette company, it failed to secure its airworthiness certificate. (Fliegerweb.com) — iv

The cover of the 1932 book, *Hitler über Deutschland*, depicts Hitler's attachment to aviation for political electioneering. Fieseler first saw Hitler alight from a plane which landed at Kassel Waldau airport in 1927. (Randall Bytwerk) — iv

Fieseler receiving a hero's welcome at Kassel Waldau airport after winning the World Aerobatics Championships in Vincennes in June 1934. (Stadtarchiv Kassel) — v

With novel foldable wings, the Fi 167 was designed to land on the sea-borne aircraft carrier *Graf Zeppelin*. which never saw service. Fieseler described the Fi 167 as 'a treat to fly.' (Sammlung Urlen) — v

The iconic and still much-admired Fi 156, the Fieseler Storch. Britain's greatest test pilot, Eric 'Winkle' Brown, described it as 'a virtuoso of slow flight' and ranked it in his top twenty outstanding planes of the 487 he flew during and after the Second World War. (Bundesarchiv, Bild 146-1977-110-05) — vi

The entrance to Carinhall, Goering's official residence, where in 1938 the Reichsmarschall ordered Fieseler and other top bosses of the air industry to prepare for war – or else. (Bundesarchiv, Bild 146-1979-175-10) — vi

LIST OF ILLUSTRATIONS

At the Führer's disposal Fieseler wearing the uniform of *Standartenführer* in the Nazi Flying Corps. (Bundesarchiv, Bild 183-R56586)	vii
A placard about the competition to identify and honour Germany's top enterprises for industrial quality and integration of Nazi ideals into the workplace. Fieseler's company won the award four times, making it one of the best run factories in Germany. (Bundesarchiv, Plak 003-017-116, designer: Christian Minzlaff)	viii
Hitler at the Greater German War Veterans Day held at Kassel in June 1939. Almost certainly just to the right of and behind Hitler is the Japanese Ambassador, General Ōshima, who in 1940 facilitated Japan's purchase of three Storch aircraft and manufacturing rights. (Bundesarchiv, Bild 183-E07050	ix
A rare photograph of the Soviet OKA-38. To celebrate the Nazi-Soviet Non-aggression Pact in 1939, Hitler gave a Fieseler Storch as a diplomatic gift to Stalin. The Soviet dictator ordered one of his brightest aircraft designers, Oleg Antonov, to make a copy of it. (Fliegerweb.com)	ix
After the defeat of France in 1940 Fieseler expected peace to break out followed by an economic boom and had this advertisement drafted promoting the Storch to major business concerns. Anticipating today's executive jets, the caption reads 'You decide when your aircraft takes off.' (Oscar Azevedo)	x
Aquatic treatment for the Fieseler work force in 1940. Fieseler's factory was one of the very first in Germany to have a full-time company doctor. (Sammlung Urlen)	xi
Fieseler apprentices in 1941 going for a run, wearing the company logo on their singlets. (Sammlung Urlen)	xii
It's June 1940, and the Luftwaffe is attacking Britain. This cartoon in the Fieseler company newspaper warns a worried Churchill that his comeuppance is nigh. The caption reads: 'The faster the production tempo, the faster our victory.' (Sammlung Urlen)	xii
Fieseler giving the Nazi salute. He would not have wished this photograph, taken in 1940, to have been widely seen after the Second World War. (Sammlung Urlen)	xiii
A remarkable photograph of a herd of reindeer sweeping past a Storch in Finland in 1942. Perhaps no other aircraft in the entire Second World War adapted so easily to such a wide range of climatic and geographic conditions. (Sammlung Urlen)	xiii
Robert Lusser, appointed in 1942 as Fieseler's development director, was the technical brains behind the V-1. He worked for the Americans after the Second World War, working at the Jet Propulsion Laboratory in California and collaborating with von Braun's rocketry team in Alabama. (Sammlung Urlen)	xiv
In August 1941 a letter was published in the Fieseler company newspaper from General Erwin Rommel praising the performance of the Storch in the desert, commending its ability to land on rock-strewn terrain. (Sammlung Urlen)	xv
Accompanying Göring, Erhard Milch, the head of the Reich Aviation Ministry, was dismissively described by Fieseler as 'an aeronautical layman.' (Bundesarchiv, Bild 146-1979-187-16)	xvi
Ernst Udet, head of procurement for the Luftwaffe. whose suicide in November 1941 was a terrible blow to Fieseler. (Bundesarchiv, Bild 146-1984-112-13, photographer: Conrad)	xvii
Göring giving the eulogy at Udet's funeral. Before long he would blame Udet for losing the Battle of Britain. (Bundesarchiv, Bild 183-B16653)	xviii
One of the Second World War's most improbable publications: the Fieseler German-Russian glossary of work terms. The company employed a few Russian slave labourers, mainly women. (Oscar Azevedo)	xviii

The first page of the glossary to help Fieseler's overseers comment on the work of Russian labourers and issue basic orders to them in rough and ready Russian. (Oscar Azevedo)   xix

Kassel in ruins as a result of the devastating air raid by the RAF on 23 October 1943. (Stadtarchiv Kassel)   xix

The Fieseler plant in the Bettenhausen district of Kassel in April 1944, showing the results of heavy bombing. (Stadtarchiv Kassel)   xx

The charismatic and alluring Hanna Reitsch, Germany's most famous aviatrix, receiving an Iron Cross 2nd Class from her adored Führer in March 1941. (Bundesarchiv, Bild B 145 Bild-F051625-0295)   xx

Otto Skorzeny, 'the most dangerous man in Europe,' with Mussolini shortly after the Italian dictator's high-risk rescue from Italian partisans in September 1943 in the Apennine Mountains. A Fieseler Storch made a perilous flight to take Mussolini and Skorzeny to safety. (Bundesarchiv, Bild 101I-567-1503C-16, photographer: Toni Schneiders)   xxi

The V-1 being taken to its catapult. Like Hitler Fieseler dreamed of the so-called wonder weapons bringing Britain to its knees, but he wanted all the glory to go to 'his' V-1. (Bundesarchiv, Bild 146-1975-117-26, photographer: Bruno Lysiak)   xxi

V-1s in production at the notorious Dora Mittelbau subterranean concentration camp. Of the 60,000 slaves who built the V weapons there, a third perished from starvation, disease, brutality and accidents. (Bundesarchiv, Bild 183-1985-0123-027)   xxii

Wilhelm Furtwängler conducting the Berlin Philharmonic Orchestra in 1942. The renowned conductor was one of the guests along with other well-known cultural figures at Fieseler's short-lived hotel around 1949. (Bundesarchiv. Bild 183-L0607-504)   xxii

A photograph taken in 1972 of the inside Fieseler's home showing his display of flying awards and trophies. (Stadtarchiv Kassel)   xxiii

The Dutchman Wim de Vries, a conscripted worker at the Gerhard Fieseler Works during the Second World War, wrote an anguished poem to mark Fieseler's death. (Stadsarchief Dordrecht)   xxiii

One of the last photographs taken of Fieseler in public at the Kassel Air Show in June 1983. (Stadtarchiv Kassel)   xxiv

Preface

My first image of Germany in or around 1949, when I was just about old enough to be taken along to the pictures by my mother, was in newsreels showing the concentration camp at Belsen. These were shocking images captured on camera immediately after its liberation by British and Canadian troops in April 1945. That same bit of newsreel seemed to be on every time we went to the cinema. I had no idea what I was looking out, but I remember feeling distinctly uneasy. 'That's what the Germans did', my mother would say.

As a school boy in the 1950s and 60s, my images of Germany were largely mediated by that splendid, if not entirely reliable source of depictions: The Great British War Film. In stirring classics like *The Dambusters, The Wooden Horse, The Colditz Story* and so on, the British were portrayed as decent, gritty and – of course – blessed with a good sense of humour. There was an intuitive understanding between well-spoken officers and the rest of the humbler fighting species, who with their not so polished pronunciation were put-upon, ever cheerful, compliant, and trusting in the greater wisdom of their officers.

There was a relatively small pool of British actors who played the officers time and again, whilst a wider pool of character actors portrayed all other ranks. A key personage in many of the films was the German actor, Anton Diffring who with his Aryan good looks and ice-cold eyes, *always* played a high-ranking and inevitably humourless Nazi officer. Whenever hapless Brits on some daring mission fell into his clutches, it was Diffring who uttered that eternally memorable incantation in his impeccable German-tinted English: 'we have ways of making you talk.'

The portrayed officers and men were united to give the Jerries, alias the Huns, a bloody nose for all the inconvenience they were causing in the world. After all what a drat it was for these chaps in 1939, because of Hitler's antics, to have to don military uniforms and put the Austrian upstart in his place. Girding them for the epic tussle ahead was the conviction that the Nazis were ruthless and, let's be honest about it, goose-stepping blockheads. For youngsters like me it was all too easy to believe that we, the British, thanks in no small way to our boffins and Spitfires, had defeated Hitler and his Nazi hordes single-handedly.

I accepted that narrative as entirely natural: just as it was natural that Britain should preside over a world-wide empire. At all events, when I went to Germany for the very first time in 1963 as a schoolboy who had been learning German for a year, I found all the Germans I met not to be in the mould of blockheads at all, nor were they without a sense of humour. However, they were, I now realise, very anxious indeed that the new Germany of the *Wirtschaftswunder* was seen to have nothing at all in common with the Nazi one. I was in Göttingen at that time and certainly not in the slightest aware that a few kilometres away was a stark reminder of the war and its continuity: namely the Iron Curtain.

Over the years I was often in Germany as student, business man and an academic. The war was never an issue for me, and it was not long before I realised that the image of the Germans *and indeed of the British themselves* as conveyed in the British war films was part of our national mythology, which even today has not been completely erased. In the late 1960s in my student days I found myself on the other side of the Iron Curtain and one day visited Dresden, which was still largely a pile of ruins. As far as I was concerned, it was a casualty of war, and that is all there was to say. No, not quite: my father, who was an RAF navigator had helped to bomb Germany on numerous occasions during the war. I remember wondering whether his squadron had been involved in that terrible bombardment of Dresden in February 1945 and hoping he wasn't; as if his missions over Leipzig, Cologne and the Ruhr were somehow less egregious.

In the mid-90s I had occasion to be in Krakow a few times. From there I once took the train to the provincial town of Oświęcim, better known as Auschwitz. I spent sombre hours walking round the former death camp. I knew what had happened there. Yet, confronted by the dread place itself, walking through that ominous portal with its bitterly sardonic slogan at the entrance '*Arbeit macht frei*' (work sets you free), I was incapable of comprehending the horror, the brutality – *the reality* – of this charnel house of utterly pointless killing and suffering.

In the early 2002 I took up an academic post in Kassel, a city in the *Land* of Hesse, a part of Germany renowned for 'its darkly forested highlands, feudal castles and half-timbered towns.'[1] I knew nothing at all about Kassel until I actually started to live there. Before long I became acquainted with the city, its history and also its near-obliteration following a major RAF bombing raid during the Second World War. On the night of 22-23 October 1943 569 bombers flattened Kassel with 418, 293 bombs, some tipped with napalm and creosote, in 80 minutes. Some 5,800 people perished that night, and it is generally held that in all 10,000 died as direct result of the attack. What tumbled out of the bomb bays was, if my calculation is about correct, a mere 0.1% of the total tonnage dropped on Germany by the Allies in the war. I was incapable of comprehending all that too.

When I started to read the full story, I discovered that during the Second World War Kassel was an important armaments centre and had as such been an inviting target for RAF bombers since 1942. One prominent manufacturer was the Gerhard Fieseler Works, which built aircraft for the Luftwaffe. My curiosity about the raid led me to a research centre in Kassel University, which specialised in the study of Hesse during the Nazi period. There I met a young researcher by the name of Thorsten Wiederhold, whose PhD thesis about the role of Gerhard Fieseler as a Nazi industrial boss of some importance had just been published as a monograph.

Wiederhold happened to show me copies of the Fieseler company newspaper, which was published from 1938 to 1943. I was no historian, but in a flash I realised that these were a treasure trove for anyone interested in the Third Reich for its insights into a totally Nazified industrial workplace. Whilst I was in Kassel, the historian Jörg Friedrich, the chronicler of the Allied strategic bombing campaign, gave a public lecture, which was delivered in the city's main church. In his 2002 book *Der Brand* Friedrich had caused a stir in Britain for having the temerity to accuse Churchill and Air Chief Marshall Arthur Harris of being war criminals. In his address to a huge audience Friedrich referred to Churchill as a 'hobby historian' and bemoaned that fact that among the dead and injured as a consequence of the British bombardment of Kassel were 'foreign workers.' I still recall his voice: low, detached, with a measured delivery and decidedly sepulchral.

Something impelled me to get up and challenge him. I started by saying that my father was a navigator with RAF Bomber Command. I then pointed out that Churchill was no hobby historian, but a holder of a Nobel Prize for literature. As for the foreign workers, it was not as if they had come to Kassel on holiday. I do not remember what Friedrich said in reply nor do I recall the reaction of the audience. I was trembling from head to foot. On a lighter note it was in Kassel too that I

---

1   *The Rough Guide to Germany,* 1998.

discovered to my wry amusement that no-one had ever heard of Colditz and that young people I spoke to about the war did not have a clue what the words *Stalag Luft* referred to.

I duly read Wiederhold's monograph and that led to an extraordinary outcome many years later: this biography of Gerhard Fieseler, the drama, shocks, twists and turns – not to mention the moments of stunning exhilaration – of whose life defied every preconception of my imagination.

Nigel Holden
9 March 2017

Introduction

Scope and overview

In the long course of his life from 1896 to 1987 the aviator Gerhard Fieseler lived through four dysfunctionally interlocking Germanys: the Imperial Germany of the erratic Kaiser Wilhelm II; the Germany of the unloved Weimar Republic; the monstrous Third Reich; and the introspective Federal Republic in awkward, divided German space.

In the first of his homelands Fieseler became a decorated and courageous fighter pilot. In the second he pushed his flying capabilities to new heights as a world-renowned aerobatics pilot as well as aircraft designer and builder. In the third he was a Nazi industrialist in Kassel, running (for a time) a highly successful aircraft manufacturing company, which built the still much-admired Storch liaison and reconnaissance aircraft – that 'virtuoso of slow flight.' He was later directly involved in the design, development and manufacture of the V-1 flying bomb. In the immediate post-war Germany Fieseler was variously a prisoner of the American occupying forces, a defendant before a denazification tribunal, and entrepreneur.

Fieseler's life follows the trajectory of aviation in general and military aviation in particular from the Wright Brothers' flight in 1903 to the production of ballistic rockets during the Second World War. But it is also shadowed by air-mindedness: the conviction that Germany's future greatness was directly bound up with releasing the potential of the greatest technological symbol of the age, the aeroplane. It is the intertwining of the events of his life with his first three Germanys, on the one hand, and the rapid development of aviation in peace and war over the same period, on the other, that make Fieseler's life so compelling a story.

From his autobiography, published in 1982, which has not been translated into English, it is indisputable that Fieseler would be very happy to be remembered as one of Germany's greatest aviators of the twentieth century, which by any standard he undoubtedly was. In handling the Nazi years Fieseler likes to convey the impression that he was essentially politically neutral, that he was just an entrepreneur who happened to be producing aircraft for his client the Reich Aviation Ministry, and that he was a very small cog in the war machine that Hitler built. It is true that he was a cog, but he was by no means insignificant as he would wish us to believe.

What is striking about Fieseler is not that he clearly benefited from the Nazi regime, but that he does not look back at those times with that deep moral anxiety which has affected so many Germans since the end of the Second World War. The point is that Fieseler was not only a committed supporter of the Third Reich, but also a large-scale employer of forced labour during the Second World War. Exactly why Fieseler had such a remarkably clear conscience and hence created such a robust sense of denial will be a topic which this book will explore.

There is certainly a good deal more to him than being the father of aerobatics (in the opinion of some) and the creator of the iconic Storch. His life, once put into perspective, reveals a man who opportunistically used events – literally some of the most important events in the twentieth century – for one overriding purpose: to further the great cause of German air-mindedness in peace and war through the medium of his own company. Therein, it seems to me, lies the *leitmotif* of his life and that idea underpins this biography. To Fieseler, so enamoured with flying since boyhood, the cause is so noble, so right that moral issues do not unduly trouble him. This also explains why his life is sometimes so unsettling to read, yet decidedly worthy of telling.

The story of Fieseler would not be complete without an account of the evolution of the legendary Storch in the 1930s and its deployment in the Second World War for reconnoitring enemy dispositions, operating as an air ambulance, and conveying senior Nazi commanders as their preferred personal mode of aerial transport. Appendix A supplies a representation of the various facets of Storch's operational career spanning some 40 years. In its own class the Storch was as fit-for-purpose and as elegant a flying machine as, say, Britain's extolled Spitfire was in its class. More to the point: just as the Spitfire can be seen to have transcended its nominal operational role, so we may say exactly the same thing about Fieseler's brain-child though for vastly different reasons.

It is fully possible to read histories of the Second World War without a single reference to the Storch, though it might occasionally be referred to as a light aircraft or reconnaissance plane without actually naming it. When it comes to that other aircraft, with which Fieseler is closely associated, namely the V-1 flying bomb, the position is completely reversed. After all, no history of the Second World War would be complete without mentioning its significant role in Germany's war effort in 1944 and 1945. The V-1 and its sister 'wonder weapon' the V-2 are subject of countless books and articles in their own right.

But, whereas mention of the V-2 readily calls to mind the name of Wernher von Braun, the V-1 does not automatically invoke the name of Fieseler as its manufacturer (let alone the name of Robert Lusser, the leading designer and development engineer). This biography makes plain that Fieseler's role in pushing ahead with a project which in his own opinion 'bordered on the fantastical' is far more significant than is generally appreciated. Seeing that Fieseler's life is intimately bound up with his two most important aeronautical creations, the Storch and the V-1, the idiosyncratic 'careers' of both aircraft occasionally take centre stage.

This book is the first complete biography of Fieseler's life in English. It is surely overdue to know more about this man who as a boy dreamed of decisively contributing to Germany's aeronautical future and found himself ensnared in a Faustian pact with one of the most diabolical regimes in world history. But it is not so much overdue as timely, because at long last the time may be approaching in which the general perception of Germany with respect to the two world wars of the Twentieth Century is becoming more nuanced, more open-minded and less judgementally preoccupied with the Third Reich. If this is correct, then this shift of attitude represents, some 70 years after the end of the Second World War, a healthy *Zeitgeist*.

Prime sources

This biography of Gerhard Fieseler will make use of three main German-language sources, none of which has been translated into English. The first is Fieseler's own autobiography. The second source is a monograph based on the PhD thesis of Thorsten Wiederhold of the University of Kassel and published in 2002. Wiederhold concentrates on a Fieseler as an industrialist in Nazi Germany. It supplies a very thorough treatment of the evolution of the Fieseler aircraft factory, explaining how all employees were not just conscientious workers, but also reliable supporters of the Nazis in thought, word and deed.

The third source is the recently published *Kassel und die Luftfahrtindustrie seit 1923* (*Kassel and the air transport industry since 1923*) by Rolf Nagel and Thorsten Bauer. This is by far the most detailed source of information about Fieseler's life as an aviator, but is evasive about his role as an employer of slave labour as well as his post-war imprisonment and indictment as a war criminal. An immense value of this book is that it is replete with key dates, which are either missing or inaccurate in Fieseler's own memoir. The Nagel and Bauer book is also an extremely good source of rare and highly informative photographs.

Three other sources of note should be mentioned. The first concerns material contained in the *Fieseler Zeitung*, the in-company newspaper of the Fieseler company, providing glimpses of a Nazified industrial workplace and revealing Fieseler as a trusted partner of the Reich Air Ministry and as a loyal servant of the Führer. Next to be noted is a short biography of Fieseler, published in 1941 and written by Adalbert Norden, a minor writer of books on aviation topics. Reportedly based on interviews with Fieseler, the book is breezy, infused with Hitler-centred *Zeitgeist*, and hagiographical. This is Fieseler as Biggles in the as yet unstoppable upswing of the Führer's new Germany. The last German-language source I should mention is Janusz Piekalkiewicz's book about the deployment of the Storch during the Second World War (this book also contains useful technical information).

Within three weeks of the deadline of my submission of my final manuscript to Helion, Herr Falk Urlen of Kassel, who had been very helpful in supplying me with photographs, sent me the copious material he had been gathering on the life of Gerhard Fieseler over the last forty years, including copies of the Fieseler company newspaper from 1940 to 1942.

Translation issues
To make life less taxing for readers without a knowledge of German, I have endeavoured to keep to a minimum the direct use of German words and abbreviations, official or otherwise, except in the case of those that require no translation such as Führer, Luftwaffe or SS. I have given an explanation of less well known words and abbreviations in the text. One main group belongs to the German of the Third Reich; another to German aeronautical terminology. Nazi German terms and expressions can often sound very clunkish when translated into English. One such word is Fieseler's Nazi title of *Wehrwirtschaftsführer*, which I have rendered as 'defence economy leader', this being the translation used in the official documentation of the Nuremburg Trails. I have also retained the title of Fieseler's rank in the Nazi Flying Corps, namely *Standartenführer*, which is held to equate with brigadier in the British army. The German actually sounds better. Beyond that, in my translations of stretches of Nazi German, I have otherwise done my best to strike the balance between banality and portentousness – which may be an impossible task. Some readers will be familiar with the German acronym, *Jasta*, a compression of *Jadgstaffel*, which a strict translation will render as 'pursuit squadron.' I have decided to retain the German term which is widely used in English-language studies of WW1 military aviation.

Several people have kindly assisted me in resolving translation issues, many of which concerned the rendering of aeronautical terms into English. I am immensely indebted to Martin Pearce as well as to German aeronautical engineers, Daniel Sülberg and Bernhard Opl, for their invaluable assistance in the translation of specialist terminology. Anne Buckley and Wolfgang Keinhorst of the University of Leeds helped to improve the translation of one particular tricky passage. Jade Douglas, a PhD student of German literature at the university, meticulously proof-read the entire manuscript and double-checked the spelling of German words in the text and in the bibliography. In the end I take all responsibility for the translation of German material in this text.

Copyright issues
I have obtained clearance from Random House Deutschland to cite material freely from Fieseler's autobiography, whilst the Gerhard Fieseler Foundation in Kassel has confirmed that they are unaware of copyright constraints. Regarding the images in this book I have made every attempt

to contact all copyright holders to secure permission to reproduce their images. After the caption accompanying the images I have indicated the source.

Acknowledgments

I would like to express warm thanks to academic colleagues for assisting me with matters great and small: Professor Sierk Horn of the University of Munich, Dr Heather Jones of the London School of Economics, Dr Felix Römer of the German Historical Institute in London, Professor Nancy Napier of Boise State University, USA. I am especially grateful to Dr Armin Grünbacher of the University of Birmingham for reading parts of the manuscript and for valuable comments on the denazification of Germany after the Second World War. The library of the University of Regensburg, where I was a visiting professor in 2015, handsomely assisted in tracking down several monographs and books unobtainable in the UK. Oscar Azevedo, a Storch enthusiast and collector of Fieseler memorabilia, has been a remarkable source of information and has generously allowed me to reproduce some rare photographs from his collection. Christopher Ailsby enlightened me on German uniforms and medals. I would also like to thank Duncan Rogers and Victoria Powell at Helion for their prompt response to my many queries and their excellent support though the entire production process.

Tony Canfer has been very helpful on explaining aspects of aircraft design and performance, whilst Martin Hall eased my struggle with WW1 aviation statistics. Eddie Flood has been kind enough to read and comment on various extracts where I needed a second opinion. Special thanks are due to Squadron Leader Steve MacFarland, who has been an excellent sounding board throughout and who first suggested that I attempt a complete biography of Gerhard Fieseler. Finally, a word of appreciation to my daughter Natalie who read several chapters and gave useful comments from the point of view of a non-specialist reader. This book is dedicated to her and to my wife Natsuko.

Part One

Aerial Gladiator

1

Unpromising beginnings

Aviation – a necessity.

German slogan 1912[1]

All of you know nothing; I alone know something. I alone decide.

Kaiser Wilhelm to his senior officials.[2]

Born a very lucky German indeed

On 10 August 1896 Otto Lilienthal plunged to his death on the Rhön Hills, some 100 kms north east of Frankfurt, in a glider he had designed and built. With Ferdinand von Zeppelin, the creator of the airship, he ranks as one of Germany's greatest aeronautical pioneers of the 19th century. Lilienthal, an engineer and known as the glider king, was 'the first person to build a gliding apparatus capable of flight and learn to fly with it.'[3] He was also notable for systematically studying bird flight as the basis for designing aircraft. Surviving photographs reveal that his gliders were elegant machines with graceful flowing lines.[4] Lilienthal was a prolific writer, for he documented his flights, of which he made some 2,000.[5] At the time of his untimely death he probably had more theoretical and practical knowledge of flight than anyone else in the world. He was the first person to build a device for measuring aerodynamic characteristics such as lift.[6] His last recorded words, which were etched on his tombstone, were: 'Sacrifices must be made.'[7]

Lilienthal was perhaps the first person to realise that, although it was a great achievement to raise a heavier-than-air machine into the air, the key challenge lay in ensuring that aircraft could maintain stability in flight. The Wright Brothers, Orville and Wilbur, acknowledged their debt to Lilienthal as the person who had done more than anyone else to 'attack the flying problem in the 19th century.'[8] Some six months before his death, on 15 April 1896, a boy was born not far from Cologne who would be fascinated by 'the new aerial science' from a very early age.[9] The boy, Gerhard Fieseler, was very conscious of a symbolic intertwining of his birth and Lilienthal's death.

---

1 W. Mühlbauer, Die Fliegertruppe entsteht, in: H. Ringlstetter, S. Krüger und W. Mühlbauer, *Flugzeug Special 12 Classic*, p.6. The original German is: *Luftfahrt tut not.*
2 J. C. G. Röhl, *Kaiser Wilhelm II*, p.58.
3 Deutsches Museum, *Aviation: A Guide to the Aeronautics Collection,* p.29.
4 See the website of the Lilienthal Museum in Anklam 200 kms north of Berlin: http://www.lilienthal-museum.de/olma/ehome.htm
5 He is most famed for his book *Birdflight as the basis of aviation* (*Der Vogelflug als Grundlage der Fliegekunst*), published in 1889.
6 Deutsches Museum, op. cit., p.29.
7 M. Eppler, *The Wright way: Seven Problems solving principles from the Wright Brothers that can make your business soar*, p.2.
8 See: http://en.wikipedia.org/wiki/Otto_Lilienthal
9 M. Gilbert, *A History of the Twentieth Century*, p.168.

Furthermore he regarded himself as having come into the world at an auspicious moment, for he could say that he was destined to live in an epoch in which he could unfold his capabilities. 'What is granted to only a few people,' he was to write as a very old man, 'was fulfilled in me.'[10] He was a very lucky German indeed to have survived the vicissitudes of that epoch – the first fifty years of the twentieth century – and to be able to hold that opinion.

Gerhard Fieseler came into this world in a mud timber-framed house in the tiny Rhineland village of Glesch, which once upon a time found itself half-way, as the crow flies, between Cologne and the ancient duchy of Jülich, which bordered the Dutch provinces. Today it lies in the *Land* of North-Rhine–Westphalia, where it has been absorbed into the town of Bergheim. At the end of the 19th century there was little work to be had on the land in that back of beyond. There were always too many mouths to feed. Gerhard would always remember Glesch as a place of 'need and poverty.'[11]

He was born out of wedlock, but the infant only remained in this socially regrettable state for a year. For whatever reason his father did the right thing and married his sweetheart Katharina Marx, the mother of his young son. Gerhard's father, August Fieseler, had been born in November 1872, the son of a pretty young widow who singlehandedly run a hotel in Koblenz, and an elderly benefactor, a man of wealth: a Prussian general no less, but otherwise mysterious. For unclear reasons he and the widow did not marry. Presumably she was retained as his mistress. A good hundred years after the birth of his father, when he was writing his autobiography, Gerhard would by sheer chance discover the identity of his grandfather, and it would stretch his incredulity.

When Gerhard's father August was but one year old, his mother, overwhelmed with the cares of the world, passed away. Her child was duly brought up in Remagen just south of Bonn in the care of a certain Frau Jonen, who had been his wet-nurse. No doubt with the approval and financial support of the elderly gentleman, Frau Jonen kept and brought up the boy August as best as she could. When he was four or five years old, August was visited by this very same gentleman. He was bespectacled and attired in a frock coat and top hat. He patted August on the head and gave him a gold coin. Such visits would take place intermittently until August was about eight years old. Then they came to an abrupt end. Frau Jonen duly broke the news to August that the old gentleman had died, also revealing that he was indeed his father. But not long after that Frau Jonen herself died of an incurable disease. She took the name of August's father to her grave.

The authorities in Remagen arranged for August to go to Bonn where he lived with foster parents. The father of the house was a roughneck who would come home drunk on pay day and think nothing of giving his wife and his new stepson a walloping for no good reason. Somehow, the authorities got wind of these goings-on and August for his own safety was sent to live with another family, where alas things were scarcely better. At least, though, he had some schooling. But, as his foster family was always short of money, August was compelled to make paper bags and try to sell them in villages in the vicinity. Come rain or shine he would make his rounds in his foster father's dog-cart. But if he returned home with too little money, he would be in for a good hiding.

The rather frail August often went hungry, so he would help his school chums with their homework to earn a piece of bread. Then, when he was fourteen years old, this German Oliver Twist had the good fortune after the tribulation of his years in Bonn to meet his Mr Brownlow. He was apprenticed to a kindly printer in Andernach on the left bank of the Rhine just north of Koblenz. Along with another apprentice he boarded at the printer's home, where he was treated as one of the family. There was always enough to eat and for the first time in his life August experienced the happiness of a well-run family home.

---

10   G. Fieseler, *Meine Bahn am Himmel*, p.10.
11   Ibid, p.11.

August at first struck the printer as somewhat timid, but once the family had taken him into its bosom, he lost his former shy awkwardness. In his four years' apprenticeship he proved to be hardworking, ambitious and quick on the uptake, learning all the ins and outs of typesetting and printing. When he had completed his apprenticeship, August spent another year under the roof of his kindly employer. Then one day his call-up papers were delivered. He reported to Trier to do two years' national service.

Life in the army was harsh; there was a severity of discipline that was unknown in other countries.[12] Every year in those days – around 1890 – there would be five or six desertions from the Trier Infantry Regiment to escape the physical brutality meted out to soldiers. Absconders would make a dash for the border into Luxemburg, from where a few would even make their way to France to join the Foreign Legion. August, it seems, never said much to his children about his younger years, but he did once tell his eldest son, Gerhard, that his sergeant-major was as pitiless as a slave-master.

August, now around 20 years old, could not take the despotic treatment any longer. After 15 months in the army he had a nervous breakdown and was despatched to a military hospital, from which he was discharged a few months later as unfit for military service. His case was taken up by the military authorities, who granted him a lifelong pension, which enabled him to pay for a furnished room with breakfast. August decided to go back to Andernach, where he had spent five fruitful and happy years. To his surprise and joy his old employer welcomed him back as it were his own son who had returned safely from war. Scarcely had August stepped in the door and a table been prepared for coffee and cakes than his former benefactor blurted out: 'It's good thing you've come back. I expect you've already heard that there's something good in the offing for you.'[13]

August was struck speechless, as his patron explained how a notary from Frankfurt had tried to contact him whilst he was away on military service. In short: 'You've come into a legacy.'[14] August headed for Frankfurt and called on the notary who told him that, when he had completed his twenty first year, he would receive the princely sum of 100,000 marks. That was the equivalent of £500 sterling at the time: around £500,000 at today's prices. "Would you kindly confirm that to me in writing', requested the stunned, unbelieving August. 'Of course', said the notary.[15] August duly learned that that the money had been bequeathed to him by that self-same old gentleman – his natural father – who had given him the occasional gold coin when he was young. But still he was not to learn his identity.

Dizzy with new-found wealth, August promptly settled in Frankfurt, where the first thing he did was to set himself up in a residence in one of the most fashionable parts of the city. But before long he fell in with the wrong sort, who cheated him out of the entire inheritance. Gerhard's mother revealed the sad story to him when he was a married man himself. Gerhard found all this hard to reconcile with the fact his father was an intelligent person, who knew in later life how to talk about literature, art, music and politics, and who, as elected chairman of various associations and societies in Bonn, showed himself to be an excellent public speaker, never needing notes and always self-assured. He was indeed a true pillar of the community. But the truth was that, when it came to money matters, his father was 'completely helpless.'[16]

Somehow August did not allow these terrible events in Frankfurt to crush him. He made off for Cologne where he found a position as a typesetter in a printing works. It was though in

---

12   B. H. Liddell Hart, *History of the First World War*, p 54.
13   Fieseler, op. cit., p.16.
14   Ibid, p.16.
15   Ibid, p.16.
16   Ibid, p.17.

Frankfurt where he met Katharina, future mother of Gerhard. Katharina Marx haled from Glesch, the daughter of a roofer. She was the first-born of the ten Marx children. Life was hard and the family often went hungry. When she was aged 18, Katharina was offered the position of a maid in a wealthy household in Frankfurt. It was a matter of some rejoicing in her family in Glesch. There would now be one less mouth to feed and Katharina would be sending money back home from her modest income.

Katharina's employers lived in one of Frankfurt's most elegant suburbs and there she learned all the good manners and habits of the well-to-do. What an eye-opener it must have been for her, remarks Gerhard, to come from humble Glesch to this imposing city of world renown on the River Main. The family treated her well and she was permitted – with a suitable lady companion, of course – to attend dances every Sunday. Katharina was something of a beauty, so there was no shortage of partners offering to take her arm and do a spin with her on the dance floor. Katharina had been working with her Frankfurt family for a year, when she met – we do not know the precise occasion – a young man with blond hair and a confident manner. This was, of course, the 23 year old August Fieseler, who was rebuilding his life after his recent misfortunes.

It was love at first sight. But, one thing, as they say, leads to another, and Katharina soon found herself in the family way. She one day told Gerhard how she, coming from her sheltered background with its strict Catholic upbringing, was completely naïve about the birds and the bees and did not understand how feelings of love could overwhelm somebody and lead to unimaginable consequences. She was indeed in her third month of pregnancy before she realised that motherhood beckoned. Without August at her side she returned to Glesch, where she broke the shocking news to her parents.

Her otherwise placid father was beside himself with rage; her equally furious mother invoked the Holy Scriptures, warning her that her transgressions would not go unpunished in the world to come; the village priest told her that she had forfeited her soul by deviating from the Church's injunctions. There was of course no way in which a scandal of such magnitude could be kept secret from the inhabitants of Glesch, so the young woman, censured by her parents and condemned by the priest, was also ostracised by the local people. But in all her tribulations never once did August send her a letter, whilst it was beneath her dignity to write to him and implore him to do the honourable thing.

In the end Katharina's parents did not repudiate her, as they had threatened to do if she brought an illegitimate child into the world. They allowed her to give birth in their house. Not that it was an occasion for family rejoicing, of course. Everyone knew that an illegitimate child, growing up without a father, would have very limited prospects in life, and then there was all the shame heaped on the Marx family. The child was baptised with the name Gerhard Marx, Gerhard being the name of Katharina's father. The months passed and there was still no word from August. He might as well be dead, as far as Katharina and her family were concerned.

Then, out of the blue, when the child was about a year old, August presented himself one day on the doorstep of the Marx family. There is no known reason for his change of heart. We can only surmise that he not only relented of his selfish behaviour, but also realised – this is what Gerhard would dearly like us to believe – that he would never again find the likes of his mother. What we do know for certain is that August was stony-broke. We are told nothing about the first, no doubt extremely tense encounter between him and Katharina's parents. It is, however, just possible that they somehow found something worthy in the young man.

The couple married, and their son Gerhard Marx became Gerhard Fieseler. They were poor, but happy, and it would even seem that Katharina's parents had taken to their new son-in-law.

The couple took a lease on a small deserted and rather run-down farmhouse. The previous owner, a widow, had recently died and her son, who lived in nearby Bergheim, allowed the young Fieseler family to move in, leaving them his mother's meagre furniture. There was no money for the many repairs that needed doing to the dilapidated dwelling. At first August tried his hand at earning a wage as a countryman. But he had no flair for tending fields, gardens or cattle. He had spent too much time in cities to adapt to the rural life of Glesch. By a stroke of luck he got a job in Bergheim, about an hour's walk away, working as a typesetter on the local newspaper. Katharina looked after the home, the small livestock and the baby Gerhard.

Advent of the balloonless airship
When he was six years old, Gerhard went to the village school. But he was only to spend six months as a pupil there. His father and mother had taken the decision to move to Bonn, where August would seek work. Bonn was a small university city on the Rhine, a residence of civil servants and especially famed as the birth place of the composer Beethoven. When they left Glesch for Bonn at the beginning of the new century, they were now a family with three children. Eventually they would have seven more, the youngest being born during the First World War.

The Fieselers moved into cheap accommodation in the north part of the city. Furniture – second-hand, of course – was purchased. Everything depended on fortune smiling on August. The young father must have calculated that he would find work in one of the city's printing works, but for all his traipsing around and knocking on doors there was no opening for him. Eventually he was offered a job as the representative of a manufacturer of sewing machines. He apparently took to this job, even though the family income depended on his skills as a salesman. But he quickly decided that he would make himself independent by setting up his own printing company. With Katharina's backing he set about studying the leaflets of companies who supplied printing machinery and other needs. Representatives were met, specifications discussed, and orders placed.

Where the money came from for this not inconsiderable investment, we are not told. Perhaps August was lent some money by Katharina's parents. As soon as the company was up and running, August would go and find customers, who were for the most part skilled craftsman and small firms, who needed brochures. These were often to be found out in the country, where he faced little or no competition. While August was collecting and delivering the bigger orders, Katharina was operating the Boston printing press, and Gerhard, as soon as he was back from school, was sent round to the customers with the printed material they had ordered, taking invoices with him. It was in principle cash on delivery: 'in principle', because it seldom happened that way. The customers would often only give a part payment or simply say that they'd pay next week.

Once, when he was eight or nine years old, Gerhard went with a delivery of invitation cards which a dance school had had printed by Herr Fieseler for a grand ball. August had given Gerhard enough money for him to take the tram to the other side of the Rhine for the journey. For the return he was to take money from the payment for the invitation cards. In the event the dancing master did not pay on the spot, saying that he only had big notes. The boy would have to come back in a few days for the exact payment. It would take him a good hour to walk home. As he approached the Rhine, Gerhard realised that he did not have the two pfennigs to pay for crossing the bridge. He had completely forgotten about this.

He did not know what to do. He knew that he would get no sympathy at the ticket office or from the bridge superintendent (no doubt a self-important man with an impressive uniform in those days). Nor did he want to ask a passer-by for money. That would be like begging. How was he to get over to the other side of the Rhine? It was time to be a daredevil. He hovered at the end of the bridge and waited for the arrival of the next tram. As it crossed the bridge he ran alongside it, keeping in the shadow. His heart pumping, he managed to cross over the bridge undetected.

This otherwise minor childhood incident, which he records vividly in his autobiography, had great significance for Gerhard. It evidently stayed in his mind as the first time in his life where he had to think fast and do something impulsive. But that is not all. In fact he attributes his forgetfulness about the money for crossing the Rhine to something on his mind. 'I must have been dreaming of my first model aircraft', he wrote.[17] This is Gerhard's first reference to the world of aviation in his boyhood. We cannot pinpoint the date, but the daring dash over the Rhine had obviously happened after 17 December 1903, when as reported in London's *Daily Mail* two days later there had taken place the sensational flight of a 'Balloonless Airship.'[18]

This referred to the wondrous achievement of the Wright Brothers who 'successfully experimented with a flying machine in Kittyhawk, North Carolina. The machine had no balloon attachment and derives its force from propellers worked by a small engine.' In the last of four experimental flights on that day the brothers were airborne for 59 seconds and covered a distance of 260 metres.[19] What we can safely deduce is that the young Fieseler was taken with the new-fangled flying machines – of the heavier-than-air variety – from a very early age. It would become a fascination that would shape his life and give it its strange destiny.

The Fieseler family business prospered after a fashion. In charge of the finances – this will be no surprise – was Katharina. When the orders stopped coming in, the Fieselers lived on dried bread and potatoes. Keeping up with the rent and paying off items bought on instalment was the priority. This was a matter of honour and very important for the standing of the business in the community. Eventually the business did sufficiently well for August to take on a young apprentice, who could assist with typesetting and printing and who, as was the custom in those days, lived in with the family, ate his meals with them and even slept in the same room with the other children. Before long there was more expansion. The Fieselers rented a house which had an annexe for the printing activities. As a further sign that things were looking up, bigger machines were ordered and then a telephone was installed in August's office.

One Christmas Gerhard received a bicycle. But it was a gift with a purpose. He would now be able to be more efficient at running messages and making deliveries. Only much later in his life did he realise that he was for his parents not just a son, but a member of the workforce. Even in old age he still held it against his parents that they did not pay enough attention to his emotional and psychological needs as a growing boy. What precisely these needs were, Gerhard does not tell us. Perhaps, if his parents had told him that the world famous Wright Brothers were once upon a time 'humble bicycle makers,' this might have had a an uplifting effect on their son's sensitivities.[20] As it happened, the renowned American aviators visited Germany in 1909. It is inconceivable that Gerhard did not know this, even though he makes no mention of the event. As often as not work carried on into the night. His mother Katharina, despite now having five children to look after, worked hard in the printing shop. Gerhard had duties allocated him: peeling carrots, doing the washing up and carrying out general housework. Every day after school he would run errands for this father.

Gerhard was of an age to notice a difference between his parents. His mother punished her children with fairness, but his father was impulsive and inconsistent. But he learnt one important lesson from his father: how to accept injustices with equanimity. If his father ruled the roost and

---

17   Ibid, p.23.
18   R. Hattersley, *The Edwardians*, p.440.
19   Deutsches Museum, op. cit., p.30.
20   D. Edgerton, *England and the Aeroplane: Militarism, Modernity and Machines*, p.3.

demanded 'absolute obedience,' it was his mother who, as Fieseler put it, 'had the stronger soul.'[21] She was somebody who with her warm-hearted worldliness always looked for the middle way. So it was that she saw through the characters of people, who with flattery and guile tried to get her husband to put his signature to orders that would prove to be not his advantage. Despite his terrible experience of being swindled in the not so distant past, he was still prone to act too fast and lose money in the process.

At all events the business slowly but surely took off, and eight years after it was founded – in or around 1910 – August was in a position to employ four assistants and three apprentices, of whom Gerhard was by now one, although he was still at school. There was a time when August went to the customers, but now they started to come to him. There was though pressure from the big ones to lower his prices, so it was a constant battle to keep enough revenue flowing in to make a profit. In the circumstances Gerhard had very little free time. Sunday was his day off as well as the occasional public and religious holiday. When he could, he would sit in the printing shop and read about aeroplanes and the men who flew them.

Gerhard memorised or quite probably noted down in a booklet what he regarded as important information about the first powered flights. He was growing up in an age – in the very first age – of a new popular hero, who 'emerged in the intrepid airman. The names of pilots such as Pégoud, Nesterov, Loieslagers, and von Hiddessen, now long forgotten, were often in the newspapers and even more often on the lips of schoolboys – and their fame would continue into the war, where they would become the first "aces".'[22]

When Gerhard was seven, the Wright Brothers had covered 260 metres in 59 seconds in 1903; in 1907, when he was ten or eleven, the Frenchman Henri Farman extended this to 770 metres in 52 seconds. As he grew older, Gerhard would see record after record collapse in the march of technical progress. He became so entranced by anything to do with aviation that he started to make sketches of model aircraft and to ponder how he could make the fuselage, made of bamboo, resistant to twisting. The power came from a wound-up rubber band, but this twisted the piece of bamboo and interfered with the flight characteristics. Gerhard says that he found the solution to the problem (he doesn't explain it), adding that he patented the idea some 20 years later.

One day Gerhard was working so hard in the printing shop that he did not notice his father come in. He suddenly stood behind him and then he spotted some of his son's sketches of aircraft. 'What's that all about?' Fieseler senior bluntly enquired, as his son tried to cover up the drawings. 'I find it exciting that there are people who are doing these flights', replied Gerhard, his voice full of enthusiasm. 'Just think. One day we'll all the able to fly through the air!' His father glowered. 'That's rubbish, a stupid idea. No-one's going to take that stuff seriously.' 'But you have to take it seriously,' retorted Gerhard hotly. 'You have other things to do here', came the stern reply. 'If you have so much free time on your hands, I'll give you some jobs that are important for our company.' Then came the parting shot, as his father disappeared into his office. 'What's going on in your head is utter nonsense!'[23]

This unhappy exchange caused Gerhard to ruminate on his life. When he thought about it, there wasn't much to laugh about and the love that a child needs was carefully rationed out to him and his brothers and sisters. He would not appreciate it until later in his life, but his mother was mindful never to show that she favoured one child more than another. If she did, then Gerhard would have surely got the lion's share. At least, he liked to think so. Yet, truth be told, he could not

---

21 Fieseler, op. cit., p.16.
22 L. Kennett, *The First Air War 1914-1918*, p.12.
23 Fieseler, op. cit., p.25.

actually say that life for him or the other children was unhappy despite the hard work and father's discipline.

After all he and his brothers and sister had a square meal every day, they were clothed and had a bed to sleep in. Of course he could not really imagine how his father and mother had battled to give them all this life, but, when he was about thirteen, he realised that he, the oldest of the Fieseler children, had from now on to take his share of responsibility and show his parents how grateful and respectful he could prove to be. This resolve gave him a great feeling of satisfaction. Suddenly, he tells us, he knew where he stood in the family. But before long his noble sentiments would be undermined in a most devastating way.

A Zeppelin and the new intellectual skyline
In the year 1908, as best Fieseler recalls, came the sensational news that a Zeppelin airship was due to fly over Bonn. All the town's school children rushed to the banks of the Rhine, for the great airship would for a time be following the mighty river. They waited hour after hour and then came a disappointing announcement: 'The Zeppelin has had to turn round owing to the strong headwind.'[24] Then, one beautifully sunny Sunday, with hardly any advanced warning, the silver giant flew low over the city. With no time to waste, Gerhard raced up to attic of his house and clambered on to the ridge of the roof. In a flash the streets filled up with people. The steerable Zeppelin – that 'masterpiece of German engineering' – glided majestically overhead and disappeared.[25] Gerhard came off the roof and rushed downstairs, almost colliding with his mother as she approached the front door with his father

'What do you say to that, my boy?' she asked Gerhard. Without thinking he cryptically replied, possibly because he did not want to provoke his father, 'Nothing will come of it.' To which, rather remarkably, his mother replied: 'Silly boy.'[26] August took no part in this conversation and did not pass any kind of comment about the sensational spectacle they had witnessed. No matter how much Gerhard strove to be unimpressed by the Zeppelin, it is hard to imagine his father August not being utterly awe-struck at the aerial leviathan – all hundred and sixty metres of it – dwarfing everything on heaven and earth and sustained in the lofty heights thanks to the 11,300 cubic metres of hydrogen contained in its gigantic frame. Who indeed would not be awe-struck even today if one floated overhead?

The Zeppelin was indeed 'an emblem (*Sinnbild*) of national greatness and technical progress,'[27] truly a 'secular miracle' in the aerial class of human achievement.[28] Perhaps more than any other artefact of the day, it symbolised the Germany of Kaiser Wilhelm, where 'everywhere one looked, one saw the contours of an economic miracle.'[29] Since around 1860, on key indicators to do with industrial production, share of world industrial production, and share of world trade, Germany had almost caught up with or had gone ahead of Britain, which had embraced the industrial revolution approximately fifty years before its rival. With Germany competing worldwide with Britain for share of world markets and using huge quantities of iron and steel with which it was building a powerful navy, Britain was in the years before the First World War all too aware of a serious threat to its status as the world's unrivalled oceanic power.

24 Ibid, p.27.
25 P. G. Neumann, *The German Air Force in the Great War*, p.9.
26 Fieseler, op. cit., p.27.
27 Mühlbauer, op. cit., p.4.
28 *The Manchester Guardian*, 25 September 1936 used the expression 'secular miracle' to describe the *Queen Mary* at its launch. Cited in: B. Rieger, *Technology and the Culture of Modernity in Britain and Germany 1980-1945*, p.1.
29 C. Clark, *The Sleepwalkers: How Europe Went to War in 1914*, p.165.

At the same time, German companies and inventors were creating new industries. Karl Benz 'constructed the vehicle from which the automobilism of the world has sprung.'[30] Friedrich Bayer helped to create Germany's – and therefore the world's – pharmaceutical industry, whilst Carl Zeiss became a leading producer of laboratory equipment, including microscopes. A factor in these and many other technological developments was the fact that science and engineering were strikingly prominent at German universities. Indeed, the Germans pioneered a completely new kind of institution of higher education: the technical university. Many of Germany's famed planemakers of the first half of the 20th century were products of the country's most illustrious engineering institutions: Willy Messerschmitt, Claude Dornier, Hugo Junkers, Ernst Heinkel. There was to be no such start in life for Gerhard Fieseler.

In science and engineering, in philosophy, theology and history as well as in the new social sciences – economics, psychology and sociology – Germany was fashioning a new 'intellectual skyline.'[31] German professors were glorified throughout the world. Add to this the lustre of the high prestige of German music: Bach, Beethoven, Brahms and Wagner; and the fact that German was the first country to introduce provisions for workers to obtain compensation during illness or for accidents at work. It can well be said that Germany, at the time of the outbreak of the First World War, was 'decades ahead the rest of the world.'[32]

But the new emerging modernity was a source of mystifying disquiet and unease. As the historian Richard Evans has observed: 'beneath its prosperous and self-confident surface, [Germany] was nervous, uncertain and racked by internal tensions. For many, the sheer pace of economic and social change was frightening and bewildering.'[33] How did these tensions play out in society? Evans tells us: 'These tensions found release in an increasingly vociferous nationalism, mixed with alarmingly strident doses of racism and anti-Semitism, which were to leave a baleful legacy for the future.'[34] Another historian has framed this tension as 'between an uncritical confidence in technical progress and a deep-rooted bourgeois fear that things would soon go drastically wrong.'[35] In the summer of 1914 that inchoate foreboding would unfold itself in the form of a conflict among nations, the scale and destructiveness of which the world had never seen before.

Being in head-long catch-up mode, Germany was keen to have colonies, to which so much emblematic national prestige – not to mention 'phantasmagoric significance' – was attached.[36] It wanted a navy to match the British one, and it was also willing to throw its weight around. Germany, as a belated great power, wanted – in Chancellor Bülow's famous phrase – its 'place in the sun' too. Kaiser Wilhelm II had a blunter term: his ambition was for Germany to become a *Weltreich* (world empire).[37] Ruling like an absolute monarch, Wilhelm was 'supreme commander of the army, the one person in whom the strands of military and political power were united.'[38]

But he was the despair of his ministers for his penchant for making policy on the hoof and keeping them in the dark – fatal tendencies in the so-called July crisis of 1914, in which the leading European powers failed to prevent the slide to war. For Wilhelm Germany was 'a giant toy created

---

30   P. Watson, *German Genius: Europe's Third Renaissance, the Second Scientific Revolution and the Twentieth Century,* p.375.
31   A. Bloom, extract from an endorsement of the book by Watson, op. cit.
32   F. Taylor, *The Berlin Wall 13 August 1961 – 9 November 1989,* p.20.
33   R. Evans, *The Coming of the Third Reich,* p.20.
34   Ibid, p.21.
35   M. Kitchen, *The Cambridge Illustrated History of Germany,* p.219.
36   W. R. Louis. The European colonial powers, in M. Howard and W. R. Louis, (eds.), *The Oxford History of the Twentieth Century,* p.91.
37   Röhl, op. cit., p.74.
38   H. Strachan, *The First World War,* p.47.

by the Almighty to please His Imperial Majesty.'[39] He could use it as he thought fit; and there were always plenty of sycophants around him who with 'unctuous insincerity' ensured that the whims and wishes of the All-Highest were indulged.[40]

It has been said that in Germany before 1914 'the nimbus of [its] world power status and world appreciation overlaid everything, producing a hitherto unknown feeling of worth', and that 'a breath of this new German feeling of worth pervaded the living rooms of the petty bourgeoisie in the remotest provincial towns'.[41] This novel feeling no doubt penetrated the Fieseler household too. For his part, though, August would know of course that his flourishing business was not entirely due to his hard work. He surely had a lot to thank the Kaiser for. The booming economy meant that he was part of the general economic upswing. His business expanded as a result of a healthy order book, meaning he had the financial resources to employ staff and invest in better equipment.

As for Gerhard, he saw the world more and more through the prism of the aeroplane. As he grew older, he was increasingly aware of rapid developments in aircraft performance and harboured a lurking sense that Germany was lagging behind France in aeronautical development. Was he somehow thinking that Germany's military leadership did not grasp the significance of powered flight in a future war? If so, he was mistaken, for, as the historian David Edgerton points out, it was *not* the case at all that 'European armies did not know what to do with aircraft in 1914, that aircraft hit them as a bolt from the blue.'[42] Before the war broke out, the French and German armies and the British army and navy were closely monitoring aeronautical developments.

In the case of Germany there was a special, unique twist. There were, on the one hand, those who supported the further development of aircraft for military purposes.[43] The most celebrated member of this for the time being less influential lobby was Helmuth von Moltke, Germany's Chief of General Staff. On the other stood those who advocated the exploitation of the Zeppelin and foresaw its use in bombing operations. It is of course most unlikely that Gerhard was aware of this division of military opinion.

When the war did come, the issue was not about any nominal shortage of aircraft relative to the size and perceived needs of the armed services in the combatant countries, but how to train enough airmen to fly them in the absence of qualified instructors. Gerhard would one day experience that reality for himself. It is incidentally interesting that he was so preoccupied with France, when, if we are to believe a British expert on the topic, it was in reality Britain that had 'the most aeronautically inclined army.'[44] In so far as the twelve year old Gerhard was foreseeing Germany engaged in some future war, he plainly did not imagine that Britain would be an adversary.

A shrewd old gaffer
A few days after the Zeppelin had so serenely floated across Bonn, Augustus told Gerhard that they, just the two of them, would go for a trek in the nearby countryside north of Bonn. It was a boiling hot day, sweat poured off them. They came across a tavern and went in for some cool air and refreshment. A group of four men were playing cards, another was chatting with the landlord. By himself was sitting a gaffer with a glint in his eye, a farm labourer by the look of him. He had a big, flowing beard and was smoking a pipe with a long stem and partaking of a glass of schnapps.

---

39   M. Stürmer, *The German Empire 1871-1914*, p.69.
40   Röhl, op. cit., p.69.
41   H. M. Müller, *Schlaglichter der deutschen Geschichte*, p.197.
42   Edgerton, op. cit., p.14.
43   Mühlbauer, op. cit., p.6.
44   Edgerton, op. cit., p.16.

The old man, turning to August, enquired in heavy dialect: 'Yer young un, eh?' 'My eldest', returned August, who finished off his beer and ordered another one. After a while the gaffer took the pipe out of his mouth, turned to August and said: 'Know wha'? He's gonna go far, that un.' For some reason this prophecy about his son made August feel uncomfortable. His reply was non-committal. 'Let's wait and see.' The gaffer did not like this for an answer and repeated himself: 'From wha' I seen, 'e's gonna go far.' When they were outside, Gerhard asked his father what the old chap had meant. 'Oh, those old folk have nothing better to do than say silly things', was the dismissive reply.[45] Yet, as the future would reveal, the old boy's prophecy was by no means misplaced.

As a teenager Gerhard spent as much time as possible making model aircraft. At first he made replicas of aircraft that he had seen in magazines. Before long he learned how to power an airscrew by tightening a rubber band with 200 to 300 twists. But he needed both money and materials to make his models, so he made a pfennig here, a pfennig there by collecting empty bottles, rags and old iron and selling the junk all to an ironmonger of his acquaintance. He also made some money, seemingly with his father's knowledge, in the form of tips for doing odd jobs for some of the clients of the Fieseler printing company. Especially lucrative was his tip from a company for whom he took large consignments to the post office twice a week. This earned him a mark, two if he was lucky.

In his spare time he built kites, which flew higher than anyone else's, and he managed to sell these to those friends who succeeded in getting the money from their parents. It amazed him, however, that none of these friends showed the slightest interest in the actual principles of heavier-than-air flight. All the money he collected went into his special fund for buying rubber bands, wheels, balsa wood, glue and other necessities. A carpenter supplied him with strips of wood made to measure. From a clockmaker, who belonged to a military association and happened to vote for his father to be its chairman, Gerhard received brass cog-wheels, solder and metal parts all for free.

In 1908, when he was 12 or 13, he was in the main park in Bonn and flying a model plane. It was a quiet Sunday morning. Suddenly a voice called out: 'Hey, you good-for-nothing, what are you up to? Can't you read? The sign says "No walking on the grass." That applies to you too.'[46] It was the park attendant. Gerhard was indignant. The last thing he wanted in his moment of triumph was an annoyance like this. Didn't the stupid man realise that he was actually witnessing a portentous moment in German aeronautical history?[47] His model had just made its maiden flight, sweeping gracefully over the greensward and making a perfect landing a hundred metres from where he had released it. Ignoring Gerhard's explanation, he unceremoniously took custody of the model aircraft, saying that he would leave it at the university, where the youngster could ask for it back in a few days' time.

Crestfallen he drifted off home, where of course he could expect no sympathy. Did no-one realise that he was a successor of the great Otto Lilienthal, and that he might one day outshine the famous French aviator, Henri Farman, who had recently built a successful biplane? Did they not grasp that the significance of what he was doing? How could he help not being fascinated by aviation, and was it not the case that his own life was running parallel to the achievements – and sacrifices – of the early flyers? He would show this nincompoop of a park attendant *and* his parents what he was capable of.

As yet he had not resolved to be become an aviator. In any case he surely assumed that flying was the exclusive pastime of the moneyed classes. For the time being he was content to devour aeroplane magazines and build model aircraft. One of these was especially innovative: 'a two-motor

---

45   Fieseler, op. cit., pp.28-29.
46   Ibid, p.9.
47   Fieseler, op. cit., p.9, describes the event in the park as a *'geschichtsträchtigen Augenblick.'*

plane.'[48] With two small drives activated by rubber bands the model could take off by itself from the ground. That led to a bigger version which had a wingspan of two metres. The young Fieseler, who was plainly irked by his father's singular lack of support for his interest in aviation, nevertheless described these days of his first experimental flights with his models as 'a wonderful time.'[49] His passion for his hobby grew, as the flights became more successful. As a result the models improved, but so far his designs were based on illustrations he had seen in newspapers. He endeavoured to understand the secrets of flight and before long got the hang of building models that had the characteristics he wanted.

Space at home was limited for making his latest model, so he worked on it in a small room in the printing shop. When it was finished, he hung it on the wall in a narrow passage. By unfortunate chance one of the young printers knocked it on his way down the passage, damaging a wing. Gerhard, who witnessed this, was beside himself. 'Couldn't you have watched out?', he exploded. The young printer just shrugged his shoulders. 'Sorry', he muttered, 'but I've got better things to do than keep an eye open for your toys!'[50]

At this point, aware of a disturbance, Fieseler *père* came along to find out what was going on. Without a word he grabbed the model aircraft and in a fury smashed it into small pieces and placed the wreckage at his son's feet. 'This damn thing has no business here', he shouted. 'You've obviously got too much spare time. Well, things are going to change from now on.'[51] His teenage son stood before him, stunned, incapable of any utterance. He looked at his father with boundless hurt on his face. His father, saying nothing, turned on his heels and went back into his office. Gerhard was choked with a terrible anguish. In that moment something between him and his father lay in ruins – their relationship had, in his words, been 'smashed to bits' (*zerbrochen*), the very word he had just used to describe what his father had done to his model. The incident left a deep wound, which never healed.

A pleasant and decidedly infectious ailment
Although daily work continued as before, a wretched atmosphere affected both the family and the business. Gerhard became enveloped in self-pity. What mother, he grieved, would not find the despondency of her fourteen year old firstborn son painful, would not regret what had come to pass, would not want to help? He was aware that his parents held serious discussions about him and once he overheard a conversation, in which his father muttered something about his son neglecting his duties. That was typical of his father, just thinking solely of the business and regarding him as cheap labour. To this remark his mother had responded, 'If Gerhard is so taken with it all, then we ought to let him have his little pleasures.'[52]

Neither his father nor his mother understood that their eldest child was suffering from what one of the first aeronautical journals chirpily called 'aeronitis', which was 'a pleasant and decidedly infectious ailment which makes its victims "flighty" mentally and physically. At times it has a pathologic, at times a psychologic foundation. It has already affected thousands, it will get to the rest of the world in time.'[53] How Gerhard would have been delighted to be diagnosed with this strange, modern malady! It would be a badge of honour with which to impress his school friends.

48 Fieseler, op. cit. p.30.
49 Ibid, p.30.
50 Ibid, p.30.
51 Ibid, p.30.
52 Ibid, p.31.
53 Cited in: Kennett, op. cit., p.12.

As much as he could, Gerhard followed the action of the world of aviation. In 1909 Blériot had flown across the English Channel in just under half an hour. Then another Frenchman, Henri Farman, had completed a non-stop 234 kilometre flight, whilst the most famous German airman around this time, Hans Grade, had made the first successful flight in his monoplane. Grade was also the first aviator to execute a flat figure of eight. Then Farman had caused a stunning sensation by flying 463 kilometres in just over eight hours. By now airfields were shooting up all over Germany with the magnet – the Mecca – for aviation being Johannisthal, an airfield close to Berlin. One aviator who knew Johannisthal very well was the Dutch pilot and aircraft designer, Anthony Fokker (1890-1939), who was the very embodiment of the 'enterprising pilot' who knew how 'to earn a living from flying in those days': he had 'panache, business acumen and not a little courage.'[54] Well before the outbreak of war Fokker remembers Johannisthal as 'lively, small cosmopolitan city' (*Weltstadt*) … Flying was a new sport, which attracted brave men, as well as ne'er-do-wells and adventurers from all over the world.'[55]

Tens of thousands of spectators – suited gentlemen in bowler hats and ladies in all their finery – would flock to newly created aerodromes to see the intrepid airmen take to the skies in what look by today's standards rickety jalopies. Fokker notes of his experiences at Johannisthal that 'many amateur aviators were sons of rich parents who were on the look-out for thrills.' The pilots themselves were lionised as Formula One drivers or world-class footballers are today. Their daredevilry 'made them the heroes of the day and' – ooh là là – 'attractive females from the theatres and night clubs were only too keen to bestow their favours on them.'[56] (The assiduous Fokker had no time for those distractions.) And, if there were a crash or fatality, this excitingly confirmed the danger of the new sport, reinforced the audacious image of airmen, and 'attracted spectators in even greater numbers.'[57]

In addition to the revelry, the cafés and even a casino as well as the air shows, Johannisthal was where serious technical knowledge was traded and patents sold. The hangars eventually became places of aircraft manufacture. Thus the airfield was a kind of cross between place of spectacle and science park. By this time there was in Germany any number of 'specialized journals or magazines … to feed the popular taste [about] anything to do with aeronautics.'[58] Aeroplane modelling became a new hobby for boys. Gerhard would have been one among thousands of young enthusiasts all over Germany.

In the meantime Gerhard's school days were coming to an end. In October 1910, half way between his fourteenth and fifteenth birthday he put aside his satchel for good. For the foreseeable future he would be working for his father full-time. He was very conscious that he had not learned a good deal at school. We have no inkling from Gerhard as to which subjects he was good at or less good at. It would, however, be reasonable to assume that he was good at mathematics. But we can be certain that he would have been educated in a curriculum that was underpinned with what was called 'a national foundation.'[59]

For generations the leaders of Germany 'had worked … to inspire their people with a patriotic conviction of the grandeur of their country's destiny.'[60] For his part, the Kaiser wanted young people – boys, primarily, if not exclusively – to be educated as 'Germans, not as Greeks and Romans.'[61]

54   A. Goodrum, *Balloons, Blériots and Barnstormers: 200 Years of Flying for Fun*, p.96.
55   A. H. G. Fokker, *Der Fliegende Holländer: Die Memoiren des A. H. G. Fokker*, p.82.
56   Ibid, p.82.
57   Ibid, p.110.
58   Kennett, op. cit., p.12.
59   C. Clark, *Kaiser Wilhelm II: A Life in Power*, p.60.
60   Liddell Hart, op. cit., p.54.
61   Clark, op. cit., p.61.

They should leave school with a strong sense of the Fatherland and a willingness to serve it – and even fight for it – to the best of their capacity. The imperatives of this 'particularly toxic nationalist mythology' were patriotism, obedience, duty.[62] Germany, in the Kaiser's view, was entering 'a new glorious era.' He, as his country's far-seeing, benevolent and exceptionally gifted ruler, 'had been called as the instrument of God to the lead the German people' into it.[63]

One day in the following spring his mother told him that the two of them were going for a walk up the Kreuzberg, a hill that overlooked Bonn. They had a heart-to-heart conversation, no doubt with her husband's approval, though possibly with his misgivings. Gerhard poured his heart out, telling her how much he loved anything to do with aviation and how he suffered because his father so strongly opposed his passion.

'You must understand your father', his mother said, adding that phrase known to all children when they can't understand why a parent is so dismissive of their enthusiasms: 'He only wants what's best for you.'[64] Father, she went on, was worried that Gerhard was wasting his time on something that had no future. Gerhard bridled at this. How could his father overlook what is happening before our eyes and refuse to speak to him about it? His mother would not be drawn into criticism of her husband, but Gerhard felt very cheered to have had this candid conversation. At least he knew that his mother always had a special place in her heart for him.

On the way back Gerhard told his mother that a school friend of his, Heinrich Döpenbacker, was going on to study at the *Gymnasium* – an academically oriented secondary school – thanks to a church scholarship. He wished that he could enjoy the good fortune of continuing his education, but he knew there was no possibility of his family affording the fees. His deeply religious mother consoled him with these words: 'Gerhard, my boy, pray to God and keep His commandments. Faith will sustain you against all setbacks. Keep educating yourself. There are always books that contain the learning you need.'[65]

Shortly after that Gerhard and Heinrich made a pact with each other. His friend would bring him books to improve his knowledge. In return Gerhard would help him with his homework and test him on his lessons. Gerhard was convinced that he was learning just as much as Heinrich despite the fact that he had to work long hours in the printing shop. Otherwise he still managed to devote time to building model aircraft. We can only assume that his mother prevailed upon her husband to turn a blind eye to their son's all-consuming hobby.

The decision of his life

The family business was now well established, and the Fieselers moved to a bigger house. With expansion of the business Gerhard's own responsibilities grew, and with the new home came a valuable advantage: he had more space for making his model aircraft. One day, at the beginning of 1912, Gerhard heard that Bruno Werntgen, who three years earlier when aged just sixteen had been the youngest pilot in the world, was bringing to Bonn both of his Dorner monoplanes (Dorner, not Dornier), and he would give a flying exhibition. The papers were full of stories about him and his wealthy mother, herself an aviatrix and co-founder in 1909 of the German Aeronautical Institute. By the time he arrived in Bonn, Werntgen had flown at air shows all over Germany. Gerhard, needless to say, simply had to see him. He made five bicycle trips to the temporary airfield, but did not get anywhere near his hero.

62 S. Anderson, *Lawrence in Arabia: War, Deceit, Imperial Folly and the Making of the Modern Middle East*, p.29.
63 Röhl, op. cit., p.74.
64 Fieseler, op. cit., p.32.
65 Ibid, p.32.

Then, one Sunday afternoon Werntgen was going to give a display. Gerhard made certain that he was as near as possible to the aircraft in order to have a close view of the take-off. Everything he observed was in a way not at all new to him. He studied the airplanes and their manoeuvres with the eye of a budding expert. As he saw Werntgen complete his flight with a perfect landing on the grass, he made the decision of his life: he too would become an aviator.

He made a further visit to the airfield in the company of his father. Given the latter's loathing of anything to do with flying, it is strange that he should bother to get so close to the objects of his violent disapproval alongside his son. Perhaps in his own way he was trying for once to show a certain parental solidarity with his youngster. That might have been his purpose beforehand, but afterwards he made no comment whatsoever until they were getting near to home. Finally he broke his silence: 'That young man won't live long. He's a show-off with a wealthy mother. When I see all that flying, it reminds me of a high-wire act in a circus, but without a safety net.'[66]

Gerhard retorted that the newspapers were always writing stories about flying records being broken, adding that there was a time when people never took the railways seriously and now everyone was going by train. It wasn't an argument that cut much ice with his father, who rounded on his son with incredulity. 'You don't actually think that there is any future in flying, do you?', he hissed. Gerhard in reply pointed to various flying achievements starting with the Wright Brothers and mentioning that the year before the Frenchman Pégoud had performed the first loop the loop. This answer vexed his father, who became very agitated. 'You are a mere apprentice', he snapped, 'and your job is follow my instructions. Show what you are capable of and clear your head of these stupid ideas.' And then came the dreaded command. 'I don't want to see any more model aircraft in my house. They are banned. You mark my words!'[67]

Gerhard was utterly downcast. His father simply refused to see the truth when it was staring him in the face, and now this preposterous ban. We do not know of his mother's reaction to her husband's decision. No doubt she, as ever a dutiful wife, supported him in public, as it were, but grieved bitterly for her son in private. But, undeterred, Gerhard would for the first time in his life blatantly defy his father. At night, when everyone was asleep, he would slip out of his bed and continue to build his model planes. But things could not go on like this. Anxiety and stress overpowered him and he fell into a raging fever. A doctor was summoned, who pronounced that the young man was suffering either from pleurisy or tuberculosis. He would have to be committed to his bed for a very long time. Treatment in hospital was out of the question, as his parents had no insurance for such an eventuality and could certainly not afford to pay the hospital fees.

It took several months for the fever to loosen its grip. Even when he was no longer confined to his bed, still Gerhard needed more weeks to recuperate. During this period he somehow kept up to date with aviation matters. He became convinced that the French had extended their aeronautical lead and were now grasping the military significance of aircraft. Germany, he worried, was slow in comparison, and under no circumstances, he wrote patriotically, should France, 'our hereditary enemy' be allowed to gain superiority in the air over the Fatherland.[68] Gerhard then, in his fifteenth or sixteenth year, plainly aware of the need for military preparedness, was beginning to develop a sense of air-mindedness: the awareness that Germany's destiny and future greatness was directly bound up with releasing the potential of the greatest technological symbol of the age, the aeroplane.[69]

66 Ibid, p.34.
67 Ibid, p.35.
68 Ibid, p.35.
69 P. Fritzsche, Machine Dreams: Airmindedness and the Reinvention of Germany, *American Historical Review*, pp.685-709.

In fact the government *was* fearful of Germany's vulnerability. Indeed, as of 1910 the Prussian War Ministry had started to step up the training of pilots and the purchase of aircraft. Two years later, at the instigation of Prince Heinrich, the Kaiser's brother – alias 'the flying Hohenzollern' – the German National Aviation Fund (*Nationalflugspende*) was set up with a subvention of seven million gold marks.[70] Not only, incidentally, did the fund support the Germany's aircraft manufacturers; it was also a boost to its motor car industry, which plainly saw scope for equipping aeroplanes with their engines.

Then in 1912, on 1 October to be precise, a truly significant event in Gerhard's aeronautical world occurred. Germany's first military air force was established. Its full name was the Imperial Prussian Flying Corps (*Die Königlich-Preußische Fliegertruppe*). Gerhard does not record this event, but it is hard to believe that he did not know about it. Around this time he might even have read in the newspapers or in a magazine that in the Balkan Wars of 1912-13 the Bulgarian air force had used a German aircraft, an Albatros biplane made by Fokker.[71] One day, it would have greatly surprised him to know, he would be flying one himself.

All the while there were more and more air shows. Airfields that originally catered for balloonists now became havens for aviators. The epicentre of German aeronautism was, as noted earlier, Berlin Johannisthal, where in 1912 half a million spectators are said to have flocked to see the acrobatic flying of the French airman Pégoud, who demonstrated looping the loop in a Blériot monoplane. Despite all this public interest in flying, the matter remained a taboo topic in the Fieseler household. Gerhard's father left his son in peace, once he was well and truly satisfied that his son was no longer building model aircraft on the premises. His son battened down the hatches and performed his duties in the printing shop. Before long Fieseler *père* began to appreciate his son's hard work and conscientiousness. 'You've got what it takes to be my successor', he said approvingly one day.[72] That in all probability made no impression on Gerhard whatsoever.

Without being able to pursue his adored hobby, Gerhard decided to embark on what he called 'a kind of education concept' with the aim of becoming a cultured person.[73] In addition to reading specialist books (which unfortunately he does not name), he took up swimming and other sports, and went to the theatre notably to attend Sunday afternoon performances by the Cologne Opera Company, which was a regular visitor to Bonn. Paying 30 pfennigs he would go up to the gallery and get to know the famous operas of Verdi, Puccini, Beethoven and Wagner. He also went to see the plays of Gerhart Hauptmann, which parts were played by actors who one day would become famous throughout Germany.

On 25 February 1913 (Fieseler is quite precise about the date) he returned home from swimming to find his mother in an agitated state. 'Have you heard?', she asked in a shocked voice, 'Bruno Werntgen was in a crash. He's been killed.'[74] Full of apprehension she looked at Gerhard, who did not respond at all as she had anticipated. 'You have to reckon on things like that,' he replied soberly; by which he meant that flying was still in its infancy and so lives would have to be sacrificed for the sake of progress. His mother didn't seem to grasp that or rather did not want to, presumably knowing by now her son's ambition to be an aviator. But he wasn't being cynical when he said that. Crashes, he knew, were part and parcel of the harsh realities of aviation. In his autobiography he made his thinking absolutely clear: 'It's a question of a task, only created for a man, who can

70 Kennett, op. cit., p.14.
71 W. Mühlbauer, Deutsche Aufklärer und Bomber bis 1917, in: Ringlstetter, op. cit., p.7.
72 Fieseler, op. cit., p.36.
73 Ibid, p.36.
74 Ibid, p.36.

commit himself utterly and completely to a cause.'[75] It reads rather like a declaration of intent; but it could easily be an epitaph.

February 1914: A moment's bliss
There are in Fieseler's autobiography some family photographs, all black and white, of course, and slightly faded. His father August is perhaps in his early fifties. His grey-white hair is receding at the front. We have portrayed him in his dealings with Gerhard as a stern father, quick-tempered, morose. Yet the photograph is a revelation. Here is a man with a kindly face, with the hint of smile on his lips and – this is unmistakable – with eyes that cannot suppress a twinkle. Opposite is a photograph of his mother Katharina in middle age, perhaps in her late forties, showing her with permed hair and wearing rimless spectacles. She is tight-lipped, is unsmiling, and looks slightly forbidding. This lady is a matriarch. There is nothing in this photograph that gives a hint of her warm-hearted worldliness, which Gerhard so much admired. Yet, comparing the photographs it is easy to see why Gerhard described his mother having the stronger soul.

There is also a photograph of Gerhard aged 16, looking very much the young gentleman, wearing his Sunday best, a thick woollen suit with wide lapels and a waistcoat. His shirt with its stiffly starched collar looks gleaming white overshadows his neatly knotted tie. This is a good-looking boy brought up in a respectable family. His fair hair is parted in the middle. He has his father's eyes, unquestionably blue. His face shows calm resolve and intelligence.

Gerhard grew up in an authoritarian household. As was the custom in those days, his father had the last word on everything. His children were there to obey him. Gerhard's relationship with him was extremely difficult. His feelings were variously marked by filial respect, out-and-out disrespect, and occasional loathing. August could not fathom out his son's obsession with the new-fangled flying contraptions. He would though live long enough to see his son achieve national and international fame as an aerobatics pilot. It would be tempting to say that August left no mark on his son, but this is not the case. Gerhard himself admitted that he had drawn a positive lesson from the unfair treatment that he father meted out to him: it helped him bear setbacks and adversity. But that is not all. August was tenacious and so was Gerhard. And one more thing: as we shall see, Gerhard inherited his father's temper.

Gerhard adored his mother. If he had not had so many brothers and sisters, then he would surely have received in his childhood more loving attention from her and especially in his teenage years, when his relationship with his father hit rock-bottom. But, as already noted, she made a maternal point of honour to distribute her love and affection to her children on equal basis. From her Gerhard unquestionably inherited a certain idealized outlook on life.

In his autobiography Gerhard's life up to the outbreak of the First World War takes up less than forty pages. He emerges as a likeable person devoid of arrogance and self-importance. The two big influences on his life are his mother and his enthusiasm for flying. But an emerging theme, once he has left school, is his determination to educate himself to make up for the fact that his family could not afford for him to go to the *Gymnasium*. In his own way therefore he is in great mould of what the Germans call *Bildung*. This key word in German culture, often translated as education, refers to the inner formation of an individual through education and the quest for knowledge to fulfil a moral purpose and make the best of one's innate talents.[76] *Bildung* then was seen as the key to the rounded person. Evidently, that is what Gerhard aspired to be.

---

75   Ibid, p.36.
76   For discussion of the term *Bildung*, see Watson, op. cit., pp.53-54.

Gerhard was fifteen when he resolved to be an aviator; but by then, and this is an important aspect of it, he had carefully studied the principles of flight without any tutoring whatsoever. We do not even know if he read Lilienthal's famous book on the topic. If his models flew higher or longer than anyone else's, it was because he had made them that way, whereby even as a boy 'technical perfection played an important role' in his designs.[77] No-one, not even his father, who ran a business completely dependent on well-functioning machinery, grasped the significance of this technical prowess. It was no coincidence, Gerhard liked to believe, that he had been born at the time when man's age old dream of flying became a reality through the invention of powered flight. He therefore saw it as his destiny to become an aviator.

In 1914, when it was the Rhineland Carnival, he went for the first time to a masked ball. He revelled in moving about in the brightly coloured costumes. But there was something he was after, and at one o'clock in the morning he had triumphed. He'd been dancing with a very pretty young woman and then he escorted her and her sister back to their home. As he bid farewell on her doorstep, he made a lunge and kissed his attractive dancing partner. Oh, that ever remembered first kiss! He was simply floating on air as he made his way home through the dark streets. Yet, so he tells us, he soon fell into a somewhat perplexed state of mind. This had nothing to do with the pretty young woman. It was, he tells us, a vague awareness that his life was about to undergo a huge transformation.

The carnival would have taken place in February 1914. If the young Gerhard Fieseler, who was seventeen at that time, had any premonition of what shape this transformation might take, it cannot have been remotely like what it was really going to happen. Neither he nor anyone else in Germany or indeed elsewhere could have imagined what horrors awaited Europe in the fateful summer of that year. In August, immediately after the declaration of war, Gerhard left home and volunteered to join the newly formed Imperial Flying Corps. But how much flying could he actually expect to do as a complete novice? After all it was common knowledge that the war would be over by the end of the year at the very latest. Indeed, the Kaiser, who knew all about these things, had proudly told his troops as they set off for battle: 'You will be home before the leaves have fallen from the trees.'[78]

---

77 R. Nagel, R. und T. Bauer, *Kassel und die Luftfahrtindustrie seit 1923: Geschichte(n), Menschen, Technik*, p.425.
78 R. MacLean, *Berlin: Imagine a City*, p.141.

2

Some damn silly thing in the Balkans

Stripped of all its high-minded justifications and rhetoric, at its core this war had many of the trappings of an extended family feud, a chance for Europe's kings and emperors – many of them related by blood – to act out old grievances and personal slights atop the heaped bodies of their loyal subjects.

Scott Anderson[1]

The incessant elaboration and development of the tactics and science of trench warfare called so urgently for the rapid development of efficient aeroplanes that might truthfully say that trench warfare was the father of the modern flying machine.

Major Georg Paul Neumann[2]

The zenith of imperialistic rivalry

After a hundred years there is no agreement among historians as to the precise sequence of events that led to the break-out of a general European war in 1914; and 'there is no danger that controversy … will ever be stilled.'[3] In the words of the eminent historian, Christopher Clark: 'The surviving sources … offer up a chaos of promises, threats, plans and prognostications – and this in turn helps to explain why the outbreak of this war has proved susceptible to such a bewildering variety of interpretations.'[4] There is, however, one fact that no-one disputes. The summer of that baleful year was delightful. The novelist Stefan Zweig recalled the weather in Vienna at the end of June: 'Throughout the days and nights the heavens were a silky blue, the soft air not yet sultry, the meadows fragrant and warm.'[5] What, unless some malevolent god of the weather were to turn summer into winter and light into darkness, could bring these balmy days to unseasonable end?

But then, on the 26 June, the Archduke Ferdinand, heir to that 'heterogeneous relic of the Middle Ages' – the Austro-Hungarian Empire – was gunned down along with his wife in Sarajevo, capital of the Austrian province of Bosnia.[6] The culprits were caught; the trail led to Belgrade, capital of Serbia. On 29 July, after a month of dithering, and having in the meantime secured tacit German support for any retaliatory action it might take to deal with its 'pestilential Balkan nuisance,' Austria moved. Austro-Hungarian artillery bombarded Belgrade. These were the very first shots of the First World War.[7]

---

1 S. Anderson, *Lawrence in Arabia: War, Deceit, Imperial Folly and the Making of the Modern Middle East*, p.70.
2 P. G. Neumann, *The German Air Force in the Great War*, pp.36-37.
3 M. Hastings, *Catastrophe: Europe Goes to War*, p.xx.
4 C. Clark, *The Sleepwalkers: How Europe Went to War in 1914*, p.xxiv.
5 Cited in: S. McMeekin, *July 1914: Countdown to War*, p.23.
6 B. H. Liddell Hart, *History of the First World War*, p.17.
7 Hastings, op. cit., p.58.

From now on 'the powder train fizzled rapidly towards detonation.'[8] For Wilhelm II – 'febrile, tactless, panic-prone, overbearing' – there could be no turning back.[9] There was a flurry of declarations of war; diplomacy had failed. The Germans set in motion the sacrosanct Schlieffen plan, which had taken 14 years to evolve, and which anticipated the eventuality of Germany having to fight simultaneously against France and Russia. Under this plan, which has been described as being 'precise to the number of train axles that would pass over a given bridge within a given time,'[10] the German army would smash the French army rapidly and then turn on Russia – 'a land of military mediocrity' – before the Tsar could properly organise his forces.[11] On 3 August the German army, 'the most formidable military machine in Europe'[12] crossed the border into 'gallant little Belgium' on its way to France.[13]

On the following day Germany, having refused to withdraw its troops from Belgium, was at war with Great Britain. The opening of hostilities caused the British Foreign Secretary, Sir Edward Grey, to deliver his famous words: 'The lights are going out all over Europe; we will not see them lit again in our lifetime.' Less remembered are the prophetic words of the former German Chancellor, Prince Otto von Bismarck, uttered in 1890: 'If ever there is another war in Europe, it will come out of some damned silly thing in the Balkans!'[14]

On all sides everyone imagined that the war 'would be an affair of great marches and great battles, quickly decided. It would be over by Christmas. Men did not debate why they were fighting. They knew. It was to defend *la patrie*, the Fatherland, or Holy Russia.'[15] It was, however, not quite the same with Britain, where its Grand Fleet would deter any invader. The British would fight 'to make the world safe for democracy'; it would be a question of 'a war to end war.'[16] The Great Powers of Europe split into two opposing alliances. There was the Entente composed of France, Great Britain and Russia. Opposing them were the Central Powers represented by Germany and Austro-Hungary. In the course of the war other countries would join one alliance or the other: the Ottoman Empire joined the Central Powers in November 1914 and the USA entered the war on the side of the Entente in April 1917.

Under the general mobilisation there would be a great gathering of men to join the colours, some 10 million in all, not to mention further millions of animals throughout the duration of the conflict. Of the latter the contending armies would, as it were, call up 20 million horses,[17] thousands of dogs (at least 20,000 of man's best friend on the British and French side), donkeys, mules (of the latter the British alone used 230,000) and, again on the British side, 100,000 carrier pigeons.[18] Neither man nor beast was to be spared the monstrous meat-grinder. So it was that 'imperialistic rivalry celebrated its zenith by persuading all the Eurasian empires to divert their enormous economic and technological resources into one vast industrial conglomerate of death.'[19]

---

8   Hughes-Wilson, *A History of the First World War in 100 Objects*, p.37.
9   Clark, op. cit., p.170.
10 B. Tuchman, *The Proud Tower: A Portrait of the World Before the War, 1890-1914*, p.94. Cited in McMeekin, op. cit., p 342.
11 Liddell Hart, op. cit., p.44.
12 Hastings, op. cit., p.26.
13 H. Strachan, *The First World War*, p.50.
14 Hughes-Wilson, op. cit., p.28.
15 A. J. P. Taylor, *The First World War: An Illustrated History*, p.22.
16 Ibid, p.22
17 A German estimates that 10 million horse shoes needed replacing every month. See: G. Krumeich, *Die wichtigsten 100 Fragen: Der Erste Weltkrieg*, p.133.
18 Hughes-Wilson, op. cit, pp., 188-191, notes that 47,000 camels were used the Imperial Camel Corps.
19 M. Glenny, *The Balkans: Nationalism, War and the Great Powers*, p.308.

August 1914: Marvellous prospects

As far as the eighteen year old Gerhard Fieseler was concerned, the war offered two marvellous prospects. First, he could join the Kaiser's Flying Corps and fulfil his ambition to become a pilot. Second, and almost as good, he could escape from his tyrannical father. It was destiny; '1914: I saw my hour come', he proudly writes in his autobiography.[20] The Dutch airman, Anthony Fokker, about whom there will be more to say, was another happy opportunist. In his inimitably buoyant language he wrote: 'The dance had begun, somebody somewhere was paying for the music, and we all joined in.'[21]

Like millions of other Europeans, Fieseler would have known very little indeed about the reasons behind the general descent into war following the assassinations in Sarajevo but a few weeks earlier. But he would of course have known about the extraordinary rash of declarations of war in the last few days. However, looking for reasons or questioning decisions made in palaces, chancelleries and ministries in Berlin and other capital cities of Europe did not seemingly cross his mind. Nor was he alone in that attitude.

The Fatherland was calling up its young men, who were not yet enlisted, to join up. Fieseler's duty as a loyal subject of the Kaiser was to offer himself for his country's defence. He saw himself as being welcomed into a wholly new brotherhood of fellow flyers. He would be deployed near the front in the grand tradition of balloon observers with one big difference: he would be surveying the dispositions of the Fatherland's enemies from on high in a new-fangled aeroplane. As a brilliant aviator he would report back accurately what he had observed to grateful superiors, and in his own particular way contribute to Germany's victory. But from the very beginning his war would not go like that at all.

When war broke out, Fieseler recalls, the citizens of Bonn were 'in a big flap' (*in heller Aufregung*).[22] People there and in other cities throughout Germany congregated on the stations and main squares to pick up the latest news intermingled with much rumour and hear-say. Stations and the roads to stations were especially thronged with people seeing off the young men on the way to catch the special trains to the front. Others would make for post-offices, where official news bulletins were posted on doors and windows, and for cafés in order to read and pass round the latest issues of newspapers.

All the while, conspiracy theories abounded, as the rumour mills went into overdrive. Spy mania was rampant. In Bonn, Fieseler tells us, 'spies' were hunted down, apprehended and taken away (he makes a point of putting the word 'spies' in inverted commas).[23] The trains conveying troops were adorned with flowers and were cheered on their way to the Belgian frontier. The carriages had slogans daubed up on the sides: 'All aboard – plenty of room', 'Declarations of war welcome' and – with German eyes fixed on Paris – 'See you on the boulevards.'[24] But after four Christmases of war the trains going to the Western Front carried altogether different slogans like: 'Cannon fodder for Flanders.'[25]

The young men of Bonn were filled with enthusiasm, Fieseler recalls. Recruiting stations were overrun and even stopped accepting any more volunteers. You heard the same thing everywhere: 'The war will be over in few months. We'll give them' – the despised French, that is – 'what for.'[26] Fieseler too

---

20 G. Fieseler, *Meine Bahn am Himmel*, p.37.
21 A. H. G. Fokker, *Der Fliegende Holländer: Die Memoiren des A. H. G. Fokker*, p.144.
22 Fieseler, op. cit., p.37.
23 Ibid, p.37.
24 S. Burgdorff und K. Wiegrefe (Hrsg), *Spiegel Special über den 1. Weltkrieg und die Folgen: Die Katastrophe des 20. Jahrhunderts*, p.32.
25 Strachan, op. cit., p.282.
26 Fieseler, op. cit., p.37.

got caught up in the general excitement. Most of people of his age were joining up. These memories of Fieseler of the public reaction to news of the outbreak of war are of considerable interest and are worth a few moments' comment. They support the received wisdom that in the countries concerned there was great jubilation at the opportunity to get stuck into unworthy enemies. Today, however, historians today are taking a far more nuanced view. They contend that the myth 'that European men leapt at the opportunity to defeat a hated enemy has been comprehensively dispelled.'[27] Indeed, according to one of the UK's authorities on the First World War, if 'the photographs of August 1914 suggest a party mood … those were braves faces for the camera.'[28]

According to the historian Jeffrey Verhey, these excited crowds were 'an urban phenomenon'[29] and 'mostly educated youths, university students and clerks predominated.'[30] He notes that 'there were three areas in Germany where there were almost no accounts of any enthusiastic or even curious crowds in the first two weeks of the war: in the countryside, in the working-class areas of large cities, and in the areas near the border.'[31] Glesch, where Fieseler was born, was a case in point. Twelve of its young men had fought against France in 1870-71 and three never returned. One of those who did return was his maternal grandfather, who had been awarded an Iron Cross for bravery. He did not like to talk about those times, only telling Gerhard and his other grandchildren that he like everyone had done his duty for the Fatherland.

In August 1914 the mothers, wives and sisters of Glesch would find themselves in silent, sombre solidarity with other anxious women throughout Germany, whether they dwelt in farmsteads, urban tenements or fashionable mansions. By no stretch of the imagination then was outbreak of war received with unalloyed jubilation in Germany. Nor, as the historian A. J. P. Taylor reminds us, should we forget that 'the German industrialists did not want war. They were convinced, and with good reason, that Germany would soon become the leading Power in Europe from sheer economic power.'[32] The Kaiser, his entourage and all other Pan-Germans had no time for that misplaced idea: 'they greeted the outbreak of war in 1914 with unbounded enthusiasm, verging on ecstasy.'[33]

A machine to ensnare men's souls
Gerhard Fieseler was not to be deterred for one moment from his grand objective. He packed his things and his mother prepared something to eat for his journey. He recalls her tenderly stroking his hair. Perhaps she had not done that since his childhood. His father accompanied him to the station, taking him to task on his unsuitable frame of mind for military life (a fine one to talk!). Needless to say, Gerhard paid no attention. The parting was brief, a cursory hand-shake, a few awkward phrases. In next to no time he was on the train with a free travel pass as a volunteer, heading for Darmstadt to join a flying unit (*Fliegerabteilung*/FA).

He tells us that there were only eight such units in all of Germany, but this seems to be an underestimate. According the well-informed Wilhelm Siegert, a major general appointed to the Inspectorate of Aviation (*Inspektion der Fliegertruppen*) in Berlin, 'the Germany army took the field in 1914 with 49 flying detachments.' It is, however, possible that Fieseler's figure of eight refers to pilot reserve units (*Fliegerersatzabteilung*/FEA), which had the task of 'securing the fresh supply (*Ersatz*) of personnel for the front, seeing to appropriate training and taking care that the supply of

27 Clark, op. cit., p.553.
28 Strachan, op. cit., p.63.
29 J. Verhey, *The Spirit of 1914: Militarism, Myth and Mobilization in Germany*, p.68.
30 Ibid, p.31.
31 Verhej, op. cit., p.91.
32 Taylor, op. cit., p.15.
33 R. Evans, *The Coming of the Third Reich*, p.67.

matériel matched requirements.'[34] As such they served as centres for selection and initial training prior to secondment to the actual flying units. However, according to Siegert, there were 15 of these entities in Germany in 1914, not eight.[35]

If Fieseler wants us to believe that 'the fundamental significance of the aeroplane' was not appreciated by the military authorities and that as a consequence Germany was under-equipped for war in the air, his fears were misplaced.[36] Consider the following statistics. According to a historian at the Centre for Military History and Social Sciences in Potsdam, the figures for German pilots 'fluctuate from 220 to 450 depending on the author.' His own considered estimate is that the Germans started the war with 'about 240 aircraft with 254 trained pilots and 271 trained observers.'[37] France's Aviation Militaire had 200 aircraft and 500 trained pilots.[38] The British began the war with around 100 military aeroplanes[39] and 197 trained pilots.[40]

At the start of the war French biplanes flew between 50 and 70 miles per hour, and 'required between thirty minutes and sixty minutes to reach an altitude of 6,000 feet.'[41] A German reconnaissance plane with a 100hp engine flew at 55 to 60mph. Its ceiling, when fully laden, was about 5,000 feet and could remain in the air for four to five hours.[42] Figures for the Royal Flying Corps are comparable, but one British aircraft, the Royal Aircraft Factory B.E. 2, first introduced in 1912, was able to attain the amazing height of 10,000 feet by the outbreak of war. This aeroplane also had a valuable property which was rare at the outbreak of war: it was 'a properly stable aircraft.'[43]

At all events it would seem that the performance of German aircraft was comparable to that of their French and British adversaries, though it is of course difficult to make an accurate comparison, given that the aeroplane 'is a particularly subtle and multi-faceted machine which is difficult to reduce to numerical indices of performance.'[44] Indeed during the war, as we shall hear, 'the organization, characteristics and evolution of German air power ... specifically that of its heavier-than-air craft ... is a complex story.'[45] Fieseler would fully experience these complexities as a pilot and have the good fortune to live and tell the tale.

It will become apparent that Fieseler did not only look upon the air as a distinctive new medium of combat, but also as a source of know-how and even wonder about the capabilities of aircraft. Furthermore, if he joined the Flying Corps because there was something glamorous about being an airman, he was to become disillusioned, but not for immediately obvious reasons. His own recollection of military aeroplanes at the beginning of the war was that they were 'unsophisticated creations (*Gebilde*), unsafe and unarmed.'[46] More graphically they were 'fragile contraptions of wood, canvas, and baling wire, fit more for the circus than the battlefield.'[47] But it would not stay that way for long, especially when it came to the question of armament. As early as 1911 it had

---

34   O. Bürger, *Die Königlich-BayerischeFliegertruppe in Schleißheim und ihre Spuren in die Gegenwart*, p.28.
35   W. Siegert, Army aeroplanes, in Neumann, op. cit., p.36-56. Confusingly, *The German Army Handbook of 1918*, p.107, gives the number as 17.
36   Fieseler, op. cit., p.39.
37   S. Rosenboom, *Im Einsatz über der 'vergessenen Front': Der Luftkrieg an der Ostfront im Ersten Weltkrieg*, p.20.
38   Hastings, op. cit., p.457.
39   Hughes-Wilson, op. cit., p.160.
40   Hastings, op. cit., p.457.
41   Ibid, p.458.
42   Neumann, op. cit., p.36.
43   D. Edgerton, *England and the Aeroplane: Militarism, Modernity and Machines*, p.11.
44   Ibid, p.52.
45   D. Stone, *The Kaiser's Army: The German Army in World War One*, p.296.
46   Fieseler, op. cit., p.58.
47   P. Fritzsche, 'Machine Dreams: Airmindedness and the Reinvention of Germany', *American historical review*, pp.685-709.

been recognised that the dropping of incendiary bombs was associated with 'the principal offensive uses of the war-aeroplane.'[48]

In fact the very first dog-fight of the First World War had already been recorded at around the time that Fieseler was hoping to be accepted into the German Air Force. This took place during the battle of Cerin in Serbia from 15 to 19 August 1914. The distinguished historian of the Balkans, Misha Glenny, describes the event, when:

> one of Serbia's three aeroplanes encountered a Habsburg plane while undertaking a reconnaissance mission over Austrian army positions. The enemy aviator waved at his Serbian counterpart who returned the compliment. Aviator Tomić, whose plane looked like a box kite on perambulator wheels, watched as the Austrian pilot took out a revolver and started firing at him. Tomić ducked and wove and made it back home. From then on, all pilots were armed with hand-guns. Within weeks, machine guns had been fitted on all Austrian and Serbian planes.[49]

We can safely assume that in August 1914 Gerhard Fieseler's vision of his aerial future did not envisage him handling guns on aircraft. Whatever his dreams were, he was abruptly wretched out of them upon arrival at the airfield in Darmstadt. 'We don't need you', he was bluntly told. 'Things are just starting up here. In any case, presumably you can't fly.' He was advised to make for the legendary Johannisthal airfield near Berlin. 'You might be accepted there,' was the parting shot.[50] He caught a train to Berlin. On the way he pictured his pilot's training in glowing colours, quite possibly thinking in raptures about the great flying displays that had been put on at Johannisthal.

Fieseler was one of thirty volunteers. Accommodation turned out to be barracks of corrugated iron with straw sacks for bedding on wooden floors. They shared two taps for washing morning and evening. So what! This was wartime now! It was all part of becoming an airman. Already he would have so much to tell his family back home. But how could he describe to them perhaps one of his first and most powerful impressions: 'the smell of an aerodrome with its mingling of petrol, oil, dope ... for stiffening and weatherproofing fabric surfaces [of aircraft], and burnt gases'?[51] In due course the recruits were distributed among six civilian flying schools. At last flying lessons were about to begin. His instructor was a certain Herr Freind. Fieseler recalls him as thin and quietly spoken, who on first acquaintance gave the young man the once-over with a critical eye. He instructed the novices on a Jannin Dove, which was named after the French designer, who had built the aeroplane, unusually for the time, with a steel fuselage. Normally at that time aircraft were built in wood and wire as their basic materials.[52]

On his second day Freind took Fieseler up on two induction flights. On both occasions his instructor let him take hold of the controls. It all came quite naturally to the young man, but unfortunately he does not tell us what actually coursed through his mind and body on this pivotal day in his life. J.D. Hunter's *The Blue Max*, perhaps the most famous novel to portray aviation in the First World War, may help us. In this extract its author conveys something of a pilot's sensations in proximity to his aeroplane: 'the wood and fabric and metal, the snarl and blatting and sighing, the provocative scent of lacquer and oil and petrol and leather that made aircraft things to ensnare

---

48 J. Ayto, *Twentieth Century Words*, p.88.
49 Glenny, op. cit., p.316.
50 Fieseler, op. cit., p.38.
51 W. E. Johns, *Biggles Learns to Fly*, p.11.
52 D. Winter, *The First of the Few: Fighter Pilots of the First World War*, p.113.

men's souls.'⁵³ On the third day the recruits were sorted out. The ten youngest, who included Fieseler, were sent home, but were told to report for duty when they were older. It was a bitter disappointment for him.

So it was that to his parents' great surprise – not to mention relief – he was back at home with a cardboard box as the only souvenir of his all too brief flying days. Exactly like prospective pilots in Britain, Fieseler's first flying experiences had been 'most unpromising.'⁵⁴ 'So are you now cured of those silly ideas about flying'? His father asked him with undisguised malice. 'Absolutely not', rejoined his son. 'I flew twice, if you must know. It was tremendous!'⁵⁵

His father's printing works were already shut, because so many if the workers had been called up, and orders were reduced to a trickle. The labour shortage meant that the eighteen year old Fieseler had no difficulty in being taken on by a well-known printer as a machine operator in Cologne, which printed the main city newspaper. Six months after he started there in or around March 1915, he chanced upon a school friend, to whom he related the sad story of his all too abrupt trip to Johannisthal. 'Don't you know?' piped up his friend, 'There's going to be an FEA [i.e. flying school] at the Butzweilerhof.' Speechless, Fieseler asked where on earth that was. 'Just the other side of Ehrenfeld', came the reply. 'There are supposed to be two hangars there already.'⁵⁶

The very next day Fieseler set out for the airfield, which was on the northern outskirts of Cologne, once again thinking that the fulfilment of his dream was in palpable proximity. In the office he learnt that volunteers were being taken on for all kinds of activities. Full of expectation he filled in the questionnaire. Four weeks later he was told to report for duty. A month later he was back and found himself in the company of about 100 other volunteers. They were assigned to one company under a commander, a sergeant and a few NCOs, all of whom were seasoned infantrymen and had no particular experience of flying. Although he does not mention it, his new FEA would have included support staff including carpenters, mechanics, fitters, saddlers, upholsterers, draftsmen, clerks, a paymaster, a tailor and a doctor.⁵⁷

The accommodation was as primitive as it had been at Johannisthal, except that this time there were straw sacks on concrete floors. Running water for all was supplied by one tap. For the next three months from morning to evening there was nothing but infantry training. It was intensive and mentally as well as physically exhausting. Anyone who had put a foot wrong got an earful from the bossy sergeant, and you were lucky if things did not go beyond that. His experiences were mirrored by those of a young Italian air force recruit who wrote: 'The shock of the discipline, the privations, the heat and the cold, all these things I could put up without difficulty. The lack of privacy in our quarters, the grime, the sometimes vulgar company, all, all that seemed as nothing compared with my desire to fly.'⁵⁸ But, in Fieseler's case there was something else that deeply wrangled him. Nobody at all spoke about flying or aircraft.

Worse of course he really seemed to have ended up in the infantry. After those three months, in which presumably he learnt the basics of soldiering, he was 'promoted', as he put it, to assistant fitter (*Monteurhelfer*) in a newly built hangar. His job was to fuel airplanes, clean them, push them into and out of the hangar, and sweep the floor. But at least he was able to get close to the objects

---

53   J. D. Hunter, *The Blue Max,* pp.241-242. Something similar was expressed by a British Hurricane pilot in Second World War with reference to the alluring smell of an aircraft: 'I breathe in the distinctive smell that is exclusive to every Hurricane; a unique combination of oil, metal, sweat, hydraulic fluid, aviation fuel and rubber. It's a potent aroma, potent and reassuring' cited In: E. Carter, *Force Benedict: Churchill's Secret Mission to Save Stalin,* p.44.
54   Winter, op. cit., p.27.
55   Fieseler, op. cit., p.39.
56   Ibid, p.39.
57   Based on the description of the airfield at Schleissheim near Munich in Bürger, op. cit., p.12.
58   Cited in: L. Kennett, *The First Air War 1914-1918,* p.129.

of his desire. 'I saw a lot', he muses, 'landings good and bad, accidents, crashes, plenty of dead bodies.'[59] But nothing dissuaded from his determination to take to the air. One day on the notice board it was announced that the volunteers could apply to be trainee flyers. Ten days later the selected couple of dozen, including Fieseler, were summoned to the office of commanding officer. Giving everyone a cursory look-over, the officer asked each one his name, age and occupation. Fieseler gave his occupation as a qualified mechanic (*Maschinenmeister*). 'Fit for service', came the brisk response.[60]

That ghastly crunch

Of that two dozen, 15 were finally selected for training at an airfield on the other side of Berlin. Of this number a further eight were dismissed. Fieseler was one of seven of the original recruits who had passed what he called 'a superficial medical examination.'[61] The selected ones were taken to quarters that had been converted from a dance hall near the airfield near Köpenick on the southeast side of Berlin. This time at least the recruits slept on camp beds. At five o'clock the very next morning they were marched to the airfield. Fieseler was allotted to a certain instructor by the name of Wenk, who only three weeks before had himself been an aircraft fitter. Wenk now found himself assigned to flight training duties in the light of the chronic need for instructors.

The aircraft chosen for training was the two-seater, the LVG (*Luftverkehrsgesellschaft*), which was powered by a 120hp Mercedes engine.[62] The two-seater configuration was not only for facilitating the training of pilots with an instructor in close proximity. At the outset of the First World War the principal role of aircraft was to conduct reconnaissance by 'serving as eyes of the commander.'[63] Aircraft were accordingly designed to accommodate a pilot and an observer, the latter doubling up as a navigator and commander. In other words, the observer, who was an officer, told the pilot, who was not, where to fly. It follows that for their own safety as well as for mission success the relationship between the two men was critical. As we shall see, Fieseler as a pilot would have both highly productive as well as disastrous – if not near-suicidal – relationships with his some of his observers.

One UK historian of the First World War claimed that the LVG trainer 'with its excellent flying qualities … proved useful for training purpose.'[64] This, however, was not an opinion shared by Fieseler and presumably his fellow trainees. According to him, the aircraft was unpopular, being regarded as 'very unsafe' (*gefährlich*).[65] During his induction period Fieseler estimates that there were three fatal crashes a week at Johannisthal. This might be par for the course, but 'a fatal crash at a training field had a profound effect on all who witnessed it.'[66] One British airman, cited by the air historian Kennett, would have spoken for many with these words about 'the ghastly crunch that an airplane can make once, and only once, in the course of its lifetime.'[67]

Only after the war would it emerge just how perturbingly high the death rate was during pilot training on both sides. According to the British military historian, Denis Winter, about a quarter

---

59 Fieseler, op. cit., p.40.
60 Ibid, p.40.
61 Ibid, p.41.
62 Fieseler states that he learned to fly on a LVG-B3, but this was not introduced until 1917. It is more likely that it was the LVG-B2 which appeared in 1915. See A. Bruce, *An Illustrated Companion to the First World War*, pp.233-234.
63 J. S. Corum, World War I aviation, in M. Strohn, *World War 1 Companion*, p.62.
64 A. Bruce, *An Illustrated Companion to the First World War*, p.233.
65 Fieseler, op. cit., p.41.
66 Kennett, op. cit., p.127.
67 Ibid, p.127.

of all German pilots were killed during training.[68] According to Kennett, Germany 'began the war with 500 airmen and ended it with 5,000.'[69] The well-informed Siegert gives the precise figures for the German fatalities as 1,399 pilots and 401 observers. These figures, he cryptically adds, 'require no comment'[70], presumably implying that this was the price to be paid in war. If we accept Kennett's figures and discount the observer losses, then German pilot losses are in the region of 28%, which is slightly higher than Winter's estimate. Of those, incidentally, 28% of airmen were lost on *Heimatdienst* (service on the home front), which meant 'flying inside Germany, much but not all of it in flying schools.'[71]

As far as Great Britain was concerned, Winter suggests that of the 14,166 pilots who had lost their lives in the conflict, a staggering 8,000 – some 56% – perished in training on home soil.[72] Not surprisingly, perhaps, the Royal Flying Corps was called 'the Suicide Club.'[73] Military historian James Corum accepts the figure of 8,000, noting that the 'very informal and haphazard' training methods were 'the biggest cause of death for British airmen in World War 1.'[74] However, a PhD thesis produced at the University of Birmingham in 2003 contends that Winter 'exaggerates the losses in training fourfold.'[75] If that is correct, then the figure of 56% is reduced to 14%; in which case German losses in training are double the British ones. Winter also estimated that in the Royal Flying Corps 'about half of all flying accidents occurred in take-off' and that '10 per cent of all crashes meant death and a further 15 per cent produced severe injury.'[76] Falling out of the sky from a great height was invariably lethal. A case recorded in Britain concerns a pilot under training in Scotland, who 'fell from a height of 2,000 feet and was killed instantaneously … His body sank through a field of three years' grass to a depth of four feet and was frightfully mutilated.'[77]

Whatever trust we put into the figures of this or that author, the fact remains that airmen on all sides faced statistically high chances of death and, if not death, severe injury during training. Like Fieseler, all of them would have witnessed ample lethal or near-lethal crashes. They must have had exceptionally high levels of motivation and courage to go aloft time after time even before setting eyes on the enemy. Causes for these training deaths were legion and applied to both sides: selection of inappropriate people for flying, bad training methods, inexperienced instructors, deficient aircraft and unsatisfactory servicing and maintenance, not to mention sheer bad luck and, notoriously, lax flying discipline. For example, the encouragement of stunt flying at fairly low altitudes was a further contributory factor on both sides.[78]

As the militarisation of the skies proceeded, God's free air was not just a medium for a totally new form of military combat, it was also a laboratory in its own right. Among other things it followed that airman needed special training. But problematically not only were there no clear guidelines as to the nature of aerial warfare, but induction programmes themselves had an ad hoc quality in wartime conditions. Both factors help explain the egregious loss of pilots well before they even encountered the enemy. They also explain why Instructor Wenk was singularly unfit to train pilots. By 1916, however, it has been claimed that Germany had 'the best aerial training programme

---

68 Winter, op. cit., p.37.
69 Kennett, op. cit., p.121.
70 Siegert, Training and Personnel, in Neumann, op. cit., pp.80-96.
71 Kennett, op. cit., p.129.
72 Winter, op. cit., p.36.
73 N. Ferguson, *First World War in the Air, 2014.* p.20.
74 Corum, op. cit., p.68.
75 http://www.theaerodrome.com/forum/showthread.php?t=64756
76 Winter, op. cit., p.92.
77 Ferguson, op. cit., p.23.
78 Rickenbacker, *Fighting the Flying Circus,* p.11.

of the major powers … pilots went through a basic training course that required 65 flying hours before assignment to the front.'[79] In short, pilot training was experiencing a steep learning curve.

Many lives might have been saved with the introduction of parachutes. Only in the middle of 1917 did the German Air Force start to use parachutes; the British did not follow suit, the official reason being that availability of such life-saving equipment 'might encourage pilots to leave their aircraft unnecessarily.'[80] For his part, Eddie Rickenbacker, America's highest scoring pilot, lamented the US aversion to parachutes in the light of the positive German experiences. In August 1918 he was moved to write:

> For the past six months the German airmen had been saving their lives by aeroplane parachutes. A parachute is a very cheap contrivance compared to the cost of training an aviator. Lufbery [an accomplished airman] and a score of other American aviators might have been saved to their country if this matter of aeroplane equipment had been left to experienced pilots.[81]

This sorry commentary about parachutes is a perfect example of what happens when military thinking remote from actual operations has no idea of what is actually happening to those at the sharp end. But, more than that, it is symptomatic of the fact that the new air weapon 'had no predecessor and no precedent. The tank, after all, had been preceded by the chariot – indeed the French still use the same word, *char*, for both; and the submarine and the dreadnought, however innovative, were nevertheless ships.'[82] As for powered aircraft, there was as yet no real body of foundation knowledge to build upon. Everything was experimental: the history of flight by heavier-than-air machines was simply too short.

In the first session in the cockpit Wenk showed Fieseler the controls. In those days the pilot under training took the front seat with the instructor seating behind. This was the same procedure in the Royal Flying Corps. A speaking tube was used to ensure some kind of communication between instructor and trainee, as shouts were not always audible in slipstream.[83] After taking him up in the front seat just twice, Wenk proposed to change position so that Fieseler could take over the controls in the back. After Fieseler had made four successful landings, Wenk was well pleased: 'You've done well. As far as I'm concerned, you can fly by yourself.'[84] Rapid progress indeed! Fieseler protested, saying that he had only been up in the air twice before.

So up they went again for two more circuits. After both landings, Wenk declared: 'From now on no problem!' Again, Fieseler protested, saying: 'No, honestly, Herr Wenk, you had your hands and feet on the controls.'[85] This Wenk repudiated, and up they went yet again with the instructor taking the front seat and gesticulating to show that he was not touching the controls at all. So it was that after just nine flights with his instructor, Fieseler made his first solo flight. In 1918 Eddie Rickenbacker, made his first solo flight after a mere 12 flights with instructors.[86] It turned out German instructors got a government premium for reducing the number of pre-solo flights. There can be little doubt that this influenced their training methods, leading to the 'manufacturing [of]

---

79 Corum, op. cit., p.68
80 C. Messenger, *World War I in Colour*, p.92.
81 Rickenbacker, op. cit., p.69.
82 Kennett, op. cit., p.21.
83 Winter, op. cit., p.33.
84 Fieseler, op. cit., p.41.
85 Ibid, p.41.
86 Rickenbacker, op. cit., p.4.

pilots on an assembly line.'⁸⁷ Fieseler was now making flights without instructor. The way was now clear for him, after he had completed some 20 solo flights, to try to obtain the necessary pilot's qualifications. He must have thought that suddenly things were going his way.

According to regulations, the would-be pilot had to pass three examinations in order to obtain a pilot's badge (*Flugzeugführerabzeichen*). The first of these was the basic pilot examination, which was 'identical with the examination for civilian pilots according to the rules of the *Deutscher Luftfahrer-Verband* (German Pilots Association).' The second must be passed in order to qualify as an army (or field) pilot (*Feldpilot*), whilst the passing of the third examination confirmed the trainee as a qualified pilot (*Flugzeugführer*) and resulted in the award of the all-important pilot's badge.⁸⁸

The first examination entailed two parts. The first part required the trainee pilot to perform five solo flights (Fieseler remembers doing six), three of which entailed landing on a marked circle of 50 metres diameter. It was also necessary, though Fieseler does not mention whether he did this, 'to climb to at least 100m and glide in [i.e. for a landing with the engine turned off].'⁸⁹ That was seen as essential training 'for an emergency landing as a result of eventual engine failure, which was always to be reckoned with.'⁹⁰ The second part required flying a figure of eight around locations 500 metres apart (Fieseler mentions a figure of 300 metres). One of Germany's most celebrated pilots, Oswald Boelcke, 'the undisputed ace of aces' until his death in October 1916,⁹¹ apparently flew 'pretzels', which were disallowed.⁹² He had to retake that portion of the test.

Looking back to this time, Fieseler was shocked by his own naiveté at actually regarding his instructor as a genuine expert and the examining officials as capable of making a sound judgement about his or anyone else's flying abilities. It was in fact rumoured that the examiners turned a blind eye to certain weaknesses on the part of the novices and often wangled things in order to fulfil their quota for ensuring that enough new pilots were reporting for duty. So it was that Fieseler considered the various sequence of tests to be 'child's play … [seeing that] the regulations harked from the time of the first generation of flyers, and anyone who was accepted at flying school, left it as an army pilot.'⁹³ In recognition of these inadequacies by January 1916 'the exercises and examinations were adapted to the much tougher conditions of air combat on the front.'⁹⁴

Fieseler easily dealt with the first part of the examination cycle. He could now proceed to the second test to become a field pilot. This test involved altitude flying. The requirement was to fly for an hour at an altitude of 2,000 metres as attested by a barometric reading. Fieseler had never experienced such a height. The test was to conclude with a glide-in landing from 800 metres.⁹⁵ He took off and attained the stipulated altitude with no idea about navigation and without a compass; these were not supplied with training aircraft. As was the way at the beginning of the war, he would have to fly 'with reference to the landscape' – and hope for the best.⁹⁶

Fieseler was required to remain within landing distance of his airfield all the time. Undeterred, he wanted to savour the experience of altitude flying all by himself. He oriented himself towards the sun and flew for about 15 minutes in an easterly direction. No doubt he was beginning to discover

87 Kennett, op. cit., p.122.
88 H. Täger, Training in the German Air Force, 1914-1918: Part 2. pages 139-141. http://www.onairpower.org/kb/Reference:Training_in_the_German_Air_Force,_1914-1918.
89 Ibid.
90 Bürger, op. cit., p.46.
91 P. Kilduff, *The Red Baron: Beyond the Legend*, p.87.
92 Täger, op. cit.
93 Fieseler, op. cit., p.42.
94 Täger, op. cit.
95 Ibid.
96 Kennett, op. cit., p.123.

the exhilaration of being a pilot, that special sensation noted by the renowned Richthofen: 'That's just the beauty of it all: you feel yourself to be completely free and be completely your own master, when you are in the air.'[97] But Fieseler was not destined to bask in this new-found freedom for long. He turned back, but only to hit a westerly wind gusting at some 80km, which was the top speed of his aircraft. He was hardly making any headway.

An hour passed in this way. Then, alarmingly, a dial told him that the main fuel tank was empty. It was imperative to land before his machine stalled. Luckily, he made a smooth landing on a cropped field, but this prudent action to save his airplane and indeed himself inevitably meant that he had failed this crucial part of the test. There was not a house, not a person to be seen. Having six to eight litres of fuel in the spare tank, he took to the air in the hope of finding a town or village, though it is not clear whether his aim was to pick up fuel (not that filling stations were exactly a common feature in those days) or get transport back to his airfield.

But that was academic. Suddenly there was a lurch as he manoeuvred the plane to land in a ploughed field near a village. Then he made a fatal mistake. He pulled on the control column with all his bodily strength. Suddenly the aircraft plunged to the ground nose-first. Fieseler remembers the ever shriller howling of the rigging. The ground surged towards him with the momentum of a locomotive at full pelt. There was a monstrous thud. He lost consciousness. He had, as German air force slang put it, 'done the firewood' (*Kleinholz machen*) i.e. smashed his plane up.[98]

Solved: the question of supremacy in the air
Fieseler would later put down the disaster to inadequate training. No-one had told him that, instead of pulling the control column towards himself, when the plane began to nose-dive – the natural reflex in the circumstance – he should in fact have done the opposite. It was 'a fundamental pilot error' which, according to him had already caused the hundreds of inexperienced flyers to crash before his own narrow escape and would cause thousands more crashes. 'In most cases', he notes, 'they fell to their deaths.'[99]

It took his rescuers three hours to recover him from the tangle of wreckage. For the next five days he was in and out of consciousness. He had been very badly injured, but he had, he knew, been very lucky. First, he had been flying in the rear seat with 80 kilos of sandbags as ballast in the front seat. These helped to limit the direct impact on his body. Next, in accordance with regulations, he had used the safety belt and was wearing a crash helmet. Third, he had landed on spongey farm land. Fourth, there was, he proudly recalls, his own indomitable spirit to survive. But lastly (he did not mention this), and by far most importantly, his fuel tank was empty when he crashed. He had been spared, to cite the wry words of America's highest scoring fighter pilot, Eddie Rickenbacker 'the slower torture of burning to a crisp.'[100] Pilots often had nerves of steel, but on all sides fire 'was always the greatest fear among pilots and orchestrator of the most sickening deaths.'[101]

The airfield commander had no alternative but to act in accordance with regulations. Fieseler was to be transferred forthwith to other duties for having abandoned the designated flying zone and for taking off following an emergency landing without authorisation. But at this point in the proceedings Wenk unexpectedly put in a good word for Fieseler. 'No, no,' pleaded the instructor, 'we can't afford to demote our best trainee pilot.'[102] Somehow he managed to persuade the commanding

97 M. von Richthofen, *Der rote Kampfflieger*, p.40.
98 Kennett, op. cit., p.127. The French language had the corresponding term: *casser du bois*.
99 Fieseler, op. cit., p.43.
100 Rickenbacker, op. cit., p.30.
101 Winter, op. cit., p.162.
102 Fieseler, op. cit., p.44.

officer to grant Fieseler six months' rehabilitation, and on 11 November 1915 it was duly confirmed that he had passed the second part of the test.[103]

So it was that he convalesced in a field hospital in Neukölln on the south-east side of Berlin. It was a very painful recovery. His parents sent him anxious letters, to which he replied reassuringly, careful to play down the severity of the crash. In particular he had sustained complicated breaks of his leg in two places. No doubt there were other injuries too. Crashes were of course a perpetual hazard and pilots who survived many crashes could accumulate a veritable portfolio of injuries.

American author Bill Bryson cites the case of French ace Charles Nungesser, who may well hold the record in this respect. His injuries leave one aghast. In a wartime career that claimed forty-four German planes and involved countless crashes, his tally included: six jaw fractures, fractured skull and palate; bullet wounds to mouth and ear; dislocations of wrist, clavicle, ankle and knees; loss of teeth; shrapnel wound to upper body; multiple concussions; multiple leg fractures; multiple leg injuries; and contusions "too numerous to list." In addition, he lost an eye in combat. Nungesser, who went so far as to list his injuries on his *carte de visite* (along with his medals and decorations), was often 'so banged up that he had to be carried to his plane by crew members and gently inserted into the cockpit.'[104] On the German side the Frenchman had a reputation for being 'undisciplined, head-strong and adventurous', so in a sense he invited some of his injuries.[105] Fieseler, for his part, having seen so many crashes from his first day as a trainee, would have been fully aware of the range of injuries, which could easily befall him and other pilots – commonly within seconds of taking a plane up.

When Fieseler could at last be helped on to his feet, every step was agony. He had to use crutches and be supported by nurses. One of them, by the name of Hilde, was attracted to the young pilot, and the feeling was mutual. A war-time romance struck up in the cheerless atmosphere of the field hospital and the couple became engaged. It was through Hilde that he heard that the female doctor who had operated on his ankle had done a botched job as a result of overwork and inexperience. It turned out that the most experienced surgeons were being assigned to the front. In fact by 1915 medical services on the Western Front were already being stretched to the limit: not only owing to the colossal number of wounded soldiers to be treated, but also to the grim fact that mechanised warfare 'was mangling flesh and bones in unrecognisable ways.'[106] Both doctors and military commanders were 'completely unprepared' for this phenomenon.[107]

Throughout his life Fieseler would suffer from this war wound. According to German aviation historians Nagel and Bauer, he remained in the hospital until 21 February 1916.[108] As his time in the hospital drew to a close, to his great joy he was not declared 'completely unfit for flying', but he was passed for service at home.[109] As soon as he was released, Fieseler grit his teeth and headed for his old flying unit. He limped into the general admin office on his crutches, where the sergeant looked askance at him. At all events he was interviewed and told to take four weeks' leave. He went to his parents' home in Bonn, where he looked after his malfunctioning leg as best he could.

Within a year of the outbreak of war aircraft were capable of stronger performance. One pilot had established an altitude record of 8150 metres; another had flown 24 hours running. The German aircraft company Junkers had produced the first plane ever to be constructed in metal.

---

103   R. Nagel. und T. Bauer, *Kassel und die Luftfahrtindustrie seit 1923: Geschichte(n), Menschen, Technik*, p.425.
104   B. Bryson, *One Summer: America 1927*, p.34.
105   H. Ringlstetter, Erste alliierte Fliegerasse, in: W. Mühlbacher, *Fleugzeug Classic*, pp.86-87.
106   Deutsches Historisches Museum, *Der Erste Weltkrieg in 100 Objekten*, p.152.
107   B. Schrep, Gebrochen an Leib und Seele, in *Spiegel Special über den 1. Weltkrieg und die Folgen*, p.58-60.
108   Nagel und Bauer, op. cit., p.425.
109   Fieseler, op. cit., p.44.

The cantilevered machine was known as the 'corrugated donkey' (*Blechesel*).[110] This was a prototype of an operational single-seater warplane, which would not come into service until March 1918.[111] Another German firm, Rumpler, and the French manufacturer, Coudron, had started to produce twin-engined warplanes.[112]

By 1915 there was another kind of innovation, which exemplified the amazing speed which drove the technological race forward in the bid to develop and get into production fighters that were faster, more manoeuvrable and better armed. This concerned a major advance in the arming of aircraft which would give them significantly greater lethal capability. At the beginning of the war a pilot might be given a rifle, a pistol and even light-weight bombs for throwing over the side. Then more powerful machine guns were mounted on aircraft. On some machines these were fixed on the top wing of planes 'over the pilot's head to shoot over the propeller.'[113] Then came a seismic shift.

The Dutch airman Anthony Fokker tilted the scales dramatically to Germany's advantage with a major innovation. Fokker had come to Germany in 1910 to learn to be an automobile mechanic, but was immediately was attracted into flying and aircraft manufacture. He founded his own aircraft company in Wiesbaden. Before the outbreak of war he had offered his expertise to the British who showed no interest. He therefore remained in Germany and developed aircraft for the German Air Force during the First World War. His achievement was to refine the interrupter gear (also known as the synchronised gear), which permitted 'blue beans' – German air force slang for bullets – to be fired through rotating propellers without shattering the blades to pieces.[114]

In April 1915 year the French aviation pioneer Roland Garros had 'achieved the first ever shooting down of an aircraft' by such a device, but it was Fokker who perfected the technique.[115] Never modest about his capabilities, the Dutchman believed that he had 'solved the question of supremacy in the air.'[116] Until this moment, as Bryson explains, 'all that aircraft manufacturers could do was wrap armour plating around the propellers and hope that any bullets that struck the blades weren't deflected backwards. The only alternative was to mount the guns away from the propeller, but that meant pilots could not reload them or clear jams, which were frequent.'[117] The aeroplane was thus transformed 'from a machine for sport and adventure into a weapon of war.'[118]

Fokker installed the interrupter gear on his new E1 monoplane, alias the Fokker Eindecker, which was the world's first aircraft to be designed as a fighter plane. The Eindecker shot down hundreds of Allied aircraft and became 'the scourge of the skies.'[119] The Dutchman's invention gave the German air force a six months' lead over the Allied air forces, whose downed airmen were known as 'Fokker fodder.' It can be truly said that the invention of the interrupter gear marked the introduction of the single-seater fighter aircraft.[120] But the invention not only changed the face of aerial warfare; it also dramatically changed the very conduct and nature of war.[121] It is almost incredible to think that only a year before at the Battle of Cerin the pilot's weapon was a 'mere' hand-gun.

110   Ibid, p.45.
111   Bruce, op. cit., p.200.
112   Fieseler, op. cit., p.45.
113   Winter, op. cit., p.41.
114   Fokker, op. cit., pp.148-165.
115   Hughes-Wilson, op. cit., pp.160-161.
116   Fokker, op. cit., p.149.
117   Bryson, op. cit., p.27.
118   Deutsches Museum, op. cit., p.38,
119   Hughes-Wilson, op. cit., p.161.
120   Bürger, op. cit., p.37.
121   Corum, op. cit., p.61.

One consequence was that this innovation in aerial armament caused the role of the observer to be redefined. At the beginning of the war the key role of the observer (or scout) was essentially two-fold: 'to look out for potential weak points to attack [in] mass movements of enemy troops and equipment; and to 'search for concentrations of troops, indicating an imminent attack.'[122] But now the pilot was getting undreamt-of fire-power, which he and not the observer had control of. However, as we shall see, this shift did not diminish the role of aerial observation per se. In the opinion of one German commentator, airplanes were no longer 'the somewhat ridiculed plaything of the officer classes … [they] had become the terror weapon of the future.'[123]

The German ace, Rudolf Stark, well captures how guns transformed pilots' view of aircraft: 'Formerly, I regarded my guns as a burden on my machine, but now my wings are only there to carry the guns.'[124] By 1918 the machine guns were capable of delivering 'a hurricane of flaming bullets.'[125] As planes could only carry small amounts of ammunition, pilots only fired in short bursts to avoid using it up too quickly. For its part, the French Nieuport could 'pour bullets at the rate of 650 per minute into the Boche machine ahead.'[126] On the German side, the twin Spandau machine-guns mounted on the Albatross D.1 fighter spat bullets 'between the rotating blades at a maximum rate of 500 rounds per minute.'[127] (In the Second World War the Hurricane 'could spit out 160 .303 bullets *each second* – enough to tear a 13-foot diameter hole in a wall at 250 yards' (added emphasis).[128]

Tremendous stuff, Fieseler

When Fieseler at length returned to his unit in or around February 1916, a significant change of policy was underway. Only after a few months of war the German military leadership recognised that there were problems in the command structure in the air force: authority was too decentralised. Accordingly in April 1915 the German Army created the post of Chief of Field Aviation and control of aircraft development, engine development and production were placed under the command of the Aviation Inspectorate of the Army. As a result the new structure 'placed all the aviation assets under a single command with its own headquarters and general staff.'[129] Not that Fieseler would have noted any efficiencies that these changes were supposed to introduce. At his unit chaos reigned, as some 30 or 40 aircraft along with some 300 personnel were being transferred to Altenburg, some 40 kms south of Leipzig, in Saxony.

There was so much general confusion that nobody seemed to notice him on his crutches. So he adopted the tried and trusted rule of every soldier since time immemorial: *just don't stand out!*[130] When the move had been completed and a semblance of normal military life established at the new airfield, Fieseler's own situation was becoming precarious. There was a pool of some 30 pilots who in the first instance were being assigned to guard duty. Among them was Fieseler. Dreading this prospect, since he could hardly stand let alone walk for a long time, he managed on three occasions to avoid being called upon. On the fourth occasion, however, he did indeed stand out, and the ill-tempered sergeant snarled a warning to him: 'Anyone who does not do guard duty,

---

122 Ferguson, op. cit., p.27
123 C. Habbe, Wettlauf der Ingenieure, in: *Spiegel Special, op cit.*, p.52-54.
124 A. Stark, *Wings of War: An Airman's Diary of the Last Year of World War 1*, p.19.
125 Rickenbacker, op. cit., p.62.
126 Ibid, p.20.
127 www.constable.ca/caah/albatros.htm
128 E. Carter, *Force Benedict: Churchill's Secret Mission to Save Stalin*, p.54.
129 Corum, op. cit., p.67.
130 Fieseler, op. cit., p.45. The German expression is: *nur nicht auffallen.*

won't be doing any flying. If you' – you being Fieseler – 'are not on the next guard duty rota, I'll be reporting you.'[131]

But standing guard was not Fieseler's only anxiety. He was also much exercised about how to handle the issue of his crash landing: should he report it to his new superiors at all? He reasoned that it might be a more sensible course to admit the offence and ask for some refresher flights with an instructor. Although he had clocked up some 20 solo flights, he had an almost fatal crash against his name and he had not been in the cockpit for a good nine months. However, even if the commanding officer at the Altenburg airfield did not have a copy of his service record, it was highly likely that the details of his case had been noted by some higher authority. He decided to keep his mouth shut and wait and see.

The sergeant did indeed keep his promise. Once he had done his stint on guard duty, Fieseler was assigned with two other pilots for flying duties on LVGs. However, flying was confined to the area around the airfield. As a preliminary each pilot was to do two circuits of the airfield in front of observers. The first plane took off. Then, a mere eight minutes later, it was Fieseler's turn. His heart was pounding. He did whatever it took to be composed. The pilot in front had completed his two rounds; Fieseler got the all-clear. He got into his aircraft, braced himself, went through the standard cockpit procedure, took off – his knees banging the sides out of sheer exhilaration – and started to increase the speed. During flight he needed to keep his knees under control, and this preoccupation made it difficult for him to complete his circuit. Luckily he summoned all his strength and made two perfect landings. The relief poured out of his body.

The next pilot to take off was a certain Paul Bäumer. Fieseler watched his aircraft as it took off. Suddenly at just 10 metres above the ground the engine cut out. Bäumer attempted to bring the LVG down on a recently ploughed field. The plane nosed over and crash-landed, bursting into flame. Rescuers managed to pull the pilot clear and get him to a field hospital for treatment of severe burns. Horror of horrors, thought Fieseler, that could have easily been my plane. Two days after this incident an orderly came into the barracks, where Fieseler was billeted. 'Pilot Fieseler', he bellowed. 'Report to the captain immediately.'[132] This did not sound like a friendly summons in the slightest, especially as the captain, who came out of the infantry to take over, was 'generally feared on account of his tyrannical manner.'[133] Fieseler, thinking of his crash a year before, saw himself charged with gross negligence or causing wanton damage to state property in the form of a LVG trainer. He therefore braced himself for a spell of detention in the guardhouse. Everything about the anteroom was brisk and business-like, unsettlingly so, as far as Fieseler was concerned.

He entered the office of the captain, who had, it seems, already studied Fieseler's service record. 'Pilot Fieseler reporting, Sir.' The captain was seated behind his desk. He looked the young pilot up and down and then, to Fieseler's utter amazement, he blurted out: 'Tremendous stuff, Fieseler! Warmest compliments! Well, keep up the good work!'[134] Outside, feeling stunned, the exonerated Fieseler could only meditate on the vagaries of human life. He could only deduce that the captain, an infantryman and, most conveniently in the circumstances, a complete novice about flying, had seen something courageous in the way he had taken up flying again after his near-fatal crash followed by the long rehabilitation.

As it happens, such officerly foibles were not confined to the German Flying Corps. Winter tells a similar amusing story concerning a pilot called Captain Billy Williams, 'one the greatest

---

131   Ibid, p.45.
132   Ibid, p.46.
133   Ibid, pp.46-47.
134   Ibid, p.47.

exponents of Avro flying.'[135] He had on one occasion taken up an Avro to practise completely stalled landings. Winter continues:

> At 500 feet [Williams] stalled until the engine and prop ceased to revolve. Then gliding down at a steep angle rather like the ascent of an autogiro, he held his machine in balance by sheer piloting skill. In attempting to land from the stalled glide, he misjudged the final movement of the elevator and fell heavily the last few feet, crashing the undercarriage. Commanding officer Smith-Barry stood out on the tarmac and without a word Williams jumped out of the wrecked Avro and into another. The second Avro also stalled near the ground and crashed. Still, the colonel stood, unspeaking. Williams went up in a third Avro and made an almost stationary landing right in front of his own hangar with the engine stopped. The colonel stepped forward. 'Good show, Williams. Good job you didn't stop trying at number two.'[136]

To both stories one can only respond with the time-honoured words: ours is not to question why; ours is but to do and die.

A wholly new species of warrior in the history of mankind
In the course of the following four weeks Fieseler passed a test in cross-country flying and landing. By now he was set to become in Major Georg Neumann's rather quaint phrase 'an aerial chauffeur:' that is to say, a pilot whose job it was to transport – and take orders from – an observer-navigator in a two-seater plane.[137] There was, as it happens, one pilot to whom the appellation 'aerial chauffer' genuinely applied. That was the renowned Eddie Rickenbacker. Before the war 'Fast Eddie' had been a racing driver and, when he arrived in France in June 1917, was a driver attached to the US General Staff before enlisting in the US Air Service. However, a rather more significant distinction can be bestowed on Rickenbacker. Of all the surviving pilots who wrote up their wartime experiences, it is surely he who more than any other airman masterfully captures in words what Bryson describes as 'the beauty and enchantment of flight as well as the fearful mayhem of aerial combat.'[138]

Neumann, whose breadth of knowledge about the development of German aviation during the First World War suggests a background in military planning, takes an almost romantic view of the pilot and observer relationship. In action, they think, act and react 'as one individual.'[139] As he explained, 'The two men were linked together by a bond of comradeship forged in many hours of common trouble and danger, and it was unwillingly that such a bond was ever severed.'[140] They developed an instinctive relationship, in which one could understand and almost foresee the wishes and actions of the other.'[141] By contrast, the German ace, Rudolf Stark, took a practical view: 'The observer puts his trust in the pilot's flying skill, the pilot in the observer's watchfulness.'[142] Given the difficulties of communicating with or without the (later produced) speaking tubes, their cooperation also depended heavily on instinct, intuition and mutual confidence in each other's respective aerial competences. In air force jargon the pilot was known as 'Emil.' The observer-navigator in command was called 'Franz.' It is not clear how these designations arose, though it must surely be the case that the names derived from actual people.

135 Winter, op. cit., p.35.
136 Ibid, op. cit., pp.35-36 (slightly amended).
137 Siegert in: Neumann, op. cit., pp.80-96.
138 Bryson, op. cit., pp.430-431.
139 Siegert in: Neumann, op. cit., pp.80-96.
140 Ibid, p.93.
141 Ibid, p.93.
142 Stark, op. cit., p.12.

Together the Franz and Emil formed what was jocularly termed 'a flyer's marriage' (*Fliegerehe*).[143] Fieseler refers to the Franz-Emil relationship as a team (*Gespann*): team as in team of horses harnessed together.[144] An enlightening British historian of aviation, David Edgerton, mentions an official report of 1917, in which it states that 'the perfect understanding and instant collaboration which spells efficiency in the air is the product of habitual intimacy and easy association during leisure hours.'[145] Very unfortunately Fieseler's autobiography make very little reference to how airmen in his experience used the informality of the mess to reinforce working relationships. (Readers of *The Blue Max* will know that the mess was a place of bonhomie, boozing, boasting and back-biting).

Fieseler recalls one of his first experiences of being an Emil. He was on his way to Halberstadt not far from Magdeburg, when an unusually violent, almost perpendicular barrage of wind dislodged the unwieldy tool bag in the pilot's compartment and jammed it between the control levers. In desperation Fieseler tried to explain to the observer what had happened, but with all the howling the latter did not understand anything. Meanwhile the situation got more dangerous when a powerful gust made the plane lurch 180º to the side. The plane was suddenly in a vertical plunge with the ground getting alarmingly close. With considerable dogged efforts and drenched in sweat Fieseler managed to right the plane just in time. The observer was gripping his seat, waiting for a sticky end. Luckily, Fieseler's flying prowess had saved them both.

Duly qualified if by an unusual route, he hoped to be sent to the front, but the well-disposed captain had other ideas. He was to be assigned to an artillery observer school in Jüterbog some 65 kms south-west of Berlin. The facility had about 25 operational aircraft and a complement of 20 army pilots along with a motley group of higher ranking pilots. Fieseler found this group 'very correct' in behaviour.[146] Even when it was fine flying weather, some of the planes never went up, meaning that pilots were often left kicking their heels. In the evening everyone read books, wrote letters or played cards. This life was for Fieseler and some of the others so tedious that they simply stayed in their own quarters. On the plus side he learned a raft of highly advantageous skills and techniques on various courses: Morse code, air-to-ground telegraphy, aerial photography, air reconnaissance, identification of enemy aircraft, and use of a machine gun. Siegert, who can be relied upon for vivid language, notes that the introduction of wireless telegraphy was seen by the faint-hearted as tantamount to 'adding an electric chair to the present dangers of the aeroplane.'[147] The truth was simpler: the electrical transmission of messages from the pilot to ground control proved faster and more reliable than the use of signalling equipment such as pistols or flashing lights.[148]

On one occasion, no doubt out of sheer boredom, Fieseler accepted an invitation from a certain corporal Pellmann to play cards in the mess with a group who were described to him as 'honourable gentlemen.' They included the airfield's deputy commanding officer and the paymaster.[149] Fieseler had never played cards in his life and before long these honourable gentlemen had fleeced him of 300 marks. Pellman was quick to console him: 'Don't worry. Your luck's bound to change.' Fieseler, though, had his suspicions about his fellow card players. Subsequently observing them like a hawk, he discovered that they were using sleight of hand when shuffling the cards.

When he felt able to, he took part in other games, being very careful to disguise his suspicions about the honourable gentlemen, whilst playing them at their own game. He made certain that he won in small amounts, as big wins could easily rouse their suspicions of him. After two weeks he

---

143 Kennett, op. cit., p.145.
144 Fieseler, op. cit., p.51.
145 Edgerton, op. cit., p.80.
146 Fieseler, op. cit., p.48.
147 Siegert in Neumann, op. cit., pp.36-56.
148 Bürger, op. cit., p.37.
149 As it happens, the German word for mess is *das Kasino*.

won back what he had lost. 'There you are', said Pellman cheerfully. 'What did I tell you?'[150] After that Fieseler did not play cards again: at Jüterbog at least.

At Jüterbog Fieseler did a lot of flying, not only gaining in confidence, but also impressing his peers and superiors with his skills. One day the captain summoned him to his office. 'I am very pleased with your abilities,' he declared, 'Congratulations. There aren't so many pilots here who are so reliable and can handle a plane with such exceptional talent.' Then came the longed-for question: 'Would you like to join me on the front? I'm putting together a new detachment' Fieseler needed no time to think: 'Without hesitation, Sir. I'd be very keen to join you.'[151] The new unit would be Field Flyer Unit (*Feldfliegerabteilung*/FFA) 243. So it was that Gerhard Fieseler was about to make the momentous transition he had dreamed of. But this was more than a shift to a more demanding activity. The captain's offer initiated a rite of passage which would in due course pave his way from pilot to a wholly new species of warrior in the history of mankind: the aerial gladiator.

---

150 Fieseler, op. cit., p.49.
151 Ibid, op. cit., p.49.

3

An airman the equivalent of three infantry divisions

Manfred Freiherr von Richthofen was a proficient huntsman who transferred his skills to the most dangerous hunting ground of all: the battlefield.

Peter Kilduff, The Red Baron[1]

Above the mud and misery of the trenches and the endless slugging matches of the First World War another contest was played out with all the military glamour, chivalric values and deadly outcome of some mediaeval tournament. This was the battle in the air between the first primitive aircraft and the intrepid pilots who flew them.

Richard Overy, introduction to the memoirs of Ernst Udet[2]

Deutschland über Allah

Squadron 243 was set up in Gotha in the Duchy of Saxe-Coburg-Gotha, which overlaps today's Bavaria and Thüringen. In the latter decades of the 19th century Gotha had become prominent as an engineering centre. Its most famous manufacturer was the Gothaer Waggonfabrik which produced rolling stock and trams and, in the First World War, the redoubtable Gotha bomber, a gigantic aircraft in its time. When in 1917 the Zeppelin's 'useful life as a raider had ended', this was the flying monster that was deployed to bomb the south coast and Midlands in Britain.[3] Gotha was also known for its flying school, which was set up in 1913 by Duke Carl Eduard, who was a grandson of Queen Victoria and Prince Albert. This flying school in all probability served as the temporary headquarters of Squadron 243.[4]

Then one day the new outfit was on the move. Some 50 or 60 pilots and ground staff, who included mechanics, electricians, welders, aerial photograph analysts, weapons personnel, carpenters, medical staff and quite probably a meteorologist, marched through Gotha to the strains of musicians towards the station. A train was waiting to accommodate them, their seven aircraft and other impedimenta for a campaign of uncertain length in unknown territory. Officers travelled in first class carriages, all other personnel were in second class. Special wagons carried the fuselages (the engines were enveloped in protective canvas) with their detachable wings lashed to the sides. Other wagons conveyed trucks, fuel, tents, medical supplies and surgical equipment as well as the all-important spare parts, including pods of propellers in their special frames. Fieseler vividly remembered the march: he was limping slightly and having difficulty keeping up. Women and

---

1 P. Kilduff, *The Red Baron: Beyond the Legend*, p.7.
2 R. Overy, introduction to E. Udet, *The Ace of the Black Cross: The Memoirs of Ernst Udet*, p.ix.
3 A. Bruce, *An Illustrated Companion to the First World War*, p.163.
4 Kilduff, op. cit., ibid, p.60.

children lined the streets, as did several war cripples. There was no jubilant cheering as there had been at the outbreak of war. One or two people waved in a subdued, joyless fashion. By now it was summer 1916. After two years of war hardship and hunger were rampant. The basic necessities of life were getting in desperately short supply.

So many women, so many women, Fieseler reflected as he passed by: someone's mother, someone's wife, someone's sweetheart. If his own mother were there, she would be weeping with them too. This thought unsettled him. There was a knot in his throat. He was close to tears. He kept swallowing hard. At last the company had reached the station. It was still not clear where they and their airplanes were heading, although by now it was obvious that they were being despatched to the front. But to which one? This, he mused, is it: the encounter with the enemy when he and all the rest of them had no clear about what war in the air would actually be like. How would he and they behave in the face of enemy shells and bullets? Before boarding the train, he had mastered his emotions. He was calm now, well, outwardly calm.

To the surprise of many, the train set off in a south-easterly direction. The men of Squadron 243 were obviously not heading for France nor to the Eastern Front to meet the Russians head-on. Perhaps they would be joining up with the Austrians, who had been fighting so dismally against the Serbs, fulfilling, as the facetious quip of the French diplomat Talleyrand had it, their 'tiresome habit of always being beaten.'[5] Speculation was put to end after three days, when Fieseler and his comrades arrived in Sofia. Never in a thousand years would he have imagined that he would end up in the Balkans. But they did not tarry long in Sofia. From there they were transported to a point on the Danube some 30kms from the Romanian border. Their task was to provide air support to two German armies, which had begun invading Romania on 3 September 1916; that of the inspirational Mackensen from the south-east and that of arch-type Prussian general, Falkenhayn, from the south. The campaign went according to plan, and the airmen of Squadron 243 were the first to land on Bucharest airport following the capture of the city itself on 6 December.

Plainly, these operations had something to do with inflicting heavy blows on Serbia, the very country that had drawn the Fatherland and other countries into this terrible war in the first place. But that was only one factor in a highly complicated geopolitical equation. German strategy did not only have an eye on Belgrade; central to the grand vision was the strengthening of its alliance with the Ottoman Empire. Briefly the context was as follows. In the first few months of the war Austria had failed miserably in its attempts to bring Serbia to heel. Then in September 1915 the Bulgarians had been persuaded to enter the war on the side of the Central Powers. In this alliance Bulgaria envisaged that it could 'inflict deep wounds on all its neighbours in retaliation for its own dismemberment and humiliation in the Second Balkan War' of 1913.[6] It was desperate to establish itself as a regional power straddling the Aegean and the Black Sea. Its armies would fight alongside the Germans to defeat the much-loathed Serbs.

In the meantime Germany was seeking ever closer links with Constantinople for several important reasons. First, the armies on the Western Front had ground themselves to a halt. They were 'in a gory quagmire,'[7] and 'a victory for either side in the Balkans could undermine the enemy's campaign on the Eastern Front, and by extension on the Western Front.'[8] Second, across-the-board cooperation between Germany and the Ottomans would have a singularly disconcerting effect on Britain. It could threaten British naval influence in the Mediterranean and, given the Ottoman influence the Middle East and Caucasus, disrupt communication between Britain and

5   Cited in: R. Bassett, *For God and Kaiser: The Imperial Austrian Army.* p.1.
6   M. Glenny, *The Balkans: Nationalism, War and the Great Powers*, p.333.
7   Ibid, p.317.
8   Ibid, p.317.

India. In other words, the German-Ottoman axis with Austro-Hungary in support could – and did – create three new fronts: in the Eastern Mediterranean, in the Black Sea, and in the Caucasus and Middle East.[9]

At the breakout of war in 1914 the Ottoman Empire, that 'sick man of Europe' was 'in a state of chaotic contraction.[10] But Enver Pasha, the Minister for War, had every reason to believe that, with its army and its navy having been modernised by the Germans and the British respectively, alliance with the Kaiser could bring several advantages to the Ottoman Empire. Thus Enver and his supporters envisaged a fresh assertion of Ottoman power in Asia and the Middle East, foreseeing a significant weakening of British influence and less Russian encroachment on the Black Sea.

In 1915 it looked most felicitously to Constantinople that the Germans had largely finished off the Russians as a fighting force. The Turkish leaders knew that they could count on the inflow of German technology, military or otherwise, as well as the wider benefits of modernization which would come with all that. No wonder Turks enthusiastic over the alliance with Germany quipped that it was all about 'Deutschland über Allah!'[11] In order to facilitate the latter benefits a key aim was the establishment of a direct railway link between Berlin and Constantinople. It would be vital therefore that the line ran its entire length without hindrance by any opposing country.

Another factor in this fiendishly complex scenario, in which 'demographic, historical, confessional, racist and economic claims were mercilessly pitted against each other'[12] concerned Romania, which 'dreamed of creating a Greater Romania by absorbing the mixed Hungarian-Romanian region of Transylvania, and eastern Moldavia (or Bessarabia).'[13] To further these aims Bucharest favoured close ties to the Entente Powers. To cut a long and exceedingly complicated story short, Romania had declared war on Austro-Hungary in August 1916. It was this act that brought the Germans sweeping into the Balkans. The resulting German occupation of Romania yielded a valuable advantage: grain and oil in abundance, two commodities urgently needed by the Fatherland.[14]

Fieseler's knowledge of strategic visions and calculations that enmeshed Germany and the Ottoman Empire was probably very limited. He gives us no clue in his autobiography. But this is not to say he knew nothing about the general course of the war. He no doubt had access to old newspapers, even though these would be censored to a greater or lesser extent and, as in the way during wartime, anything that could be proclaimed as a success, victory or triumph of German arms would invariably be broadcast far and wide. Furthermore, we can assume that the he and his comrades picked up through air force networks, formal and informal, information specifically about airborne operations, the performance of various kinds of aircraft, both German and enemy, new developments in aircraft design, and the accomplishments of flyers on other fronts.

So it was that the time had now come for the twenty year old Fieseler as a loyal member of the Flying Corps to convert his months of training and preparation into action as an Emil on the front line. As already noted, observers were officers and held right of command on board. This was a case of a regulation deriving from peace-time conditions when the basic task of the Franz to search the ground, use his map and make his notes more freely. It would, however, be mistaken to regard the

9   J. Hughes-Wilson, *A History of the First World War in 100 Objects*, p.92.
10   Glenny, op. cit., p.319.
11   Ibid, p.324.
12   Ibid, p.335.
13   Ibid, p.339.
14   L. Mayerhofer, Making Friends and Foes: Occupiers and Occupied in First World War Romania, 1916-1918, in H. Jones, J. O'Brien, and C. Schmidt-Supprian (eds.). *Untold War: New Perspectives in First World War Studies*, pp.119-149.

pilot as doing all the hard work. Aerial navigation was more exacting than might be thought. It required 'steady, precise flying to enable the observers to photograph important ground positions.'[15]

The following extract from *The Times* published on 19 January 1915 provides an excellent overview of what aerial reconnaissance entailed and what skills and aptitudes a good observer needed:

> Aerial reconnaissance is not work which can be carried out by everyone. The really first-rate observer must possess extensive military knowledge in order to know what objects to look for and where to look for them; he must have very good eyesight in order to pick them up; and must have the knack of reading a map quickly, both in order to mark correctly their positions and find his way.
>
> To reconnoitre is not easy even in fine weather: but in driving rain or snow, in a temperature perhaps several degrees below zero, or in a gale, when an aeroplane travelling with the wind rocks and sways like a ship in a heavy sea and may attain a speed of 150 miles an hour, the difficulties are immense. In these circumstances, and from the altitude at which it is necessary to fly in order to escape the projectiles of anti-aircraft guns, columns of transport or of men are easily missed. Indeed, at a first attempt an observer will see nothing which is of military value, for it is only after considerable practice that the eye becomes accustomed to scouring a great stretch of country from above and acquires the power of distinguishing objects upon it.
>
> The temperament of an observer is of the greatest importance. He must be cool and capable of great concentration in order to keep his attention fixed upon his objective in spite of all distractions such as the bursts of shells close to him, or the noise of rifle bullets passing through the planes of his machine. Many men are absolutely unfitted for such duty, and even trained observers vary in their powers of reconnaissance.[16]

Adding to those points; first, terrain as viewed from the air did not correspond to the information on maps. Richthofen himself acknowledged this truth: 'I compare nature with my map, but it's in vain.'[17] He would have agreed with the British pilot, who commented: 'You could get lost in the air as easily as in a forest.'[18] In a similar vein, Rickenbacker pointed out that a pilot can 'easily' get lost in the air, 'notwithstanding a clear sky and a brilliant sun shining in its proper position.'[19]

Second, it was one thing to fly over regions in which it was possible to follow roads and railway lines, and quite another when there was an absence of such clearly visible landmarks. Besides, if the tracks were there, they could not be readily made out from the air.[20] Furthermore, 'to swoop low' to get a clearer view of some kind of landmark was 'often a risky manoeuvre,'[21] especially if the enemy were lurking nearby and viewing you from on high. In the Balkans, where Fieseler was destined to operate, there were rarely highways, but rather 'beaten tracks loosely covered with pebbles and

---

15   Kilduff, op. cit., p.130.
16   The value of aerial observation, *The Times*, 19 January 1915. Reproduced in *The Times* on 19 January 2015, p.29.
17   M. von Richthofen, *Der rote Kampfflieger*, p.114.
18   D. Winter, *The First of the Few: Fighter Pilots of the First World War*, p.93.
19   E. Rickenbacker, *Fighting the Flying Circus*, p.55.
20   S. Rosenboom, *Im Einsatz über der 'vergessenen Front': Der Luftkrieg an der Ostfront im Ersten Weltkrieg* p.41.
21   B. Bryson, *One Summer: America 1927*, p.69.

clay.'²² He was to spend well two years in this part of the world, where the mountain ranges 'had been left undisturbed since time immemorial by all but a few shepherds.'²³

A punch-up at 2,000 metres

As for the regulation that the observer was aircraft commander, Fieseler regarded this as 'completely wrong.'²⁴ He saw an urgent need for new regulations to replace the current ones which in his view were 'patchy (*lückenhaft*) and primitive.'²⁵ These simply did not suit 'a new type of war which involved constant high-speed manoeuvre in an unbounded three-dimensional medium for which there were no manuals or established rules.'²⁶ It made complete sense him to appoint the pilot as commander of a two-seater aircraft. He was justified in his opinion on the basis of many unhappy experiences in Romania.

The first of these involved an observer, a certain Lieutenant G, with whom Fieseler had flown in Jüterbog. G was of Prussian military stock and had been in the cadet corps; which possibly suggests that he took the view that observation on an aeroplane had distinct similarities to the time-honoured tradition of cavalry reconnaissance. At all events, on one occasion, they were flying in an AEG C4, a versatile and well-regarded reconnaissance plane, under orders to help the artillery to home in on targets by means of air-to-ground telegraphy. This led to Fieseler's very first encounter with an enemy fighter.

Lieutenant G as Franz had ordered Fieseler as his Emil to fly in a homeward direction, but Fieseler knew that this would have given the enemy fighter a golden opportunity to open fire on them with his machine-gun blazing. Ignoring G's order, he put the plane into steep dive. The enemy fighter was duly robbed of the chance of getting the AEG in his sights, whilst G could ward it off with bursts of his machine gun. When they got back safely, Fieseler let his Franz have it: in future he would have complete freedom of action in combat situations. No doubt relieved to have escaped with his life, the Franz was more than happy to oblige.

Fieseler notes that in Romania the fighting was becoming more intensive. In particular French fighter pilots were showing increasingly stiff resistance in the air. Before long Fieseler would also find himself in combat with British pilots too, who had been transferred from Alexandria. By way of brief explanation: as of October 1915 the French and British had installed themselves in Salonika with the acquiescence of the Greeks, who saw participation on the Entente side as the path to Greece's great dream of straddling 'two continents and five seas.'²⁷ Another problem for German airmen was Russian flak, which they feared on account of its accuracy. At that time the Russian armies were pressing from the north, having scored a series of victories just north of the Romanian frontier over the Austrians, who had surrendered in their thousands.²⁸

In all the general mayhem each of the Balkan countries made calculations about which of the major warring alliances to hoist its petard to. They were not so much motivated to support some nominal higher cause espoused by the Entente, on the one hand, and the Central Powers, on the other, as to have the opportunity with a powerful military ally to settle old scores with their neighbours as brutally as possible. Fieseler can surely be excused for not outlining the Balkan situation in which he found himself. He certainly did not understand it at the time nor in all probability ever later in life. Unfortunately for posterity Fieseler does not specify precisely where

22 Rosenboom, op. cit., p.41.
23 Glenny, op. cit., p.353.
24 G. Fieseler, *Meine Bahn am Himmel*, p.51.
25 Ibid, p.51.
26 Winter, op. cit., p.25.
27 Glenny, op. cit., p.349.
28 A. Palmer, *The Gardeners of Salonika*, p.71.

he was based in Romania, but an on-line search led to the German version of Neumann's book on the German Air Force in the First World War, which we have already cited from the abridged English translation. From Neumann we learn that Squadron 243 was operating in Dobrudja, then disputed territory straddling Romania and Bulgaria.[29] It is likely that it was supporting Bulgarian and German ground forces to effect the total transfer of Dobrudja to Bulgaria.

It is possible that for a time at least Fieseler could enjoy a valuable privilege. In common with German troops passing through Bulgarian territory, he may have been permitted to send home five kilogrammes of food per week.[30] The practise, however, was virtual plunder. If his family in Bonn were indeed receiving regular food supplies from their son in the Balkans, this would have been very warmly received, and especially in the 'extraordinarily cold' winter of 1916-17, known in Germany as 'the turnip winter' (*Steckrübenwinter*), when the population was on starvation rations.[31] Winter 1916-1917 was a bad time for the Balkans too; 'millions of people' were 'homeless, diseased, wounded, avoiding shelling or genocidal assaults, undernourished and frozen.'[32]

On one occasion Fieseler was piloting another Franz. Their task was to take reconnaissance photographs near the enemy lines. Mission accomplished, they were returning to base at an altitude of 4,000 metres, when suddenly they found themselves bombarded with heavy flak from three artillery batteries. The air around them crackled with explosions. The Franz started to dictate the flying manoeuvres using their agreed code. He alternately tapped Fieseler once or twice on his right and left shoulder. One tap told him to make a 45 degree curve and two meant 90 degrees. All this proved completely disconcerting for Fieseler, who glanced round and saw complete panic on the face of his Franz.

In all this aimless manoeuvring, they were still within range of the flak. He fixed the plane in a homeward direction, throttling at top speed and gaining considerable altitude. The Franz tapped him twice on the shoulder. Fieseler shook his head in a gesture of disobedience. This prompted the Franz in his panic to punch his refractory Emil. Fieseler, now enraged, was not going to be put off. He continued to let the plane plunge downwards. At last they were free of the flak and therefore no longer in immediate danger. Then the Franz punched Fieseler for a second time. That did it. Fieseler turned right round and struck the Franz full in the face. They were then about 2,000 metres above the enemy lines.

They limped towards their own airstrip. Miraculously Fieseler made a smooth landing. Fitters and riggers rushed to the stricken plane aghast at the punishment it had absorbed. Shrapnel had completely chewed up one of the wings. To our eye, the First World War fighter aeroplane 'might seem a flimsy structure of wood and wire' but in fact 'engineers constructed machines of deceptive strength using materials and skills most readily available – those of the coach builder and farm machinery manufacture.'[33] Even so it was a near-miss for Fieseler and his Franz on that day.

Fieseler must have surely very quickly realised the implications of what he done. He had struck an officer. He could be court-martialled and dismissed from the Flying Corps in disgrace. Be that as it may, he did not have to wait long for the consequences of his behaviour. 'You've had it, Fieseler', snapped the Franz, 'I'll be reporting you for disobeying orders in the face of enemy action.' To this Fieseler rejoined: 'Do me a favour! I'm going to the captain to have you transferred. I'm never going to fly with you again.' It was Fieseler's self-styled 'choleric temperament,' evidently bequeathed from

---

29 G. P. Neumann, G.P. (1919). *Die Deutschen Luftstreitkräfte im Weltkriege*, p.509. Accessed at Google Books.
30 Glenny, op. cit., p.338.
31 G. Krumeich, *Die wichtigsten 100 Fragen: Der Erste Weltkrieg*, p.90-91.
32 Glenny, op. cit., p.345.
33 Winter, op. cit., p.112.

his father, that was doing the talking.³⁴ He then let rip with an outburst of language that hit home, but was, he admitted, completely unacceptable. Still in a frenzy, he stormed off to find the captain. However, the Franz was in close pursuit, caught up with him, tried to appease him and dissuade him from taking things any further.

'Fieseler, please. You don't have to go that far. Don't bring the captain into it,' the Franz jabbered, adding, 'my nerves were in shreds up there.' His voice sounded pathetic. By now Fieseler had calmed down somewhat. He stopped and pondered. 'All right then, Lieutenant. I'm willing to fly with you again, but on one condition …' The Franz smiled sheepishly. 'On condition', Fieseler continued, 'that I'm in charge, not just in combat situations, but during the entire flight.' The Franz relaxed. 'Of course, of course. It'll be better like that.'³⁵ It is very likely that it suited both of them not to mention the incident to anyone. The Franz might emerge as either a coward or useless officer; Fieseler could might acquire an unlooked for reputation for insubordination.

Despite the fracas, Fieseler and Lieutenant G continued to fly together for some time. The latter kept to their agreement and the former could get on with things as he thought best. There was no more friction between them. Indeed, Fieseler seemed well contented with his new life as a flyer. We must assume that he was getting plenty of flying and was respected by his fellow airmen, notably the officers. His next Franz was a lieutenant from the infantry, a rather weedy type. In combat and at high altitudes he crawled into his seat and frequently vomited. This officer, comments Fieseler laconically, was not only unfit for aerial combat, but was also a danger to airplanes and their crew.³⁶ After flights, whenever there had been vomiting as a result sheer fear or acute airsickness, fitters had the unpleasant task of removing the detritus. On the Western Front Richthofen reported the case of pilots who took their dogs – their treasured mascots – on board with them. (Other mascots included one attested case of 'a lucky teddy bear.')³⁷ The hapless fitters had to clear up any resulting 'unpleasant things.'³⁸ They no doubt complained; presumably to no avail. Richthofen's canine mascot was a Great Dane, which to the certain relief of the fitters was too big for his master's aircraft.³⁹

These less than happy experiences of 'flyer's marriage' were taking place at the end of 1916 or the beginning of 1917. For several weeks the pilots of Squadron 243 had been operating on the fast receding front line. But then, as on the Western Front, the war on the ground had acquired a static character. Fieseler, who was regarded as a competent flyer, received 'a by no means straightforward assignment, but one that was even so a distinction.'⁴⁰ His task was to fly with a Franz directly behind the front line as a forward scout. In this new capacity he was to become subordinate to the command headquarters. This required a change of location. He was shown a landing strip on a map and told to proceed there. When he landed there, a tent for his plane had already been erected. But his quarters were located nearly an hour away, which meant an arduous walk over rough terrain.

Two fitters assigned to him fixed up their own accommodation in the tent and guarded the plane at all times. It was winter and the night-time temperature sank to -40°C. Sometimes it could take an hour to crank up the engine of his aircraft. Nevertheless Fieseler was up in the air practically every day performing the vitally important reconnaissance flights unless 20 or 30cms of snow covered the runway. When it was impossible to take off, it was the job of his Franz to inform

---

34 Fieseler, op. cit., p.55.
35 Ibid, p.55.
36 L. Kennett, *The First Air War 1914-1918*, p.127, writes that one British medical officer coined the term 'aerosthenia' for such reluctant flyers, a condition he regarded as permanent.
37 Kilduff, op. cit., p.183.
38 Richthofen, op. cit., p.96.
39 Kilduff, op. cit., p.200,
40 Fieseler, op. cit., p.52.

command headquarters. It was well said that that in regions like the Balkans with their extremes of temperature it was more challenging for flyers to get to grips with 'the treachery of the climate' than the actual enemy.[41]

In the autumn and winter there were long spells of weather which made flying unsuitable. As one pilot wrote to his parents in December 1915, 'the continual waiting for good weather gets on everyone's nerves.'[42] In the summer Central Europe was prone to electrical storms, which flyers preferred to avoid. The hot months brought another irritation: infestations of insects and other vermin that got into bedding as well as flying suits. Far more than on the Western Front the conduct of aerial warfare in the Balkans and across the Eastern Front in general was 'weather-dependent.'[43]

Fieseler was learning an unexpected truth: that the actual enemy was but one of many adversaries with which one has to contend. Major Wilhelm Siegert, a knowledgeable contributor to Neumann's book, pondered this point too. He wrote: 'The word "flying" has always been synonymous with fighting, first against prejudice' – Fieseler's own father exemplified that – 'then against wind, weather, and the malice of inanimate matter, then for laurels of records, height, speed, and duration; and finally against a host of enemies.'[44] But the fractious Emil-Franz hostility that Fieseler experienced may have even taken the knowledgeable Siegert by surprise.

A Russian pounding
One day some 200 bedraggled Russian prisoners were herded on to the airstrip by some German reservists who were armed with obsolete-looking guns. Fieseler, who happened to witness this shambolic spectacle, enquired what the prisoners were doing here. One of the reservists replied: 'No idea. We were told to report to this airstrip.'[45] What sort of an answer is that, mused Fieseler. There was an icy wind. The Russians, many with rags on their feet, were flapping their arms about and stamping on the ground. The poor devils, he thought, feeling genuinely sorry for them. Seeing this doleful sight, he might have thought that on God's earth no group of people could look more wretched than wretched Russians; he might well have been right.

Suddenly, he had an idea. He lined the Russians up in groups of twenty, formed them into ten rows and gesticulated to them by pounding the ground with his feet. The Russians grasped what they had to do. They started to trample the frozen snow, getting a bit warm in the process, whilst Fieseler got what he wanted: a serviceable runway for take-off and landing. That had to suffice until his outfit could be transferred to a proper airfield. On the Western Front infantry columns were used to pummelling mud to create airstrips.[46] Here, in the glacial Balkans there were no German booted feet at his disposal; it had to be hardy feet broken in by many a Russian winter.

Around this time Fieseler learned that he had been promoted to NCO. He now held the rank of corporal (*Unteroffizier*). In due course he received a further promotion as number two to an airfield commander. This singular achievement involved a transfer to one of the newly formed fighter squadrons (*Jagdstaffel*), known in German by the abbreviation *Jasta*. Fieseler welcomed this because he did not enjoy a very easy relationship with his commander, a certain Captain Wentscher, towards whom he had been blunt almost to the point of insubordination in requesting a transfer. This would not be the first time that Fieseler would strike his superior officers as a trouble-maker. The new *Jasta* was commanded by the well-respected Captain Denk. It impressed Fieseler with its

---

41   Rosenboom, op. cit., p.39.
42   Ibid, p.39.
43   Ibid, p.37.
44   W. Siegert, Army aeroplanes, in: P.G. Neumann, *The German Air Force in the Great War*, pp.36-56.
45   Fieseler, op. cit., p.52.
46   Winter, op. cit., p.62.

comradely and confident atmosphere. It happened though that the otherwise well-regarded captain could not actually fly; which perhaps was not such a big surprise to Fieseler. At all events he, as the youngest pilot, was beginning to find himself looked upon as an expert in everything to do with flying and, for the first time in his life, his opinion was sought and listened to. He tells us that around this time he was 21 years old; which means that we are in the spring of 1917. The war had been going on for nearly three years. It had a year and a half to run.

With his new *Jasta* Fieseler found himself flying in tandem with a new Franz. This was Lieutenant Hotz, who was brave, intelligent and reliable. You only had to tell him something once. Everything went like clockwork. Indeed, it was a pleasure to fly with him. When flying over potential targets and telegraphing the artillery with information for the gunners, they could expect to be attacked by enemy fighters. But with Hotz on board Fieseler, relying on his increasing experience of front-line aerial combat, felt confident enough take on the enemy in dog-fights, using his mounted machine-gun. But his successful cooperation with Hotz was to come to a sudden end for a completely unexpected reason.

One day Denk requested Fieseler to meet him. He came straight to the point. 'My dear Fieseler, I'm facing a large difficulty. Recently I've turned down two requests from general command to second one of my pilots to operate as a fighter pilot. I've now got another request and I've got to cave in and release someone.' Fieseler knew what was coming. Before Denk resumed, he asked: 'Do you have me in mind, Sir?' 'I do', rejoined Denk. I know that you are well-suited for that. I'm sorry, but I've got to ask you: do you want to become a fighter pilot?' The answer came without hesitation. 'Indeed I do, Sir. That's just the move for me.'[47]

Hotz for his part took the news of his Emil's departure badly. 'Without you I'm done for,' he grieved. 'Really, Lieutenant Hotz,' Fieseler tried to reassure him, 'You will be fine with another pilot.' This only made things worse. 'If you go away', whimpered Hotz pathetically, 'It will be the death of me,' Again Fieseler tried to console him. 'Lieutenant Hotz, please, there is no need for that,' adding 'We all have our own destiny, and mine is beckoning me to become a fighter pilot.'[48] The next morning Fieseler left for his new posting, carefully avoiding another meeting with Hotz. This made him feel guilty, for Hotz was someone in whom he had had complete trust. He did, though, share a bottle of *Sekt* with Captain Denk, whose solemn words upon parting were: 'May the good Lord protect you on the path ahead.'

The cavalry to the rescue

Let us take stock of Fieseler in the context of military aviation after three years of war. As soon as he could, after the conflict broke out in August 1914, he joined the colours with millions of other patriotic young Germans. His destiny was to fly for the Fatherland. He saw himself as reporting on enemy dispositions from a lofty height. He no doubt imagined that he would be doing his duty on the Western Front to support the military effort against Germany's perpetual enemy, the French. But, whether he liked it or not, he was in the Balkans. He was by now flying planes that already made the 1914 machines look feeble in comparison with respect to power, clime, speed, versatility and armament. A good example of the awesome rate of technical change is given in a picture caption referring to a German Pfalz fighter in the 1990 edition of Richthofen's brief memoirs: 'At the beginning of 1917 the Pfalz factory produces the D III fighter biplane. Although it was an immediate operational success, by the end of 1917 it had already been technically overtaken'[49]

---

47   Fieseler, op. cit., p.56.
48   Ibid, p.57.
49   Richthofen, op. cit., p.41.

Although by 1916 dog-fights with machine guns blazing were dominating encounters between contending air forces, combat tactics were still underdeveloped. You picked things up from a few old hands or, as in Fieseler's case, you were self-taught in the art of aerial combat. So it was that each and every fighter pilot had his own method of confronting the enemy. At the same time the skills of pilots had to change along with all the technical developments. It was certainly no longer sufficient 'to love flying.' One had to be exceedingly brave, calm under monstrous pressures, and, for want of a better word, laconic. In the words of American air ace Eddie Rickenbacker: 'An airman's daily duties surround him every moment with the possibilities of death.'[50] Ernst Udet, a leading flying ace during the First World War and later high-ranking official in the Reich Aviation Ministry, was even more to the point: 'one does not think, one acts – or perishes.'[51]

Pilots might never talk about death and ways of dying, but all were conscious of it. German pilots did not wish each other good luck as they set off on missions from which they might not return, After all, the very utterance of those two words could charm misfortune. Rather than tempt fate with ill-chosen words, the pilots used the taboo-lancing formula '*Hals- und Beinbruch*', to be roughly translated as 'here's wishing you a broken neck and broken leg.' In other words: 'I hope it won't be your turn today.' Fieseler would have used this expression and had it wished on him countless times throughout the war.

That Fieseler was exceptionally brave is not in dispute. He had got into the cockpit again after a crash that nearly killed him, he had shown himself to be imperturbable when exposed to enemy fire, and had safely brought down stricken airplanes with observers who were a positive danger to him in the air. Thus, he was regarded as an outstanding pilot. In all this he acquired authority and stature. But his manner of putting observers and fellow flyers in their places suggests a wilful, confident personality, of which there were few if any signs before the war. Whether Fieseler was actually popular with his fellow flyers, we cannot say. At the very least we can say that he was not one to court popularity. Certainly his autobiography makes clear that he rather resented those, whether his peers or his superiors, who did not share his enthusiasm for flying. He was probably not very good at disguising his animosity; which, if true, would not have endeared him to his fellow flyers.

When Fieseler accepted the opportunity to become a fighter pilot, it surely was not just a case of wanting to embark on an even more dangerous form of life in the air. There can be no doubt that he anticipated the possibility of flying in Germany's most advanced fighter aircraft. This would unquestionably have been a massive incentive. But no doubt too he saw his new role as a golden opportunity to finish with aerial chauffeuring and to be free from anyone else on board. 'If I'm going to be killed', he might well have said to himself, 'it's going to be as a result of enemy fire, not because of some cowardly liability of a Franz.'

By 1915 it was clear to all sides that the airplane had a notable role to play in the war. Volunteers were needed to join the German Air Force as a matter of urgency. Specifically, there was said to be 'a chronic shortage of *aggressive* fighter pilots' (added emphasis).[52] One particular group who jumped at the offer to become pilots were the cavalrymen, who had been made increasingly redundant in the static war along the Western Front, where 'extensive barbed-wire entanglements and trench emplacements rendered tradition-rich mounted fighting and reconnaissance obsolete.'[53] The most famous of these aerial warriors by far was Manfred von Richthofen, who joined the Flying Corps in June 1915. At that time the airplane plane was still primarily viewed as an instrument of reconnaissance. This well suited to the likes of Richthofen, who saw his previous experience as a

50 Rickenbacker, op. cit., p.84.
51 Udet, op. cit., p.121.
52 Kilduff, op. cit., p.71.
53 Kilduff, op. cit., p.8.

cavalry officer as making him 'ideal as an observer.'[54] Indeed, 'my happiest time has come' he wrote. 'It had great similarity to my life in the cavalry. Every day, in the morning and afternoons, I could go on reconnaissance missions.'[55]

Rudolf Stark, who was also 'a recycled cavalryman,'[56] even admitted to 'patting the silver skin of my plane – just as I used to pat my horse,'[57] whilst on one occasion he actually likened his Fokker to a blood-stock animal![58] It is surely Richthofen, Stark and their ilk who more than any other group 'recreated the possibility of warfare between high-status combatants: a "cavalry of the clouds" … like "knights of the air" – looked after by loyal retainers, cheered on by grateful plebeians.'[59] Certainly they would have completely identified with a British officer who wrote in 1917 – not 1914, note – that 'flying is perhaps a little easier than riding a horse because you sit in a comfortable armchair in a quiet machine instead of a slippery saddle on a very lively horse.'[60] More prosaically, the horsemens' experience of spills from the saddle was said to toughen them for rough landings in aeroplanes.[61]

As for Ernst Udet, who did not have an equestrian background, the form of transportation that he thought about as he was being buffeted by the clouds was the toboggan.[62] But it was not just the perceived similarity between riding and flying that drew the cavalryman to take to the air. It was, writes Fieseler, simply below their dignity to join the infantry.[63] Very true, no doubt. Like Udet, Fieseler did not share that particularly gentlemanly romantic view of the airplane. Indeed, what emerges from his autobiography is that he appears to be one of the very few pilots – perhaps on any side in the conflict – who came with some sort of appreciation of aeronautics. He also got intensely frustrated with his peers and superiors for their indifference, and even ignorance about, the technical aspects of flying. For him it was a question of possessing 'an innate feel for flying' (*ein angeborenes fliegerisches Gefühl*), which in his opinion he had patently had and many others patently had not.[64]

At all events the problem of the shortage of pilots was very quickly resolved. The irony now was that, although new flying schools were sprouting up, there was a dearth of competent instructors. Fieseler, of course, had strong reason to know how inadequate pilot training had been. Nevertheless fresh influxes of pilots were coming through and were transferred to the front, joining the new *Jasta*. All well and good, thought Fieseler, but the flying examinations were still outmoded with the result that unsuitable men received their pilot's badge. Furthermore, in those days very little was known about desirable psychological attributes of good future pilots. 'Mere flying capability'[65] was certainly not a sufficient indicator of the capacity to cope with the intense – at that time unimaginable – stresses of being a pilot in wartime conditions. Fieseler was going to learn all about those stresses.

A local shortage of matadors

It was now May 1917 and Fieseler had been promoted to the rank of vice-sergeant-major (*Vizefeldwebel*).[66] In the course of his journey from his old outfit in Bucharest to his new one,

---

54 Richthofen, op. cit., p.38.
55 Ibid, p.38.
56 Kennett, op. cit., p.116.
57 A. Stark, *Wings of War*, p.16.
58 Ibid, p.150.
59 D. Edgerton, *England and the Aeroplane*, p.73.
60 Winter, op. cit., p.19.
61 Kilduff, op. cit., p.25.
62 Udet, op. cit., p.30.
63 Fieseler, op. cit., p.59.
64 Ibid, p.59.
65 Ibid, p.60.
66 R, Nagel und T. Bauer, *Kassel und die Luftfahrtindustrie seit 1923: Geschichte(n), Menschen, Technik*, p.424.

Jasta 25, somewhere over the border in Macedonia, Fieseler learnt – it is not clear how – that Lieutenant Hotz, his former very reliable Franz, had been killed in action. That was what Hotz himself had prophesied. This deeply affected Fieseler. Why him and not me, he asked himself? He found himself philosophising. 'Are there supernatural forces', he pondered, 'that we are unable to perceive with our senses?' Then he partly answered his own question: 'Much of what I've experienced points in that direction.'[67] Writing those words, when he was more than 80 years old, he must have thought many times that he had cheated death so often in his long life. How was it that he survived, when millions – literally millions – did not?

It turned out that *Jasta* 25 was based on the Salonika Front not far from the then Serbian-Greek border in Macedonia. According to a Macedonian source, it had taken up its duties there on 28 November 1916.[68] Was he to do his duty for the Fatherland here of all places? When he arrived at his destination, the summer heat, 40º in the shade, was overpowering. He found himself surveying an improvised airfield on untended farmland not far from the town of Kanatlarci, some 15 kms from the regional capital, Prilep and some 100 kilometres south of the capital, Skopje. Fieseler passes no comment on Prilep, but when it fell into French hands in September 1918, it was found to be a 'picturesque little town, with its white minarets, low wooden houses, and rows of black cypresses, plane trees and almonds ... [having] an enchantingly oriental atmosphere.'[69]

Wherever he looked, as he approached the airfield, there was not a single tree or bush; no human being was to be seen. A factor accounting for the absence of people is offered by the German military historian Sebastian Rosenboom: 'Since most of the indigenous people were by all accounts superstitious, they were as a rule profoundly impressed with the modern flying machines and to some extent in awe of them. At the sight of them, they would cross often themselves in amazed wonder.'[70] Perhaps the local people of Kanatlarci wanted nothing to do with these diabolical machines and the ungodly men who flew in them. As for the airfield all he could see were a few tents and wooden sheds, into everyone had crawled to escape the heat. It was depressing. He found his way to the camp office.

However, the camp at Kanatlarci was quite possibly not as godforsaken as his brief description suggests. There was a German field bookshop (*Deutsche Feld-Buchhandlung*) for the use of German troops stationed in the vicinity. This is an intriguing place. It was not just a bookshop, but would have also served as a post-office, from which German soldiers could despatch food parcels to their starving families back home. It was also a place where soldiers could buy newspapers and other small items as well as being something of an 'improvised recreation point', seeing that several German infantryman were based in nearby Prilep.[71]

'We've been expecting you, sergeant', said the orderly, adding morosely. 'In case you've not noticed, the climate here in the summer is terrible. About a third of the lads are sick: malaria, dysentery, typhus.'[72] What sort of ghastly posting was this? How Fieseler would have liked to return to Captain Denk forthwith. Enquiring about his quarters, Fieseler was taken by the orderly to a ramshackle shack of about five metres square. The roof and walls were covered with tar paper. In the middle was a battered bed. 'There's nothing else available just now,' said the orderly. 'I'll make do', replied the Fieseler resignedly.[73] When the orderly had cleared off, Fieseler squatted on the bed, deeply regretting that he had not resisted this posting to the back of beyond. He dozed off only to

67 Fieseler, op. cit., p.61
68 www.oldprilep.com/vojna-mir/neboto-nad-prilep.
69 Palmer, op. cit., p.216.
70 Rosenboom, op. cit., p.85.
71 Dr Heather Jones, LSE; private communication.
72 Fieseler, op. cit., p.61.
73 Ibid, .p. 62.

be awoken by some voices. Out of nowhere or so it seemed there were some fitters and supervisors as well as pilots. Fieseler emerged from his shack. There were handshakes and greetings for the newcomer.

The chief was a certain Senior Lieutenant Burckhardt, who had been in charge since the previous December. One of the more talkative of the pilots by name of Pinkert described the chief as 'a professional officer, 28 years old, who had already learnt to fly in 1912, friendly with a sense of humour, but rather weak and indecisive.'[74] His informant added that Burckhardt was careful not to get too close to people and kept himself to himself. On his first meeting with him, Fieseler found that that this estimation summed him up to a tee. This was a bitter disappointment, for he had expected the leader of a group of fighter pilots to radiate confidence, clarity and energy. It turned out that the key role in the set-up was played not by the other pilots, but by an erstwhile infantryman. This was a certain Wiesner (not his real name), who with four aerial victories was, in Fieseler's phrase, 'the squadron matador', a position he plainly relished.[75] Fieseler found him unpleasant and shifty.

Another dubious character was a small, nervous type, a man from Bavaria named Bauhofer, who had once suffered the disturbing experience of being caught by flak coming from a German artillery unit. Blind with rage, he had thrown his plane into frenzied dive and even sprayed the unit with a burst of machine-gun fire. All this made Fieseler think that this bunch of pilots, although they had been on the front for more than a year, were probably a rather useless lot. He was right. In that time they had only managed to bring down twelve planes in addition to the matador's modest tally. Those twelve victories were thanks to two pilots who had spent half a year on the Western Front before being transferred to the Balkans. Needless to say, these two clashed with Burckhardt. 'There have been some right bust-ups', confided the knowing, talkative Pinkert.[76]

Together with these two there were fourteen pilots in all. Fieseler describes them all as 'calm, straightforward and decent fellows,' even if they were not exactly covering themselves with glory.[77] He put that down to the poor leadership. All his cherished preconceptions about being a fighter pilot were wiped away. He had expected the chief to have conversations with him about enemy aircraft, about how to operate on the front, about aerial tactics and formation flying. Nothing! No wonder there was hardly any *esprit de corps* among his new comrades. He mused over these things. He accused himself over being prematurely sceptical about his key outfit. Once he had been on the front, he would have a better picture of things.

The *Jasta* was equipped with Roland DIIs, which gave pilots a restricted field of view and came equipped with two machine guns, which were prone to jamming. These aircraft were not popular and found service on the less well-known Eastern Front.[78] Fieseler took one up for the first time. Something was not right. He gingerly made a circuit of the airfield and promptly brought the machine down. He called over the supervisor of the fitters and mechanics. 'The body of this machine is either warped or there's too much tension – in fact probably both.' 'Can't be', the other retorted. 'It was thoroughly checked.' Fieseler shook his head. 'Look, this thing is a danger to anyone flying it. No pilot should touch it.'[79] The supervisor pretended not to know anything about it. The reason for that was simple: it was common practice for any newcomer to any kind of flying unit to get the worst aircraft. In this case the aircraft assigned to Fieseler could have cost him his

74 Ibid, p.62.
75 Ibid, p.62.
76 Ibid, p.62.
77 Ibid, p.62.
78 H. Ringlstetter, Kampfeinsitzer der ersten Jahre, in *Flugzeug Classic Special 12*, pp.54-59.
79 Fieseler, op. cit., p.63.

life. That machine duly went in for a further service and he was given a different machine (whether it was a DII or a different type altogether is not clear.) There was no problem with this one.

The whole Balkan Front was 400 kilometres long. Fieseler's squadron was responsible for about 150 kilometres. The terrain was roadless and there were mountains up to 3,000 metres high with steep sides. Two more German flying squadrons were in the vicinity of his camp near Prilep, which was the headquarters for an army group under General von Scholtz, consisting of seven Bulgarian divisions and the staff of two German army corps.[80] On the enemy side there were three French fighter squadrons along with an Italian one backed up by four French reconnaissance units. Every now and again British fighters were in the skies. German headquarters were in telephone communication with their three units and it was up to the duty officer of each of them to give the order for take-off. In this case regulations stated that a minimum of three aircraft was to take to the air. Fieseler's first three weeks passed uneventfully. Then both Wiesner and Bauhofer went on leave (the latter with nervous exhaustion induced by the blazing heat.) Pondering the rather ad hoc approach to formation flying, Fieseler asked himself how exactly he was supposed to stick to in formation, when enemy aircraft got near.

One day, around breakfast time at 6.30 in the morning, there was an alarm. Six or seven pilots took off in random order without any attempt at formation. But it was too late. A group of nine British bombers, supported by three fighters, had overflown the German-occupied zone, dropped their bombs over Prilep and headed back the way they came. None of the pilots in Fieseler's *Jasta* got remotely close to the British planes. How on earth was that possible? Did they not know that manoeuvres executed in isolation were nothing and that what counted was the capacity to cling to the enemy in small numbers?[81] Fieseler was not the only one who wanted answers to that. So did headquarters, which fired Burckhardt with the questions, which he found excruciating. Fieseler himself asked his fellow pilots what the problem was. They were silent or evasive, muttering that the British were a big threat. Then on the evening of the same day there was another bombing raid by the British. As before, the alarm had been given, there had been no clear instructions, there had been no sign of leadership.

On this occasion, however, Fieseler was among those who took off. At least they were quicker on the draw this time. When though Fieseler found a suitable position to attack one the British planes, he discovered that not a single comrade of his was in the vicinity. He swept in on the highest of the enemy formation. The pilot veered off immediately. Then two of the British planes set on him with their machine guns. Fieseler had only one option. He put his DII into a steep dive and eventually landed safely. One of his fitters came up to him and reported: 'The chief had a tough fight. He was almost shot down.'[82] It turned out that all the manoeuvring to keep safe had totally exhausted Burckhardt, who upon landing had taken himself to the make-shift sick-bay.

Fieseler could hardly believe his ears. Then his suspicions were aroused. He made a point of inspecting the chief's plane. There was not a single bullet hole to be seen. The chief, it quickly dawned on him, had cut and run, and so had all the others. Although he was the most junior member of the squadron, Fieseler gave his version of events to his fellow pilots in no uncertain terms. This was hardly a way to make himself popular with them. Then one of them rounded on him; 'You just said that there isn't much going on here. Well then, just you show us what you can do!'[83]

---

80   Palmer, op. cit., p.199.
81   Winter, op. cit., p.135.
82   Fieseler, op. cit., p.65.
83   Ibid, p.65.

On the very next morning, on Fieseler's suggestion, a group of planes was ready for take-off at 6.00am under the command of the most senior pilot. They approached the oncoming British planes, having the advantage of height to swoop down on them. But the pilot in the lead pretended not to see them and carried on, taking his small squadron with him – all except Fieseler, that is, who broke away from the main group and attempted to signal to it the whereabouts of the enemy. His comrades paid no attention. The British planes headed off for their own lines. Fieseler left the other German pilots to their own devices, intending to make an attack on the enemy. At one point he was joined by one of his own formation. Fieseler signalled to him that they should proceed to disable one of the British planes jointly.

To his frustration the machine gun on the right-hand side of his plane jammed. 'Same old problem', he might well have muttered to himself. Despite that handicap he confronted one of the British bombers only to discover that his comrade in arms had cleared off. Fieseler was now in single combat with the British airplane. He outmanoeuvred it. His finger squeezed the trigger of the one operational machine-gun. This too jammed, but not before it had managed to propel a solitary bullet which 'unbelievably'[84] smashed into the head of the British pilot – the proverbial 'inhuman goggled figure',[85] a comrade of sorts who happened to be your sworn enemy.

Fieseler put his plane into a downward spiral, almost striking the propeller of his assailant's aircraft in the process. He saw a cloud of dust as the British plane crashed. It should have been his first air victory, but there was no-one on his side to corroborate it. Nevertheless, with his first aerial victory – or kill – he had joined 'a handful of men [who] fought in a virgin medium' – the air – 'seeming to personify skill in arms, individual judgement and sustained ferocity in single combat leading to a calculated killing.'[86]

This was Fieseler's first aerial victory, which according to a Macedonian source, took place on 20 April 1917.[87] Fieseler himself confirms that his victim was a certain Major Bamford, who according to him was the squadron leader of the British force. A British website provides two eye-witness statements of his death, which were quoted in the Belfast Newsletter of 1 October 1917 under the headline 'Airman falls 12,000 feet.' The first is the commanding officer of Lieutenant – not Major – Joseph Bamford, an Ulsterman born in 1894, who had won the Croix de Guerre in 1917. According to this account:

> He, together with another pilot, each on single-seater scout machines, escorting a bombing formation to (Prilep). On the return journey our machines were attacked by a considerably numerical superiority of the enemy. [Your son] fought brilliantly for a long time, guarding the rear of the formation, on several occasions helping other of our machines out of extremely tight corners. In the course of one of his engagements he had obtained position behind an enemy machine and was firing at it, and would undoubtedly have brought it down in a few seconds, when another hostile scout dived on him from a considerable height, firing as he came down. Your son's machine was seen immediately to fall completely out of control, giving the impression that its pilot had been killed. This machine fell thus until it reached ground, and on the morning of the 21st we received confirmation of his death from two captured German aviators.

---

84   Ibid, p.66.
85   Winter, op. cit., p.132.
86   Ibid, pp.132-133.
87   www.oldprielp.com?vojna-mirr/neboto-nad-prilep

In the words of the second account, Bamford

> was killed in an air fight on 20th August. He was fighting one Hun when another came up behind, and then, of course, it was all up. He must have been killed instantly, for his machine came down entirely out of control. They fought at 12,000 feet, and he fell in the Hun lines. He has already been avenged, as we brought three of them down yesterday. He died as I know he would have wished, swiftly and fighting as only brave men can fight. He was a star pilot and fully recognised as such by his comrades.[88]

Fieseler – the Hun in question – mentions that he was attacking British bombers. However, according to the Macedonian source, he in fact shot down a French Nieuport 17, a well-regarded French biplane fighter which were ordered in considerable number by the Royal Flying Corps. There were immediate consequences of his first aerial victory. First, the British, wary that they had lost such an accomplished airman, avoided that sector in future. Second, Fieseler found myself in a extraordinary situation on terra firma, which given his very recent brush with death in the sky he calls with unwitting irony 'dangerous.'[89] He was the junior member of his *Jasta* and he had just exposed his fellow pilots as faint-hearted. Many consequently avoided him like the plague.

Once his anger was stilled, Fieseler decided to see Burckhardt, who was still laid up in the sick-bay. 'Sir, I can't stand it here anymore,' he pleaded, 'I want to go to the Western Front. There's *esprit de corps* there. I could get killed any day here.' The chief sought to calm him down: 'My dear Fieseler, no, no. Please wait until Wiesner and Bauhofer return from leave. Things'll change. You wait and see.'[90] Fieseler looked at the chief, 'a desperate, helpless man, who was not up to the job.' 'Please stay, Fieseler.' The young flyer, probably against his better judgement, let himself to persuaded not to put in for a transfer. 'All right, I'll stay then,' he conceded, adding with undisguised lack of respect for rank. 'I expect you to replace the cowards and whip things into shape!'[91]

Fieseler left the sick-bay with a sense of gloom. His long-cherished dream of joining a fighter squadron and being initiated into the arts of aerial combat was in tatters. Until being stuck in this obscure corner of the Balkans, he could not have imagined that German fighter pilots would avoid confronting enemy aircraft. He found himself with pilots for whom flying weather (*Flugwetter*) was never preferable to so-called 'flyers' weather' (*Fliegerwetter*), when the poor weather meant that pilots – often to their great relief – were under orders not to take their planes up. He really could not believe that things would get any better. Twenty of so years later he might have read the memoirs of Rudolf Stark, who wrote of his own experiences: 'The first weeks in a fighter squadron are always the most dangerous.'[92] However, Stark had in mind the dangers that spring from flying over unfamiliar territory or not spotting the enemy in time, not the threat posed by one's fellow flyers.

It has been argued by a German source that pilots were reluctant to confront the enemy because 'very many' ... knew each other from the [pre-war] flying shows and were more interested in their opponents' aircraft than engaging in mutual attempts to shoot themselves down.'[93] But it seems hard to credit this. Whilst the first phase of aviators did join their nations' respective air forces, they would have constituted but a small number of the total numbers of pilots who enlisted in 1914: in Germany's case 'some 4,000,' the vast majority of whom would not have been civilian pilots.[94]

88   http://www.magherafeltwardead.co.uk/persondepth.asp?cas_id=877
89   Fieseler, op. cit., p.66.
90   Ibid, p.67.
91   Ibid, p.67.
92   Stark, op. cit., p.19.
93   Deutsches Historisches Museum, *Der Erste Weltkrieg in 100 Objekten,* p.128.
94   Ibid, p.128.

There were simply not enough mutually acquainted pilots to go round. But we can be certain that the introduction of the interrupter gear in 1915, whereby aircraft became genuinely lethal weapons of war, created natural fear among pilots. Even so, Fieseler's accounts of the timorous attitudes of his fellow flyers right up to the end of the war would seem to support his opinion that officers failed a key test of military leadership: that troops must have confidence in their commanders.

Richthofen's death: An unmentionable topic

Since 1916 'German aerial supremacy was starting to crumble, [as] 'new allied fighter planes proved themselves to be superior to the Fokker and Pfalz monoplanes.'[95] All the exuberance which had accompanied the outbreak of war had evaporated. Every soldier knew how grim it was on the front. Just about every family at home had lost dear ones and feared more heart-ache. Everywhere in Germany was indescribable suffering, misery, poverty. For his part Fieseler was doing his duty for the Fatherland far beyond its borders. He knew that he was an exceptionally talented aerial gladiator, but here in Macedonia he was largely surrounded by cowards.

But by summer 1917 he had strangely enough softened his attitude towards them. After three years of terrible war Germany's losses and casualties were mounting into millions; of the latter hundreds of thousands of the wounded would be crippled for life. However much the authorities in any belligerent country appealed for the supreme effort or dished out medals and decorations, there was simply less and less willingness to fight. The very dread of not surviving the war, says Fieseler, 'created an even stronger counterforce, which, because it was all-present, was never quite suppressed and conquered. No-one spoke about this fear, which was primordial (*kreatürlich*) in nature, and of which everyone was aware.'[96]

He goes on: 'Every soldier, whether in the trenches, on the high seas or in the air, was exposed to the same kind of dangers.'[97] But he qualifies this with the observation that airmen, unique among the armed services, had the opportunity to artfully avoid both danger and direct confrontation with the enemy. Beyond that, the pilot 'had no need to march long distances with heavy packs, then hurl grenades or fight with bayonets at close quarters.'[98] So, given that asymmetry the life of pilots was often seen as a soft option by the armies fighting on the ground. Yet, taking off to encounter the enemy could be in its own way as nerve-shredding as it was for infantrymen going over the top. You could not be certain that you would survive any day's encounter with the enemy.

Fieseler was aware of all the dangers and had a determined attitude that set him apart from his comrades. Some of them viewed him as a troublemaker, others saw in him a useful outsider and even a welcome daredevil (*Draufgänger*), yet others simply assumed he would be dead before long, which in any case was a high statistical probability. In the event it happened that he became a pilot who fought alone; he was simply better off without such unreliable comrades in his vicinity It has been written that 'fighter pilots were the most isolated of fighting men, and necessarily so.'[99] Fieseler would spend much of the rest of the war largely living out that truth.

After the first ten or so aerial combats he was able to make shrewder assessments of his opponents. He learned how to outmanoeuvre them, to come out of the sun at them, to make rapid escapes. These were the essential flying skills with which he managed to survive the war. Another factor was his relentless drive to do his duty for the Fatherland and to engage courageously in aerial combat. Throughout his life he would never be able to explain this drive. As with all other

95   H. Ringlstetter, Fokker D.I-V, in: *Classic Flugzeug Special 12*, pp.42-47.
96   Fieseler, p.68.
97   Ibid, p.68.
98   Winter, p.133.
99   Winter, op. cit., p.174

fighter pilots he knew that is in essence a matter of kill or be killed. To cope with that, according to the American air ace, Eddie Rickenbacker, you needed a 'quick-thinking, unburdened mind.'[100] Fieseler would have agreed.

Fieseler was adamant that some of his more disconcerting experiences in the Balkans were replicated on the Western Front, where in his uncompromising opinion 'a clear majority of the fighter pilots (*die weitaus meisten Jagdflieger*) were unsuitable.'[101] However, there were also commanders who could not be called cowards by any stretch of the imagination. They would go at the enemy hammer and tongs, but this led to heavy losses. Even Richthofen's famous Flying Circus, which consisted of four squadrons (*Staffeln*) famed for their bright red livery, had been 'decimated' (*aufgerieben*) on no less than three occasions.[102] Many of Germany's best pilots were losing their lives. But no death matched in impact that in April 1918 of Richthofen himself, whose name was considered by Ludendorff, Germany's military leader, to be 'the equivalent of three infantry divisions.'[103] It foreshadowed something ominous for Germany. It may not be entirely outlandish to equate the death of Richthofen with the assassination fifty years later of President J F Kennedy: you know where you were when you heard about it.

Perverse as it may sound, the titanic – the totemic – Richthofen was so greatly admired as a pilot – as 'a genius' (*Alleskönner*)[104] – that, when he was felled in April 1918, the British and the French buried him with full military honours. On that day

> six pilots of 209 Squadron carried the black wooden coffin out of the hanger to the gun carriage. Over 10 British and French pilots followed it. They had come from every squadron on the front. They walked behind the coffin down the road to the cemetery at the end of the road.

A machine took off that evening from Bertangles with a container wrapped in bunting. The lights were still burning in the Richthofen Squadron H.Q. When the officers opened the container they found a photograph of the late commander's grave and a sheet of paper giving the following information:

> To the German Flying Corps. Captain Freiherr Manfred von Richthofen was killed in an air battle on 21st April, 1918. He was buried with full military honours.[105]

Richthofen's solemn and respectful burial befitted the curious sense of chivalry in the air observed by flyers on all sides as a sign of respect to an honourable and gallant adversary. There are even incidents of pilots who refrained from shooting down the enemy when an unfair advantage intervened. Perhaps the most celebrated case involved the French ace, Guynemer, who had a perfect opportunity to kill Ernst Udet, who as a member of the Flying Circus would finish the war as Germany's second highest scoring fighter pilot after Richthofen. In a frantic dog-fight Guynemer could see that Udet's gun had jammed. The Frenchman considered it unchivalrous to kill a fellow airman who could not protect himself through no fault of his own. He raised his arm, waved and disappeared in the direction of his own lines.[106] Thus did Udet, with 62 victories to his name by the

---

100   Rickenbacker, op. cit., p.34
101   Fieseler, op. cit., p.69.
102   Ibid, p.69.
103   Winter, op. cit., p.133.
104   Krumeich, op. cit., p.50.
105   H. Herlin, *Udet: A Man's Life*, pp.55-56.
106   Udet, op. cit., pp.61-63.

end of the war, live on to become Richthofen's 'real successor … in terms of air combat successes.'[107] In the case of all the honours lavished on Richthofen it is as if his adversaries had exonerated the famed Red Baron of downing 80 of their fellow airmen. As far as the British were concerned, Manfred von Richthofen was, in a manner of speaking, the Rommel of the First World War.

Fieseler remembers when the official announcement of Richthofen's death reached Kanatlarci. No-body discussed it. This was consistent with attitudes to death among pilots. They grieved for fallen comrades in private. The death of one pilot 'gave survivors experience of their own death.'[108] One therefore kept silent. The French ace Guynemer, who had died in September 1917, had written a Latin tag in his diary: '*Hodie mihi, cras tibi*' (me today, you tomorrow).[109] No pilot needed to be reminded of that.

At this point in his tale Fieseler introduces a remarkable, if not highly intriguing conversation with Ernst Udet. who was, like Fieseler, a stunt pilot in the 1920s and early 1930s. The two became close friends, but the friendship came to an abrupt end in November 1941 when Udet, by then Director-General of Equipment for the Luftwaffe, committed suicide. There is no doubt that Richthofen fascinated his fellow flyers. He was among all the fighter pilots of the First World War the legend of legends. But Fieseler and Udet do not discuss Richthofen with dewy-eyed awe, but as professionals with comparable experience.

The conversation begins with a discussion about the air war on the Western Front. Fieseler asks Udet for his opinion about Richthofen. He was, replies the gregarious Udet, 'a rather unapproachable chief … No-one could get behind his uncommunicativeness (*Verschlossenheit*).'[110] Udet's observation is consistent with the verdict that Richthofen 'did not attempt to be "one of the boys", even though he socialised with his men in off-duty hours in the mess.'[111] Indeed his mother was conscious of 'his moroseness and aloofness to the point of being almost unapproachable.'[112]

As far as Udet was concerned, his former commander 'was a typical Prussian cavalry officer.' Fieseler, who presumably knew what that meant, makes no comment and asks a question that had no doubt intrigued him for many years about Richthofen: 'What about him as a flyer? How could he notch up so many victories?' Udet, giving a gesture of indifference, responded: 'In the beginning he had a few crashes, but his intuition as a pilot (*sein fliegerisches Gefühl*) took a long time to develop. Then he joined Boelcke's squadron, with whom he was on good terms and who taught him the basics. There was nothing mysterious about our tactics. You had to have the guts (*Schneid*) to fly into a hail of machine gun fire … and shoot better than your adversary. If you caught an enemy fighter unawares, your job was to get in the first rounds. If you didn't manage to do that, then you'd be in a life or death spin. Whoever was the better at manoeuvring was the winner.'

'There's nothing special about that', Fieseler comments. 'You take each combat as it comes,' adding that 'a good pilot has to be able to make quick decisions in a split second and must have a specific predisposition for flying.' To which Udet rejoins: 'and lots of courage and plenty of luck.' Thinking of some his own precarious disastrous experiences, Fieseler adds another factor: 'cover from another fighter.' Between them Fieseler and Udet then seem to be saying that as a fighter pilot Richthofen was not out of the ordinary. Fieseler is even more explicit. Richthofen was, he concedes, Germany's was most decorated and lionised soldier, but the legend became more important than the man. Udet agrees, but concedes that, although Richthofen often landed with his plane shot to

---

107 Kilduff, op. cit., p.219.
108 Winter, op. cit., p.159.
109 Ibid, p.159.
110 Fieseler, op. cit., p.70.
111 Kilduff, op. cit., p.77.
112 Ibid, p.174.

ribbons, he was an indisputably courageous flyer. But again Fieseler is not very impressed. 'There is nothing special about that either,' he chips in.

On the point about Richthofen being closely protected in the air, it has been noted that 'the aeroplane-maker Fokker thought that a wingman in attendance was the chief reason that Richthofen survived so long.'[113] If that sounds somewhat belittling, in his memoirs Fokker points out that Richthofen flew using his brain and had a rare capacity to analyse fast-moving situations in combat conditions.[114] He also had the rare achievement of being among the very few pilots who were 'specialists in peripheral hovering.'[115] In addition Richthofen was, in the words of one of his new recruits – young hares (*Häschen*) in German airforce slang – 'unequalled as an instructor.'[116]

Fieseler told Udet that he had heard that Richthofen had claimed victories that really belonged to other people. This was not so startling, as there was intense rivalry – and dirty tricks – amongst pilots for securing victories to obtain the coveted *Pour le Mérite,* Germany's highest decoration for an individual act of gallantry. The problem concerned ensuring independent witnesses from one's own side. When pilots and observers flew together before one-to-one combat, verification 'for personal statistics' was easier.[117] However, when it came to 'noted fighter pilots' and no-one was more illustrious than Richthofen, it was common knowledge that such luminaries 'either gave away victories or took credit for the work of their subordinates.'[118] So why not Germany's most famous airman? To this Udet replied nonchalantly that he had heard similar stories. He did not know for certain, he said. In truth, he probably did. It is in the end an open question. What though is inescapable that there were rumours about his claim to all his aerial victories. Indeed one airforce lieutenant specifically claimed to 'have heard from various sources that the number of machines shot down by the entire circus was claimed by [Richthofen] personally.'[119]

This conversation between Fieseler and Udet is certainly intriguing. They are not saying that Richthofen lacked courage, but both are unmistakably suggesting that he was overrated as a pilot. But was there perhaps some professional envy on their part? We shall never know, but we can speculate. Concerning Udet, he may well have thought himself to be a better pilot than his famed commander; which was probably the case. As for Fieseler, he might have felt that too much glory attached itself to Richthofen and that he, for his singular achievements on the Macedonian front, deserved far more fame.

That Richthofen was the highest-scoring German fighter pilot of the First World War is not in doubt, but whether he was the best is a different matter. Fieseler and Udet plainly did not believe that he was not outstanding in all respects. That is confirmed by another pilot of that era, Antonius Raab, who will play a short, but important role in Fieseler's life in the 1920s. According to Raab, Richthofen never mastered the art of landing. He may well have damaged a dozen or so aircraft. Given this propensity, there were always 'two or three red birds' standing in reserve.[120]

Part of the Richthofen legend refers to his chivalry. In the words of one biographer: As far as the public were concerned, 'Manfred *Freiherr* von Richthofen was the 20th century incarnation of the mediaeval knight ... a model of courage and discipline for other Germans to emulate.'[121] Indeed Richthofen reigned *and reigns* supreme among Germany's 'aviator heroes [who] became military

---

113 Winter, op. cit., p.142.
114 A. Fokker, *Der Fliegende Holländer: Die Memoiren des A. H. G. Fokker,* p.221.
115 Winter, op. cit., p.103.
116 Kilduff, op. cit., p.168.
117 Rosenboom, op. cit., p.74.
118 Kilduff, op. cit., p.187.
119 Ibid, p.187.
120 A. Raab, *Raab fliegt: Erinnerungen eines Flugpioniers.*, p.20.
121 Kilduff, op. cit., p.73

and national symbols. Indeed "branded articles" and whose 'portraits and names came to stand for the nation itself and another (victorious) war.'[122] The potency and durability of the Richthofen brand is beyond dispute. In August 2016 – a hundred years after he shot to fame – *The Times* newspaper described him as 'the world's most celebrated pilot.'[123]

Echoing these sentiments, in the introduction to the 1990 edition of his short memoirs, first published in 1917, former NATO Secretary-General, Dr Manfred Wörner, describes Richthofen as 'a symbol of chivalry, unblemished conduct and flying capability.'[124] There are many who see him that way. Wörner adds that Richthofen, had he lived, would have distanced himself with loathing from the atrocities of the Nazis.' Really? Consider how in his own words Richthofen describes his doings on the Russian Front in 1915:

> He and his pilot 'sought out military camps, as it is special fun to worry (*beunruhigen*) the people below with machine guns. Such half-wild Asiatics have a good deal more fear that the educated English'[125]

and

> My observer steadily fired his machine gun at the [Russian] brothers, and we found that hilarious (*hatten wilden Spass*)[126]

It is impossible not to conclude that on both occasions Richthofen's plane was liberally spraying bullets at Russian troops who were an easy target. It would not have been fun otherwise. That Richthofen relished in these cannonades is confirmed by his own words. This is *Schadenfreude*, not chivalry. Chivalry, it seems, was reserved for the fighting worthy adversaries such as the French and the British; it was not needed against worthless 'Asiatics.' With his aristocratic Prussian background, his illustrious flying career, his international renown, his racial disdain for Russians, there is little doubt that Richthofen would have been highly promising material indeed for the Nazis. It would be left to his ruthless first cousin Wolfram to bear the Nazi mantle as a field marshal of the Luftwaffe during the next war. This Richthofen was 'an avid believer in the power of aerial bombardment', for whom civilian casualties were 'simply a by-product of war,'[127]

These comments are not for one moment to suggest that Richthofen would have gone along with the Nazi programme of annihilation of so-called 'sub-humans.' But we can be absolutely certain that, if he had lived, the Red Baron would have been cultivated for higher things by Hitler and Göring. This after all is exactly as happened to Udet, who did not refuse the opportunity to help build up the Luftwaffe into a war-machine fit to avenge the sham defeat of Germany in 1918. Indeed within a few weeks of Hitler coming into power in January 1933, Fieseler himself joined the Nazi Party. He for his part was not going to lose the opportunity to build aircraft for the Führer. But in his case he did not have vengeance on his mind.

---

122   F. Esposito, *Fascism, Aviation and Mythical Modernity*, London, Palgrave Macmillan, p.208.
123   *The Times*, Families to toast Red Baron and his "kills," 30 August 2016.
124   Richthofen, op. cit., p.6.
125   Ibid, p.65.
126   Ibid, p.66.
127   D. Sloggett, *A Century of Air Power: The changing Face of Warfare, 1912-2012*, p.150.

4

Tiger of Macedonia

Der Starke ist am mächtigsten allein' (The strong man is at his mightiest alone).
                                                Friedrich Schiller, *Wilhelm Tell*.

Fly he would; excel he must. The war itself was simply a means to that end.
                                                Jack D. Hunter, *The Blue Max*.[1]

Ersatz: no substitute

Fieseler knew that after three years of war most of his fellow flyers on the Macedonian Front were unlikely to demonstrate any real preparedness for combat. They simply did not find aerial combat with its much-vaunted 'romance and glamour' to be 'thrilling to the point of addiction'[2] – that high-octane elation which jumps from the pages of the memoirs of von Richthofen, Udet, Fokker and Rickenbacker. So it was a great consolation for Fieseler when his unit received the latest version of the Albatros biplane, which had the great advantage of properly functioning machine guns. This would have been the Albatros D.VII, which Fieseler rated very highly.

But unfortunately for Fieseler, within a few weeks, he and his Albatros were destined to be separated from each other for nearly two months. On or around 21 September 1917 he found himself suffering from a raging fever and could hardly stand on his own two feet. 'You've got typhus', the field doctor casually told him. 'You need proper treatment straightaway.'[3] Typhus, along with malaria, was a major scourge across the Balkans.[4] Fieseler was taken to a field hospital for infectious diseases in Prilep, which once upon a time had been a barracks and which now was so crammed with patients that tents had been erected to deal with the overflow. Fieseler would never forget the scenes of suffering and death. He spent three weeks there, delirious and apathetic, wasting away and passing through all the stages of the disease on the slow road to recovery. After those three weeks he was discharged and told to take home leave.

He went all the way back to Bonn on a variety of trains. Back in Germany, wherever he looked, he was confronted by the misery of war. People queued in long, dispirited lines in front of the few shops that were open to get meagre rations. By now people were making coffee from acorns and tea from ground raspberry leaves, clothing and underwear from paper.[5] There was even vegetarian meat (then known as 'meatless meat'), which almost a hundred years on has been ranked by a BBC's news reporter in Berlin among the '10 inventions that owe their success to World War One', the other

---

1   J. D. Hunter, *The Blue Max*, p.50.
2   B. Bryson, *One Summer: America 1927*, p.18.
3   G. Fieseler, *Meine Bahn am Himmel*, p.72.
4   A. Palmer, *The Gardeners of Salonika*, p.23 and p.32.
5   N. MacGregor, *Germany: Memories of a Nation*, p.420.

nine being sanitary towels, paper handkerchiefs, the sun lamp, daylight saving time, tea bags, the wristwatch, zips, stainless steel and ground-to-air communications.[6]

Fieseler stood aghast in front of his family house. It looked utterly desolate. As he entered, his mother, care-worn and haggard, greeted him in tears. She showed him a new sister, Maria, whimpering in a cradle. Maria was six months old, more than twenty years younger than him, which he found somewhat incomprehensible. His mother told him that, if he had not been sending back biscuits from the front, the little one would have not survived. Fieseler began to realise that it was the Entente Powers' blockade of food imports that was crippling Germany, not defeat on the battlefield, horrific as trench warfare had become. In fact it was not only the blockade. On the home front 'food distribution had been a disaster, with rampant price inflation and an even more exorbitant black market.'[7] In short the German civilian population was the victim of 'permanent mismanagement of the economy (*Misswirtschaft*) above all in the cities.'[8]

His father, who had joined the home guard (*Landsturm*), had got special permission to take leave in order to spend time with his son. He was embittered and pessimistic, declaring flatly 'we've had it', adding that he – once the great optimist – could not be bothered with his business these days.[9] Although Herr and Frau Fieseler were happy to have Gerhard with them for a few weeks, they were troubled about their second son, August, who was fighting on the Western front. There had been no word from him for some time. Then, one day before Gerhard returned to Macedonia, a letter arrived from his brother. 'He's alive', gasped Fieseler *père* with joy and relief. August had scribbled a few reassuring lines. He was at Verdun, he wrote, and would be home before long.

After four weeks with his parents, it was time for Gerhard to leave for Salonika. Even though he had still not fully recovered from the bout of typhus, he was privately glad to be returning to the front and to be flying again. He could not stand any more of the enforced idleness. His mother accompanied him to the station. Perhaps, as was expected of German mothers, she carried the burden of his departure 'with grace and her head held high.'[10] But then perhaps not. As the train was pulling out, he tried to cheer her up: 'It won't last forever', he said, 'All wars finish one day.'[11] He hung out of the window and watched his mother as she vanished into a tiny dot. On the journey he could not put out of his mind her face wreathed with sadness.

When he finally made contact with his old *Jasta* in Macedonia at the beginning of November, he was still shaky on his feet. While he had been away, Wiesner, the squadron matador, and Bauhofer had both secured an aerial victory each, but this brought no elation at this stage in the war. There was a weird stillness overhanging the front even though there was no real lull in hostilities. Besides, there was now a persistent rumour that the Allies were planning a major offensive on the Balkan Front, whose purpose was to wipe out the opposition of the Central Powers. Back in the cockpit Fieseler downed three military aircraft in single combat.

One day he was flying with his squadron at an altitude of 400 metres. He became aware and then suspicious of three dots slightly behind the German formation. He broke away, got a better view and established that these dots were very fast fighters of a type he had not encountered before. Suddenly they were approaching the main formation of German fighters undetected. Fieseler raced to catch up his comrades, but he was being outpaced. In a daring manoeuvre, putting his Albatros

---

6   http://www.bbc.co.uk/news/magazine-26935867, posted on 13 April 2014.
7   N. Stargardt, *The German War: A Nation Under Arms, 1939-1945*. London: The Bodley Head, p.53.
8   G. Krumeich, *Die 10 wichtigsten Fragen: Der Erste Weltkrieg*, p.18.
9   Fieseler, op. cit., p.73.
10   C. Siebrecht, The *Mater Dolorosa* on the Battlefield – Mourning Mothers in German Women's Art of the First World War, in: H. Jones, J. O'Brien, J. and C. Schmidt-Supprian, (eds.) *Untold war. New perspectives in First World War Studies*, pp.259-292.
11   Fieseler, op. cit., p.74

into full throttle and climbing fast, he managed to position himself vertically above the fighters, which he identified as French.

By this time those planes were firing rounds on a certain Lieutenant Rose who was flying alongside Wiesner. Fieseler engaged the nearest of the enemy fighters, peppered it with bullets, and hung on its heels. The two of them went into a spiral, both attacking and evading each other. Rickenbacker records such a moment, when two planes 'only a few yards apart [were] sparring around one another like two prize-fighters in a celestial ring.'[12] But, as they dropped from 4,000 metres to a few metres above a plateau, Fieseler had made it impossible for his opponent to rectify his position as they hurtled downwards. He knew all too well that 'killing in the air was always a matter of millimetres and milligrams.'[13] The Frenchman's plane was smashed to bits on the plateau.

A self-confessed *Schwein*
Fieseler mentions that this was his longest dog-fight to date, but does not say how long it actually lasted. The American flyer, Eddie Rickenbacker, mentions one such combat which lasted forty minutes, during which time he and his opponent 'soon came to know each other's idiosyncrasies.'[14] Such an event was truly an adrenalin-pumping experience, which 'defies description.'[15]. In his very first duel Ernst Udet recalls his blood turning to ice and his mind being in a whirl.[16] Sheer experience might eventually calm the nerves, but every pilot knew that every combat could end in death. In the memorable words of Udet: 'death flies faster.'[17] The British air historian Denis Winter noted that in dog-fights 'the emotions experienced by pilots involved were as extreme as those of infantry going over the top.'[18] This author gives a vivid description of a dog-fight, with which Fieseler would have immediately identified:

> The dog-fight might well seem like a confused whirlpool, like a cluster of bees swirling round a honey jar and losing height gradually as they turned. The whole mass would drift with the wind leaving in its tracks plumes of tracer and exhaust fumes which hung in the air like corbels and combine with anti-aircraft puffs to trace a delicate grid which recorded every manoeuvre and every shot.[19]

Later, a German search party found the body of the Frenchman whom Fieseler had shot down. In his pocket was a newspaper cutting, saying that he, Lieutenant Sonné, had shot down five German aircraft in three weeks. Plainly, Fieseler wanted to make certain that the victory was attributable to him. Before he landed, it had already been announced on the German airfield that an enemy plane has been brought down in a combat earlier that day. Wiesner, it would seem, turned to Rose and said: 'You did that. Well done.' Rose, however, demurred; 'No, that's impossible.'[20] But he proved no means averse to being congratulated by the other pilots on this specious victory. As soon as Fieseler landed, Wiesner came up to him and told him that the victory had gone to Lieutenant Rose. Fieseler was choked. To him it was another example of his fellow flyers' incompetence and envy. Somewhat out of character, he did not for once lose his temper. He chose to bide his time. He

12 E. Rickenbacker, *Fighting the Flying Circus*, p.27.
13 D. Winter, *The First of the Few: Fighter Pilots of the First World War*, p.141.
14 Rickenbacker, op. cit., p.42.
15 Ibid, p.27.
16 E. Udet, *Mein Fliegerleben*, p.31
17 Ibid, p.44.
18 Winter, op. cit., p.103.
19 Ibid, p.103.
20 Fieseler, op. cit., p.75.

did, however, make his way to the weapons officer who confirmed that neither Wiesner nor Rose had opened fire; their aircraft had merely suffered some grazes.

After that episode the squadron commander, Burckhardt, was posted to Saarbrücken to take over a squadron on the home front. Shortly after that, Wiesner and Bauhofer were transferred. Then Rose himself got a new posting. As was customary, there was a farewell drink in the mess. Rose, a gregarious fellow, got well lubricated. As he bid Fieseler *au revoir*, Rose blurted out that he was a dirty swine (*Schwein*) and should not have played that mean trick on Fieseler. 'No, one shouldn't do things like that', he prattled on, 'Please forgive me.' 'Don't waste your words', retorted Fieseler.[21]

'Anyway, Fieseler', replied Rose. 'You'll quickly shoot down another plane to make up for that one.'[22] So much for 'the cavalry of the clouds' and all that so-called chivalry. Fieseler turned and spat on the ground. This unpleasant episode, almost certainly not an isolated one of its type, suggests that sometimes more chivalry was accorded to the enemy than to one's own fellow flyers.

Lieutenant Rose's replacement was a certain Lieutenant Bender. He had been a member of Richthofen's flying circus with its planes, which spurned camouflage and presented themselves to the world with their 'beautiful scarlet noses,'[23] Bender had been shot down on the Western front. In common with other survivors of air crashes, he 'had entered into and emerged from a death zone,'[24] an experience which had shredded his nerves. So, it came as no surprise at all to Fieseler, who was not much younger than Bender, when the new man told him: 'This damned war – you can't count on me in combat!' Fieseler, a fellow flyer, would no doubt have had sympathy for Bender's highly nervous disposition, but it would probably been unfathomable to him why this damaged man had been given a position of command.

He had, it turned out, been a cavalry officer who had applied to become a pilot when his regiment had been disbanded. He introduced Fieseler to chess and was the only person with whom he could discuss philosophy. It is not all clear when Fieseler acquired his philosophical interests. Bender had, as Fieseler put it, a pronounced awareness of reality, but as for his flying abilities, these were pitiful. Regarding the other pilots, Fieseler's relationships were in a professional sense appropriate all things considered, but, although they often shared moments of mortal danger, there existed no comradeship, as he understood that term, between them and him. In a way he pitied them. In his two years with them there had never been a leader to set an example and to encourage them to take risks. Whenever enemy planes appeared, they invariably made themselves scarce. Fieseler recorded grimly that they used up lots of precious fuel in these antics, but what they did not use up was ammunition for their machine guns. No wonder *Jasta* 25 had not experienced a single loss!

Fieseler came to the view that it was pointless to be in the air with them. Indeed that was actually dangerous. He learned that things were no better at *Jasta* 38, which was stationed 150 kilometres to the east. In a matter of weeks four commanders had been abandoned by their men in combat conditions and all had died. His experience of commanders was they could play being the boss on the ground, but they did not know how to be that in the air.

As he dwelt on these things, Fieseler had heard that *Jasta* 25 was to get a new commanding officer. He turned out to be a Flying Officer (*Oberleutnant*) by the name of Heidamer. He wore thick glasses, had a jovial manner, and struck everyone as thoroughly decent. The snag was, as Bender told him, that he knew very little about flying. Learning that Fieseler was the best pilot, Heidamer ordered him to take general responsibility for things in the air while he was learning

---

21 Ibid, p.76.
22 Ibid, p.76.
23 Rickenbacker, op. cit., p.72.
24 B. Rieger, *Technology and the Culture of Modernity in Britain and Germany 1980-1945*, p.130.

the ropes. In the meantime the new commander was improving his flying abilities by taking his plane up and doing circuits around the airfield. Fieseler was curious to see how he would put his stamp authority on the squadron. According to Bender, Heidamer had been considering this very question himself, and he had come up with a pathetic, cunning and certainly face-saving solution, of which he happened to be very proud. 'Fieseler', he said to his best pilot, 'You are in charge in the air. In future I will be flying 100 or 200 metres above you just to check when things get hairy (*brenzlig*)!'[25]

In the light of all these shenanigans among his fellow flyers, it might have amazed – or even shocked – Fieseler to learn that among the British pilots their German counterparts were seen as 'a force altogether more precise and professional than the RFC/RAF.'[26] In a similar vein the German aviator was seen by his British counterparts as 'disciplined, resolute and brave and … a foeman worthy of our best.'[27]

Alan Palmer, the chronicler of the Macedonian Front, supplies a rare and illuminating vignette about Anglo-German cross-cultural perceptions. It concerns a British officer who in 1916 had fallen into the hands of the German Flying Corps (it was not made clear how this actually happened.) Noting that the conflict in the Balkans was 'a gentlemanly and leisurely war, very different from the ferocity of France', Palmer comments that 'even the German airmen seemed a chivalrous crowd; they were prepared to drop messages over the British flying-field giving information about the fate of airmen shot down behind the lines.'[28] Then he quoted from a letter written by the British officer to an RFC major about his captivity. 'I have just dined with the German Flying Corps', he writes, 'They have been very kind to me. I am going to Philoppopolis tomorrow. The Germans have asked me to ask you to throw them over some coffee on Drama which they want in the Mess.'[29] Even after three years of war, it seems, there still lingered that bizarre chivalrous bonhomie, which enabled sworn enemies, whose compatriots were otherwise slaying each other in their thousands in Flanders, to treat each other in a civilised way in non-combat conditions.

Antonius Raab remembers the notices that German airmen wrote about British pilots who had crashed along the lines:

Your pilot X … dead.
Your pilot Y … landed alive.
Your pilot Z … slightly injured.[30]

As the British reciprocated in a similar way, it meant that both sides were quickly informed of their respective losses. Raab adds that any British pilot who survived crashing or being shot down would be taken to the German mess before the military police came to escort them to a prison camp. Fellow pilots were not a hated enemy as such. They were seen as fellow aerial combatants, who had to do their duty.[31] Udet, for his part, found British pilots to be 'young, plucky lads' as opponents.[32] In the mess captured airmen were treated as 'guests.' One had convivial conversations about 'horses, dogs and aeroplanes', and certainly not the war, the very thing that brought the foes together.[33]

25 Fieseler, op. cit., p.81.
26 Winter, op. cit., p.75.
27 Ibid, p.74.
28 Palmer, op. cit., p.144.
29 Ibid, p.144.
30 A. Raab, *Raab fliegt: Erinnerungen eines Flugpioniers,* p.21.
31 Ibid, p.21.
32 Udet, op. cit., p.52.
33 Ibid, p.58.

Back at Kanatlarci, when the pilots of his *Jasta* took to the air, they were invariably lagging behind Fieseler. On one occasion he spotted six or seven dots in the sky. He motioned his pilots to follow him. He decided to attack not head-on, but from below. All his planes stayed together until the actual attack. Then, as usual they vanished. Fieseler brought down one plane with a burst of machine gun fire. He saw it plunge in flames into a rocky defile. The enemy planes scattered. On another expedition Fieseler with his retinue behind him started to engage some French fighters. He had his sights on one and had his finger on the button ready to shoot, when suddenly he heard the crackle of machine gun fire behind him. He made an immediate evasive dive and proposed to reposition himself to engage with his attacker. To his horror realised that his 'attacker' was none other than Heidamer. The new commander had obviously wanted to be able to say afterwards that he had been in on the action. What he did not know is that he could have easily been Fieseler's tenth kill!

On landing and in great fury Fieseler told a fellow flyer to please tell Flying Officer Heidamer that, if anything else like that happened again, he – Fieseler – would shoot him down without compunction. This extraordinary message was actually delivered to Heidamer and the whole episode became a sensation. Inexplicably Heidamer took no retaliatory action, but the result was a permanent stand–off between the two of them. But there was an immediate, conspicuous consequence: Heidamer never flew again and, in the absence of any instructions to the contrary, Fieseler retained command in the air. Nothing else changed. He remained the only pilot to engage the enemy in aerial combat.

The Tiger is with me

It is not clear when, but at some point in 1918 his comrades gave Fieseler the nickname of 'Tiger.' He would duly become known as the Tiger of Macedonia, a title he relished for the rest of his life. By this time the Tiger found that he was becoming a model for some of his comrades. On one occasion a flyer called Eggebrecht asked him how he could achieve something. Knowing that Eggebrecht might not be able to cope in actual combat, Fieseler proposed that he shoot down a barrage balloon. He, Fieseler, would keep enemy fighters at bay. Eggebrecht did shoot down a balloon, but suddenly found himself in hot pursuit by some Nieuports. He overcame his nerves by saying to himself aloud: 'Keep calm, the Tiger is with me!'[34] This success gave Eggebrecht a boost of confidence and led to another young pilot by the name of Schott making a similar request of Fieseler. In his case he could not bear the thought of returning home without having earned an Iron Cross – an Iron Cross First Class, to be precise.

Again, Fieseler proposed that Schott disable a balloon, but when it was close to the ground at twilight. That, thought Fieseler, would be safer. Properly briefed, Schott set off, but failed to return. For a time his disappearance remained a mystery. Some time later Fieseler guided in a crippled French fighter plane. It turned out that the captured pilot was able to explain what had happened to Schott. The young German had indeed fired shots into the balloon, but it had burst into flames. It turned out that French soldiers were in the vicinity and they brought down Schott in a hail of machine fire. Schott had been granted Iron Cross First Class, but lost his life. His commanders arranged for his posthumous medal to be sent to his parents. Fieseler was mortified with guilt for his part in Schott's death.

The Macedonian Front would produce another outstanding flyer, who, like Fieseler, was given a majestic nick-name for his heroic exploits. This was Rudolf von Eschwege, who was killed in November 1917, aged twenty two. He was dubbed 'the Eagle of the Aegean Sea' and even 'the Red

---

34   Fieseler, op. cit., p.32.

Baron of the Balkans.'[35] As with von Richthofen, the British buried him with full military honours. Fieseler certainly knew of Eschwege, whose death he notes in his memoirs, but they appear never to have met. Eschwege also died, as he attempted to cripple a balloon. As his bullets tore into it, it exploded and ripped him and his plane to pieces. It turned out that the French had used a dummy observer packed with high explosives. Death by booby-trap: yet another mode of extinction for pilots. This event brought back to Fieseler unhappy thoughts of Schott's death.

Heidamer still refrained from flying, but despite all impression to the contrary he had in fact acted when Fieseler had caused a sensation with his unheard-of warning to his superior. He had contacted high command, seeking their advice. High command was based in Gradsko, 'the communications junction that co-ordinated the activities of the German troops in western Macedonia with the Bulgarian armies in the centre and western region.'[36] They were having increasing problems with their Bulgarian allies, who were losing the will to fight. According to the well-informed Bender, the generals were plunged into confusion and there was a division of opinion about Sergeant Fieseler's 'huge threat (*massive Drohung*).'[37] The result was, in Bender's words, a Solomonic judgment. *Jasta* 25 would be merged with *Jasta* 38 on the River Varda, though where precisely is not clear. The new formation would have a new commander. Heidamer and everyone, except Fieseler, Bender and a new recruit called Waldvogel, would be transferred to the Varda. These three were to remain in Kanatlarci. As there was serious shortage of fuel on the Varda, this suited Heidamer and the rest perfectly. There would be less flying.

For months Fieseler had wanted to become an officer, but he lacked the necessary educational certificate, as he had left school so young. Throughout this time at the front he somehow crammed as much as he could into his head without neglecting his flying duties. He even found someone to teach him mathematics and English, whilst the helpful Bender arranged for him to take leave in order to attend a secondary school (*Gymnasium*) in Cologne for five weeks where he could get tuition prior to taking the all-important examination. In the event he did get his longed for promotion; but not in ways he could have imagined, and he did not have to go to Cologne

We are in July 1918. Around this time Squadron 38 received two brand-new Fokker D VIIs, one for his commanding officer, the other for Fieseler, as the acknowledged best fighter pilot. By now the British and French planes were superior, but the Fokker – the one described by Rudolf Stark as 'a bloodstock animal'[38] – had a better performance than any other German aircraft. The British air historian, Denis Winter, is another admirer of the Fokker D VII, describing it as 'perhaps the best fighter of the war.'[39] Fieseler had the plane painted and camouflaged as he wanted it to help him fly undetected by enemy aircraft flying higher than him. The topside of the plane was painted in traditional khaki, the nominal colour of the ground; the underside was painted in sky blue.

It was becoming common practice to camouflage aircraft in distinctive colours. On the Western Front as of 1917 air engagements could involve a hundred or more planes. It was critical to give squadrons striking colours so that each side could clearly identify which side planes were on. It is well-known that Richthofen's Flying Circus had their livery painted in 'glaring red.'[40] In August 1918 Stark recalled the thrill of waiting for the fuselage of his new Fokker to be painted with coloured bands that were individual to him and equipped with streamers as the insignia of

---

35 http://hubpages.com/education/About-World-War-1-Rudolf-von-Eschwege-Sole-German-Fighter-Pilot-in-the-Balkans
36 M. Glenny, *The Balkans: Nationalism, War and the Great Powers*, p.354.
37 Fieseler, op. cit., p.84.
38 A. Stark, *Wings of War*, p.150.
39 Winter, op. cit., p.156
40 P. Kilduff, *The Red Baron*, op. cit., p.69.

leadership. Only when the plane was in his colours – like a knight of old or professional jockey – did he regard the plane as really belonging to him.[41] It is hard to imagine that Fieseler did not experience similar elation when his Fokker emerged in 'his' colours.

Fieseler took part in several patrols with Bender and Waldvogel, in which they perfected a communication system, whereby certain movements of the aircraft – as opposed to mere waves of the hand from one cockpit to the other – conveyed the necessary signals. On one occasion they encountered a formation of French Spads, who were bent on attack. Fieseler veered away, indicating to Bender and Waldvogel that they should follow him. Unfortunately, they took his signal to mean that he had engine trouble. With considerable skill Fieseler brought the two of them back in line, keeping one of the Spads firmly in his sights. He then signalled Bender and Waldvogel to disperse, leaving himself to finish off the French fighter in a blaze of machine gun fire. When they were back on the ground, a sheepish-looking Waldvogel expected a severe reprimand from Fieseler. Fieseler, though, had taken a shine to his younger comrade and said: 'Now, Waldvogel, do you get the point?'[42]

By the end of June 1918 Fieseler's tally of aerial victories stood at five. Between then and the end of August this had increased to 14.[43] He now ranked with Eschwege as one of the two by far highest scoring German fighter pilots on the Macedonian Front. As the summer wore on, Fieseler was less worried by the numbers of aircraft that the enemy were able to put in the air than by the technical superiority of their new fighters. Behind this lay a factor of which he was completely unaware. By 1918 the Germans were simply not able to 'match the Allied production levels due to the policy of building too many aircraft prototypes and models, more than 600 during the war, which diffused the production effort.'[44] Exactly the same criticism about production planning could be made about the rapid development of the Luftwaffe during the 1930s. One such superior aircraft was the French single-seater Spad XIII, which Fieseler had already encountered. This was impressive on account of its considerable fire power and 'its ability to lose most pursuers in a dive – not only because of its speed, but because of the wing cellule's ability to hold up to the stress.'[45] For his part Richthofen had been complaining as far as back as July 1917 that German aircraft were 'ludicrously inferior' to their British counterparts.'[46]

Fieseler's Fokker could not match this performance. In his frustration he began to push himself to the limit and take risks. The trusty Bender was aware of this. 'Tiger', he said in a cautionary voice one evening. 'On the Western front I saw some of our greatest pilots. They streaked into the sky like rockets. Then one day they didn't come back.' He went to the crux of things. 'I'm worried about you. Think about it. Just one small mistake and you're finished.'[47] Fieseler knew his friend was speaking sense. Yes, he would take more precautions in future.

A new secret weapon
But then came a restraint on his flying activity, which was caused by an acute shortage of fuel. From now on he and the other two could only go out as a threesome every other day. This restriction was, according to Fieseler, due to the fact that their sector was judged to be of secondary importance. However, the ban did not appear to stop him from making solo flights. That well suited him, for

41   Stark, op. cit.,134
42   Fieseler, op. cit., p.86.
43   http://www.oldprilep.com/vojna-mir/neboto-nad-prilep.html
44   J. S. Corum, 'World War I aviation' in M. Strohn, *World War 1 companion*, p.68.
45   Holmes, T. Spad XIII in: *Famous Fighters of World War 1*, pp.49-56.
46   Kilduff, op. cit., p.137.
47   Fieseler, op. cit., p.87.

he had the opportunity to develop further his combat skills. Alone, he could develop ways of using surprise to greater tactical effect in the face of the superior performance in speed, versatility and climb of the enemy aircraft. At the same time he was aware of being at a severe disadvantage against those planes especially 'in longer dogfights with a skilled and cold-blooded fighter pilot.'[48] With their forward-facing machine guns the more versatile enemy planes had a decided edge whenever they bore down on him.

It could no longer be denied: his chances of being shot down by superior planes had increased considerably. He had to do something to reset the balance of forces in his favour: he would need to convert his plane into 'a flying rifle,'[49] not metaphorically, but in actual practice. His life now depended on it. After many nights of pondering on his paillasse in his mosquito-netted bunk he came up with the solution. He needed to equip his plane with a new kind of armament. What he had in mind was a *third* machine-gun so mounted on the underside of the fuselage that it pointed at an angle upwards. In this way he would be able to fire at the enemy from below in dog-fights, whilst very importantly giving himself greater protection. That solved the theoretical problem, but could this otherwise ingenious solution be put into practice?

The nub of the problem was that the German machine-guns were heavy, unwieldy things and the arrangement of the ammunition belts meant that the guns could not be easily remounted and still be capable of firing. Fieseler was for a time at a dead-end. Then, out of the blue – in fact literally out of the blue – the solution presented itself. It happened that, as he was mulling these things over, he had shot down a French reconnaissance plane, a new Bréguet, which was equipped with two, rear-mounted and movable fast-firing Lewis machine guns. These had got slightly damaged upon impact on the ground. It was customary to obtain mementoes from downed enemy aircraft; Richthofen, for example, had a walking stick fashioned from a broken propeller removed from an adversary's aircraft.[50] But for Fieseler the Lewis guns were more than mementoes. After days of work his armourer succeeded in creating from them a single fully functioning machine gun. The ammunition had to be sent from a depot for requisitioned munitions in Mainz, which took ten days to arrive.

The ground crew then fashioned a steel-tube support, onto which the new hybrid machine-gun was mounted at a 45° angle. Thanks to this innovation involving a British-made Lewis gun, his plane was now equipped with three machine-guns, one being his own improvised weapon. At all events he could now engage in dog-fights and manoeuvre without fear of being defenceless. Once the enemy had worked out the nature of the new tactic, he knew that they would be after him with a vengeance and in great numbers. This eventuality, which could mean being attacked from several angles at the same time, made it necessary for him to be able to look behind without restriction in the cockpit. Fieseler dispensed with his shoulder strap and belted himself in at the waist only; which meant breaking a regulation 'which no doubt started life on a desk of some bureaucrat, from which the occupant would not risk being shot down!'[51] But who would be bothering about that at this stage in the war, he must have thought.

Fieseler's comrades on the Macedonian Front coined the verb *fieselieren* ('to fieseler'), which referred to his technique of shooting at enemy from below.[52] This technique was highly effective: 'his slanted MG rarely missed its target.'[53] This technique became known as '*schräge Musik*' (lit.

48   Ibid, p.88.
49   Winter, op. cit., p.134.
50   Kilduff, op. cit., p.214.
51   Fieseler, op. cit., p.89 (slightly modified).
52   J. Piekalkiewicz, *Der Fieseler Fi 156 Storch im Zweiten Weltkrieg*, p.9.
53   J. Piekalkiewicz, *The Air War 1939-1945*, p.301.

'harsh music') in the Second World War, referring to how Luftwaffe pilots trained their new upward firing twin cannons at their British bombers on night raids over Germany. One author claims that *schräge Musik* was first introduced in 1942.[54] But Fieseler was in the lead by nearly a quarter of a century. The verb *fieselieren* had no currency beyond his own *Jasta* and passed away into obscurity at the end of the war.

In the air he kept a look-out like a hawk and always flew 'only in a serpentine line' i.e. he never kept to a straight course for long. At all times it was a question of keeping his eyes peeled. As he knew only too well, there were plenty of things that could conspire against a pilot's concentration: 'blind spots in a biplane's configuration, engine noise, cold and air rush, which always vibrated the goggles.'[55] He knew too that skilled pilots could come at you as if out of nowhere (he did this himself often enough), and then you always had to keep your eye on the sun, 'where the greatest danger lurks, whence sooner or later an enemy must make his appearance.'[56] Not for nothing did the British pilots quip: 'Beware of the Hun when in the sun.'[57]

As if he did not have enough to preoccupy himself with, Fieseler had not given up the idea of qualifying for promotion to officer rank. Given the precarious situation facing the German troops in the Balkans, he knew that this was not the time to petition high command for leave. That view was quickly confirmed, when Bender told him that his request for educational leave had in fact been turned down. Fieseler was nevertheless furious. He told Bender in no uncertain terms that as a result of this decision he was 'not going to continue to play my role as "Tiger of Macedonia,"' whatever that was supposed to mean.[58] Bender, who for reasons of tact did not have convey that hot-headed message word-for-word to the high command, relayed nevertheless Fieseler's extreme disappointment with the decision. At this point the commander-in-chief intervened personally. Bender received the following message: 'Fieseler to be promoted. Keep up the good work.'

Fieseler saw Bender rushing towards him with a beaming smile and arms flourishing. 'Tiger', he called,' You've got your promotion!.'

'Well, what are we waiting for!', yelped the new officer.[59]

It was now August 1918. In whatever theatre of war the soldiers of the Reich operated, they 'were worn out, hungry, badly equipped and shaken in their morale, and there was a sharp increase in the numbers of them surrendering.'[60] In Germany itself there were strikes and the threat of revolution. The hard-liners on the left, jubilant after the Russian Revolution of November 1917, vividly foresaw the end of Germany's monarchical-capitalist order and anticipated popular acclaim for a communist form of society. The big question was: could, as in the case of Russia, the disillusioned soldiers returning from the bloody battlefields be counted upon to support the revolution? Was there not every possibility they would want to do away with a Germany that in any way resembled that of the unpopular, blustering Kaiser? The signs, from the point of view of those of a Marxist persuasion, were most encouraging. As the Kaiser's biographer explains: 'To the starving population and the army itself the Kaiser seemed an impediment to the end of the war for which they longed; a revolutionary mood developed with astonishing speed both at home and at the front.'[61] But, while

---

54   J-D. G. G. Lepage, *Aircraft of the Luftwaffe, 1935-1945: An Illustrated Guide*, p.59-60.
55   Winter, op. cit., p.71-72.
56   Stark, op. cit., p.112.
57   Raab, op. cit., p.21.
58   Ibid, p.90.
59   Fieseler, op. cit., p.90.
60   M. Stürmer, *The German Empire 1871-1914*, p.94.
61   J. C. G. Röhl, *Kaiser Wilhelm II*, p.176.

the war continued, Germans faced 'the spectre of slow enfeeblement ending in eventual collapse.'[62] That scenario too, of course, played into the hands of the left.

But the war was destined to last for another three months. Germany's high command, knowing that the war was lost, handed over power to a civilian administration in a bid to deflect from itself 'the opprobrium of accepting national defeat.'[63] Army leaders were also casting around for scapegoats for Germany's betrayal (betrayal being a key word in this context). Jews and Bolsheviks were ideal fiendish aliens for this duplicitous end and so was created the notorious myth of a 'stab in the back' (*Dolchstoß*), whereby an insidious enemy within had allegedly deprived the German Army of rightful, glorious victory over its enemies. Before long this myth would become a central axiom in the Nazi catechism and bring about the most terrible consequences imaginable.

More recently another twist on Germany's defeat has been offered by the German historian, who has suggested that 'only America's sudden intervention at the Allies request had saved England and France from the coup de grace of the spring invasion of 1918. Put simply, the Americans had stolen Germany's victory.' This intervention in April 1917 had instantly converted the other European nations into 'second-rate powers,' but Germany for its part 'had not been subdued in and by Europe.'[64] It goes without saying that Germany's military leaders were in a severe state of denial about several miscalculations including the infallibility of the Schlieffen Plan, the entry of first Great Britain and then the United States into the war as well as the poor military capabilities of their major ally, Austro-Hungary, and their minor ally, the Bulgarians. As a coda to the American entry into the war, US politicians had all too evidently recognised the significance of the new aerial weapon. In May 1917 the US congress passed the aviation bill which poured $640 million into the coffers of the US army 'to enable [it] to quickly build up an air arm equal to that of the other major powers.'[65]

Had you asked Fieseler, a young fighter pilot, in the summer of 1918, about his view on Germany's pending defeat, he would not an offered a mealy-mouthed explanation. He would have pointed to the superiority of Allied aircraft and the poor leadership among German air force commanders. In August 1918 he was braced for the grand Entente offensive. All around him he witnessed the relentless build-up. There were ever more enemy planes in the sky. If he saw a heavily armed plane – possibly a Nieuport Ni-9 – at 4,000 metres, it would protected by up to 15 Nieuport fighters. Once he came across a loose formation of enemy aircraft at a height of some 3,500 metres near the front. They used huge banks of clouds, perhaps 15 kilometres long, to keep themselves out of danger. Fieseler stalked above them. Using a compass and stop-watch, he estimated the distance of the enemy from him and their flight-path. With perfect timing he came at them out of nowhere and scattered them like a fox among chickens.

On another occasion he saw off a Nieuport that tried to ram him. By now Fieseler had gained such a reputation among the enemy that he, like von Richthofen though of course on a much smaller scale, became a known quantity (*Begriff*).[66] Even though he was in his own words 'feared' among French pilots for his capacity to vary his style of attack,[67] he could not harass the enemy as much as he wanted. Besides, before long he was restricted to one flight a day owing to the critical shortage of fuel. In time the commanding officer heard of Fieseler's successes and immediately granted him a reward of 150 litres of fuel for every enemy plane he brought down.

62   B. H. Liddell Hart, *History of the First World War,* p.589
63   M. Fulbrook, *History of Germany 1918-2000: The Divided Nation,* p.20.
64   W. Schivelbusch, *Die Kultur der Niederlage*. Berlin: Alexander Fest Verlag, 2001. Cited in Watson, *German Genius: Europe's Third Renaissance, the Second Scientific Revolution and the Twentieth Century,* p.566.
65   Corum, op. cit., p.74.
66   Fieseler, op. cit., p.91
67   Ibid, p.92.

Hardly a side-show

The big build-up continued on the Entente side. The German field telephones supplied an endless stream of reports about their aircraft movements. Ranged against Fieseler's small squadron on the other side of the front line were no less than six enemy fighter squadrons. Some days, no sooner had he landed, than he was ordered to take to the air again. Even Fieseler found things stressful. He was on the point of exhaustion. This could lead to lack of concentration and even induce drowsiness in the air, and pilots needed their full of sleep, 'the food of the nerves' for the next day's combat.[68] At night in the barracks his right arm would suddenly twitch upwards. He wasn't alone in these reactions. Winter cites a British pilot, V. Yeates, who in a well-regarded autobiographical novel about his wartime experiences 'wrote of men waking up at night covered in sweat, men jerking up in bed with twitching faces, men walking about their huts smoking.'[69] Fieseler would know all about that.

As he lay on his paillasse, unprompted questions would fill his mind. Will you be lying here tomorrow? Will you survive this war at all? Then an inner voice would remind him that French pilots were in fear of him. That thought gave him a psychological boost. But then came more dark thoughts. Yet, when he awoke, his anxieties would be swept aside. He went into attack mode, asking himself whether this sense of invincibility was really manifestation of some atavistic aggression within himself which he could not control.

Fieseler says that in the last weeks of the war he was enjoying an 'almost legendary reputation.'[70] He threw himself into aerial combat with gusto. On one occasion he encountered a British fighter formation of seven SE5s. These, 'the first British single-seat fighters to mount two machine guns'[71] were flying over 'German' territory as if to say to Fieseler personally: 'We're not putting up with the likes of you.'[72] This was too much. Fieseler would take them on. His plan was to isolate the leader of the squadron by appearing to attack others, but without losing sight of him. He calculated that, if the leader had seen him, he would turn round to help his own men. This is exactly what happened. The squadron lost its formation. It was suddenly every man for himself. Fieseler broke off from the sham attack and pursued the leader. Flying beneath him, Fieseler now had the Britisher squarely in his sights, but he (the Britisher) found it impossible to get Fieseler into his line of fire. He found himself in a hail of machine gun fire. He crashed on the crags below that made up 'the 30 unhospitable kilometres of my (Fieseler's) front, upon which the human foot has never set.'[73] His *Jasta* squadron made a bolt for it. This victory for Fieseler was, however, not corroborated.

It is a striking feature of Fieseler's narrative about being a fighter pilot in the First World War that he *never* shows any compassion for the enemy flyers he brings down. Not for him, like Rudolf Stark after enjoying 'a wonderful victory', ever to confess: 'I have committed murder.'[74] It is perhaps in the word of Bill Bishop, the high-scoring Canadian attached to the Royal Flying Corps, that we find resonances with Fieseler's seeming lack of empathy with his victims:

> The excitement of the chase had a tight hold on my heart strings and I felt that the only thing I wanted was to stay right at it and fight in the air. It seemed that I had found the one thing that I loved above all others. To me it was not a business or profession but a wonderful

---

68   Winter, op. cit., p.180.
69   Winter, op. cit., p.146, citing Yeates's novel, *Winged Victory*, which was published in 1934.
70   Fieseler, op. cit., p.93.
71   Holmes, op. cit., p.44.
72   Fieseler, op. cit., p.93.
73   Ibid, p.94.
74   Stark, op. cit., p.164.

game. To bring down a machine did not seem to me like killing a man but more as if I was just destroying a mechanical target with no human being in it at all.[75]

In that passage we surely get close to the real Fieseler. He sees as his task the disabling or destruction of mechanical targets, whereby feelings of guilt slide into denial. He never says that seeing an enemy hurtling to the ground in flames gave personal satisfaction, but perhaps it did. Every time he brings down an enemy we can almost hear him say: 'Job done.' Besides, he could always tell himself that he was doing his duty for the Fatherland, and duty, as Winter points out, could dispense 'benediction to a killing without guilt.'[76]

By October 1918 the Bulgarians, who formed the majority of the fighters representing the Central Powers, were caving in under the Allied assaults. At the end of their tether they threw aside their weapons and made off. According to Fieseler, the German view of the Bulgarian participation in the war was that it was a miracle that they had held out for so long. Their soldiers by now had no boots; their feet were wrapped in rags. Fieseler heard a story that for him summed up the wretchedness of the Bulgarians' plight. Once a Bulgarian officer took his dog along with him to visit front-line troops, but the four-legged friend was never to be seen again. The ravenous soldiers had caught it and made a meal of it.

Glenny notes that it was during this confused Bulgarian retreat that 'British aviators opened a new chapter in the history of modern warfare. They caused havoc by carpet-bombing and machine-gunning the narrow files of undernourished and ill-clad Bulgarians. Air power meant that a hasty retreat would no longer guarantee the safety of a defeated army.'[77] In his peerless narrative of the Macedonian Front, Palmer writes that the Bulgarians, trapped in steep-sided ravines, 'were mercilessly bombed and machine-gunned by the RAF.' As far as the British were concerned, he suggests, 'there was little time for sad heart-searching.'[78]

Following the Bulgarian departure, the few strategic points held by the Germans now had to be vacated. The Germans too were in tactical retreat. Fieseler found himself in Üsküp, Skopje today, where he met up with several old comrades in arms, including of all people Flight Lieutenant Heidamer. He heard talk of a new front to be established by the Germans some 200 kilometres north of the Greek border. That came to nothing. In the meantime, on the Western Front German troops were powerless to prevent the Allied advance. In these desperate times it amazed Fieseler that his fellow flyers seemed to be quite indifferent to this state of affairs. He knew the answer to that paradox: everyone just wanted the war to end. There was only one person who did not share in the general gloom. That happened to be Heidamer. He was from Alsace, so he was probably hoping that the province would become French once more and that he would find himself on the side of the victors.

For his part Fieseler knew from first-hand, if brief, experience how deeply the British naval blockade had reduced the Fatherland to military impotence. Beyond that, he knew as much as anyone just how superior was the war machine of the Allies. He calculated that on 'his' front alone the Allies' air supremacy had within a matter of months increased some thirtyfold. It seemed to him though that there in Kanatlarci he and his fellow flyers could retain dominance in the air. Before that particular hypothesis could be put to the test, the command for full-scale retreat had been issued.

75 Winter, op. cit., p.168.
76 Ibid, p.167.
77 Glenny, op. cit., p.354.
78 Palmer, op. cit., pp.213-214.

Fieseler too had to discontinue combat. When some sixty years later he was writing about the end of the First World War in his memoirs, he could not forget his emotions at that time when he departed from Macedonia along with his treasured Fokker. 'I find it hard', he wrote, 'to describe how I felt back then. It was a combination of self-reliance, pride and dismal despondency. Behind me lay a phase of my life that was so full of metamorphosing experiences and impressions that no other event in my long life ever eclipsed.'[79] In the light of what would befall Fieseler during and immediately after the collapse of the Third Reich, that is quite a remarkable statement.

The Macedonian Front has received disproportionately little attention by military historians. At the time it was seen as 'a side-show' which exposed combatants 'to boredom, extremes of weather, and disease – above all malaria.'[80] The French commander, General Maurice Sarrail, was mocked in France for fighting the war on two fronts – 'one in Macedonia, the other in the bedroom.'[81] As for Britain, the Macedonian Front even became a popular music-hall joke in 1917 as the favoured place for skivers in search of a holiday. In Germany it was 'scornfully ridiculed … for being [the Allies']"largest internment camp"'[82] – a reference to the 160,000 soldiers restricted to their huge base at Salonika, a city which Palmer calls 'an Aegean Verdun' with defences 'out of proportion to the danger of enemy attack.'[83] But, as Balkans specialist, Misha Glenny, has observed: 'The image of the Macedonian Front as one enormous holiday camp could not have been further from the truth. Not only was Macedonia a much tougher posting than the journalists of France and Britain appreciated, it was on this front and not in France that the military breakthrough essential for the defeat of the Central Powers was made in the autumn of 1918.'[84]

An officer for a day or two

Fieseler alas is sparing with dates in general and only rarely gives names of locations, where he engaged enemy planes. However, a website devoted to German air aces of the First World War lists his 19 confirmed victories and one unconfirmed one during his service with *Jasta* 25,[85] whilst the Macedonian source mentioned earlier suggests that the number of confirmed victories is 21 (see Appendix B). His first victory, south of Prilep, was on 20 August 1917; his last one was confirmed on 20 September 1918 at Troyatsi.[86] (On 22 September Prilep fell to the French). Impressive is that he scored sixteen victories as of 5 July 1918. Fieseler easily outstripped his fellow fighter pilots. The next highest score belonged to a pilot named Treptow with six victories to his name; his former commander, Burckhardt, had a tally of six, whilst Rose, that 'dirty swine' had four. It has been suggested that Fieseler was in fact Germany's highest scoring ace throughout the entire eastern theatre of war.[87]

The war was coming to an end 'with a speed that scarcely could have been imagined mere weeks earlier.'[88] By this time Fieseler had already been awarded the Iron Cross First Class and Second Class for his gallantry in the air. Then in the very final days of the conflict he was awarded further distinctions. From His All-Highness, the Kaiser himself, he received notification of his promotion to lieutenant for gallantry before the enemy. Not only that: the Kaiser bestowed upon him the

---

79   Fieseler, op. cit., p.96.
80   H. Strachan, *The First World War*, p.315.
81   Glenny, op. cit., p.346.
82   Liddell Hart, op. cit., p.591.
83   Palmer, op. cit., pp.52-53.
84   Glenny, op. cit., p.346.
85   http://www.theaerodrome.com/aces/germany/fieseler.php, accessed on 15.11.2014
86   http://www.oldprielp.com?vojna-mirr/neboto-nad-prilep
87   R. Meredith, *Phoenix: A Complete History of the Luftwaffe 1918-1945. Vol. 1 – The Phoenix is Reborn*, p.347.
88   S. Anderson, *Lawrence in Arabia: War, Deceit, Imperial Folly and the Making of the Modern Middle East*, p.1.

Kingdom of Prussia's highest military award, the Golden Military Merit Cross, which was otherwise the NCO version of the much coveted *Pour le mérite*. That two distinctions should be granted to him on the same day so close to the end of the war must have struck him as rather incongruous. However, and this might have come as slight disappointment, it was the NCO version of the much coveted award. This was no doubt due to the fact that the actions for which he was being honoured had taken place while he retained the rank of sergeant. Now, at last he was an officer, if only – almost literally – for a day or two. When he died in 1987, Fieseler would have been one of the oldest surviving recipients. In addition the Golden Military Merit Cross, he had also been awarded the Austrian Merit Cross in Silver with Crown and the Bulgarian Soldier's Cross First, Second, Third and Fourth Class.[89]

More than once Fieseler said that he did not know what drove him on to excel as a fighter pilot. But there can surely be little doubt about that: he *deeply* craved recognition for his heroic exploits and also relished his fame among the enemy. On the basis of the adage that all is fair in love and war Fieseler, we may say, deserved this recognition. He had proven himself to be a highly successful fighter pilot on account not only of his aerial victories in a relatively short period of time, but also of his considerable skills at dispersing numerically superior forces in aircraft which outclassed his own in all important respects – speed, versatility and rate of climb. He had what Richthofen in his short air combat operations manual published in April 1918 regarded as that all-important 'absolute will … to do battle.'[90] As a result he struck fear in his enemy's hearts to the extent they changed their tactics as a precaution.

Beyond that, his skill as a pilot – even when he was a 'mere' Emil – had saved the lives of many of his comrades, including his immediate superiors. This skill – this versatility and quick-thinking behaviour – manifested itself in the critical ability 'to make immediate use of an opponent's error or weakness in … lightning duels in the air.'[91] It revealed itself in another striking way. In his discussion about Richthofen with Udet, Fieseler mentions that his plane was never once struck by an enemy bullet (*'ich brachte nie einen einzigen Treffer mit'*).[92] There is no doubt that his technique of shooting at the enemy from underneath with his slanted machine gun meant that he could 'stand up to overwhelming odds' without receiving a hit in return.[93] This is an altogether more remarkable achievement, given that Fieseler, round 1926 admitted that as a fighter pilot it was all about being a 'daredevil without thinking twice [and] success at any price.'[94]

The ability to evade enemy fire at close quarter reveals flying skills of the highest order. By way of comparison, France's highest scoring ace with seventy-five confirmed aerial victories, René Fonk, 'was adroit at knocking down enemy planes, but even more incomparably skilled at eluding damage himself. Fonk's own plane was struck by an enemy bullet just once.'[95] Even against Fonk's achievement, Fieseler's is truly remarkable, given the mental stresses he was under towards the end of the war and the fact that he was for months in combat – specifically in dog-fights – with enemy planes that were technically superior to his Fokker.

To appreciate the true significance of that last point, it is appropriate to turn to Winter for what we might term the context of these stresses:

89   T. Treadwell, *Knights of the Black Cross*, p.285.
90   Kilduff, op. cit., p.233.
91   P. G. Neumann, T*he German Air Force in the Great War*, p.39.
92   Fieseler, op. cit.,p. 71.
93   Pielkalkiewiecz, op. cit., p.301.
94   http://www.illustrierte-presse.de/die-zeitschriften/werkansicht/dlf/73350/27/0/http://www.illustrierte-presse.de/die-zeitschriften/werkansicht/dlf/73350/27/0/.
95   Bryson, op. cit., pp.23-24.

The basic structure of the fighter war was … one of daily fluctuation between the most violent combat and total idleness, between depths of terror and the most generous ease, yet with periods of being grounded by bad weather or of flying without meeting the enemy. Mixing predictability and confusion in a Russian roulette. Such a rhythm was unlike any other branch of the fighting services and made air a war apart in mind as well as medium.[96]

One of the handicaps facing pilots and air forces in general was that commanders at headquarters, almost all of them infantrymen of a previous era of human warfare, had no comprehension of these pressures: to put it bluntly, these commanders were 'out of their depth.'[97] We do not know how many of these 'contextual' factors about Fieseler's prowess as a flyer as opposed to the tally of his victories were conveyed from his commanding officer to a committee attached to the War Ministry that vetted applications for the granting of military honours. There is, however, one factor that almost certainly would *not* have been brought to the notice of that committee. Fieseler's combat experience was overwhelming acquired in the Balkans, where he had to cope with the challenge of unchartered, inhospitable and often mountainous terrain as well as brutal extremities of climate. There can be no doubt that operating here was significantly more difficult than on the Western front. It was not an environment for run-of-the-mill pilots, as he in fact discovered.

For an independent commentary of Fieseler's prowess as a fighter pilot, it is worth quoting aviation authors Nagel and Bauer at some length:

Several German pilots engaged in aerial warfare as it were a duel. They flew more or less into the enemy head-on, and the one whose nerves held out to shoot the other plane down with the best hits was the victor. These pilots were proud that their machines had been hit with enemy fire and in spite of that managed to land at their own airfield.

Fieseler by contrast developed a particular technique. He tried to creep up on the enemy and then unnoticed let his machine guns rip. He always kept a wary eye open to ensure that he was not attacked from behind. Through moving sinuously he always tried to guard the air space to his rear … On one occasion he even managed to force an enemy plane to make a landing uninjured instead of shooting him down.[98]

Nagel and Bauer suggest that he acquired the nickname Tiger precisely because like the predator itself he attacked from behind, as its prey was always a threat until dead or disabled. These various comments on Fieseler's prowess as a fighter pilot lead to another point of interest. Had he had the good fortune to be deployed on the Western Front, he may well have been talent-spotted by Richthofen, who 'was always looking for out for new promising material [and] had a free hand to take in all the successful pilots into his squadron.'[99] In that case he would have definitely been more widely known as an aerial gladiator. At the same he would have had outstanding pilots to learn from and emulate. The point is that Fieseler in the complete absence of mentors was almost completely self-taught, which makes his achievements all the more remarkable.

But it was also his misfortune to see combat on that least glorious and least known of fronts in Macedonia. Furthermore there was a perception among those who did not fight on the Eastern Front in general that air warfare there was 'far and away less dangerous' than on the Western

---

96   Winter, op. cit., pp. 82-8.
97   Liddell Hart, op. cit., p.58.
98   R, Nagel und T. Bauer, *Kassel und die Luftfahrtindustrie seit 1923: Geschichte(n), Menschen, Technik*, p.425.
99   Herlin, op. cit., p.38.

Front.[100] That is surely a moot point. All this has ensured that Gerhard Fieseler for nearly a hundred years has never been ranked among the very greatest of German fighter pilots of the First World War. Yet by any measure he is unquestionably among them.

Defeat and apprehension
Fieseler does not tell us precisely when and how he returned to his home town of Bonn in faraway Germany. He tells us that he was in Kanatlarci, when the order came for withdrawal, and that he left with his cherished Fokker; which suggests that his and the other aircraft of his *Jasta* were dismantled and packed for transportation back to Germany. No doubt his journey took several days with little to eat or drink and involved countless train journeys with long waits on frontiers and on stations. At some point he would have had to bid farewell to his plane, which may well have been a bitter experience.

Later he would hear about the terrible human losses that the First World War had brought about. One of Germany's experts on the conflict cites a figure of between 10 and 11 million for the total number of fallen. Germany lost just over 1.8 million with some 4,248,000 wounded (for Great Britain, excluding the Empire contribution, the corresponding figures are 908,000 and 2.09 million).[101] Not only had Fieseler survived the war, which for an airman was statistically noteworthy in its own right. His only serious injury had been the one that he had sustained in his crash in 1916, resulting in a slight limp. As far as we can tell, he was not unduly psychologically traumatised.

The Kaiser, who does indeed 'bear a heavy responsibility – perhaps the heaviest overall – for having brought about Europe's great catastrophe,' was not in Germany to welcome the remnants of his armies.[102] On 9 November 1918 – two days before the armistice – he had been forced to abdicate – he, who only that August had assured his war-weary, starving, people in his usual crass way that the worst was over. The following day he fled with a small entourage over the border to the Netherlands where he spent the rest of his life in exile. Upon arrival, on 11 November, the former Kaiser requested – preposterously – 'a nice cup of English tea.'[103] But far worse, in 1920 he referred to the German people, not least his soldiers – the dead, the damaged, the crippled, the disfigured – for their 'betrayal, downright felony, cowardice'[104] as 'utter filth.'[105] The disdain was completely mutual.

In November 1918 Fieseler was for his part oppressed by the thought of what might befall the German nation. His subconscious told him that after this momentous, savage struggle among nations Germany would face stark times ahead. With hindsight no-one would dispute the general soundness of his premonition, but no-one could have foreseen what kind of ruination what actually befall Germany and how that ruination would 'dramatically shape – and drastically truncate – the lives of millions of people, Germans and non-Germans' later in the twentieth century.[106] While Fieseler was vaguely contemplating this ominous future, its contours were already taking shape in the imagination of an obscure Austrian corporal, Adolf Hitler, who arrived back in Munich on 21 November, having just recovered from the effects of mustard gas. He regarded Germany's defeat as intolerable – 'the greatest villainy of the century.'[107] It would have to be avenged. Among other things, the accursed communists and the verminous Jews would have to be eradicated from Germany.

100   S. Rosenboom, *Im Einsatz über der 'vergessenen Front': Der Luftkrieg an der Ostfront im Ersten Weltkrieg*, p.82.
101   Krumeich, op. cit., pp.140-142.
102   Röhl, op. cit., p.163.
103   H-U.Stoldt, "Schamloser Verrat!" in: A. Grossbongardt, U. Klussman and J. Mohr, (eds), *Der Erste Weltkrieg: Die Geschichte einer Katastrophe*, pp.266-273.
104   Röhl, p.186.
105   The actual word he used was *Schweinebande*, lit. 'herd of pigs.'
106   Fulbrook, op. cit., p.xi.
107   I. Kershaw, *Hitler 1889-1936: Hubris*, pp.96-97.

Part Two

Hardship and Triumph

5

Weimar, Versailles and Atlantis

You'll be under the earth one day. Get off it!!!
Flying display poster, Boston, UK, 1923[1]

Der Friedensvertrag von Versailles zählt zu den am heftigsten angefeindeten Dokumenten des 20. Jahrhunderts. (The Treaty of Versailles ranks among the most vehemently invidious documents of the 20th century.'
Klaus Wiegrefe[2]

The edge of a volcano

Germany was crushed and humiliated in November 1918. The old Reich was no more. Defeat meant a shattering break with the past. Things had to change, but 'cautious moves for reform from above were swept away by a revolutionary tide on the streets.'[3] Wherever you looked, there were 'strikes, uprisings, mass demonstrations and the breakdown of governmental authority.'[4] Soldiers came home from their various fronts to a hungry, disillusioned, embittered homeland. They belonged to a generation of young men, who were 'tough, spirited individuals, rootless and restless.'[5] This was the beginning of 'the intermezzo between the authoritarian Kaiserreich and totalitarian dictatorship.'[6]

The airman Rudolf Stark recalls flying back over a Germany that was 'seething and raging within.'[7] Two days after Germany's defeat he was back in his home town of Munich, where he discovered that he and air force comrades did not receive 'the sort of welcome we had imagined.' They were shunned. 'Home has become a strange land to us,' he lamented, 'Our home – our home is dead.'[8] Ernst Udet, Germany's highest scoring surviving air ace, had his unpleasant experiences too. He recalls one particular day in November 1918:

> The day was wet and dismal. The man stared at me offensively. He was wearing a grey-green military greatcoat, a peaked cap without a regimental badge ... He was a member of the Soldiers' Council. At length he reached out with his hand, and touched the *Pour le Mérite* which hung at my throat. "So much old iron!" He jeered.'[9]

---

1 A. Goodrum, *Balloons, Blériots and Barnstormers: 200 Years of Flying for Fun*, p.141.
2 K. Wiegrefe, (2004). Der Unfriede von Versailles. *Spiegel Special: Die Ur-Katastrophe des 20. Jahrhunderts*, p.132
3 M. Fulbrook, *History of Germany 1918-2000: The Divided Nation*, p.21.
4 Ibid, p.11.
5 R. Overy, introduction to E. Udet, *The Ace of the Black Cross: The Memoirs of Ernst Udet*, p.ix, p.xii.
6 G. Mai, *Die Weimarer Republik*, p.11.
7 A. Stark, *Wings of War: An Airman's Diary of the Last Year of World War 1*, p.226
8 Stark, op. cit., p.225-227.
9 E. Udet, *The Ace of the Black Cross: The Memoirs of Ernst Udet*, p.125.

Later, on a tram a passenger took exception to Udet, and 'a hairy paw reached for my throat, and tugged at the order: "Aren't you going to take this bit of tin off", he growled.'[10] Then, to add insult to injury, he and ex-airman friend, Ritter von Greim, who would end up as the last commander of Hitler's Luftwaffe, were thrown out of a tavern.

Adalbert Norden who wrote a short biographical sketch of Fieseler, which was published in 1941, says that Fieseler too had the experience of people wishing to 'tear off his military decorations earned for bravery fighting the enemy.'[11] Fieseler for his part does not record any incidents of this nature.[12] Assuming, however, that these experiences were by no means isolated, it is hard to reconcile these humiliations with the conviction that aviators were seen as 'individuals who miraculously reappeared after encounters with death.'[13] There was, it would seem, no return for Germany's aerial gladiators as heroes.

In the case of Britain 'the mood on aerodromes was ... one of resentment at the loss of four years, resentment at the uneven way in which the burdens had been shared.'[14] As one pilot recorded: 'On news of the armistice, the thin spread of enthusiasm which bound the fighting services together seemed to snap. I remember the next three months with greater horror than all the rest of my experience – the depression, the demoralisation.'[15] Even Britain's Air Minister wrote that 'we would appear to be on the edge of a volcano.'[16] But it was perhaps an American airman who more than any other captured the strangeness of the transition from aerial warfare to civilian life. He grabbed Eddie Rickenbacker by the arm and 'shouted almost incredulously, "*We won't be shot at any more!*"'[17]

When Gerhard Fieseler returned to his home in Bonn, he was, according to Norden, 'broken in body and soul.'[18] This suggests that his physical and psychological condition were delicate, though Fieseler himself does not imply that. It is, however, probable though that his reunion with his mother was a good deal more emotional than he himself suggests. One of the first things his mother said to him was 'How much older you look – a proper man now.'[19] In the air force you looked young and old at the same time. A case in point was Richthofen. As an acquaintance noted in September 1917, lines had etched themselves in his 'motionless face from cheekbone to chin.'[20] Rudolf Stark knew this gaunt look all too well. He wrote this when the Germans were making their last desperate push in the Western front in 1918:

> We are not much further on in years now. But we are so old. We no longer belong to the younger generation ... Our faces are still smooth, but one has wrinkles round the eyes, another a sad drawn expression about the mouth and a third deep furrow on the forehead. But one thing we all have in common, one thing we shall never lose – the serious look about the eyes.[21]

The air historian Denis Winter also discusses how faces changed under the accumulated strain of facing death every day – sometimes many times a day. It was noted among British airmen 'how old

10 Udet, op. cit., p.125.
11 A. Norden, *Das Herz muss dabei sein: Der Flieger Gerhard Fieseler und sein Werk*, p.76.
12 Norden, op. cit., p.76,
13 B. Rieger, *Technology and the Culture of Modernity in Britain and Germany 1980-1945*, p.133
14 D. Winter, *The First of the Few: Fighter Pilots of the First World War*, p.192.
15 Ibid, op. cit., p.192.
16 Ibid, op. cit., p.192.
17 E. Rickenbacker, *Fighting the Flying Circus*, p.107 (original emphasis),
18 Norden, op. cit., p.76.
19 Fieseler, *Meine Bahn am Himmel*, p.97
20 P. Kilduff, *The Red Baron: Beyond the Legend*, p.155
21 Stark, op. cit., p.168.

the faces of young pilots suddenly became after a short experience of active service work.' A man of twenty-four might have the face of a man of forty. The faces of young airman would acquire a 'new seriousness', even 'the loss of his former carefree boyishness with a single tour.' Winter goes on:

'At the bottom of such changes were facial muscles which maintained a posture during each patrol suited to depth of anxiety, uncertainty and fear unknown to most men since infancy. Not death but the waiting for death and the undignified, self-destructive thoughts which went with the waiting carved on the skin those sustained tensions which a later wartime generation were to see in the urgent press photos of first-wave combat troops or perhaps of liberated concentration camp inmates.'[22]

Like so many other airmen then Fieseler almost certainly returned home with the horrors of war etched on his cheeks and brow. If so, Frau Fieseler could not have conceivably imagined what had brought about the physical changes to her son's face, the outward sign of which suggested a kind of premature ageing. To her comment about his gaunt appearance Gerhard drily responded: 'The war has changed us all and everything.'[23] He realised that his days as an aviator were over. His life had suddenly become what Stark likened to 'an empty void.'[24] There was no other possibility for Gerhard but to work for his father and help rebuild the family business.

The crippling of the German Air Force

Germany's new leaders, against a background of street-fighting notably between the Left and the para-military groups on the Right, sought to introduce democratic principles into German life. This meant among other things defanging 'militaristic, authoritarian, imperial Berlin, which had led Germany to war and failure.'[25] A new National Constituent Assembly debated a new constitution in Weimar, the city of two of Germany's greatest literary giants, Goethe and Schiller, in the conviction that 'the cosmopolitan humanity of their Weimar classicism, arguably Germany's supreme cultural achievement, would shape and inspire the new Weimar Republic with their intellectual and ethical authority.'[26] It was perhaps inevitable that the Weimar Republic, which was inaugurated in 1919 and swept away with the Nazi seizure of power in 1933, has been seen as 'a tumultuous interregnum between two disasters.'[27] But it was also a period of remarkable efflorescence in science, design, philosophy and the arts.

One of the first tasks of the new government was to sign a peace treaty with the victorious powers of 1918. In the following June its representatives would sign the fateful Treaty of Versailles. The eminent British military historian, John Keegan, had described the Schlieffen Plan as 'the most important government document written in any country in the first decade of the twentieth century.'[28] There can be no doubt that its counterpart in the century's second decade was the Treaty of Versailles, signed in June 1919. It concluded the First World War, but it also helped to bring about 'the next big war [in] 20 years and 64 days.'[29]

Germany was forced to accept 'the sole guilt' for the outbreak of war in 1914. The reparations were crippling: 226,000 million marks – around $850bn in 2014 prices – plus 12 per cent of

---

22   Winter, op. cit., p.144.
23   Fieseler. op. cit., p.97.
24   Stark, op. cit., p.209.
25   N. MacGregor, *Germany: Memories of a Nation*, p.355.
26   Ibid, p.355.
27   P. Watson, *German Genius: Europe's Third Renaissance, the Second Scientific Revolution and the Twentieth Century*, p.568.
28   J. Keegan, *The First World War*, p.31.
29   T. Darnstädt, Stunde der Abrechnung. In: A. Großbongradt, U. Klußmann, und J. Mohr. *Der Erste Weltkrieg: Die Geschichte einer Katastrophe*, p.265.

German exports until 1962. Germany's Rhineland territories – a source of historical friction with France – and the Ruhr, the industrial heartland, were to be occupied by French, British and American troops. The country lost a seventh of its territory and its few overseas colonies; its once huge army was reduced to 100,000 regulars; its naval fleet and parts of its merchant marine were handed over to the British.

Nor were aircraft to be exempted in the rout. Effective from 10 January 1920 the Treaty of Versailles 'prohibited for a short time the manufacture and import of aircraft, parts and equipment.'[30] As for military aircraft, Germany destroyed or handed over to the Inter-Allied Aviation Control Commission 'approximately 15,000 aircraft, 28,000 aircraft engines, and 16 airships, and dismantled 1,000,000 square metres of hangers.'[31] The German Air Force was demobilised, though a few pilots were transferred to the army. In passing we should mention that after the end of the war the ever-enterprising Anthony Fokker managed to spirit away across the border to his native Holland 350 good trains containing some 200 of his aircraft as well as engines, propellers and 'the thousands of bits and pieces needed in aircraft construction.'[32]

Civil aircraft production was to be banned for six months until June 1920, whilst the future for military aviation looked bleak. Indeed it would be throttled for the foreseeable future. One of Germany's leading air war planners, Lt.-Col. Wilhelm Siegert, whom we have cited earlier, vividly likened the Treaty of Versailles to 'the tightly-knotted meshes of [a] net which has been cast over the young eagle's head.'[33]

In 1919 he wrote elegiacally that 'the dream of a German Air Force has faded away. Henceforth it will survive only as a memory and in heroic story.' He consoled himself by imagining the future of aviation, which he believed belonged to 'the giant aeroplane' in a pacific world. This wondrous machine would one day supersede the airship and 'undertake transoceanic flights, which are at present are so rare and phenomenal.' If, God forbid, his country should be involved in another European war, then it would be the French who would start it. He predicts that aeroplanes will transform life in ways that frankly must have seemed utterly hair-brained a hundred years ago. They will assist the science of surveying of rivers and coastal regions and in the production of town maps. They will support fisheries and whaling. One day, he predicts, there will even be 'unoccupied' [i.e pilotless] machines' on long-distance flights which will be 'directed on their way by wireless … controlled only by electric waves.'

He foresees the day when airplanes will undertake 'special transport work such as carrying fresh flowers, combating forest and prairie fires [with] fire-extinguishing bombs.' They will even 'save time in business on journeys which would otherwise have to be made on the backs of donkeys or camels.' Most desirable. They can watch over herds of cattle in huge countries such as Australia and those of South America; they can melt dangerous packs of ice or 'snowdrifts in railway cuttings and sunken roads by employing "flame-throwers;"' they could be used for advertising purposes and dropping propaganda leaflets.[34] But the idea that 'aeroplanes will take the place of the express train or the liner, just as the locomotive took the place of the horses of mail coaches' is frankly 'mistaken'. He avers confidently: 'No apprehension need to be felt on that score for another fifty years.' Noting that aircraft have a role to play in policing, surveillance and the compilation of crowd statistics, Siegert suggests that aeroplanes could be used 'for dispersing forbidden assemblies without bloodshed at a low altitude. The sound of the propeller would drown all speechmaking.'

30   E. L. Homze, *Arming the Luftwaffe: The Reich Air Ministry and the German Aircraft Industry 1919-1939*, p.1.
31   Ibid, op. cit., p.2.
32   A.H. G. Fokker. *Der Fliegende Holländer: Die Memoiren des A. H. G. Fokker,* p.249.
33   W. Siegert. A glance into the future.' In P. G. Neumann, *The German Air Force in the Great War*, p.287-297.
34   The word 'flame-thrower' is in inverted commas in the cited extract.

Siegert's sense of woe at the seemingly irretrievable loss of Germany's aerial capability is wonderfully expressed in this extraordinary *cri de coeur*:

> Imperial German Air Force. A pebble I cast into the sea of memory creating waves that joined, swept on towards the shore, and were then turned back. To-day the waters of that sea lie calm and mirror-like, pitilessly reflecting the image of the past. Below there in the depths one's eye can see the sunken city of his dreams; far off one hears the ringing of bells. Atlantis![35]

In 1919 German aviation, civilian and especially military, was all but facing doom. In the recent war the airplane, as Homze explains, had 'developed from the oddity of 1914 to the necessity of 1918.' Furthermore, 'everywhere military thinkers were keenly aware of the potential of the air weapon for the next war: that is why the victorious Allies sought to crush German aviation through the peace treaties concerning World War I.'[36] Gerhard Fieseler, who had never shown himself to be politically minded, would have known that. Thus, when he heard about the terrible prohibitions under the Treaty of Versailles, that must have reinforced his conviction that he would never get into a cockpit ever again. His life's prospects looked singularly dismal. He had given everything for the Fatherland, and what was his reward? Absolutely nothing except to work once again for his father. He could not imagine a grimmer future.

Old hostilities break out

Before 1914 Gerhard had no clear idea about how the First World War came about. As a twenty three year old, when the Treaty of Versailles was signed, he probably did not grasp the full perspective of events. But, when writing his memoirs some sixty years later, he recreates his attitude at the time he has just returned from Macedonia. He begins by saying that the Treaty of Versailles was sheer vengeance. It was intended to blame Germany for the war, humiliate it and bring about the ruin of its economy. Its harsh terms suited the British, who felt so threatened by German economic power in 1914, and they suited the French too who could at last wreak vengeance on Germany for their humiliating defeat in the 1870-71 Franco-Prussian War.

Fieseler is though critical of the Kaiser's sabre-rattling, all the 'hurrah patriotism' that went with it and 'the stupidly arrogant behaviour of Germans abroad.' The conduct of Germany's pre-war foreign policy was 'to put it mildly inept,' because it led, he recalls, to 'the encirclement of Germany.'[37] Presumably by that he is referring to the fact that Germany had found itself sandwiched between France and Russia as military allies. He admits that there are other factors, which is indeed true. As for the question of encirclement, he may not have grasped – and the peacemakers at Versailles definitely hadn't – that 'in geostrategic terms Germany was stronger after the war than before, since for the first time in thirty years France had no substantial ally in the east to contain German energy.'[38]

Fieseler says no more about the First World War and its causes. When he casts his mind back to the time just after Germany's defeat, he is right to suggest that the one thing on people's mind was simply how to survive from one day to the next. The defeat had been so sudden and demobilisation so swift that the labour market was bloated with young men seeking non-existent jobs. In his own family everything depended on how quickly his father's business could get going again. Unless the war had actually changed his father in some fundamental way so that he would now be more easy-

---

35   Siegert, op. cit., p.96.
36   Homze, op. cit., p.1.
37   Fieseler, p.98.
38   M. Stürmer, *The German Empire 1871-1919*, p.103.

going and less despotic, Gerhard feared that their relationship would be uneasy. For a while there was an unspoken truce between father and son and then a few weeks after Gerhard's return, his father rounded on him. 'Why aren't going to church?,' he snapped. 'The front changed my outlook', came the reply. 'In that case', rejoined his father, 'if you are not going to church every Sunday, don't expect a roof over your head here.'[39]

Gerhard avoided getting into an argument, whilst his father did not take things further on this occasion. A year passed, and slowly but surely a few of the old customers started to come back. Then one day his father excitedly announced that he had received a major order to supply a small publisher with a supplement called *The Bonn Illustrated* which would be distributed to seven or eight regional newspapers. The publisher, to break even, needed another ten or fifteen customers. To reduce his own financial risk, he succeeded in driving down the Fieseler prices. This was a severe blow because the family printing company lacked capability and even the space to cope with such a large order against the deadline which Gerhard's father had agreed to.

Worse, his father had given him the responsibility for seeing the project through. Not for the first time his father had entered into a risky business venture. 'A fine mess this is',[40] thought Gerhard. He told his father of his misgivings, who responded: 'You acquitted yourself very well in the war, but your job is to carry out this task to the best of your ability, and you can put out of your mind any idea about flying.' Gerhard pleaded with mother, who indeed entreated her husband not to over-commit the family business. It was a waste of time. 'I am in charge', he hissed, 'I'm the boss here. I give the orders and that's that!'[41]

In any case it was impossible to break the contract, but luckily a month's extension was granted. Out of obligation, and mainly for the sake of his mother, Gerhard shouldered the task, slaving away all the hours that God gave. He managed to print off the copies in time. In the end the Fieseler company did rather better than expected. As a result, and with credit and a mortgage from the bank, it was possible to expand the production area and invest in better equipment. The income also helped the family to weather the catastrophe of the hyper-inflation of 1923, about which there will be more to say presently.

Somehow, the Fieseler family business survived. *The Bonn Illustrated* went from strength to strength. Gerhard's success put his father on the defensive for a time, but before long he was his old, dictatorial self. There were further clashes between them, and then came the tipping point. Gerhard invited his fiancée Hilda, the nurse who had cared for him after his crash in 1915, to meet his parents. She had come all the way from Stettin. When she had left, his father came straight to the point: 'She's not the woman for you.'[42] A furious row broke out between them. Gerhard carried on as best he could, but there were always arguments, many of which turned on his brother August, who equally miraculously had survived the war in the trenches. August, who was also working for the family business, had no aptitude for or interest in the work, but, as Gerhard knew only too well, their father always protected his younger brother.

Bonn at this time was in a zone occupied by the British. This brought home to Fieseler in a directly personal way the humiliation of defeat: *their* uniforms in *his* Germany with all the restrictions on movement, the interdictions and regulations. He witnessed British troops assaulting his fellow citizens if they were not shown due respect and, according to Norden, also witnessed how French colonial troops from Africa 'kept tabs on (*kontrollierten*) the German population.' All

---

39   Fieseler, op. cit., p.100
40   Ibid, p.100
41   Ibid, p.100
42   Ibid, p.102

these foreign occupiers 'pestered and tyrannised (*drangsalierten und knechteten*)' good Germans.[43] It goes without saying that the myth of mass rape of German women by French colonial troops would be exploited by the Nazis as yet another national humiliation.[44] The memory of these times permanently stayed in Fieseler's mind. You can feel his cold anger, vented at the British and not at anyone else, in his brief description.

Wages by the cartload
Realising he could not for his own sanity remain much longer under his parents' roof, Gerhard sought a way-out. It never seemed to cross his mind to approach the Reichswehr, which as of 1920 was building up its permitted handful cadres of flying officers. The former Tiger of Macedonia may well have been very promising material. Having endured a year or so of unpleasantness under his father, Gerhard followed up an advertisement which was seeking a purchaser for a printing works in Eschweiler, a small town some 80 kms from Bonn and not far from Aachen. He agreed a price with the seller, but he needed financial support from his parents.

His mother was reasonable, but his father took his intention to set up a business on his own account as an act of betrayal. For days an oppressive atmosphere pervaded the entire family. Finally, no doubt after much pleading by his mother, his father relented and asked to see the set-up in Eschweiler for himself. Father and son set off together, not speaking to each other throughout the entire journey. In Eschweiler Fieseler senior held a private conversation with the seller. To Gerhard's surprise, his father had made himself the owner, though he would be managing director.

For the next six years – between 1920 and 1926 – Gerhard worked between 60 and 70 hours a week and never took one day's holiday. He would take on any work, no matter how dirty or difficult, with the one ultimate aim in mind: to earn enough in order to repay his father and be free of him. The former owner of the business admired his relentless labours. 'I've never seen anyone get stuck into things like you do. There's nothing you can't do!'[45] His hagiographical biographer Norden describes these years as the time when Fieseler 'worked, waited, believed.'[46] When he speaks of Fieseler 'believing', Norden is attributing to him a messianic expectation of the pending transformation of German destiny under the great Führer.

Not long after he starting to work on his own account, he received a devastating letter from his fiancée, Hilda. They had evidently not given up their plans to marry when one day Gerhard could afford a wife and family and ignore his father's total opposition to their union. Hilda wrote to say that she had been diagnosed with an incurable illness. Under the circumstances, she wrote, Gerhard should consider himself released from his pledge to marry her. Gerhard was downcast by this terrible news. For days, he says, he did not know how to react. Stettin was far away, he could not leave his business unsupervised even for a few days, and besides the journey was complicated. 'It's my destiny to bear this misfortune', he wrote: his destiny, note, not hers.[47]

He wrote a long letter, doing his best to comfort her and give her renewed hope. In it, though, he carefully avoided any reference to their engagement. He tells us that he was in a depressed state for weeks, but his business affairs left him little time to dwell of the sadness of it all. He was so downcast that the family with whom he lived as a tenant treated him with special consideration. To distract him from his woes, the eldest daughter of the family obtained for him an invitation to

---

43 Norden, op. cit., p.77.
44 R. J. Evans, *The Coming of the Third Reich*, p.187.
45 Fieseler, op. cit., p.104.
46 Norden, op. cit., p.76.
47 Fieseler, op. cit., p.104.

attend a song recital in Eschweiler. He found himself sitting near the two Oidtmann sisters, whom he already knew by sight. Their house was not far Fieseler's lodgings.

The prettier of the two, Helene, immediately took his fancy, exactly as intended by his landlord's daughter. She, it turns out, had seen him 'every midday', when he cycled home for something to eat. But Gerhard is at pains to tell us that he was not looking for a new romantic involvement. Thus, 'so as not to appear impolite' he engaged the two sisters 'in as much non-committal conversation as possible during the interludes,' and evidently promptly disappeared after the recital. It so happened that soon after that he bumped into Helene, and, seeing that they lived quite close to each other, escorted her to her home. He did not want to appear 'impolite once again.'[48] But the dénouement to all the melodrama was swift. Hilda, it seems, was rather quickly forgotten and Gerhard and Helene were soon married. That was at the beginning of 1922. Before long two children were born of the marriage. First came Manfred in November, who in character reminded Gerhard of his maternal grandfather. He was followed in February 1924 later by Katharina, who, he records with pride, would develop into an elegant and beautiful woman.

It is perhaps as well that he found a wife when he did. Not only did Helene breathe womanly warmth into life, but was also at his side when during 1923 and 1924 German currency 'nose-dived into worthlessness', creating the scourge of hyper-inflation that struck Germany and every German.[49] It seems hard to imagine that Fieseler and his wife pulled though this catastrophe and that the family business in Bonn seemingly had enough money – or rather enough money and ingenuity – to cope with the catastrophe.

The cause of German inflation 'lay in the earlier financing of war by bonds and loans rather than taxation increases … its explosive growth was fuelled by, among other factors, the printing of paper money for the payment of reparations, and for the financing of heavy social expenditure (on pensions, for example). This sent the value of money totally out of control.'[50] There were rising lay-offs everywhere, as production slumped and as the volume of money circulating in Germany grew astronomically … in improbable denominations from nearly two thousand printing presses operating around the clock.'[51] The following figures starkly reveal the inflation in barely credible perspective:

> In July 1914 the US dollar cost 4.20 marks. In January 1922 one dollar would cost 191.80 marks. In January 1923 the dollar cost 17,972 marks. In August 1923 the rate was 4,620,455 marks to the dollar, and 15 November 1923 the dollar worth 4.2 billion [not million] marks.[52]

The German government brought inflation under control in November 1924. At its height 'paper notes were simply stamped with a new increased value; people were paid their wages by the cartload; prices doubled and trebled two or three times a day, making shopping with money almost impossible; and the savings, hopes, plans, assumptions and aspirations of huge numbers of people were swept away in a chaotic whirlwind.'[53]

Fieseler, his wife and his business survived that terrible time, which haunts Germany to this very day and whose memory still exerts a sober influence on German monetary policy to ensure

---

48 Ibid, p.105.
49 N. Ferguson, *Kissinger 1923-1968: The Idealist*, p.38.
50 Fulbrook, op. cit., p.28.
51 M. Burleigh, *The Third Reich: A New History*, p.56.
52 H. M. Müller, *Deutsche Geschichte in Schlaglichtern*, p.242.
53 Fulbrook, p.28.

economic stability.⁵⁴ In due course normal business conditions returned, and he was soon doing well for himself. He acquired a small paper-making company, employed fifteen people and had two vans for deliveries to customers. Then the day came when he could repay his loan to his father, and he did so handsomely. It made him happy for his mother's sake to be so generous. So it was that by the mid-1920s Fieseler's life was transformed. He had a wife and family, he had a thriving business, and he had something else which, looking back over all his life, he never had before: spare time in which to please himself.

But in the seven or so years since the war he had never entirely forgotten about his childhood passion for aircraft and his experiences as a pilot in the First World War. The time had come to bring himself up-to-date with the world of aviation. He hired an engineer who had studied aeronautics to give him what he had never acquired: a proper theoretical grasp. He was now one of any number of former wartime pilots like himself, who in his words 'would resort to anything'⁵⁵ to take to the air again. He took up gliding.

The special path of German aviation in the Weimar years
The first years of the Weimar Republic until 1924 had been marked by revolution, civil war, foreign occupation, and inflation. These had been years of great hardship for almost the entire German population. There was scarcely a single German family that escaped the ravages of hyper-inflation. However, the years 1924 to 1929 – until the Wall Street Crash, to be precise – Germany enjoyed a remarkable degree of economic stability. But after that the years 1929 to 1933 saw a return to political violence, culminating in the installation of the Nazi regime under Adolf Hitler.

Extraordinarily, the Weimar years produced 'a golden age of twentieth century physics, philosophy and history' as well as a subculture of decadence.⁵⁶ It was a culture that subverted – sometimes healthily, sometimes not – many traditional values. The 1920s produced major new trail-blazing writers such as Thomas Mann, Hermann Hesse and Bertolt Brecht. The Bauhaus was a major force in design and remains influential to this day. German cinema was world-class and film stars became 'the new aristocracy of a rootless society.'⁵⁷ Fritz Lang's *Metropolis,* which was released in 1927, is one of the most iconic films of all time. There was cabaret and jazz. There was a rage for new-fangled dances. In addition to film there was another exciting mass medium: radio. One day Hitler would give one to every German family to hear his speeches.

Gerhard Fieseler has not a word to say about this extraordinary resurgence of German creative energy and culture, but it is hard to imagine that he felt himself to be detached from it. It has been noted that Weimar culture with its 'fascination with criminals, embezzlers, gamblers, manipulators, thieves and crooks of all kinds' created 'a cynical edge [which] made many people eventually long for the return of idealism, self-sacrifice and patriotic dedication, derived from the disorienting effects of the hyperinflation.'⁵⁸ Had you asked Fieseler in 1925 if he welcomed a reassertion of those three values, he might have said 'yes' with a particular qualification. In his case his aim in life would be resume his boyhood dream: that of contributing to Germany's aeronautical future. For him it was an article of faith that Germany should be restored to its rightful place among all the world's

---

54   See MacGregor, op. cit., Money in Crisis, pp.418-437.
55   Fieseler, op. cit., p.106.
56   Watson, op. cit., p.595.
57   Stürmer, op. cit., p.123.
58   Evans, op. cit., pp.111-112.

nations as a leader in aviation. But he had never been in the cockpit of an aircraft since 1918. But what had actually happened to German aviation since signing the Treaty of Versailles? How did he fit into the big picture, if indeed there was one?

After the signing of the Treaty of Versailles, any air-minded German – that is to say, any German who considered the restoration and expansion of aeronautical endeavour to be of national importance – would have regarded the future of German aviation as utterly bleak. Yet within 10 years Germany had flourishing airlines, there were several aircraft manufacturers with national and international customer and supplier networks, gliders were in vogue, and stunt flying was a national fad. How did this come about?

In 1919 Germany had two options in addressing the aviation-related provisions of the Treaty of Versailles : 'either [Germany] could comply strictly with its provisions, thereby losing her technical proficiency and falling from the ranks of major air powers, or she could develop her civilian aviation as a stand-in for prohibited military aviation.'[59] Germany chose the second course. For its part, however, civil aviation got off to a slow start in the immediate post-war years. Things began to improve in 1922, when Germany was again empowered to design and build civil aircraft, but with stringent restrictions as to speed (170km per hour), payload (600kg), ceiling (4,000m) and range (300km).[60] Over the course of the decade the restrictions on German aircraft manufacture were, however, lifted across the board. Indeed by 1926 manufacturers 'obtained complete sovereignty in civil aviation,'[61] but it never went further than that, as the Allies were wary of the efflorescence of Germany military aviation. Throughout the decade civilian development got the lion's share of the Ministry of Transportation's budget – 35 million out of 40 million Reichmarks.'[62]

Restrictions on aircraft performance imposed by the Treaty of Versailles, the rampant inflation of 1923-24 and the chaotic political situation 'made normal business virtually impossible.'[63] As a consequence many wartime aircraft companies had shut down, whilst the AEG, and Siemens, two of Germany's biggest industrial concerns, both closed their aviation departments. Meanwhile, though, some aircraft companies opened offices in other countries to maintain their competences and develop innovative ideas. Hugo Junkers, whose company opened a branch office in Malmö in addition to the one it retained in Moscow, rapidly broke new ground in the early 1920s by producing the world's first all-metal passenger plane and developing blind-flying instrumentation.[64] In 1921 Claude Dornier formed a production company where his developments included his famous Wal flying boat.[65] For his part, Ernst Heinkel founded a design company in Sweden and worked on catapult-launched sea-planes for the Imperial Japanese Navy.[66] By 1938 the companies of these three renowned aircraft builders would employ about 40% of the Nazi airframe workforce.[67]

Germany's first commercial airline had been established in 1917 by AEG. After the war various services came into operation: Dessau-Weimar, Munich-Vienna, Königsberg-Moscow. Along with AEG the other big player was the Deutsche Luftreederei (German Air Transport Agency). To meet the increasing demand for aircraft throughout the 1920s, new manufacturers emerged. They offered to the market airliners, cargo planes, mail planes, sports planes, sailplanes, trainers;

---

59   Homze, op. cit., p.48.
60   Ibid, p.3.
61   Ibid, p.19
62   Ibid, p.48.
63   Ibid, p.11.
64   Deutsches Museum, *Aviation: A Guide to the Aeronautics Collection.* p.51 and 57,
65   Deutsches Museum, p.54.
66   https://en.wikipedia.org/wiki/Ernst_Heinkel
67   Homze, op. cit., p.198.

one company even built small flying boats.⁶⁸ Even Zeppelins were making a come-back: one made its first commercial flight in 1928 to New York and another a round-the-world flight in the following year.

As for military aviation, if the Reichswehr wished to develop capability, it would have to do so very largely by stealth. For example, in 1922 Germany signed the Treaty of Rapallo with the Soviet government, whereby under secret protocols the two countries 'granted one another most favoured nation treatment.'⁶⁹ Among other things, two German aircraft companies, Albatros and Junkers, signed agreements about setting up aircraft and engine plants in Soviet Russia, whilst in Lipetsk, two hundred miles south-east of Moscow, there was also 'an operational center that would train the future top-echelon commanders of the Luftwaffe.'⁷⁰

In 1923 the Allied restrictions on sports flying were lifted. This gave the Reichswehr and its various agencies more opportunity to use civil air activities as a cover for its own purposes. For example, under one ruse schools for sports flying often received 'black' funds indirectly from the Reichswehr administered through the Ministry of Transportation, whilst 'active and inactive flying officers from the army received training to maintain their proficiency.'⁷¹ Then in 1927 the German Commercial Flying School *(Deutsche Verkehrsflieger-Schule)* was founded to provide specialist – and secret – training programmes for pilots.

A new, more urgent, much more sharply defined and ultimately catastrophic form of German air-mindedness was being doggedly forged. This was no longer an air-mindedness associated with the precarious flying machines of the First World War. Thanks to the stunning aeronautical and ballistic advances witnessed in the recent conflict, the new air-mindedness was focused on the necessity of military aircraft for robust defence of the Fatherland *and* for destructive retaliation – in, of course, the extremely unlikely case of outbreak of another war (which only the French would be mad enough to provoke.)

To hell with aero engines

In the early 1920s the limitations on powered flight had an important consequence. Those who wished to see Germany develop as a significant aviation nation acquired 'an attitude of defiance which released an improbable amount of energy.'⁷² The national mood was summed up thus: 'If we can't fly with an engine, then it will be without one – but fly we will.'⁷³ This gave crucial impetus to gliding.

An exemplar of this defiance was an aviation and glider enthusiast by the name of Oskar Ursinus who organised possibly Germany's first post-war flying event in July 1920. This was held in the Rhön hills, which were popular with glider pilots, including in his day Otto Lilienthal, on account of their 'strong upwinds and thermal updrafts.'⁷⁴ That event recorded 44 flights; in the following year there would be 122 and in 1928 no less than 1,007.⁷⁵ As a result of Ursinus's initiative in 1920, 'all over Germany aircraft would be drafted, designed and built.'⁷⁶ 1922 saw a book of poems about gliding, of which the following – in very free translation – captures the general mood:

68 http://en.wikipedia.org/wiki/Category:German_civil_aircraft_1920%E2%80%931929
69 M. Kitchen, *The Cambridge Illustrated History of Germany*, p.238.
70 Homze, op. cit., p.10.
71 Ibid, p.13.
72 E. Sauer, *Absturz im Kinzigtal: Die Luftfahrt im hessischen Kinzigtal von 1895 zu 1950*, p.14.
73 Ibid, p.14. The original German reads: *Fliegen wir nicht mit, dann eben ohne Motor – aber geflogen wird!*
74 Homze, op. cit., p.14.
75 Ibid, p.17.
76 Ibid, p.14.

> No need for props anywhere
> When flying through the upper air,
> We are the glider-men of the Rhön hills
> And need no engines for our thrills![77]

These sentiments square with those of Edward Homze, a key source on German aviation after the First World War, who wrote that 'glider flying typified, in many respects, the state of German aviation in the early 1920s. So obvious a sport as gliding was not considered important enough to be banned by the Allies. The Germans, however, immediately perceived in it a means of instilling air-mindedness in German youth and advancing the science of aviation.'[78] Homze goes on: 'The ultimate development was today's glider with a long, thin wing and a graceful fuselage. Gliders taught Germans better ways to distribute weight and deal with vibrations through structural design and opened the entire field of meteorology to the dangers of hidden turbulence, the use of the jet stream, and, of course, thermal currents.'[79] It was not fully recognised at the time, but 'knowledge and experience gained in glider design … had a tremendous impact on the technologies in the world of powered flight.'[80]

Fieseler himself noticed how gliders, in the hands of skilful pilots and in the right meteorological conditions, could do 'something sensational.'[81] In a strong enough wind pilots could keep gliders in the air for hours at a time. So it was that German aviators worked out how to build aerodynamically superior motorless aircraft. In the 1930s Fieseler would become increasingly intrigued by the characteristics of slow flight and the design implications for powered aircraft. In the meantime German gliders found customers all over the world for their excellent performance. He also observed that the development of gliders would one day lead to 'a wholly new aviation discipline,' namely aerobatics.[82]

Gliding attracted enthusiasts very quickly after the First World War. But once the restrictions on powered flight were eased and once the German economy began to stabilise itself after the hyperinflation of 1923-24, sports planes were produced in great number, and sports flying, including stunting, became a highly popular activity, which brought thousands of people to see daring flying displays in what were at that time in Germany the fastest airplanes.

In the year 1925 German sports flying was boosted by the reinstatement of the Round Germany Air Race (*Deutschlandflug*).[83] Not only did this development lead to the setting up of flying clubs and associations along with civilian flying schools (often attended by military personnel, of course), but it also helped to create the new aviation discipline of aerobatics. In 1926 Germany rejoined the Paris-based Fédération Aéronautique Internationale, the principal body for sports flying and verifying air records. The prime body for all aspects of aviation was the German Air Transport Association – Deutsche Luftfahrt-Verband – hereafter DLV, which had been established in 1902. This body 'acted as an umbrella organisation for the various clubs and associations that appeared before the Great War and its aftermath.' Sports flying came within its remit.

---

77 Ibid, p.16. The original German is: *Wir brauchen keinen Propeller mehr – beim Fliegen durch das Aethermeer – Wir sind die Segler von der Rhön – wir Machen kein Motor-Gedröhn.*
78 Homze, op. cit., p.13.
79 Ibid, pp.14-15.
80 Deutsches Museum, op. cit., p.120.
81 Fieseler, op. cit., p.106.
82 Fieseler, op. cit., 106.
83 R. Meredith, *Phoenix: A Complete History of the Luftwaffe 1918-1945. Vol. 1 – The Phoenix is Reborn*, p.348.

By 1930 the DLV would have 40,000 members linked to 250 local associations and clubs.[84] It was a major organiser of flying events and annual air shows so-called 'flying days' (*Flugtage*) in larger towns and cities. These events were 'a valuable stimulus to aircraft design and development.'[85] As such the DLV was a major catalyst for promoting and sustaining air-mindedness from the end the First World War until it was disbanded under the Nazis and reconstituted as a paramilitary body concerned with sports flying.[86]

As for stunting, which would evolve into the professional sport of aerobatics, this was a popular diversion for pilots in the First World War. The US pilot Rickenbacker mentions that he did stunting for the entertainment of visiting senior army commanders.[87] In the 1920s the fancy tricks were performed by pilots – those 'surplus airmen' in various countries, who had been accustomed to flying as warplane pilots.[88] They had experience of manoeuvring aircraft at speed, plunging them into sudden dives and letting them rip skywards: not only in combat, but on occasions when they got new aircraft and wanted to put them through their paces *before* combat.[89]

Germany's new breed of sports fliers not only executed new, exciting turns, but they also, according to Fieseler, symbolised 'the suppressed national consciousness' about flying as a respectable activity.[90] Both America and England were ahead of Germany in making aerobatics a major spectator sport. For example, in England as early as 1923 air displays offered 'stunt and crazy flying' and even the daring feat of 'walking on the wings.'[91] In the USA Charles Lindbergh, who would earn eternal fame for the first solo flight over the Atlantic in 1927, had flown nearly a thousand times since learning to fly in 1922.[92] No small number of those flights had been at stunting events, known as barnstorming in the USA.

A man whose moment has come
In the mid-1920s two of Germany's best known German aerobatics pilots were Ernst Udet and Paul Bäumer. Both they and Fieseler had all born within a few weeks of each other in 1896. In September 1925 it happened that the former two were scheduled to take part in an aerobatics display in Düsseldorf. Fieseler would join the other 20 or 30,000 spectators to see them do their turns. Udet, as we have already noted, had been a much-celebrated fighter pilot in the First World War. After the war he had set up with a business partner an aircraft factory near Munich. One of his aircraft, the Udet 8b, built in 1925, was the first airplane to be equipped with both flaps and slats.[93] But he tired of this venture and devoted his energies to stunting. In the mid-1920s he was certainly Germany's best known exponent of aerobatics. He was 'a colourful and charming character,' but 'a restless free spirit.'[94] He was to play a major role in Fieseler's life until his untimely death in 1941.

In October 1919 Udet had taken part in a flying display in Augsburg. The local newspaper announced the following events, which would surely attract a huge number of spectators especially at a time when there was very little in the nature of popular entertainment in the immediate post-

---

84   W. Schwipps, *Kleine Geschichte der deutschen Luftfahrt*, p.103.
85   Meredith, op. cit., p.351.
86   Meredith, op. cit., p.348.
87   Rickenbacker, op. cit., p.11.
88   A. Goodrum, *Balloons, Blériots and Barnstormers: 200 Years of Flying for Fun*, p.134.
89   Such an event is described in J. D. Hunter's novel, *The Blue Max*, p.118.
90   Fieseler, op. cit., p.106.
91   Ibid, op. cit., p.143 and p.146.
92   B. Bryson, *One Summer: America 1927*, p.71.
93   Deutsches Museum, op. cit., p.46,
94   Homze, op. cit., p.102.

war period: 'Aerobatics, mock aerial combats, parachute drops and passenger flights during the performances.'[95] There would be raffles for five passenger flights and all or most of the proceeds of the day would support the People's League for Prisoners of War.[96] The newspaper report makes clear how brilliant a pilot Udet was: 'In a power zoom Udet's machine reached looping height; he turned over on his back, flew upside down and came out of this position in a half-roll. Then he descended in a power dive to within a few feet of the spectators' heads. He spent ten minutes 'throwing the red machine about the sky with loops, rolls, spins and all manner of turns.'[97] Since 1919 he continued to perfect his technique and produce ever more daring turns. This was a massive head-start on Fieseler.

Bäumer for his part was a decorated wartime pilot, gaining the nickname 'the Iron Eagle.' After the war he had become a dentist, but also ran a glider training school and did stunt flying in his spare time. Fieseler specifically went to see Bäumer and Udet in order to compare their abilities with his own. When he watched the two of them in action, he felt 'a bit disappointed.' They were, in his opinion, not as good as they were cracked up to be. An inner voice said to him: 'You can do better than that!'[98]

In the weeks that followed the idea of taking up flying never left Fieseler's mind. Then came the resolve: he would fly again, come hell or high water. His wife Helene, who presumably knew absolutely nothing about flying, gave her husband's plans her blessing. In the coming weeks he wrote letter after letter, followed up advertisements, visited various places, entered serious business discussions – all in a bid to find an opening in the admittedly underdeveloped world of aviation. In 1926 he was on the point of giving up, when he renewed his acquaintance with wartime pilot he'd got to know briefly in 1917.

His name was Kurt Katzenstein, who had been a member of Richthofen's Flying Circus and who was now a pilot with a small manufacturer of sports aircraft and trainers in the Bettenhausen district of Kassel, where they had acquired two production halls of the German Works, a defunct munitions factory. Katzenstein had teamed up with a fellow pilot, Antonius Raab, to form their own company, which was said by Raab in his 1984 memoirs to be Germany's biggest aircraft manufacturer in 1928.[99] Fieseler put it to Katzenstein that, if he could join them, he would be willing to put his own money into the Raab-Katzenstein Aircraft Company – Raka, as it was known. Raka designed and produced its well-regarded Grasmücke (Warbler), which at 7,500 Marks was seen as value for money, especially as it was cheap to maintain.'[100] In 1926 the company developed its most successful sports biplane called the Schwalbe ('Swallow').

Although the two of them were joint managing directors, all the commercial decisions were made by Raab; Katzenstein preoccupied himself with being chief pilot. Raab was not very interested in having Fieseler as a pilot, but the possibility of attracting his capital was a major incentive. He could use every Mark of someone else's money for designing and building sports planes, improving repair facilities, building up the flying school, organising flying shows and paying for advertising. Raab drew up a draft contact, which Fieseler showed to his lawyer in Eschweiler, who expressly warned his client not to accept its terms. But Fieseler, choosing to follow his heart and not his head, ignored the advice. He sold up his entire business and all its assets along with a new car he had just bought himself. Virtually all the proceeds went into the Raab-Katzenstein company as cash.

---

95   *Neue Augsburger Zeitung*, 15 October 1919. Cited in: H. Herlin, *Udet: A Man's Life*, p.94
96   Herlin, op. cit., p.94
97   *Neue Augsburg Zeitung*, 16 October 1919. Cited in: Herlin, op. cit., p.94
98   Fieseler, op. cit., p.107.
99   A. Raab, *Raab fliegt: Erinnerungen eines Flugpioniers*, p.14.
100 Schwipps, op. cit., p.104.

It wasn't long before Fieseler found that the company – that is to say Raab – was not keeping to the conditions of their contract. Not only that: he discovered that Raab's business methods were less than honest. In his initial position as head of purchasing Fieseler found that he was expected to fob off creditors with excuses. In the meantime his family was waiting to move from Eschweiler to Kassel, where suitable accommodation was proving hard to find. Fieseler switched to becoming one of the company's flying instructors, which involved imparting practical instruction with some theory. This suited him better. However, it was no consolation to learn subsequently that quite a few pilots, very keen to get jobs in aircraft companies and with some cash in hand, had likewise been taken for a ride by dubious business partners. For the moment he had to hope for the best. Did it ever cross his mind, one wonders, that he just made the kind of misjudgement that his father had been so guilty of?

Collision course

Fieseler now needed to bring his flying skills up to scratch. He made use of a Schwalbe and soon on almost every Sunday he would head for flying displays, where he could do some circuits and put on some stunts. Raab created an incentive scheme for Fieseler, but as usual it was himself the former who ended up being the bigger beneficiary. Fieseler's first year in the world of civil aviation had been in many respects a big come-down. Then in early 1927 he received a request from Raab to do something he would find truly irksome. He was single-handedly to organise the company's own flying events. By now Fieseler had already been involved in several flying displays and himself conceived of holding major one in Kassel in the spring of 1927 in conjunction with a local flying club. Raab rejected the proposal out of hand, maintaining that people in Kassel would have no great interest and that the city did not have suitable viewing facilities at the small Kassel-Waldau aerodrome. When Fieseler said that he would underwrite the entire event, Raab relented. Fieseler knew that they would not be able to afford the services of Udet and Bäumer, so it was a question of coming up with 'a quite special attraction,'[101] a sensation to bring in spectators in huge numbers.

Before long he hit upon the idea of using one of the old aircraft that had seen service in the war – a LVG B3 with its 100hp engine – as a tug to lift a glider off the ground, take it to a certain height and release it. The glider would make an elegant descent and land in front of the public. Although Anthony Fokker had as far back as 1912 started to toy with this idea, nothing like it had yet been seemingly attempted in practice. The episode of the sensation takes up no fewer than twelve pages in Fieseler's memoirs. It is a story of subterfuge and skulduggery culminating in – how shall we put it? – a sudden change of employment status for Fieseler. In short, the unstoppable aviator was out on his ear. This is how things came to such a sorry pass.

The scheme raised question after question: how long should the tow rope be, and how strong? How was it to be connected to both aircraft and how exactly was the glider to be released? Would not any arrangement mean that the centre of gravity of the two machines in harness would need to be located in the tug i.e. the aircraft pulling the glider? How would the tug stabilise itself when the glider was released? And, upon release, might the tow rope swing about and disrupt the flight of the tug? His colleagues were highly sceptical about the whole business. However, as Fieseler explained to the RaKa designers how these challenges could be overcome, they came round to his way of thinking and produced a coupling according to his ideas.[102] In the meantime at the end of February a press conference had been arranged with the flying club, at which local journalists would learn

---

101 Fieseler, op. cit., p.110.
102 R. Nagel und T. Bauer, *Kassel und die Luftfahrtindustrie seit 1923: Geschichte(n), Menschen, Technik*, p.39.

more about the programme of the planned flying event, which had been scheduled for the 18th April, Easter Monday. Unwittingly, a colleague of Fieseler's had dropped hints about the sensation to be unveiled at that event. The press rounded on Fieseler. He was so bombarded with questions about it that he confirmed the rumours.

The day after the press conference everything was all in the papers. Raab, having read the reports, was beside himself with anger. 'Our firm', he ranted, 'will have nothing to with this matter. I immediately forbid any more work on this stupid scheme. I don't want my firm to be ridiculed because of this lunacy.'[103] He stormed off, but Fieseler remained unfazed, determined to push ahead with his pioneering initiative. He prepared drawings at home and paid one of the Raab-Katzenstein designers on the side to assist him, telling him 'the bosses aren't to know anything about my plan.'[104]

In the meantime Fieseler ran his idea past a certain Gottfried Espenlaub, known as Espe in local aviation circles. Espe, originally a carpenter by trade, had his own company building gliders. He had of course already got wind of Fieseler's scheme. After much to-ing and fro-ing Espe threw his lot in with Fieseler, agreeing to fly the glider which would be towed by Fieseler in the LVG. But when they did test runs one afternoon, Espe prematurely activated the release mechanism when the glider was but a few metres above the ground. That happened on three occasions. Fieseler gave him a piece of his mind, but could get no sense out of him. Then, as it was getting dark, Espe simply vanished into thin air.

Later on the true picture emerged. Espe, having read of Fieseler's plans about towing a glider, had himself applied for a patent for a release mechanism of his own design. Then, it was announced in the local papers that he, Espe, the famous glider pilot, had made the world's first glider tow in conjunction with Herr Fieseler of the Raab-Katzenstein company. He would now perform the operation himself in full public gaze. This brought Antonius Raab into things, who, keen to promote his company name and side-line Fieseler at the same time, announced that he would fly the plane which would take Espe's glider into the air. Fieseler was in no position to oppose Raab. On the appointed day, a rudder on Espe's glider actually fell off and he was forced to disconnect from the tug at low altitude. However, this was good enough from the press (some journalists had even come from Berlin). The first tow flight in the world was widely reported. In a bid to consolidate his Raab's own claim the RaKa company newspaper '*Der Sportflieger*' announced the 'sensation' in its issue of 15 April 1927 – three days before the airshow – under the prophetic headline: 'The tow flight: what does towing mean for the future of the world's air transport?'[105]

There was nothing Fieseler could do, but he persisted in crediting himself with the achievement. Raab, though, in his memoirs published in 1984, disputes that claim, saying that he and Katzenstein had been the pioneers, using the ideas of Fokker which the Dutchman had had patented in 1912.[106] According to him, Fieseler's memory was plainly at fault. It was just 'one of the many errors that Fieseler committed' as an associate of Raab.[107] Things would get worse between them.

Fieseler and his collaborators worked feverishly on the preparations for the Kassel air display. On the day itself, Easter Monday, there was formation flying, an acrobatics competition, an air race, a demonstration of a glider tow and – another idea of Fieseler's – a parachute drop. A fellow called Geck had volunteered for that particular stunt. As a novelty Fieseler had distributed with the programme a form, allowing participants to vote for the best acrobatics pilot. The choice was

103   Fieseler, op. cit., p.113.
104   Ibid, p.113.
105   Part of the front page of *Der Sportflieger* is reproduced in Nagel and Bauer, p.41.
106   Cited in: T. Wiederhold, *Gerhard Fieseler – eine Karriere: Ein Wirtschaftsführer im Dienste des Nationalsozialismus*, p.26.
107   Wiederhold, op. cit., p.25.

between Katzenstein, who was Kassel-born and the presumed favourite, and Fieseler, the not so well known outsider. The score line was 88-12 per cent in Fieseler's favour, much to his surprise and his rival's indignation. After that event Fieseler was scheduled to demonstrate an Immelman turn (Immelmann was a famous wartime pilot, who was killed in 1916). He took off, but at an altitude of a mere 100 metres the engine cut out. The plane hurtled to the ground. The onlookers – some 30,000 of them – screamed cries of horror. There was only one calm person: Fieseler himself. Using all his hard-won flying skills from the war, he managed to leap from the plane seconds before the plane crashed.

Undeterred he jumped into the plane that was to take up Geck. With the greatly alarmed parachutist already in it Fieseler – himself in trepidation – performed various rolls and turns in front of cheering crowds. And if all that were not enough the spectators were finally treated to the sight of a glider being towed and released in mid-air. The events of the flying display were the talk of Kassel. Fieseler became a local celebrity. Furthermore, the day had been a great financial success. He anticipated that Raab and Katzenstein would like to congratulate him with a show of generosity. But he was to be severely mistaken.

Two days following the display, on 20 April 1927 he received a letter, signed by the two of them, in which he was informed in no uncertain terms that his services were no longer required: 'Seeing you have damaged in such an egregious way the aeronautical standing of Messrs Raab and Katzenstein, you are dismissed with immediate effect.'[108] As soon as he read the letter, he realised that the two of them had begrudged his successes, which had so completely eclipsed their abilities as fliers. Nevertheless, Fieseler conceded that from their point of view he had put their noses out of joint and so they had no choice but to get rid of him. As for the two flight tows, there was 'a concatenation of wrangles' between Fieseler, Raab and Espenlaub over who could actually claim to have pulled it off.[109] In fact, as we shall see, the dispute was to bubble up well after the Second World War.

Fieseler gives the impression that Raab and Katzenstein got rid of him for reasons of professional jealousy. But Raab's memoirs reveal another factor not mentioned by Fieseler. After that crash Fieseler apparently fobbed off the misfortune on a faulty aircraft. Raab though considered that Fieseler had been guilty of a near-lethal blunder: he had been flying so low that the wings touched the ground. After Fieseler's dismissal the matter was put to the adjudication of the important Deutsche Versuchsanstalt für Luftfahrt, the German Research Institute for Aviation – hereafter DVL[110] – which was responsible for certifying designs and carried out applied research on behalf of aircraft manufacturers.[111] No doubt to Fieseler's dismay the DVL found in favour of Raab and Katzenstein. As far as Raab was concerned, Fieseler's flying style was 'over-confident and frivolous' and he had even warned him about flying too close to the ground.[112] It happens that Raab's memoirs were published in 1984 two years after Fieseler's own autobiography came out. It is tempting to think that Raab had read the Fieseler book and promptly decided to write his own memoirs to put the record straight, as far as he was concerned.

In so far as he could claim to be the first person to have made glider towing possible, Fieseler was gratified to note that his invention (if it were his) had found military applications in the Second World War. Gliders, carrying heavier loads than otherwise, could be towed to where they were needed and operate at night without making any noise. He referred specifically to the Wehrmacht's

---

108 Ibid, pp.120-121.
109 Nagel und Bauer, op. cit., p.40.
110 Not to be confused with DLV (Deutsche Luftfahrt Verband), mentioned above.
111 Meredith, op. cit., p.118 and p.140.
112 Raab, op. cit., p.25-26.

invasion of Belgium and the Netherlands in 1940, their operations on the Eastern front, and the daring mountain rescue of Mussolini in 1943.[113] All that lay in the future. But in 1927 Fieseler's summary dismissal was a very serious kick in the teeth. On the other hand, he had been reunited with the world of aviation, and there could be no turning back.

---

113 Fieseler, op. cit., p.123.

6

The alpha and omega of flying

I flew in order to live. But at the same time I nourished a hope that through my work I might be contributing to German air-mindedness.

Ernst Udet[1]

Most of the people who acclaimed him at the Sportpalast in 1930 would have probably avoided giving a light to this man [Hitler] on the street.

Sebastian Haffner[2]

A sensational victory

Fieseler had very little money and in 1927 it seemed to him that economic conditions in Germany were getting worse. Not surprisingly he pondered how he could get back at least some of the money that he had given to Raab. He was reluctant to take him to court, which would in any case be an expense he could not afford. He calculated that, despite what had happened, Raab still needed him. After all he had been successful flying the Schwalbe sports planes, which had significantly promoted the company's name. Could a deal be struck? In the end it was.

Through a third party Raab was approached with a request from his former employee. Would Herr Raab be willing to hire to Herr Fieseler a Schwalbe, but without a power plant? If so, Fieseler intended to install a more powerful Siemens SH 12 engine with 120hp and wanted to deal with the manufacturer direct. The point was that Raab already bought engines from Siemens and did not have a reputation for prompt payment. Siemens could at any point easily refuse to have more dealings with the unreliable Raab, thus leaving Fieseler cut off from his preferred engine supplier. That was a risk that he was not prepared to take, if he used a plane that happened to be owned by the Raab-Katzenstein Company.

When he received the indirect request, Raab realised that Fieseler was going to branch out on his own as an aerobatics pilot. Plainly, if Fieseler were using the successful RaKa Schwalbe, then that could only be good publicity for his company. A deal between Raab and Fieseler was struck, but there was one condition: Fieseler had to renounce his shares in RaKa. That, however, was not so onerous, as they were virtually worthless anyway. To all intents and purposes Fieseler and Raab went their separate ways and would not be on speaking terms again. There was also a valuable concession to Fieseler. As a Schwalbe pilot he could have access to the firm's mechanics and designers. As all these things were being settled, Fieseler quite by chance heard that there was to be a major flying event at Essen on Whit Sunday, 5 June. He resolved to take part in the aerobatics competition, even though he was up against strong competition in the form of that redoubtable pair, Udet and

---

1   E. Udet, *Mein Fliegerleben*, p.191.
2   S. Haffner, *Geschichte eines Deutschen: Die Erinnerungen 1914-1933*, pp.88-89.

Bäumer. Fieseler would not be underestimating these two, especially Udet. It was one thing to think he could emulate and even outclass them, but to do so on a public occasion was quite another.

As the plane promised by Raab was not ready, Fieseler hired a Schwalbe from an owner in Hamburg and, having picked it up, set about practising for the big event. After making an unscheduled landing en route to Essen from Hamburg, which involved an overnight in a farm house and a tricky take-off from a very muddy field, Fieseler and his mechanic, Willi Welle, reached the aerodrome at Essen in the nick of time. There were eight competitors, each of whom took part in obligatory flying events in addition performing their own special tricks. The jury consisted of former wartime pilots, who, in Fieseler's view, were not necessarily the best people to make informed judgements about aerobatic flying. It turned to be a grand occasion, attracting some 50,000 spectators with sponsors from the local government as well as prominent firms from the Ruhr. The prize money was very attractive, though Fieseler does not say what this amounted to.

Just before it was Fieseler's turn, a young competitor was killed in a crash. Not for the first time Fieseler, who was completely smitten with flying, reflected that 'you have to accept that there will be accidents, however tragic and regrettable they are.'[3] Some twenty years earlier he had said the same thing to his mother, and since then he had witnessed many a flyer's death. The crash did nothing to dampen his enthusiasm. On the contrary, he felt 'sovereign and confident.'[4] Unfazed, he executed his figures, some of which had never been seen before. He now had to await the judges' verdict.

This would be announced at an evening ball along with a prize-giving ceremony. Ladies attended in long dresses; gentlemen came in tails or dinner jackets with their orders and decorations on display. Fieseler had not been forewarned about all this formality. Even if he was not dressed for the occasion, he certainly took part, wearing a business suit which bore scruffy witness to his 'rural intermezzo' en route.[5] At 9.00 the result was announced: 'By unanimous decision of the jury the winner of the aerobatics competition is Gerhard Fieseler!'[6]

There was an eruption of spontaneous applause, as a very stunned Fieseler was showered with congratulations and accepted the prize money. He looked around for his rivals. There they were, Udet and Bäumer, smilingly sheepishly, doing their best to disguise their incredulity and disappointment. Later Fieseler learnt that the organisers, to spare either of those distinguished flyers public embarrassment, had allocated prize money for them both as joint winners. They did not dare choose between them. What an apple cart he had upset! It was his first victory in an air contest outside Kassel, and it would not be a flash in the pan.

In 1941 Fieseler was at a similar banquet in Bad Kissingen in Bavaria. There he found himself in the company of Thea Rasche, a well-known aviatrix, Germany's first licenced female pilot who had been one of the few female aerobatics pilots in the 1920s and 30s.[7] Rasche had at one point been a pupil of Fieseler's in the early 1930s. She had attended that air show in Essen, which had occurred a few weeks earlier. Indeed the British air magazine *Flight Global* published a photograph of Udet, Rasche and Fieseler standing together on that occasion.[8] More to the point: Rasche was at the time of the event in Essen a pupil of Bäumer. According to her, Udet had managed to stifle his dejection, but losing out to Fieseler had hit Bäumer especially hard and he never recovered from the shock. Feeling wretched, he had told her that he could have performed the same winning turns, if only a

3   G. Fieseler, *Meine Bahn am Himmel*, p.129.
4   Ibid, p.129.
5   Ibid, p.129.
6   Ibid, p.129.
7   E. Zegenhagen, *Schneidige deutsche Mädel: Fliegerinnen zwischen 1918 und 1945*, p.255.
8   *Flight Global* (1928), 19 April, p.272, Available at: http://www.flightglobal.com/pdfarchive/view/1928/1928%20-%200300.html

plane he was having built had been ready for the occasion in Essen. 'What am I say to my sponsors?' He whined. 'What do I tell my plane makers?'⁹

In July 1927 Bäumer died in an air crash in his new machine at a flying event in Copenhagen, attempting to perform a tail-spin. Presumably, as far as Fieseler was concerned, this was another case of *c'est la vie*: just another tragic and regrettable death of a fellow airman. Meanwhile, Fieseler's victory at Essen was hailed as a sensation among flying circles. Who was this outsider who had beaten Udet and Bäumer, hitherto Germany's greatest aerobatics pilots? Raab, for all his distaste for Fieseler, was quick to realise the publicity potential for his planes and ordered his workers to go flat out and build a new sports plane for the new star of the skies.

By now it was nine years since the end of the war, and in the intervening years German aviation had, Fieseler knew, lagged considerably behind developments in other countries; by which he invariably means European countries. Oddly, he never mentions the USA. Yet in May, a few weeks before the air meeting in Essen, the American aviator, Charles Lindbergh, had flown his monoplane, Spirit of St. Louis, non-stop and single-handedly, from New York to Paris. This was surely the most famous aerial achievement to date. When Lindbergh returned to the USA, there was public ecstasy. The New York Evening News called it "the greatest feat of a solitary man in the records of the human race", whilst another rag eulogised it as "the greatest event since the Resurrection."'[10] Like many other flyers in the 1920s Thea Rasche had been bowled over by Lindbergh's epic transatlantic flight and was determined to emulate him.[11]

It is curious that Fieseler has nothing to say about Lindbergh's triumph, all the more so as the American was a very accomplished stunt pilot. In fact, shortly after he arrived in Paris, Lindbergh took up a Nieuport, which he had never flown before, and 'executed a series of loops, rolls, corkscrews, barrel turns and other aerial aerobatics.'[12] In the 1930s Lindbergh was in Germany on two occasions, where he was lionised by the Nazis. He liked Hitler's uncompromisingly anti-semitic view of the world.

Humiliation in Zürich

Fieseler's next challenge was the international air meeting to be held in Zürich in August 1927. It turned out that the Swiss organisers sent a letter to the German Aero Club, inviting its participation. Fieseler was asked to represent Germany and take part in the aerobatics competition. The Aero Club was a venerable institution, tracing its origins to 1881.[13] Its prime purpose was to 'promote aviation-related links with other countries.'[14] The Aero Club's nomination of Fieseler was a singular honour: not only because he had evidently eclipsed Udet and Bäumer, but also because since the end of the war in 1918 'no German plane had ever flown in another country.'[15]

That, however, was not true unless Fieseler was specifically referring to sports planes. German planes were being clandestinely test-flown in Russia, but at the time Fieseler would almost certainly have known nothing about that. Furthermore, by the mid-1920s there were German-made planes plying commercial routes to other European countries. More to the point, though: since the end of the war Germans had, in Fieseler's words, been 'treated like pariahs in the rest of the world.'[16] So

9   Fieseler, op. cit., p.130.
10 B. Bryson, *One summer America 1927*, p.141.
11 R. Italiaander, *Drei deutsche Fliegerinnen: Elly Beinhorn, Thea Rasche, Hanna Reitsch; drei Lebensbilder.* p.53.
12 Ibid, p.145.
13 G. Brütting, *Fliegen ist unser Sport: Geschichte des Deutschen Aero Clubs e.V,* p.278.
14 W. Schwipps, *Kleine Geschichte der deutschen Luftfahrt*, p.103.
15 Fieseler, op. cit., p.131.
16 Fieseler, op. cit., p.131.

here was his chance for him to salvage something of his country's reputation, if he could overcome some redoubtable challenges.

He would be up against the world's leading competitors in their very latest aircraft. He therefore had to come up with some novel stunts. He scoured international air magazines to get an idea of the state of the art. After much careful thought, he decided that he would execute something really spectacular: an inverted loop, which involved flying upside down at the top of a loop (when the pilot is 'inverted') and for longer than a few seconds. But it was one thing to have the idea, yet quite another to actually pull off the actual manoeuvre.

Fieseler's brain was now in overdrive. He had to find solutions to an array of important and for the time highly novel problems. Could his Schwalbe be designed so that the engine functioned satisfactorily when the plane was flying upside down? Is so, would the wings and steering equipment be strong enough to cope with the forces acting on the plane as it performed the unusual manoeuvres? Was it aerodynamically possible for the wings to carry out the inverted loop? What was the maximum blood pressure acting on the head that a young pilot could take? On the last point Fieseler had made already experiments on tail-spinning which had entailed horrible consequences. He found that after eight complete rotations, as the blood drained from his brain, his head was swimming. It took precious seconds until he had recovered his normal vision, by which time he was a mere 100 metres above the ground, and that was perilous. All the while every twist and turn he had developed in the First World War to achieve advantageous offensive or defensive positions was now being exploited in his pioneering aerobatic routines.[17]

Regarding the demands of inverted looping on the engine, Fieseler went to Berlin to meet flight engineers from Siemens. For a few minutes they did not take his plans seriously. Smiling patronisingly, they pointed out that their SH12 engine was not designed to be flown upside down. Before long the discussion was joined by the chief designer himself, who proposed that they could manufacture a new oil pump, but let Fieseler know that he would need a different kind of carburettor, which was not commercially available. 'Not yet,' retorted Fieseler, adding, 'One day you'll see what I mean.'[18]

His next point of call was to the Sum Carburettor Factory in north Berlin. Herr Sum, evidently an acquaintance of Fieseler, and a man only too happy to oblige, told him that he needed an injection carburettor. He added that some time ago his company had produced one, but it never worked reliably. 'Can I see it?' asked Fieseler. Sum disappeared and came back with it. His eyes twinkling, Fieseler said that he would like to buy it. 'Good heavens, no', came the reply, 'I'll give it to you!'[19] Back in Kassel, he set about creating his modified Schwalbe with the unstinting assistance of the mechanics and fitters at RaKa. Fieseler helped to design a spherical fuel tank suitable for inverted flying. It was equipped with an air pressure pump, a pressure ventilator, manometer and level gauge. His highly reliable fitter Welle had the key task of replacing and installing the normal carburettor with the injection one. The new device did not work immediately; there was no ignition. Fieseler had it equipped with four nozzles with boreholes of various sizes.

After considerable perseverance and much experimentation, there was suddenly a loud roar, some explosions and an eruption of black vapour. Then there was ignition at last. This led to the discovery that too much fuel was being forced through the carburettors. That meant modifying the sparking plugs and making the nozzles smaller. All this took days of work, resulting in many bruised and aching fingers. In the end the engine worked perfectly in the workshop and then in the air. Fieseler then spent hours every day putting the new Schwalbe through its paces, carrying

17   R. Nagel und T. Bauer, *Kassel und die Luftfahrtindustrie seit 1923: Geschichte(n), Menschen, Technik*, p.425.
18   Ibid, p.132.
19   Ibid, p.133.

out various manoeuvres upside down. He next set about perfecting his inverted loop, which had seemingly never been attempted before and which was considered to be highly dangerous: there was a risk of blood veins bursting in the eyes in addition to giddiness. Not surprisingly perhaps many people in aviation circles actually considered this manoeuvre to be impossible. Fieseler, who these days was far less reckless than when he had been a fighter pilot, had a second seat belt fitted to his plane.

The figure would be his star turn for the meeting in Zürich. He spent countless hours practising it until everything came quite naturally to him. In the meantime word was getting around about what he was up to. He even had imitators. One was the chief test pilot of Junkers. In an experimental flight at around 1,000 metres he turned his plane over, but he was flying too fast. He lost control and may have been severely giddy as well as far too close to the ground to stabilise his plane. The plane crashed and the pilot was killed. Would-be acrobatics pilots in Germany took very careful note. Only the most skilled would try the inverted loop from now. According to Fieseler there was never a second tragic death as a result of mismanagement of that particular manoeuvre.

In the meantime, and possibly to prevent his practice flights being observed by rivals, he started training at four o'clock in the morning. But even this ruse apparently did not deter would-be copy-cats. Wind of what he was up to reached the all-important DVL. The considered opinion of the institute's experts was that the inverted loop was aerodynamically a complete impossibility in a Schwalbe. But, when Fieseler repeatedly succeeded in demonstrating his achievement to the DVL inspectors, they were stunned into silence. Once he had perfected the principal manoeuvre, he developed five new variants, including one called 'the screw,' three twists along the axis of flight without losing height.[20]

Fieseler and Welle arrived in Zürich two days before the meeting was due to begin. The event took place at the aerodrome at Dübendorf, a few kilometres to the east of the city. Several stands had been specially built for the occasion. Fieseler's rivals came from nine other countries. Around 5.00pm on the day before the competition he made a test flight, going through his manoeuvres, which gave some a foretaste of his prowess. In the newspapers it was announced that neither Udet nor Bäumer would be there to represent Germany. Fieseler was nonetheless disappointed, as he had hoped to test himself against them for a second time. Apart from him, there was only two other Germans in attendance, a minor government observer and a former pilot called Major Hildebrand, who was Germany's sole newspaper correspondent based in Switzerland. Even before the flying events got underway, Fieseler found himself cold-shouldered. He was an unwelcome German, from whom in any case nothing noteworthy was to be expected.

The following morning Welle was getting the Schwalbe ready for the compulsory events, which were scheduled for the afternoon. When he arrived at the hanger, Fieseler could hardly believe his eyes. Welle was surrounded by sundry military officials speaking to him in melodic, half-comprehensible German. What was the name of the pilot they'd seen practising the day before? How exactly was sustained inverted flying achieved? Was it possible to inspect the engine? And so forth. In the meantime the hotly tipped French pilots were nowhere to be seen. They suddenly realised that they were up against a serious competitor and had to think through their manoeuvres. At the end of the compulsory events Fieseler was exactly where he wanted to be: in the lead with two French rivals. The next day, a Sunday, would determine the winner. The three pilots who acquitted themselves best in their chosen routines in the morning were chosen for the run-off in the afternoon. Fieseler found himself among them.

20 Ibid, p.137.

In the afternoon the stands and spectator areas were packed. It was a sunny day, perfect for flying. At two o'clock a three-gun salute for the three final contenders announced the start of the main event of the entire meeting. Stretched out on the grass, Fieseler attempted to convey a picture of calm nonchalance, but inside he was in a state of nervous agitation. At last it was his turn to take to the air. He performed all his manoeuvres impeccably, introducing 'his negative loop, triple slow roll, 360 degree negative-g turn, figure of 8 negative-g turn, vertical 8 and horizontal 8 into his freestyle sequence.'[21] When he landed, the cheering of the crowds completely overwhelmed him. In a flash he was surrounded by other flyers, mechanics and military men. 'That was a revolution in aerobatics', a jubilant Dutch officer told him. 'What you did was magnificent!'[22] Fieseler had seen the flights of his two rivals and knew that he had easily left them behind. He now had to wait for the result.

In the evening there was a gala dinner in one of Zürich's most exclusive hotels. Fieseler had never seen food like it, but was too tense to touch it. Then the result was announced: First place: Fronval, France with 93.25 points. Second place: Fieseler, Germany with 92.25. Third place: Doret, France, with 90.75.[23] Fieseler was astounded. He immediately sensed that politics was behind the result. A pilot from Germany could not be seen to have won. A Swiss pilot, who he had got to know him slightly, came up to him and said, 'I'm ashamed.'[24] Humiliated, Fieseler left the dinner, having eaten nothing. Press coverage revealed that even the French pilots admitted that it was an unjust result. By way of doing the honourable thing, they implored him to take part in the next major French aerobatics event in Reims.

Twenty one years hence – after the Second World War, of course – Fieseler by chance encountered one of the Swiss members of the international jury in Zürich in June 1927. In a conversation with him Fieseler's suspicions were confirmed. The judge told him that he and his Dutch and Czech counterparts had ranked Fieseler first, but they had come under political pressure, presumably from the Swiss authorities, not to declare Fieseler, as a German, the winner so as not to offend the French government. 'It was wrong,' I admit, said the Swiss, adding awkwardly, 'I wouldn't do the same again today.'[25] Galling as this episode was for Fieseler, his impressive flying in Zürich made him into an internationally acclaimed aerobatics pilot.

Local hero
Cutting his loses and completely crestfallen, Fieseler sent a telegram to Helene, telling her to get the train to Zürich. They would go on a belated honeymoon, which would help him to wind down from all his exertions of the last few months. While waiting for Helene's train, Fieseler bumped into the journalist Hildebrand, whose opinions on aviation carried weight in Germany. 'I will write about these dirty tricks (*Schweinerei*),' Hildebrand assured him, which was a kind of consolation prize for Fieseler.[26] Helene arrived and she and her husband spent some happy days at the Vierwaldstättersee. After that they made their way to the aerodrome at Dübendorf. Fieseler would fly his wife back to Kassel. As he was taking his Schwalbe out of its hangar, a member of the aerodrome staff told him to send a telegram to Kassel-Waldau to confirm his arrival time.

When he and Helene arrived at the aerodrome, there was an official reception party waiting for him. Top officials of the city of Kassel, including the mayor himself, were there to greet him.

21 R. Meredith, *Phoenix: A Complete History of the Luftwaffe 1918-1945. Vol. 1 – The Phoenix is Reborn*, p.351
22 Fieseler, op. cit., p.139.
23 Nagel und Bauer, op. cit., p.427.
24 Fieseler, op. cit., p.139.
25 Ibid, p.140.
26 Ibid, p.140.

Already it was common knowledge in Germany that Fieseler's triumph had been taken from him in an underhand way. If anything, his shoddy treatment enhanced his standing in Germany and especially in Kassel, where he was now a local hero. Hundreds of people flocked to the Kassel-Waldau aerodrome. A band was on hand. Raab, never one to forgo a publicity opportunity, made certain that several of his planes were there for all too see. To everyone's delight Fieseler complied with a request to do some turns in a Schwalbe. The mayor gave a speech in his honour and presented him with a silver cigarette case. Fieseler pondered what he believed was a change in public mood as a result of the fiasco in Zürich. Were the people happy, he asked himself, that Germany's long-standing enemy, France, had been defeated by a person from Kassel in a sports competition or was their reaction a sign that there was under the surface a revival of some subdued, but no longer repressible patriotic impulse?

When Fieseler returned home, there was a letter waiting for him. It was from Rudolf Böttger, the well-regarded commandant of Tempelhof Airport in Berlin. Böttger invited him to take part in a major flying event to be held there in September. The deadline was close and Fieseler immediately confirmed his participation. The fee was ten times that what he had received at Zürich, which made the invitation even more irresistible. He flew to Tempelhof for the event, where he was most warmly received. His Schwalbe was inspected with awe and admiration. Böttger, on greeting him, said, 'Thanks to your achievement in Zürich, we can at last demonstrate what we are capable of.'[27] He presented Fieseler with a copy of the programme. Skimming though it, Fieseler noticed that Udet was also taking part and then saw his own name and a photograph of himself spread over two pages. This would be a demotion for Udet, Germany's most celebrated aerobatics pilot!

Seeing Fieseler's shock, Böttger reassured him. 'Don't worry about Udet. As long as he's paid, that's the most important thing to him.' In flying circles it was well known that Udet liked to live life lavishly. 'The thing is', Böttger went on, 'when it comes to aerobatics, it's all about living responsibly and not getting distracted.'[28] It was Berlin's very first such air show and people came in their thousands. Udet arrived and did his turn, which entailed picking a handkerchief off the ground with the tip of his wing and performing a daring loop. Fieseler remembered watching this display with unalloyed admiration. Then it was his turn. He had been engaged to perform for ten minutes. The loudspeaker announced him as if he were 'a fairground sensation.'[29]

Mindful of a motto he had devised for himself 'keep a cool head and have something up your sleeve,'[30] he went through his paces, flying first upside down very close to the ground and then sweeping alongside the spectators. As he taxied to the hangar, people swarmed towards the Schwalbe – journalists, photographers, radio reporters and newsreel cameramen. Just about managing to clamber out of his plane, he saw a familiar face and an outstretched hand. 'Well, Fieseler, old chap, if I'd have known you were destined for all this greatness, I would have treated you with far more respect!'[31] It was no other than one of his old commanders from the war, Captain Wentscher, of whom he did not harbour especially warm memories.

As Fieseler was being photographed and bombarded with questions, there was an announcement over the loudspeaker: Herr Udet will challenge Herr Fieseler to an aerobatic duel, in which they will exchange planes. This took Fieseler completely by surprise, though this practice was not uncommon between rival stunt pilots. He knew that this was Udet's way of proving his supremacy in the sport. As far as Fieseler was concerned, this was a pathetic challenge. He was determined to

27   Ibid, p.142.
28   Ibid, p.143.
29   Ibid, p.143.
30   Ibid, p.143.
31   Ibid, p.143.

beat his rival and he in fact did. This caused a sensation. His photograph with stories about him appeared in the newspapers.

By now it was clear to Fieseler that he should devote himself to aerobatics. This was a serious sport in which 'the pilot must be in complete control of his aircraft at every moment and be able to master critical situations at any time.'[32] And had not Fieseler shown himself to be such a pilot? Whilst aerobatics gained huge numbers of followers – for instance an event in Berlin in which Fieseler and Udet took part reportedly attracted huge crowds, it was not a sport to be appreciated by mere sensation seekers. It was all very well for spectators to gawp at daring individuals walking on wings in flight and jumping on other planes in the air, but there was no discipline in those antics.[33]

Since September 1927 until the end of the year Fieseler took part in eleven flying events in Germany, which brought in personal earnings of 17,000 Reichsmarks.[34] In the following year he received more and more invitations to fly in other European countries. The whole time he devised new manoeuvres to delight the public and test himself and his plane, but always within the margin of safety. His celebrity opened up other avenues. For example, the DVL asked him to help them provide guidelines on aircraft performance. The authorities had noticed that Fieseler was pushing his plane to new limits and a formal description of these limits could assist German designers, as and when restrictions on German aviation were further relaxed.

At the same time the DVL introduced two new licences for aerobatics pilots, the second being a requirement for those performing more advanced, in other words more dangerous, manoeuvres. This body was keen for future fighter pilots to obtain the second licence to certify their proficiency in advanced flying. So it was that Fieseler received an invitation from Junkers to give their pilots a three weeks' course in aerobatics. After that he received a request from the German Aero Club to assist with compiling regulations by which to judge aerobatic performances. This was a very difficult task because there were no such things as weightings or handicaps nor did any country have guidelines which could help Fieseler. We may of course assume that he was being well paid for these consultancy activities. His involvement with national bodies as well as notable aircraft manufacturers, not to mention suppliers of engines and specialist parts, meant that he was acquiring a very useful network of contacts across the entire gamut of German aviation.

'The world's finest exponent of stunting'

A slightly different kind of invitation came from of all places England. His successes in Germany and Switzerland had come to the notice of the Royal Aero Club in London. Would Herr Fieseler kindly consider writing an article for their official organ, the weekly magazine *Flight Global*? Launched in 1909, the magazine was 'devoted to the Interests, Practice, and Progress of Aerial Locomotion and Transport.' As might be expected, Fieseler seized this particular opportunity to promote himself and German aerial endeavour to a much wider audience. He wrote the article and it was published in English translation on 5 January 1928. The editor, introducing Fieseler in the most flattering terms, wrote as follows:[35]

> When, therefore, we publish this week an article by Herr Gerhard Fieseler on 'Aerobatics,' we do so because we regard the evolutions carried out by that famous German pilot as something ranking a very long way higher than mere 'stunts,' although for brevity we have

32 Schwipps, op. cit., p.105.
33 Ibid, p.105.
34 Nagel und Bauer, op. cit., p.428.
35 G. Fieseler, Aerobatics, *Flight Global*, No. 993, Vol, XX, pp.3-6. Available at: https://www.flightglobal.com/pdfarchive/view/1928/1928%20-%200001.html

used the word 'stunt' in the article as a translation of the German word *Figur*, since it was thought that, the word having unfortunately got into the English language, it would perhaps be better understood than a literal translation of some of the expressions used in the original German text by Herr Fieseler. Let it be admitted at once that Herr Fieseler's 'stunts' deserve the name to this extent that they are spectacular. It is no use trying to deny it. They are very spectacular, as those who have seen his low rolls and loops will admit.

The editor continues:

But as the author of the article, and inventor of many of the new "figures," there are certain evolutions the accurate carrying out of which can be guaranteed, and which are not therefore, dangerous to carry out at a low height. There are others which cannot always be guaranteed to be carried out perfectly, and these should always be done at a safe height, and well away from the public enclosures. By way of an example of how Herr Fieseler's work differs from many purely "stunt" exhibitions, we may mention that recently he has been carrying out his evolutions with a special cinematographic camera mounted on his machine in such a way that during the "aerobatics" a film is taken which afterwards shows what deflection, if any, of the wings takes place during any particular manoeuvre.

His words continue in this glowing vein:

Of 'stunts,' in the usual sense of the word, we have always disapproved, but the work carried out by Herr Fieseler has a very real practical value … Herr Gerhard Fieseler has become famous on the Continent as a 'stunt' pilot. We have not personally had the privilege to see his 'aerobatics,' but several British pilots who have seen him fly in Germany hold view that he is the world's finest exponent of stunting. As pilots are conservative folk, and not given to unduly praising one another's performances, this is praise indeed.

The editor urges members of the Royal Aero Club not to delay in extending invitations to Herr Fieseler to give demonstrations in the UK, as he is 'busy booking engagements.' He would be only too happy to provide members with Herr Fieseler's address. All communications to the effect should be made to the editor's London club. The encomium concludes:

Herr Fieseler was a 'Jagdstaffel' pilot during the war, and as he says in the concluding paragraph of his article, he would like personally to meet some of the British pilots about whose skill he was able to gain first-hand knowledge during the war. Perhaps it might be possible to arrange for a match against some of our 'stunt' pilots.

In his own article Fieseler is quick to point out that the effects of the Treaty of Versailles, on the one hand, and the impact of the recent hyper-inflation, on the other, had dealt aviation in Germany a terrible blow. One consequence was 'that the old stock of "stunt" pilots disappeared, and newcomers were not trained.' Despite all the setbacks, he notes that Germany 'leads the world' in commercial aviation, which may have taken some of his British readers by surprise. Turning to stunting, he opens with points of importance. First, 'a well-executed evolution in the air presents an aesthetically beautiful spectacle.' Second, 'stunting has great value as a sport' because 'it requires the closest cooperation between man and machine found anywhere.' Third, 'the heavy stressing of the [stunt] machine … brings to the general public a sense of the unquestionable safety of our commercial machines which are flown in a straightforward manner only.' In other words, the general public, which 'must be given confidence in our most modern form of transport', can see for itself in the stunt flying how safe an activity flying has become.

Fieseler gives a revealing explanation of second point about the co-ordination of man and machine: 'The legs operate the rudder; the right hand the elevator and ailerons; the left hand the throttle and ignition controls; the eyes observe approximately eight different instruments; and the ears are constantly listening to the sound of the engine. But the alpha and omega of flying is a certain "feel", consisting in a ceaseless concentration of all faculties, and which cannot be described.'

We sense that this passage, which is far more complete statement of his approach to flying than anything we find in his autobiography, brings together everything he thinks and knows about flying in war and peace. Of considerable interest is his reference to that certain 'feel.' He used the phrase 'feel for flying' a good deal in his description of his wartime experiences and notably in his recollection of his discussion with Udet about Richthofen. Fieseler plainly divides aviators into two classes: those with 'feel' and those without it. Not that he says it, but he plainly regards himself as a supreme exemplar of the first category.

Fieseler then goes on to describe how it took him 'several weeks' to fly with his old confidence after a break of some seven and a half years. Then, having briefly introduced his seven 'new figures' (i,e. stunts) with his Raab-Katzenstein Schwalbe, he explains how rigorously he practiced with it, flying it 'day and day out … until I felt thoroughly at one with it.' Only then did he attempt upside-down flying, mentioning that he made use of a scale model to 'study the different control movement. He made short flights at first and could eventually 'make upside flights of 4 to 6 minutes without feeling any special bodily effects.' As for his show-piece, the inverted loop, many experts had considered this to be 'impossible.' He had proved them wrong by minutely thinking through every manoeuvre and experimenting accordingly. In his own words: 'I ascertained this slow and deliberate procedure to be the correct one. After I knew quite definitely how my machine behaved at various speeds, how the controls were, and last but not least how I myself felt, I proceeded to attempt the second half of the inverted loop, independent of the first half.'

What, it might be asked, did he have to say about blood rushing into the head? First of all it did not happen as people expected. He was conscious of an increase of pressure, but it was tolerable. Of greater concern were spells of giddiness or black-outs which sprang from unusual pressures on the body and senses. For example, in performing a complete inverted loop blood drains from the head and is then forced in it. Fieseler found that moments of 'everything going black' were of short duration; sometimes 'I tore my helmet and googles off, and rested by head on the cockpit coaming, in the slip-stream, and opened my mouth wide.' A one point he did consult a doctor about headaches. The doctor could find nothing wrong and merely advised him 'to fly in a normal attitude.' It was advice that Fieseler politely ignored.

On matters of safety, he warns against undertaking aerobatic manoeuvres at unsafe heights i.e. too close to the ground. Before each flight he notes down on a sheet of paper the precise height at which each stunt is to begin. These notes are attached to his knee immediately below the altimeter. 'With adequate height,' he writes, 'the pilot will, in 90 out of 100 cases, be able either to get his machine under control again or to remove the cause of the trouble.'[36] Even so there is human error and the worry of technical defects during flight. He gives two examples. On one occasion he attempted to correct a manoeuvre, but could not control the rudder. It turned out that his mechanic had inadvertently forgotten to remove a 20 inch long tommy bar (which was used for

36   Fieseler, op. cit., *Flight Global*.

taking off propellers) from the cockpit. It had lodged itself between the footbar and the cockpit floor, making the rudder inoperative. On that occasion Fieseler, who had dropped from 800 to 300 feet, was able – just in time – to discover the cause of the problem and kick the bar away. On another occasion the petrol supply to the engine suddenly cut out. He was able to put his aircraft into a spin and 'just in time reach the aerodrome and land without the engine.'[37]

Then consciously writing as a former fighter pilot, Fieseler concludes the article with these words: 'I should be particularly happy to have an opportunity of meeting English pilots, of whose outstanding abilities I was able to convince myself during the war. Perhaps an opportunity to visit England may occur before long.' Perhaps, as he wrote those words, he was thinking of Lieutenant Bamford, over whom he achieved his first aerial victory in 1917.

If at the start of his aerobatics career Fieseler was wary about performing stunts too close to the ground, a few years later he appeared to have abandoned his caution. A photograph of him at an airshow in Berlin in 1932 shows him flying in inverted mode at a mere 25 metres above the ground.[38] But this feat would of course have only been executed after meticulous preparation of himself and his machine.

Descending from the sky like a god

Fieseler was not the only person in Germany making a name for himself in the skies in the late 1920s. Another was Adolf Hitler, who had a genuine interest in flying and aviation technology before he came to power in 1933. Hitler had made his first flight in 1927 with Udet's friend Ritter von Greim as pilot. Hitler never liked flying as such, but was keenly aware of its political advantages for publicity and electioneering. Indeed, in April 1939 an article in the newspaper *Der Adler* it was noted that 'with acute perception, Adolf Hitler recognized the airplane as a hugely dynamic instrument to wage the political struggle with unprecedented speed and hitherto unsuspecting intensity.'[39] As the first German politician therefore to use an airplane extensively in the late 1920s, Hitler dramatically raised his profile by 'taking to the skies in a hired plane, American-style.'[40]

At all events, when Hitler with a small entourage in two planes – a Junkers 52 and a Junkers F 13 – landed at Kassel-Waldau aerodrome in 1928 to address a mass rally in the city, that would have been among his first flights. At that time Hitler did not yet have complete dominance over the Nazi Party, but he was a big enough name to bring prestige to the Kassel branch. Fieseler witnessed the arrival of Germany's future master, which is interesting in itself. An intriguing question at this point is: did Fieseler happen to be there on the day Hitler arrived or did he make a point of being there to get a close view of the man who in his own words 'had made himself into such a talking-point' (*der schon so viel von sich reden gemacht hatte*),[41] and whose crowd-pulling oratorical style was bringing him 'patrons, money and followers.'[42]

The modest airport was empty when the erstwhile 'beer-hall agitator' and the few other Nazis stepped out of their planes.[43] According to Fieseler, the entourage walked a respectful five to eight metres behind Hitler. Already a car was waiting to take the Nazi leader to his venue in Kassel where a huge tent, capable of accommodating 10,000 people, had been erected and where SA storm troopers had taken up positions. Fieseler, however, could not help admiring the slick organisation of the entire day starting with Hitler's arrival to his departure. Indeed, everything proceeded 'with

37   Fieseler, op. cit., *Flight Global*,
38   Meredith, op. cit., p.9.
39   Cited in: F. Esposito, *Fascism, Aviation and Mythical Modernity* p.348.
40   I. Kershaw, *Hitler 1889-1936 Hubris,* p.363.
41   Fieseler, op. cit.,166-167.
42   G. Mai, *Die Weimarer Republik ,* p.43.
43   Kershaw, op. cit.,p. 129.

military precision.'⁴⁴ As they drove into Kassel, more cars joined Hitler's entourage along with two lorry loads of SA men. Fieseler lets us know that he was among the last to gain entrance to the venue. Perhaps he does not want us to think that he was too keen to see the future Führer harangue the masses.

As for the speech itself, which he evidently heard, Fieseler vividly recalls it being 'clear, correct and convincing', but when Hitler got on to the topic of the Jews, that was distasteful. After all, says Fieseler, the Jews had lived in Germany for generations; it was inappropriate to call them 'guests.' Even so, he had to admit that the 'demonic' Hitler had a way with audiences: 'the best actor would not have been able to exert such fascination,' he observed.⁴⁵ The future Führer was rapidly learning how to appeal to 'the disgruntled, disenchanted and dispossessed middle classes.'⁴⁶ Not only did he have a way with the German language – that 'glorious but all too powerful instrument', with which he secured a magnetic grip over virtually the entire German nation,⁴⁷ but he also had become 'so magnificent a handler of the German mind.'⁴⁸ Much has been made of Hitler's mass appeal and his powers of oratory, whose 'overall effect was like being whirled around inside a warm wave of unfathomable emotions.'⁴⁹ A sharp insight into Hitler's technique is offered by one of Germany's leading historians of the Third Reich, Joachim Fest:

> Those who think [his] success was entirely due to the unbridled, almost sensual extravagance of his delivery are mistaken: what it really was, was the calculated intermingling of frenzy and rationality. Standing always deadly pale and gesticulating in the light of projectors … hoarsely hurling his accusations and tirades, or almost whispering his declarations of faith and love for his listeners, he was always unfailingly in control.⁵⁰

One of Britain's leading historians of Germany has noted that his 'lack of polish was an essential precondition of his uncanny ability to connect with the masses'⁵¹ On this lack of polish the distinguished historian and journalist Sebastian Haffner lets rip. Everything about Hitler, he writes, 'was for the normal German thoroughly repellent … the spivvish haircut, the tacky elegance, the Viennese twang; above all the many, long speeches, not to mention the jerky movements, the wild gesticulating, the salivating, the gaze at one moment flickering and at another fixed. And as for the contents of those speeches: the relishing of threats, the relishing in violence, the blood-thirsty, murderous phantasising.'⁵² No wonder perhaps that Fieseler's first impression of Hitler is that he was 'downright disagreeable (*ausgesprochen unsympathisch*),' behaving like a 'narrow-minded dictator' (*kleinbürgerlicher Diktator*).⁵³

On that Hitler rally in 1928, by future standards a modest one, Fieseler looked around: everyone was in thrall, hypnotised, stunned. (Was he one of them?). Only at the end was there deafening applause. Fieseler states that if in the crowds any doubters, sceptics and political opponents had the courage to protest, they would be unceremoniously ejected by the SA men. Writing of that day more than half a century later, it is hardly surprising that he describes Hitler as 'obnoxious.'

44   Fieseler, op. cit., p.166.
45   Ibid, p.167.
46   C. Bielenberg, *The Past is Myself: An Englishwoman's life in Berlin under the Nazis*, p.28.
47   T. Garton Ash, *The File: A Personal History*, p.201.
48   W. Shirer, *The Rise and Fall of the Third Reich*, p.903.
49   M. Burleigh, *The Third Reich: A New History*, pp.114-115.
50   Cited in: G. Sereny, *Albert Speer: His Battle for Truth*, p.98.
51   R. Evans, *The Coming of the Third Reich*, p.188.
52   S. Haffner, op. cit., p.88.
53   Ibid, p.166.

Fieseler's retrospective impression of Hitler would have been in tune with that of countless others after the Second World War, when no German would wish to appear to have been an admirer of the man whose folly had cost so many lives.

Be that as it may, there may well have been something special about Hitler, which drew Fieseler's reluctant admiration. Here was a politician, who exactly like himself was in his own *pioneering* way furthering German air-mindedness. Hitler's association with the aeroplane would be exploited in Leni Riefenstahl's celebrated – and notorious – propaganda film about the Führer, *Triumph of the Will*, which was premiered in 1935. The Canadian writer Rory Maclean recalls one of the most potent and memorable sequences in the film:

> The three-engined Junkers dropped through towers of cumulus clouds, its shadow sweeping over mediaeval rooftops and cathedral spires. The Führer descended from the sky like a god, his arrival on earth cheered by shouting, ecstatic crowds. Eager women and children near to tears raised their arms in fervent salute.[54]

The eclipsing of Udet

In 1928 an illustrated magazine in Germany requested Fieseler to describe himself as human being and aviator. Fieseler takes the opportunity to explain in a paragraph why, because he is not a poet, he does not have the gift of describing the exhilaration of flying.[55] This prompts the magazine to request a few paragraphs on his greatest flying experience. He reflects on his wartime experiences, which 'will sound incredible today.' He contrasts himself as a one-time fighter pilot and as an aerobatics pilot now, saying that the intervening years have changed him. In the war he was 'a dare-devil without a second thought': it was all about 'success at any price.' Now he is reflective; all risks are calculated; safety must not be compromised; self-control.' As an aerobatics pilot his way is always to run an aircraft in, as one did in those days a brand-new motor car.

In July 1928 Germany organised its first national aerobatics championships. The venue was Düsseldorf. Making a stop-over at Tempelhof on his way from Kassel. Fieseler met Böttger, who told him that he was sorry that his aerodrome was not running the event. More to the point, he mentioned that Udet was using a new English stunt plane and was practising all the time for Düsseldorf. By now Fieseler was no longer disconcerted by Udet. He regarded himself and his great rival as outstanding pilots, but noted that were polar opposites in their approach. He rated Udet highly for his 'skills at improvisation and his unfettered, uninhibited manner.' As for himself, he characterised his own style as 'inventive, versatile, precise, difficult and exacting.'[56] German aviation historians Nagel and Bauer have compared their respective flying styles. According to them Udet was a pilot who flew with gut feeling ('*Bauchflieger*'). He engaged more emotionally with the public, treating them to a display entailing 'a certain risk.' By contrast Fieseler was as a pilot who flew using his head ('*Kopfflieger*'), noting that he focused on precision and kept himself 'rather distanced' from the public.[57]

The Düsseldorf air meeting assembled a jury of Germany's leading experts on aviation. The big Berlin newspapers made a point of only sending former wartime pilots as correspondents. Ullstein, one of Germany's biggest publishers, commissioned the well-known artist, Theo Matejko, to produce drawings for *Berlin Illustrated*. The announcer for the loudspeaker was also a former pilot and well-known for his turn of phrase. The event attracted ten aerobatics pilots. Once again

54 R. MacLean, *Berlin: Imagine a City*, p.228.
55 http://www.illustrierte-presse.de/die-zeitschriften/werkansicht/dlf/73350/28/
56 Fieseler, op. cit., p.146.
57 Nagel und Bauer, op. cit., pp.429-430.

Fieseler defeated Udet. He was now Germany's first ever national aerobatics champion. At the celebratory dinner the two of them sat together. The whole evening Udet drank, but the alcohol did nothing to lighten his depressed and pensive mood. At one o'clock in the morning Udet turned to Fieseler and said. 'Because of you I've now got to do my stuff upside down!', adding that 'the best thing to do is stay out of your way!'[58]

Did Udet actually record his own reaction to this string of devastating defeats at the hands of Fieseler? Apparently not. In 1935 Udet's memoir *Mein Fliegerleben* (My life as an aviator) was published.[59] It covers his life as a wartime pilot in von Richthofen's Flying Circus, his life after the war when he turns to aircraft manufacture and then seeks his fortune abroad. It is an upbeat account of his stunting life in the USA, notably in Hollywood, and his adventures as pilot for film crews in Africa and Greenland. But there is absolutely no reference to his participation in competitive air shows in a Germany and other European countries. Nor are his defeats by Fieseler mentioned by Udet's enthusiastic German biographer, Hans Herlin. They may have been too painful for him as well. Indeed the name of Fieseler does not feature in the biography at all.

The absence of references to Fieseler are a strange omission, seeing that Udet and he were already great friends. As Nagel and Bauer explain: 'In the last year [1928] they had got to know each other very well at flying events and to value each other. There was a rule between them: 'a hard fight in competition, afterwards a friendly get-together.'[60] In a few short years Udet would emerge as a very senior official in the Hitler's new Reich Aviation Ministry; and that proved a very useful connection for Fieseler after he had turned his attention to aircraft design and manufacture. Before then Udet always remained in high demand for solo demonstrations in Germany and other European countries. In one memorable stunt in 1928 he landed a Klemm sports plane on the snow-covered Zugspitze, Germany's highest mountain.[61]. He also acted as a pilot in the making of films in Switzerland, Africa and Greenland. Just for the record: in 1928 he liquidated his company and it was taken over by a young aircraft designer from Augsburg by the name of Willy Messerschmitt.

In one film, *The White Hell of Pitz Palu*, which involved landing on the Mont Blanc glacier, he had an actual part. He was starring alongside Leni Riefenstahl, then an actress. Udet, as Germany's most lionised pilot in the 1930s, was personally chosen by Göring to give a demonstration of his prowess at the Berlin Olympics in 1936. Fieseler might have had grounds for thinking that he had been unfairly passed over. But no-one could hold a candle to Udet for panache and glamour. Not even Fieseler had landed a sea-plane on an ice-flow. Udet's earnings were substantial. To put that in context: when he agreed in 1936 to join the Luftwaffe as a colonel at Göring's insistence, his officer's salary of 13,000 Reichsmarks a year was a nominal pay-cut of 187,000 Reichsmarks.[62]

Blackpool welcomes Herr Fieseler

In his autobiography Fieseler mentions that in the course of his aerobatics career he made several visits to other European countries, especially France, Italy and England. In 1928 he flew from Kassel to Rheims to attend an air meeting. As he approached the former battle grounds of the Western Front, he dropped his altitude to about 100 metres to see what remained of the trenches and dug-outs, which only a few years before had been an 'obscenity of the square miles of mud, barbed wire, broken trees and shattered bodies.'[63] All the trenches and shell holes had been filled

---

58   Fieseler, op. cit., p.147.
59   The title of the English version of his memoir is 'Ace of the Black Cross.'
60   Nagel und Bauer, op. cit., p.429.
61   Deutsches Museum, *Aviation: A Guide to the Aeronautics Collection*, p.52.
62   Ibid, p.195.
63   S. Williams, preface to: V. Brittain, *Testament of Youth*, p.11.

in, but from the air he could see their tracery. According to his own testimony Fieseler, a guest of a French organisation, was seemingly the first German to fly over that terrible place of slaughter. Many of his flights to France took over this beautiful, fertile land and over the vast war cemeteries. The same questions pressed on his mind. How on earth did it come to this? Who was to blame? What was the point of it all? Today the same questions are being asked, the answers still contested.

For the most part Fieseler does not mention all the flying events he attended. Writing as an old man, he simply could not recall every one. In addition to those meetings he mentions, there is a very valuable supplementary source in the form of the on-line archive of *Flight Global*. The issue of 12 July 1928 describes his participation in an event which surprisingly he does not refer to, namely the Blackpool Air Pageant on 6-7 July. This was his first visit to England and it almost certainly sprang from his article in *Flight Global*. This was a very substantial event, as it was aimed to promote Blackpool as a thoroughly modern resort, and 'what could be more modern … than an aerodrome to serve the symbol of the modern age: the aeroplane.'[64] The great gathering was also special in that it took place at the very same venue which had hosted Britain's very first flying meeting in 1909, where people had flocked to see the novelty of the age, described by the *Daily Mail* as 'aerial motor cars.'[65] The pageant attracted no less than 250 officials from the Air Ministry, and some 200 civilian pilots would take part. According to the programme, the displays would include 'races, fancy flying, parachuting, sky writing, and the usual manoeuvres.'

The programme states that 'many foreign noted pilots, such as the German air "ace", Herr Fieseler who will come from Germany and perform his extraordinary stunts which he ably described in FLIGHT January 5 1928.' The leading French aerobatics pilot would be M. Marcel Doret, who Fieseler had outclassed the year before at Zürich. In addition to their own specialities both Herr Fieseler and M. Doret would take part in a flypast along with other prominent pilots, including Sir Alan Cobham, former wartime pilot, chief test pilot of de Havilland and barnstormer *par excellence*, and A. V. Roe, whose aircraft company would one day build the legendary Lancaster bomber.

The 12 July issue of *Flight Global* reported that 'Herr Fieseler's performance, the first in England, was eagerly awaited by expert and inexpert.' This statement makes clear that Fieseler, still a relative newcomer to aerobatics, had built up a remarkable international reputation for himself in a short space of time. At Blackpool he flew a Schwalbe, described as 'a small cantilever biplane fitted with a Siemens 112 h.p. air-cooled radial engine.' At about 1,500 feet he commenced aerobatics. The journalist records his performance in the following words:

> From the purely expert point of view, he was not exceptional until he performed the vertical figure of eight, and the stirring feature of this was the slow struggle to bring the tail level with the nose at the end of the outside loop following the ordinary loop above it. The movement finished at a fairly low altitude, thus clearly revealing the spectacular climb to normal. His flying is very graceful … Most of his flying is done upside down, in which position he has made himself equal to many of the manoeuvres performed in normal position. That, one suggests, is his particular flair.

The spectators were impressed. Indeed, 'all our pilots considered that he had put up a very good show, and they gave him a deserved ovation.' *Flight Global* reports that Fieseler received £300 as a fee.' That would be around £10,000 at today's prices.

---

64 S. Seabridge, *Blackpool's Aerodromes 1928-1936: Politics and Local Media*, p.8.
65 Ibid, p.5.

Less than two weeks after his Blackpool success Fieseler's took part in an airshow in Rotterdam from 22 to 22 July 1928, where, according to *Flight Global*, 'a number of friendships were formed that are bound to endure.' The competing pilots apparently received petrol and oil ' free, gratis and for nothing' thanks to 'a certain number of wealthy people who show their interest in flying in the very practical form of a substantial donation.' As a further sign of Fieseler's celebrity, the magazine even noted the actual time when he arrived at the aerodrome. In fact that was just before the gala dinner at which the Dutch host welcomed the visitors in English, French, German and Dutch. The journalist covering the air show noted that in an exhibition event Fieseler's 'upside down circuits of the entire aerodrome proved the most attractive feature.'[66]

When Fieseler returned to Kassel after his success in Blackpool, there was once again an enthusiastic reception waiting for him. At the aerodrome the mayor presented him a special testimonial on behalf of the joyous city of Kassel, afterwards inviting him to him a dinner along with a few selected persons of high standing in business and politics with an interest in air transport. One of the guests gave Fieseler a laudation on behalf of the industry. By the end of 1928 Fieseler had taken part in 25 air shows and given some 95 displays and his earnings for the year were 80,000 Reichsmarks.

Into the aircraft business
During the flying season, that to say from April to November, Fieseler's schedule became increasingly demanding. The more events he won, the more his fame grew, and the more invitations he received both to give aerobatics demonstration and take part in competitions. But, during the autumn and winter months he had time not only to think and try out his routines, but also to make decisions about his future. By now he was in his early thirties. He knew that he could not expect to engage in aerobatics flying for his entire career. But knowing that he would forever be smitten with flying, it seemed logical him to go into aircraft manufacturing. Indeed the time was approaching fast when he would have to build his own aircraft to suit his style of flying with its penchant for new aerodynamically demanding manoeuvres.

Besides he was all aware that not only Udet but also his foreign rivals were flying in new or modified planes that would one day outclass his 'old' Schwalbe. As of 1928 Fieseler developed designs for a more powerful version tailor-made to his needs as a practitioner of aerobatics with a reputation to protect. This plane would be known as the Raka Tigerschwalbe ('Tiger Swallow'). Raab evidently allowed his staff to work on the new plane, whilst approving the change of name, knowing full well that Fieseler was harking back to his old nickname from the First World War. It made its maiden flight at the end of March 1929 with Katzenstein as test pilot. Then Fieseler made his first flight. After that one of the two RaKa designers involved with the project by the name of Richard Bauer asked to be taken up. Fieseler obliged as pilot. This flight resulted in a crash, from which both men emerged without serious injury. They were very lucky because the new Tigerschwalbe was a write-off. Raab not surprisingly blamed the mishap on Fieseler's devil-may-care attitude, whereas the latter was convinced that a defect had crept in during manufacturing. At all events the Tigerschwalbe was subject to a major overhaul, and there was no reoccurrence of the problem.

By the end of 1929 Fieseler had taken part in twelve flying events, performed 36 displays of aerobatics and earned a further 93,000 Reichsmarks. As a result of his high earnings from prize money Fieseler was taken with the idea of having an aircraft manufacturing company of his

---

66   *Flight Global (1928)* The Rotterdam Meeting, p.645-651 (26 July). Available at: http://www.flightglobal.com/pdfarchive/view/1928/1928%20-%200707.html

own. However, he did not want to build up a company from scratch. It suited him to take over a company which in his view had the potential to be built up into a viable business. He would want to influence what it produced: from design and performance, from selection of suppliers to sales. He also had ideas – very advanced for the time – about building gliders in serial production. So it was that that in April 1930 he bought Kegel-Flugzeugbau Kassel, a manufacturer of gliders, most of which were exported. It happened that the works manager, Erich von Knüpfer, had been an employee of RaKa and was known to Fieseler.

Some six months earlier Knüpffer had lost his job at RaKa and was on the bread-line. Fieseler had taken Knüpfer into his confidence about his plans and sent him occasional food parcels, in return for which the grateful Knüpfer kept his ear to ground about local aircraft companies. When he had started to work for Kegel, which was located in Ihringshausen on the north side of Kassel, Knüpfer told Fieseler that Fritz Ackermann, the biggest shareholder in the company, had little idea about management nor was he much respected by his 30 or so employees. Beyond that the finances were not in good shape. 'Keep me up to date, Herr Knüpfer', Fieseler asked him, undeterred by this not exactly encouraging assessment.

Then, at the beginning of 1930, Fieseler told Knüpfer to mention to Ackermann that he might be interested in making an investment in his company. A visit was arranged. Fieseler's first impression was favourable, but there was something about Ackermann's manner that nonplussed him. It turned out that Ackermann had plans to take over a business in the Ruhr, so was more than willing to discuss the sale of his company to Fieseler. A purchase price was agreed 'with astounding speed' after a cursory inspection of its finances.[67] Fieseler paid in cash. That was in April 1930.

Within a fortnight Fieseler realised that he had been duped. The company debts exceeded the actual purchase price, the order book was a piece of fiction, and the employees had no proper work. Fieseler could not believe how he had allowed this to happen, especially as he found Ackermann to be a shifty character. In the circumstances the best thing might have been to cut his losses and wind up the company. No, he was, come what may, going to make a success of it. He hung in, even though friends and relatives were urging him to throw in the towel. What made things even worse was that the 1929 Wall Street Crash had been devastating for the German economy. At that time German incomes were about what they what they had been just before the outbreak of war in 1914. Now all those gains had been lost. Fieseler took stock.

What was the point of democracy in the midst of all this economic mess? And wasn't it the fault of so-called democrats who had so submissively signed the Treaty of Versailles and accepted all the terms about restricting the development of German aviation? Unemployment was rising alarmingly. No wonder that there was 'near civil war on the streets'[68]. But it wasn't a question of clashes between those who were respectively for or against the government. The violence on the streets of German cities was between supporters of Hitler and his left-wing opponents.[69]

Was it not a sign of the times that it was risky for respectably attired people like himself – in other words, members of Kassel's 'traditionally conservative-authoritarian bourgeoisie' – to walk through the city's old town at night? [70] He deplored that fact that anyone with a car would be branded 'a capitalist.' Indeed, in his case, his car 'had been pelted with stones by the children of communistically minded parents.'[71] Not that he produces the slightest evidence to confirm the

67   Fieseler, op. cit., p.164.
68   M. Fulbrook, *History of Germany 1918-2000: The Divided Nation*, p.50.
69   Haffner, op. cit., p.88.
70   D. Krause-Vilmar, Die nationalsozialistische Machtergreifung 1933 der Stadt Kassel, in: *Arbeitsgemeinschaft, Arbeit und Leben: Kassel und nordhessen in der Zeit der Nationalsozialismus. Dokumentation einer Vortragsreihe Kassel*, p.7-18.
71   Fieseler, op. cit., p.166.

ideological position of the parents of his young assailants. What was Germany coming to if children were ambushing law-abiding citizens? Who was going to put an end to all this? The country needed law and order.

The aircraft companies in Kassel, of which there were seven or eight, were badly hit. RaKa was one that went out of business. Its demise showed all too clearly that 'idealism and an enthusiasm for flying were not enough to sustain a company' quite apart from 'Raab's financial dealings and his underhand way of management.'[72] As for Fieseler's small business venture, in its first year of operation it employed about thirty people and managed to export 80% of its output: some '30 gliders were sold to America and there were even sales in China.'[73] But he could scarcely cover his costs, so its output was being sold at a loss. Then, ever the innovator, he had the idea of building gliders on a rolling production line rather like Henry Ford made cars. He realised that it was a way of saving on the costs of production. According to Nagel and Bauer, Fieseler's glider manufacturing company became the first aircraft maker in the world to use serial production techniques.[74]

By and large serial production was used for building gliders destined for customers in other countries. For customers in Germany the novel technique had less attractions for the simple reason that many glider pilots simply bought drawings from manufacturers and then had them built in their clubs and associations. However, an important seed had been sown. In the meantime Fieseler continued his appearances at air shows in 1930, but with all the pressures associated with keeping his company afloat he only managed to take part in eight. His earnings from aerobatics displays amounted to 60,000 Reichsmarks, a drop of some 30,000 Reichsmarks over the previous year.

In June 1930 one of his gliders, flown by well-known glider pilot Robert Kronfeld, had set a new all-comers record for a duration flight of 3 hours and 15 minutes.[75] Gratifying as that was, Fieseler knew that the time had come for him to branch into the manufacture of motorised aircraft. For a start he needed a new plane, incorporating his specific requirements, if he were to increase his chance of winning at airshows, earn sufficient money to make further investment in his company and pay his employees. In the same year Fieseler appointed Emil Arnolt to his design team. Arnolt had been working on a free-lance basis and his clients had included Kegel. This proved to be a very advantageous move on Fieseler's part.

Another significant person entered Fieseler's life at around this time was one of Germany's budding aviatrixes, Vera von Bissing. She was well-heeled and had her own Schwalbe. Fieseler, busy as he was, agreed to instruct her in aerobatics. Bissing proved to be a successful pupil and became one of the first women in Germany to secure the necessary certificates. Not only did she become one of Europe's leading woman aerobatics champions, but was also the first aviatrix to perform one of Fieseler's signature figures, the inverted loop. In the next few years she and Fieseler would often take part in airshows together. She often acted as his interpreter at international events.

Despite the fact that new customers had been found in the USA, South America, South Africa and British India, Fieseler's company still had to struggle. Then came a potential life-line. Kronfeld, who had had a great success with a Fieseler glider in England, asked the company to build a glider with a 30-metre wingspan, which was unheard of at the time. Fieseler was keen to get the business, as he knew that a glider of these proportions could generate valuable publicity. Fieseler was even willing to sell the final product as close as possible to cost price and even cover start-up costs.

It all back-fired. It turned out that Kronfeld was a wily character who had no money even for a down-payment. His plan was to earn money with his 'super glider' and eventually pay for its

---

72 Nagel und Bauer, op. cit., p.67.
73 T. Wiederhold, *Gerhard Fieseler – eine Karriere: Ein Wirtschaftsführer im Dienste des Nationalsozialismus,* p.29.
74 Nagel und Bauer, op. cit., p.92.
75 Ibid, p.93.

production. Fieseler only had himself to blame, being overkeen to secure work for his employees. The losses to himself were painful. Not that this was occasion the first time that he had miscalculated the motives and goodwill of business associates. How could he be so like his father, he might have asked himself in an exasperated way. He vowed there and then to be much more circumspect in his commercial dealings after that. Had he not said that to himself before? As usual, the next time would be different.

Masterpieces of aircraft construction
In all these ups and downs Fieseler showed a certain flair for publicity and used testimonials from well-known glider pilots to promote his company. One such pilot was none other than Kronfeld who praised the Fieseler aircraft for 'such careful workmanship and fine attention to detail that has never been seen before.' Another, Wolf Hirth, billed as 'one of the world's most successful glider pilots' stated that his Fieseler-built gliders were 'masterpieces of aircraft construction in wood finish', whilst Carli Magersuppe, the holder of the English glider endurance record, wrote that the Fieseler gliders were the best that he in ten years' experience had ever flown.[76] Even though the company was not prospering as a business, the testimonials nevertheless helped establish it as a manufacturer of gliders of exceptional craftsmanship and performance.

It was probably in 1930 when three young engineering students from Kassel Technical College came to see Fieseler and asked for a job. He explained to them how difficult were the times for his company at the moment. He simply could not afford to employ more staff, no matter how well qualified. A few weeks later, just before their final examinations, they were back, this time with drawings of aero engines. If only Herr Fieseler could take them on so that they could learn from him. They did not even want a wage. They just wanted to be involved in aircraft manufacture. Fieseler was touched by their enthusiasm. He liked these young men and their determination. 'And what might be your salary expectations?', he asked, relenting. They proposed a derisory sum, explaining that they could satisfactorily exist as they were now: helping out a farmer and living in his barn. 'Please, give us a job to do. Please help us', they pleaded.

'Very well', rejoined Fieseler. 'I'll give you a job to do, and I'll pay you the going rate.' The three young men were overjoyed. Fieseler never forgot their names – Pfeiffer, Holstein and Hackenschmidt, and he recorded with much pleasure they all went on to have 'brilliant careers.'[77] In its own way it is an inspiring story. It shows Fieseler at his magnanimous best, admiring young people who do not give up in and are prepared to accept hardship today for a better tomorrow, and giving them a chance in life. He may not have realised it at the time, but this small episode, which he recalled so vividly after neatly fifty years, laid a notable foundation in his philosophy as an industrial manager.

In 1930 Fieseler had come up against the redoubtable Michel Détroyat, the French aerobatics champion. If he were to do battle with against his greatest rival at forthcoming international competitions, he needed a sports plane of enhanced performance and versatility. He turned to his by now much valued designer Emil Arnolt, who confirmed that he could help build the aircraft that his boss had in mind. There was, however, a snag in that Fieseler had only a limited formal appreciation of aerodynamics. He knew the principles, but he had to rely on his qualified designers and trained engineers to develop precise drawings based on actual calculations using statistics. In short he could not design, though he was not lacking in imagination or creativity. On the other hand, he knew precisely the flight characteristics and performance capabilities he was after.

---

76   Ibid, p.226.
77   Fieseler, op. cit., p.169.

Fieseler worked almost daily with Arnolt who in a manner of speaking converted his boss's experience and aspirations into the engineering drawings out of which one day a new aircraft would emerge. Every point of detail was discussed between them. There was never a clash of opinion; everything was thought through together. It was a relationship that Fieseler cherished. He had considerable admiration and respect for Arnolt, who more than anyone else he had ever met 'combined fundamental capability with striking modesty.'[78] The new plane flew for the first time in March 1930 and was known as the F1 Tigerschwalbe. It was a land-mark development for the fledgling company, and Arnolt was promoted to chief designer in a few months. Significantly the new aircraft bore the new Fieseler logo, a tilted F set in a light blue circle. Fieseler himself designed the logo and therefore created a brand based on his own name.[79] Whilst looking rather dated by today's standards, it is easy to imagine that in the 1930s its unmistakable resemblance to an arrow would have readily been associated with speed and modernity.

---

[78] Fieseler, op. cit., p.170.
[79] See plates xii and xviii.

7

1933: new spirit, new hope

We have a new government every year. I wish we had a Hitler.
Michel Détroyat, French aerobatics champion, 1934[1]

Wilhelm II was a novice compared to the present master.
Victor Klemperer[2]

The shape of things to come, but not yet

In 1931 Fieseler played around with the title of the Kegel Flugzeugbau Kassel and renamed it Segel-Flugzeugbau Kassel (*Segelflugzeug* being the German word for sail-plane or glider). It is unlikely that the change of name made any significant change to the company's never quite secure position. However, as work progressed on his new Tigerschwalbe sports plane, Fieseler received a most unusual commission, which he found irresistible.

In 1931 the Haus Bergmann cigarette company of Dresden approached him with a request to manufacture an aircraft that they could use for advertising: not just for trailing advertising banners, but as an attention-grabbing aerial mascot in its own right.[3] The company, better known as HB to generations of German smokers, wanted to have three models in time for the 1932 Deutschlandflug, the round-Germany air competition. On the face of things it is certainly a mystery why the cigarette manufacture should approach Fieseler. His company was at that time not especially well known and only had experience of building gliders. The facilitator of the arrangement, improbable as it may sound, was almost certainly Vera von Bissing. This is how how the commission must have materialised.

It so happened that RaKa had had a side-line in promoting aerial advertising. The company sold planes to large companies and then recommended pilots from his own training school. RaKa planes did not just haul streamers bearing company names. Those names were actually painted on their fuselage and wings. Many were well-known brands at the time, two of whom still exist today, namely Opel and Nivea. Raka also produced a small airship, one of which floated about displaying the name Trumpf, a leading chocolate producer in those days.[4] (This form of aerial advertising, incidentally, reached a low point in 1935, when an unnamed, but reportedly wealthy young woman purchased a Schwalbe and had an anti-semitic slogan painted on it: 'The Jews are our misfortune.')[5] One of Raka's recommended pilots was none other than their former trainee, Vera von Bissing,

---

1   Michel Détroyat, French aerobatics champion, quoted in G. Fieseler, *Meine Bahn am Himmel*, p.201.
2   Klemperer, V. (1998). *I Shall Bear Witness: The Diaries of Victor Klemperer*. London: Weidenfeld & Nicholson, p.155.
3   http://adl-luftfahrthistorik.de/dok/Fieseler_Wespe_Teil1.pdf.
4   R. Nagel und T. Bauer, *Kassel und die Luftfahrindustrie seit 1923: Geschichte(n), Menschen, Technik*, p.45
5   Ibid, p.52

who flew for HB.[6] It is very likely that Herr Bergmann happened to mention to her that he was interested in a new aircraft and she used the opportunity to put in a good word for Fieseler as an up and coming designer and manufacturer.

As with the Tigerschwalbe Fieseler could not himself design the new plane, but he could conceive of it. What he had in mind was for the time truly sensational: a two-engined tailless aircraft with swept-back wings in the general form of a triangle.[7] The specific design he envisaged was for an aircraft with the thrust of the two engines centrally positioned in the longitudinal axis of the stubby fuselage. The major challenge he identified concerned the matter of controlling the machine in flight. This particular problem he could not solve without expert help from outside. Not for the first time Fieseler tapped into his extensive network. The person he contacted was Alexander Lippisch.

Lippisch at the time was the technical director of the 'extremely influential' Rhön-Rossiter Society, which had been founded in 1924 for promoting gliding in Germany.[8] He had already considerable experience as a designer of gliders, a field of aviation in which Germany led the world. More importantly, he had been experimenting with tailless gliders. When they met, Lippisch gushed with enthusiasm, affirming that the problem of stability had been 'long solved,' adding emphatically, 'I'm prepared to put my head over the parapet.'[9] Fieseler jumped at this. Would Herr Lippisch be willing to take complete responsibility for the design? Indeed, he would and after discussion of various points of detail they came to an agreement, which presumably involved a consultancy fee.

Within two months the new plane, give the name F3 Wespe, was entering production. With its foldable 'delta wings, canards and an engine and propeller mounted in both the nose and tail', it was truly of 'unorthodox design.'[10] The two nine cylinder engines, imported from England, each delivered 90 hp and were the lightest in their class. From existing photographs it is clear that this was futuristically looking aircraft. Before long it was ready for its inaugural flight. Despite Lippisch's assurances Fieseler still had his anxieties about the stability in air. Fieseler himself was going to make the maiden flight and he could not rid himself of these qualms. Suppressing these, he clambered into the cockpit and took off. He was only three metres in the air, when the machine crashed nose-first on the ground. He clambered out unhurt. 'Badly designed', he declared. 'We must start from scratch again.'[11]

With Lippisch's help Fieseler set about building a modified version of the F3. On two following occasions the plane crashed again. These mishaps resulted in the third major modification. This period as a test pilot he described as the most difficult and dangerous times of his flying career – a description hitherto reserved for his experiences on the Macedonian Front in the First World War. As Lippisch worked on all the redesign, so Fieseler was beginning to feel that he had become an unofficial member of his aeronautical society. He was also beginning to have doubts whether 'a good average pilot' could ever fly the thing.[12] To add to his misfortune, all the costs of modification and the repair work were being borne by himself. He really should have scuppered the whole project after the second or third aborted attempt.

He was further disconcerted to learn from his staff that Lippisch was so nervous that, when he saw Fieseler taxiing the plane to take off, he was said to make involuntary 'jerking movements and

---

6   https://de.wikipedia.org/wiki/Vera_von_Bissing
7   J. Ayto, *Twentieth Century Words*, p.270.
8   R. Meredith, *Phoenix: A Complete History of the Luftwaffe 1918-1945. Vol. 1 – The Phoenix is Reborn*, p.349
9   G. Fieseler, *Meine Bahn am Himmel*, p.171.
10   https://en.wikipedia.org/wiki/Lippisch_Delta_IV.
11   A. Norden. *Das Herz muss dabei sein: Der Flieger Gerhard Fieseler und sein Werk*. p.22.
12   Fieseler, op. cit., p.173.

even tore out tufts of grass.'[13] This odd behaviour (if true) confirmed Fieseler's fears: there *was* a major design flaw. He eventually realised that the critical weakness, which directly affected flight stability, was due to the two engines being positioned too far apart. What, he must have wondered, was Lippisch up to? Once again Fieseler sees himself 'as the victim of the confidence that I had placed in other people.'[14]

By this point Lippisch, who had run out of ideas, was reluctant to concede that his design was at fault. This intransigence caused Fieseler to remind the great designer that he, Fieseler, was the only person to have flown the plane. Fieseler ordered the installation of a dual control system and then requested the appropriate testing authority – the DVL – to submit the F3 to a formal inspection. By this time he had made some fifty test flights, risking life and limb on every occasion. Another person intrepid enough to fly the new aircraft was Vera von Bissing.

In Fieseler's view the plane would never obtain an airworthiness certificate. But he needed formal confirmation of that from the DVL in order to claim compensation from the Rhön-Rossiter Society. When a DVL test pilot by the name of Knoetsch arrived, Fieseler explained the whole sorry saga. But when he was told that the F3 was too dangerous even for a first-class pilot, Knoetsch took this as a personal insult. Fieseler managed to assuage him and they finally agreed to take the plane up together. At a height of 600 metres he handed over control to Knoetsch. As soon as the test pilot took over, the plane careered upwards. Immediately Fieseler, well familiar with this reaction, grabbed the controls and stabilised the aircraft. After they had landed, Knoetsch confirmed Fieseler's opinion: there was no way that the DVL could issue a certificate of airworthiness. Knoetsch, as it happened, joined Fieseler in 1936 as his chief pilot.[15]

Deciding to seek compensation from the Rhön-Rossiter Society, Fieseler met its director, Professor Georgi, who was irritated with Lippisch's involvement in the whole affair and wanted to brush it under the carpet. He decided to press his claim harder, but foolishly did not hire a lawyer to assist him. In a subsequent meeting 'six very adroit negotiators' representing the interests of the Society outmanoeuvred him, and he had no choice but to agree to sell the latest version of the F3 to them for modest fee and to take on all the other costs regarding modifications, repairs and all other outstanding costs concerning the second and third versions.[16] In this way the Rhön-Rossiter Society maintained its dignity, whilst he 'once again had been done in the eye.'[17]

Despite this set back, Fieseler felt duty-bound to write to Professor Georgi, formally informing him that the plane was dangerous and should not be flown. This warning was not heeded. A few months later one of Georgi's most experienced test pilots took the plane up. It was his last flight. It crashed and he was killed. We can be certain that this outcome gave Fieseler, who otherwise viewed pilots' death as the unavoidable price of aeronautical progress, no particular satisfaction.

Such was the fate of an innovative aircraft that Fieseler considered to be the world's first twin-engined delta aircraft. It appears that documentation on the F3 is 'extremely rare.'[18] The records were destroyed when Kassel was severely bombed in October 1943. There can, however, be no doubt that the F3 Wespe is a highly important aircraft in the history of aeronautical design. In the fiasco there was one crumb of comfort, financially speaking. The managing director of the cigarette company, realising that he had commissioned an experimental aircraft, took a reasonable stance and did not press for reimbursement of his advance payment. Fieseler gives no idea of the losses

---

13 Ibid. p.172-173.
14 Ibid, p.173.
15 http://adl-luftfahrthistorik.de/dok/Fieseler_Wespe_Teil1.pdf
16 Fieseler, op. cit., p.174
17 Ibid, p.174.
18 http://adl-luftfahrthistorik.de/dok/Fieseler_Wespe_Teil1.pdf

he sustained directly and indirectly with development of the Wespe. Not only did he have to pay the wages of the employees, but he also purchased new production machinery, test equipment and specialist parts which his company did not manufacture on site. The true cost of everything was in effect carried by his substantial earnings as an aerobatics pilot.

The preoccupation with the F3, on the one hand, and the development of the Tigerschwalbe, on the other, dominated Fieseler's 1931. But in September there was an event that would have even diverted Fieseler from all his cares, when a Graf Zeppelin airship landed at the aerodrome at Kassel-Waldau. Fieseler does not mention this event. Yet, if he were present, it is tempting to think that he might have reflected on the twenty or so years since a Zeppelin had flown over Bonn when he was a boy. At that time he made model aircraft and dreamed of flying. Now he was building real aircraft of a sophistication unthinkable in the first decade of the twentieth century. Not only that: he was among the very best aerobatics pilots in the world. How extraordinary his life path had been. He had after all more than fulfilled any dream of his boyhood. If only Germany could have some stability, he might have thought, then he could run his company on a secure footing, build innovative aircraft, and improve the livelihoods of his employees.

Somehow Fieseler managed to attend 22 flying events in 1931, of which seven were held in France, where he no doubt did battle with his great rival, Détroyat. In all he performed some 37 exhibition flights. Nagel and Bauer estimate that his earnings for the year were 110,000 Reichsmarks, with which he could offset his company losses.[19]

The big time

Fieseler does provide a general clue about the scale of this income, describing himself as 'the best paid airman in the world' in 1930.[20] At the height of his fame he was being paid for 10 minute exhibition flights between 3,000 and 5,000 Reichsmarks in Germany and up to 10,000 Reichsmarks abroad. He does not include winnings at competitive events. The air historians Nagel und Bauer estimate that Fieseler's total earnings between 1928 and 1934 as an aerobatics pilot amounted to 670,000 Reichsmarks, which would be about £48,000 at the time or around £1m at today's prices.[21] In addition he would have obtained money for consultancy services to government agencies and private firms. As an indication of the scale of Fieseler's earning power, in 1931 the hourly wage of skilled industrial worker (*Facharbeiter*) was one Reichsmark, whilst a fully qualified craftsman could expect to earn 1.40 Reichsmarks.[22]

We already know that his great rival Ernst Udet earned 200,000 Reichsmarks a year from flying activities. If the respective figues for Fieseler and Udet are correct, then this would appear to dent the former's claim about being the best paid aviator in the world. Bearing in mind that a high proportion of Udet's income had been earned in the USA for film work as well as exhibition flying, it may be safer to describe Fieseler as 'the best paid airshow pilot in Europe.'[23] As such he was in the early 1930s was one of Germany's top earners in any branch of life. In its own way all the prize money he was winning in the 1930s must have seemed as astronomical to him as the value of banknotes printed in 1923-24 during the period of the notorious hyper-inflation.

In April 1932 a modifield Tigerschwalbe named the F2 Tiger was ready for its test flight. Fieseler, who took it up for the first time, was satisfied that it was a big improvement on its predecessor. The

---

19 Nagel und Bauer, op. cit., p.96.
20 Fieseler, op. cit., p.165.
21 Nagel und Bauer, op. cit., p.109.
22 Ibid, p.95.
23 http://www.britannica.com/EBchecked/topic/1409585/Gerhard-Fieseler. Entry by K. Koessler; accessed 28.01.2015

positioning of the engine, the fuel tanks and the pilot's seat made for a favourable distribution of weight. He could accomplish figures with this plane which had not been possible before. It took some six weeks and countless test flights for Fieseler to feel at one with it. As he knew that that the Tiger with its 400 hp engine would be a difficult plane to fly, he decided to produce a cheaper, lighter version. This was to emerge as the F4, a low-wing, two-seater monoplane. But somehow this plane did not please the ever fastidious Fieseler, who ordered its discontinuation and immediately started to work with Dr Arnolt on the design of a successor.

The resulting F5 was also a low-wing, two seater, but it was very different in concept. The F5, having a wooden fuselage covered with fabric, was lighter. Its engine was 60 to 70 hp, but the F4 had excellent capabilities and was easy to fly. Its top speed was around 200 km/hour and could take and land in short distances. Fieseler and Arnolt were thrilled to be breaking new ground in terms of aircraft design and performance. Commercially, it was imperative that the F5 should be a big hit because the development costs of the abortive F3 Wespe and earlier versions of the Tiger. The more Fieseler flew the F5, the more he liked it. It was indeed 'a poem.'[24] Yet, before it went on the market, he demanded more improvements, not least a bigger engine, which meant expenditure on new equipment. All the while he was aware that his earnings as an aviator could not be sufficient to cover all his costs.

In short, Fieseler's company was still not on a secure financial footing. Yet he refused to team up with investors who would have a say in the running of his company. He had to believe that fortune would smile on him, and luckily it did. His chief test pilot was enraptured with the F5. It was 'fabulous', he said. 'I've never flown anything like it.'[25] With that word got around the industry about the F5. Fieseler allowed pilots to do test flights and before long the orders flowed in. This took all the financial pressure off him. Then he found that the F5 had been approved to take part in the 1933 in the Deutschlandflug. After there followed a personal invitation to become a member of the DVL. This was exceptional, as membership was restricted to people representing companies who were in receipt of government contracts.

This recognition duly turn led to Fieseler being summoned to appear as an expert witness in a court case, in which a pilot had been charged with negligence as a result of a crash-landing resulting in the death of two passengers. Fieseler was able to demonstrate, using aerodynamic explanation, that the crash was the result of a design failure, which should have been detected by the licencing authority. Fieseler, who hitherto had been making his reputation as an outstanding aerobatics pilot, found himself being regarded as an aeronautical expert in his own right.

The Duce takes an interest

In the meantime there was no let-up in Fieseler's international commitments. One destination was Prague; another, surely to his great surprise, was Bucharest. He was due to land at the very same airport he had once visited in December 1916 as a budding military pilot. The journey, which involved flying over the Transylvanian Alps, proved truly hazardous. First, an hour or so from Bucharest his petrol feed broke and he was also running out of fuel. Sepp, his mechanic on board, did a temporary repair, but it was essential to take on fuel. There was no alternative but to make an emergency landing. Fortunately they found themselves near habitation. Somehow and with the help of Romanian currency, the curious locals cooperated. A man arrived in an indescribable jalopy and offered Fieseler a small barrel of petrol. Sepp took a whiff, screwed his face up and said, 'Our motor ain't gonna go for that stuff.'[26]

24   Fieseler, op. cit., p.178.
25   Ibid, p.179.
26   Ibid, p.158.

Fieseler had to get to Bucharest before nightfall, and it was already getting dark. He took on enough fuel for the last leg of the journey. The take-off would be tricky. The local men helped remove rocks on his ad-hoc runway for some 50 or 60 metres. But he also had to clear a metre wide ditch. There was nothing for it but a flying start. Fieseler revved up the engine, whilst Sepp and the Romanians restrained the F5 from moving until he gave the all-clear and then he surged forward. He took to the air, leaving Sepp behind with instructions to get a train to Bucharest. The motor spluttered. Sepp was right. It was low-grade fuel. Fieseler sped on eastwards with the mountains behind him. But by now he was flying in total darkness and could not read his compass nor his altimeter, although they were centimetres in front of him. He could no longer be certain that he was still flying in an easterly direction. For once Fieseler found himself gripped in terrible fear. As always in such precarious situations, he forced himself to keep calm and think rationally.

He pressed on for a further half hour. Then below he saw lights, which he took to be the oil-fields of Ploeşti. Thanks to the fact that he had flown over this territory in the First World War he knew exactly where he was. He made a ninety degree turn and headed for Bucharest. In another ten minutes he made out the lights – petrol flares in all probability – of the city's airport. Somehow he was spotted and a vehicle with dazzling headlights guided him to the runway. Seldom had Fieseler been more relieved to jump out of an aircraft.

Not long after that adventure he was in another dangerous situation. He was flying back from Milan with Sepp over the Alps. He knew from previous flights that from on high the Alps were commandingly breath-taking to behold: 'You had the feeling that you were closer to God.'[27] On this occasion there had been a bad weather warning, but he dismissed it, wanting to return to Kassel as soon as possible. Soon they were enveloped in a barrage of snow clouds. He took the plane down as close as possible to the ground, following a line of telegraph poles and then, at a height of 20 or 30 metres, a river. At one point they appeared to be on a collision wall with the sheer wall of a mountain. The normally imperturbable Sepp was getting very edgy. Fieseler knew that there was no turning back.

They had to fly dangerously close to the mountain side. It was a kind of slalom that lasted 14 hair-raising kilometres. He refused to yield to fear, although even his nerves were getting seriously frayed. At last the mountainous terrain gave way to a broad valley. The cloud cover had lifted to about 50 metres and the snow had turned to rain. Eventually Fieseler brought safely his plane into Friedrichshafen. Once on terra firma he discovered that he was trembling from head to foot. Sepp for his part was incapable of speech. Forget all that closeness to God. They had just been through hell.

1931 saw Fieseler in Milan for a flying meeting, which had been planned to show off Italian expertise in military aviation. The event took place in the presence of Marshal Balbo, the Minister of Air Transport and second most powerful man in Italy. Balbo was an airman and had once commanded a squadron of flying boats, which had flown across the Mediterranean. Fieseler was the only foreigner at the event, and the high-point of the programme was an aerobatics contest between himself and the Italian champion, Colombo. Surrounded by his fawning retinue of 200 of officers and other hangers-on the Marshal observed all the events on a specially built tribune. He was periodically telephoning the Duce, for whom 'aviation stood for the dawn of an eternal order,'[28] had taken flying lessons in the early 1920s and stated that 'Italy should take back air supremacy.'[29] Balbo boomed his statements to the Duce to make certain that all those in earshot felt themselves to be highly privileged to overhear a conversation between the two most powerful men in Italy.

27   Ibid, p.160.
28   F. Esposito, *Fascism, Aviation and Mythical Modernity*, p.273.
29   Cited in S. Seabridge, *Blackpool's Aerodromes 1928O1936: Politics and Local Media*, p.21.

After the duel with Colombo, Fieseler was approached by a senior officer who told him and his Italian rival that they were both to immediately present themselves to the Marshal. Colombo managed to convey to Fieseler that he (Fieseler) was to receive a special Italian medal. Both the German and Italian champions made their way into the august presence of Balbo with an appropriately unassuming demeanour. Through an interpreter Balbo told Fieseler that he wished to see him and Colombo repeat their performance, but they should exchange planes. Colombo could scarcely disguise his horror at this suggestion. He simply could not refuse the Marshal. However, Fieseler could and did so. As this was being translated, Balbo's face darkened. He disdained to look at Fieseler, who without much regret had to forego the special medal.

On 5 June 1932 Fieseler took part in an air show at Saint-Germain-en-Laye near Paris, where the event involved 'interesting exhibitions of aerobatic and stunt flying by leading international aces, parachute jumping, the presentation of several new planes and the attendance of a number of prominent aeronautical personalities.'[30] One notable attendee was none other than the famous American aviatrix, Amelia Earhart. A photograph of them together was featured on the front page of the *Stuttgarter Illustrierte* magazine dated 26 June 1932.[31] Another in attendance was the French pilot, René Fonck, who had been France's leading ace in the First World War with some 75 victories to his name. The 17 June 1932 issue of *Flight International* reported that in the stunting event Fieseler flew 'his new two-seater biplane, the Tiger F.2, which was built at the Kassel Areoplane Works from his own designs ... The plane was equipped with a 340-h.p. , nine cylinder radial Walter air-cooled motor. It has a speed of1 55 m.p.h (250km./hr) and can climb 1,000 m. in 1 min. 20 sec.'[32] There is a photograph in the magazine of Fieseler flying upside down. The caption reads: 'he appears to be equally at home either side up.'[33]

In 1932 Fieseler had taken part in 21 events and earned 145,000 Reichsmarks in fees. It is tribute to his determination that he could deliver sich consistently high performances, engage in long hours of preparation for each event and run a company at the same time.

A fatal vote
As already noted, the Wall Street Crash of 1929 had devastating consequences for the Germany economy, which was so dependent on American loans. Industrial production had halved between 1928 and 1932. During the same period unemployment had quadrupled from 7% to 30.8%. Throughout Germany the picture was the same: 'deepening recession, growing cohorts of unemployed, communists fighting anti-communists on the streets, indecisive elections, and endless cabinet crises.'[34] As a result, 'economic misery weighed on people like a nightmare,' Fieseler recalls.[35] In Kassel itself wages fell by between 10 and 15% in January 1932. In May 23,416 people, of whom slightly more than 40% were long-term unemployed, were on state aid.[36] Fieseler, thanks to his substantial earnings as an aerobatics pilot, was just able to keep his company going. But it had not been easy. Things could not continue like this, he realised. Where was salvation for Germany to come from?

In the fourteen years since 1918 Germany had had some 20 governments. The so-called 'golden years' of the Weimar Republic with its 'deceptive appearance of normality' of the mid-1920s were

30 *Flight International* (1932). Saint-Germain-en-Laye international meeting, pp.535-536. Available at: https://www.flightglobal.com/FlightPDFArchive/1932/1932%20-%200583.PDF
31 Fieseler, pp.316-317.
32 *Flight International* (1932), pp.535-536.
33 *Flight International* (1932), p.536.
34 N. Davies, *Europe: A History.* Oxford, Oxford University Press, p.967.
35 Fieseler, op. cit., p.178.
36 http://www.erinnerungen-im-netz.de/aw/home/Zeitliste/Unterkategorie_Zeit-vg/1930er-Jahre-1932/

over.[37] There were thirty different political parties angling for the people's votes. In 1932 there was yet another election in Germany. As Fieseler saw things, a lot of people with nothing to lose would either vote communist for the hell of it, whilst others would just turn their back on politics in disgust. But then there were others, who, like himself, were looking increasingly to the Nazis, though with some misgiving, as the only party that could 'save our country.'[38] To make significant gains for his Nazi Party, Hitler that year flew criss-cross over Germany, using the slogan 'the Führer over Germany' – a subtle or perhaps not so subtle inversion of *Deutschland über alles*. In one week he addressed twenty huge audiences, totalling perhaps a million people.[39] The air historian, Edward Homze, claims that in a four weeks' period the Nazi leader visited 96 cities. He writes:

> Once, twice, sometimes three times a day Hitler's plane would descend, bringing the Führer to speak to the gathered thousands of the party's faithful. Hitler beautifully exploited the thrill and adventure of flying. The picture of the dashing young politician alighting from an airplane, dressed in a long leather coat and a distinct, snug-fitting flying helmet, became commonplace to millions of German newspaper readers. The artfully contrived image of the simple, brave, common soldier turned politician flying across the country became one of his trademarks.[40]

On 20 April 1932 – his 43rd birthday – just five days before the elections Hitler arrived out of skies to descend upon Kassel. The Nazis organised a huge rally. Hitler was, of course, the main speaker. He 'so impressed the citizens of Kassel that they voted for him and his party.' In an 85.5% turn-out, the Nazis received 46,000 votes.[41] One of them belonged to Gerhard Fieseler. For him the choice was between the communists and the Nazis. Fieseler is ever careful to leave the impression that he was no lover of Hitler, but in this hour of Germany's need he recalls seeing him as the lesser of the two evils.

It was around this time that one day one of his employees, a certain Herr Haak, happened to present himself at work wearing a Nazi Party badge. This angered Fieseler, who called the man over. 'What's this all about, Herr Haak?' He asked. 'You are inciting people who happen to think differently from you. In this company people are paid to work, not to play politics.'[42] Yet, in just a few short years there would be at his company a fusion of work and politics with one way of thinking – the Nazi way of thinking – overarching everything. The entire enterprise would be honed to serve the megalomaniac aims of Germany's Führer, Adolf Hitler. He, Fieseler, would preside over the process with, it must be admitted, exemplary commitment to the cause.

Fieseler had, it seems, been courted by the Nazis, but had always rejected their overtures, which included conversations with some locally prominent ones. He rebuffed the Nazis, contending: 'I don't want have anything to do with politics. I can't permit myself to join any political party even the Nazis.'[43] He even claimed to have 'pacifist attitudes.'[44] These overtures from the Nazis may well have intensified after Hitler assumed power. From the point of view of Kassel's party worthies, Fieseler, as a local and indeed international celebrity, would have been regarded as an excellent catch indeed.

37   G. Mai, *Die Weimarer Republik*, p.51.
38   Fieseler, op. cit., p.178.
39   I. Kershaw, *Hitler 1889-1936 Hubris*, p.363.
40   E. L. Homze, *Arming the Luftwaffe: The Reich Air Ministry and the German Aircraft Industry 1919-1939*, pp.50-51.
41   http://www.erinnerungen-im-netz.de/aw/home/Zeitliste/Unterkategorie_Zeit-vg/1930er-Jahre-1932/
42   Fieseler, op. cit., p.166.
43   T. Wiederhold, *Gerhard Fieseler – eine Karriere: Ein Wirtschaftsführer im Dienste des Nationalsozialismus*, p 223.
44   Ibid, p.224.

Hitler had visited Kassel again in November 1932, and his next visit took place in February 1933. This was a matter of weeks after his appointment as Chancellor on 30 January 1933; for Nazi believers their idol's elevation heralded 'the coming of the Messiah.'[45] By summer 1934 one could say that with his appointment as Führer and Reich Chancellor, he had virtually *conquered* his adopted country. His position was unassailable. In the words of Henry Kissinger, Hitler's 'advent to power marked one of the greatest calamities in the history of the world.'[46] Yet, Hitler and his Nazis 'did not march on Berlin at the head of an army of unemployed; there was no "seizure of power". Hitler did not have to topple a weakened government as the Bolsheviks did, nor threaten the head of state, like Mussolini. He came to power through participation in Germany's democratic process, and at the invitation of the lawful authorities.'[47] But those who helped him 'all knew that Hitler wanted nothing less than the transition from an authoritarian state to dictatorship.'[48] In 1932 he has been interviewed by *The Times* of London, in which he said he hoped for 'the Third Reich, which would have as its cornerstone the conception of the people and the national idea.'[49] Perhaps not so many *Times* readers would quite understand what he meant by that. But they were not to remain benighted for too long.

The invitation to Hitler was extended by the incumbent, but politically weakened Chancellor von Papen, who is reported to have said, speaking for Germany's right-wing groups, that 'we have hired him. In two months' time we'll have pushed Hitler so far into a corner that he'll be squeaking.'[50] Note that von Papen spoke about hiring and not appointing Hitler. Von Papen and the rest of them were going to tame Hitler and keep him in check. But before long it would be Hitler who would be taming *them*. He duped everyone, as this snippet of conversation reveals. It takes place among three Jewish residents of Kassel, who have just bought a copy of a special issue of a newspaper announcing Hitler's victory. The one says: I don't give him more than six months.' The second responds: 'Not even that.' The third: 'A still-born child.' But before long they'd be hearing the SA bully-boys coming down the street with one of their many anti-Semitic chants:

And when our knives drip with Jews' blood,
Oh, then, how life once again is getting good.[51]

Before the actual Nazi take-over in 1933, Fieseler in common with other Weimar industrialists had 'overall distaste for the rabble-rousing Hitler', but he almost certainly shared 'their anti-republicanism, their anti-communism, and their support of authoritarian solutions to the economic and political crisis of the early 1930s.'[52] Besides, with Hitler in charge, he reasoned as one who had been stung by anti-Germanism abroad, that Germany would now earn a good deal more respect from other nations. But perhaps there was surely another personal element in his vote: it may well have occurred to him that, Hitler with his burning ambition to further German air-mindedness might actually be good for the country's aeronautical future. After all, one of Hitler's

---

45 H. Schulze, (2013). *Kleine deutsche Geschichte,* München, Deutscher Taschenbuch Verlag, p.165.
46 H. Kissinger, (1994). *Diplomacy*, New York: Touchstone, p.288.
47 Davies, p.966.
48 Mai, op. cit., p.121.
49 J. Ayto, *Twentieth Century Words*, p.246.
50 Schulze, op. cit., p.165.
51 V. Senger, In: U. Schneider, K. Boehm, P. Grünewald, U. Krause-Schmidt, R. Neuhaus und R. Winkler, (eds.) (1983). *Hessen vor 50 Jahren – 1933*. Frankfurt am Main: Röderberg Verlag, p.59.
52 S. J. Wiesen, *West German Industry 1945-1955 and the Challenge of the Nazi Past*, Chapel Hill, University of North Carolina Press, p.12.

key accomplices was none other than Hermann Göring, a member of Richthofen's Flying Circus and a known enthusiast for aviation.

Gleichschaltung: an innocent-sounding German word in other circumstances

According to Fieseler, when Hitler was appointed chancellor, the country was infused with a new spirit. 'After the long years of deprivation and uncertainty the German people had their hope restored', he rejoiced, adding: 'From now on things could only go upwards.'[53] New jobs were created; unemployment dropped. Adalbert Norden, Fieseler's hagiographical biographer, was even more gushing. 'The dam has burst', he rejoiced, gloating that 'the interim Reich', which was incapable of giving people work, bread and work, has foundered under the swell of the NS movement. A feeling of relief goes through the people. There will be soon the opportunity to work! The restoration of economic life must be tackled *(in Angriff nehmen)* step by step.'[54] Many a German at the time felt like Norden: utterly fed up with the unloved Weimar Republic and wishing for its demise regardless of the consequences.

Once in power Hitler and his cronies lost time with the 'forceful seduction of the German people', the 'stripping the country of human values, step by step' and the planning of a new new European order with Germans elevated as the master race. Such ambitions could only mean 'war, conquest, annihilation, and reshaping German and European society.'[55] But that did not bother Hitler, for whom 'war was not a moral issue but the physical means to a social end: the survival of the superior Germans.'[56]

When Hitler visited Kassel on 11 February 1933, the occasion was to celebrate the opening of the Nazi campaign in the November referendum and to inaugurate of the Adolf Hitler House in the centre of the city which would serve as the headquarters of the Gau of North Hessen-Nassau. The accompanying rally attracted some 80,000 people, for whom a 'Hitler tent' was especially erected.[57] After that event local Nazis had put on a torch procession, at which Hitler, surrounded by uniformed SA men, was the centrepiece. This would be an occasion for anti-communist and anti-Jewish taunting and thuggery with singing of the Horst Wessel song.

A photograph in a local newspaper shows Hitler standing in his Mercedes, flanked by his SA escort. One of them is Kassel's new police chief; another is SA General von Ulrich, who will be a victim of the night of the long knives in 1934, when the Nazis 'take out' (as the euphemism goes) the leadership of their SA rivals. There was a march past by sundry groups: railway and tram workers in their uniforms, students from the university in Marburg (some 90 kms south-west of Kassel), and 6,000 school children and their teachers.[58] (For innocent, impressionable children Hitler rallies 'were just about as important as Christmas.')[59]

Even if Fieseler was not present at the time, it is impossible that he heard nothing about the anti-Semitic chanting and thuggery that accompanied Hitler's visit, let alone the 'anti-Semitic excesses' which took place in Kassel in November.[60] He may have read in the local newspaper about an

---

53   Fieseler, op. cit., p.181.
54   Norden, op. cit., p.28.
55   J. Foerster, The Relations between Operation Barbarossa as an Ideological War of Extermination and the Final Solution. In D. Cesarani, (ed). *The Final Solution: Origins and Implementation.* London: Routledge, p.86.
56   Ibid, p.455.
57   http://www.lagis-hessen.de/en/subjects/xsrec/mode/grid/setmode/grid/current/8/pageSize/50/page/2/sn/bd?q=YToxOntzOjY6InBlcnNvbiI7czoxMzoiSGl0bGVyLCBBZG9sZiI7fQ==
58   Kassel und die 'Machtübernahme': Verfolgung von Andersdenkenden/Schwarz-weiß-rot neben dem Hakenkreuz. HNA, 29 January 1983.
59   Cited in: H. C. Täubrich, *Fascination and Terror.* Nuremburg: Documentationszentrum Reichsparteitagsgelände, p.77.
60   R. Gross, *November 1938: Die Katastrophe vor der Katastrophe.* Munich: C.H. Beck.

violent SA attack on a Jewish visitor in January 1933, some four weeks before the Nazi take-over.[61] Writing some 50 years after these events Fieseler records how in the 1930s Nazis carried out 'their idiotic progroms against Jews and political opponents, which almost all citizens condemned in the strongest possible terms' (*aufs schärfste verurteilten*).[62] Did they? In the early days of the regime, he admits, Nazi 'elements' had a free hand 'even in Kassel', their misdemeanours going unpunished.[63] Hitler did not visit Kassel again until 1939.

Within weeks of the Nazi take-over, Roland Freisler, a prominent Nazi lawyer based in Kassel, and his henchman began their purges in local administration in earnest. A historian of Kassel during the Third Reich crystallises the procedure: Freisler and the local Gauleiter (regional Nazi party boss) would 'discuss things' with heads of departments, whilst outside SA and SS 'waited' with much parading up and down the street and hoistings of the Nazi flag. So it happened all over Kassel, so it happened all over Germany. In the case of Kassel 'countless' local bodies, including the city hall, labour department, various banks and even high schools received these intimidatory visitations in just two days.[64] No wonder the Nazi propaganda chief, Joseph Goebbels, marvelled how 'quickly the [Weimar] Republic had left the scene (*das Feld geräumt*).'[65] All these ominous actions, which were being replicated throughout Germany, 'came under the dynamic-sounding, but ominous Nazi umbrella term *Gleichschaltung* ('forcing into line')', which would leave no institution, no family, no person untouched.

In February and March alone there were a flurry of new laws, regulations and decrees which laid the quasi-legal foundations of the Nazi state. In Kassel at the beginning of March thugs and supporters of the Stahlhelm, the right-wing ex-servicemen's association, smashed the headquarters of the local trades union organisation, an all too obvious lair of reprehensible left-wingers. The destruction of furniture and chucking out of windows of banners, files and photographs was the writing on the wall. Then on 9 March the local Nazis announced a boycott of Jewish shops.[66] Remarkably, this thuggery in Kassel too place some four weeks before the *official* nation-wide boycott of Jewish businesses, when posters were stuck up saying: 'Germans! Protect yourselves. Don't buy anything from Jews!' On 22 March the Dachau concentration camp for detaining political opponents of the new regime.

'Amazing as it may sound today' the Nazis did not keep their excesses secret.[67] Rather they wanted to make certain that local newspapers reported the measures so that nobody should doubt that the Nazis meant business. People, including Fieseler, would be under no illusion about what a spell in so-called 'protective custody' meant. Fieseler must have known all about the excesses – the purges, the mindless thuggery, the Jew-baiting. He only refers to them obliquely. However, we can safely assume that he was privately horrified. But the speculation about Fieseler's attitude to Germany's new leaders can stop here, because on 1 May 1933 he joined the Nazi Party of his own volition.[68] This momentous decision he omits to record in his autobiography. So how can we account for this change of mind?

61   Kasseler Tageblatt (1933). SS-Leute überfallen Jüdische Reisende, 5 January, Accesses at: http://digam.net/dokument067e.html?ID=3381, 21 July 2015
62   Fieseler, op. cit., p.182
63   Ibid, p.182
64   Photocopied text of D. Krause-Vilmar, Die nationalsozialistische Machtergreifung 1933 in der Stadt Kassel. Delivered at the Volkshochschule Kassel, 27 October 1999.
65   Ibid.
66   Ibid
67   D. Krause-Vilmar, M. Rügheimer und C. Wicke, Das KZ Breitenau 1933-1934. In: U. Schneider, K. Boehm, P. Grünewald, U. Krause-Schmidt, R. Neuhaus und R. Winkler. (Hrsg.) *Hessen vor 50 Jahren – 1933*. Frankfurt am Main, Röderberg Verlag, 1983.
68   Wiederhold, op. cit., p.222.

In the first few weeks of 1933 he knew that that the Nazi state would be supporting a major expansion of the German aircraft industry. Just four days into his chancellorship Hitler appointed Göring to head the new Reich Commission for Aviation. This move was more than a signal about the importance of aircraft in Hitler's Germany. It also sent an explicit message to the army and navy: that aviation development in those branches was to be brought under centralised control. Army and navy chiefs knew that the ambitious Göring 'would never restrict himself to civilian aviation.'[69] Powerless, they promptly agreed to the establishment of a new Air Defence Office and merged their respective aviation offices. In April the Reich Commission for Aviation achieved ministry status, took over the Air Defence Office and on 1 May 1933 became the Reich Aviation Ministry.

In the previous year British Pathé had reported that 'The boys of Germany are living in a state of air-mindedness today. Out of school they stream to their model flying grounds.'[70] This, of of course, only augured too well for the Führer's new Germany. But it is unlikely that the air-mindedness of the boys of Germany corresponded to the true vision of Nazis, which envisaged aviation as not just the paramount expression of technology and modernity, but also (in a manner of speaking) as the wings upon which Hitler's thousand year Reich would sweep in.

A few weeks earlier in March the German Air Sports Association, which had originally been set up after the First World War for training civilians as glider pilots in deference to the Treaty of Versailles, assumed a new role. From now on it would act as an umbrella organisation for various aviation bodies and have responsibility for training future military pilots. This too came under the control of the Ministry, acquiring a new status and raison d'être in the process. In 1937 it was dissolved and became yet another paramilitary organisation, the National Socialist Flying Corps, which, as we shall learn, played a significant role in Fieseler's life.

Faustian pact
To what extent Fieseler through his contacts in German aviation circles was aware of the military significance of these dramatic organisational changes is a moot point. However, he must have looked upon these developments on the surface with considerable approval, but he was careful – years later, of course – to claim no special interest in the Nazi regime. After the Second World War, when he was arraigned before a denazification tribunal, Fieseler described his attitude to the Nazis with these words: 'I was rather apathetic. When I saw injustice, I was against it. But politically speaking I was no opponent of the state or the party.'[71] At the same time Fieseler's lawyers played down his party membership, arguing that 'both as an industrialist and private citizen he was nothing more than nominally associated' with the Nazis.[72] Nominally associated! Not for one moment do Fieseler's statement or his lawyers' arguments carry any weight. The point was, as we shall see, that Fieseler was not only willing to give the Nazis the benefit of the doubt when they came to power, but also ready supported the war effort until the very end.

There can be no doubt that Fieseler as an entrepreneur decided to join the Nazi Party for the benefit of his company. Whilst we may concede that he was never a totally committed Nazi – in other words, a completely blind follower of Adolf Hitler – he was nevertheless about to become one of many entrepreneurs who were groomed and harnessed by the Nazi state 'as a specific form of untapped resources ... to implement the war economy.'[73] It was a Faustian pact, whereby Fieseler in common with countless other entrepreneurs chose to 'seize the chance of a meteoric

69   Homze, op. cit., p.48.
70   http://www.britishpathe.com/video/air-mindedness
71   Fieseler, op. cit., p.225.
72   Ibid, p.222.
73   L. Budrass, *Flugindustrie und Luftrüstung in Deutschland 1918-1945,* p.5,

Fieseler's boyhood hero, Otto Lilienthal, perhaps the greatest aeronaut of the 19th century. Fieseler had a photograph of Lilienthal on display at home until he died. (Otto-Lilienthal-Museum)

An outstanding fighter pilot in the First World War, Fieseler was awarded the Golden Military Merit Cross, Prussia's highest award for bravery for non-commissioned officers and the Iron Cross First and Second Class. He also received awards from Austria and Bulgaria. (Oscar Azevedo)

Manfred von Richthofen, the most celebrated fighter pilot of the First World War, who had 81 aerial victories to his credit. But was Fieseler with his 19 confirmed victories a better pilot? (Bundesarchiv, Bild 183-S54131)

The battle cruiser *Goeben*, named after a Prussian general who was Fieseler's mysterious grandfather. It was transferred to the Ottoman Navy in 1914 and finished its days as the flagship of the Turkish Navy until decommissioning in 1950. (Bundesarchiv, Bild 134-B0030)

Fieseler in plus-fours, at the Berlin Air Show in September 1927, aside his Raab-Katzenstein RK-26 Schwalbe with his name on the fuselage. (Bundesarchiv, Bild 102-04780, photographer: Georg Pahl)

Fieseler arm-in-arm with his French rival Marcel Doret in October 1927 at an unidentified venue. At his first international competitive event Fieseler had outpointed Doret at the Zürich Air Show in August 1927, but he was cheated out of first place on account of being German. (Oscar Azevedo)

The F3 was an early form of delta-wing aircraft, which Fieseler's company built in cooperation with Alexander Lippisch in 1932-33. Commissioned by the HB cigarette company, it failed to secure its airworthiness certificate. (Fliegerweb.com)

The cover of the 1932 book, *Hitler über Deutschland*, depicts Hitler's attachment to aviation for political electioneering. Fieseler first saw Hitler alight from a plane which landed at Kassel Waldau airport in 1927. (Randall Bytwerk)

Fieseler receiving a hero's welcome at Kassel Waldau airport after winning the World Aerobatics Championships in Vincennes in June 1934. (Stadtarchiv Kassel)

With novel foldable wings, the Fi 167 was designed to land on the sea-borne aircraft carrier *Graf Zeppelin*. which never saw service. Fieseler described the Fi 167 as 'a treat to fly.' (Sammlung Urlen)

The iconic and still much-admired Fi 156, the Fieseler Storch. Britain's greatest test pilot, Eric 'Winkle' Brown, described it as 'a virtuoso of slow flight' and ranked it in his top twenty outstanding planes of the 487 he flew during and after the Second World War. (Bundesarchiv, Bild 146-1977-110-05)

The entrance to Carinhall, Goering's official residence, where in 1938 the Reichsmarschall ordered Fieseler and other top bosses of the air industry to prepare for war – or else. (Bundesarchiv, Bild 146-1979-175-10)

At the Führer's disposal Fieseler wearing the uniform of *Standartenführer* in the Nazi Flying Corps. (Bundesarchiv, Bild 183-R56586)

A placard about the competition to identify and honour Germany's top enterprises for industrial quality and integration of Nazi ideals into the workplace. Fieseler's company won the award four times, making it one of the best run factories in Germany. (Bundesarchiv, Plak 003-017-116, designer: Christian Minzlaff)

Hitler at the Greater German War Veterans Day held at Kassel in June 1939. Almost certainly just to the right of and behind Hitler is the Japanese Ambassador, General Ōshima, who in 1940 facilitated Japan's purchase of three Storch aircraft and manufacturing rights. (Bundesarchiv, Bild 183-E07050

A rare photograph of the Soviet OKA-38. To celebrate the Nazi-Soviet Non-aggression Pact in 1939, Hitler gave a Fieseler Storch as a diplomatic gift to Stalin. The Soviet dictator ordered one of his brightest aircraft designers, Oleg Antonov, to make a copy of it. (Fliegerweb.com)

After the defeat of France in 1940 Fieseler expected peace to break out followed by an economic boom and had this advertisement drafted promoting the Storch to major business concerns. Anticipating today's executive jets, the caption reads 'You decide when your aircraft takes off.' (Oscar Azevedo)

Aquatic treatment for the Fieseler work force in 1940. Fieseler's factory was one of the very first in Germany to have a full-time company doctor. (Sammlung Urlen)

Fieseler apprentices in 1941 going for a run, wearing the company logo on their singlets. (Sammlung Urlen)

It's June 1940, and the Luftwaffe is attacking Britain. This cartoon in the Fieseler company newspaper warns a worried Churchill that his comeuppance is nigh. The caption reads: 'The faster the production tempo, the faster our victory.' (Sammlung Urlen)

Fieseler giving the Nazi salute. He would not have wished this photograph, taken in 1940, to have been widely seen after the Second World War. (Sammlung Urlen)

A remarkable photograph of a herd of reindeer sweeping past a Storch in Finland in 1942. Perhaps no other aircraft in the entire Second World War adapted so easily to such a wide range of climatic and geographic conditions. (Sammlung Urlen)

Robert Lusser, appointed in 1942 as Fieseler's development director, was the technical brains behind the V-1. He worked for the Americans after the Second World War, working at the Jet Propulsion Laboratory in California and collaborating with von Braun's rocketry team in Alabama. (Sammlung Urlen)

Steckschlüssel, den wir auf dem Bilde sehen, werden die Spannbacken, die den Bohrer halten, festgeschraubt. Der Schlüssel hängt an einer Kette an der Maschine.
Während unser Schlosser den Bohrer mit dem Schlüssel festspannte, wurde er von einem Kameraden angerufen. Er ließ den Schlüssel los und drehte sich nach dem Anrufer um. Etwas später schaltete er die Maschine ein, **ohne an den im Spannfutter steckenden Schlüssel zu denken.**
Emsig in eine größere Arbeit vertieft, stehe ich mit zwei Kameraden an der großen Richtplatte (waagerecht aufgestellte Platte zum genauen Ausrichten von Werkstücken). **Plötzlich stößt der eine Kamerad einen gurgelnden Schrei aus** und greift sich an den Hals. Wir schrecken zusammen. Was war geschehen?
Als die Bohrmaschine anlief, drehte sich der im Futter steckende Schlüssel mit. Die Kette, an der der Schlüssel befestigt war, wickelte sich zunächst um die Bohrspindel. Sie war natürlich nur kurz und daher bald zu Ende. Da sie ihrerseits ja an der Maschine festhing, gab ihr in diesem Augenblick die Kraft der sausenden Spindel einen gehörigen Ruck. Sie wurde gesprengt und gab den Schlüssel frei, der nun mit großer Gewalt durch den Raum flog und meinen Kameraden am Kehlkopf traf.
Obwohl wir zehn Meter von der Maschine entfernt standen, war der Anprall des weggeschleuderten Schlüssels so stark, daß die getroffene Stelle erheblich anschwoll. Der Kamerad hatte geraume Zeit unter ziemlichen Schmerzen zu leiden. Außerdem bewirkte die Schwellung eine Atemnot, die auch nicht von Pappe war.
Trotzdem verlief der Unfall noch verhältnismäßig harmlos. Was wäre wohl geschehen, wenn der Schlüssel jemand ins Auge oder an die Schläfe geflogen wäre? Er hätte das Auge verlieren oder sogar getötet werden können.
Aus so kleinen Ursachen, wie in dem hier geschilderten Fall, entstehen manchmal die schlimmsten Folgen. Darum denkt immer daran: **An Maschinen soll man nur mit höchster Konzentration arbeiten. Niemals darf man einen Kameraden an der Maschine stören.**

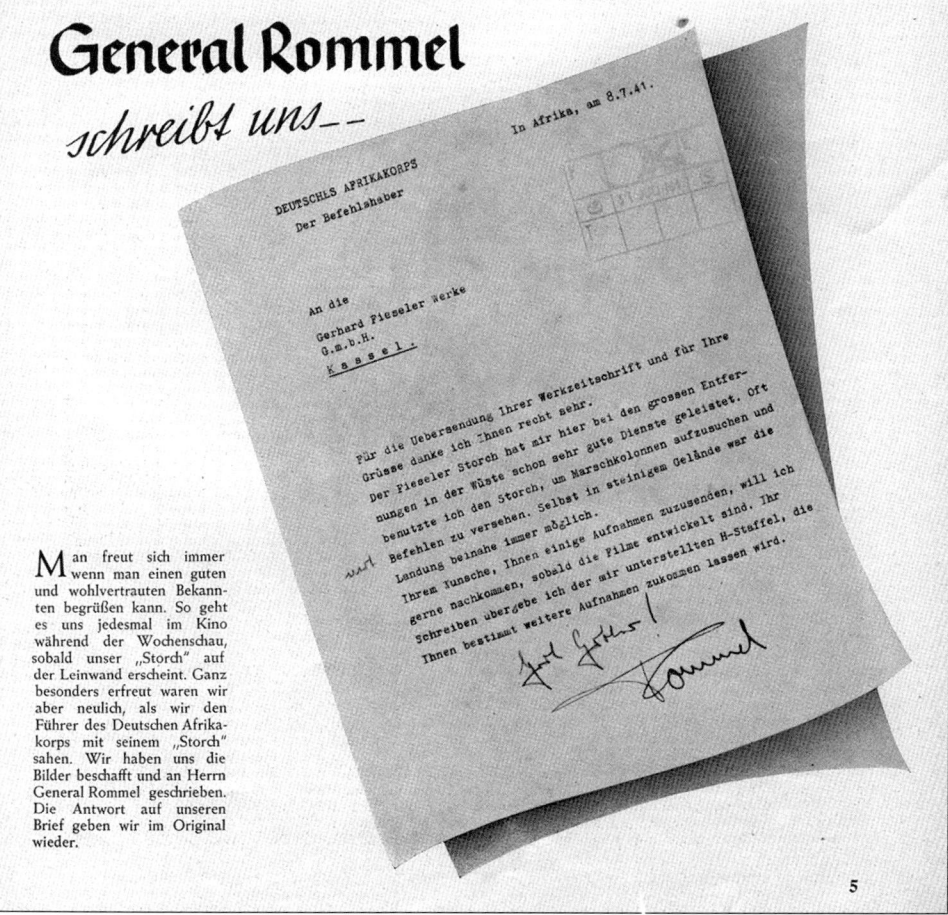

In August 1941 a letter was published in the Fieseler company newspaper from General Erwin Rommel praising the performance of the Storch in the desert, commending its ability to land on rock-strewn terrain. (Sammlung Urlen)

Accompanying Göring, Erhard Milch, the head of the Reich Aviation Ministry, was dismissively described by Fieseler as 'an aeronautical layman.' (Bundesarchiv, Bild 146-1979-187-16)

Ernst Udet, head of procurement for the Luftwaffe. whose suicide in November 1941 was a terrible blow to Fieseler. (Bundesarchiv, Bild 146-1984-112-13, photographer: Conrad)

Göring giving the eulogy at Udet's funeral. Before long he would blame Udet for losing the Battle of Britain. (Bundesarchiv, Bild 183-B16653)

One of the Second World War's most improbable publications: the Fieseler German-Russian glossary of work terms. The company employed a few Russian slave labourers, mainly women. (Oscar Azevedo)

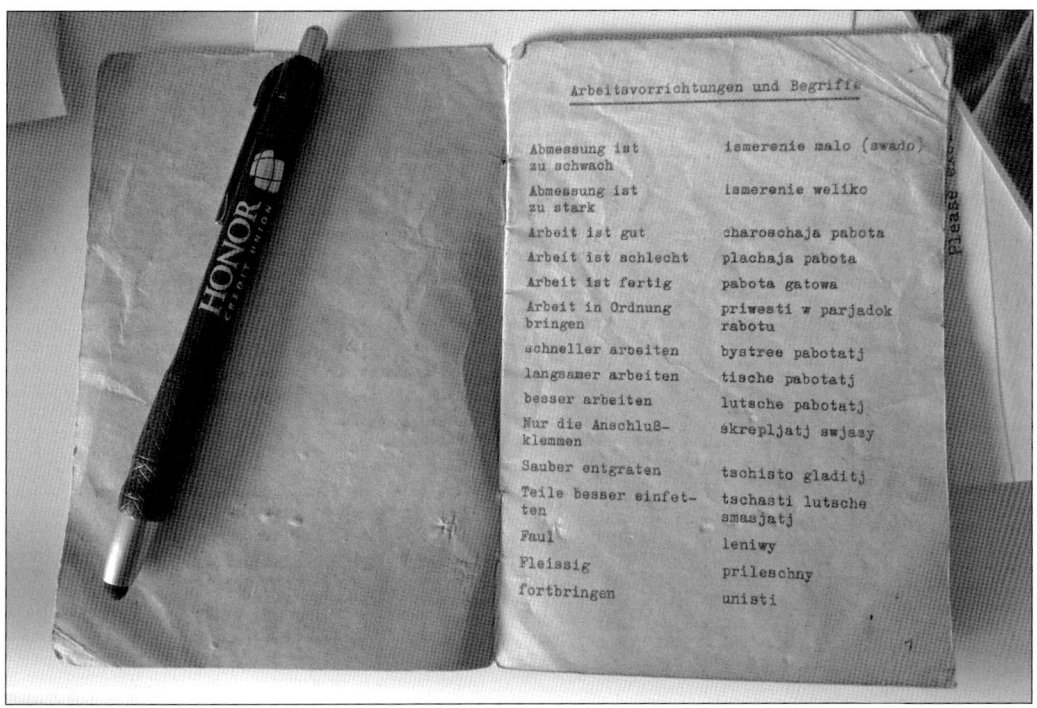

The first page of the glossary to help Fieseler's overseers comment on the work of Russian labourers and issue basic orders to them in rough and ready Russian. (Oscar Azevedo)

Kassel in ruins as a result of the devastating air raid by the RAF on 23 October 1943. (Stadtarchiv Kassel)

The Fieseler plant in the Bettenhausen district of Kassel in April 1944, showing the results of heavy bombing. (Stadtarchiv Kassel)

The charismatic and alluring Hanna Reitsch, Germany's most famous aviatrix, receiving an Iron Cross 2nd Class from her adored Führer in March 1941. (Bundesarchiv, Bild B 145 Bild-F051625-0295)

Otto Skorzeny, 'the most dangerous man in Europe,' with Mussolini shortly after the Italian dictator's high-risk rescue from Italian partisans in September 1943 in the Apennine Mountains. A Fieseler Storch made a perilous flight to take Mussolini and Skorzeny to safety. (Bundesarchiv, Bild 101I-567-1503C-16, photographer: Toni Schneiders)

The V-1 being taken to its catapult. Like Hitler Fieseler dreamed of the so-called wonder weapons bringing Britain to its knees, but he wanted all the glory to go to 'his' V-1. (Bundesarchiv, Bild 146-1975-117-26, photographer: Bruno Lysiak)

V-1s in production at the notorious Dora Mittelbau subterranean concentration camp. Of the 60,000 slaves who built the V weapons there, a third perished from starvation, disease, brutality and accidents. (Bundesarchiv, Bild 183-1985-0123-027)

Wilhelm Furtwängler conducting the Berlin Philharmonic Orchestra in 1942. The renowned conductor was one of the guests along with other well-known cultural figures at Fieseler's short-lived hotel around 1949. (Bundesarchiv. Bild 183-L0607-504)

A photograph taken in 1972 of the inside Fieseler's home showing his display of flying awards and trophies. (Stadtarchiv Kassel)

The Dutchman Wim de Vries, a conscripted worker at the Gerhard Fieseler Works during the Second World War, wrote an anguished poem to mark Fieseler's death. (Stadsarchief Dordrecht)

One of the last photographs taken of Fieseler in public at the Kassel Air Show in June 1983. (Stadtarchiv Kassel)

career, enormous profits and business expansion' in league with the big-talking Nazis.[74] For a time Fieseler might have thought that he had all things concerned made a good decision. Of course, not everything about the Nazis and their methods was to his liking, but things could never get as bad as they had been in the Weimar years. Besides, now that he was Chancellor, Hitler 'enjoyed great prestige abroad.'[75] Fieseler decidedly approved of that.

Writing about the events of 1933 over eighty years later, it is easy – especially if you are not German – to adopt a very moral tone about people like Gerhard Fieseler who threw their lot in with the Nazis. But we should not judge his actions then about what we know about the Nazis as of 1945. This is a false prism through which to judge him and by extension millions of other Germans. One of Britain's most accomplished historians of Germany, Richard Evans, has written that it is 'arrogant and presumptuous' to 'indulge the luxury of moral judgment.' He adds: 'I cannot know how I would have behaved if I had lived under the Third Reich, if only because, if I had lived then, I would have been a different person from the one I am now.'[76] Evans goes on to quote fellow historian Ian Kershaw, writer of an internationally acclaimed biography of Hitler, on this troubled theme. Kershaw notes: 'For an outsider, a non-German who never experienced Nazism, it is perhaps too easy to criticise, to expect standards of behaviour which was well-nigh impossible to attain in the circumstances.[77]

When the Nazis assumed power in January 1933, 'Hitler and Göring were committed to a massive build-up of civilian aviation under the control of Göring and the establishment of a cabinet-level ministry as a preliminary to further military expansion in aviation.'[78] If Fieseler had any doubt about the Nazi commitment to *military* aviation (which is most unlikely), then by the summer he is likely to have heard through his contacts in aviation circles that Göring and Blomberg, the minister of defence, 'formally approved [plans] for the construction of a combat force of 600 planes in 51 squadrons by the fall of 1935.'[79] He must have sensed that for an ambitious designer and manufacturer like himself that before long the Air Ministry would be issuing tenders for new aircraft. Before, however, we return to Fieseler's main activities, namely aerobatics flying and running his company, we should note two perturbing Nazi-inspired events that took place in Kassel in 1933, both of which Fieseler must have heard about.

It is not clear whether the first took place before or after he joined the Nazi party. Hitler fanatics erected in the centre of Kassel a 'symbolic concentration camp', consisting of a small enclosure girded with barbwire. Inside was a donkey. A photograph shows SS men in attendance, whilst the enclosure is thronged by a large crowd, many of them children. The Nazis supplied the following *bons mots* for the occasion: 'If you don't know that Adolf Hitler is *Führer* of the German people and he must bring about his Reich, then you belong in a concentration camp.'[80] Fieseler must have heard about this crude display of sardonic humour which would have been on everyone's lips. No-one could mistake the message, and to reinforce it, 'an early "classic" concentration camp' was opened near Kassel in June 1933.[81] This was Breitenau, a former Benedictine monastery, which had served as an institution for Germany's young tear-aways of both sexes who were deemed best locked away for their own and

---

74   G. Knopp, *Hitlers Manager*, München, Wilhelm Goldmann Verlag, p.7.
75   Wiederhold, op. cit., p.204.
76   R. J. Evans, *The Coming of the Third Reich*, p.xx
77   Kershaw, cited in Evans, p.xx.
78   Homze, p.54.
79   Ibid, p.55.
80   D. Krause-Vilmar, M. Rügheimer und C. Wicke, Das KZ Breitenau bei Kassel 1933-1934. In: Schneider et al., op. cit., pp.68-70.
81   http://www.gedenkstaette-breitenau.de/1933.htm

society's good. It had a reputation for being 'one of the Hesse's harsher reformatories.'[82] Reinvented as a concentration camp, it was not to be compared with Dachau or Buchenwald in their ghastly systems of terror. Even so, unfortunates held at Breitenau could expect to fully feel 'the rage of the people' (*Volkswut*) as administered by unsympathetic SA wardens.

The second event is equally bizarre, but also weirdly prophetic. As we know, since the end of the First World War, flying events as mass spectacles were a highly popular form of outdoor entertainment for thousands of enthusiasts. What had started life as so-called flying days (*Flugtage*) became Nazi flying days (*Nationalsozialistische Flugtage*) by the end of the 1920s. Kassel had started to hold one every October. On 22 October 1933 another one, billed as a 'National Socialist grand flying day' took place at Waldau airport in Kassel. For completely mystifying reasons the event was promoted under the motto 'Bombs on Kassel.'

The organisers had built a replica of the city's old town out of wood and paper. Both the conclusion and high-point of the day would be, in the odd words of the *Kasseler Post* newspaper, when the model would 'come to grief under bombs.'[83] But this peculiar spectacular culmination of the day's flying never took place. A rain storm put paid to that. This event might seem too trivial to mention except for the fact that eleven years later to the day Kassel would experience the real thing: in 80 minutes an armada of 569 RAF bombers would drop 1,500 tons of bombs on the city, causing a firestorm and killing some 10,000 people. No wonder the German chronicler of the devastation of Kassel, which will be described in chapter 10, characterised the 1933 flying day as 'macabre.'[84]

In 1933, which was yet another intensive year for Fieseler, he had managed to attend 20 airshows and earned 120,000 Reichsmarks in fees. He began to ask himself how long he could pursue this double life as aerobatics pilot and aircraft manufacturer. In any case he would have known, as he was now in his late thirties, that he could not expect to retain for much longer the massive concentration and capability for split-second reaction. His company was now around 35 people strong, and he realised that he needed somebody to support him in matter of organisation. He appointed the 27 year old Erich Bachem to the post of technical manager. Bachem was a qualified engineer and had experience of flying gliders and motorised aircraft. Before joining Fieseler's company, he had worked for the DLV in Berlin. When Fieseler was preparing for and taking part in flying events, Bachem was the man who held the company together. It proved to be a very advantageous appointment.

Triumph and euphoric collapse

In October 1933 Fieseler increased his workforce some threefold to 200. Needing more space for production he transferred his company to the Bettenhausen district of Kassel, where he took over the Deutsche Werke, an old munitions factory. Advantageously his new site was much closer to the aerodrome at Waldau; it also had an existing infrastructure for workshops. The next year would push him and his small company to the limit. Thanks to all his conspicuous and well publicised successes at air shows, Fieseler's company started to receive orders for the F5 Tiger. Furthermore, at the end of 1933 he received a commission from the Aviation Ministry to submit a design for five totally new aircraft to take part in the 1934 Europa-Rundflug (the Round Europe Air Race), which would run from 28 August and 16 September. The resulting aircraft would be known as the Fi 97, Fi being the ministry's own short designation for the Fieseler company.

The Europa-Rundflug was the most famous of all international competitive events for amateur pilots in light sports planes. Its sponsoring body by the Paris-based Fédération Aéronautique

---

82 N. Stargardt, *The German War: A Nation Under Arms, 1939-1945*, p.62.
83 W. Dettmar, *Die Zerstörung von Kassel im Otober 1943: Eine Dokumentation*, Fuldabrück, Druckerei Hesse GmbH, p.17.
84 Ibid, p.17.

Internationale (FAI), the official governing body for racing and world records. Both a technical competition and a flying race, it was a two-weeks' event involving 'technical inspection, performance events, a 6,000 mile tour of the principal cities of Europe and North Africa, and a closed circuit race. The winner was declared on the basis of accumulated merit points.'[85]

The commission from the Aviation Ministry was indeed a sign of its high regard for Fieseler aircraft. If a contract resulted, that would transform the finances of his company. He could then plan his business on a much surer footing than ever before. Besides, he was aware that his days as an aerobatics pilot were coming to an end. He certainly admitted to Norden that he was aware that 'one day his strength would fail.'[86] From now on he would consciously reduce his aerobatics activities and devote himself to designing and building the five sports planes commissioned by the Air Ministry.

The Rundflug organisers instituted an exceptionally thorough technical inspection – it lasted ten days – which focused matters of design, seating, baggage arrangements, strict conformity to weight and wing-span requirements as well as the foldability of wings. On this last point each aircraft 'had to be towed through an inverted U-shaped gate 11.5ft high and 14.7 ft wide and, if folded within one minute, rated 12 points.'[87] Performance factors included take-off speed, landing distance take-off over an obstacle, fuel consumption over a 385 mile course and top speed over a 185 mile course. By 1934 the contest had gained such international prestige that governments were giving direct subsidies to manufacturers to build and enter new airplanes. For the same purpose money was raised by popular subscription. In that year some 90 contestants took part from 'some half a dozen countries.'[88] In their national teams they would fly some 31 different aircraft.

After receiving the commission for five aircraft from the Aviation Ministry, there had been weeks of internal discussions at the Fieseler company about the specification for the new plane. They would be up against Europe's top sports planes manufacturers: the Areo from Czechoslovakia, the RWD from Poland, not to mention the German Messerschmitts which combined high speed and low fuel consumption. For weeks Fieseler's company had nothing to show but 'a mountain of technical drawings.'[89] Decisive for Fieseler was his excellent working relationship with his highly capable chief designer Arnolt. As on previous occasions, he would tell Arnolt what performance capabilities he wanted within the constraints laid down by the FAI; Arnolt would convert his demands, aspirations and ideas into an aeroplane.

After some ten weeks of feverish activity, the drawings containing the design for the new plane could be taken to the Air Ministry for inspection. The well-regarded Erich Bachem went to Berlin, where he learnt that through a bureaucratic mix-up the original commission had been sent out to the Fieseler company two months after the other selected German firms, Messerschmitt and Klemm, had received theirs. Bachem put up a very strong case for the Fieseler design. As if to make good the blunder, the Ministry rang through the order in a matter of days, confirming that the company could immediately apply for advance payments to cover production costs.

The order also made it imperative to take on more staff, one being a new chief statistician, who was a 'non-Aryan who had been dismissed by another well-known aircraft manufacturer.' Fieseler notes that he 'saw no reason to submit himself to racist prejudices' when it came to employing

85   R. G. Naugle, (1948). The Europa Rundflugs. *Flying Magazine*. August, pp.29-30, 50-52, 53. Accessed on 23 July 2015 at: https://books.google.co.uk/books?id=MSTJFFMHS9oC&pg=PA29&lpg=PA29&dq=europe+rundflug+naugle&source=bl&ots=O4Og92vFQJ&sig=jN27HLZb0TflKUqY5qh-3SjaLVs&hl=en&sa=X&ved=0CCEQ6AEwAGoVChMImLiiosjxxgIVyKNyCh2mWQUI#v=onepage&q=europe%20rundflug%20naugle&f=false
86   Norden, op. cit., p.19.
87   Naugle, op. cit. pp.29–30.
88   Ibid, p.29.
89   Norden, op. cit., p.30.

competent people.⁹⁰ At that time it was no small act of courage to take on Jewish employees. In the meantime he had to identity and appoint an effective production director as well as a head of the company's commercial department. With so much to do and think about, his 'wife and family had to be kept out of the way'; which was probably no change of status, as far as they were concerned.⁹¹

Then, one day in March 1934, he received out of the blue an invitation from the Aero Club of France to take part in the world aerobatics championships scheduled for June. This was the first such event and the prize money was 100,000 francs. The timing was extremely bad for Fieseler given how busy his company was and the fact that he was very much a hands-on boss at this key stage in the company's development, but the invitation was irresistible. As for the money, Fieseler's first biographer Norden wrote that victory would enable him to build up his company to continue 'on the same path that other, bigger firms have abandoned' in the light of the 'Versailles diktat.'⁹² He noted that eighteen aircraft manufacturers had been bankrupted in the Weimar years.

When he read the conditions, Fieseler immediately recognised that these had been written by his great French rival, Michel Détroyat, and favoured the Frenchman's aircraft. After careful thought Fieseler wrote to the Aero Club, saying that he would take part in the championships, but only if the evaluation scheme was more objective. This created consternation in Paris, but in the end of the conditions were modified. This change of heart confirmed to the self-regarding Fieseler that the event 'would lose its appeal in the absence of Fieseler, who were so well known in France.'⁹³ Around the time of that bit of haggling – on 21 April, to be precise – resumed training with one of his F5 Tigers, which had not only been through a complete overhaul and had been decorated with a swastika on the port side and the back, white and read Reich flag on the other side.⁹⁴ No doubt Herr Haak, not so long ago reprimanded by his boss for wearing a swastika armband on company premises, was delighted to see that his boss had identified with the new Germany.

Fortunately Fieseler had few other flying commitments at the time, so he could concentrate on his preparations for Paris championships. His participation would be the culmination of all the previous seven years, during which had been building up to 'day after day, year upon year' experience as an aerobatics pilot.⁹⁵ But the intensity of these preparations at the same time as running his company proved exhausting. Fieseler pushed himself to the limit, so made a point of flying to Paris two days ahead of schedule. He booked a room in a quiet hotel, drew the curtains and devoted two days to 'sleep therapy' (*Schlafkur*); after which with his batteries recharged he felt unencumbered and high in confidence.

The championships took place on the eastern suburbs of Paris at Vincennes, which had hosted its first air show in 1911, in the days when pilots risked their lives on every flight. A sand-covered airfield had been laid out on an army drill-ground close to woods. On this gleaming June day in 1934 the competition, which would be Paris's sporting highlight of the summer, attracted 150,000 people – 200,000, according to Norden – who packed the stands bedecked in flags and bunting. The cream of Parisian society was also in attendance: representatives of the government, including the French minister for aviation, business leaders, military officers, members of the diplomatic corps. A band was playing, the champagne was flowing. Europe's best aerobatics pilots from nine countries were there. They included the Briton Christopher Clarkson with his Tiger Moth, D'Abreu from Portugal with his British-made Avro, the Italian Colombo with his Breda and the French champion

---

90 Fieseler, op. cit., p.188
91 Ibid, p.188.
92 Norden, op. cit., p.11.
93 Fieseler, op. cit., p.194.
94 Nagel und Bauer, op. cit., p.105
95 Norden, op. cit., p.11.

Détroyat with his red Morane-Saulnier with its 500hp Gnome-Rhône engine. Fieseler's Tiger was silver-white with deep blue flashes on the upper fuselage. On the side was his trademark oblique white F in a blue circle. Vera von Bissing was at hand to time his various flights with a stop-watch as well as assist in some interpreting.

The event began with some formation flying followed by some stunts by military pilots. Then each of the competitors performed a fixed sequence of demanding compulsory routines involving various figures (rolls, a half-horizontal screw, an inverted loop) all within ten minutes. Everything depended on the pilot's 'precision of execution, elegance, ease of transition from one figure to the next [and] temperament.'[96] Fieseler showed 'the smooth continuous form' for which he was so much admired.[97] The first day's flying concluded with Fieseler slightly ahead of Détroyat. When they had met each other a year earlier at Vélizy-Villacoublay on the south-west side of Paris, the contest had been declared a draw. This year, though, he knew that there would be no draw: the champion would be him or the Frenchmen. The best the other pilots could hope for was to be in a respectable position behind them.

On the second day of the competition the pilots had to perform 38 figures of their own choosing within a given number of minutes. Not only had he rehearsed his routines day after day, he also spent evenings at home with a model Tiger to concentrate his mind. The heat in Vincennes on that day was overpowering. Twelve aircraft were drawn up, each one guarded by the pilots' assistants. Before the start of the competition a young French pilot André Bourré had taken his plane up and inadvertently grazed the ground with a wing-tip. His plane crashed and he was killed outright. Some of the wreckage landed five metres from Fieseler's plane. 'How many times have I seen that', mused Fieseler, adding darkly, 'But this time it really perturbed me.'[98] The wreckage was quickly removed so that neither pilots nor spectators would dwell on the fatal crash.

Shortly afterwards at 2.00pm guns announced the beginning of the contest. Fieseler was by now relaxed and inwardly prepared. 'Only his face betrayed him', wrote Norden, referring to that reflex from his fighter pilot days.[99] First off is Clarkson. He does his turns, lands. Next is D'Abreu, the Portuguese champion. His figures are breath-taking, executed with passion. But in the seventh minute in an attempt to pull out of an inverted flight, his plane suddenly plunges to the ground. D'Abreu is 'consumed in fire and smoke, he is burnt to death.'[100] Is this a grim foreboding? A second pilot has died in the space of an hour. Thousands of throats scream in horror, thousands of eyes unable to avert their gaze from the scene, women faint. There is pandemonium. Some members of the jury as well as German diplomats break through the barrier, their faces full of anguish, and make their way to Fieseler. 'How was that possible? How could that happen? D'Abreu was his country's finest pilot.'[101]

Fieseler deflects the questions. In half an hour he must take off. He cannot afford to be 'to be under the sway of a subdued atmosphere.'[102] Twenty paces away sits D'Abreu's engineer, a broken man, sobbing. 'Pity about D'Abreu', says Détroyat to Fieseler, fiddling with a cigarette. Like his German rival the French champion is calm. Fieseler replies 'It was a fine death worthy of a pilot' (*ein schöner Fliegertod*). 'Oui, mon camarade,' Détroyat rejoined.[103] Denain, the French aviation

---

96   Ibid, p.9
97   *Flight Global* (1934). Aerobatics at Vincennes (21 June). Available at: http://www.flightglobal.com/FlightPDFArchive/1934/1934%20-%200612.PDF
98   Fieseler, op. cit., p.195
99   Norden, op. cit., p.12
100 Ibid, p.13
101 Ibid, p.12.
102 Ibid. p.13
103 Ibid, p.13.

minister, immediately convenes a meeting of the president of the Aero Club, organisers, members of the jury and pilots and asks whether or not the event should continue. Fieseler speaks up: 'Such a misfortune could happen to anyone of us. If the pioneers of aviation had stopped flying, only because there had been an accident, where would be today?'

The contest continues in the dazzling sunshine. The pilots take off, starting with the Italian champion Colombo, who flew over the public, which was against the rules, banked, lost control and nearly crashed into woods. Some twenty metres above the ground his engine cut out. There was a crash not far from where D'Abreu had come to grief. Miraculously he emerged from it more or less unscathed. His airplane had a branch of a tree embedded in its landing gear. According to Fieseler, the Italian plane had not been properly put through its paces for such an important competition. Colombo himself was so nervous that before take-off he had forgotten to open his petrol tap; which nearly killed him.

Next comes Novak, the Czech champion. Soon it is the turn of Détroyat, who has achieved the highest score so far. Next is Fieseler. All his team back in Kassel have put in supreme efforts for this moment. Everything has been thought through up to the very last second. Fieseler now has to execute 32 figures as an integrated whole (*zum einzigen Guß*).[104] Everything has been performed again and again against a stop-watch, everything calibrated, recalibrated. Every kind of weather was put into the equation.

Fieseler is ready for take-off. His puts his sunglasses on. A marshal with a flag gives the starting signal. At 200 metres he executes the first figure and passes smoothly into the next ones, many of them not in Détroyat's repertoire. He carries out a completely new one, designed especially for this occasion. Only the knowledgeable members of the jury can clearly distinguish one figure from another. Six minutes have passed. He and his Tiger are as one. Then, for a split-second, inexplicably the plane is out of control. Only the jury notices that something is amiss. The buckle of Fieseler's safety belt had sprung open just before he is about to go into a loop. This is very dangerous. There is a clatter of metal on metal that 'threatens to disorientate me', writes Fieseler.[105] While his brain is racing like mad, he manages to stabilise the plane.

But critically he has lost speed. He and those in the know realise that he is under severe pressure to keep to the deadline. He lands one minute and ten seconds too late. The crowd, not appreciating what has happened, think the French champion has triumphed. 'Vive Détroyat,' they cheer, 'Le champion du monde!'[106] According to the rules of the contest, the judges cannot assess Fieseler's last three figures, because these were executed outside the allotted time. Even so Fieseler nearly has a 23 point lead over Détroyat, 645.5 to 622.9. He is world champion for Germany. But for a good ten or twelve minutes Fieseler is incapable of coherent speech, so overwhelmed was he by his ordeal, of which the vast majority of spectators had not the slightest inkling.

As he recovered from this state of euphoric collapse near his Tiger, the German ambassador, Dr Roland Köster, approached him with warm words of congratulation. Fieseler fulsomely described this urbane, cultivated man as 'this most accomplished personage' who generated a 'radiated a beneficent imperturbability.'[107] Köster said in soft voice, 'I am so grateful you. Today's events have done valuable work for our mission in France,' Referring to his embassy, he added. 'We cannot achieve in one year what you have pulled off in one day. After the political upheavals in Berlin and the unfathomable nature of German policy' – an unmistakably critical reference to the Nazis' – we have a difficult position here.'

104   Ibid, p.15.
105   Fieseler, p.194.
106   Ibid, p.199.
107   Ibid, p.199.

He then said that on the following evening he planned to mark Fieseler's success as a diplomatic coup and hold a banquet. Would Herr Fieseler be able to attend? To his deep regret Herr Fieseler would have to decline the invitation, explaining 'I must get back to my company in Kassel. We're up against a deadline for our new aircraft.'[108] He then explained to Köster the importance of the Fi 97 under development now that he was at the end of his flying career. Fieseler's conversation with the ambassador was interrupted by a French officer in a resplendent uniform. 'The Minister of Aviation would greatly like to speak to you. Be so kind as to follow me.' Bidding farewell to the visibly disappointed German ambassador, Fieseler found himself in the presence of Minister Denain, who was attired in a black frock coat and a top hat. The adjutant was about to formally introduce Fieseler, when Denain interrupted him and addressed the new world champion in passable German. 'No need for an introduction, as I already know you very well, Monsieur Fieseler.' He explained that during the First World War he had been a commander of Allied airmen on the Balkan Front and that he, Fieseler, had shot down many of his aircraft. Fieseler was completely taken aback and was about to express his regrets, when an inner voice told him: *'You can't say that.'*

He answered tactfully: 'Your excellency, that was war and we fought in the air with machine guns. Today there is peace and we fight each other for points.' No doubt Köster, the seasoned diplomat, would have been well pleased with this remark. Minister Denain certainly was. He congratulated Fieseler on his victory 'with Parisian charm', shook his hand and wished him all the best.[109] The next day French newspapers wrote lengthy articles about the world championships at Vincennes, then the German press, who had shown no interest beforehand, picked up the story and was in raptures about Fieseler coming first and the other pilot German flyer Achgelis coming third. According to Norden, Fieseler's fame was 'glowing around the world', his achievement being discussed in columns of newsprint.[110]

Fieseler rejoiced. Suddenly, 'it meant something to be German!' gloated Norden all the more so now that 'Hitler was at the helm, whose words and actions were being observed with keen interest throughout the world.'[111] During the event at Vincennes he had a conversation with his rival Détroyat. The French champion, tall, elegant and some ten years younger than Fieseler, told him: 'We have a new government every year. I wish we had a Hitler.'[112] One wonders what both would have said on that topic in a few years' time.

On the evening of the following day Fieseler was greeted at the Waldau airport in Kassel by rapturous crowds with cries of congratulation and strewn with flowers. He was raised on the shoulders of his well-wishers, including all or most of his workforce. Erich Bachem gave an address on his behalf in front of all the company's employees, saying how proud everyone was to have the honour of working with and for Herr Fieseler.[113] Weary as he was, the hero of the hour had to play the part: show a radiant smile, wave and, as he modestly put it, 'pretend to be the great victor, whether I liked it or not,'[114] According to Norden, he told the ecstatic crowds: 'From now on my life belongs to my company.' The next day he was of course main news in the local newspapers. One carried the headline: 'Fieseler to stop aerobatics.'

---

108   Ibid, p.199.
109   Fieseler, op. cit., p.201.
110   Norden. op. cit., p.19.
111   Fieseler, op. cit., p.201.
112   Ibid, p.201.
113   Nagel und Bauer, op. cit., p.106.
114   Fieseler, op. cit., p.202.

Over mountain ranges, the sea and the African desert

Whilst Fieseler had been concentrating on his participation for Vincennes, there was no let-up in the production of the five light sports planes for the Europa-Rundflug. Around the time that Fieseler received the invitation from the Aero Club of France in March, a mock-up of the new aircraft emerged. It was a low-wing, cantileveres aeroplane with a four-seater retractable canopy cockpit, fabric-covered tubular steel fuselage and rudders made of electron. An innovative arrangement of flaps running along the whole wing was to limit landing speed to a minimum.[115]

Then in April the first prototype of the new plane, the Fi 97, saw the light of day four months after the issuing of the contract. Fieseler, as much as possible, was on hand to be in day-to-day charge, although his immediate task was to prepare for Vincennes. His men would often work very late or even through the night, snatching sleep as and when. Sometimes Fieseler actually ordered them to go home. The company canteen could not keep up with the demand for food and drink on almost a 24 hour basis, so wives brought victuals for their husbands.

The Fi 97 offered excellent visibility from the cockpit and ease of boarding; the seats were comfortable. Everyone admired its general technical neatness. Only one person was not satisfied: the ever meticulous Gerhard Fieseler, who detected that something was not quite right with the undercarriage. He ordered his engineers and statisticians to redo their calculations. They spotted nothing amiss and became vexed. His chief statistician told him that 'technology will sink back into the Middle Ages', if people do not trust numbers.[116] 'I don't doubt it', rejoined Fieseler, 'but I trust my eyes and my intuition.' In the end Fieseler was shown to be right. His staff had been basing their calculations on loads on an existing undercarriage but not for the cantilevered undercarriage of the Fi97. It is a nice story, showing how in Norden's description his engineers think of aircraft in terms of calculations, whereas Fieseler sees them as 'living beings.'[117]

In August 1934, lashed by wind and rain, the five brand-new Fi 97s take off from Kassel for Warsaw, where the competition will start and end. When they arrive in Warsaw, the planes have exceeded the maximum weight permissible. The excess weight is a result of the dried rain on the wings. Fortunately, this is readily solvable. At last the flying competition begins. The route has scheduled stops in Berlin, Paris and Madrid. That summer the planes encounter unusual amounts of wind, fog and rain. Leaving European airspace, they head for North Africa, stopping over in Casablanca, Tunis, Algiers and Biscra. Severe sandstorms force the pilots to fly over mountains.

Then the planes cross the Mediterranean, flying northwards across Italy before crossing the Adriatic. Between Rimini and Zagreb the flying is perilous. Planes are buffeted by huge masses of cloud, they pass over mountain tops, where they are chased by the Sirocco 'with unexpected vehemence.'[118] At any second a plane could smash against the mountains. Of the 31 starters, only 18 make it back to Warsaw. All five Fi 97s complete the course, the only team to return to Warsaw with their full complement. They have flown 'over mountain ranges, the sea and the African desert'[119] and have taken places in the first ten. One of Fieseler's pilots, Hans Seidemann, was the highest scoring German pilot.[120] It was a tremendous result for the Fieseler company, which has never competed in this kind of event before. 'Novice firm pulls off sensation', sings a newspaper headline.[121]

---

115 Norden, op. cit., p.29-30.
116 Ibid, p.31.
117 Ibid, p.32.
118 Ibid, p.35.
119 Fieseler, op. cit., p.192-193.
120 Meredith, op. cit., p.547.
121 Fieseler, op. cit., p.193.

The triumph at Vincennes was, however, not quite the end of Fieseler's aerobatics career. Major flying displays were to be held in Cologne and Frankfurt, to which he was invited to give a solo performance. He simply had to fly a few figures and no doubt pick up a handsome fee. No intense preparation was involved. In Cologne the local Gauleiter (Nazi Party boss) had speedily transformed the old Butzweiler Hof airport, which he recalled from the First World War. It had been equipped with a brand-new railway station. Fieseler could not help being impressed with Nazi efficiency and organisation. On the day of the event trains were arriving every five minutes, bringing some 250,000 spectators to see him. He went through his figures, feeling 'free, detached as if in another world,' In front of such a huge expectant crowd he had the sensation of making 'rhythmical music' in the air. The newspapers were ecstatic: 'Daring aerobatics', 'Dicing with life and danger' and 'Virtuoso control of an aircraft.'[122]

A few weeks later in Frankfurt some 100,000 spectators came to see him perform. In the air he experienced the same sensations as at Cologne – until he landed. Then he was overwhelmed by a feeling of irreplaceable loss in his life. In the last seven years he had given as much energy and personal commitment as possible to achieve his status as the world's greatest aerobatics pilot. He had of course always known that devoting himself to flying whilst not neglecting his company involved him a kind of double life. His strength would surely give way one day. Yet, although he had known for a long time that in the end he would have to give up flying, when the time to quit that part of double life actually came – on this day in Frankfurt – he was overcome with an awful anguish. But it had to be. Ernst Udet for one knew what a wrench it was for Fieseler to bid farewell to aerobatics. He drew a cartoon of his former rival and now friend chained to his factory with a handkerchief in his hand, waving at an aeroplane that is executing twists and turns in the sky. Great tears are dropping from Fieseler's eyes, splashing into a great puddle of their own making.[123]

Shortly after he returned to Kassel, he suffered a nervous breakdown. All his exertions had taken their toll. His doctors ordered complete rest for six weeks. It was then just as well that Fieseler had in Erich Bachem a reliable deputy, who kept things ticking over.'[124] In the meantime the Aviation Ministry had offered to sell his triumphant Tiger to a young, gifted aerobatics pilot (which strongly indicates that the Ministry regarded the plane as their property). Three keen fellows apparently came forward, did some test flights and decided not to take things further. To Fieseler this was inexplicable. 'No-one wanted to have it, not even as a gift!', he laments.[125] The Ministry took charge of the Tiger and accorded it a place of honour in the Berlin Air Museum. In September 1943 the museum was almost completely destroyed in an RAF bombing raid. The Tiger finished its days in a fire-ball.

The year 1934 marked the culmination of Fieseler's career as an aerobatics pilot as well as his departure from that branch of aviation. He was now world champion, having already been crowned European champion on two occasions and German champion five times. He pioneered new turns in the aerobatics repertoire, for which he remains known in those flying circles today. Few would disagree that Gerhard Fieseler 'was the creator of modern aerobatics.'[126]

On 18 September 1934 there was a grand reception of the German Aero Club in Berlin, at which Fieseler was the guest of honour. The president of the club presented him with a silver cup on behalf of the French Aero Club to commemorate his victory at Vincennes. The Aero Club was more than it sounds. It had founded in 1907, but Göring as the Reich's for aviation 'turned

---

122   Ibid, p.203.
123   Ibid, p.204.
124   Nagel und Bauer, op. cit., p.109.
125   Fieseler, op. cit., p.205.
126   Nagel und Bauer, op. cit., p.108.

it into a social club and lobbying association for his aviation empire [and] high-society meeting place … [to] provide opportunities for making contacts in a relaxed atmosphere – in short, to cultivate camaraderie among flyers.'[127] It membership list was said to 'read like a *Who's Who* of the prominent politicians of the time' in addition to leading figures in aviation. Its members included 'all the government ministers … together with twenty secretaries of state and about sixty high-ranking members of the diplomatic service.'[128] As one of Germany's leading aviators, Fieseler was a member of the Aero Club (an obituary makes this clear). There can be no doubt that he exploited his membership to the advantage of his company.

1934 had been a year of triumph and fame for Fieseler and his company. His work force had expanded as had been his production facilities. He had taken on key senior personnel especially in design and engineering functions. But the time had come for him to appoint competent people who could help him negotiate with the Air Ministry and support the general management of the company. All these things were not unusual in themselves. Every small company, when it begins to grow, faces the challenge of creating a robust management system, when the founding entrepreneur reaches the point when he cannot control every aspect of his company. In 1934 Gerhard Fieseler had reached that critical point even before his nervous breakdown.

But there was one significant difference about corporate development in the Third Reich. A company like Fieseler's, that was gaining from orders from the government, was expected to run its affairs in conformity to Nazi ideals and requirements about creating companies worthy of the Führer and his explicit aim to restore Germany to world greatness. Or to put that in another way, though admittedly with the advantage of hindsight: companies – indeed every kind of organisation in Germany – whether they realised it or not – were to put themselves at the complete disposal of 'the corporal of the last war' so that he could 'prove what he could do as a conquering Generalissimo in the next.'[129] In practice, this meant far more than bedecking the workplace with de rigueur photographs of the Hitler, sprays of Nazi flags and insignia, and festoons of slogans. Every company was to become a place of fealty and submission to the Führer. But this did not happen as a result of 'large-scale social engineering' after the Nazis came to power. Germany's new masters first aimed at 'a revolution of feeling', whereby the population at large could feel itself swept along by a new, revitalising energy that left no part of society untouched: neither one home nor one's place of work nor anywhere else.[130]

The Ministry would now like a Stuka, Herr Fieseler

The success of the Fi 97 in the Europa-Rundflug had been truly remarkable. It was now one of the finest aircraft of its type in the world. The fact that the Fieseler company had only had two years' experience of the design and production of motorised aircraft had been duly noted by the Aviation Ministry. Commissions came to build under licence three aircraft for Heinkel: a trainer, a fighter and a spotter aircraft. Fieseler's membership of the Nazi Party was also said to have stood in his favour.[131] He was also to build another training aircraft for the Klemm company, which was well known for sports aircraft. It was necessary yet again for Fieseler to increase his production capacity and purchase equipment, but Air Ministry contracts financed the expansion and these purchases. By the end of 1934 his workforce expanded to 500 from around 150 in 1933. So it was that all the skills

---

127   M. Steber and G. Gotto (eds.), *Visions of Community in Nazi Germany: Social Engineering and Private Lives.* Oxford: Oxford University Press, p.207.
128   Ibid, p.207 and p.208.
129   A. Beevor, *The Second World War,* p.19.
130   Stargardt, op. cit., p.12
131   http://www.abnachkassel.de/ge/fieseler.php

that Fieseler and his workforce had developed in making high-performance aircraft for competitive aerobatics over the last few years would be harnessed by the Nazi regime for their ends.[132]

Fieseler learnt at the end of August 1934 that a condition for government finance was that he had to convert his firm into a limited liability company. He was duly visited by Alois Cejka, the Air Ministry's head of finance and contracts, who told him that another condition was that, when his company purchased materials, equipment, machinery and the like to fulfil the Ministry's contracts, these assets would belong to the state. These were the first steps in an attempt by the Nazis to secure the dependence of his company. Fieseler, who 'wanted to remain master of his own house and continue building trainers and sports planes,'[133] had limited ground for manoeuvre. Without capitulating completely, he made himself and his wife the sole shareholders, appointing himself managing director with a management built around himself with directors responsible for technical matters, for commercial activities and production. The capitalisation of the company was 300,000 Reichsmarks, of which 255,000 had been contributed by Fieseler and the balance by his wife.[134] The company was renamed Fieseler-Flugzeugbau GmbH, (Fieseler Aircraft Construction Company Ltd), hereafter FFB. This, however, was not the end of the matter, as far as the Ministry was concerned.

By 1934 then, when it began the manufacture of the trainers, the Fieseler company was already 'in a relationship of close dependency on the Reich Ministry and involved in rearmament of the Luftwaffe.'[135] However, before the post-war denazification tribunal Fieseler would declare that 'in 1934/35 no-one was talking about rearmament. As far as my company was concerned, we had nothing to do with that.'[136] Yet, according to Wiederhold, half of the Heinkel and Klemm aircraft would be used for training pilots for the Luftwaffe. It seems inconceivable that Fieseler did not know that some of the planes were required for military purposes. In his defence he offered two main reasons for cooperating with the Air Ministry to help build a strong Germany under the Führer. First, the orders from the Ministry guaranteed employment for his loyal workforce, who had endured so much hardship in recent years. Second there was no alternative. As he put it: 'I only two options: either comply with the request or go to a concentration camp.'[137]

As work proceeded on the training aircraft, the Fieseler company was commissioned in 1935 with the designing and building of dive-bomber, for which the German acronym Stuka (short for *Sturzkampfflugzeug*) would become synonymous with Nazi aerial terror in the Second World War. This was the company's first explicitly military contract. Fieseler's design office based their work on the Curtiss Hawk known as the Helldiver, two specimens of which Ernst Udet had ingeniously, though legally imported from the USA with the discreet connivance of the Air Ministry. Once the Ministry's specification was in their hands, Fieseler's company started work on the dive-bomber.

Called the Fi 98, it crashed during trials in April 1936, whereupon the ministry halted further development. A rival manufacturer, Junkers, was all the more successful, creating the feared Ju 87 Stuka, notorious for its screaming Jericho trumpets. It seems that the Aviation Ministry was not unduly perturbed at Fieseler's failure to design and produce the dive-bomber, seeing that other commissions were in the pipe-line. After the end of the war his denazification tribunal asked Fieseler about this abortive dive-bomber in the context of Luftwaffe expansion. Not for the first time denied that his company had anything to do with armaments manufacture. His reply was breath-takingly unconvincing: 'It wasn't a weapon of attack. It was a single-seater Stuka, from which it was possible

---

132 Meredith, op. cit., p.351.
133 Nagel und Bauer, op. cit., p.122.
134 Ibid, p.108.
135 Wiederhold, op. cit., p.46.
136 Ibid, p.46.
137 Ibid, p.46.

to drop a bomb' – one bomb, note. He then added disingenuously: 'That's easy to do from any single-seater.'[138] In the mid-1930s Fieseler was not to know that Stukas would before long be acting as 'the flying artillery of the panzer spearheads'[139] in war-torn Europe. Even so he surely knew in the mid-1930s that they were attack aircraft; it was not as if they were being developed for Sunday air shows for the family.

138 Ibid, p.47.
139 Beevor, op. cit., p.90.

Part Three

Companion to Catastrophe

8

Industrialist of consequence

Nothing is impossible for the Fieseler men.

Adalbert Norden.[1]

We can stand Hitler, but there are all those little Hitlers.

Sebastian Haffner[2]

All the threads in his hands

In May 1933, when the Reich Aviation Ministry was established, some 4,000 people were engaged in aircraft production in 14 enterprises.[3] In July 1934 a long-term programme envisaged the manufacture of more than 2,000 fighters, 2,000 bombers, 700 dive bombers, some 1,500 reconnaissance aircraft and thousands of training aircraft by the end of March 1938.[4] In 1933 German industry built 328 aircraft. In 1934 the figure increased to 1,968 and in 1935 to 3,183.[5] In the latter year the industry was employing 72,000 workers.[6] By 1939 the aircraft industry was employing 325,000 people. Some 24 firms were manufacturing aircraft and 42 were engaged in the production of parts from propellers to fittings. Other firms specialised in repair work, whilst others supplied various industries and not the aircraft sector exclusively.[7] All the military aircraft commissioned by the Aviation Ministry as of 1933 were being built for the Wehrmacht, but with the creation of the Luftwaffe in 1935 with Göring as commander-in-chief it was hard to keep secret the fact that this was being created as an independent offensive force.

Fieseler's company, FFB, which was a direct beneficiary of these dramatic developments, acquired a new complexion in the six years building up to the outbreak of war in 1939. Its workforce increased from 150 to around 5,000. It ceased to be a producer of sports aircraft and began to design and build a range of military aircraft, including several under licence for the Reich Aviation Ministry. The licenced production commenced in 1936 with aircraft from the drawing boards of Heinkel: the He 51 biplane fighter and the He 72 biplane trainer. The company enlarged its facilities accordingly: but not only to reflect the greater demands of production, but also, as we shall see, to provide amenities for its workers which would be beneficial to their physical and mental well-being. It also acquired land that it could use to build a runway. In terms of comparative size FFB was never in the same league as Junkers, Heinkel, Dornier or Messerschmitt, but it nevertheless became a very significant supplier of aircraft right up to the end of the Second World War.

---

1 A. Norden, *Das Herz muss dabei sein: Der Flieger Gerhard Fieseler und sein Werk*, p.42.
2 S. Haffner, *Germany: Jekyll & Hyde – 1939 von innen betrachtet*, p.61.
3 R. J. Evans, *The Third Reich in Power*, p.364.
4 Ibid, p.364.
5 R. Nagel und T. Bauer, *Kassel und die Luftfahrtindustrie seit 1923: Geschichte(n), Menschen, Technik*, p.114.
6 Ibid, p.339.
7 T. Wiederhold, *Gerhard Fieseler – eine Karriere: Ein Wirtschaftsführer im Dienste des Nationalsozialismus*, p.35.

Alongside these developments, the Fieseler company, like all other enterprises and organisations in Germany experienced nazification of the workforce, a process which touched every single employee regardless of occupation and position. Presently we will discuss this process in some detail, which led to Fieseler's company acquiring a distinctly quasi-paramilitary character well before the outbreak of war. But first we need to draw attention to the appointment in the mid-1930s of three influential men who would serve as Fieseler's right-hand men. With Fieseler they constituted a top management team of considerable intellect as well as practical and theoretical aeronautical experience. What is more Fieseler maintained very good relationships with each of them, which was crucial for the future development of the company. So who exactly were they?

On the technical and engineering side a key appointment was that of Karl Thalau, who had a PhD in mechanical engineering and a higher postgraduate qualification – the German *Habilitation* – in aeronautical engineering. Thalau had been a professor at the Technical University of Berlin and had also worked as a statistician at the DVL. He had relished the opportunity to switch from theory to practice. He would play a crucial role in the further development of the firm. Thalau, wrote Fieseler, possessed the gift of rigorous thought, whereas 'I had a more creative turn of mind (*mehr konstructives Denken*). What Thalau could do, was beyond me; what I could do was alien to him. It was a fortunate mix for the firm.'[8]

The key post of financial expert was filled by Tobias Göbel, who also had a PhD; in his case, in law. He functioned as finance director and chief accountant. According to Norden, Göbel 'knew how much everything and everyone cost.'[9] His skills made it possible for the Fieseler company to become the first aircraft builder to conclude sales on the basis of fixed prices. The third member of the team was Walter Banzhaf, who held a PhD in engineering. Previously he had been a manager responsible for aero engine manufacture at the Bayerische Flugzeugwerke, which in 1938 would evolve into Messerschmitt AG with the famous aircraft designer in charge. Upon joining the Fieseler company, Banzhaf was responsible for general management with an emphasis on training and integration of new employees. Part of his brief was to put into practice new methods and new work plans. In this set-up Fieseler was the managing director with Thalau and Göbel as his deputies.

We should also add that as of the mid 1930s the company was attracting highly qualified engineers, aerodynamicists and statisticians, many from the top technical universities, as well as highly competent test pilots. This reflects the excellent reputation that the company now enjoyed as a stimulating place to work, where new and exciting aircraft were being built or developed. However, January 1935 saw the departure of Fieseler's immensely reliable chief designer Emil Arnolt, who left FFB to work for an aircraft company in Berlin which was 'intensively engaged in helicopter technology.'[10] Fieseler does not mention Arnolt's departure, but it must have come as a considerable disappointment to him.

It might seem remarkable that the most senior managers of the Fieseler company, namely Thalau, Göbel and Banzhaf, all had doctorates. But this was – this still is – Germany through and through: packing a lot of brain-power into a small company. What is even more striking, when we consider the members of his management key team, is that Fieseler himself had no formal education in engineering whatsoever. In this he differed dramatically from his contemporaries like Hugo Junkers, Hans Klemm, Willy Messerschmitt, and Claude Dornier, all of whom came from reasonably wealthy backgrounds and had a sound technical or engineering education in the universities. Some had PhDs in engineering, whilst Junkers and Messerschmitt even doubled as university professors.

8   G. Fieseler, *Meine Bahn am Himmel*, p.208.
9   Norden, op. cit., p.42.
10   Nagel und Bauer, op. cit., p.110.

The general motley of men running Germany's major aircraft manufacturers were said to be 'vain, ambitious, intensely suspicious of each other, and extremely gifted.'[11] Fieseler was certainly ambitious and was definitely gifted, but vanity and a suspicious nature were largely alien to him. At all events he was plainly considered by his peers in his company, and perhaps especially by Thalau (German professors being a very pedantic species), as totally competent in the sense that he understood from his exceptional experiences as a fighter pilot and aerobatics champion the ins and outs of aircraft design and performance.

That he possessed the competences to be general manager of a large industrial firm, namely 'the personal, compulsive attention to detail and the bureaucratic virtues of patience and orderliness', is not in doubt.[12] But there was more to it than this. Fieseler would have been viewed as a boss who knew what's what, an expression which carries far more potency in German (*Bescheid wissen*) than its nominal English translation conveys. In German the expression means to know *exactly* what's what to the extent that others can *absolutely* depend on it. Without this capability Fieseler could never have secured the respect and confidence of its managers and staff in general.

In short, as managing director of the company he was an exponent of that German forte: 'management by highly specialised knowledge' (*Führung durch Fachwissen*).[13] It was in fact one of the greatest achievements of his life to project his authority through his specialist, highly empirical – one might even say intuitive – knowledge of aeronautics, on the one hand, and his evident grasp of managerial and commercial complexities, on the other. In German engineering culture there was – and is – no other way. According to Nagel and Bauer, Fieseler gained these competences through 'iron-like willpower' and the drive to educate himself in the necessary fundamentals.[14] But there was another extremely important factor in his managerial make-up: He was also 'a man who relished decision-making (*ein Mann der Entscheidungsfreudigkeit*).'[15]

Fieseler was completely in tune with the working environment of those years, which is well described by the American aviation historian, Edward Homze. It is worth quoting him at length on aviation development and design, in which:

> the Germans showed as much originality, progress, and achievement as any comparable country. Design and development are essentially engineering processes in which drawings, tolerances, mechanics, and strength of materials are blended with production designs for assembly-line needs, economic choices of materials, adaptations of machines, and hundreds of practical other matters. Once aircraft leave the drawing boards of the design engineers, they undergo a process of refinement in which their basic design is enhanced by incessant testing and production. Omissions and deficiencies are discovered, corrections made, and models perfected. Long, tedious work is needed until a model is ready for use, and the process is, of necessity, never ended. In this area, traditional German virtues of pride in work, love of execution in detail, and the desire for precision and completeness were displayed to their best advantage.[16]

---

11   E. L. Homze, *Arming the Luftwaffe: The Reich Air Ministry and the German Aircraft Industry 1919-1939*, p.63.
12   Ibid, p.264.
13   H.D. Ganter and P. Walgenbach, Middle Managers: Differences Between Britain and Germany, in: M. Geppert, D. Matten, and K. Williams, *Challenges for European Management in a Global Context: Experiences from Britain and Germany*, p.170.
14   Nagel und Bauer, op. cit., p.103.
15   Nagel und Bauer, op. cit., p.175.
16   Homze, op. cit., p.212.

Fieseler's special skill in a technical sense was his unquestioned knack for identifying omissions and deficiencies. He then went about rectifying them by setting arrays of specialists in motion to create a first-class flying machine. In Norden's words, in his company Fieseler 'has all the threads in his hands, creates the foundation of the company based on confidence so that all the mutually enriching work of individuals and departments can flourish.'[17] With competent lieutenants at his side, Fieseler ensured that he spent the minimum amount of time in his office, making a point of visiting a different department every day 'so as not to lose perspective.' On these visits, as he put it: 'I spoke to workers and their immediate superiors. Thus I saw and heard what was good and not good, what to change and what to improve.'[18] But, as we shall see, some of his colleagues thought that Fieseler's proneness to intervention was counterproductive.

From what we have learned about Gerhard Fieseler so far, his sheer drive and determination stand out. But you need more than those qualities to run a company which is employing arrays of talented people. So what qualities might those be? As we know so little about his private life, it is hard to get a rounded picture of the man himself. However, German aviation authors Nagel and Bauer come to our assistance with the following description which they claim is based on people who knew him in his professional and personal capacities. They write:

> He had firm ideas about how things were or how they should be. He could express these clearly and when necessary could get his ideas implemented with enormous authority. He had a completely level-headed, rational and blunt philosophy of life. He was exceptionally direct (*gradlinig*) and could hurt people. He possessed a special flair for judging people. Even if those people did not actually work for him, he could after a conversation with them form conclusions about their character or professional development. Future events showed an astonishingly high hit rate in his judgments.[19]

One of his former colleagues found Fieseler to be high-handed, obstinate and dogmatic, adding that he had his good points, which he did not actually specify.[20] Somebody who knew him in his later years described him as being 'no push-over', noting that he was 'excessively arrogant.'[21] From those statements and from we know about Fieseler already it is hard not to come to the point of view that he was a man who did not suffer fools gladly; who frequently got his way by sheer personality; and whom one respected rather than liked. It is in fact hard not to come to the conclusion that he inherited more of his father's DNA than his mother's. He does not come across at all as man of wit or humour. For him life was, ever since his wartime experiences as a fighter pilot in the First World War, a serious business to be pursued with dogged determination.

Exactly what kind of relationship he had with his wife and children, we do not know, but in 1935 Fieseler resolved to spend more time with them, taking them out for outings on Sundays with the families of his close colleagues such as Bachem and Göbel.[22] The next year he moved house to the refined Wilhelmshöhe side of Kassel so as not to be on the company doorstep. No doubt this was much to the approval of his wife. It is indicative of his wealth that he commissioned an architect to design his new house. This architect was also invited to design houses for Bachem

---

17   Norden, op. cit., pp.42-43.
18   Fieseler, op. cit., p.230.
19   Nagel und Bauer., op. cit., p.443.
20   Ibid, p.443.
21   According to a personal informant in Kassel.
22   Ibid, p.112.

and Thalau; which suggests that FFB was paying for the private accommodation of at least some of its senior managers.

Difficult birth, wondrous offspring

One of the key designers on the abortive Stuka project was an over-confident engineer called Reinhold Mewes. He and Fieseler had clashed on various occasions. Nevertheless, Fieseler still rated him as a highly competent aircraft designer and invited him to develop a concept for a liaison aircraft for which the Aviation Ministry issued tenders in September 1935. FFB found itself with competition with two other aircraft manufacturers Bayerische Flugzeugwerke and Klemm, both having been identified by the ministry's Technical Office as having the necessary expertise. This aircraft was required to be capable of slow flight, be light-weight and able to take off and land in short distances. It was envisaged for use by military commanders to give them an advantageous aerial view of military operations as they unfolded and facilitate radio communication with subordinates on the ground. There was no precedent for such an aircraft.

Since the crash of the Stuka, Reinhold Mewes had become noticeably contrite. Even so Fieseler had to handle him tactfully. Having a psychological advantage over his temperamental colleague, Fieseler told Mewes that he could work on the new design provided that 'every drawing that leaves your office is signed off by me.'[23] He gave Mewes a day to think it over. The next day Mewes, making an awkward face, confirmed his acceptance of the condition. It was now all hands to the pumps. As with the Fi 97, which had done so well in the Europa-Rundflug in 1934, the designers, engineers and of course Fieseler himself were all up against tight deadline. But this time there was a difference. The company facilities were bigger and better. There was more brain power to draw on and Fieseler, who had ceased any kind of aerobatics flying, was now omnipresent. Mewes and his team set about things with gusto and before long a design emerged that, as far as they could see, needed no further modification.

The new plane was designated the Fi 156. Mewes and his team, including a long-standing collaborator Viktor Maugsch from his old company, referred the major design decisions to Fieseler, who after much thought considered that for the wings the best option was a so-called Göttingen aerofoil. But that would require tests in a wind tunnel for which there was simply not enough time. Given the time pressure, Fieseler offered Mewes and his team a reward if they could design the plane to meet the requirement for weight empty. In the meantime Fieseler had requested some modifications to the proposed undercarriage. Mewes exploded: 'First you promise a reward for sticking to the required weight, now you want an undercarriage that weighs 15 or 20 kilos more!'[24]

As before, Fieseler allowed his designer to stew in his own juice. But the next day there were more wrangles, as Fieseler made requests for further modifications. Mewes and his like-minded deputy Maugsch fretted yet again. It was perfectly obvious that they regarded themselves as experts in plane design. Fieseler was, as far as they were concerned, a layman who should concentrate on running the company and not impose ill-informed demands on them. Evidently, they had had a free hand in their old company and were not used to a boss who got so intimately involved in their work. Fieseler again requested other modifications to the undercarriage, wing slats and rudder. The squabbling went on for weeks, but after much expenditure of patience and nervous energy interspersed with common sense Fieseler got his way.

In December a mock-up emerged. A clutch of inspectors from the Aviation Ministry came to Kassel, but to general consternation they refused to accept the Fieseler concept. They requested

---

23 Fieseler, op. cit., p.209.
24 Ibid, p.211.

improvements to visibility in the cockpit, which itself would have to be redesigned from four-man to three-man occupation for a pilot, observer and radio operator. This was a hard blow to the FFB team, but it nevertheless motivated them to introduce the features as required. At this juncture Fieseler came to the conclusion that Mewes was not the man to be in charge of the expanded design office which the modifications to the Fi 156 would necessitate. There was a far more suitable person recommended by Thalau, a certain Dr Hermann Winter, who had previously worked in Bulgaria, where he helped lay the foundations of that country's aircraft industry. He joined FFB in January 1936 and proved to be an ambitious man of great energy.

On 24 May 1936 the modified Fi 156 made its maiden flight with, of course, Gerhard Fieseler in the cockpit. It was a high-winged plane with 250HP engine. Built for a three-man crew, the glassed-in cabin provided the pilot with maximum visibility. Its top speed was 175kms/hr, but could land at just 45 kms/hr. With its maximum load it could reach 1,000 metres in four minutes. It could fly as slowly as 50 km/h, take off into a light wind in less than 45 m, and land in 18 m. These figures outclassed those for autogiros, which had 'a conventional engine-powered propeller but deriving its lift from a system of freely rotating horizontal vanes, and capable of landing in a very small space.'[25] It stood on unusually long legs, whilst the very robust landing gear could absorb the impact even if the plane dropped to the runway in a controlled stall.[26]

It could take off and land anywhere: on roads, on open fields, meadow or tracts of land where virtually any other plane would come to grief. In the hands of a good pilot it could even hover in the air in a strong enough head-wind. Fieseler was very pleased that it had only taken six months after the setbacks of the previous December for the Fi 156 to take to the air. It was a company record, for competitors in the bid had required a year to design and build their models. Whilst Winter is often credited with the design of the Fi 156, that was strongly disputed by Mewes and Maugsch. The episode bears out the truth that aircraft design 'depends on teamwork by a collection of experts', making it 'difficult to a lot responsibilities for individual aspects of any aircraft to a particular designer.'[27] In fact the wrangles over the claim over who designed the Storch continued until well after the Second World War.

In 1937 Fieseler dubbed the Fi 156 'the Storch' (stork) not only because of the posture of the aircraft on its stilt-like legs, but also because of the way it landed almost vertically. It would be nice to be able to say that the name was chosen partly to honour his boyhood hero, Otto Lilienthal, who had made a point of studying storks in the Baltic.[28] But, as far as can be ascertained, Fieseler did not make that particular connection. There is no doubt that among aviation specialists the Storch was regarded as among the finest aircraft of its type and to this day it remains a very well regarded aircraft. Here is a description of a British expert:

> So excellent were the flying characteristics of the Fieseler Fi 156 Storch ... that it seemed as if it was capable of breaking the aerodynamic laws governing flight ... it was almost impossible to stall and could fly at very low speeds.' The Fi 156 owed abilities to its wings full-span fixed slats and slotted flaps, a high stalky undercarriage.[29]

No-one seems to have disputed the aptness of the name Storch for such an innovate-looking aircraft. But, there is a curious exception to be found in a novel by Les Cartwright about certain

---

25   J. Ayto, *Twentieth Century Words*, p.126.
26   Deutsches Museum, *Aviation: A Guide to the Aeronautics Collection*, p.63.
27   F. Vann, *Willy Messerschmitt: First Full Biography of an Aeronautical Genius*, p.52,
28   Norden, op. cit., p.48.
29   C. Shepherd, *German Aircraft of World War II*, p.19.

Larry Hanson, a Canadian weather man, who is intrigued by the similarity between a Fieseler Storch and a crane fly, which has been sucked into the air system of his car. The crane fly, of the family tipulidae, is indeed described as having 'a slender body and stilt-like legs.'[30] Larry, happening to be an aeronautics fanatic, coaxed the insect onto the back of his hand and delicately placed it on the seat beside him:

> You're a little beauty.' He said, 'You'd make a lovely brooch for the lapel of a lady's business suit.' But, through his inner voice, he told himself, 'Those Germans, when they designed the Fieseler Storch … they may have had one of these sitting on the desk in front of them.'[31]

This is a nice piece of imagination, but there is no evidence that a crane fly ever inspired the Storch design team.

The Richthofen of the Spanish Civil War
By the mid-1930s Fieseler already had a very good relationship with the Reich Aviation Ministry. His lines of communication would improve as of January 1936, when his erstwhile aerobatics rival and now close friend, Ernst Udet, had started to work for the Ministry at a very senior level. In January of that year he allowed himself – and against his own better judgement – to receive on Göring's instigation a commission as colonel in the Luftwaffe and became the Ministry's Inspector of Fighter and Stuka Pilots.[32] In the following June the post of head of the Aviation Ministry's Technical Office fell vacant. This important body 'had a decisive influence in determining the aircraft to be ordered for quantity production.'[33] When offered the position, Udet quaked at the thought of all the bureaucracy, but accepted it primarily as an opportunity to promote his pet project, dive-bombers.[34]

With special responsibility for research, development and supply, Udet became one of the most powerful men in the Aviation Ministry and a major influence on the Nazi's aircraft building programme. In fact Udet's unalloyed enthusiasm for fighter planes led him to neglect of the production of bombers, an omission that would cost the Luftwaffe – and Germany – dear in the Second World War. Fieseler never expressly states that his company received government contracts thanks to his friendship with Udet. He says, however, that he was often in Berlin in the 1930s and it was agreed between them that he should make a pointing of meeting Udet '*every time*.'[35] (new emphasis). At the very least we can be sure that through his frequent meetings with Udet Fieseler was kept informally up-to-date with aircraft policy and priorities.

It is by no means certain, but Udet may have been influential in ensuring that the Storch received its baptism of fire in military operations. Within months of the outbreak of the Spanish Civil War in July 1936, Germany's new Luftwaffe was supplying air support to General Francisco Franco, the republican military leader and later dictator of Spain. There was more to this than one Fascist regime providing military assistance to another. Spain created a golden opportunity for Germany's new, well-armed Luftwaffe – in the form of the specially assembled Condor Legion – to test its latest aircraft and give its pilots operational experience. Göring excitedly declared that the Spanish Civil War was 'the greatest exercise ground of all time.'[36]

30 https://en.wikipedia.org/wiki/Crane_fly.
31 L. Cartwright, *If Winter Comes,* p.21. Accessed on Google Books.
32 Homze, op. cit., p.195.
33 Vann, op. cit., p.48.
34 H. Herlin, *Udet: A Man's Life,* p.196.
35 Ibid, p.244.
36 J. Piekalkiewicz, *Der Fieseler Fi 156 Storch im Zweiten Weltkrieg,* p.13.

The Condor Legion included Heinkel and Dornier bombers, Messerschmitt fighters, Junkers dive-bombers as well as reconnaissance aircraft, including 10 Storchs.[37] It is not clear when these Storch aircraft joined the Condor Legion or where they were deployed. By the time the war in Spain came to an end in 1939, the Condor Legion had 'dropped nearly 2.7 million pounds of bombs and fired more than 4 million machine-gun bullets.'[38] All in all the impact of the German experience in Spain on 'aircraft development, production planning and general aviation theorizing was … profound.'[39] It can be safely assumed that details of the Storchs' performance were duly reported back to the Fieseler company, as the Luftwaffe had set up 'a special combat reporting team … [which] … sent reports directly to Berlin for analysis and evaluation.'[40] It goes without saying that the thousands of Spanish citizens who were the sacrificial lambs in the Luftwaffe's experiment in aerial terrorism constituted not the slightest threat to Hitler's Reich.

Mysteriously, in March 1937 a British newspaper, the *Sunday Chronicle*, ran an article headlined 'Nazi air ace killed in Spain.' Its correspondent, who claimed to have had 'ten interviews with officials, great and minor' reported that Fieseler, bizarrely described as 'the Richthofen of the Spanish war', had been 'shot down fighting for Franco's Nationalists against the Spanish government in February.' Nor is that the end of the journalistic preposterousness. Fieseler was said to be 'commander of a German air detachment in Seville.' Readers are led to believe that 'Berlin has done its utmost to hush the matter up, not even Fieseler's relatives being told.' Berlin, in the form of Ernst Udet, sent Fieseler a copy of the article waggishly offering his commiserations on his friend's apparent untimely death.[41] According to Norden, a press report actually announced: 'Fieseler is dead.' Despite official denials, there was 'no hushing up' the rumour in Germany until Fieseler turned up at an airshow in Paris two days later.[42]

Fieseler himself gave the first public demonstration of the Storch at the Zürich Air Show, an important showcase for the latest aircraft, in July 1937. In fact the event was a great success for German manufacturers. The new Messerschmitt 109 fighter and Heinkel 111 bomber were unveiled to an international public, giving rise to 'considerable worry for the Air Ministries of the other European countries who were rightly apprehensive about Hitler's intentions in the long term.'[43] As for the Storch, Fieseler's friend Ernst Udet performed some tricks with it, taking off, rising to ten metres and landing three times along the length of the 200-metre tribune. Udet's performance created 'gales of laughter.' Fieseler himself found his antics 'really too funny for words.'[44]

The Storch was immediately recognised as being superior airplane to the de la Cierva, the most modern autogiro at the time. Indeed it was one of the hits of the Zürich Air Show. According to the ever enthusiastic Norden, 'Germany's latest innovation is announced to all countries in press reports and photographs.'[45] For Fieseler the success of the Storch must have been especially sweet. Ten years earlier he had been humiliated in Zürich, having been cheated of his victory in his first aerobatics contest outside Germany.

As a result of all this very favourable publicity about the Storch, the Nazi leadership found a novel purpose for the Storch: as a diplomatic gift. One was presented to Mussolini.[46] In

37   Nagel und Bauer, op. cit., p.248.
38   R. Andrews, *The Storm of War: A New History of the Second World War*, p.5.
39   Homze, op. cit., p.172.
40   Ibid, p.171.
41   Nagel und Bauer, op. cit., p.124.
42   Norden, op. cit., p.45.
43   Vann, op. cit., pp.60-61.
44   Fieseler, op. cit., p.214.
45   Norden, op. cit., p.49.
46   Fieseler, op. cit, p.218.

Fieseler's autobiography there is a somewhat indistinct photograph showing Hitler, Göring, Hess, Udet and Mussolini all peering into the cockpit of a Storch. The photograph was taken during military manoeuvres – the biggest in Germany since World War 1 – in Mecklenburg in north Germany in September 1937. On that occasion 'air ace Ernst Udet landed his Storch plane almost perpendicularly from the tree where the two dictators were watching the event ... it made a considerable impression.'[47] As we shall see, Mussolini was not the only dictator to receive a Storch as a mark of Nazi esteem. In the meantime another Storch was given by Göring to Italo Balbo, the governor of the Italian colony of Libya since 1933. When he heard of that, it must have afforded Fieseler wry amusement. It will be recalled that he once to stood up to Balbo in his aerobatics days and so forsook the opportunity to receive the Duce's aviation medal.

Air-mindedness and the reinvention of Germany
In the First World War Gerhard Fieseler had wanted to make a great contribution to German airmindedness, which he conceived in terms of enhancing Germany's greatness through the superiority of German pilots and their aircraft in the event of combat with those of other nations. If he saw airmindedness as Germany's destiny, the national humiliation as a result of the First World War called for a new variation of it. With the restrictions on aircraft production and development required by the Treaty of Versailles, it was clear to the 'air-minded' that a seriously weakened Germany was especially vulnerable to onslaughts by bomber aircraft unless it could build up its air defensive capability. In the 1920s, as we have seen, air-mindedness for national defence took the form of using various forms of subterfuge to build aircraft and test engines in other countries, train future military pilots under civilian guise and to divert 'black funds' from the Reichswehr to the Ministry of Transportation for maintaining such clandestine activities.

However, as of 1933 this expedient form of air-mindedness was not only openly appropriated, but also transmogrified by the Nazis into a major national project, which was nothing less than 'the reinvention of Germany' driven by 'an ideologically infected diagnosis of danger and opportunity.'[48] With the Storch not to mention the V-1, as history would show, Fieseler would make his mark on this resurgent, Nazi-influenced form of air-mindedness. In 1936 he, as ever the entrepreneur, seized his opportunity. The danger, of course was not yet apparent to the German population at large. By 1942 it certainly would be in all its starkness, when the Royal Air Force began to attack targeted industrial sites in Germany and the manpower base engaged in war production. In Fieseler's case, as we shall see, he got a chilling advance warning of the danger in 1938.

With all the previous aircraft he had built, starting with the F3 Wespe, he has always wanted to produce something that was innovative in design and performance. With the Storch he duly achieved his ambition 'to build an aircraft that could fly unlike any other.'[49] But actually there was more to it than that. In years to come aeronautical designers and engineers from 'at least ten countries', including the USA and USSR, tried to produce imitative versions and failed.[50] Fieseler's supreme achievement lay in developing, building and putting into service an airplane that had *intrinsic uncopiability* – the holy grail of all technology companies to keep ahead of competition. This achievement, completely unnoticed then and perhaps even now, may well rank him among the world's greatest aircraft builders in the first half of the twentieth century.

The secret of the Storch's intrinsic uncopiability was due to the way in which Fieseler was able to inspire his hard-nosed designers and engineers to build the mystery of his years of experience

---

47   S. Corvaja, *Hitler and Mussolini: The Secret Meetings*, p.49.
48   P. Fritzsche, Machine Dreams: Airmindedness and the Reinvention of Germany, pp.685-709.
49   *Deutsche Kampfflugzeuge des Zweiten Weltkriegs*, p.76.
50   Ibid, p.77.

and intuitions into an aircraft with unique operating characteristics. All too evidently Fieseler thrived in this intense form of collaboration. This dynamic process evolved through the conversion and interplay of his 'soft' (or tacit) knowledge into their 'hard' (explicit) knowledge. Nearly fifty years later two eminent Japanese professors would proclaim such a process of industrial knowledge creation as distinctively Japanese and uniquely characteristic of world-class firms such as Honda, Canon, Nissan and Matsushita Electric. They argued that among other things the 'ambiguous nature of the Japanese language' vouchsafed the sharing of the all-important tacit knowledge among experts.[51] It would surely surprise those professors and their thousands of worldwide readers to know that completely analogous processes were taking place during the Third Reich in the Fieseler's company, in which the operating language was forthright, ambiguity-shunning German.

The instant success of the Storch led to major contracts from the Aviation Ministry, and here the company faced three significant challenges. First, Fieseler and his key colleagues realised that they would have to adopt American-style mass production techniques, which would entail extending current facilities and introducing new kinds of production equipment. Fieseler had already experimented in a modest way with serial production techniques to build gliders, but there was in Germany at large very little home-grown experience to tap into. Not for the first time his company would need to be innovative. Second, it would prove very difficult to source – locally at least – engineers and operatives who knew anything about mass production. Third, the switch over from traditional manufacturing with all the new equipment to buy would require colossal investments.

As Fieseler wrestled with these problems, in 1936 the company received a substantial order to produce Messerschmitt 109 fighters under licence. By this time it was also building the Arado 68 biplane fighter in addition to the aircraft for Heinkel. In 1937 FFB delivered 90 Me 109s; by 1941, when it had ceased to build them, the company produced 1,075 models of the Me 109 and Me 109T.[52] In 1938 FFB began building, also under licence, the Focke-Wulf 58, a training aircraft for the Luftwaffe. When the company pointed out to the Aviation Ministry that the company lacked specialist labour, its officials told it to provide proper training facilities. Technical discussions took place in Berlin, but the matter of who would actually pay for these facilities was not raised. But then it became apparent that the fighter production would need a new factory. When Fieseler asked Dr Göbel how they could possibly fund these developments, his financial director replied: 'He who places the order pays up.'[53] And that is what happened. Thus the company secured substantial funding from the Aviation Ministry which helped Fieseler equip it with mass production facilities as well as a company training establishment.

In the process the FFB acquired two more sites in Kassel, one in Lohfelden and the other in Waldau not far from the aerodrome, which was used for test flights. These sites were known in the company as No 2 Works and No. 3 Works respectively. But it was a good investment, as far as the Ministry was concerned. The first Messerschmitt 109 took to the air just fifteen months from the placing of the contract. Normally preparation for serial production was 'two and half years with one year for prototype construction and another year for testing.'[54] There can be no doubt that the capacity to build reliable aircraft in relatively fast times had helped make Fieseler's company a favoured supplier to the Aviation Ministry. The failure with the Stuka was seemingly a thing of the past.

51   I. Nonaka, I. and H. Takeuchi, *The Knowledge-Creating Company: How Japanese Companies Create the Dynamics of Innovation*, p.31.
52   Nagel und Bauer, op. cit., p.232.
53   Fieseler, op. cit., p.219.
54   Homze, op. cit., p.118.

In the meantime in 1938 the Storch went on show far beyond Germany. With the company's chief pilot at the controls, the novel aircraft headed for Poland, the Balkans and Turkey. A well-known pilot, Emil Kropf, took one to the USA, where the newspapers were full of reports about the famous 'slow-speed aircraft.'[55] This tour was followed by a tour of Scandinavia. The Storch was even used in Spitzbergen for a scientific expedition, where – good practice for the coming war – it had to land and take off on floating ice sheets.[56] By now the Aviation Ministry, satisfied that the Storch had an unassailable technical lead, had granted permission for it to be sold abroad, but sales were not permitted to the British Empire, France, the Soviet Union, Lithuania, and Czechoslovakia.[57] In 1937 the first orders were placed by Italy, Yugoslavia and Sweden.[58]

In November 1936 the Fieseler company was commissioned to build a seaplane for an aircraft carrier under construction. The ship in question was the *Graf Zeppelin*, which had been laid down at the end of 1936. Mewes led the design team and this time, Fieseler notes with pleasure, his working relationship with this 'too confident and difficult man' proceeded without a hitch.[59] In November 1937 the Fi 167 with its novel foldable wings made its maiden flight.

Based on the Storch, it was designed to land almost vertically on the moving vessel. If the plane inadvertently came into contact with the water, the pilot could release the undercarriage in order to give the plane more buoyancy and so increase the chance of rescue for the pilot, if he had not made use of the instantly inflatable rubber dinghy. In comparison with the hundred or so aircraft that Fieseler had flown, the Fi 167 was described as 'a wonderful machine' and 'a treat to fly (*eine fliegerische Delikatesse*).'[60]

The Aviation Ministry was impressed too and ordered a limited production run of 15. But it never came to a contract to supply the Fi 167 in quantity. According to Fieseler, this was because the *Graf Zeppelin* was destroyed by bombing at the beginning of the war. This was not correct. In 1940 the building of the aircraft carrier was abandoned, when it was 90% completed, and towed to the East Prussian port Gotenhafen, today's Gydnia.[61] At the end of 1947 it saw its last days in the Baltic Sea, where the Soviet military finished it off as a target for weapons testing.

The saving of Herr Wilhelm David and his family

In the summer of 1936 Fieseler's secretary informed him that a certain Herr Wilhelm David had come to see him. For a moment Fieseler did not recognise the name. Then his secretary explained that David was a member of the Order of the Prussian Golden Military Merit Cross, the highest award for bravery in the First World War for NCOs and enlisted men. The penny dropped. David and he were both members of the order, so Fieseler did know him slightly. The point was that Fieseler, 'at the insistence' of unnamed people, had taken over the chairmanship of the local branch for award holders. David was Jewish, but as a recipient of that august decoration was exempt from the general anti-Semitic harassment.[62] He explained that in his small town of Grebenstein, where he ran a shoe and textile store, there were five Jewish families and two had been forced out the previous night. David, looking pale and with doleful eyes, was now fearful for himself and his own family.

---

55 Norden, op. cit., p.49.
56 Nagel und Bauer, op. cit., p.138.
57 Ibid, p.127.
58 Ibid, p.248.
59 Ibid, p.220.
60 Ibid, p.220.
61 Ibid, p.159.
62 Ibid, p.216.

Fieseler said he would take up the cudgels on David's behalf. He would write a personal letter to the Gauleiter and request clarification. A sceptical Herr David left Fieseler's office with his head lowered, bracing himself for certain impending misfortune. Fieseler wrote to the Gauleiter 'in expectation of a positive decision.'[63] No reply came and before long David paid a second visit to Fieseler. Forlornly he explained that his family was now the last Jewish one in Grebenstein and that his customers only dared buy from him at night time. By now there was a virtual boycott on buying things from Jewish-owned shops. Culprits in Nazi eyes could face reprimand not to mention social stigmatization for infractions. After all no respectable citizen would not want a sign outside his house bearing the ominous words: 'I have disgraced Christianity.'[64]

'They'll soon be knocking on my door,' said David in desperation. 'It's the end of us.'[65] Fieseler, completely flummoxed, offered David some money. 'There's nothing I can do', moaned David. Fieseler saw himself 'confronted with an incomprehensible injustice' and racked his brains for a solution, but then he had an idea, admittedly a risky one. 'Come back in half an hour.' Once David had gone, Fieseler dictated and signed a letter on his personal correspondence paper:

> It is hereby certified that in accordance with the instruction of the Deputy Führer, Rudolf Hess, it is not permissible to boycott the business of Herr Wilhelm David, the bearer of this letter, or to take adverse action (*nachteilige Maßnahmen*) against him in any way. The undersigned is a Knight of the Prussian Golden Military Merit Cross.[66]

Fieseler made copies of the letter, which had of course no authority whatsoever, though David appears not to have appreciated that. David repaired to Grebenstein, showed the letter to the mayor of Grebenstein who was equally taken in, and had one posted on the window of David's shop. David then went to the local Nazi authorities, who, vastly impressed at a letter invoking the instruction of the Führer's deputy, proceeded to congratulate Herr David for his conspicuous service to the fatherland.

In due course Fieseler received a non-committal letter from the Gauleiter, which prompts him to say something which prompted a frankly preposterous comment in his autobiography. 'The case of David', he recalls, 'was for me the first sign that something was not quite right in the Third Reich.'[67] If this is his first sign of something rotten in Hitler's Germany, we have to wonder what he has been doing for the last few years. On the positive side, however, if the incident with David did take place as described, Fieseler took an exceptionally courageous step. A more fanatical Gauleiter might have made life for him seriously uncomfortable.

It happened that David and his family managed to live for two more years without harassment. Then they made for Breslau, where they must have hoped that life would be safe or at least safer.[68] From there were taken away to a concentration camp. Even there, it seems, they were protected by Fieseler's letter. David and his family survived the horrors of incarceration and he, full of gratitude, could subsequently tell Fieseler about their miraculous salvation when they moved back to Grebenstein after the war. Fieseler then told David the truth behind the letter. It was a ruse, he told him, pure invention. David could scarcely believe that a letter which some ten years he held

63 Fieseler, op. cit., p.216.
64 R. Chotjewitz-Häfner. Juden haben keinen Zutritt: Die Auflösung der jüdischen Landgemeinden in Osthessen. In: U. Schneider, K. Boehm, P. Grünewald, U. Krause-Schmidt, R. Neuhaus and R. Winkler. (Hrsg.). *Hessen vor 50 Jahren – 1933*, p.143.
65 Fieseler, op. cit., p.216.
66 Ibid, p.217.
67 Ibid, p.217.
68 Wiederhold, op. cit., p.242.

to be genuine carried no authority whatsoever. But it was a piece of deception that saved him and his family from a gruesome fate. Fieseler was scarcely in the same league as Oskar Schindler, but not every German in Nazi Germany would have dared to counter injustice against Jewish acquaintances.

There is one more aspect of this story which requires comment. Fieseler tells us that he accepted the chairmanship of the local association of the Order of the Prussian Golden Military Merit Cross as a result of emphatic local encouragement. That source can only have been the Nazi Party. The Nazi world-view the veterans of the First World War, of whom the greatest of them all, Adolf Hitler, was one, were accorded special glorification. They were the loyal ones who had been betrayed – stabbed in the back – in 1918 and were an inspiration to the new Germany, which would in the fullness of time remove the stain of the Versailles Treaty. From the point of view of the local Nazi party bosses Fieseler was an excellent catch for the chairmanship: a highly-decorated fighter pilot, a world-famous aviator, a builder of aircraft for the new Germany, and, of course, a member of the Nazi party himself. But perhaps Fieseler simply welcomed the opportunity to serve Germany as a local dignitary in this particular way. It presumably allowed him to support one particular cause of the Nazis, with which he identified with genuine fellow-feeling.

Industrial life Nazi-style

By the time war broke out in Europe in September 1939, FFB was producing the Storch in substantial numbers and building various other aircraft under licence. The company had a reputation for aircraft that were extremely reliable, value for money and delivered on time, if not ahead of schedule. At every level in the company the watchwords were 'discipline, hard work and trustworthiness.'[69] Fieseler regarded himself as a boss, who was happy to delegate responsibility to his key colleagues, but saw himself as the person who in the end had to act and make decisions. But in practice he could not quite control the company in the way that suited him temperamentally because he was required to run its affairs in conformity with the prevailing Nazi ideology. This led to occasional clashes within the company with self-important party stalwarts appointed by the German Labour Front – *die Deutsche Arbeitsfront* – hereafter DAF – which was charged with the Nazification of the workplace. The DAF people were little experienced in the world of industrial production and so made the daily management of the company 'hard going.'[70]

In practice Nazification of any kind of endeavour in the Third Reich meant subservience to Nazi convictions about Germany as a sacred entity under the beneficent guidance of the Führer and compliance with Nazi ideals. It follows from this that the place of work in Nazi Germany was an extremely important place for the coercive, dynamic inculcation of Nazi ideals under the sinister portmanteau term *Gleichschaltung* ('forcing into line'), which we have already encountered. But it was not enough for the Nazis to just control people: they 'wanted to transform them into a cohesive, racially pure "national community" (*Volksgemeinschaft*), whereby 'community aliens' (*Gemeinschaftsfremden*) such as Jews, gypsies, homosexuals, those hereditary diseases, and "a-social" people' and other '"pollutants" of the social body' could be excluded.[71] In line with this policy Fieseler's company, as we shall see, operated a recruitment scheme, one aim of which was to ensure that it only took on people from the 'national community.'

By the mid to late 1930s FFB was fully in tune with the direction of things and acquired the big-sounding Nazi jargon to go with it. Fieseler himself refers to his company as 'an enterprise community' (*Betriebsgemeinschaft*), created out of management and the mass of employees. This

69 Fieseler, op. cit., p.228.
70 Fieseler, op. cit., p.222.
71 M. Fulbrook, *History of Germany 1918-2000: The Divided Nation*, p.61.

enterprise community was ultimately at the disposal of the National-Socialist movement under the Führer Adolf Hitler, whereby:

> Owners and managers alike bought enthusiastically into the rhetoric of *Führertum'* – the blessed state of being under the supreme leader. It meshed all too well with the concept of *Unternehmertum* (entrepreneurial leadership) that had become increasingly fashionable in business circles, an ideological counterpoint to the interventionist tendencies of the trade unions and the Weimar welfare state.[72]

The corresponding German for employees in this context is *Gefolgschaft*, a collective noun meaning literally 'retinue,' 'entourage' or 'followers', implying a large number of them. But historically the word has connotations of fealty and allegiance. In practice then the company *Gefolgschaft* is loyal and obedient to its leader just as the entire German people is (in principle) loyal and obedient to its leader. Fieseler habitually referred to his employees as his *Gefolgschaft*. Thus in its ideal form the Nazi enterprise was one that evolved into 'a living powerfully symbolic entity, infused with [Nazi] politics and the spirit of the times and ultimately explicable in terms of the state' (*eine lebendige, stark symbolhaltige, geistespolitisch geprägte Einheit, die ihren letzten Sinn im Staate hat*).[73]

In line with this everyone who worked for the Fieseler company (until foreign compulsory labour was drafted in in 1940) shared the same fate and helped to create what Wiederhold describes as 'a stylised community, in which according to National-Socialist ideology it was not possible for there to be contrasting interests based on social or class factors.'[74] In short, FFB was a place where everyone, whatever his position or skill, was expected to serve the Führer to the best of his or her ability.

William Shirer has aptly described the status of the German worker in the Third Reich – 'deprived of his trade unions, collective bargaining and the right to strike' – as 'the serfdom of labour.'[75] Under the Law Regulating National Labour of 20 January 1934, 'the employees and labourers owe [to the employer] faithfulness.' That means, as Shirer reminds us, 'they were to work hard and long, and no back talk or grumbling, even about wages.'[76] Throughout the land it was an uncompromising approach to management, but it would be mistaken to see it as unfair in its operation. The fundamental premise was that every worker would wish to *display* the all-important virtues of discipline, hard work and trustworthiness. It would be un-German – not just unNazi – to do otherwise. Interestingly, a study, published in 2002, characterised German management as 'a tough on the issue, tough on the person' leadership approach,' adding that 'compassion is low and interpersonal relations are straightforward and stern.'[77] That could have been said of FFB in the late 1930s. After all Fieseler himself described management (he used the word *Führung*) in his company as 'firm-handed, goal-centred and authoritarian' (*straff, zielbewusst, autoritär*).[78]

A key person in Nazi industrial organisation was the *Obmann*, which translates variously as chairman, foreman or shop-steward. The senior *Obmann* – the *Betriebsobmann* – was certainly not a chairman in the sense of company chairman, but he was definitely more than a foreman. He worked directly below the *Betriebsführer* (i.e. Fieseler) in such a way that the latter was never quite master of his own house. A Party appointee, he acted as a political commissar, having responsibility not only

---

72 A. Tooze, *The Wages of Destruction: The Making and Breaking of the Nazi Economy*, p.102.
73 Cited in Wiederhold, op. cit., p.89.
74 Wiederhold, op. cit., p.79.
75 W. Shirer, *The Rise and Fall of the Third Reich*, p.327.
76 Ibid, p.328
77 F. Brodbeck, M. Frese and M. Javidan, Leadership made in Germany: Low on Compassion, High on Performance, *Academy of Management Executive*, Vol. 16, No. 1, p.16-29.
78 Wiederhold, op. cit., p.129.

for 'the political goings-on and social needs' (*das politische Geschehen und die sozialen Belange*), but for also 'the eradication from the company community and tracking down (*zur Strecke bringen*) of politically unclean, asocial elements.'[79] Reporting to the *Betriebsobmann* was the so-called *Werkschar* (lit. works horde), the storm troopers of the company – the active face of the Nazi propaganda machine at the FFB. They would take part in uniformed parades on special days to mark Hitler's birthday or to welcome Nazi dignitaries. When the company employed foreign labour in wartime, the *Werkschar* were on hand to cajole, intimidate and mete out beatings.

The *Werkschar* was in turn divided into a *Werktrupp* and a *Stosstrupp*. The *Werktrupp* was especially responsible for the political well-being and monitoring of the workforce (*politische Betreuung*), whilst the *Stosstrupp* was broken down into three 'task forces' (*Arbeitsgruppen*) for training, health at work and for the activities of the Strength-through-Joy movement (*Kraft durch Freude*). The KDF was a large state-operated organization, whose mission was to promote and support affordable leisure, cultural and sporting activities, whilst infusing them Nazi values. In its day it was one of the world's biggest tourist operators. The *Stosstrupp* was also at hand to ensure that the loud-speakers for company mass meetings and rallies were in good order, that everyone knew the words of the Nazi battle songs, and that the Nazi flag fluttered conspicuously. Overall then the *Werkschar* was responsible for anything to do reinforcing the Nazi message among the workforce. In the words of the company newspaper in 1938, the *Werkschar* is 'the bearer of National-Socialist thought (*Gedankengut*) in the company.'[80]

In common with other Nazi enterprises FFB employed *Unterführer* (lit. 'sub-leader(s)'. This title was accorded to master craftsmen and department heads who had particular responsibility for the education of apprentices. But it was also task of the *Unterführer* to monitor 'order, attitude and readiness for responsibility.'[81] At their disposal were the contributions to the company suggestion scheme (*Vorschlagswesen*), which in FFB attracted more than a hundred suggestions a month.[82] The scheme may well have been a useful source of good ideas and 'a safety valve for positive criticism', but it may have also served as a mechanism for identifying ideological malcontents.[83]

Overall the management system at the Fieseler company, as in all enterprises in Nazi Germany, was also reinforced daily with the visual symbols of Nazism: uniforms, flags, the Hitler salute and greeting, and the parades. Throughout all the enterprises in Germany, on the basis of the almost feudal obedience, undisguised use of menace, the manipulation of language, and the concomitant emphasis on subordination to the ideals of Nazism, the industrial leader could become a cameo of the Führer himself. Fieseler was indeed a well-developed example of *betriebliches Führertum* (industrial 'führerdom') in thought, word and deed.

But, however much he was keen to build aircraft for the Luftwaffe, Fieseler did not always take kindly to the way in which the Nazis influenced behaviour at work. The key body for introducing change was, as noted, the DAF. The problem for Fieseler was that the DAF people had no experience in the day-to-day running of an industrial plant, and that made things difficult for owners like Fieseler. Worse, many of them had been nobodies before 1933 and were intoxicated with power. Where possible, Fieseler would get Thalau or the reliable Bachem to sort matters out with the DAF, though there were times when he intervened when one or other of them 'lacked the necessary

---

79 Ibid, p.142.
80 Ibid, p.139.
81 Budrass, op. cit., p.814.
82 Norden, op. cit., p.72.
83 Budrass, pp.814-815.

competences.'[84] All too often Fieseler to feel undermined, finding DAF interventions 'wrong, not to say damaging.'[85]

In other words, just as the Nazi state was guided by the Führer himself, so Nazi enterprises were to be commanded by top managers who were themselves lesser Führers, who eagerly imbibed the Nazi discourse and used it explicitly as a management communication tool. For such mini-Führers their employees were a consciously nurtured as a *Volksgemeinschaft* in its own right and were required – just as in the Nazi armed services – to perform their duties with 'order and discipline, command and obedience' for the glory of Hitler's Germany, and woe betide those who stood in the way.[86] No wonder a rather risqué quip was doing the rounds: 'We can stand Hitler, but there are all those other little Hitlers.'[87] And there was no shortage of those.

Aquatic therapy for the Fieseler workforce
Fieseler, who 'from the outset had managed his company in a paternalistic manner (*patriarchalisch*) and placed great value on the wellbeing of his workforce,' set about introducing amenities and facilities for his employees.[88] There was enormous emphasis on a sense of belonging and 'social achievements' (*soziale Errungenschaften*), that is to say amenities for the workforce ranging from purpose-built subsidised accommodation (not least as a recruitment incentive to workers who would have to move to Kassel from other parts of Germany), in-house medical care and leisure activities, all of which helped to reinforce Nazi ideology in the workplace. There was, Germany being a land of music, a company choir, a string orchestra, a brass orchestra and a harmonica group. There were sports clubs, clubs for chess players, photography enthusiasts and, of course, builders of model aircraft as well as staff trips to the theatre and concerts.

With all this going on one wonders how the workforce found the time to build aircraft! Needless to say, all these activities were exploited to promote the ideals and advantages of National Socialism as well as to maintain a committed workforce. In the summer of 1939 all these activities were described in the company newspaper as achieving 'systematic' social cohesion.[89] 'Systematic' can only refer to one thing here: *Gleichschaltung* in its (more or less) perfected industrial form in the Fieseler company.

On the matter of accommodation, the company build housing for employees. This was an incentive to attract new employees with their families from afar to Kassel. It is also a reflection of the rapid growth of Fieseler's company since the early 1930s. A total of 341 families were offered accommodation in two company residences near Kassel. Many families lived in apartment blocks, whilst senior managers were offered detached houses. Accommodation was always reserved for foremen and especially engineers, critically important staff who had to be sourced from all over the German Reich. Applicants were subject to medical examination, one purpose of which was to ensure that they were 'of healthy stock' (*erbgesund*), showing no unacceptable blood line or other hereditary deficiency from the Nazi point of view.[90] Through this practice the Fieseler company in its own way subscribed to 'the notion of the blood community (*Blutgemeinschaft*) and an underpinning biological concept of people (*Volksbegriff*), according to which Germans through innate racial superiority had evolved into the master race (*Herrenvolk*).[91]

84 Fieseler, op. cit., p.222.
85 Ibid, p.225.
86 Wiederhold, op. cit., p.134.
87 Haffner, op. cit., p.201.
88 Nagel und Bauer, op. cit., p.125.
89 Wiederhold, op. cit., p.151.
90 Ibid, p.152-153.
91 V. Dahm, Die Blutgemeinschaft. In: V. Dahm, A. Feiber, H. Mehringer und H. Möller, *Die tödliche Utopie: Bilder, Texte, Dokumente, Daten zum Dritten Reich*, p.247.

Fieseler, ever aware that the success of FFB depended on a satisfied and well-motivated workforce, regarded as 'especially important' the health of his workers.[92] A healthy worker was more alert and therefore likely to produce sustained high-quality work and not cause or be involved in accidents in the production areas. Crucial was Fieseler's appointment of a certain Dr Mehren as his head doctor. Mehren, who headed a team of three other doctors on site, readily took to the environment of the factory as his practice and introduced medical examinations, syringed ears and when necessary referred people to specialist doctors. He and his colleagues were also on hand to treat accidents at work. A company poster produced in 1938 showed that 33% related to fingers, 15% to hands and 12.7% to eyes.[93] No doubt the high proportion of injuries to fingers and hands were a result of mishaps with machinery and contact with metal without proper protection.

Apparently in-company health-care was at the time so unheard of and so deeply associated with 'going to a doctor, waiting around for hours and in overcrowded, poorly ventilated waiting rooms' that the medical support had to be introduced with considerable sensitivity. Fieseler did not want to put anyone under pressure.'[94] His approach worked. By the outbreak of war, according to Norden, medical care was costing 70,000 marks a year (rising to 100,000 in 1940). He records, presumably on the basis of his conversations with Fieseler, that 1,000 men and women went to the company doctor *every month*. Hundreds of others availed themselves of the solarium, röntgenoscopy tests and diathermic treatment.[95] There is a remarkable photograph, appearing in the July 1940 issue of the Fieseler Newspaper, showing some twenty cheery FFB employees thrashing around in a shallow pool near a company building. Men have their trousers rolled up and women their dresses hitched up over their knees. The hectic activity is being supervised by two gentlemen in white coats, no doubt the company doctors.[96]

If recommended by Mehren, FFB might even send people on cures. Lacquerers, being habitually exposed to noxious vapours, as well as apprentices, received free milk and even got meals recommended by the company's dietician. Fieseler's attitude was expressed in the company newspaper: 'The challenge of health management is not about making sick people healthy, but making certain that healthy people don't get sick.'[97] The company doctor had various assistants and dentists and could even call upon the *Werkschar*'s own first aiders. Care was not just limited to Fieseler personnel. It was extended to members of their families.

Nor was care limited to physical well-being. Fieseler, being a believer in motivation, was keen to establish rates of satisfaction – and dissatisfaction – among his workforce. He helped create a scheme for managing discontented employees (*Unzufriedenenbetreuung*), which he claimed 'bore beneficial fruit.'[98] It took two years to devise and implement the scheme which required people to rate their own satisfaction and dissatisfaction on a questionnaire. The idea was that immediate superiors could deal with dissatisfied workers. By means of the scheme the company could establish whether dissatisfaction sprang from internal factors such as fractious relationships in the actual place of work or external factors such as unsatisfactory accommodation or even problems with debts.'[99]

According to his secretary, writing in the company newspaper in 1942, the scheme 'came into being on the personal initiative of the managing director [i.e. Fieseler] and has shown its worth over and

---

92 Wiederhold, op. cit., p.145.
93 Nagel und Bauer, op. cit. p.134.
94 Fieseler, op. cit., p.229.
95 Norden, op. cit., pp.55-56.
96 Nagel und Bauer, op. cit., p.135.
97 Wiederhold, op. cit., p.146.
98 Fieseler, op. cit., p.233.
99 Wiederhold, op. cit., p.158.

over again.'¹⁰⁰ It is, however, more than plausible that the cases of some malcontents would be referred to the *Betriebsobmann*, who was ultimately responsible for dealing with matters which compromised Nazi ideology and policy. After the Second World War a witness in Fieseler's denazification tribunal said that there were cases of malcontents 'who ended up at the Gestapo or in jail.'¹⁰¹

Fieseler was certainly very proud of the social achievements of his company. He told Norden of his personal motivations and his concept of the workplace:

> If I am to find solutions to the tasks presented to me, then I must have a willing, hard-working and enthusiastic workforce. When for whatever reason this condition is disturbed, then I must know about it and remove the cause. I will not have unsatisfied people in the ranks of my workforce. I will do whatever is my power to see to it that unsatisfied people are removed. Everyone must do his work with a sense of freedom, without undue pressure and with joy (*Freude*). The workplace is where he spends the greater part of the day and it should be like a home to him. It is a piece of ground in which he takes root and to which he feels connected. He should be proud of his company.¹⁰²

There can be little doubt that the entire system created both high levels of motivation and a powerful sense of identification with the company and its achievements.¹⁰³ It is also incontestable that Fieseler himself was a driving force behind the socio-technical development of his company. Where they were straightforward, he put the DAF guidelines into practice, even presenting himself as the actual initiator of some of the innovations. In his mind the task of a leader was to look after employees, provide them with the best possible working conditions, and motivate them all from top to bottom. In the context of the Third Reich prior to the outbreak of the Second World War, Fieseler outstandingly exemplified these leadership principles, whilst going along with and occasionally ignoring Nazi expectations.

All this raises an interesting, if perturbing point. With all the knowledge we have today of Nazi Germany, it is easy to condemn everything about the regime in the harshest terms. But, if for once we can overcome our customary shock and repugnance, then surely the achievements of Gerhard Fieseler as an industrialist alone ought to elicit at least some admiration on our part.

That impudent Fieseler

In February 1937 Fieseler found himself in further discussions with the Aviation Ministry about the relationship between FFB and the Nazi state, including the issues of funding and investment. The Ministry was once again represented by its finance chief Alois Cejka who on this occasion noted that Fieseler was 'an unusually difficult personality', adding spiffily that it was one thing to build sports planes, but quite another thing to produce military aircraft.¹⁰⁴ The not so distant disaster with the Stuka was proof enough for Cejka. However, it seems that Fieseler was able to exploit a breakdown in communication between Cejka's department and that of Ernst Udet, which had a much greater regard for the prowess of FFB. For the time being Cejka was thwarted.

Around this time Fieseler found himself on a collision course with the DAF people who, knowing that FFB paid good wages, pressed for higher rates. Fieseler resisted their appeals, which he did not find reasonable, as much as he could. Then one day he was paid a visit by a regional

---

100   Ibid, p.158.
101   Ibid, p.162.
102   Norden, op. cit., p.63.
103   Wiederhold, op. cit., p.155.
104   Nagel und Bauer, op. cit., p.123.

DAF organiser in uniform. Fieseler was not to be browbeaten over the issue of wages. There was a violent argument between him and the DAF man, who, red in the face, declared that he would report Fieseler to the Gauleiter.

This particular incident did not appear to lead to reprisals, but it was not the end of troubles for Fieseler. On at least one occasion a DAF representative was selling *Der Stürmer*, a vehemently anti-Semitic Nazi weekly newspaper, on the company premises. Fieseler had him removed. Then he noticed a man with a gold party badge hanging around in a production bay. The production manager told Fieseler that he had been forced to take the man on and not give him a job that made him look unskilled. Making enquiries with his personal department, Fieseler discovered that the DAF had connived to get three veterans – a protected species in Nazi Germany – recruited and given nominal jobs.

Then one day Fieseler was asked to dismiss two employees and a further two shortly after that. He resisted the request, finding that there was no satisfactory justification to dismiss them. He appeared to enjoy a victory there. Then shortly after that incident came the case of a certain Major Ziegler, who was by all accounts a very competent worker, and thus Fieseler saw no reason to dismiss him. This was at a time when Fieseler's 'most difficult problem was finding workers with appropriate qualifications' in and around Kassel.[105] Unfortunately Ziegler, who was a reliable employee (we do not know what his job was), had been a member of the socialist party after the First World War and he was as such in the eyes of the DAF particularly suspect. Once more it came to a tussle, but before long the matter came to the attention of 'the all-powerful Gauleiter and State Counsellor Weinrich', who had duly received from the DAF certain 'allegations' about Fieseler.[106]

On hearing these charges Weinrich struck his table with his fist and declared that he would 'once and for all show that impudent Fieseler who was in charge of things.'[107] He would be paying Herr Fieseler a visit on such and such a day. On the appointed day Weinrich arrived with four SA heavies, his personal adjutant and his trade-mark accessory, a Hitler moustache. They entered Fieseler's office with five bulging files of documents, all of which indicated that Ziegler was not a suitable person to be working in an aircraft factory carrying out important work for the country. The conversation dragged for an hour. Fieseler had no difficulty rebutting Weinrich's case about Ziegler's alleged unsuitability and demonstrated that the Gauleiter's information was completely false. Weinrich, having been shown up in front of his minions, lost his temper. He brought down both his fists on Fieseler's table, accusing Fieseler for being such a fanatical stickler for the truth (*der reinste Wahrheitsfanatiker*).[108]

This was praise indeed from such a man, who was by now screaming at Fieseler at the top of his voice, whereupon Fieseler's own explosive temper was unleashed. Almost bursting out of his uniform, the most powerful Nazi in the Gau, Hitler's representative, then stood up and yelled: 'You dismiss those people. I insist on it.' To which Fieseler, again pointing out how specious were the allegations against Ziegler, rejoined: 'It is within your power to dismiss people from my company. You had better get rid me of me first.'[109] At that Weinrich, choking with anger, left with his obsequious entourage. He would be recommending Fieseler's dismissal to a higher level. Word about this explosive encounter quickly got round the company: 'The boss gave that big shot what for!'[110] But behind the approving whispers there must have lurked fearfulness for the boss's fate. Taking top Nazis down a peg or two was by no means advisable.

---

105   Fieseler, op. cit., p.223.
106   Ibid, p.226.
107   Ibid, p.226.
108   Ibid, p.227.
109   Ibid, p.227.
110   Ibid, p.227.

About a week later Fieseler heard from a reliable, but unnamed source that Weinrich – propaganda minister Goebbels described him as 'no shining light' around this time – had given instructions for Fieseler to be left in peace in future.[111] There was no dismissal. Fieseler's colleagues assumed that he had 'a good friend' in Berlin who stood by his 'civil courage.'[112] It is more likely, however, that Fieseler company's designation as a 'development firm' (i.e. one recognised as having a key role to play in German rearmament) in a key industry meant that he enjoyed special protection from the top against an over-zealous local Nazi satrap.

After all, as Fieseler himself records at this specific juncture, Hermann Göring, commander-in-chief of the Luftwaffe and Minister-President of Prussia, had visited Kassel twice and was seen by the public in conversation with Fieseler. The first of these visits had taken place in early June 1933, by which time the build-up of the Luftwaffe was already in motion. The conversations between the two former ace fighter pilots then or on the later occasion were surely not just limited to exchanging their wartime experiences. Göring would have had far weightier things to discuss with Kassel's most famous aviator and well-regarded aircraft builder, Herr Fieseler. Here after all was a man who was in the mould of the new up-coming industrial leader so prized by the Nazi leadership: 'dynamic, hands-on (*handsärmelig*) ... unhesitatingly enthusiastic' for their cause.[113] Göring, as we shall discover, had things in mind for Fieseler.

Fieseler's use of the expression 'civil courage' requires comment. It was famously used by the 19th century German Chancellor Bismarck who remarked that it denoted something rare in German society and 'deserted a German the moment he put on a uniform.'[114] Perhaps Fieseler is trying to persuade us that he was in fact a man who was not lacking in civil courage at least on this occasion. But let us allow him his moment of self-glorification. There were countless other Germans who showed no civil courage at all during the Third Reich (which again raises the question: what we, in the face of the intimidatory machinery at the disposal of the Nazis, have done in their place?)

In the meantime FFB continued to grow. At the end of 1937 the company had a turn-over of 13 million Reichsmarks and employed 4,200 people, including 100 designers. In addition to the Storch it was building aircraft under licence for Messerschmitt, Arado and Heinkel. In 1937 350 new aircraft left the FFB production lines.[115] This expansion, which eventually included the building of a 100-metre long firing range, was accompanied by injections of new staff.[116] A notable addition in 1938 was Willy Fiedler, who had qualified in engineering from the Technical University of Stuttgart, was a qualified pilot, had worked on aircraft design projects and had obtained one of the new DVL qualifications in aircraft production. Before joining FFB he had worked for the British Aircraft Manufacturing Co. Ltd as assistant to the chief designer. A letter of recommendation from the company dated 9 October 1935 described Fiedler as 'an extremely clever engineer.'[117] He then worked for the prestigious aircraft research establishment at Rechlin in north-east Germany. He became responsible for prototype testing at FFB and would become greatly valued by Fieseler, and not only him.[118]

---

111 T. Schattner, (undated). 'Der gute Weinrich ist keine Leuchte' – vor 80 Jahren wurde Karl Weinrich Gauleiter der NSDAP von Kurhessen. Accessed at: http://www.gedenkstaette-breitenau.de/rundbrief/RB-26-59.pdf.
112 Fieseler, op. cit., p.227.
113 K-D Henke, *Die amerikanische Besetzung Deutschlands,* p.451.
114 Beevor, op. cit., p.4.
115 Nagel und Bauer, op. cit., p.130.
116 Ibid, p.131.
117 https://ritstaalman.files.wordpress.com/2014/09/willy-fiedler.pdf
118 Nagel und Bauer, op. cit., p.127-128.

Accolades and honours

By now Fieseler, whether he have would admitted it or not, was an accomplice of Nazi pomp, swagger and arrogance. It is unclear exactly when this irreversibly happened, but two events in 1937 are of great significance. If in 1933 he joined the Nazi party in order to secure orders for his growing company, in 1937 he received two marks of favour which immediately identified him with the Nazi cause. They far outweighed his role as chairman as a local war veterans' association in significance. The first of these distinctions Fieseler plays down, only referring to it in the context of what happened to him after the defeat of Nazi Germany. The second event he does not mention at all.

The first mark of favour is linked to the transformation in April 1937 of the innocent-sounding German Air Sports Association into the National Socialist Flying Corps. As was the way in the Third Reich, the Nazi Flying Corps dropped the previous sporting activities in favour of paramilitary ones befitting the new, resurgent Germany. Not only did it conduct military aviation training, it also provided a pool of air enthusiasts for enrolment in the Luftwaffe. Being a paramilitary organisation and Germany being Germany, the Flying Corps had a hierarchy of full-time officers and honorary officers, who were awarded ranks and entitled to wear a uniform. In December 1937 Gerhard Fieseler, who had completed the First World War with the rank of lieutenant, now found himself elevated to the honorary rank of *Standartenführer*, which roughly equated to colonel in the British system and was also in use in the SS.[119]

The rank of *Standartenführer* entitled him to wear Nazi insignia as well as his decorations from the First World War. Photographs show him on his company premises wearing his uniform with all the regalia. Oak leaves encrust his lapels, an array of medals, an aviation badge and his Iron Cross embellish the left breast of his uniform, decorated epaulets enhance his authority. He may not have worn it every day, but was frequently seen in it in the presence of Nazi dignitaries. He would have no doubt worn it on notable days such as the Führer's birthday. It is hard to imagine that he did not like the extra authority it gave him especially as he could wear his decorations from the First World War. Against that, it would have been unthinkable for Fieseler, as one of Germany's most famous aviators, to decline membership of the Nazi Flying Corps. Such a step would have been tantamount to displaying disloyalty to the Führer and betrayal of the Fatherland, both unforgivable sins in the Nazi world view, as Fieseler would have definitely known.

The other elevation, unmentioned by Fieseler, took place in December 1937, when his contribution to German rearmament was recognised with his designation by Göring to the appointment of *Wehrwirtschaftsführer*, for which the general rendering in English is defence economy leader. This title was reserved for around 100 industrialists in charge of 'armament-important firms who would be 'made aware of the significance of national defence and prepared for the requirements of a possible mobilisation.'[120] In fact Fieseler was among one of 24 heads of aircraft manufacturers to receive this appointment in 1937. Other equally enhanced air industry leaders included Claude Dornier, Ernst Heinkel and Willy Messerschmitt. Commenting on Fieseler's appointment, the *Kasseler Post* newspaper noted that his new status was a result of having rendered exceptional services in the material build-up … and material readinesss …of the armed forces.' The chosen ones 'commit themselves … to an exceptional extent to be loyal to the state and armed forces (*im besonderem Maße zu einem Treue-Verhältnis zum Staat und zur Wehrmacht*)'.[121]

As a mark of their exclusive status these honoured industrial leaders were all entitled to wear a special gilded badge – nowadays an 'extremely rare' item for collectors of Nazi memorabilia – with

---

119 Wiederhold, op. cit., p.226.
120 M. Pabst, *Willy Messerschmitt: Zwölf Jahre Flugzeugbau im Führerstaat*, p.18.
121 *Kasseler Post*, 15.12.1937. Cited in Wiederhold, op. cit.p.227.

a design depicting 'a factory complex belching smoke'.[122] Among other things, the members of this industrial élite were granted exceptional authority to ensure that items required by the state (i.e. aircraft) would be delivered on time and of the right quality. For example, they could order night work and switch personnel around 'without seeking permission from the relevant bodies,'[123] notably the DAF. To secure such autonomy at the workplace was a considerable mark of favour and would accordingly have been granted only to those whose loyalty to the Nazi regime was not in doubt. By 1937 Gerhard Fieseler had of course shown himself to be worthy of Nazi trust. Like other favoured industrialists Fieseler 'maintained considerable power to make … business decisions without governmental interference, even during the war.'[124]

Whilst Fieseler was receiving personal awards, his company began to receive accolades too. In 1938 FFB earned a national achievement award after being judged to be an exemplary occupational training establishment (*Berufserziehungsstätte*). In the previous year the DAF had announced a nation-wide competition to recognise firms which organised work and working conditions both in terms of best general practice and, of course, integration of its Nazi ideals into industrial life. Evidently Fieseler and his management team 'must have identified with the goals of the competition and so it was decided that they would take part.'[125]

FFB's success in 1938 was marked by company celebrations including parades with accompanying martial music (supplied by the company orchestra), the hoisting of flags, and an address by Fieseler himself in front of the acclaimed apprentices and dignitaries, including Gauleiter Karl Weinrich, presumably now assuaged. In his speech Fieseler thanked the DAF for facilitation of the award and then proceeded – mindful of his audience, which also included the commander of inspection for the military industries no less – to emphasise the importance of apprentices in the Nazi state.[126] This was a theme close to Fieseler's heart; it also fitted in with Hitler's masterplan for Germany, in which the young were seen as 'the guarantors of the future shape of [Nazi] polity and the maintenance of the Third Reich.'[127]

There can be no doubt the Fieseler company in the 1930s was seen as a highly attractive place to work, not just because of its prestige, but also because of the apprenticeship scheme. As just indicated, the company 'placed especial value on apprenticeships to secure its human capital for the future (*Nachwuchs*).'[128] Apprentices learnt their craft in workshops which were equipped with the latest technology. The company created its own vocational training school to underpin the four-year programme of instruction, which was strictly regulated.

According to Norden, FFB apprentices were so enthusiastic that you could see the blaze in their eyes.[129] However, one former apprentice recorded that everything was 'organised along military lines' (*militärisch organisiert*), adding that 'at midday we were escorted to the canteen for something to eat and in the evening escorted to the main exit. If anyone went to the toilet in work time, he had to sign out and it would be recorded on a card.'[130] The formal entry requirements for apprenticeships were a school leaving certificate and, not surprisingly, membership of the Hitler Youth. By this time apprentices knew the way the wind was blowing. In the words of August Meier, a press operator at the Zeppelin factory at Germany's southern extremity. 'You could think whatever

122 C. Ailsby, *A Collector's Guide to German Nazi Party Awards,* pp.154-156.
123 Wiederhold, op. cit., p.226.
124 Wiesen, op. cit., p.15
125 Nagel und Bauer, op. cit., p.125.
126 Wiederhold, op. cit., p.111.
127 Ibid, p.138.
128 Ibid, p.155-155.
129 Ibid, p.78.
130 Ibid, p.155.

you wanted. But woe betide anyone who did not raise his arm in a Hitler salute.'[131] Gerhard Fieseler knew which way the wind was blowing too.

The achievement award for training excellence in turn enabled the Fieseler company to take part in a nation-wide competition to secure the prestigious and emulative title of National-Socialist Exemplary Enterprise (*NS-Musterbetrieb*). In all 80,559 firms entered the competition. The Fieseler company was one of just 73 to receive Nazi Germany's highest award for industrial achievement, which was bestowed not only for technological performance but also for its application of Nazi ideals at the workplace. In April 1938 Dr Thalau and the Betriebsobmann Wilhelm Stahlhut accepted the award at a ceremony in Berlin presided over by Deputy Führer Rudolf Hess.[132]

Nazi exemplary enterprises were those 'in which the thought of the national socialist industrial community (*Betriebsgemeinschaft*) had been realised at the highest level of perfection.' In accordance with Nazi aspiration these outstanding firms maintained 'the survival and viability (*Lebenssicherung*) of our German people' … [through] … 'the highest possible productive performance', requiring in turn 'the highest possible input (*Krafteinsatz*) of very single skilled worker (*Schaffenden*) to be set even higher.'[133] Fieseler had the satisfaction of knowing that his young company ranked among the absolute best industrial firms in the land. Indeed his company went on to win the prize for four years in row until the competition was discontinued in the war.

FFB was now entitled to use a celebratory plaque on his its premises and fly the specially designed 'golden flag' with its gold braiding showing a swastika enclosed inside a cogged wheel. To mark the momentous occasion, on 30 April – the Führer's birthday – there was a gathering of the great and the good on the company premises with speeches by Dr Thalau (Fieseler was apparently ill at the time) and a no doubt beaming Gauleiter Weinrich. There was a KDF film about Norway. After the film there was a special rendition of Strauss's Blue Danube by the company orchestra and choir. Then at last Fieseler's hard-working staff were treated to an evening of festivities with dancing, tombola and prize-giving. The first prize of the tombola was KDF motor bike; the second prize was a KDF cruise to Madeira.

On the next day, 1 May, National Work Day, the official standard, topped by a Nazi eagle above the Fieseler logo, was borne first through the streets of Kassel which were festooned with Nazi flags and then, to the strains of military music provided by the company orchestra, it was paraded around Number One Works. There the golden flag was officially hoisted on the company flagpole.[134] Fieseler marked the occasion with a message to his staff in the company newspaper:

> With great pleasure I can today make it known to my members of staff that, to mark this year's festive National Work Day, our enterprise been declared by the Führer and Chancellor 'a National Socialist Exemplary Enterprise … We shall not allow other successes to elude us … we can look with pride on our joint effort for our Führer and our greater German fatherland (*unser grossdeutsches Vaterland.*)
>
> Heil Hitler![135]

The Fieseler company, being regarded as one of the best run enterprises in Germany, was for sure a model for other companies. In 1937 as a further innovation it had inaugurated its so-called

---

131 Citation from a display in the Zeppelin Museum in Friedrichshafen.
132 Wiederhold, op. cit., pp.111-112.
133 Proceedings of the award ceremony, cited in Wiederhold, op. cit., p.211.
134 Nagel und Bauer, op. cit., pp.136-137.
135 Wiederhold, op. cit., p.115.

'customer service house', where guests were received and where pilots could spend time in pleasant surroundings as they waited to pick up an aircraft. In June 1938 the facility was christened the Udet House with no doubt great approval by the eponymous one himself.[136] As befits a source of inspiration and ideas to the regime, FFB attracted a fair share of Nazi dignitaries; one of the most notable being was Robert Ley who was head of the DAF. There is a photograph of Ley and a widely grinning Fieseler in his Nazi uniform and regalia.[137] In May 1945 Ley was captured by American troops. In October he was indicted at the Nuremburg Trials, being charged among other things for maltreatment of prisoners of war who were serving as slave labour in Germany. He committed suicide in his prison cell. Ley was one of three prominent Nazis, known personally to Fieseler, would take their own lives in or immediately after the end of the war in 1945.

In July 1938 FFB was closely involved in another kind of public event. It was a sponsor of the Nazi Air Day, which attracted some 70,000 spectators. Fiedler and other FFB pilots showed off the new Messerschmitt 109 fighters. Vera von Bissing delighted the crowds with an aerobatics display, but it was perhaps Germany's most famous aviatrix of the 20th century, Hanna Reitsch, who gave a dazzling display in her aerobatics glider. A woman of allure and charisma, Reitsch was one of several highly intelligent German women to be in complete thrall to Hitler. Another performer was Germany's current aerobatics champion, Albert Falderbaum. Fieseler himself did a turn in a Storch, following a display by the de la Cierva autogiro, the plane that came the closest to the Storch in performance. Now the public could see for themselves 'which advantages the Fieseler plane possessed over the autogiro.'[138] Afterwards all the performers were entertained in the Udet House. Fieseler had good reason to feel well satisfied with the success of his company and the acclaim that he was personally receiving. Besides that, he was confident that under the Führer the welfare, prestige and fate of Germany were in very good hands.

---

136 Nagel und Bauer, op. cit., p.126 and p.138-139.
137 Wiederhold, op. cit., p.137. On 22 July 2015 *The Times* published of photograph of Ley with the Duke of Windsor during the latter's much disapproved of visit to Germany in 1937.
138 Nagel und Bauer, op. cit, p.141.

9

If we lose this war

Only he [Hitler] knew where Providence was leading him; the people were simply expected to follow.
Michael Burleigh[1]

Germans did not have to be Nazis to fight for Hitler, but they would discover that it was impossible to remain untouched by the ruthlessness of the war and the apocalyptic mentality it created.
Nicholas Stargardt[2]

The Grand Vizier holds court

Fieseler was by now no minor figure in the armaments sector of the Third Reich. He was one the country's top industrialists in the aircraft construction sector. As a further mark of favour, in July 1938 Fieseler received a personal invitation from Hermann Göring, commander-in-chief of the Luftwaffe among other appointments, to attend a gathering of senior aircraft company managers. The venue was at Carinhall, Göring's fabled hunting lodge located in the Schorfheide Forest north of Berlin. Named after his deceased first wife, the extravagant residence was not only his hunting lodge, but also his imperial palace, where he wined and dined Nazi Germany's most important foreign guests. The invitation card, which Fieseler received, was of the finest hand-made paper and, befitting the potentate himself, 'unduly large.'[3] At the entrance to the drive was a guard house and Fieseler estimated that there were a good hundred Luftwaffe men on hand in the grounds to protect Nazi Germany's 'crown prince,'[4] alias 'Grand Vizier' in the apt formulation of the British historian, Hugh Trevor-Roper.[5]

On either side of asphalt drive there were enclosures where Göring kept exotic animals, including a herd of large cattle which had been cross-bred in a bizarre attempt to restore the extinct aurochs to Europe. The drive finally opened out into an ample forecourt for parking vehicles. Drivers were instructed to proceed to the parking area. There was a building for them where they could relax and get something to eat and drink. Fieseler was ushered into a spacious reception room eight metres high and occupying some 300 to 400 square metres. This was the famed baronial hunting hall (*Jagdhalle*), all hammerbeams and antlers.[6] There he found himself in the company of 22 dark-suited men, many of whom he already knew by sight. There could be no doubt about it. Göring had brought together his chosen élite of armaments industry leaders, who were tasked with building up

---

1   M. Burleigh, *The Third Reich: A New History*, p.156
2   N. Stargardt, *The German War: A Nation Under Arms, 1939-1945*, p.7.
3   G. Fieseler, *Meine Bahn am Himmel*, p.236.
4   Ibid, p.236.
5   H. Trevor-Roper, *The Last Days of Hitler*, p.13.
6   For photograph, go to https://www.google.co.uk/search?q=carinhall+jagdhalle&espv=2&biw=1366 &bih=643&source=lnms&tbm=isch&sa=X&ved=0ahUKEwil9--Ks9HLAhWGBBoKHfEqAx8Q_AUIBygC&dpr=1#imgrc=XOkDaLFxc9OcIM%3A

the Luftwaffe. They were all huddled together, whispering. Wherever he looked, Fieseler saw in the faces of the other guests 'awe, curiosity and anticipation.'[7] He noted that he was the youngest in the party and that his company was the smallest among those represented.

It is impossible not to conclude that he is trying to persuade us that he was the least significant person there – not just a small cog in the Nazi war machine, but a rather insignificant one in comparison with the others. But there was no such thing in Nazi Germany as an armaments industry leader who was somehow a small cog. It is also extremely likely that Fieseler was much better acquainted with his fellow guests than he would have us believe. As for being the youngest person present, that was not true. Willy Messerschmitt, who was two years Fieseler's junior, was in attendance too. We might add that Göring himself was only three years older than Fieseler. But more to the point: Fieseler, Messerschmitt and the other industry bosses at the Carinhall gathering represented a new generation of the Nazi-influenced managers, namely the all-important 'technocrats of rearmament, who Hitler was putting his money on' for the greater glory of the Third Reich.[8]

After a while a flunky in a uniform from the time of Frederick the Great ascertained that everyone was present and correct, and then disappeared. Fieseler and the rest stood around, taking in the opulence of their surroundings. It occurred to nobody to sit down. 'The lord of the manner will be here soon,' whispered somebody knowingly to Fieseler. By now there was a palpable tension in the air. Then, at last, the over-large master of Carinhall himself made his entrance through a massive door, which was swung open for him. A master of ceremonies struck the floor three times with a staff to call everyone to attention. In his left hand Göring bore what Fieseler describes as 'a two metre long ceremonial staff.'[9] This may well have been his 'stick shaped like an ancient Germanic spear', with which he liked to impress his guests.[10] He was attired in a white leather uniform with a wide belt and golden buckle, and puffed sleeves. He had a jewelled dagger and exuded charisma and aloofness.

Göring passed imperiously through the midst of the industrialists without deigning to glance at anyone. Pausing at the end of a ten metre long table, he made a sweeping gesture of command. All sat. Fieseler tells us that he had difficulty suppressing a smile at the preposterous appearance of the second most powerful man in Germany, who was among other things the creator of the feared Gestapo. His comment is surely *ex post facto* phantasy. In the presence of such an intimidating man the very idea of smiling would never have crossed his mind. Göring began by saying that the Führer had bestowed on him responsibility for equipping the Luftwaffe for its future tasks and he would not fail the Führer in this. He then addressed his guests directly. 'All of you here are charged with building up the Luftwaffe', he said, adding menacingly' 'That means that your personal interests take second place.'[11]

There followed a 15- 20 minutes' diatribe, in which 'The Corpulent One' then lashed firms for not grasping the new realities of life under the Führer.[12] Let no-one misunderstand, he intoned: other countries will begrudge Germany for its massive upsurge of strength in all directions and their ill-will will one day lead to military confrontations (*kriegerische Auseinandersetzungen*).[13] For this reason Germany must arm itself and explore all possible avenues to keep up the momentum of

---

7   Fieseler, op. cit., p.236.
8   K-D Henke, *Die amerikanische Besetzung Deutschlands,* p.479.
9   Fieseler, op. cit., p.238.
10 I. Kershaw, *Making Friends with Hitler: Lord Londonderry and Britain's Path to War,* p.135.
11 Fieseler, op. cit., p.238
12 Göring was nicknamed '*Der Dicke*', the fat one or fatso. 'The Corpulent One' is my own rendition. Albert Speer, cited in Sereny, p.586, says that Göring was known as *'der Fette',* the fat – if not obese – one.
13 Fieseler, op. cit., p.239.

rearmament. Germany shall prevail! Every person, Göring went on, must realise that the capacity of any country to survive depended on the dedication of its people to equip itself to handle threats and to draw the necessary conclusions. He then laid down the law:

> I should not hesitate for one second to relieve anyone of his responsibilities, if I had the feeling that he wasn't getting the point. Such a man, who only serves the interests of his own firm and does not see the bigger picture (*und nicht darüber hinaus blickt*), commits a grave error. That man will have to be swept aside. At the stroke of a pen he will be deprived of his property and his assets.[14]

Fieseler realised, and so presumably did every other person present, that Göring was preparing them for war and that anyone who did not comply with the Reichsmarschall's injunctions would be jeopardising himself and his family. There was absolutely no doubt about that. The industrial leaders listened to Göring in stunned silence. Nobody dared look at anyone else in the eye. Nobody is recorded as having protested to Göring. Yet Fieseler's horrified reaction to Göring's unsettling harangue can only strike one as naïve.

Fieseler was not only as a member of that select military industry grouping, he was also a close friend Udet who held one of the top jobs at the Aviation Ministry. It therefore seems hard to believe that he had no inkling that Hitler and Göring were preparing Germany for war. Surely he had not forgotten that his own Storch had already had its military baptism of fire in the Spanish Civil War. Did Fieseler somehow think that the Luftwaffe really wanted the Storch as an airplane for recreational stunting? Had not his company once been invited to design and build a Stuka, which by no stretch of the imagination could be classified as a civil aircraft? Was the recently installed firing range at one of his factories there as an innocent amusement for shooting enthusiasts among his staff?

After his harangue, and when the atmosphere was more relaxed, Göring mingled affably with his guests. At some point, Fieseler tells us, Göring heard someone mention his name. At this the Reichsmarschall turned to Fieseler and proceeded to engage him in conversation, telling him in an almost confidential manner how many Stuka squadrons and parachute regiments he had set up. At the end of the evening Göring bid Fieseler goodbye, offering 'his soft, almost spongey hand.'[15] Fieseler appears to give the impression that Göring made his way to him only at the mention of his name. We can dismiss that with a pinch of salt.

As we have already heard, Fieseler had met Göring on two previous occasions in Kassel. Besides it seems most unlikely that Göring had even momentarily failed to recognise him, Germany's lionised and much photographed world aerobatics champion As if he did not know his own guests on such an occasion! Again Fieseler wants us to believe that he is actually a peripheral figure in the Nazi armaments programme. This is completely disingenuous. He was attending in his capacity as an armaments industry leader favoured and selected by Göring himself, as he obviously knew only too well.

After that encounter at Carinhall Fieseler asked himself: 'what is going on the heads of the likes of Hitler, Göring and Hess?'[16] On his way back to Kassel, Fieseler felt certain that war was imminent. 'But what should I do – what must I do?'[17] He found himself helpless faced with that question. Well, there was one thing he could do: he could build bomb-proof air-raid shelters for

14 Ibid, p.239.
15 Ibid, p.239.
16 Ibid, p.239.
17 Ibid, p.239.

his workforce. In great agitation and uncertain of what to think and what do, Fieseler reported to his senior managers what he had seen and heard at Carinhall. To his bafflement those colleagues listened to this description with surprising calmness. Perhaps they, unlike him, had already read the runes properly. In the meantime just three days after the conference, Göring ordered Luftwaffe commanders to make preparations for Operation Green (*Fall Grün*), the attack on Czechoslovakia.[18] The Storch would have a role in that.

The year 1938 was a difficult one for Fieseler for personal reasons. He and his wife Helene separated after some 16 years of marriage. The breakdown of the relationship was, in Fieseler's rather stiff description, a result of 'a phase of alienation.'[19] He claims that he and Helene had tried to sort out their marital problems, but all attempts were in vain. When they had married in 1922, Fieseler was a struggling entrepreneur. But a few years later he was back in the cockpit, taking part in air shows first in Germany and then in several European countries. He was forever on the go. Then things surely got worse from Helene's point of view, when he set up his own company. He had almost bankrupted them until he could stabilise the business. At the same time he was risking life and limb week in week out during the flying season as an aerobatics pilot. She quite possibly found his flying activities more stressful than he did. Helene moved to Schleswig-Holstein, taking her fifteen-year old daughter with her. Katharina attended a boarding school there. Her fourteen year old brother Manfred was also placed in a boarding school; in his case in the Harz mountains.[20]

By the end of 1938 the turn-over of FFB had increased to 18 million Reichsmarks. The company now employed a workforce of 5,300 people, including 100 designers, which represented a 4,000 increase since 1934. It was of course the capable Bachem rather than Fieseler who was the organising genius in creating the actual work structures. The company was by now manufacturing at his three factories in or near Kassel. Although in 1938 FFB produced 99 Storchs, the greater portion of its output concerned Messerschmitt 109 fighters, of which 187 were assembled. The company also continued to build Focke-Wulf and Heinkel training aircraft under licence. It was by any standards a formidable achievement to manage so effectively such a rapidly expanding organisation that was producing technically sophisticated machines, whilst recruiting, deploying, training and even housing new staff. In an innovative bid to keep the technical and personnel functions operating as smoothly as possible – and in anticipation of today's computers – FFB introduced a punched card system to improve materials management and organisation of the payroll. It is quite remarkable that the growth was maintained in such harmony with Nazi ideals and purposes.

Sledgehammers, synagogues, shock-waves

In March 1938 Hitler had already annexed the country of his birth, Austria. On 1 October 1938, within two days of the signing of the Munich Agreement, the Wehrmacht marched into Czechoslovakia to take control of the Sudetenland. Generally the occupation proceeded smoothly from the German point of view despite road blocks put up by the Czechs and some isolated shooting. The next day the Luftwaffe proceeded to seize all the airfields in their newly acquired territory. However, the Czech patriots had dug up the runways to make them inoperable. The first Luftwaffe plane to land on such a runway, undeterred by the hazards, was a Fieseler Storch.[21] Of all its remarkable capabilities, its ease of landing and taking off from uneven, restricted surfaces was one most valued by pilots as well as military commanders. If the Nazi action in Czechoslovakia

---

18   E. L. Homze, *Arming the Luftwaffe: The Reich Air Ministry and the German Aircraft Industry 1919-1939*, p.158.
19   Fieseler, op. cit., p.296.
20   R. Nagel und T. Bauer, *Kassel und die Luftfahrtindustrie seit 1923: Geschichte(n), Menschen, Technik*, p.136.
21   J. Piekalkiewicz, *Der Fieseler Fi 156 Storch im Zweiten Weltkrieg*, p.15.

paralysed Britain and France, it was an event in Germany itself in November that caused even greater shock. It was a direct attack on the country's Jewish population.

Once he had donned his *Standartenführer* uniform in December 1937, Fieseler was clearly more symbolically attached to the Nazis and their ambitions. But, if he thought that his main task was to concentrate on designing and delivering planes for the Luftwaffe, attend various functions at which he had to say 'Heil Hitler' and generally say the right things for the good of his company, the encounter with Göring had surely put things in perspective. He was by now a personage of no small significance in the Nazi war machine however much he tried to play this down in later life. But if he actually thought that he could remain detached from all that to him anti-Jewish unpleasantness, that luxury was shattered – one might say literally shattered – on the night of 9-10 November 1938. If before that date Fieseler had managed to put out of mind any inconvenient thoughts about the Nazi avowed aim to 'deal with' the Jews, if he wished to pretend that the bullying and baiting of Jews would fizzle out, then that particular night would completely disabuse him. It has gone down in history as 'the night of broken glass' in English – *Kristallnacht* in German.

It was a pogrom, one of its main aims being to destroy every synagogue in Germany. In that night of mindless, vengeful thuggery 'an estimated 7,500 [Jewish-owned] business premises were damaged or destroyed.'[22] Among other things, SA gangs 'destroyed anything not easily removable – slashing paintings, breaking furniture and pianos, or shattering marble and porcelain with sledgehammers – while stealing cash, cameras, jewellery and so forth.'[23] In Kassel, 'seat of one of the oldest and most distinguished Jewish communities in Germany,'[24] things got under way (according to the official police report), when a Jewish-owned café was 'completely destroyed.' Then a throng of perhaps a thousand strong headed off for the synagogue, where they 'completely devastated the interior.' The mobs then smashed up and looted some 20 Jewish-owned businesses.[25] The police stood by and did nothing.

The Jews were rounded up and some 300 and their rabbis were sent to Buchenwald concentration camp, which had been established in August 1937.[26] It so happened that two nights before Kristallnacht itself local Nazis, incensed at the murder of a German diplomat in Paris by an alleged Jewish assailant, vented their anger by entering the synagogue, dragged out the Torah and other ceremonial objects and set them on fire. So it was that Kassel has the unenviable reputation for being as 'the birthplace of Kristallnacht.'[27]

There is no reference in Fieseler's autobiography to these grim events. But, whether he liked it or not, he was a uniformed member of the national organisation, whose leaders had instigated the pogrom. The distinguished journalist and chronicler of Nazi Germany Gitta Sereny confronted Albert Speer, Hitler's armaments minister, about his recollections of Kristallnacht. When Speer professed a certain amount of amnesia, this vagueness provoked Sereny to retort: 'It happened right in front of you, all around you; you cannot simply have not seen it.'[28] The same uncompromising charge could be levelled at Fieseler too.

---

22   Burleigh, op. cit., p.328.
23   Burleigh, op. cit., p.328.
24   G. Sereny, *Albert Speer: His Battle for Truth*, p.176.
25   A. Steinweis, *Kristallnacht 1938*, p.24.
26   https://www.jewishvirtuallibrary.org/jsource/judaica/ejud_0002_0011_0_10811.html, accessed on 26 July 2015.
27   O. A. Popa, *Bibliophiles and Bibliothieves: The Search for the Hildebrandslied and the Willehalm Codex (Schriften zum Kulturgüterschutz) (Schriften Zum Kulturgüterschutz/Cultural Property Studies)*. Berlin: De Gruyter, p.40.
28   Sereny, op. cit., p.164.

Serving an incomparably higher purpose

In the meantime Fieseler was also behind another scheme which supported social and ideological cohesion at the work place, namely the introduction of a company newspaper, the *Fieseler-Zeitung (FZ)*, in 1938. This was almost certainly an idea he had picked some ten years earlier when he worked for RaKa, which published a company newspaper called the Sports Flyer (*Der Sportflieger*), but an additional source of inspiration might have been the company newspaper of Junkers, *Der Propeller*, which first came out in 1935.[29] *FZ* served the purpose of instilling esprit de corps and promoted the idea of the company as a Nazi-style industrial community. The publication was also, as we shall see, generally informative about many aspects of company life. It can be read today as one of the most illuminating sources of insight into life at FFB. Indeed it is a goldmine for anyone interested in the nature of industrial life and management in Nazi Germany's medium-sized enterprises.

FZ originally appeared once a month, but this dropped to ten issues in 1939. In 1942 it came out in four issues, but was discontinued in 1943 with the final issue being published in early 1944. Gerhard Fieseler took a strong interest in the magazine which he used to put his personal stamp on his workforce. Introducing the very first issue, boss Fieseler wrote that the new bulletin aimed to strengthen the close bond (*Fühlungnahme*) 'between *my* workforce (*Gefolgschaft*) and *me*' (added emphasis), serving 'an incomparably higher purpose' by 'creating joy about our common endeavour.' It would also prepare the workforce for 'hard work and self-sacrifice', reminding them of the 'vigour of our Führer, who has restored to our fatherland the freedom to bear arms (*Wehrfreiheit*) ... Thus .... let our new company newspaper', proclaims Fieseler, 'be a source of comradeship and company commitment.' In that self-same first issue Vera von Bissing wrote an article about Fieseler under the title 'The Tiger, from the life of our managing director.' Bissing was not an employee of FFB, but her use of the word 'our' suggests that she was viewed in the company as having a close association with it.

The list of contents for all the issues of 1938 breaks topics down into 22 categories. The number in brackets after each title refers to the number of articles devoted to the topic in that year:

1. Working comrades as artists (4)
2. Enlightenment and teachings (13)
3. Company music life (7)
4. Company sport (7)
5. Flying (10)
6. Visits to the company (7)
7. German Labour Front (11)
8. Festivals and celebrations (4)
9. Fieseler worker accommodation (6)
10. Fieseler Storch (15)
11. Company history (12)
12. Health and safety (19)
13. Bulletins of the publicity department (4)
14. Personal (22)
15. Trips and holidays (11)
16. Reportages (15)

---

29 http://www.worldcat.org/title/propeller-werkszeitung-fur-die-gefolgschaft-der-junkers-flugzeug-und-motorenwerke-aktiengesellschaft/oclc/183232338

17. Saving (3)
18. Spying and sabotage prevention (4)
19. Technical contributions (14)
20. Our company education system (8)
21. Our employees write to us (21)
22. Entertainment, poems, etc.

Although the workforce were 'were encouraged to take part with their own contributions,'[30] in the end, as Thorsten Wiederhold argues, the publication existed to reinforce 'order and discipline, command and obedience as the fundamental structures in the work processes.'[31] But that is not entirely so. *FZ* is not awash with photographs of Hitler or snippets of his speeches or of other high-ranking Nazis. In fact, when you read the war-time features, it is clear that *FZ* served the very important function of morale-building without lashings of Nazi propaganda. It is true, however, that articles written by Fieseler show that he had absorbed the tone and swagger of Nazi Germany which 'concretized' Nazi-approved aspiration as to German racial, cultural and technical pre-eminence.[32] But overall we can say that the corporate culture of Fieseler's company was not only one imposed by the management under Fieseler, but one that was also quite literally empowered by Nazi discourse, which Fieseler himself both articulated and embodied.

To be avoided: a rift with Fieseler

In the spring of 1939 the Reich Aviation Ministry once again despatched its chief of finance, Alois Cejka, to meet Fieseler and cajole him into creating a limited liability company and transferring his assets to state ownership. As in the past Fieseler resisted these moves as much as possible, fearing loss of control of the enterprise he had built up from scratch. However, the ministry had a clear motive: it was seeking a recapitalisation of the company to place it on a solid financial footing for future development. As a sweetener Cejka offered an attractive financial inducement. Fieseler declined to go along with the Ministry's request and for a year there was 'a tug-of-war' between him and Cejka.[33] It was perfectly clear that 'by means of a new contract the goal of the ministry was to secure the greatest possible influence over the FFB and to keep Fieseler's influence to the least possible.'[34]

But eventually Fieseler and his senior colleagues realised that they could not in effect risk making an enemy of Cejka and being forced out of business (not to talk of other baleful consequences facing opponents of the Nazi state). His company had no alternative but to go the same way as other aircraft manufacturers. At one point, accordingly to Wiederhold, Fieseler in his frustration even offered to sell out to the state and volunteer for military service. However, 'the seriousness of this offer is open to question.'[35] In the end Fieseler agreed to 'a miserable arrangement', whereby he changed his company to limited liability status, yielded the majority of his own shares and transferred No 1 Works at Bettenhausen and No 2 Works at Lohfelden to the state.[36] On 1 April 1939 the company changed its name to Gerhard-Fieseler-Werke, hereafter GFW. So it was that the Nazi state became a majority shareholder, owning 60% of the shares of the new company. As a sop Cejka had given Fieseler an option to buy back shares from the state at an agreed price. But if he thought that Fieseler would cease to be an irritant, he had another think coming.

30 Nagel und Bauer, op. cit., p.133.
31 T. Wiederhold, *Gerhard Fieseler – eine Karriere: Ein Wirtschaftsführer im Dienste des Nationalsozialismus*, p.134.
32 H. James, *A German Identity 1770 to the Present Day*, p.151.
33 Fieseler, op. cit., p.235.
34 Wiederhold, op. cit., p.66.
35 Ibid, p.70.
36 Fieseler, op. cit., p.235.

With his commercial director, Dr Göbel, Fieseler concocted a scheme, supported by his bank, to buy back a sufficient number of shares so that he became a majority shareholder. Acting in complete consistency with the contract, Fieseler's bank transferred the requisite funds to the Aviation Ministry to secure a 51% share in the company. This completely unexpected, seemingly legal move infuriated Cejka, who refused to accept the payment. 'We were stunned', wrote the surely insouciant Fieseler, who duly requested a meeting with Field Marshall Milch, the head of the Aviation Ministry, to solve the matter.[37]

In Berlin Fieseler quickly got to the point: 'I have come to ask you, Herr Field Marshall, if our state keeps to its contracts it has concluded or not.'[38] Of course the state honours its contracts, retorted Milch, adding 'admittedly under the condition that keeping to a contract does not harm the interests of the state.' This mealy-mouthed reply confirmed Fieseler's unfavourable impression of this former squadron leader. At length Milch confirmed that he would make a personal decision in the matter and communicate this to Fieseler. A few months later Milch made it clear in a letter that the terms of the contract were valid. According to Fieseler, if Milch had supported Cejka's unilateral actions, this would have the effect of invalidating the disputed contract.

In this letter Milch writes that his decision was guided by 'exclusively objective considerations' and not influenced by 'various personal factors in the discussions conducted with you [that] were of no consequence.'[39] This latter statement suggests that Milch was prepared to overlook Fieseler's unmasked indignation in the presence of his august self. If so, that supports Wiederhold's conviction that Milch's accommodating behaviour was influenced by the fact the Fieseler was in charge of a National Socialist Exemplary Enterprise and was as such a proven supporter of the Nazi state. Besides, Fieseler's company was building the Messerschmitt 109 fighter under licence. A rift with Fieseler and his company could not be permitted to disrupt production of an aircraft that was the best regarded fighter of the Luftwaffe. Throughout the entire protracted saga Fieseler had once again challenged Nazi authority at a senior level and got away with it.

Führer Imperator Maximus

In May 1939 Fieseler represented his company for the award of the title of National Socialist Exemplary Enterprise, which it had won for the second year running.[40] The ceremony took place in the new Reich Chancellery and the Führer himself would be doing the honours. If he was not impressed by the building from the outside, Fieseler was favourably struck by its awesome internal appearance: the expanse of marble, the spaciousness, the imposing staircase which led to the rooms in which the Führer himself lived and conducted the affairs of state. With the other 200 or so industrial leaders Fieseler was ushered into a 600 square metre reception room. Everyone was standing to attention like soldiers on parade. You could hear a pin drop. No-one dared not so much as to whisper, cough or clear his throat. All eyes were on the massive doors, through which the Führer was expected to make his entrance.

Hitler was due to appear at 11.00am. Ten minutes passed, then twenty. The atmosphere relaxed a bit. Then at 11.30 some folding doors near the huge staircase opened. Through it came Hitler in a brown jacket and black trousers. In his wake came retinue of Nazi party big-wigs as well as high-ranking members of SA, SS and Wehrmacht. Hitler came down the steps and stood a mere two metres from Fieseler. According to Fieseler the Führer looked haggard and drawn and was bent slightly forward. Fieseler had seen Hitler close-to on three or four occasions, but this time the most

37 Ibid, op. cit., p.236.
38 Ibid, p.236.
39 Wiederhold, op. cit., p.72.
40 Fieseler, op. cit., pp.240-241.

powerful man in Germany made 'a downright shocking impression' on him. Hitler's speech befitted his unprepossessing appearance: it was 'meaningless twaddle.'[41]

According to Fieseler, no-one attending had any idea what was being said. He and others in attendance were actually witnessing Hitler not as the great orator, but as the man who to his innermost circles was noted for his rambling disquisitions. The Führer himself may have been all too conscious that this was not one of his greatest performances. In a menacing tone and with a gesture of displeasure, he told his audience to make certain that not a word of his address appeared in the next day's newspapers.[42] He did not need to add 'or else.'

On 1 March 1939 'Luftwaffe Day,' took place in Kassel, the high point of which was a display by a Storch which landed in one of the main squares of the city. Around two weeks later Berlin hosted 'Wehrmacht Day', when a Storch took off and landed in Unter den Linden at the very heart of the city. Then in June Kassel was the venue for one of the most important events in the Nazi calendar for 1939: the Greater German War Veterans Day (*Großdeutscher Reichskriegertag*), culminating in the day when Hitler would address a mass rally. On this occasion Fieseler, as a prominent citizen of Kassel as well as an armaments industry leader, is likely to have attended some function or other.

Some 200,000 veterans of the First World War attended the occasion. The veterans were accommodated in schools (some 30,000 beds had been brought in) and in 15 tent cities (*Zeltstädte*), whilst a convoy of 120 trucks provided the field kitchen. Several high-ranking Nazis accompanied their Führer, including SS chief Heinrich Himmler; the head of the Chancellor's office, Martin Bormann; and various Wehrmacht generals including head of the armed forces, Wilhelm Keitel and head of the army, Walther von Brauchitsch. Guests of honour included foreign dignitaries such as the assiduous Japanese ambassador, General Ōshima, of whom we shall hear more. Kassel was festooned with Nazi flags. There were wreath-laying ceremonies and torch processions. In his speech Hitler, in addition to performing the standard oratorical obsequies to Germany's fallen heroes of the First World War, used the occasion to set the mood for the next phase of Germany's restoration to greatness. After the ovations, the celebrations concluded with 'a gigantic firework display.'[43]

At this occasion, the last Hitler rally in Kassel, Fieseler simply can have been under no illusions about the massive military preparations build-up, if not the warlike intentions of the Nazi regime. But if he expected war at any time, he cannot have expected the sudden rapprochement between the Third Reich and the Soviet Union. In August Hitler pulled off 'perhaps the greatest coup of his career' by sealing a deal with the wily Stalin, the so-called Nazi-Soviet Non-aggression Pact.[44] This event stunned the entire nation not to mention the rest of the world. Across Europe faithful followers of Stalin were especially perplexed and plunged into ideological confusion. The fundamental aim of the deal, which began life as innocent-sounding trade talks in June, was to create two spheres of influence, which would split Europe in two, premised on the carving up of Poland between the two totalitarian regimes (though 'carving up' is far too genteel a word for what would befall Poland in the impending war).

Not of course that there was much non-aggression about this very nasty piece of horse-trading, seeing that the Nazis and Soviets merely agreed to refrain from attacking each other ' in the full expectation that they could commit aggression with impunity in other directions.'[45] Not for nothing has the deal been called 'perhaps the most astounding ideological reversal of the

---

41   Ibid, p.241.
42   Ibid, p.241. Hitler's words, according to Fieseler, were: 'Aber nicht, daß mir das wieder in der Presse steht.'
43   *Hessische Niedersächsische Allgemeine.* (1997). Reichskriegertag Kassel: Stimmungsmache für das neue Völkermorden, 13 April.
44   A. Roberts, *The Storm of War: A New History of the Second World War*, p.9.
45   I. C. B. Dear, and M. R. D. Foot, *Oxford Companion to the Second World War*, p.781.

twentieth century.'⁴⁶ Stalin, with his greedy eyes on the eastern part of Poland, the Baltic states and Finland, tacitly agreed that Hitler's anti-Bolshevik rants in *Mein Kampf* should not be made to block the mutually advantageous territorial aggrandisement. Now Hitler could attack Poland, knock it out without provoking the Soviets, and turn on France to avenge the hated Diktat of Versailles. He would not waste any time setting about this.

One incidental outcome of this diplomatic chicanery is that Stalin was given a Storch as a mark of esteem. The Soviet dictator was said to be 'so impressed with the aircraft that he ordered Oleg Antonov' – one of the USSR's brightest aircraft designers – 'to produce a non-licensed copy of the aircraft.' The resulting prototypes, powered by equally non-licensed Renault aero engines, were known as the Oka-38 Aist (*aist* being the Russian word for stork), but full production never got underway. The factory in the Baltic charged with manufacturing the Aist succumbed to the Wehrmacht's onslaught on the Soviet Union in the summer of 1941.⁴⁷

On 1st September 1939 Hitler ordered the Wehrmacht to invade Poland in the face of an entirely specious incursion of the Reich by its eastern neighbour. But this time Hitler had overreached himself. The British, shamed by their previous appeasement of the German leader, declared war on Germany two days later. This time there was no jubilation on the streets of Germany; indeed the outbreak of war was 'deeply unpopular.'⁴⁸ The general public accepted the official line that Britain, which repeatedly stymied the Führer's peace-making efforts in the last two years, had provoked their Polish allies to attack the Reich. The Germans closed ranks, being 'convinced that war had been forced upon them.'⁴⁹ There was 'no great soul-searching.'⁵⁰

Hermann Göring, who bore no small responsibility for its outbreak, said: 'If we lose this war, may heaven have mercy on us.'⁵¹ On the day of the invasion of Poland the entire Fieseler workforce gathered to hear loudspeakers delivering the Führer's announcement. Fieseler claims to have cursed Hitler under his breath: 'Why don't you blow your own brains out? What is going to happen now to the people of Germany?' It was a seemingly Damascene moment for Fieseler, for he realised 'in a flash' that Hitler was no more than a reckless gambler who was playing with the lives of millions of Germans and who 'without any scruple was going to plunge entire peoples into wretchedness and misery.' Then he asked himself: 'What can I do, what must I do?⁵²' He confesses that in that moment he had no answer. He was simply overwhelmed by the realisation that Germany was at war.

Fieseler himself did not address his workforce on the outbreak of war, but used the October issue of *FZ* to affirm his and his company's commitment to the Führer's great cause. Germany finds itself at war, he began. It was a war 'against injustice and acts of outrage, against British arrogance and provocation.' The Fieseler workforce with its powerful sense of community would fulfil its duty to Führer and Fatherland. Faith and work were to be the watch-words. But woe to any habitual moaner, any doubter or any self-seeker. There was no place at GFW for such people. We are ready, he went on, to obey in blind faith. We are ready and determined to do our utmost for final victory. He urged his workforce to remember their comrades who had obeyed the Führer's command and already joined the colours. There was, of course, unstinting praise for the Führer, who has 'liberated us from the yoke of the British masters and their associates. He has torn up that disgraceful treaty (*Schandvertrag*) and thrown it bit by bit at their feet.' He will know how to confront Germany's enemies. He will determine whether in future our people can work and live

46 R. Mitter, *China's War With Japan 1937-1945: The Struggle for Survival*, p.212.
47 J. Rickard, *OKA-38 Aist/ ShS*, http://www.historyofwar.org/articles/weapons_oka-38_aist.html
48 Stargardt, op. cit., p.15.
49 Ibid, p.34.
50 Ibid, p.15.
51 A. Beevor, *The Second World War*, p.27.
52 Fieseler, op. cit., p.241.

in peace or whether 'we must still witness how England's masters control the world's wealth, which they have plundered for themselves.'[53]

Fieseler concludes on this rousing note: 'If millions of German soldiers must say to themselves: it is unimportant that we live, the important thing is that Germany lives; so we must say to ourselves: it is unimportant if things are going well for us … we must bear hardship, it is important that we build as many aircraft as possible for our airmen.'[54] For a man who would like to give the impression to posterity that he was a reluctant Nazi, then this article does not exactly support his case. He could of course have been dissembling or reading what Nazi hacks had prepared for him. But neither possibility sits easily with a man with belief in the Fatherland and conviction that Germany had been deeply wronged by the victors of the First World War and that Hitler was the man to restore German honour. Besides he probably *did* think that it was the British who had shattered the peace. He was at this momentous hour at one with his workforce. Whether, however, in his heart of hearts Fieseler really had that *blind* faith in the Führer must remain open to question. But it is nevertheless safe to say that ever since he joined the Nazi Party in 1933 he had never given any outward sign of being disloyal or disaffected.

In October new regulations under the draconian War Economy Decree were introduced concerning factory workers during wartime, including of course the GFW workforce. There were restrictions on holiday allowances, new rates of pay applied nation-wide, working hours increased from fifty to sixty hours. In his rousing article of Fieseler had stressed need for sacrifice for the sake of the Fatherland. This was little comfort to the parents of Lieutenant Alfons Jens, a legal specialist with a PhD, who had the dubious honour of being the first member of the GFW workforce to sacrifice his life for Adolf Hitler.[55] Readers of the *FZ* would see more obituaries about their colleagues who had fallen fighting for the Fatherland.

By the end of the 1939 GFW had delivered 652 aircraft, of which 299 were Me 109s. Its turnover was 32 million Reichsmarks, an increase of 14 million over 1938. It was employing 5,000 employees, which represents a loss of 300 over the previous year.[56] Almost all of those 300 would be young men called to serve the Fatherland in the battles ahead. No small number of these men who would joined GFW in the years of rapid expansion as of 1935 and would have been highly skilled industrial craftsman: in other words, difficult to replace. In December 1939 it would not have clear to Fieseler, but the scene was being set for a huge, irreversible shift in the composition and competences of the company's work force.

By the end of the year too the company had formed its own 'industrial protection squadron' (*Industrie-Schutzstaffel*), composed of its own groups of pilots, who mainly owing to age were not actually serving in the Luftwaffe. Their task was to help protect GFW in the event of any kind of aerial attack. A photograph shows Fieseler in an unposed take addressing the eight-man squadron shortly after its formation. He is in his black Nazi Flying Corps uniform, wearing a greatcoat with a ceremonial dagger attached to a decorative tassle. In the background is one of the new Messerschmitt fighters. Directly above Fieseler's head is a large disc atop a factory building bearing the famous tilted F of the Fieseler logo.[57] There may be no other photograph of Fieseler that simultaneously reveals him as a pilot among fellow pilots, an entrepreneur and duly attired Nazi praetor. Anyone seeing the photograph without prior knowledge might well assume that the great-coated figure was a high-ranking officer in the SS.

53   Wiederhold, op. cit., p.236.
54   Wiederhold, op. cit., pp.236-237.
55   Nagel und Bauer, op. cit., p.155.
56   Ibid, p.157.
57   Ibid, p.156 and photograph, p.157.

On 20 April 1940, announced *FZ*, General Field Marshall Göring had promoted Fieseler to the rank of *Oberführer* in the Nazi Flying Corps, which had no military equivalent and is generally referred to as senior colonel.[58] Evidently Fieseler was well regarded by the Nazi leadership. In the same issue there appeared a lionising feature about Fieseler: 'Everyone who knows Gerhard Fieseler senses the effect that he gives out. His face, with the keen, shining eyes and his firm, jutting chin, conveys the impression of a personality of exceptional character.'[59]

If Germans in general and any of Hitler's military commanders had grave misgivings about the aims and direction of the conflict, these were largely dispelled in June 1940 when after a seven week campaign France surrendered. There was rejoicing in Germany. Hitler was 'hailed as "the greatest military commander of all times" and magnanimously appointed a dozen new field marshals under his – for the time being – unassailable supremacy.[60] He entered Berlin in triumph as general of generals, avenger of wrongs, master of Europe, *Führer Imperator Maximus*.[61]

But behind the jubilation of the adoring masses was joyous anticipation that this victory would hasten the end of the war.[62] In such hope Fieseler had a new advertisement drafted, which was presumably never used, showing a line drawing of two hatted men in business suits, each carrying briefcases, walking towards a Storch. The caption reads as having an uncannily modern ring about it: 'You decide when your aircraft takes off.' The blurb begins: 'The leaders of major enterprises in particular can find it difficult to keep to air travel plans. Something always crops up at the last minute …'[63]

Indeed, at the time of drafting that advertisement, that unexpected something would be precisely what most Germans at home feared: a continuation of the war. Unbeknown to them the subjugation of France was but one step in the Führer's master plan. He was not to be satisfied with the mere avenging the Treaty of Versailles. For a start he had to deal with those dogged British. But that part of his master plan for that crashed in a literal sense over the south of England and the English Channel in the summer. In its first major engagement with a powerful enemy in the air, the Luftwaffe was outmanoeuvred by the Royal Air Force. If anyone else but Göring had been in charge of the Luftwaffe, Hitler would have sacked him. Britain, the Führer decided, would have to wait for its comeuppance. In any case other visions were swirling in his mind.

In anticipation of a crushing victory that was not to be, the June 1940 issue of *FZ* published a cartoon Churchill attired as an admiral cowering before an unstoppable onslaught of Luftwaffe aircraft. Another cartoon in the September issue depicted the Luftwaffe flying over a defenceless London. Despite the devastating defeat for the Nazi leadership, Fieseler is shown in the December 1940 issue of the company newspaper with his armed raised in the Hitler salute in the midst of his workers. It is a photograph that Fieseler would not have liked to enter the public domain after the defeat of Germany in 1945, when he like some many others were at pains to distance themselves from the Nazi regime and its crimes.

Forced labour: 'a complete success'

After the outbreak of war one of the first changes to life in GFW was the extension of the working day from eight to ten hours. That could be tolerated, but it was nothing compared to the consequences of the haemorrhaging of talented staff who had been called up to join the Wehrmacht. Many

58 https://en.wikipedia.org/wiki/Oberführer
59 *Fieseler Zeitung*, April 1940. Sammlung Urlen.
60 G. Mann, *Deutsche Geschichte des 19. Und 20. Jahrhunderts*, p.924.
61 Führer Imperator is taken from the title of chapter 2 in Roberts, op. cit., pp.48-86.
62 Mann, op. cit., p.923.
63 Nagel und Bauer, op. cit., p.162.

were master craftsmen who had been nurtured by the Fieseler company over many years. How on earth were they to be replaced? The gap was initially filled to some extent by German women, but eventually labour compulsorily conscripted from the territories under the Nazi jackboot would form between 40 and 50% of the entire GFW wartime workforce of around 10,000 people.[64] In the Nazi ideology the role of women was seen as that of 'racially pure bearer of offspring (*rassereine Erbträgerin*)' and not as a factory worker.[65] But in wartime conditions this was wholly unsustainable. So it was by 1940 that GFW started to take on women.

For their part, German women often resisted industrial employment for one practical reason: who would look after their children? But many did take up work in factories, whereby in a certain ideological sleight-of-hand 'the traditional "female space" of the home was thus enlarged to include the home front', while their menfolk fought for the Reich on foreign soil.[66] Fieseler, pragmatic as ever, ordered the provision of a spacious kindergarten on site with four attendants. The kindergarten was equipped with children's furniture and toys. Around 75 children on average were looked after every day. They received a square meal with milk. Ailing children were cared for by the company doctor.[67]

In the first place women were given simple, routine jobs and were called 'female factory helpers' (*Werkshelferinnen*).[68] They received training and, having passed a medical examination, were employed variously as 'lathe and milling machine operators, welders, electrical fitters not to mention carpenters and lacquerers.'[69] There were some work procedures in which women proved to be particularly adept. In such cases tools were adapted to suit their hand size and bodily strength. But, overall the benefits of employing women proved to be 'dubious and patchy.'[70] A more radical solution was called for. In common with all other industrial enterprises in wartime Germany, Fieseler's labour shortages would have to be satisfied by the wholesale deployment of compulsory labour from the occupied territories. Given the Nazi emphasis on racial purity 'the influx of foreign workers could be at best be tolerated as a wartime expedient, a rational but unpleasant necessity.'[71]

In 1940 and 1941 various issues of *FZ* discussed the role of women in the workplace, though the June 1942 issue poses the ever topical question 'can women do men's jobs?' [72] In the issue of July 1940 it is pointed out that even before the war there was a 'palpable lack' of men in the workforce owing to the large scale recruitment into the Wehrmacht. But once the war had started, not only were women needed in greater numbers, but also for the heavier kinds of work. Accordingly, the company placed great emphasis on the successful integration of women into the previous male domains and on the importance of keeping healthy. In the same issue there was a report of a speech of Fieseler to his women workers 'in a densely packed assembly hall.' He tells them that there was no job that a man can do and that a woman can often do 'better and faster' than men. He adds that 'the home front is just as important as the front facing the enemy.'[73]

By the end of 1940 the first batches of conscripted foreign labour arrived for work at GFW. But Fieseler's company in common with other German employers was not at all happy to receive them. The foreigners were viewed as 'slack (*leistungsschwach*) and unskilled,' whilst 'mixing them

---

64   Wiederhold, op. cit., p.189.
65   Ibid, p.173.
66   Stargardt, op. cit., p.140.
67   A. Norden, *Das Herz muss dabei sein: Der Flieger Gerhard Fieseler und sein Werk*, p.72.
68   Wiederhold, p.175.
69   Ibid, p.176.
70   Ibid, p.178.
71   Stargradt, op. cit., p.293.
72   *Fieseler Zeitung*, June-July 1941, Sammlung Urlen.
73   *Fieseler Zeitung*, July 1940, Sammlung Urlen.

thoroughly' (*Durchmischung*) with the German workforce would be bad for production and company morale.[74] The greater portion of the compulsory workers, both men and women, came in the first instance from the Netherlands. But in the course of the war there were influxes of Belgians, Poles, Ukrainians, a few Russians – mainly women, and Italians. German authors, Nagel und Bauer, in their otherwise lengthy description of GFW in the war years keep the discussion of these unfortunate souls to an absolute minimum, at one point delicately referring to them as 'civilian workers.'[75]

The foreign conscripted workers were kept in some locations around Kassel, where they lived in improvised barracks, empty factories or redundant school buildings 'with the crudest sanitary arrangements and degrading conditions'[76] and quite possibly at the mercy of a pitiless warden.[77] The accommodation would be deloused every so often. It should, however, not be forgotten that many Germans up and down the country who worked alongside forced labourers did show common humanity and smuggled food to them to ease their plight. There were some, however, who provided food 'as a way of making money out of them.'[78] No doubt in GFW there were instances of both motives, noble and base.

The working week was 60-72 hours, and the workers were subjected to harassment and beatings. When later in the war the racially despised *Ostarbeiter* i.e. workers who had been transported from the Eastern Europe (Poles, Ukrainians and, Russians) were taken on, they were found to be 'useless.'[79], being regarded as 'racially worthless.'[80] It was generally agreed that the treatment was more brutal 'the further East a man had come from.'[81] The foreign workers were of course paid much less than German workers, had no legal protection, no right to sick pay or bonuses and were subject to fatal diseases.[82] Their wretched lives were fully in keeping with the aim of Fritz Sauckel, the Plenipotentiary General for the Reallocation of Labour, who was responsible for the entire slave labour machine. Foreign workers, he callously declared, were 'to be treated in such a way to exploit them to the highest possible extent at the lowest conceivable degree of expenditure.'[83]

By the end of the war there were some 8 million forced labourers in Germany or around 20% of the entire workforce. In certain industries, such as armaments and aircraft manufacture they often made up '40% or more.'[84] In 1943 the aircraft industry employed some 317,000 forced labourers, including prisoners of war and inmates of concentration camps. Of these 'more than 100,000' were forced to live and work in underground facilities such as caves, tunnels large-scale bunkers, where 'the majority died of exhaustion and ill-treatment.'[85] As might be expected, productivity of forced labourers was low: 'In metal-working industries such as aircraft production, male compulsory worker productivity was around 40% of German productivity, whilst the figure for women exceeded 60%.'[86]

---

74 Wiederhold, op. cit., p.188.
75 Nagel und Bauer, op. cit., p.178.
76 Wiederhold, op. cit., p.196.
77 G. Knopp, *Hitlers Manager*, p.248.
78 K. Lowe, *Savage Continent: Europe in the Aftermath of World War II*, p.96.
79 Ibid, pp.195-201.
80 J. Stephenson, *Women in Nazi Germany*, p.33.
81 M. Middlebrook, *The Peenemünde Raid 17/18 August 1943*, p.31.
82 R. J. Evans, *The Third Reich at War: How the Nazis led Germany from Conquest to Defeat*, 351-357.
83 W. Shirer, *The Rise and Fall of the Third Reich*, p.1168.
84 Lowe, op. cit., p.96.
85 Deutsches Museum, *Aviation: A Guide to the Aeronautics Collection*, p.62.
86 A. Tooze, *The Wages of Destruction: The Making and Breaking of the Nazi Economy*, p.535.

Anyone caught slacking at work or fomenting of industrial unrest faced the threat of being sent to a concentration camp.[87] Not that ruthlessness made for efficiency: Nazi planning was simply 'too bloodthirsty to be really practical.'[88] In GFW foreign workers were treated as inferiors, subjected to harassment and beatings and were permanently undernourished.[89] Anyone deemed to be a slacker or in violation of workplace regulations ran the risk of being reported to the Gestapo and arrested. There were reputedly 'special rooms' on the Fieseler premises where wrongdoers could be detained before being delivered to the enforcement agencies.[90]

One former Dutch worker at GFW described his experience living in a wooden barracks in Waldau, where in the winter there was always a shortage of fuel. The toilet was a trench with a board over it and would become periodically usable. In the absence of light in the evening 'you shit where you stand.' The food was so terrible that on one occasion the Dutch prisoners protested. This resulted in a visitation by company and DAF representatives, who responded with 'that curious mixture of callousness and punctiliousness so characteristic of the Nazis.'[91] Somewhat extraordinarily the inmates scored a victory, if only a very temporary one. The Dutch were praised as 'first-rate people, good workers' and should accordingly be well fed. They promptly received good food: potatoes, vegetables and meat, but only on that day. Immediately after that things reverted to normal: they were given the usual cabbage soup.[92] So much for the Dutch 'being regarded as essentially "Germanic" people who needed to be led "back to the Germanic community."'[93]

In his autobiography Fieseler, as we shall learn in greater detail, was at pains to give the impression that he did all he could to alleviate the living and working conditions of his compulsory workforce. In repudiation of that Wiederhold cites a speech given by one of Fieseler's senior managers, Richard Freyer, to aircraft industry representatives held in Kassel in June 1943. At one point Freyer discusses the advantages of deploying foreign labour in GFW:

> The greatest advantage of employing foreign labour … lies in the fact that we only have to issue orders. No-one contradicts them, there is no necessity for discussion … The foreigner is always available when he is required to do overtime or work on Sundays … The task of deploying foreign labour in the German armaments industry for the war effort, initially an experiment, has been a complete success.[94]

According to Wiederhold, what Freyer describes is a system of slave labour that Gerhard Fieseler must not only have known about, *but which he was also responsible for.*[95] It seems inconceivable to Wiederhold that Fieseler could not have known about the content of Freyer's talk, bearing in mind that he was addressing such an important audience. There is no proof of this and there is, for obvious reasons, no reference to the talk in Fieseler's autobiography. In the absence of countervailing evidence the balance of probability must lie with Wiederhold. All that we can say on Fieseler's behalf is that in comparison with other industrial sites in wartime Germany there is no record of a single member of his forced labour force being actually worked to death in his factories. In the meantime the Fieseler company newspaper gave a positive ring to life at GFW. There were uplifting letters

---

87   R. J. Evans, *The Third Reich at War: How the Nazis led Germany from Conquest to Defeat*, p.353.
88   T. Snyder, *Bloodlands: Europe Between Hitler and Stalin*, p.166.
89   Wiederhold, op. cit., p.195-201.
90   Ibid, p.162.
91   N. Ferguson, *Kissinger 1923-1968: The Idealist*, p.75.
92   Wiederhold, op. cit., pp.198-199.
93   Lowe, op. cit., p.36, citing SS boss Heinrich Himmler.
94   Wiederhold, op. cit., pp.203-204.
95   Ibid, p.205.

from the front, upbeat features about apprentices, advice on keeping one's teeth healthy, items on sport as well as on the success of the Storch. There is even an item on 'how I stopped smoking.'[96] In the June 1941 issue there was a feature with the cheery title: 'we'd like a bit of a laugh too.' But laughter was going to be in very short supply before long.

The death of an alter ego

In his autobiography we learn a lot about Fieseler's relationships with certain people. Certainly we get a clear picture of his attitude to his parents. Mostly, however, he talks about individuals who come and go in his life. Sometimes the relationships are antagonistic. One thinks here of the aircraft builder Raab, the aircraft designer Lippisch and Alois Cejka, the finance chief of the Aviation Ministry. But for the most part there is every sign that despite his proneness to outbursts of temper Fieseler was well-regarded by his colleagues and he certainly enjoyed working very closely with people such as his chief designer Arnolt and his fellow director, Dr Thalau. That Fieseler built up a very substantial network within aviation German circles is not in doubt and he could not have exploited this, if he had not come across as both professional and personable.

Apart from his parents there is only one other person, about whom he writes at length, and that is Ernst Udet. The two were evidently very close. It may not be an exaggeration to call them kindred souls, bound by a life-long love of aircraft and both admiring the other as a highly capable pilot. Certainly Fieseler did not, as far as we know, indulge in a hedonistic, pleasure-loving lifestyle to compare with Udet's lavish ways. Perhaps they attracted each other as opposites. Udet was debonair, indiscreet, given to recklessness and adored by beautiful women. By contrast, Fieseler was level-headed, patient and single-minded. He appears not to have been a womaniser.

Fieseler and Udet had first met each other in 1927 when both were budding aerobatics pilots. Fieseler eventually branched into aircraft manufacture, whilst eventually Udet allowed himself, against his better judgement, to accept at Göring's coaxing a senior post in the Aviation Ministry. Before long he was appointed as head of the Aviation Ministry Technical Office, where he found himself too much governed by deadlines and paperwork. He and Fieseler met frequently in Berlin. We can therefore safely assume that Udet kept Fieseler well informed about aviation developments and may well have been influential on his friend's behalf within the Aviation Ministry and even with Göring. It is by no means impossible that Udet had a hand in the appointment of Fieseler as an defence economy leader in 1938.

A general judgement is that Udet was an incompetent crony of Göring. Furthermore he was frequently at odds with the head of the ministry, Erhard Milch who wanted to oust him from control of aircraft production, and who, unlike the dangerously insouciant Udet, was a master political operator. On 17 November 1941 Udet was found with a self-inflicted bullet in his head at his expensive apartment in Berlin. But it was not 'office politics' that drove him to kill himself.[97] It has been suggested that he did away with himself 'after failing repeatedly to convince Hitler and Göring that aircraft production in Britain and America was growing so fast that German planes would face overwhelming, impossible odds within a few months.'[98] But that may not be the full story.

This event rocked the Nazi establishment, who hushed up the circumstances of his death. The newspapers reported that he had 'tragically met his death … while testing a new weapon', adding that he 'died of his injuries on the way to hospital.'[99] Hitler ordered a state funeral for Udet. It

---

96   *Fieseler Zeitung*, June 1940, Sammlung Urlen.
97   Tooze, op. cit., p.506.
98   Evans, op. cit., 2008, p.325.
99   H. Herlin, *Udet: A Man's Life,* p.9 and p.244.

took place on 21 November in the Aviation Ministry's Hall of Honour. Prominent persons from the Nazi Party, state and Wehrmacht attended. Fieseler does not indicate whether he was present, but he almost certainly did attend, seeing that he received a formal invitation from Göring as 'Reichsmarschall of the Greater German Reich and Commander-in-chief of the Luftwaffe' with instructions as to attire and the laying of wreathes.[100] If so, he would have heard a section of the Berlin Philharmonic Orchestra play the funeral march from Wagner's Götterdämmerung and Göring give the eulogy, culminating with the words: 'Farewell, my best friend.'[101] These were crocodile tears if ever there were. Before long the egregious Göring was conveniently able to lay the blame for the failed Battle of Britain exclusively on Udet.[102]

Fieseler was devastated when he heard of his friend's death. It would also seem most likely that he quickly picked up through the grapevine that Udet's death was suicide. Fieseler devotes some seven and half pages, which include two half-page cartoons drawn by Udet, to his friend. No other person receives this amount of attention in his autobiography. The first cartoon depicts Udet on a scooter racing around his spacious office in the Aviation Ministry building. He is holding a file under one arm, from which pages of documents are fluttering to the ground. As a smile is discernible on his face, we may assume that Udet was not too bothered about mislaying bits of information.[103] The second cartoon is more revealing. It shows him padlocked to a desk which is piled up with files, his head bent grimly over it. Above him is a glider soaring under a sunny sky. Sprawled in the cockpit, with his legs dangling over the fuselage, is a happy looking man. The cartoon is captioned 'The two souls in the breast of Udet, as portrayed by himself.'[104]

When as of 1933 'the intelligent Göring' started to court Udet intensively for a post in the Aviation Ministry, this placed Udet in a dilemma.[105] He hankered after his life as 'an uninhibited Bohemian', but a senior military position had attractions: not least because he knew that he had but two years left as a aerobatics pilot and he needed the money.[106] Joining the Ministry as Inspector of Fighter and Stuka Pilots with the rank of colonel and as of 1936 Head of the Technical Office, he belonged to Göring's inner circle, was a frequent visitor to Carinhall, when 'he played the court jester' and amused Frau Göring as a ladies' man and wag.[107] Fieseler recalls that Udet divided opinions: some people adored him, whilst 'there were those who were so disillusioned with him that they hated him.' Fieseler makes it plain that he belongs to those who had 'basked in his company.'[108]

Although Erhard Milch was the Secretary of State at the Aviation Ministry, Udet reported directly to Göring. When Udet became the Head of the Technical Office, this embittered Milch; which is possibly what the scheming Göring wanted. From Udet Fieseler received a good deal of information about the workings of the Nazi state with his imitations of Hitler haranguing the masses. Fieseler found these 'astoundingly good.' On one occasion Udet told him how 'the bastards are performing experiments on innocent people', a reference presumably referring to the Nazis' notorious euthanasia programme, which murdered more Germans than 'any other group of domestic victims of Nazi persecution.[109] Udet knew all the top Nazis and told Fieseler the most dangerous of the lot was Reinhard Heydrich, one of the main architects of the Final Solution. He

---

100 Nagel und Bauer, op. cit., p.169.
101 Herlin op. cit., p.246.
102 P. Kaplan, *Fighter Aces of the Luftwaffe in WWII*, p.51.
103 Fieseler, op. cit., p.245.
104 Ibid, p.249.
105 Ibid, p.244.
106 Ibid, p.245.
107 Ibid, pp.245-246.
108 Ibid, p.242.
109 Stargardt, op. cit., p.153.

even told Fieseler – it is not certain when – that his life was pointless and prattled on about 'putting an end to it all.' Fieseler also noted how Udet was drinking heavily.

On other occasion Udet told Fieseler about how Göring summoned him to Carinhall and berated him for not meeting aircraft production targets. Put out, Udet explained to Göring that delays were due to difficulties in implementing technical changes. The Reichsmarschall was having none of it. He turned on Udet in a rage: 'Difficulties! Don't talk to me about that! Do you think I appointed you to the post of Director-General of Equipment for the Luftwaffe to be told that production schedules can't be kept to?' As he told this to Fieseler, who was no doubt being reminded of Göring's vehement tirade when he had been at Carinhall in 1938, Udet pronounced that 'that swine Milch is behind this. He wants me out of the way.'[110]

In January 1941 Fieseler was in Udet's company once again. He noted that a distinct change had come over him. Something serious was rattling him. They were in Udet's apartment, sitting by a blazing fire. Udet stood up to get a cigarette and bent down to whisper in Fieseler's ear: 'Hitler's going to attack Russia!' Fieseler's blood ran cold. 'We've lost the war now!' he gasped. Hitler's plan was unfathomable to Fieseler. Germany, he reasoned, was on the point of winning the war. Why risk everything in a bid to subdue Soviet Russia? At that time only a very few Germans close to Hitler knew that he was about to attempt to unleash a 'messianic racial war … on Europe, Eurasia *and the whole of the world.*' (original emphasis).[111] This incident reveals Udet's proneness to indiscretion, passing on top secret information he was privy to. There can be little doubt that, as he made his way back to Kassel, Fieseler's mind was dominated by this shocking revelation. He does not say whether he told it to anyone else. If he were wise, he would keep his mouth firmly shut.

Fieseler records that he was again with Udet in his apartment just two days before he killed himself. Udet was completely distracted, saying that he was at the end of this tether. Fieseler tried to steer the conversation to cheerier topics over a drink. Suddenly Udet turned to him and said; 'Do you hear something? By the window.' Fieseler walked over to a window at the furthest end of room, opened it, heard nothing, and told this to Udet. But moments later the same thing happened. Fieseler had occasion to recall this conversation with Milch, who said that Udet had been suffering from a persecution complex. But Fieseler tells us that he himself is not convinced of this, being certain that Udet was feigning these hallucinations. The real truth, he suggested, was that Udet could not bring himself to see that he had been a failure. It seems then that several factors rather than one overriding one were the trigger for Udet's suicide.

After the war Carl Zuckmayer, a well-known author and playwright, who had spent the entire war in exile in the USA, had written a play – 'The Devil's General (*Des Teufels General*)' – in which a senior Nazi officer, who happens to be in the Aviation Ministry and a bon viveur, commits suicide. It is generally believed that this general is based on Udet. In the play the general is harassed by the Nazis and his apartment is bugged by the Gestapo. It is not impossible that Udet's place was bugged. But whatever the truth, when he was writing his memoirs some forty years after the event. Fieseler regards the good of name of Udet as restored. It is 'surrounded with aura' (*von einem Nimbus umgeben*).[112] That is surely stretching a point. In his mind Fieseler was still viewing Udet as a gallant, daring flyer, having no sense of danger in the air – a sort of alter ego.

It was perhaps around the time of Uder's death that Fieseler chanced to meet in Berlin a young man of his acquaintance by the name of Kai Karstensen.[113] It happened that Karstensen had some years earlier, when he was eighteen, visited Fieseler in Kassel, hoping to learn how to fly at the

110   Fieseler, op. cit., p.250.
111   Burleigh, op. cit., p.236.
112   Fieseler, op. cit., p.242.
113   Ibid, pp.275-276.

GFW flying school. The young man evidently impressed Fieseler, but he was dissuaded from his ambition by his father, a wine grower in the Rhineland, who looked upon his son as his successor and saw flying as a dangerous activity. After that Karstensen, who was well educated, had been imbued with Nazi ideology and taken up a post in the Party, where he acquitted himself well. He was promoted to a position in the propaganda ministry; indeed he worked very closely with Propaganda Minister Goebbels himself. When they happened to bump into each other in Berlin, Fieseler invited Karstensen to spend a relaxing weekend as his guest in Kassel. Indeed he proposed that they do a spot of hunting together, evidently a pursuit that both men indulged in.

Karstensen accepted the invitation and before long the visit took place. Fieseler's initial good impressions were confirmed, but he noted that the young man was troubled in some way. They engaged in a frank conversation, in the course of which Karstensen dropped his guard. He said sufficient unpleasant truths about the regime to cause Fieseler to admit that he too was 'informed about some crimes.' Fieseler appears to have revealed to the young man some of his own confidential views about the Nazis. So it was that the two men became united in a bond of trust, meeting on various occasions, presumably in Berlin. 'Every time I spoke to him,' says Fieseler, 'I could detect increasing dissatisfaction.' At some point Karstensen admitted that he was very uneasy with the sort of work he had to do at the propaganda ministry. It turned out that he had been requested to perform certain tasks which for moral reasons he felt unable to perform. This hesitation had led to a dispute between himself and Goebbels. The crux of their differences was unknown to Fieseler, or so he said. The upshot was that Karstensen was told that 'there was only one solution:' he would have to perform military service. The young man went to a military flying school, obtained a pilot's licence, and was posted to North Africa, where he was killed in action.

That is the account as recorded by Fieseler, but it only rings true in its general outline. A handicap is that Fieseler does not specify any dates, but, seeing that the German army in North Africa was defeated in May 1943, we can assume that Karstensen was killed around then at the latest. The fact that he and Fieseler met with some frequency suggests that Karstensen was forthcoming about what he knew about the regime. If that were not the case, the two men, otherwise enjoying a bond of trust with each other, would not have much to talk about. If that supposition has a basis in fact, then it almost certainly follows that Karstensen *did* reveal to Fieseler the nature of that unpalatable task that Goebbels wanted him to undertake.

However, even if the young man actually restrained himself from that admission, it is highly likely that Fieseler learnt from him a good many unsavoury things about the Nazi state. We may therefore conclude that Fieseler, informed by the indiscreet Udet, on the one hand, and the possibly more circumspect Karstensen, on the other, was for sure privy to highly sensitive matters that the average citizen would never get to know. For someone who professed to be politically neutral, Fieseler was freely delving into the murkier politics of the Nazi state through two well-placed sources. It is as if in revealing these conversations with Karstenstein that Fieseler could not resist passing on to his readers the hint that he knew a good deal about some very unsavoury aspects of the Nazi regime.

A loyal companion and helper.
In addition to Storch production in 1941, which had increased from 207 to 426, GFW turned out 35 Klemm trainers and 154 Me 109s. From 1937 to 1945 the company produced nearly 3,000 Storch aircraft for the Luftwaffe, but the year 1942 saw a notable change concerning production. Assembly commenced at the factory of the Morane Saulnier Company in Puteaux in the western suburbs of Paris. The connection with France brought some unexpected cheer to GFW or to a

few lucky ones, once arrangements were underway to transfer the production of the Storch to Morane-Saulnier in France. This resulted in the establishment of the GFW Paris office and a good deal of commuting by a twin-engined Caudron, a French aircraft. In next to no time the plane was bringing to Kassel 'coveted French articles like perfume, ladies fashions and sumptuous foodstuffs.'[114] Whenever the Caudron landed at Waldau, there was always a reception party eagerly waiting for it.

The Storch was also manufactured at the Beneš Mráz aircraft Company in Shoken in Nazi-occupied Czechoslovakia. In the course of the war 138 Storch would be built by Beneš Mraz and 141 by Morane-Saulnier. There was also production under licence in Romania, a Nazi ally at the time, at the ICAR airplane factory in Bucharest, but only 16 came off the assembly line before the end of the war.[115] Fieseler does not comment on these developments, but it is hard to imagine that he relished the idea of his beloved Storch being assembled in other countries.

Aeronautically speaking, Fieseler's greatest triumph was the Storch. No telling of his life would be complete or even justifiable without recounting how this remarkable aircraft, so perversely versatile, fared in the context for which it was first conceived by Aviation Ministry planners in 1936: war. It might be argued that there is no need in a biography of Fieseler to chronicle the role of the Storch in war because it had, as it were, a life of its own quite independent of its actual creator. But, without recording the story of the Storch, we are not able to grasp Fieseler's singular contribution to German air-mindedness and indeed to world aviation in the first half of the 20th century. Therefore, let it not be thought that there can be nothing special about a slow-moving, vulnerable, lightly armed aircraft. Despite being on the losing side, it might be said that the Fieseler Storch had (as they say) a good war. If the British can say that about Spitfires, Hurricanes and Lancasters, why should Germans or indeed anyone else not be able to say that about the Storch?

The point is that in its own class the Storch was as fit-for-purpose and as nimble a flying machine as, say, Britain's extolled Spitfire was in its class. Just as the Spitfire has been transformed into a symbol of heroic resistance in British memory and in the memory of its allies, so in its own way Fieseler's brain-child, with its almost mysterious slow speed and astoundingly short take-off and landing capability, can be seen to have equivalently transcended its nominal operational role, though for vastly different reasons. In the case of the Storch, it can best be likened to a minor actor in a major theatrical production who manages to be on stage in the presence of various leading actors at several epochal moments in the unfolding of the drama and, as we shall, at its eventual climactic conclusion. The leading actors *so far* have included Hitler, Göring, and Mussolini, not to mention Stalin. Other parts, as it were, will be played by other major presences as well as some of the most loathsome specimens thrown up by the Nazi regime.

We can go further. No other aircraft in the entire Second World War can hold a candle to the Fieseler Storch in combined terms of geographical spread of deployment, exposure to climactic range, and personalities associated with it. Furthermore, it may well be that the Storch was the only German aircraft that lasted the entire duration of the Second World War without being bettered by anything developed by the Allies. Wherever it was in service, it was considered 'a loyal companion and helper,' performing outstandingly in reconnaissance, liaison and rescue.[116] Twenty one different variants of the Storch were produced between 1936 and 1945, each variant being a response to new technology such as improvements in engine performance or communications equipment or to operational requirements. One variant was produced for purely civilian use. There was an ambulance version. Another – in limited series – was designed for operations in the 'tropics' (i.e.

---

114 Nagel und Bauer, op. cit., p.176.
115 Ibid, p.248.
116 Piekalkiewicz, p.28.

North Africa), whilst a highly specialised version was produced in 1942 as a 'police aircraft for countering partisans and secret missions.'[117]

When war broke out in September 1939, the Storch had already been in support of the Condor Legion in the Spanish Civil War (1936-1939) and in the invasion of Czechoslovakia in 1938. With the commencement of the Polish campaign in September 1939, it displayed its true worth. Wolfram von Richthofen, who was in charge of the Blitzkrieg against Poland, used a Storch to go behind enemy lines. His plane received shots through the fuel tank, but Richthofen skilfully brought it down on the German side. The Storch saw action throughout Poland, where again it showed its adaptability in the face of enemy fire. Not only that: it was used to detect where 'dispersed groups of insurgents hiding in forests, which would not be seen by war planes roaring by at great height.'[118] These experiences quickly confounded 'the pessimists at the top of the Luftwaffe', who believed that reconnaissance flights with unarmed Storch were highly risky.[119] The very first day of the war had squashed their prophecies about 'a blood bath' awaiting such a slow-moving plane.[120] In fact the Storch was remarkably doughty throughout the entire conflict. According to one assessment: 'Despite audacious missions in full view of the enemy, it suffered amazingly few losses, its front-line life being (as was said) 10 times that of the Bf [Messerschmitt] 109 fighter.'[121]

As the Polish campaign got underway, one Storch was actually flown ahead of German lines. Thus in a matter of days it was proving to be a very useful adjunct to Wehrmacht operations on the ground. One consequence of the Polish campaign was a surge of orders for the Storch from Nazi Germany's allies, notably Bulgaria, Croatia, Hungary and Romania. The Aviation Ministry in Berlin restricted the number to so-called 'prestige deliveries', as the Luftwaffe was the priority customer.[122] Keen interest was shown by Japan, which was heavily involved in its war with China. In January 1940 the Japanese Embassy offered to purchase three Fi 156 machines for 67,500 Reichsmarks and to acquire for a further 150,000 the rights to manufacture their own version in Japan. In the event the Japanese build two variations. The first one, built by Nippon Kokusai Kōgyō and redesignated as the Ki 76, was designed for submarine detection and was equipped with four bombs – a good example of the Japanese penchant for modifying a sophisticated foreign product for hitherto unexploited purposes. The other variation, called the Te-Gō, was designed for artillery observation, but development was discontinued in 1942 when a prototype crashed.[123] But even in Japan the Storch proved uncopiable.

Links between Axis partners Nazi Germany and Japan in the field of military aviation may have been much closer than is generally assumed; certainly the Japanese Ambassador, Baron Ōshima, who had a good command of German, was well-informed on the basis of regular conversations with top Nazis, including Hitler and foreign minister Ribbentrop.[124] Willy Messerschmitt, whose aircraft had been delivered to Japan in the 1930s, sent his chief pilot to Japan in 1941 to discuss cooperation, whilst the Japanese, who were evidently informed about some top-secret projects through their embassy in Berlin, became 'extremely interested' in the Me 163 and 262 prototype

---

117   Ibid, p.164.
118   Norden, op. cit., p.51.
119   Piekalkiewicz, op. cit., p.28.
120   Ibid, p.28.
121   P. Eden (ed.) (2008). *The Encyclopedia of Aircraft of WWII*. London: Amber Books, p.170.
122   Piekalkiewicz op. cit., p.124.
123   Ibid, pp.125-126.
124   M. Hastings, *The Secret War: Spies, Codes and Guerrillas* 1939-1945, p.396. My wife, who is Japanese, found a Japanese website that revealed that Ōshima had been taught German as a boy by a German tutor and that as ambassador in Berlin he was considered to be 'more German than the Germans.'

jet fighters. Remarkably in December 1943 there were even direct discussions between Willy Messerschmitt and Baron Ōshima about possible secondment of his company's experts to Japan.[125]

In 1940 and 1941 the Storch supported operations in Europe, when Belgium, Luxembourg, the Netherlands, Denmark, Norway and France found themselves under the control of the Reich. Notable from the point of view of military aviation is the attack on Belgium on 10 May, when 100 Storch aircraft in relays dropped 400 men – two per plane – of the Grossdeutschland Infantry Regiment behind the Belgian frontier. This was said to be the Storch's 'greatest and at the same time most audacious operation in the entire Second World War.'[126] In May 1940 France itself capitulated. Paris was spared destructive attacks by Stukas which would have killed and injured hundreds of people and damaged countless buildings. Instead, Parisians had to endure the lesser humiliation of watching the smallest and least armed of German aircraft, namely a couple of Storch aircraft, land and take off from La Place de la Concorde: a feat which was '"nothing special" for their pilots.'[127]

By May 1940 the fighting had spread to North Africa. Rommel was a frequent passenger and used an issue of *FZ* to praise the performance of the Storch in desert conditions, noting that 'it was almost always possible to land it on stony terrain.'[128] This was of course a tremendous celebrity endorsement for the Storch. In the North African campaign a Storch fell into the hands of the British and was used by Montgomery, who would not be the only commander on the Allied side to appreciate this versatile aircraft. When in June 1941 Hitler unleashed Operation Barbarossa, his assault on the Soviet Union, this massive operation would prepare the ground for 'his greatest project of all, the destruction of Jewish Bolshevism.'[129] The Wehrmacht with Luftwaffe support ripped its way deep into that country's vast territory. Wherever the Wehrmacht campaigned in the Soviet Union, the Storch was on hand.

One memorable deployment involved Germany's best known and much lionised female pilot, Hanna Reitsch, who in November 1941 accepted a request 'to undertake a morale-boosting visit to the men on the Eastern. For three weeks she enthusiastically and courageously toured Luftwaffe units, some very isolated, in her Storch, 'sometimes sharing a tin of sardines with the men' and learning 'to distinguish between the sounds of German and Soviet fire.'[130] Reitsch, incidentally, was not the only notable German aviatrix of the Nazi period to appreciate the superb flying qualities of the Storch. Equally remarkable was Melitta von Stauffenberg, the sister-in-law of Claus von Stauffenberg, one of the leading members of the failed July 1994 plot to remove Hitler from power. Melitta, an outstanding and intrepid Luftwaffe test pilot with a PhD in aeronautical engineering, ranked the Storch with Messerschmitt and Focke-Wulf aircraft as being 'particularly interesting from a flying point of view.'[131] Being based at Rechlin, the Luftwaffe testing station (*Erprobungsstelle*), she had wide access to a considerable range of military aircraft, including the Storch. Later in the war she learnt how to fly it at night.[132]

By early autumn it looked as if the USSR were a spent power. The Japanese were so certain of this that it was a factor in the most fatal decision in their history to attack the US Pacific fleet in Pearl Harbor in December 1941. They reasoned that with the USA eliminated as a military threat

---

125   H. Ebert, J, Kaiser and K. Peters, *Willy Messerschmitt – Pionier der Luftfahrt und des Leichtbaues*. Bonn: Bernard & Graefe, p.272,
126   Ibid, 33.
127   Norden, op. cit., p.51.
128   *Fieseler Zeitung*, July 8 1941.
129   Beevor, op. cit., p.150.
130   C. Mulley, *The Women for Flew for Hitler: The True Story of Hitler's Valkyries*, pp.197-199.
131   Cited in Mulley, op. cit., p.116.
132   Mulley, op. cit, p.236.

they could expand their military operations in Far East without fear of Soviet reprisals. Within days of Japanese warplanes crippling the US fleet, Hitler declared war on the US. By this time, however, the Soviet Union had repulsed the Wehrmacht at Moscow. That rebuff and the entry of the USA into the war 'made December 1941 the geo-political turning-point' of the entire Second World War.[133] No-one could have seen that at the time. Hitler though still remained completely convinced of his military genius. His will, as articulated in German fighting power, discipline and adoration of their Führer, would conquer all.

In 1942 Hitler ordered the Wehrmacht to conquer Stalingrad. Not only would its capture ensure German access to the oilfields of Baku beyond the Caucasus, but the city named after his arch-enemy would be obliterated. On 19 June a Fieseler Storch was shot down behind Soviet lines. Its passenger was Major Joachim Reichel, a German staff officer who was carrying the plans for the entire German offensive in South Russia. This, in a manner of speaking, was a very inglorious moment for a Storch. Hitler was furious, but Stalin, suspicious to a fault, believed the documents were fakes to lull him into thinking that the true target of German strategy was Moscow.[134]

On Sunday 23 August the German armies and their allies set about crushing Stalingrad. The Storch performed reconnaissance duties and was used by the overall German commander, General Friedrich Paulus as personal transport. Wolfram von Richthofen, commander of the Fourth Luftflotte began to carpet-bomb the city. On 25 August he 'flew over the ruined city in his personal Fieseler Storch spotter aircraft and pronounced it totally destroyed.'[135] If this pronouncement were to imply that Stalingrad was for the taking, Richthofen was going to be proved severely wrong. Some of the most savage fighting of the entire Second World War would take place in Stalingrad.

As the snows came and the temperature plummeted, the Soviet Army and its fighters – including civilians in the city – were aided by a redoubtable force of nature, which Russians call 'General Winter' and which literally froze the Nazi onslaught to a standstill. In Germany information about the epic battle being waged by the Wehrmacht 'slowed to a trickle.'[136] On 2 February 1943 the Germans surrendered. The defeat of the Wehrmacht at the epic battle of Stalingrad had cost the German army and its allies nearly half a million men, killed and captured. It was not just a shattering event in its own right; it undermined Hitler's standing as a military leader. At home, 'the population reacted with utter shock, dismay and an anger made all the greater by the optimistic reports which had circulated so recently.'[137] By now 'only Nazi fanatics still believed that the war could be won.'[138]

In the meantime *FZ* had run various features in its 1941 and 1942 issues about the Storch and its exploits. Photographs depict the Storch in various locations. Some show Storchs 'all over in Tobruk', whilst another captures a Storch 'in the front with the panzers in Russia.' A rather stunning, if grainy, photograph taken in 1942 in the wilds of Finland shows a Storch with a herd of reindeer charging past it. An article by a pilot in Russia writes that how the Storch was indispensable for 'delivering munitions, spare parts, mail and food to the soldiers on the front line and returning with the wounded.' The Storch, he adds, had proved its mettle in all weather conditions, including the Russian winter.[139]

Less obvious to the German public for a time was the systematic implementation of Hitler's ghastly, genocidal vision to exterminate (*ausrotten*) the Jews in Europe. This was now happening on a scale of murderous ruthlessness that still staggers the imagination. Indeed, 'at the beginning

133 Ibid, p.257.
134 Beevor, op. cit., p.333.
135 M. Bourne, *The Second World War in the Air: The Story of Air Combat in Every Theatre of World War Two*, p.115.
136 Stargardt, op. cit., p.329.
137 Stargardt, op. cit., p.322.
138 Beevor, op. cit., p.400.
139 *Fieseler Zeitung*, June 1941; August 1941; April 1942; July 1942. Sammlung Urlen

of 1942', writes historian Nicholas Stargardt, 'most of Europe's Jews were still alive; by the end of the year, the majority were not.'[140] To cite one mind-numbing statistic: in the horrific Treblinka extermination camp some 700,000 Jews and smaller number of Roma perished in the gas chambers in July 1942 and August 1943 alone.[141] Fieseler, not surprisingly, has nothing to say about the genocide. This is not to say that he was oblivious to certain terrible things happening to the Jews 'in the East.' Not only were reports about mass killings, not necessarily precise, but pointing in the right direction, seeping back into Germany, but also Fieseler himself was operating in privileged circles, in which the better informed passed among themselves well-sourced information in low whispers.

Throughout 1942 GFW work continued to be hampered. To add to the increasing woes of material shortages, disruption of supply lines and the limitations of employing forced labour, Kassel had been the target of RAF bombing raids, the earliest of which, causing little damage, had taken place in July 1940. So far the Fieseler factories had not been severely affected by what was seen in Germany as British aerial terrorism. There was nothing to indicate that the Aviation Ministry were in any way dissatisfied with performance at GFW in the increasingly demanding wartime conditions. In 1943 GFW produced 493 Storchs. By this time 181 had been exported to various friendly countries, the biggest customers being allies, namely Hungary, Romania and Italy. In addition two neutrals, Sweden and Spain, purchased small numbers.[142]

In 1942 the company had commenced building the Focke-Wulf 190 under licence, production of the Messerschmitt 109 having been discontinued in 1941. Until March 1945 no fewer than 2,461 Fw 190s would leave the Fieseler production lines.[143] So it was that GFW was a major builder under licence of the two planes which formed the backbone of the Luftwaffe fighter capability. Later in 1943 Fieseler became a leading light in the creation of a wholly new species of aircraft, a pilotless projectile, which today would be called a weapon of mass destruction. Could this be the weapon so desperately needed by Hitler, after defeat at Stalingrad a deeply tarnished military figurehead around the world and not just in Germany, to regain the initiative and knock out Britain?

The path to Peenemünde

It happened that in 1936 the Argus company, which was the major supplier of V-8 piston engines for the Storch, developed a system for controlling aircraft at a distance. In 1939 the company sent a preliminary design to the Aviation Ministry. The aircraft envisaged was called an 'aerial torpedo' (*Lufttorpedo*) capable of carrying a payload of 1,000kg to an operational altitude of 5,000 metres. This aircraft would be equipped with an engine with pulse-jet mechanism and have a cruising speed of 700km/h.[144] In this revolutionary type of engine 'fuel is injected into a combustion chamber where it is mixed with air and then ignited, with the resulting jet exhaust directed back through an exhaust tube.'[145] Details about the engine were formally presented to the Aviation Ministry in 1940, but officials there did not wish to fund further development. At this stage in the war everything was overwhelmingly going Germany's way. Hence there was no pressing urgency to think about developing aerial weaponry of enhanced lethal capabilities. That conviction would change dramatically when as of 1943 German cities were being pulverised by British and American bombers.

---

140   Stargardt, op. cit., p.233.
141   https://www.jewishvirtuallibrary.org/jsource/Holocaust/chron.html#42
142   Nagel und Bauer, op. cit., p.248.
143   Ibid, p.232.
144   Mantelli-Brown-Kittel-Graf, *The V1, the V2, the V3*, p.8.
145   S. J. Zaloga, *V-1 Flying Bomb 1941-1945: Hitler's Infamous "Doodlebug,"* p.4.

According to Fieseler, his own interest was sparked in the winter of 1941-42, when he heard of the highly innovative aero engine being developed by Argus. He recalls that he had probably been put in the picture by the managing director of Argus, Dr Kloppenburg.[146] He immediately saw possibilities for creating a new kind of high-speed aircraft that could 'fully automatically carry a ton of explosive between 200 and 400 kilometres to hit a target with the highest possible precision.'[147] He admits that in January 1942 the project 'bordered on the fantastical, but I was convinced intuitively and aeronautically from the outset of the possibility of making it happen.'[148] He adds: 'I regarded the solution to the challenge was virtually self-evident (*fast als eine Selbstverständlichkeit*)', reasoning that 'when a load is to be transported into enemy territory, the only possible bearing element is the atmosphere.'[149]

Never one to let the grass grow under his feet, Fieseler arranged to discuss his ideas with General Roluf Lucht, the chief engineer in the Aviation Ministry, who Fieseler knew from pre-war days when he was chief test pilot for the Luftwaffe.[150] However, there was something else on Fieseler's mind that January 1942, The highly reliable Erich Bachem, with whom he had worked so closely for the last ten years, had recently told him that he was leaving FGW to set up with the approval of the Aviation Ministry his own company which would supply parts to the aircraft industry. This was a major blow to Fieseler. In Berlin he decided to take the opportunity to enquire whether there were talented people available to fill the vacancy of technical director at his company.

Lucht showed immediate interest in Fieseler's 'fantastical' scheme. In the course of their conversation Fieseler mentioned that at his company none of his otherwise highly capable designers or engineers had experience of Argus's new engine technology. By good fortune, Lucht promptly identified a candidate. A well-known designer, Robert Lusser, who had until recently been working for Heinkel, had apparently left the company amid much rancour. At all events Lucht had high regard for Lusser's expertise, but warned Fieseler that he was not an easy man to work with.

Ignoring that, Fieseler realised that Lusser might indeed be the very man to succeed Bachem. In reality Lusser had very strong credentials. He had qualified as an engineer at the Technical University of Stuttgart. He had also worked at Siemens, Klemm, and Bayerische Flugzeugwerke, where he collaborated with Messerschmitt on the design of the Me 109 and other notable aircraft. He was therefore one of Germany's brightest aircraft designers; hence a very good catch indeed for Fieseler. Furthermore he was also a qualified pilot. In between times he gave lectures in his alma mater in Stuttgart. From past experience Fieseler could sense that he and Lusser could work well together.

On 22 January the two of them held a very productive meeting. Fieseler offered Lusser the opportunity to work on the new project as an inducement. Lusser immediately accepted, as already he had been turning his mind to the possibility of designing a low-cost bomber (*Billigbomber*).[151] Within five weeks he was in Kassel and in next to no time in contact with the Ministry. At the end of February he visited Argus, who no doubt welcomed Fieseler's initiative. *FZ* of June 1942 published a profile of Lusser to GFW, describing him as 'one of the most German successful sports flyers in the 1920s and 30s.'[152] No doubt this shared background with Fieseler was a factor that helped the two men to bond together so promptly.

---

146   Fieseler, op. cit., p.252-253.
147   Ibid, p.253.
148   Ibid, p.252.
149   Ibid, pp.252-253.
150   Piekalkiewicz, op. cit., p.15.
151   Fieseler, op. cit., p.252.
152   *Fieseler Zeitung*, June 1941. Sammlung Urlen.

Fieseler, not wanting to wait for official ministry approval, authorised Lusser to set the project office to work on developing a flying bomb. His independent initiative is a striking example of the remarkable discretion which could be exercised by an defence economy leader even during wartime. In GFW the project received the designation 'P5 Project Erfurt.'[153] As for Bachem, he left GFW in July. In 1944, with SS backing, he developed a vertical take-off manned rocket, *der Natter* (Adder). The project foundered in March 1945 after the pilot was killed in the first manned test flight.

In the meantime the ministry, having been persuaded by Lusser of the project's potential, had a change of heart and set up a project evaluation committee. The criteria it was seeking in the proposed missile were these: it had to relieve the pressure on Luftwaffe fighter command, save flying personnel and substitute expensive bombers.[154] In June 1942 it issued GFW with a development contract under the project designation Fi 103, for 'a long-range missile in the form of an aircraft' (*Ferngeschoss in Flugzeugform*).[155] Aviation Ministry chief Milch granted the project highest priority status and 'shortly after that was able to inspire Hitler and Göring about the whole project.'[156] In the Aviation Ministry the flying bomb project was code-named 'cherrystone' (*Kirschkern*).

As far as Fieseler was concerned, it was now a question of designing and building a body to accommodate the engine and a warhead packed with a ton of explosive which would be detonated upon impact with the chosen target. The device would need to be launched from specially constructed catapults and have an operating range between 200 and 400 kilometres. The whole thing, he thought, be 'a simple affair', requiring 'a primitive design,' but making it fit for purpose was a different matter.

Lusser proved to be another ideal collaborator for Fieseler.[157] There was never any disagreement between them. Not only was Lusser a very competent aircraft designer with flying experience, he was also a focused and energetic leader of men. As with Emil Arnolt, Fieseler was 'astounded' how promptly and positively his new colleague dealt with his questions, doubts and suggestions.[158] In the meantime he set about building up the project team. One of the first appointments was that of Reinhold Mewes. Another recruit was the highly capable Willy Fiedler, who relinquished his position of chief test pilot. But, as work progressed, unforeseen problems arose, all of which required their own solution. For example, it was discovered that during a catapult launch the sudden kick-back could be so powerful that the aerofoils snapped backwards. So a way had to be found to prevent deformation of the aerofoils during take-off and ascent at full speed.

Another challenge concerned the best way to measure the distance to the target and ensure that the flying bomb hit it. Lusser and Fieseler opted for 'a pre-set automatic guidance system,' which had been developed by the Askania Werke in Berlin and was being assembled by 'slave labourers in underground prisons.'[159] The device comprised a magnetic compass, two gyroscopes incorporating an accelerometer (a type of speedometer), a barometer to gauge altitude and a small propeller on the nose to measure the distance travelled. This propeller 'was pre-set to trip a switch arming the warhead, and when this was reached, a tachometer switched on an electromechanical device which cancelled the gyroscopes and caused the weapon to swing into an uncertain dive.'[160] Until one of the missiles fell into their hands, the British thought mistakenly that the device was radio-

---

153   Nagel and Bauer, op. cit., p.175.
154   Ibid, p.177.
155   Ibid, p.252.
156   Ibid, p.178.
157   Ibid, p.253.
158   Fieseler, op. cit., p.253.
159   R. MacLean, *Berlin: Imagine a City*, p.135.
160   P. Haining, *The Flying Bomb: Contemporary Accounts of the VI and V2 Raids on Britain 1942-45*, p.15.

controlled. In short, there was a good deal of technological sophistication in the device's operating system to ensure that the engine cut out at the appropriate height and position with respect to its target.

Yet another challenge crossed Fieseler's mind: how could the flying bomb overcome the barrage balloons that the British had strung up along their coastline as a major form of aerial defence? He asked Lusser to consult with experts, who came up with a solution. It transpired that it would be necessary to equip the leading edges of the aerofoils with square holes, which being sharp could cut through cables tethering the barrage balloons. As work progressed on Project Erfurt, Kassel was the target of an RAF air raid on the night of 27/28 August 1942. Some 250 bombers dropped 567 tons of incendiaries and high explosives. A few incendiaries fell on No 1 Works in Bettenhausen, but the overall damage was light.

Throughout that year the Wehrmacht continued to call up even more skilled workers from German industry, whilst the agents of Fritz Sauckel, Hitler's Plenipotentiary for Labour, 'brought 34,000 foreign workers to the Reich each week.'[161] Although key armaments factories enjoyed a certain amount of protection from these levies of their best workers, FGW found itself taking on more and more compulsory workers. For example, in November it was assigned 150 Russian women. As problems of intercultural communication across the complex linguistic *and* ideological divide were so acute, 'a small Fieseler dictionary' was produced for work leaders.[162] In fact, this most improbable of war-time publications was a modest glossary focusing on the quality of work ('work is good', 'work is bad'), general commands ('work faster', 'work more slowly') and commands concerning specific technical procedures ('grease parts better', 'remove flash properly'). The Russian appeared not in the Cyrillic alphabet but in transliteration, allowing the overseer to say – or shout – the phrases in not always so intelligible Russian.[163] It is most unlikely that this practical aid did much to reduce on-site misunderstandings or alleviate mutual mistrust between 'superior' Germans and 'inferior' Russians.

By this time in the war Fieseler – if of course we accept his version of events – was far more involved in design problems of the Fi 103 than it is normally appreciated. For a start, 'it was often impossible to determine which of the sub-systems had been responsible', whilst the crashes were often induced by the pulse-jet engine.'[164] He was working with Lusser and his team in the way that characterised his involvement with the creation of the Storch: he discussed, reflected, proposed solutions and overcame objections on the basis of his very considerable intuitions. In other words, Fieseler did more than just provide his company as a manufacturer of the flying bomb. In reality, GFW had an explicit innovative role in its development. Thus, by the end of the year the missile 'had changed dramatically' in form and performance.[165] What was being created was a weapon that was difficult to classify. It was not a rocket in so far as that was not being designed to leave the atmosphere. Equally, it was not a plane owing to its guidance system which did not require a pilot. It could be best described as 'a winged but pilotless fuel propelled flying bomb.'[166] The time had come to put it through trials.

The location was the top-secret Army Research Establishment (*Heeresversuchsanstalt*) at Peenemünde, a fishing village on the Baltic some sixty miles east of Rostock on the island of Usedom. Strictly speaking Usedom was really a peninsular: a 'ragged-shaped area of land … than twenty five

---

161 Stargardt, op. cit., p.273.
162 Nagel und Bauer, op. cit., p.180.
163 I am indebted to Oscar Azevedo for his scan of the first page of the glossary.
164 Zaloga, op. cit., p.7.
165 Ibid, p.180.
166 http://www.historylearningsite.co.uk/world-war-two/world-war-two-in-western-europe/the-v-revenge-weapons/the-v1/

miles long', separated from the mainland by a river.¹⁶⁷ The facility had been established in 1937 and was where a rocket programme was being developed under SS General Walter Dornberger and Wernher von Braun, who was overall technical director and 'the outstanding spirit in the whole rocket project.'¹⁶⁸ Some 10,000 engineers, scientists, administrators and secretaries were employed here, many living in purpose-build housing and enjoying a life-style that was a good deal safer than other parts of Germany subject to bombing by the British and Americans. Indeed one of the secretaries recalled 'a lovely time, so completely untroubled with world's affairs.'¹⁶⁹ But it was not a lovely time for the 10-12, 000 forced labourers, a high proportion from nearby Poland, who lived in camps surrounded by watchtowers. 'Undernourished and subject to harassment, they did the unskilled heavy work – 'the digging, fetching and carrying, pulling and pushing.'¹⁷⁰

The facility's work was being conducted in conditions of absolute secrecy. It is probable that Fieseler had known nothing about the programme to develop the rocket code-named A-4, unless of course the indiscreet Udet had told him about it. In October 1942 one of von Braun's A-4 rockets had been shot to a height of about 60kms and achieved a speed of 1,200m per second. The first test flight of the Fi 103 was scheduled for 24 December, being launched from a Focke-Wulf 200. Fieseler was on hand to observe its aerodynamic qualities in flight. The test proved successful, the device 'covering the predetermined path without difficulty.'¹⁷¹ It was a perfect Christmas present for the Fieseler team.

The Fi 103 was first launched from a ramp at the beginning of April 1943 some ten months after the Aviation Ministry issued the contract. It was 'a considerable achievement': a tribute to Lusser and his team, and all the more so given the wartime conditions, which by now included the massive bombing by British and American bombers.¹⁷² Every single test flight was being filmed in order to observe performance and behaviour in flight. All the while progress of the Fi 103 was closely monitored by Aviation Ministry chief Erhard Milch, who often asked Fieseler for updates. Fieseler would have told him that Lusser and his team were having problems with launches. For example, no complete solution had yet been found to stop the aerofoils from bending backwards on every launch. The result was that 'one flight was a success and the next one a failure.'¹⁷³ A member of Lusser's team was one of GFW's most capable engineers, Willy Fiedler, who served as Fieseler's eyes and ears at Peenemünde.

If in April 1943 Milch was monitoring the progress of the Fi 103, in that same month the Royal Air Force undertook three reconnaissance sorties over Peenemünde, suspecting that it was the hub of a rocket programme or of some other 'diabolic project the Nazis were fomenting.'¹⁷⁴ This was eleven months after a Mosquito on a reconnaissance flight over Peenemünde had photographed three large circular embankments, which the specialist photographic interpreters in Britain were at a loss to explain.¹⁷⁵

To put that in context: since 1942 the Royal Air Force had been taking high-quality reconnaissance photographs of the entire territory of Germany. This activity was being closely monitored by a special committee which had been appointed by Churchill to probe rumours about a suspected German rocket programme. The cameras provided photographs of exceptional detail.

167 Middlebrook, op. cit., p.14.
168 R. V. Jones, *Most Secret War: British Scientific Intelligence 1939-1945*, p.347.
169 Cited in: Middlebrook, op. cit., p.28.
170 Ibid, p.29.
171 H. D. Hölsken, *Die V-Waffen: Entstehung – Propaganda – Kriegseinsatz*, p.38.
172 Fieseler, op. cit., p.255.
173 Ibid, p.258.
174 M. Hastings, *The Secret War: Spies, Codes and Guerrillas 1939-1945*, p.421.
175 Ibid, pp.420-421.

The British developed a technique for creating 3 D images by overlapping the photographs, which were minutely scrutinised by expert photograph interpreters to help identify objects of military significance and of special interest.

The embankments remained a mystery, but in 1943 the British had bugged a conversation between two captured German generals, in which they referred to a new top-secret weapon. This was a major breakthrough of intelligence, which could be added to other fragments, some emanating from Polish intelligence in Warsaw. Then, on 23 June 1943, London received 'from a well-placed official in a technical department of the German High Command' a report about 'a secret weapon' to be used against the British capital. It was said to be 'an air mine, with wings, long distance steering and a rocket drive.'[176]

In the meantime work on the other major advanced project, that of the Wehrmacht-backed A-4 rocket, had been progressing at Peenemünde. No doubt von Braun and his men regarded the Fi 103 project as a pointless distraction and inferior from the technical point of view. By early 1943 the rivalry between the Wehrmacht and Luftwaffe was said to have flared into 'a smouldering conflict.'[177] According to Fieseler, Milch was hell-bent on 'thwarting the mammoth rocket.'[178] In February a Development Commission for Long-Range Shooting' (*Entwicklungskommission für Fernschiessen*) was established to bring together senior representatives of the Wehrmacht, Luftwaffe and members of the development teams. It is likely that Lusser represented GFW on this body, whose task was to further mass production of the rocket for the army and the flying bomb for the Luftwaffe.

All the while Willy Fiedler, who had been working at the top-secret site at Peenemünde, proved to be a very reliable informant about developments there. He reported to Fieseler that the Army Weapons Office in Berlin was not very impressed with the Fi 103 and ordered von Braun himself to identify the problems with its development. Von Braun, it seems, was not very complimentary; which is perhaps not surprising. He may well have thought that the Fieseler device was unwelcome competition with his A-4, which was not without its own teething problems and which would later be known to the world as the V-2. It is normally assumed, by the way, that a remark of Propaganda Minister Goebbels gave rise to the notion V-weapons, whereby the V stands for the German word *Vergeltung*, meaning vengeance or retribution. However, at least as far as the V-2 is concerned, the V 'originally stood for *Versuchsmuster*, meaning 'experimental type.'[179]

Despite the inter-service rivalry, the outgoing Fiedler struck up friendly relationships with some of the army weapons people and through them he acquired a lot of information about the A-4. From him Fieseler learned that the weapon weighed 14 tons. Fuel alone accounted for two-thirds of that weight: methyl alcohol, hydrogen, pure alcohol and liquid oxygen. Almost all the remaining weight was accounted for by precision instruments, motors, relays, pumps and other technical equipment. The warhead proper weighed just 560kg, which was about 4% of the total weight. If that stunned Fieseler, then he could hardly believe his ears when Fiedler told him that around 10,000 people were working on the A-4 at the facility at Peenemünde. Half were engineers and scientists, all working on how to lift half a ton of explosive in vertical ascent and guide it to its target.

Fieseler estimated (without indicating the basis of his calculation) that that the phenomenal costs of developing the A-4 'were bound to outweigh umpteen times (*um das Zigfache*) the damage

---

176 Middlebrook, op. cit., p.38.
177 Ibid, p.43.
178 Fieseler, op. cit., p.259.
179 According to Middlebrook, op. cit., the A in A-4 stood for *Aggregat*, meaning 'machine unit' or 'assembly of machine parts', p.19.

inflicted on the enemy.'[180] It was blindingly obvious to him that of the two devices the Fi 103 would prove to be the more cost-effective. Indeed, according to one estimate, an A-4 rocket cost 'about a hundred times' as much as the Fieseler device.[181] However, by summer 1943 the truth was that his pet device was still a long way from being seriously considered to be an actual weapon.[182]

---

180   Fieseler, op. cit., p.257.
181   D. Irving, *The Rise and Fall of the Luftwaffe: The Life of Luftwaffe Marshal Erhard Milch*, 1973, p.236.
182   Hölsken, op. cit., p.52.

10

The redesigning of aerial terror

So many people were clamoring for Hitler's attention and approval, and authority was divided so much, that rivalries for the Führer's favour created bottlenecks with the German war effort.

Peter Watson[1]

In the tally of non-combatant deaths caused by twentieth-century warfare, German losses to Allied bombing in the Second World War do not demand explanation in the way that the Holocaust or the use of atomic bombs do.

Hew Strachan[2]

The Storch: brilliant plane, sullied brand

For the entire conflict the Fieseler Storch was regarded as an operationally outstanding aircraft, supporting in its own particular way the conquest and subjugation of the enemies of the Reich. But it should not be forgotten that Hitler's grand plan required the wholesale elimination of the Jews and other racially inferior peoples. The Storch was put to service in that cause too. Janusz Piekalkiewicz, who has written the most complete account of the Storch in the Second World War, omits any reference to that horrific aspect of the conflict. Yet it is a matter of record that the Storch came face to face, as it were, with the shocking realities.

On 26 February 1943 a Storch was shot down near Kharkiv. Along with its pilot its high-ranking Nazi passenger was killed. This was Theodor Eicke, commander of the SS Totenkopf Division of the Waffen SS. In 1934 Eicke had been a commandant of Dachau before being appointed Inspector of Concentration Camps. Himmler approvingly described him as 'the father of the concentration camps', such was his influence over the development of the entire ghastly system.[3] We may confidently say that the Storch was a much greater loss to humanity than its passenger.

Another passenger in the same vile line of business as Eicke was Odilo Globocnik, who in the middle of September 1943 flew in a Storch to the death camp at Treblinka, where truly unspeakable horrors took place.[4] Of Globocnik, 'one of the very worst of the Nazi criminals,' it may be said that he was the most despicable specimen of mankind ever to have flown in a Storch.[5] A few weeks later Jakob Sporrenberg, Globocnik's successor as SS- and Police Chief in Lublin, flew in a Storch over the zig-zag air raid trenches, watching as forty-five thousand Jews were massacred. All the

---

1   P. Watson, *The German Genius: Europe's Third Renaissance, the Second Scientific Revolution, and the Twentieth Century,* p.697.
2   H. Strachan, Strategic bombing and that question of civilian casualties up to 1945. In: P Addison, and J. A. Crang, *Firestorm: The Bombing of Dresden, 1945,* pp.1-17.
3   P. Johnson, *Reuter Reporter in Divided Germany 1955-58.* p.77.
4   http://www.tenhumbergreinhard.de/taeter-und-mitlaeufer/treblinka-proze/a-vi-19.html.
5   G. Sereny, *The German Trauma: Experiences and Reflections 1938-2000,* p.195.

while 'loud music was broadcast to drown out the gunfire.'⁶ This cynical event, cheerily known as 'Operation Harvest Festival' must rank as one of the most macabre spectacles in the annals of military aviation (not to mention military music-making.)

One more infamous Nazi can be mentioned in this context. Since 1941 Klaus Hanke had been the fanatical Gauleiter of Lower Silesia, when on 29 April 1945 he was appointed by Hitler as Reichsführer and Chief of Police, replacing the 'disgraced' Heinrich Himmler. A Storch spirited him away 'in its glassy dome' from Breslau hours before it capitulated to the Soviet Army on 6 May 1945.⁷ He was perhaps the very last of the senior Nazi die-hards to fly in a Storch. Globocnik was captured by the British in Austria at the end of May 1945 and committed suicide before being interrogated. Hanke was captured and killed by Czech partisans in June 1945.

There is another macabre story in this general area. In the former Sudetenland there was in Graslitz (Kraslice) one of the 100 or so sub-camps of the Flossenbürg concentration camp. There French women prisoners nicknamed a particularly vicious overseer 'Fieseler Storch' on account of her being 'so long-legged and thin and spindly (*dürr*).'⁸ For those who over the years have admired the Storch for its outstanding performance and innovative design features, its anthropomorphosis into a female overseer at a concentration camp is a chilling, unsettling, but necessary reminder of the true ghastliness of the Nazi regime, which was the godfather of Fieseler's brain-child.

There is a rather different kind of story associating the Storch with two other concentration camps, namely Buchenwald and Sachsenhausen. Remarkable as it may sound, it involves flights not above, but *to* these notorious locations, and they had a humanitarian mission. It will be recalled that the leading Luftwaffe test pilot, Melitta von Stauffenberg, was the sister-in-law of Claus von Stauffenberg, who had attempted to assassinate Hitler in the failed July 1944 plot. In the aftermath her husband Alexander, a Wehrmacht officer, had with hundreds of others been arrested for complicity and interned. In the closing months of the war Alexander was imprisoned in Buchenwald. Melitta, intent on seeing Alexander, had somehow managed to secure a special permit to make a short visit to her husband, who was detained in a compound for special prisoners: that is to say, prisoners who could be used as bargaining chips with the Allies upon Germany's defeat.⁹

Shortly after that Melitta, again using her privileged status, made a second such humanitarian flight in a Storch to visit an uncle of Alexander's who was being detained at Sachsenhausen. Remarkably she secured permission to have him released and she flew off with him to safety in so far as there was safety for anyone in Nazi Germany at this time. En route she touched down near Buchenwald to make the second of eight such brave visits to her husband.¹⁰ Alexander was never to see Melitta again; she was shot down – not in a Storch – and killed by the US Air Force in April 1945.¹¹ We can perhaps conclude that Melitta's flights to Buchenwald and Sachsenhausen associate the Storch with a truly noble purpose and a remarkable personality.

A consequence of the defeat of Nazi Germany is that the victors are able to glorify their own achievements on the field of arms, whilst post-war Germans do not have the luxury of this indulgence. Britain of course has created a complete national myth around the evacuation of Dunkirk, the Battle of Britain, the convoys to Murmansk, the Dambusters Raid and the D-Day landings, not to mention the cryptoanalytical brilliance of Bletchley Park and the indefatigable pugnacity of

6   M. Burleigh, *The Third Reich: A New History*, p.656.
7   http://magazin.spiegel.de/EpubDelivery/spiegel/pdf/76574301, accessed 31 July 2015.
8   P. Cziborra, *Frauen im KZ: Möglichkeiten und Grenzen der historischen Forschung am Beispiel des KZ Flossenbürg und seiner Außenlager*, p.153
9   C. Mulley, *The Women Who Flew for Hitler: The True Story of Hitler's Valkyries*, pp.299-301.
10 Ibid, pp.301-302.
11 Ibid, pp.312-313.

Churchill. With respect to the air war, the British can lionise the Spitfire and Lancaster, of which some of the last ones flying still traverse the skies on notable national occasions. Yet, if there is one German plane in the service of the Luftwaffe that pulled off a truly spectacular feat, which can still awake the admiration of airmen and aviation enthusiasts, it must be the Fieseler Storch for its part in one particular operation: the rescue of the deposed Italian dictator Benito Mussolini from Gran Sasso, the loftiest peak in the Apennine mountains in September 1943. For some reason Fieseler does not have a word to say about this celebrated episode. Here in brief is the story.

In July 1943, after the start of the Allied invasion of Italy, King Victor Emmanuel III had Mussolini arrested in Rome. The deposed dictator was spirited away to various secret locations, the last of which was Campo Imperatore, a plateau in the Abruzzo region in the Gran Sasso massif. Immediately after Mussolini's detention, Hitler wanted 'his ally and dear friend', the Duce – 'the incarnation of the ancient grandeur of Rome' – to be rescued and brought to Germany before he was captured by the Allies.[12] A redoubtable snatch squad was assembled with Otto Skorzeny designated with Hitler's personal blessing to lead the actual rescue attempt. However, the Germans had no idea where Mussolini was being held. It took them two months to deduce that he was being confined in the resort hotel at Campo Imperatore, but even then it was only conjecture. But the evidence was strong enough for Skorzeny, dubbed 'the most dangerous man in Europe' by General Dwight Eisenhower, to plan a rescue attempt with the assistance of a company of paratroopers and a unit of SS commandos.[13]

Campo Imperatore is the highest plateau in the Apennines, alias Italy's 'Little Tibet', at an altitude ranging from 1,500 to 1,900 metres. As the location could only be accessed by cable car, the plan was that the main rescue party would be dropped by gliders near the hotel and disable any Italian military personnel. Skorzeny would enter the hotel and rescue Mussolini. A Fieseler Storch with Captain Heinrich Gerlach in the cockpit had accompanied the gliders. It would circle over the plateau and await a command to land and whisk the rescued Duce to safety. The paratroopers encountered no real opposition from the Italians. Skorzeny rushed in the hotel to get the Duce. The rescue had taken just twelve minutes. Skorzeny signalled to Gerlach that he must land. Table clothes were removed from the hotel and spread out on the rugged terrain to indicate where Gerlach should touch down. The spot chosen was on 'a steep, uneven slope … a 100 to 120 metres long … strewn with boulders and flecked with snow melt.' Ominously, 'take-off would have to be only effected down the slope in the opposite direction to landing.'[14] Gerlach also had to reckon on being buffeted by winds at that height.

Once the Storch had landed and inspected the landing strip, Skorzeny told him that he must fly off with him and that most precious of loads, Mussolini. Gerlach was horrified, as between them both men weighed around 180 kilos. 'Almost on his knees', he implored Skorzeny that their combined weight would dangerously overburden the Storch, especially as the air was so thin.[15] Besides that, the take-off run 'was dangerously short' and overlooked a ravine.[16] Skorzeny threatened to blow Gerlach's brains out if he did not comply.[17] Gerlach gave in. Into the Storch clambered Skorzeny and the decidedly unsettled Mussolini. Gerlach revved up the engine, whilst German paratroopers held on the wings until there was maximum power for take-off.

---

12   O. Szorzeny, *Szorzeny's Special Missions: Memoirs of Hitler's most Daring Commando*, p.46.
13   C. Whiting, *Skorzeny: The Most Dangerous Man in Europe*, p.3.
14   J. Piekalkiewicz, *Der Fieseler Fi 156 Storch im Zweiten Weltkrieg*, p.111.
15   Ibid, p.112.
16   R. Forczyk, *Rescuing Mussolini – Gran Sasso* 1943, p.53
17   Whiting, op. cit., p.41.

As it moved forward, the plane was twice jolted by rocks struck by its wheels. It was at the very end of the improvised landing strip before Gerlach took the Storch upwards. It 'shot over the edge of the ravine and started a dizzying descent.'[18] Until they cleared the Apennines, it was 'nerve-wracking low-level flight.'[19] Gerlach duly delivered Skorzeny and Mussolini to the German-held airfield at Pratica di Mare near Rome, where a Heinkel 111 was waiting to take the Duce to Vienna and then on to Germany to be greeted by Hitler. Skorzeny was awarded the Knight's Cross and promoted to *Sturmbannführer* (major) in the Waffen-SS for his part in the rescue. As for Gerlach, he 'had to content himself with knowledge that he had flown well.'[20]

One of many websites devoted to the Gran Sasso raid notes that it 'had all the right elements for a truly epic tale – except for the fact that it performed by the bad guys.'[21] But that is not entirely true. In the British Parliament Churchill conceded that the rescue was 'a stroke of great daring.'[22] But it was of course than that; the mission had been daringly planned and brilliantly executed. At all events the rescue of Mussolini was the most celebrated rescue of its kind of the entire Second World War, and it is certainly true that it succeeded by virtue of the extraordinary capabilities of the Storch as a short take-off and landing aircraft in the hands of an outstanding pilot. As might be expected, the rescue was given the full propaganda treatment in Germany especially at a time when Hitler's vaunted Thousand Year Reich was becoming a mere chimera. It received top billing on the front-page coverage in the *Völkischer Beobachter,* the official newspaper of the National Socialist movement, under the headline 'Out of Gran Sasso with the Fieseler Storch'.[23]

Winged rockets with remote control and launched by catapults

Back at Peenemünde joint tests of the rival weapons, Fieseler's Fi 103 flying bomb and von Braun's A-4 rocket, took place on 26 May 1943. According to Fieseler, the suggestion for the comparison was put by Milch to 'his friend', Armaments Minister, Albert Speer.[24] The event was witnessed by several notable Nazi eminences in addition to Speer and Milch, including the chief of the general staff Keitel, two senior generals, namely Olbricht and Fromm, as well as Grand Admiral Dönitz. But it was not a happy day for the Fieseler team. The two Fi 103s crashed into the sea shortly after being launched. Beyond that, he had found it galling that Milch, whom he described as 'an aeronautical amateur (*Laie*),' had directed Lusser and his team to speed things up for the event without consulting him.[25] Concerning the two A-4 rockets, the first launch went according to plan; which caused Milch no joy. The second resulted in a crash in the sea; which was said to cause the smile to return to Milch's face.[26] The advocates of the A-4, including Speer, felt 'disappointed' as they were driven back from the testing ground.[27] Fieseler would have to wait until September to witness the launch of the A-4.

The outcome of the tests was unexpected as far as Fieseler was concerned. The senior Nazis representing the two rival groups decided that Germany's best interests were served if the go-ahead were given for both projects. It was not then a straightforward case of one or the other. Rather it was realised that the two projectiles complemented each other in that the Fi 103 was 'more vulnerable

18 Whiting, op. cit., p.41.
19 Forczyk, op. cit., p.53.
20 Piekalkiewicz, op. cit., p.112.
21 https://strikehold.wordpress.com/2010/06/07/rescuing-mussolini-gran-sasso-1943/, accessed 11.09.2015
22 Whiting, op. cit., p.44.
23 R. Nagel und T. Bauer, *Kassel und die Luftfahrtindustrie seit 1923: Geschichte(n), Menschen, Technik,* p.195
24 G. Fieseler, *Meine Bahn am Himmel,* p.259.
25 Ibid, p.259.
26 D. Irving, *The Rise and Fall of the Luftwaffe: The Life of Luftwaffe Marshal Erhard Milch,* p.221.
27 Fieseler, op. cit., p.259

to interception, but far less expensive to manufacture and much simpler to operate; the A-4 ballistic missile was invulnerable to interception, but was very expensive to manufacture and complicated to operate.'[28] Not only that: the Fi 103 'promised to tie down a significant proportion of British air defences when it was employed, while the A-4 rocket … being invulnerable to attack, would not.'[29] Furthermore, the A-4 took ten times as many man hours as the Fi 103 to build, and the pressure was on to get as many of the weapons operational as possible for bombarding Britain.[30]

Progress on the Fi 103 was made in a few weeks, when on 19 June it made its first successful catapult launch. In a series of test flights in June only 28 launches out of 68 proved successful, whilst an internal Fieseler report noted that, although speeds up to 600km/h were being recorded, the projectiles were falling well short of attaining their trajectory.[31] However, in July the first 'extremely successful flight of a Fi 103' took place, but overall results remained 'disappointing.'[32] Around 70 test flights took place at the end of July, but 'about of third of all flying bombs did not leave the catapult or did a 90° turn upon take-off and crashed.'[33] It turned out that the crashes into the sea had established that, when its fuel tanks and air-pressure tanks were empty, the Fi 103 remained buoyant. This was an undesirable outcome, as a more or less intact flying bomb would be very valuable if one fell into enemy's hands. The countermeasure was to install an explosive charge that would be detonated upon impact with the sea.[34]

At the beginning of July Milch summoned Fieseler to discuss the prospects for the Fi 103. Among other things Milch asked Fieseler's opinion about the countermeasures the British might take to repulse attacks. Fieseler's first thought was radar, which could blunt surprise. Against that, he went on, the Fi 103 had the advantage of being launched day and night from around a 100 launch pads, alternating not only flight paths but also targets; which would require the enemy to 'continuously man batteries and search-lights.'[35] However, there was always the possibility of enemy fighters bringing down the flying bombs by tipping their wings (which actually happened). To counter that, suggested the ever creative Fieseler, one could provide the wings with detonators.

'If I may express a purely personal opinion, Herr Field Marshall', ventured Fieseler, 'My fear is that the enemy will bomb our launch pads and their fighters will eliminate our gun crews.' Milch's response, writes Fieseler dismissively, was worthy of Göring: 'We're ready for them. If those gentlemen cross into our territory, then they'll live to see something!'[36] These words, recalled all those years later, bring Fieseler to a frenzied state of retrospective indignation. It is worth quoting his rant verbatim, for his words may well reflect exactly what was going through his mind in the fourth year of war:

> How about that for spurious optimism, how about that for self-delusion! Just half a year earlier we had lost an entire army at Stalingrad, our troops were on the retreat in Russia, our Luftwaffe was being worn down. We failed to defeat Britain. British fighters had proved that it was possible to halt bombing raids. Yet Hitler ordered the building of more bombers at the cost of fighters. The attitude of the dictator was: combat terror with more terror! As one German city after the other was reduced to rubble and ash, because our defences were too

28 S. J. Zaloga, *V-1 Flying Bomb 1941-1945: Hitler's Infamous "Doodlebug"*, p.8.
29 Irving, op. cit., p.236.
30 P. Haining, *The Flying Bomb: Contemporary Accounts of the VI and V2 Raids on Britain 1942-45*, p.17.
31 H. D. Hölsken, *Die V-Waffen: Entstehung – Propaganda – Kriegseinsatz*, p.45.
32 Hölsken, op. cit., p.45.
33 Ibid, p.47.
34 Nagel und Bauer, op. cit., p.197.
35 Fieseler, op. cit., p.260.
36 Ibid, p.260.

weak against the streams of bombers, Hitler stuck to his "strategy" of pushing ahead with bomber construction.

But that is not the worst of it, according to Fieseler. 'Messerschmitt had come out with a twin-engined jet-powered fighter' – the Me 262 – 'which put all the rest of the world's fighters in the shade. This was 200 kilometres an hour faster than any enemy fighter. Yet Hitler orders it to be converted into a bomber. No-one could understand this mad command, which a few people' – no doubt Fieseler one of them – 'took as a sign of the mental state of the hard-pressed despot.'[37] Indeed the Me 262 was a redoubtable aircraft. Eric 'Winkle' Brown, the UK's most experienced test pilot flew in one shortly after the end of the war and pronounced it to represent 'a quantum jump in fighter performance.'[38]

Fieseler recalled how he flew in a Storch from Kassel to Peenemünde in order 'to be able to convince myself of trouble-free flying capabilities of the Fi 103.'[39] He was flying in the Fi 256, the so-called Super-Storch. Flying across Germany was increasingly hazardous, as enemy aircraft were beginning to fly over the country virtually unmolested. As it happens, this particular journey reminded him of his fighter pilot days in Macedonia, when he had to always keep a look-out behind him. Today, nearly thirty years on, but this time over war-torn Germany, attack could come at any moment.

In the meantime British scientific intelligence had, as the joint test launches were being undertaken in May, established that a new kind of aircraft was being developed at the top-secret facility in Peenemünde. Reconnaissance images revealed a slender metal tube of an estimated 14 metres in height. This led to deductions about the location of development and testing of the top-secret projectile. However, it was not known until June that in addition to this device another one appeared to be under simultaneous development: namely, 'a 'winged' rocket with remote control and launched by catapult.[40] This was confirmed later in August 1943 when what turned out to be 'a small pilotless plane' crashed on the Danish island of Bornholm in the Baltic Sea. A Danish naval officer took a photograph and made a sketch, which duly found their way to London. This was the first time that the British had visual evidence of the Fi 103. But for the time being the British were not certain what they had found.

As of summer 1943 Fieseler was paying frequent visits to Peenemünde, on each occasion of which he would need the highest security clearance in the forms of three separate special passes.[41] On one of his visits, in September he witnessed the launch of an A-4 rocket, which he recorded with these words: 'The vertical take-off of a 14 ton rocket, in a column of flaming gases and with the prodigious roar of its engines, was a breath-taking sight and an unforgettable experience.'[42] However, all wonder aside, Fieseler still could not justify to himself the boundless use of skilled people (he does not refer to forced labour) and precious materials to build the A-4. Pursuing von Braun's project 'simply made neither military nor economic sense' in the fourth year of war. When he later learned from Fiedler that the A-4 was going into mass production, Fieseler described this as 'incomprehensible decision … an utter ineptitude of the first order … a scandal as none other in the history of warfare.'[43] That particular rant of course smacks of hindsight and long smouldering

---

37   Ibid, p.261.
38   E. Brown, *Wings on my Sleeve*. p.229.
39   Fieseler, op. cit., p.261.
40   Jones, op. cit., p.339.
41   Ibid, p.351.
42   Fieseler, op. cit., p.257.
43   Ibid, p.257.

bitterness. What plainly remained at the back of his mind for many a long year was that *his* project had been irresponsibly starved of resources.

For German civilians the war entered a new, destructive phase at the end of July and beginning of August 1943, when over eight days and seven nights the RAF despatched hundreds of bombers to destroy Hamburg. Codenamed 'Gomorrah', the operation led to the deaths of some 40,000 people, thousands from incineration in the firestorm that reached temperatures of 800°C. This horrific bombing, which also destroyed more than half of the city's dwellings and left some 900,000 homeless, 'dealt a severe blow to civilian morale, already weakened as it was by the catastrophic defeat of the German army at Stalingrad.'[44] The bombing of Hamburg and other cities in 1943 not only severely shook morale, it also led to the equation of these horrors with 'what we did to the Jews', however much Germans at home lacked precise information about the true scale of the killings 'in the East.' The indiscriminate bombings were even called 'Jewish terror raids.'[45] This apparently wide-spread, openly discussed guilt-tinged sentiment laid the foundation for what Germans have come to call *Vergangenheitsbewältigung* (lit. 'coping with the past'), the still troubling coming to terms with the history of the Third Reich and the Holocaust.

Since the summer of 1943 the Fi 103 and A-4 devices were needed more urgently than ever, as they were 'miracle programmes that were offensive in nature ' and 'appealed to the propagandist need for vengeance.'[46] Armaments Minister Albert Speer obtained from Hitler approval for ultimate charge of the A-4 programme. This immediately lead to tugs-of-war between suppliers of machine tools and precision instruments, on the one hand, and tussles for securing ample numbers of workers, on the other. At the same time 'there was no consensus on how best to deploy the new missiles.'[47] The situation was, according to a possibly gloating Fieseler, 'absolute mayhem' (*unkontrollierbares Durcheinander*).[48] Even so the Fi 103 was also destined for mass production. Milch fought tooth and nail for 'his' flying bombs and as a result of 'turbulent negotiations' secured for the Fi 103 the same priority status as the A-4. However, notes Fieseler gloomily, this did nothing to advance the cause of the Fi 103.

There being little doubt that the Peenemünde complex 'was the focus of highly dangerous German activities', the British took the decision to mount a major bombing raid.[49] This took place on the night of 17/18 August 1943 and involved an armada of 596 RAF bombers – Lancasters, Stirlings and Halifaxes – which dropped 1,924 tons of bombs on the site.[50] In June British air intelligence, having treated with great caution earlier claims of new weaponry being developed there, at last received incontrovertible photographic evidence of 'of a V-2 lying on a trailer.'[51] The attack, which killed around 150 German personnel on site, including the scientist in charge of rocket design, and some 600 inmates of a nearby forced labour camp, set back production for up to six months and forced the Wehrmacht to relocate rocket development and production to new, secure and highly secret site.[52] However, it was decided to press on with testing the smaller and easier to hide V-1 there.[53]

---

44 R. J. Evans, *The Third Reich at War: How the Nazis led Germany from Conquest to Defeat*, p.449.
45 N. Stargardt, *The German War: A Nation Under Arms, 1939-1945*, p.6.
46 A. Tooze, *The Wages of Destruction: The Making and Breaking of the Nazi Economy*, p.620.
47 Zaloga, op. cit., p.9.
48 Fieseler, op. cit., p.264.
49 Hastings, op. cit., p.423.
50 M. Middlebrook, *The Peenemünde Raid 17/18 August 1943*, p.69.
51 D. Richards, *RAF Bomber Command in the Second World War: The Hardest Victory*, p.198.
52 I.C.B. Dear. and M. R. D Foot, *Oxford Companion to the Second World War*, p.872
53 Haining, op. cit., p.21.

Fieseler, as we have seen, had anticipated that the British would eventually bomb the launch pads of the Fi 103, but even he had not imagined that the enemy would attack Peenemünde, the top-secret location for flying bomb and rocket development. Unaware of the serious intelligence breakthrough, the guiding spirits of the two projects fixed a date for the first flying bomb attack on Britain: 15 December 1943. The company was issued with 'utopian' production targets, which envisaged an increase from 100 machines in August 1943 to 5,000 a month by June 1944.[54] Production was scheduled to begin at the Volkswagen plant at Fallersleben and at Fieseler's factory in Kassel-Bettenhausen.[55]

At the end of August 1943 Lusser received a letter from his former boss and close collaborator, Willy Messerschmitt, among other things a fellow defence economy leader with Fieseler. In this opaquely worded letter Messerschmitt says that he considers the Fi 103 project to be 'so extraordinarily important.' In one sentence he writes: 'I really do not want to involve myself in your work'; in another he would be very willing to come and see Lusser and support him 'with advice and practical help.'[56] In other words: he would be ready to join Lusser at any time! A week later Messerschmitt wrote to Albert Speer full of praise for the 'self-piloting aircraft, such as Fieseler has developed' and expressing great reservations about 'the A-4 device [which] is unacceptably expensive if only on account of fuel costs.'[57] He allegedly urged the Armaments Minister to approve the production of one million Fi 103 flying bombs a year![58]

That judgement from Germany's most innovative and productive aircraft designer would have been music to Fieseler's ears, all the more so as Messerschmitt presumably knew of Speer's commitment to von Braun's rocket. It must surely be the case that Lusser informed Fieseler of Messerschmitt's approach, and it would be illuminating to know his reaction. Messerschmitt had in fact demonstrated outstanding aeronautical talent in identifying three highly advantageous areas for perfecting the Fi 103: reducing wind resistance, cutting down on aircraft weight, and simplifying design.[59] However, as nothing came of the letter, we can only assume that Fieseler, who must have known Messerschmitt reasonably well, did not take things further. Perhaps he feared that, if Messerschmitt joined the Fi 103 team, it could become a project associated more with Messerschmitt than himself.

In the meantime in London the Bodyline committee was renamed 'Operation Crossbow', and on 27 August there was a highly significant breakthrough. A report by Duncan Sandys 'recognised that the Germans were developing two different weapons, but fierce arguments persisted about the weight of explosive either might deliver.'[60] Then, on 14 September Reginald Jones, one of Britain's leading scientific military intelligence experts, reported that: 'It is probable that the German Air Force has been developing a pilotless aircraft for long range bombardment in competition with the rocket, and it is very possible that that the aircraft will arrive first.'[61] A week earlier he had learned through an Enigma intercept of the existence of a device known as FZG 76, which roused his suspicions. This was the Wehrmacht designation of the Fi 103 and stood for *Flakzielgerät* (flak aiming device). It would have surely shaken the German military establishment to the core, had they known that the British had not only acquired so much information about the development

---

54 Hölsken, op. cit., p.49.
55 Zaloga, op. cit., p.9.
56 F. Vann, *Willy Messerschmitt: First Full Biography of an Aeronautical Genius,* p.172.
57 Ibid, p.173.
58 Irving, op. cit., p.236.
59 J. Kraus, *Willy Messerschmitt – Flugzeugbauer, Pionier und Forscher*. In: H. Ebert, J. Kaiser und K. Peters, pp.13-17.
60 Hastings. op. cit, p.424.
61 Jones, op. cit., pp.358–359.

of both top-secret weapons, but had also deduced that they were the objects of inter-service rivalry. But Jones had no idea at this time that the Fi 103 was equipped with 'a completely new engine.'[62] Then, on 21 October 1943, Jones 'received word that the Fieseler aircraft factory in Kassel was producing the same secret aircraft' that was being tested at Peenemünde.[63]

A few weeks later, on 4 December, reports reached London of areas of ground in the Pas de Calais and northern France being converted into what looked like ski sites. It was assumed that these 'were designed for the pilotless aircraft.'[64] On 21 December large-scale bombing of the sites were instigated. Two days later Jones circulated 'a fairly comprehensive report,' in which he suggested that 'the whole V-1 programme had been hastily conceived, probably by the Luftwaffe in rivalry with the German Army which was developing the A4 rocket.' Indeed the accuracy and reliability of the missiles were still so poor … only one in six would have hit London.'[65] No wonder British intelligence had the feeling that they were 'in a ringside seat at all the trials of the flying bomb.'[66]

It might be wondered why it took British intelligence so long to piece together what had been happening at the top-secret facility at Peenemünde, given that the British cryptoanalysts were having so much success – or rather so much relative success – at decoding German military communications. Military historian Max Hastings provides the answer: 'all German exchanges about the technical aspects of V-weapons were conducted on paper or by landline, and thus remained impenetrable by Bletchley Park,' Britain's leading code-breaking centre.[67] This explains why in his view, and surely rightly so, 'the V-weapon saga remains one of the most fascinating intelligence studies of the war.'[68] It was only when the first V-1s began to land on Britain in the summer of 1944 that the British could understand the precise nature of the weapon and the peril it represented.[69]

Kassel: A single sheet of flame

Despite set-backs for the development and testing of the two weapons, production of the Fi 103 aircraft themselves continued in Kassel but only until October 1943, when the city was the target of a mammoth RAF bombing raid which ripped out its 'genuinely mediaeval heart' and caused some 10,000 deaths.[70] The attack severely disrupted production at GFW plants. This horror made Fieseler more resolute than ever to bring *his* weapons to bear on the abominable British on their stubborn island. Kassel, with its population around 216,000, was no stranger to RAF bomb attacks. The first took place in July 1940, causing little damage. Between then and the devastating bombardment of October 1943 there were twelve raids, of which the most destructive one had occurred in September 1941.

On that occasion some sixty bombers dropped 270 high-explosive bombs and more than 6,000 incendiaries. This caused 15 deaths and damaged buildings and infrastructure, including the railway station. By the end of 1942 Bomber Command in the UK had identified Kassel as a target requiring closer attention. In a report 'not to be taken in the air', it was noted that Kassel 'is one the best railway towns in Europe, but its importance is due to the presence of the Henschel works, the largest locomotive works on the continent of Europe, rather than to the volume of traffic passing

---

62   Jones, op. cit., p.370.
63   Piekalkiewicz, p.303.
64   M. Hastings, *The Secret War: Spies, Codes and Guerrillas 1939–1945*, p.426.
65   Jones, p.367.
66   Ibid, p.360.
67   Hastings, op. cit., p.425.
68   Ibid, p.421.
69   Ibid, p.426.
70   F. Taylor, *Dresden Tuesday 13 February 1945*, p.270.

through the town.'⁷¹ In addition to locomotives, Henschel was evidently to be a key strategic target in a major raid, was also building 20, 35 and 50 ton tanks for the Wehrmacht. Other targets included a subsidiary of Henschel that was manufacturing aero engines, a subsidiary of the plane maker Junkers and the Gerhard Fieseler Works.

In May 1943 Kassel had a different experience of British bombing. On the 17th of that month there took place, according to a British author, 'possibly the best-known single operation in the history of aerial warfare', the Dambusters Raid.⁷² One of Germany's authorities on the bombing war regards the attack 'as the most brilliant air operation ever.'⁷³ The waters of the breached Eder Dam erupted in 'a tidal wave of 160 million cubic metres nine metres high at its peak … in the direction of Kassel.' The torrent surged into the Eder and then into the Fulda, which flowed through Kassel.

Word reached Kassel of impending inundation before dawn. In the afternoon flood waters, carrying all manner of flotsam including animal cadavers, two metres deep surged into the old town. 'Dwelling houses and recreational facilities were 'swamped', but 'the Henschel railway works and factories making aeroplane engines and military vehicles were not.'⁷⁴ Reuter's special correspondent in Zürich reported that morale among the people of Kassel was at a low ebb: 'Their only desire is that the war should end, whatever the result.' He added: 'The danger was heavier than in the worst air raid.'⁷⁵ However, this assessment was said to belong to a genre of 'imaginative articles of apocalyptic achievement', the report about the despondency of the people of Kassel being 'possibly the most notorious of which.'⁷⁶

Fieseler's factories suffered no material damage as a consequence of the Dambusters Raid, but they were less fortunate a few weeks later. On 28 July 50 RAF bombers dropped some 1,000 high-explosive bombs and incendiaries. 129 people were killed and production was hit at a number of industrial installations, including one of the Fieseler factories.⁷⁷ After that there was a lull. A week before the massive October attack Kassel scarcely looked like a city in its fifth year of war. Indeed in that week life looked relatively normal. People packed the trams and went about their daily business. A picture palace showed 'Munchhausen', one of the first colour films. Theatres played to full houses. Opera lovers – perhaps Fieseler among them – were treated to the Barber of Seville and the Walküre. All last performances began at 17.30 so that people had time to get home well before any bombs might fall.

On the evening of Saturday 23 October, as they left their various places of entertainment, an armada of 569 RAF bombers – 322 Lancasters and 247 Halifaxes – nearly a hundred miles long, was heading for Kassel with it quaint narrow streets and timber-frame houses. Just two days earlier Air Marshall Arthur Harris had received the report about the Fieseler company in Kassel producing one of the two mysterious secret air weapons. Faced with this evidene he 'immediately' took the decision to obliterate Kassel.⁷⁸ Two days later a massive mock raid involving 486 heavy bombers took place over Frankfurt to divert German homeland defences and emergency services from the real target, which was only 150 kms away.

71 W. Dettmar, *Die Zerstörung Kassels im Oktober 1943: Eine Dokumentation*, p.80.
72 J. Sweetman, *The Dambusters Raid*, p.xi.
73 J. Friedrich, *Der Brand: Deutschland im Bombenkrieg 1940–1945*, p.104.
74 Sweetman, op. cit., p.157.
75 Ibid, p.165.
76 Ibid, p.209.
77 Dettmar, op. cit., p.73.
78 J. Piekalkiewicz, *The Air War 1939-1945*, p.303.

THE REDESIGNING OF AERIAL TERROR 223

The raid began with the 'the largest concentration of target flares ever used in the war.'[79] A total of 418, 293 bombs of various kinds – a mere 0.1% of the total tonnage dropped on Germany in the war – were released from the bomb-bays over Kassel at 20.45 that Saturday evening. The incendiaries – all 386,747 of them – were especially horrible, containing mixtures of phosphorus, magnesium, benzole, creosote and napalm. Indeed these vicious bombs 'were dropped in such quantities that the entire central part of the city was on fire inside 15 minutes.'[80] It was a cloudless night, and the British planes had done their job by 22.10. When the sirens had first sounded, people either went into the cellars under their homes or joined others in the air-raid centres. One woman joked: 'Just look at that. I've just made everything tidy, and now the Tommies are coming for us!'[81] It was a night of hell. One dweller in a cellar recalled the noise: 'You would think it was the end of the world … the whistle and gurgling sound of the heavy bombs and mines with their ear-shattering crashes was gut-wrenching.'[82]

The citizens of Kassel and the thousands of forced labourers who swelled the population were experiencing a fire-storm. The pattern is described by Antony Beevor with reference to the bombing of Wuppertal on 29 May 1943:

> The Pathfinders … dropped incendiaries to get fires going before the high-explosive bombs from the next wave blasted open buildings. The blazing buildings soon created an inferno which sucked in air from all around. Many citizens were asphyxiated by smoke or lack of oxygen, and in many ways they were the lucky ones. Tarmac melted on the streets so that people's shoes stuck fast. Some ran down to the river to protect their bodies from the heat.[83]

Crushed, entombed, asphyxiated and baked, 5,830 people never survived that night in Kassel, whilst a further 8,084 were wounded. Of the latter, no fewer than 7,682 had sustained damage to their eyes as a result of contact sparks, cinders and superheated debris. Nearly three quarters of the victims that night were women and children. The final death toll was put at 10,000. I was told one story about the immediate aftermath of the bombardment of Kassel, though its veracity cannot be proven. On the morning after firemen spotted a young woman swaying about the rubble, moaning in inconsolable anguish and carrying a small valise. One of the firemen took it from her, opened it and saw inside a charred roundish object, black and flecked with pink. The woman screamed 'my baby!' and collapsed to the ground in helpless convulsions.

One eyewitness who ventured out after the Tommies had gone described the old town as a 'sea of flames',[84] whilst another found himself confronted by 'an advancing wall of fire.'[85] The heat was unbearable, eyes were stung by smoke, many people had sustained severe burns. When day broke, the scale of the devastation became apparent. Entire buildings, entire streets were blackened, smoking rubble. The emergency services were laying out bodies on the streets, nearly a third of them charred beyond recognition, some as a result of self-ignition. Desperate mothers and wives looked for children and husbands. A woman lamented that she lost everyone. 'Give over', said a

79 Piekalkiewicz, op. cit., p.303.
80 Ibid., 303.
81 Dettmar, op. cit., p.219.
82 Ibid, p.221.
83 A. Beevor, *The Second World War*, p.450.
84 Ibid, p.218
85 Ibid, p.222

man nearby. 'We've all lost everything.'[86] One eyewitness recalled a man bemoaning the loss of his expensive cigars, commenting that it was as if they were a greater loss than his own home.[87]

British aircrews reported that, as the bombs struck, that they saw an orange flash that rose some 4,000 feet above the ground. One pilot reported that Kassel 'was a single sheet of flame from which violent explosions were erupting. You could see smoke up to an altitude of 16,000 feet.' 'The extent of the destruction in Kassel,' he concluded, 'must virtually match that of Hamburg.'[88] The glow, that cloudless night, was to be seen as far away as Hanover, Frankfurt and Cologne. From Göttingen, some 40 km away, the sky over Kassel was 'blood red.'[89] A young worker for the emergency services, surveying the smouldering remnants of his once fair city, wrote in a trembling hand:

Kassel is no more

The bombing caused 3,000 fires, of which 815 were described as 'major conflagrations.' Some 155 industrial premises were severely damaged and 26,000 dwellings were destroyed. Seven days after the raid British reconnaissance photographs showed that the fires were still burning.[90] Kassel has the unpleasant distinction of ranking seventh among German cities which lost most citizens as a result of Allied bombing during the Second World War. There and back the RAF had lost 44 aircraft: 'not considered unduly high for the results achieved', chippily pronounced the *Daily Express* on 24 October.[91] If you saw aerial photographs of Kassel taken at the end of the war, you would readily think that it was another shot of Berlin or Dresden in 1945.

One person who saw Kassel the morning after the attack was Gerhard Fieseler, who drove from his own bomb-damaged home on the Wilhelmshöhe district of Kassel, which was relatively unscathed, to his works in Bettenhausen. He describes his horror: 'I saw hideous sights, which I can still see clearly today.'[92] Fieseler's factories were badly hit, but not 'severely damaged' as British reconnaissance photographs suggested.[93] Even so production dropped to 40% owing to the disruption of supplies and the effects of dislocation on his workforce, who had been bombed out of their homes; or, in the case of forced labour, out of their barracks. A final count showed that 34 of his German workers had been killed, with a further 12 classed as missing. Of his entire workforce 630 were 'totally' and 800 'partially' affected by the bombing.[94] For the record Fieseler's factories fared worst in bomb attacks in April and September 1944. Fieseler would have guessed that the disabling of his factories was a major aim of the RAF raid in October 1943. But the just recently discovered existence by British intelligence of his V-1 production facilities ensured that the assault on Kassel had been designed to be utterly devastating. He could not have known that.

An immediate consequence was that production and all other activities were dispersed over 65 different locations: purchasing was in Eschwege not far from Kassel; some production was switched to Thüringen and Westerwald, whilst a commissar from the Armaments Ministry requisitioned dance halls which could serve as depots for spare parts. Lusser, who was working on the Fi 103 rocket plane, was promptly transferred along with his engineering team to Wolfsburg, a major factory complex

---

86   Ibid, p.222–223.
87   Ibid, p.223.
88   Piekalkiewicz, op. cit., p.274.
89   As described to me by a Göttingen acquaintance.
90   Piekalkiewicz, op. cit., p.303.
91   Dettmar, op. cit., p.151.
92   Fieseler, op. cit., p.255.
93   Piekalkiewicz, op. cit., p.303.
94   Wiederhold, op. cit., p.216.

near Berlin where, if war had not intervened, Volkswagen cars would have been coming of the assembly lines. Instead the plant was producing the *Kübelwagen* ('bucket-seat car'), the equivalent to the American Jeep, along with tank chains, mines, airplanes and military equipment.

The dispersal of all these operations meant that the plants in Kassel were deprived of further skilled workers. Fieseler records bitterly that the replacements came in the form of forced labour from six Nazi-occupied countries. Among them were 500 Russian women, who had to be trained immediately. By now only Nazi fanatics still imagined that the war could be won. Fieseler, although he was still officially a member of the Nazi party along with some six million other Germans, was definitely not in that particular minority. But it was not in his nature to give up. He still must do his best for the war effort. Furthermore he still had high hopes of the Fi 103 as a war-changing weapon to get even with 'the filthy Tommy', who had so mercilessly incinerated Kassel.[95] In December 1943, perhaps when he was at a low ebb or simply seeing the need to share his life with another, he remarried. His second wife's name was Ruth (née Manss) and she was ten years younger than Fieseler. This marriage, although it was destined to last longer than his first one, also ended up in divorce.

A saboteur and defeatist

In 1943 the war was swinging to the advantage of the Allies: 'It was the year Rommel began to lose in North Africa, the Allies won in Tunisia and landed in Sicily, and in Russia Manstein lost the great tank battle for Kursk. In Italy Mussolini was ousted and much of southern Italy joined the Allies.'[96] On the home front the carpet-bombing of Hamburg and other cities dealt a 'shattering blow to German morale.'[97] By the end of 1943 Hitler's attention switched from the Eastern Front to the new threat presented by a possible invasion of Europe by British and American troops in the West. If in the Nazi leadership there were anxieties that the Allies in the West would use their European foothold to widen their bombing of German industrial centres, there were those who proclaimed that that the Wehrmacht could yet deliver a crippling blow to the invaders. Accordingly, Nazi propaganda played down the threat in the West. The up-beat mood was captured in a statement by an agent of the security service (SD). 'Fear of the invasion is scarcely being registered,' he said confidently, adding, 'Rather people are anticipating a heavy defeat for the enemy.'[98]

But that was scarcely the thinking of the German population at home. Many were beginning not only to fear military defeat, but of what fate would befall Germany if the war was lost. Forbid the prospect. Fieseler himself, not a natural pessimist, conceded that 'as of the middle of 1943 the news from the front was more and more alarming.'[99] The lurking anxiety was well expressed by a German general in July 1943, who wrote that it was clear that 'there must be no defeat in this war, since what would come afterwards is not to be thought of. Germany would go under, and we ourselves with it.'[100]

It so happened that in early 1944 a neighbour of Fieseler told him that he was being watched. The person allegedly observing Fieseler happened to be a lodger at the neighbour's house and turned out to be a security officer, who was carrying out his duties in civilian dress. Whereas other citizens might have quaked at the thought of coming to the attention of state security in guise or other, Fieseler, as he put it 'took the bull by the horns and invited the SS man in for a glass of

---

95 Stargardt, op. cit., p.358.
96 G. Sereny, *Albert Speer: His Battle with Truth*, p.370.
97 Ibid, p.370.
98 K-D Henke, *Die amerikanische Besetzung Deutschlands*, p.79.
99 Fieseler, p.268
100 R. Evans, *The Third Reich at War: How the Nazis led Germany from Conquest to Defeat*, 2008, p.500.

wine.' In the ensuing conversation it turned out that the man blindly believed Nazi propaganda, and Fieseler ascertained that his guest 'could only be working for the SD,' the security branch of the Gestapo. The man revealed that his superiors in Berlin had indeed told him to keep a close watch on Fieseler. When they came to discuss 'the strategically decisive role of secret weapons' at 11.00pm (which suggests several glasses of wine), the security man admitted that 'we have lost the war.'[101] Fieseler saw no reason to disabuse him.

If in 1943 Germany suffered misfortune after misfortune, 1944 would prove to be 'a year of catastrophes.'[102] Fate had something unpleasant in store for Fieseler in that year too. It began during 1943, but it is not clear exactly when. A senior engineer by the name of Derdau, who was an Aviation Ministry inspector attached to the Fieseler Works, filed report to his superiors, accusing Fieseler himself of 'sabotage and defeatism: he 'was not exerting his total energy' to fulfil the required production quota.[103] This was a serious charge, and there were for Fieseler dramatic consequences.

At all events, on 2 March 1944, Gerhard Fieseler received a letter signed by Field Marshall Erhard Milch, head of the Aviation Ministry, that he was to be replaced as de facto managing director of the Gerhard Fieseler Works by his deputy, Professor Thalau. The Aviation Ministry had decided that Fieseler's company had not been able to maintain the required production schedules. The letter noted that 'the arguments and excuses for these delays as presented by Fieseler were not recognised.'[104] This sentence makes clear that this letter cannot have come out of the blue. Plainly, Fieseler had evidently been already confronted by charges as to his zeal and commitment and had stated his side of the case.

In the new arrangement, which would take immediate effect, Thalau would become a specially appointed commissioner (*Kommissar*) of the German Reich, whereby he would of course be bound to the Ministry rather than to GFW. Henceforth Thalau and not Fieseler would be directly responsible to the Ministry for keeping production schedules. Whilst this move might be seen as advancement for Thalau, it was also a poisoned chalice. Production was still spread over more than sixty locations, foreign labour was unskilled and for obvious reasons demotivated. The virtual non-stop bombing by RAF at night and by the USAAF by day was not only crippling German industrial sites, but also playing havoc with infrastructure, notably railways and supplier networks.

The upshot of the Milch's directive was that on 31 March 1944 the assets of the Gerhard Fieseler Works were placed at the disposal of the Aviation Ministry. In short, the company had been requisitioned. On 1 March 1944, the day before Fieseler had received Milch's letter, the so-called Fighter Staff (*Jägerstab*) programme had been established. Under this urgent and draconian programme, to be implemented under the direction of senior officers of the Air Ministry and the Armaments Ministry, there would be a dramatic step-up in the production of fighters which were urgently needed to repel British and American bombers from devastating Germany.

Under the Fighter Staff 'incompetent managers were dismissed, the rubble was cleared, temporary building erected and a seventy-two hour working week was proclaimed throughout the industry.'[105] The initiative envisaged the construction of six huge underground bunkers for aeroplane construction. Each bunker 'was to be an area of more than one million square feet, to which the main aeroplane factories were to be transferred to escape the bombs.'[106] This was being proposed at a time when 'the factories had no spare labour, no construction workers and

---

101   Fieseler, op. cit., pp.280-281.
102   Henke, op. cit., p.79.
103   Nagel und Bauer, op. cit., p.201.
104   Wiederhold, op. cit., p.205.
105   Irving, op. cit., p.272.
106   Sereny, op. cit.,p. 426.

scarcely any transport.'[107] The whole monstrous undertaking envisaged a labour force increase of 90,000 workers seconded from concentration camps and a further 100,000 to build underground production facilities.

Fieseler's company was about to be absorbed into the Fighter Staff initiative, which was jointly headed by Albert Speer, now the Minister of Armaments, and Milch, as head of the Aviation Ministry and representative of Göring, commander-in-chief of the Luftwaffe. However, in practice the Fighter Staff programme was run by Speer's ambitious deputy, Karl-Otto Saur, an utter devotee of Hitler who was known for having 'the aggressiveness of the born yes-man.'[108] On 15 March 1944 Fieseler was summoned to a meeting with Saur.

The very summons was ominous enough. In the early hours there was a knock on his door, As he opened the window, a senior officer of the Kassel Munitions Inspectorate told him that he must report immediately to its head, General Schindke. An affable man, Schindke apologised for having requested Herr Fieseler to present himself at such an ungodly hour. However, he was under orders. 'I have just come from a meeting of the newly established Fighter Staff, presided over by the Führer's special representative Saur. At ten o'clock you and your directors are to appear before the Fighter Staff at the AGO Aircraft Works in Oschersleben.'[109] Schindke told Fieseler and his colleagues would be driven to Oschersleben, which was 200kms north-east of Kassel and in the vicinity of Magdeburg. He, Schindke, would accompany them.

The formalities over, Schindke took Fieseler aside and informed him of 'the unbelievable methods' that Saur used in meetings with the leaders of the aircraft industry. Only the evening before, Schindke confided, the technical director of one particular company had been arrested during a meeting. 'Herr Fieseler', he went on, 'Let me give you some good advice. Be very cautious. That man is very dangerous.' [110] Heavy snow on the way delayed the journey to Oschersleben. Schindke, Fieseler and the others were shown to the AGO canteen, where the Führer's special representative was loudly berating senior managers of a company that had evidently not met its production quota.

True to form, Saur's behaviour, which Fieseler likened to that of 'a malicious tyrant', 'defied every description.'[111] He shouted everyone down, letting nobody finish a sentence. He ranted and raved, relishing his role as a plenipotentiary of the Führer. Perhaps he had seen the Führer when he had unleashed his temper on his (mainly) submissive and obsequious generals. Fieseler adds that all this went on for a good ninety minutes, during which time he could size up 'the small, tubby choleric' Saur and decide how to handle the inevitable accusations.[112] The more he witnessed 'the proletarian behaviour and cheap treatment of the leading industry figures', the more his fighting spirit grew. When that session was all over, Saur bellowed: 'A meeting in five minutes with Fieseler company in my special train at the station!'[113]

It was a direct result of the first bombings by the American Airforce in February 1944 that Saur and Milch took it upon themselves to 'to tour all the aircraft factories in a special train, code-named Hubertus, from which they dispensed summary justice to plant managers they considered to have failed in their duties.' In Regensburg they had, for example, 'court-marshalled two German contractors for allegedly holding up construction of the Messerschmitt plant.'[114] Milch had already made crystal-clear that nobody 'should be surprised if we ruthlessly interfere anywhere at any time.

107 Irving, op. cit., p.271.
108 Ibid, pp.299-300.
109 Fieseler, p.269.
110 Ibid, p.270.
111 Ibid, p.270.
112 Ibid, p.270.
113 Ibid, p.271.
114 Tooze, op. cit., p.628.

It doesn't matter if Herr X or Herr Y are spared. It's all about fighters coming out according to specification and in the right numbers.'[115] For his part, when on his tour of aircraft factories he came across 'difficulties', Saur had no compunction about ordering executions, withdrawal of ration cards, arrests and hauling before military tribunals.'[116]

Fieseler, Thalau and unspecified others represented their company for the meeting with the panjandrum, who on this occasion was not accompanied by Milch, but by Karl Frydag, who was directly responsible to the former for airframe companies. Saur was the epitome of the hated 'little Hitler', if ever there was one.[117] He was a man who conducted his affairs with 'brute force and iron hardness.'[118] The meeting took place in the dining car. It began without formalities. Saur, addressing Fieseler, did not mince his words: 'I understand that the job of managing director has got too difficult for you. That's the only explanation I can find for your fighter production being below par. The war situation requires the highest exertion from everyone, For that reason the Fighter Staff find it necessary that you cease to lead your company.'[119]

Fieseler mentioned the various reasons for the production delays, adding that in any case he and Thalau had agreed a year before that Thalau would take on sole responsibility for production. Indeed this arrangement had been promptly approved by Field Marshall Milch. Not only did that information take Saur by surprise and therefore irritate him, but Fieseler had raised his voice when saying it. A slanging match took place between the two men. Those attending watched open-mouthed. No-one had ever dared shout back at Saur, whose face was by now red 'with swollen veins.' 'Is that true?' he screamed at 'the intellectual Thalau', who calmly explained the situation: 'over seventy percent of foreign labour unskilled, bottlenecks in the delivery of materials and spare-parts, 65 production sites, commercial departments and storage depots dispersed all over the country, difficulties to do with accommodation and feeding of the workforce, erosion of morale, not to mention the loss of 150 people through bombing raids.'[120]

The discussion between Thalau and Saur was, in Fieseler's word, 'grotesque': his deputy was composed, pale, but unflinching, the enraged Saur shouting at the top of his voice. When Thalau described the situation with production as 'impossible', Saur retorted: 'Don't use that word again or I will show you what is possible.' It was an undisguised threat. Thalau capitulated, blurting out that he had four children, saying that he wasn't shirking responsibility, but that even so he could not promise to increase production. Fieseler knew that it would have been only too easy to give Saur the promise he was after. Turning to Fieseler, Saur demanded: 'Are *you* going to give the promise?' Fieseler's response was heated. 'A few moments ago you demanded that I give up my position and now you expect me to stab him in the back. What kind of person do you think I am?' At that moment there was an air raid alarm. Saur jumped up, left the dining car and yelled: 'We're off in two minutes.' In an equally loud voice Fieseler turned to his men: 'Let's get out of this hole!'

There is an odd coda to Fieseler's telling of this bruising encounter. He says that a few days later he heard from a member of the Fighter Staff, a young colonel, who he does not name, that Saur had said of Fieseler: 'He was nothing like how people described him to me.'[121] Evidently no-one had told him that Fieseler could be such a difficult person to deal with. It is hard not to come to the conclusion that Fieseler exaggerated events somewhat to show that he was a man to stand up to

---

115 M. Pabst, *Willy Messerschmitt: Zwölf Jahre Flugzeugbau im Führerstaat*, p.66.
116 Ibid, p.66.
117 S. Haffner, *Germany: Jekyll & Hyde*, p.61.
118 Pabst, op. cit., p.65.
119 Fieseler, op. cit., p.271.
120 Ibid, p.272.
121 Ibid, p.273.

the Nazis, when it was necessary. That in turn feeds into the narrative spun by Fieseler's lawyers at the denazification tribunal that their client was someone who put up resistance to the Nazis.

As far as we know, he did not request of Milch or Saur a reconsideration of the decision to replace him. He knew these were dangerous men, but perhaps he was in a way glad to be relieved of some of the stresses that came with his role as managing director and defence economy leader. But he now knew that the 'great personal commitment and fair amount of good fortune' that helped to build up his company over the years had come to nought.[122] Two weeks after the bust-up with Saur the requisitioning of Fieseler's company by the state was confirmed. It had to all intents and purposes come under 'definitive *Gleichschaltung* with all the uncompromising draconian scrutiny that that implied.'[123] Thalau duly became the state's appointee for production at GFW. But more than that: he acquired in effect complete control of the company. And that, reveals Fieseler, is precisely what Thalau had for a long time been dreaming about. It is, however, impossible to prove it either way. If his deputy had long cherished the idea of taking over GFW, it is unlikely that Thalau would have been delighted at its coming to pass in the present circumstances. There would always be Saur or one of his equally unpleasant minions breathing down his neck.

Another toppled figure at this time was Willy Messerschmitt, who was similarly demoted by Nazi fiat.[124] He was condemned by Milch 'for possessing the allure of a prima donna and beyond that acting like an absolute autocrat.'[125] He merely retained control of his company's technical operations.[126] Both he and Fieseler had been toppled from leading their companies, but neither had been ousted. A slight irony in all this is that Fieseler's company had once upon a time been building the Me 109 under licence. Both men were in effect victims of powerful figures in the Nazi firmament who saw their own positions as under threat if the aircraft manufacturers failed to meet the output targets; which explains why the manufacturers' explanations were so readily swept aside by the likes of Saur.

Predictably, the aircraft manufacturing industry 'hovered between mute acceptance and continued resentment against forced labour.'[127] If industry leaders had objections, these were brushed aside. Humanitarian considerations did not of course figure in the attainment of Saur's goal, which was: 'fighters, fighters and nothing but fighters.'[128] The new arrangements involved the installation of one of Saur's minions at GFW, who bore an uncanny physical resemblance to his master. The fighter programme was based on the principle of carrot and stick or rather – to use the more vivid and here far more applicable German equivalent expression – on 'dainty morsel and whip' (*Zuckerbrot und Peitsche*).[129]

Saur's man duly arranged for the supply of cigarettes, canned sardines, coffee beans, chocolate, spirits and other rare foodstuffs – absolute luxuries in wartime Germany – as well as new clothing. Fieseler's foreign workers put in double shifts to secure more treats, but incentivised zeal had a negative consequence. Many became seriously fatigued, would collapse at their workplace and even fall asleep. Even so there was an 'enormous increase' in aircraft output at the Fieseler plants, as is attested by these figures for the Focke-Wulf 190. In February 1944 the company only had produced 42 aircraft against a target of 100; in July and August output actually slightly exceeded the targets

---

122 Ibid, p.278.
123 Pabst, op. cit., p.78
124 Wiederhold, op. cit., p.212.
125 Pabst, op. cit, p.42.
126 Wiederhold, op. cit., p.212.
127 Pabst, op. cit., p.71.
128 Ibid, p.65.
129 Pabst, op. cit., p.30, uses as a section heading *Zuckerbrot und Peitsche: Luftfahrtindustrie unter dem Hakenkreuz* (Carrot and stick: aviation industry under the swastika).

of 180 and 200 respectively.[130] In 1944 Fieseler's total production was 1,146 aircraft, which almost doubled the figure for 1942, which was 671.[131]

According to Fieseler himself, all the Fighter Staff initiative was 'completely pointless', even though the air industry was producing between 2,000 and 3,000 planes a month.[132] It was nevertheless a 'Phoenix-like resurrection of the fighter aircraft industry from the ashes of the factories.'[133] The British and American bombing campaign was still destroying the industrial infrastructure and there was a perpetual shortfall of Luftwaffe. Fieseler furthermore estimated that around 50% of all the new aircraft 'broke down at the front.'[134] He referred specifically to the Me 109, which was being built under licence at GFW. Once the mainstay of the Luftwaffe, this famed fighter-interceptor, had 'the horrible tendency to swerve during take-off and landing.'[135] Then, as the Allied armies drew closer and closer, bad decisions became more prevalent. He cites an example about his own company.

He had heard that there was a plan to make No. 2 Works the company's main storage depot for metal. Previously metal had been stored in a modern, 30,000 sq.m. facility in Wildungen, which so far had evaded heavy bombing by the enemy. It made no sense whatsoever to Fieseler that the storage of such a critically important resource as metal should be transferred to a location that every day faced destruction. Furthermore, the facility in Wildungen had very good links to the railway for efficient loading and unloading, using up to 60 wagons. As it happened, No. 2 Works was not to be heavily bombed, but when the American occupation forces arrived in Kassel in April 1945, it was promptly requisitioned.

A science fiction horror

Once he had been relieved of his position as managing director of the company that bore his name, Fieseler could devote himself to other things. In his autobiography he gives the impression that he could improve the working conditions and general welfare of his foreign workers. Precisely what he did will be described later. To what extent Fieseler remained involved in his flying bomb project, the Fi 103 after his eclipse is impossible to determine.

With Milch championing the Fi 103 and behind him Hitler dreaming of the wonder weapons as the uncrushable deliverer of retribution to the British, GFW was under great pressure to keep to production deadlines. The greatest pressure was on Lusser in Wolfsburg to produce drawings for the mass production of the Fi 103. In the beginning of 1944 Fieseler made a point of visiting the huge plant. 'What I saw', he writes', was beyond my imagination.' But what he saw is described in a few lines, which merely hint at the horrors before him. He describes how in one working bay forced labourers wearisomely assembled sheets of metal using 'primitive apparatus' and then spot-welded them.[136]

Was Fieseler somehow expecting the forced labourers, sick with 'the tedium of factory work, the shame of labouring for the enemy, and the physical discomforts of sleeping in freezing and verminous barracks', to be going about their tasks *with enthusiasm*?[137] In a wooden booth Fieseler spots a German overseer reading a newspaper. Is that supposed to be overseeing? Then in another location he notices how the workers are hanging around, doing nothing and waiting for consignments to

---

130 Wiederhold, op. cit., p.218.
131 http://regiowiki.hna.de/Gerhard-Fieseler-Werke_GmbH.
132 Fieseler, op. cit., p.274.
133 Irving, op. cit., p.272.
134 Fieseler, op. cit., p.274.
135 Ibid, p.274.
136 Ibid, p.265.
137 I. Buruma, *Year Zero: A History of 1945*, p.4.

come from a neighbouring area. They are hanging around because on the previous night a four-engined bomber, which had been shot down, had crashed through the roof and virtually destroyed that entire area of plant.

In that grim setting did it perhaps cross Fieseler's mind that that the Nazi regime had for years been 'trapping the whole population as its accomplices, willing or not, in its own crimes, and its own insanity?' Did he not appreciate that he, a member of the Nazi Party, a senior honorary officer with the Nazi Flying Corps, and a defence economy leader and builder of terror weapons, was himself a good deal more than a naïve supporter?[138] But what is truly extraordinary about Fieseler's description of Wolfsburg is his complete indifference to the fate and conditions of the forced labourers and his indignation with a German overseer who has no more interest in his job than those in his charge.

He almost seems to blame those workers who can do nothing thanks to the inconvenience of a bombing raid the previous night. Can this the same Gerhard Fieseler who was, as he would later claim, so preoccupied with the welfare of the forced labourers at his Kassel plants? Furthermore, was he not witnessing scenes of confusion after the bombing raid? Was nobody removing the bomber and reorganising the affected workplaces? Perhaps, as an afterthought, some of the unfortunates were *enjoying* the disruption caused by the bombing raid. Be that as it may, Fieseler's visit to Wolfsburg in early 1944 may well have been his last direct involvement with the flying bomb. Perhaps, as far as the Aviation Ministry was concerned, he had served his purpose.

In the spring of 1944 trials took place of a manned version of the V-1 with one specific target in mind: British navy targets in the Channel. According to Fieseler, the trusted Willy Fiedler was closely involved in the project at the Rechlin aeronautical research facility and made at least one test flight in a prototype.[139] The bizarre idea behind the project was that the modified Fi 103 would be borne skywards under the wing of a Heinkel bomber, from which it would be released with the pilot at the controls during the mission. Having guided his air torpedo into the vicinity of an enemy vessel, the pilot would bail out by parachute just before impact and land safely in the sea. Some 150 of the projectiles were built, but none was operationally deployed. It was known as the Fi 103 Reichenberg (Fi 103R for short). For his part Fieseler saw no reason in principle why the Fi 103 should not be capable of 'destroying the British navy' (*die englische Flotte*). On the other hand, he reasoned that only fanatical members of the Hitler Youth would actually volunteer for any suicide mission (*Himmelfartskommando*).[140]

One person who was won over by the project was that 'fabulous creature,' Hanna Reitsch, Hitler devotee and Germany's best known aviatrix.[141] Fieseler described her as possessing a feel for flying that was 'unusually powerfully developed', and having 'a rare capacity for enthusing herself and others for a cause.'[142] According to one military historian, 'the most notorious version of the Fi 103' was the brainchild of Hanna Reitsch and Otto Skorzeny, her equally enthusiastic accomplice.[143] After trial flights which nearly killed the test pilots the Aviation Ministry terminated the project. Reitsch, it is said, 'could scarcely hold back her tears.'[144] Ignoring the Ministry's decision, on the very next day she strapped herself into a prototype and was hurtled from under the wing of a Heinkel bomber. She reached a cruising speed of 375mph before bringing the Reichenberg down

138 Beevor, op. cit., p.400
139 Fieseler, op. cit., p.263.
140 Fieseler, op. cit., p.263.
141 Brown, op. cit., p.114.
142 Fieseler, op. cit.,p. 263.
143 Zaloga, op. cit., p.38.
144 Mulley, op. cit., p.230.

safely on its skids. She was to perform that manoeuvre in a further ten or so test flights.[145] Skorzeny who witnessed these scintillating and exceptionally courageous flying performances rejoiced that 'the idea and the machine had been vindicated.'[146] The project might have got back on track, but once the Allies had secured their foothold on contintental Europe after D-Day in June 1944, Germany's entire strategic position dramatically shifted. The manned V-1 project was dead. A bitterly disappointed Hanna Reitsch had to concede that the decisive moment for the manned V-1 had been missed, roundly 'blaming Göring and the Nazi leadership' for their blinkered incompetence.[147] The whole concept, muses Fieseler, may have served as an exemplar for the Japanese kamikaze pilots.[148] This is not so quite outlandish as it sounds.

In fact the University of Tokyo was around the same time experimenting with a piloted rocket plane under the innocent code-name 'Cherry Blossom, *baika* in Japanese.'[149] According to Max Hastings, one of Britain's leading military historians, the well-informed Japanese ambassador in Berlin, Baron Ōshima, appears to have been told about some important weapons being developed in Germany – in order to keep up Japanese morale – but not to have been given concrete details.[150] According to one website, the Japanese device was powered by an Argus pulsejet engine, which suggests actual German-Japanese cooperation[151] At all events it would appear to be case that the Cherry Blossom was loosely based on the Fieseler flying bomb.[152]

Following the D-day landings in June 1944 Hitler ordered the immediate launch of V-1s. By now 'in his world of delusion' he had 'convinced himself that the V-1 flying bomb … would bring Britain to its knees, and that the jet fighters would soon destroy the Allied air forces.'[153] Minister of Propaganda Goebbels memorably described the two much-vaunted weapons as *Vergeltungswaffen*, 'weapons of retribution', from which the designations V-1 for the Fi 103 and V-2 for the A-4 are popularly derived. These then were the wondrous and long-awaited 'weapons of unequalled power', speculation about which had been percolating into German society for months.[154] At last Germany could wreak revenge on the 'criminals from across the Channel.'[155]

As for the proposed flying bomb, when it finally became operational, it was said to be 'the first weapon used offensively to be driven by jet-propulsion.'[156] When the British aviation experts first examined a V-1 in 1944, they were taken aback by 'the ingenious nature of the engine.'[157] Until the attacks 'the British had scant idea either of the precise nature of the weapon, or how serious a peril it represented.'[158]

The V-1s would be launched from some 100 launch pads in northern France. Each weighed two tons, of which the warhead itself containing a mixture of TNT and ammonium nitrate weighed nearly a ton. They would cross the English Channel at around 2,500 feet at a speed of around

---

145 Ibid, p.231.
146 Ibid, p.231.
147 Ibid, p.232.
148 Fieseler, op. cit., p.263.
149 Yokosuka MXY7 *Okha*. See: https://en.wikipedia.org/wiki/Yokosuka_MXY7_Ohka
150 Hastings, op. cit., p.245.
151 http://www.militaryfactory.com/aircraft/detail.asp?aircraft_id=1485
152 http://www.historyofwar.org/articles/weapons_kawanishi_baika.html
153 Beevor, op. cit., p.585.
154 Stargardt, op. cit., p.464.
155 Ibid, p.353.
156 *Jane's Fighting Aircraft of World War II*, p.180.
157 R. V. Jones, *Most Secret War: British Scientific Intelligence 1939-1945*, p.370.
158 Hastings, op. cit., p.42

340mph. At the height of the campaign the crews manning the ramps 'managed to fire a V-1 every half hour, and the usual rate was around fifteen per site per day.'[159]

On the night of 12-13 June the first ten V-1s were launched. (Fieseler says that 250 were already operational and waiting). Only four hit the British mainland, of which one reached its target – London – a railway bridge in Bow, to be precise. Six people were killed, thirty people were seriously injured, 200 people were made homeless, whilst damage was done to railway track, some houses and a pub.[160] Within days of the first attack V-1s had delivered 647 bombs, killed 499 people, seriously injured 2,000 people and had damaged some 137,000 buildings. By the 6th July the figure for people killed had risen to 2,752. It was predicted that 'if attacks continued at the same rate, within two months London would suffer the equivalent destruction as in the whole nine months of the Blitz.'[161] That would have music to Hitler's ears and indeed to Fieseler's too.

Hitler was so enraptured with the early successes that he ordered all available resources to support the V-1. Within a matter of days the 2,000th flying bomb was launched to strike London. But for all its promise the V-1 could not live up to expectations as a result of being 'rushed into combat and mass-production without adequate testing.'[162] So much then for all the Nazi propaganda about the 'V-weapons at the decisive moment transforming everything for the better.'[163]

Londoners were horror-struck, but remarkably there was no mass panic as such. One London woman matter-of-factly recorded on 25 June how 'the pilotless aircraft, or as they are being called here, those "flitter-bombs" have been causing interest and excitement this past week.'[164] A member of the Women's Auxiliary Air Force reports how she and her mother heard 'a queer sound – a sort of crackling noise' and, when she instinctively looked up, found herself beholding 'right over the top of us like a huge black whale's head.' There was a loud explosion and she and her mother 'were thrown into the air and blown about ... like waste paper.'[165] Another person observed that 'many people found [the V-1] a particularly scary form of warfare, an unreckonable mechanical monster impervious to human interference, a science fiction horror.'[166] However, of all the appellations and word portraits applied to the V-1, nothing quite matches the incongruity – from the German point of view – of the one that described how 'from the ground it looked like a half-sized Spitfire.'[167]

By August, when 'between 100 and 150 V-1s a day were aimed at London,' the new aerial menaces caused morale to 'hit rock-bottom'; it was as if victory, despite the Allied landings in Normandy in June, was as elusive as ever.[168] The War Office, the Aviation Ministry and politicians 'were now completely obsessed' by the V-1 that they were neglecting the threat of the V-2.[169] Fieseler for his part writes that 'life in London was becoming 'intolerable,' adding:

> There were nights on which more than 300 1,000kg bombs flew to London. Colonel Wachtel – commander of the flak regiment responsible for deploying the V-1 – heard from his agents that the mass evacuations were causing the authorities major concern and looting was the order of the day. Many inhabitants were leading a hellish existence in the overcrowded

159 J. Gardiner, *Wartime Britain 1939-1945* p.641-642.
160 Ibid, p.638.
161 Ibid, p.640.
162 Tooze, op. cit., p.612.
163 Henke, op. cit., p.817.
164 S. Garfield, *Private Battles: How the War Almost Defeated Us*, p.434.
165 Gardiner, op. cit., p.646.
166 Ibid, p.642.
167 Ibid., p.641.
168 Ibid, p.643.
169 Jones, op. cit., p.425.

underground stations. The agents report that consideration was being given to the use of poison gas by way of retaliation.[170]

The possible use of poison gas can be dismissed as fanciful, but in one respect Fieseler was right. Life was becoming extremely difficult for hard-pressed Londoners. In that summer up to 20,000 houses were damaged every twenty four hours, as a result of which the Post Office registered more than a million changes of address; the main railway stations were overwhelmed with people leaving the capital.[171] Wachtel's mysterious agents were reporting mass evacuation and the ransacking of shops,[172] All the time 'there was a heightened, edgy awareness with everyone's ears permanently cocked for the distinctive sound of a flying bomb.[173]

In total nearly 10,000 V-1s were launched against London and south-east England. Nearly 4,000 were shot down before reaching their target. Just over 3,500 quarter reached London and other key targets such as Southampton and Portsmouth not to mention Antwerp, where '211 landed within the designated vital area.'[174] As the Allies started to overrun the launch pads along the north coast of France as of March 1945, the onslaught weakened. The V-1 caused 6,184 deaths and 17,981 cases of injury. As for the V-2s, a total of 1,054 rockets hit London between September 1944 and March 1945, causing 2,700 deaths.[175] Yet for all that death, destruction and chaos, the V weapons did not remotely achieve the grand aim of forcing the British to sue for peace.

In his autobiography Fieseler is uncompromising in his assessment of the V-1 and its role in the Second World War. He is worth quoting at length:

When the Allies had got a firm foothold in France, the V-1 could no longer play a militarily decisive role. Without a doubt the V-1 strikes taught the British about war by bombardment for a time … But this was nothing in comparison with the after-effects of the Allied carpet bombing of our cities. 20 times more bombs were dropped on V-1 launch pads than the number of V-1s, that actually took off. At least those bombs could not fall on German cities. The number of casualties, which were the equivalent of what the enemy achieved in an attack on German cities in half an hour.

This is the voice of sweet revenge. He goes on to cite General Eisenhower:

If the Germans had succeeded in deploying their weapons six months earlier, that would have made the invasion of the European continent considerably difficult, if not impossible.' Evidently pleased with this accolade – this professional recognition from the Supreme Allied Commander himself – Fieseler responds:

Our Fi 103 would have been ready six months or more earlier, if we had only received 20% of the resources available to the A-4. But not only that: it would have been possible to build more accurate flying bombs under less pressure, against more realistic timetables. That would have meant none of that catastrophic hustle and bustle and running around like headless chickens.[176]

170 Fieseler, op. cit., p.266.
171 Gardiner, op. cit., pp.648 and 649.
172 Fieseler, op. cit., p.266.
173 Gardiner, op. cit., p.643.
174 http://www.dtic.mil/dtic/tr/fulltext/u2/733387.pdf
175 Dear and Foot, op. cit., p.1249-1253.
176 Fieseler, op. cit., p.267.

When he was building the Storch – and before that his aerobatics planes – Fieseler was on the spot and constantly badgered his engineers and technical staff to ensure that the emerging aircraft were as fault-free as possible. In those days he was exerting all the pressure. In 1943 and 1944 the pressure ultimately came from the Führer himself, who wanted results sooner rather later. At best, from Fieseler's point of view, the V-1 was a mixed success. Even so it is with great self-satisfaction that Fieseler refers to '*our* Fi 103' (new emphasis). He takes undisguised pride in the fact that *his* weapon of death and destruction brought retribution, even if it were not proportionate, to the recalcitrant British for their bombing of Germany. But is Fieseler actually saying that the V-1 *alone*, if properly funded from the outset, could have finished off London? If so, he made at least two serious miscalculations.

First, by September 1944 British scientific military intelligence had established that between January 1941 and 10 September 1944 there had been no German photographic reconnaissance of London, let alone Britain. This meant that there was no strategic plan behind the deployment of the V-weapons apart from the vague hope of bringing Britain to her knees. This incalculable German blunder was described by one of Britain's experts in scientific intelligence as 'one of the biggest surprises of the whole war.'[177] The military historian Max Hastings gives a very persuasive explanation for this miscalculation: 'Hitler never wished to use intelligence as a planning or policy-making tool. He recognised its utility only at the tactical level: the Nazis were strikingly incurious about Abroad.'[178]

Second, if V-1s alone – that is to say, without simultaneous deployment of the V-2 – had actually forced a British capitulation, Hitler would have needed to send hundreds of thousands of German troops to occupy the British Isles and maintain order there. In late 1944 such a measure would have required catastrophic down-sizing of the Wehrmacht on either the Western Front or Eastern Front for that task, if not on both; which would have reduced the Reich to virtual defencelessness. All in all Gerhard Fieseler suffered from severe self-delusion about the war-winning potential of 'his' V-1

If Fieseler admits making at least one visit to the Volkswagen works and finding himself shocked, he omits all reference to another place where the V-1 was being built in the latter stages of the war. If he did go there, then he would surely wish to obliterate all memory of it from his mind. This was the notorious underground concentration camp at Dora Mittelbau. Since it was opened in December 1943, the Nazis had employed some 60,000 slaves to build V-2s and then, as of January 1945, V-1s. A senior doctor described the facility as Dante's Inferno to munitions tsar Albert Speer, who in turn claimed to be 'outraged' when he saw it for himself, describing the food as 'an inedible mess.'[179] A former inmate describes what it was like:

> The missile slaves … from France, Belgium, Holland, Italy, Czechoslovakia, Hungary, Yugoslavia, Russia, Poland and Germany … toiled eighteen hours a day … for many weeks without tools, just with bare hands … ammonia burnt their lungs … they slept in the tunnels in the cavities which were hollowed out: 1,024 prisoners in hollows on four levels which stretched for hundreds of yards …

The same author continues:

---

177 Jones, op. cit., p.422.
178 Hastings, op. cit., p.66.
179 Sereny, op. cit., pp.404 and 405.

> The deportees saw sunlight only once a week at the Sunday rollcall. The cubicles were permanently occupied, the day team following the night team and vice versa ... no drinkable water ... you lapped up liquid and mud as soon as the SS turned their backs ... dysentery ...[180]

Every one in three missile slaves died: approximately one life for every V weapon that was launched against Britain. Some 7,500 V-1 aircraft were assembled at Dora from August 1944 to April 1945.[181] The number of slaves who perished in the inhuman process of production of V-1s alone runs into many hundreds, perhaps as many as two thousand, though the precise number can never be computed. Of course, Fieseler had absolutely no control over the creation of Dora and its abominable operations nor could have conceivably have made any modest interventions to improve the ghastly lot of the inmates. However, the fact remains that 'our Fi 103' is indelibly linked to a truly hellish place that has been grimly called 'an Auschwitz in the Harz mountains.'[182]

It is impossible to read Fieseler's autobiography without coming to the conclusion that, as far as he was concerned, the V-1 was for him an even greater triumph than the Storch, the aircraft most associated with his name. The reason for this is surely that the V-1 was the most technologically advanced aircraft he had been directly involved with from its very inception. Indeed the British expert in scientific intelligence, R. V. Jones, acknowledged 'its technical excellence as a weapon', noting that it was cheap to produce, hard to shoot down and 'designed to exploit the extraordinarily favourable situation in which the Germans found themselves able to shoot at such a large target as London from an entire 90° arc running from east to south.'[183]

The fact was that the V-I 'was the most widely used guided missile of World War II.'[184] Furthermore, after the war American, British and Soviet scientists all attempted to make copies of the V-1.[185] It is also surely the case that, if Goebbels had not rechristened the Fi 103 with the designation V-1, the name Fieseler would certainly be much better known in Britain today. It may not be too outlandish to suggest that Goebbels' coinage has spared the name of Fieseler from certain infamy in the country he wanted so much to punish.

It seems to be a little noticed fact that Fieseler had been involved in the design and manufacture of two extraordinary aircraft which stood in a curious asymmetry with each other: on the one hand, the Storch, magnificently slow-flying, amazingly versatile and climactically adaptable; on the other, the V-1, one of the fastest aerial devices of its era. Furthermore, the Storch was to all intents and purposes non-lethal, whereas the V-1 had been designed to help bring Britain to its knees by dint of its enormous capacity for delivering death, destruction and demoralisation. The Storch was a creation which derived in good measure from Fieseler's manifold experiences as a fighter pilot in the First World War and later as an acclaimed aerobatics pilot. By complete contrast the V-1 did not spring from the past. Everything about it was *futuristic* from its design to its exceptional lethal capability.

As far as Fieseler was concerned, the V-1 took on a new significance after the horrific bombardment of Kassel in October 1943. From that moment on the V-1 was for him truly a weapon of vengeance, in fact well before it became fashionable to apply that term to embrace both the Fieseler device and von Braun's rival V-2. As of October 1943 Fieseler was committed to bringing the V-1 to operational readiness. But in this ambition he was *not* blindly serving what

---

180   Ibid, p.405.
181   http://xn--untertage-bertage-c3b.de/Mittelwerk.html
182   http://www.zeit.de/2005/04/A-Auschwitz
183   Jones, op. cit., p.429.
184   Zaloga, op. cit., p.3.
185   Ibid, p.39-43.

he once held to be some incomparably higher purpose of the Führer. This was about something infinitely more precious, namely the fate of Germany, not the Führer's Germany, but that Germany fundamental to all Germans, a beloved land of culture, decency and hard work, where Nazism was both alien and repellent.

Part Four

After the Storm

11

Time of reckoning

Enjoy the war; the peace will be terrible.

Victor Sebestyen[1]

The terrible price paid by the German population, flight and expulsion from the east, and the destruction of cities like Hamburg and Dresden, are a second memory which the Third Reich has bequeathed to almost all Germans.

Neil MacGregor[2]

Victory or Siberia

If Fieseler is not always a reliable guide regarding chronology, one date we can be absolutely sure of is 6 June 1944, D-Day. Fieseler had particular reason to remember it, for his only son, Manfred, who was a Luftwaffe pilot, was shot down by the British over the North Sea on that day. Manfred's squadron consisted of some 40 fully operational aircraft, and he managed to shoot down one enemy plane on what was apparently his first experience of frontal attack. But, as Fieseler grimly records, it was the fate of him and his comrades 'to be unscrupulously sacrificed one after the other to a force a hundred times greater than their own.'[3] He is for once remarkably candid about his feelings:

> All my life I never got over the loss of my boy – such a fine boy. With his father's inheritance he could have achieved great things, for everything in his nature predestined him to that. Particularly in old age there is a bitter feeling when there is nobody who can take hold of and keep together everything you have worked for, fought for and saved.

It is unclear exactly when, but at some time in 1944, and quite possibly as a result of Manfred's death, Fieseler's life became in his words 'a burden which bore down on me.' He became lethargic and was on the point of collapse. Illness seized him and he was confined to bed for a month. But a trigger for his malaise may have been connected with the loss of his company and the sudden release of years of built-up stress. There is no definitive answer. However, the rest did him a power of good. He returned to his office, where he felt he had been solely missed, refreshed in body and soul. Back in harness, he described himself as 'a stabilising element, which radiated certainty and strength.'[4]

As he mourned his son, the entire German population, Fieseler notes 'apart from a few exceptions' – in other words, Nazi fanatics – had lost 'its fighting spirit.' Propaganda to the opposite persuaded nobody. There was little or no faith in Nazi leadership in Germany at large. The relentless bombing

---

1   V. Sebestyen, *1946: The Making of the Modern World*, p.41.
2   N. MacGregor, *Germany: Memories of a Nation*. London: Allen Lane, p.496.
3   G. Fieseler, *Meine Bahn am Himmel*, p.279.
4   Ibid, p.279.

campaign had virtually broken civilian resistance. Even 'the most successful fighter aces', he wrote, valued their lives above trying to win the war without adding the obvious: precisely as happened towards the end of the 1914-18 War.[5] Naturally enough, points out Fieseler, no-one spoke openly about things. But his own conversations with certain unspecified senior military figures readily confirmed his opinion. They could hardly be blamed for thinking like him.

When in 1939 he used his company newspaper to motivate his workforce to support the Führer, there can be little doubt that Fieseler privately supported his great mission to avenge the bitterly hated Treaty of Versailles. He vividly remembered the 'bitterly angry' (*bitterböse*) Weimar years. Only 'an insignificant minority' (*verschwindend wenige*) had not supported Hitler as Germany's saviour. The Wehrmacht had smashed its way through the redoubtably fortified Maginot Line, defeating France, sweeping aside a British army and within two years 'had conquered almost all of continental Europe.'[6] Fieseler, we can be sure, was fully behind these triumphs. But, when in January 1941 Ernst Udet whispered those fateful words: 'Hitler's going to attack Russia', he 'could not grasp how this man, who had created work for seven million Germans, had removed the internal strife (*Zerrissenheit*) and general uncertainty, had declared the Treaty of Versailles to be void, and had in a few years made the country flourish again, was going to jeopardise all those achievements.' It was now clear that Hitler's true purpose was to use the resurgent Germany as a means for subduing other countries. His successes had gone to his head and now 'in his megalomania he was gambling *va banque*.'[7]

After the Allied landings in Normandy in June 1944, it would only be a matter of time before British and American troops would cross the Rhine and set foot on Germany. For those Germans who longed for an end to the war, the prospect of occupation by those forces coming from the west was infinitely preferable to the stark alternative: occupation by the Soviet Army. If soldiers battling to hold up the Russian onslaught on the Eastern territories of the Reich as of the middle of 1944 suffered from 'a desperate fear of being overrun by the Red Army', German civilians dreaded retribution at the hands of 'the Asiatics': it was a stark choice between 'victory or Siberia.'[8] Somehow the euphonically grim German – *Sieg oder Siberien* – makes the choice sound even more cataclysmic.

As the Soviet Army, which 'had broken the back of the Wehrmacht at an appalling cost', passed through Pomerania and Silesia in the middle of January 1945, terror seized the German population.[9] Fieseler himself does not refer to that particular choice between victory or Siberia, but he admits that 'after nearly five years of barbarous war the victors would wreak considerably more revenge than after the First World War.' He adds gloomily: 'I could scarcely imagine what would happen to us hated Germans.'[10] He had of course expressed similar thoughts in 1918, but like almost all Germans in 1945 he knew that the war against the Russians had been unspeakably savage and that the Soviet Army was not poised to enter the territory of the Reich offering olive branches. No fewer than 58 countries were at war with Germany in 1945. The prospect of defeat spelt fears of apocalyptic annihilation, as was summarised by a Nazi official in August 1944: 'If we lose the war, it means slavery for every German – for every member of the [Nazi] Party certain death.'[11]

---

5   Ibid, p.274.
6   Ibid, p.275.
7   Ibid, p.275.
8   K-D. Henke, *Die amerikanische Besetzung Deutschlands*, pp.674-675.
9   A. Beevor, *The Second World War*, p.609.
10   Fieseler, p.279.
11   R. Blank, Kriegsende im Westen. In: A. Surminski, (ed). *Kriegsende in Deutschland*, p.64.

Not exactly philanthropic heroism

In the summer of 1943 the works council reported to Fieseler a complaint about his behaviour on-site. The word among his German workforce was that 'our boss is more interested in the foreign workers than us.'[12] Fieseler explained to the works council and later to a larger gathering of his workforce, which presumably excluded the foreign workers, that nobody took the concerns of his entire workforce to heart more than he did. As for the foreign workers, they had no protection and no support. There being no one else willing to stand up for them, Fieseler saw it as his 'duty' to take up the cudgels on their behalf. On both occasions he also said that there were cases of foreign workers being beaten by their overseers. Appealing to his colleagues' finer feelings, he added that; 'I don't think that any German worker will approve of such things.'[13] With that, he sweepingly claims, he had 'convinced' his people of the correctness of his actions.

After his demotion in 1944 Fieseler could, he tells us, devote himself 'almost exclusively' to the interests of his hundreds of foreign conscripted workers. He recalls that he did what he could to improve conditions for them at their places of work and in their accommodation. Before long he got to know their cares and needs and they began to put their trust in him. As a consequence, he says, they sent 'numerous reports and complaints' about their maltreatment to his office. Above all he now wanted to ensure that they received 'decent treatment.'[14] But this was difficult because beating up the foreign workers had become a part of company culture. Fieseler knew all too well that many foremen wreaked their cravings for power on defenceless foreigners, but it took 'much time-consuming research' on his part before the number of indiscriminate beatings diminished.[15] Presumably the time-consuming research involved his tracking down the main culprits who evidently relished the power they had over those unfortunates. However, interviewing the victims was not often productive, for they feared more punishment if they reported a German overseer.

If we are to believe him, he performed a minor miracle of care in an industrial system based on 'coercive violence to the armaments economy [which] extended across the board to German management, to the German workforce, but most of all to the various grades of foreign labour employed in Luftwaffe production.'[16] Although Fieseler claims that his efforts to improve the lot of the foreign workers had the approval of Thalau, it should not be forgotten that the Fighter Staff programme had their appointees at the Fieseler Works. Thalau could not risk giving the impression to Saur and Milch that he was encouraging Fieseler to be soft on the foreign workers.

In short, it is difficult to accept without reservation everything about Fieseler's 'almost exclusive' preoccupation with his foreign labour force in what would be the last months of the war. He claimed to visit unannounced the barrack kitchens of the foreign labourers and made a point of tasting their food, but he does not say if he could improve it or increase the meagre amounts of it. After all the civilian population was facing deprivations. When you read his account of these doings in his memoir, it might be easy to form the impression that Fieseler was performing acts of philanthropic heroism for some of the Reich's downtrodden victims. However, the probable truth is that, when these actions took place, the workers were actually receiving – at least for a time being – better food under the Fighter Staff programme. He may well have wanted to ensure that the state was fulfilling its promise to his workers. If not, he would have grounds for putting pressure on Saur's appointee to improve quantity, quality or both. That would explain why Fieseler and Thalau did not, as far as we know, have disagreements on the matter of welfare of compulsory labourers.

---

12   Fieseler, op. cit., p.277.
13   Ibid, p.278.
14   Ibid, p.277.
15   Ibid, p.277.
16   A. Tooze, *The Wages of Destruction: The Making and Breaking of the Nazi Economy,* p.628.

As it happens, in April 1986 'an extraordinary event took place', when 120 former GFW forced labourers from the Netherlands and their wives met up in Kassel. The event was widely covered in the local press and led to a 60-page monograph, now available on-line, which contains many contributions by those unfortunates about their deportation to Kassel, their experiences there in the war and their repatriation to the Netherlands after the war. Some Dutch voices speak of working twelve hour shifts with little or no food, of beatings, of primitive and humiliating living conditions in barrack-like accommodation, of medical neglect and oppressive supervision. Other voices speak of acts of kindness on the part of Germans – even of friendships with them. One even had 'no complaints', simply because it was 'possible to survive.' Another bore no hatred towards the Germans, only against Hitler. What is noticeable in these personal testimonies and subsequent newspaper reports is that there is no reference to any single act of kindness on the part of Fieseler towards his oppressed foreign workers.[17] In the end we are forced to agree with the German commentator who concluded that regarding, Fieseler's behaviour towards his press-ganged workers, 'we will never get to the bottom of it.'[18]

Ever wishing to establish his credentials as a fair-minded man, Fieseler tells of an occasion – probably in early 1945 – when he even had one of German workers followed and searched on suspicion of having stolen meat from the foreign workers. The man in question was instantly dismissed. As a coda to this incident Fieseler adds that such cases were extremely rare, seeing that 'theft was severely punished in the Third Reich.'[19] That of course did not apply to the property of deported Jews, whose 'households ... left behind in Germany became sought-after spoils' and realised billions of Reichsmarks.[20] Fieseler appears to have forgotten that.

Fieseler, who had built up his company over the last fifteen years, now saw it 'sink in rubble.' When he had been barred from running it, he knew that he could 'got into serious danger', if he had rebelled in any way.[21] He had to accept what had happened, painless as it was. Thus, his attempts to improve the lot of his foreign workers were a great consolation to him, or at least so he would have us believe. In March 1945 the last planes left the FGW production line: 50 Focke-Wulf 190s.[22] By this time 'the once mighty Luftwaffe had been reduced by both combat attrition and bombardment to a mere shadow of its former glory.'[23] It is therefore uncertain how many of these fighters ever saw service.

It was around this time that Fieseler, in common with all male citizens between the ages of 13 and 60 years old, was called upon to take up arms against the Reich's invaders. He was summoned to a training area in countryside near Kassel famed for its natural beauty to take part in training as a member of *Volkssturm*, the German Home Guard. The *Volkssturm* had been created by Himmler as a mass militia. Its members were equipped with 'a variety of very old rifles captured from different armies earlier in the war, and the Panzerfaust shoulder-launched anti-tank grenades.'[24] In other words the *Volkssturm* would be no match for powerful armies entering the territory of the Reich from all sides.

It was a Sunday morning when Fieseler put in an appearance at his local unit. In fact he had already failed on two occasions to take part in these exercises. The local *Volkssturm* leader, a retired

17 G. Richter, Niederländische Zwangsarbeiter während des 2. Weltkriegs in Kassel.' Kassel: Verlag Winfried Jenior. Available at: http://www.gedenkstaette-breitenau.de/publikat-Dateien/zwangsarbeiter.pdf.
18 http://www.erinnerungen-im-netz.de/aw/Testseiten/~bma/Gerhard-Fieseler-und-seine-Werke/
19 Fieseler, op. cit., p.278.
20 N. Stargardt, *The German War: A Nation Under Arms, 1939-1945*, p.241.
21 Fieseler, op. cit., p.278.
22 R. Nagel und T. Bauer, *Kassel und die Luftfahrtindustrie seit 1923: Geschichte(n), Menschen, Technik*, p.263.
23 A. Weir, *The Last Flight of the Luftwaffe: The Suicide Raid on the Eight Air Force, 7 April 1945*, p.14.
24 Beevor, op. cit., p.641.

former lieutenant colonel by the name of Steinhoff, asked Fieseler to account for these absences. Steinhoff, not failing to notice the indifferent expression on Fieseler's face, rounded on him: 'Various gentlemen have referred to this error on your part and are asking questions, which I am not able to answer. I am under obligation to report to the Gauleiter every instance of refusal to serve.'

'That's fine with me', responded Fieseler casually, 'Let the Gauleiter know that I am prepared to clean the toilets at the Wilhelmshöhe Schloss, if that would help to win the war!' Steinhoff, choosing to ignore this, changed tack: 'Herr Fieseler, I suggest you refer to your war injury. But at least make a point of making yourself seen.' Steinhoff had, it seems, overlooked what others might take as insubordination or defeatism, presumably not wanting to report Fieseler to the Gauleiter. But Fieseler in high dudgeon stuck his heels in: 'Herr Steinhoff, I will not turn up at the *Volkssturm*!'[25] Once again he had managed to avoid complying with a Nazi imperative. But this time the lack of retaliation was increasingly symptomatic in a Germany where, as defeat loomed, the Nazi writ was fast losing its draconian rigour.

A further incident around this time concerned a GFW employee by the name of Hohmann, who was in charge of the Fieseler's company's apparently still functioning market garden. Hohmann had ignored 'a strict prohibition' of Fieseler's about taking it out on foreign labour. But a Pole had complained about 'further acts of mistreatment,' which had taken place on the railway line extension at Number Two Works, where Hohmann was overseeing the unloading of wagons carrying vegetables, which were part of the special food consignments to workers under the Fighter Staff Programme. He had beaten up some workers who were, according to Fieseler, 'on the awkward side.' Confronted by this allegation, Hohmann reacted angrily: 'What am I supposed to do? I had to unload the waggons in next to no time and send them on their way. The kitchens require a daily delivery of fresh vegetables. Then these so-and so's start skiving.' Fieseler clearly understood why Hohmann had lost his temper, but even so he should have complied with the ruling about not mistreating foreign workers. He then appealed to Hohmann's 'reason, his humanity' and then to 'the consequences of his actions, if – purely theoretically of course – the war should be lost.'

Fieseler had no idea if that had the desired effect on Hohmann, but there was a swift consequence. On the day before the Americans occupied Kassel and 'our people ceased to turn up at work' – in other words, at the beginning of April 1945 – Frau Hohmann reported that her husband had not returned from work. It turned out that he had been murdered by bullied foreign workers at Number Two Works.[26] The writing was on the wall about what Germany could expect when – no longer if – the war was lost: furious revenge. At the same time his murder was symptomatic of all manner of violence that was now happening all over Germany, as liberated foreign workers in their hundreds marauded the streets, as victims of concentration camps were herded in their wretched remnants across the Reich and as ethnic Germans poured panic-stricken by the million into their ancestral homeland from the East to escape the retribution of the Soviet armies. One such shocking event, not necessarily unique of its kind, took place in Kassel at the end of March, as American troops were poised to take the city.

At that time around 50,000 Germans, about a quarter of its prewar population, lived in the ruins of the city, and some 25,000 male and female foreign workers were stuck in various outlying locations, awaiting repatriation. On 31 March Kassel Gestapo chief, Franz Marmon, received reports of the plundering of a goods train at the city's main station, which was reportedly transporting tinned meat, butter, margarine, cigarettes and other coveted items. Not only foreign workers but also German citizens were engaged in the looting. Among the foreign offenders were

25   Fieseler, op. cit., p.281.
26   Ibid, p.280.

Italian labourers as well as some compatriots who were prisoners of war and had refused to fight in the Wehrmacht after Mussolini's downfall in 1943. Marmon ordered the execution of the Italians, which was carried out by SS soldiers. In all 79 were shot.[27]

In the meantime Berlin the Führer fretted in his bunker. His state of mind was well captured by the German historian, Golo Mann. In his refuge, as Germany's foes pushed on towards Berlin and the entire country resembled 'a burnt-out volcano', Hitler was enraged that 'he had sacrificed his health for his people, had renounced the pleasures of life for the last five years, had not been to the cinema nor to a concert, and this was all the thanks he got! Betrayal, nothing but betrayal had been surrounded him, on all sides, he alone was supposed to be the cause of his well-intentioned war, which moreover not he, but the Jews had begun … If the nation did not know how to be victorious then it had not passed the test and should not live on. As it was, the best had fallen and only the inferior were left.'[28] The German race had simply not been up to the great mission he set them, had not shown itself worthy of his leadership; now it could fester and rot. Kaiser Wilhelm had said much the same thing after World War 1.

The Storch's last wartime flourishes

As already stated, the Storch operated in every theatre of war where the Wehrmacht fought. Towards the end of the war, it was not only German commanders who were using it. Captured versions were conveying leading figures on the enemy side, including Montgomery Eisenhower and Churchill, who found the Storch to be an ideal liaison aircraft. As for Churchill, after the landings in France in 1944, he is said to have 'frequently hopped in a captured Storch between the tents of his generals for breakfast meetings.' It was indeed well said that the Storch was admired by 'friend and foe' alike.[29] When the Americans arrived in Kassel, the war in Europe had a few weeks to run. In those final weeks the Storch was still taking to the skies. In two famous cases it was directly linked with the drama and turmoil surrounding the collapse of the Third Reich at the heart of Berlin. There is a third episode too, which would have a special place in the entire history of the Second World War.

The first episode took place concerning war-torn Berlin on 23 April 1945, when armaments minister Albert Speer flew from Hamburg for what would be his last meeting with Hitler. The two-seater Focke-Wulf trainer took him as far as the airport at Gatow to the west of Berlin. From there a Fieseler Storch brought him 'into the centre, landing at dusk short of the Brandenburg Gate on the east-west axis.'[30] Hitler, Speer found, 'was calm, like an old man resigned to death,' but when they parted a few hours later he was 'both brusque and distant. Speer, his former favourite, had ceased to exist in his mind.'[31] Of course, the role of the Storch is completely overshadowed by the happenings inside Hitler's bunker. However, without a Storch at his disposal Speer may never have made it there. It is the only aircraft of the Luftwaffe capable of evading enemy fire in the centre of Berlin and taking off and landing in very short distances amidst all the rubble.

The second – truly dramatic – episode involved the aviatrix Hanna Reitsch on 26 April 1945. The Luftwaffe general Ritter von Greim had been summoned to a personal meeting with the Führer in his bunker. Greim asked Reitsch to fly him in a helicopter from the Rechlin aircraft test centre some 70 miles to the north of Berlin. They found that the helicopter had been destroyed in an air raid. A Luftwaffe pilot flew them to the airfield at Gatow, where they clambered into a Fieseler Storch with Greim as the pilot and Reitsch as passenger for the last, perilous stage in their journey.

27   http://www.gedenkstaette-breitenau.de/rundbrief/RB-24-67.pdf
28   G. Mann, *Deutsche Geschichte des 19. und 20. Jahrhunderts*, p.960.
29   *Der Spegiel*. Flugzeuge: Lustiges Ding, 1978, pp.148-151.
30   A. Beevor, *Berlin: The Downfall 1945*, p.288.
31   Ibid, p.290.

It appears that there was no necessity for Reitsch to go beyond Gatow, but evidently she decided that she would present herself to the Führer as a sign of loyalty and devotion. Not that she was unfamiliar with the perils of flight in and out of bomb-wrecked Berlin. Indeed she 'was reputed to have flown her Fieseler Storch on and off the roof of the German Air Ministry in the last days of the Third Reich, acting as a courier to the Hitler bunker.'[32]

As they flew across Berlin, the Storch was hit by a hail of Russian artillery shells and bullets. Greim was struck in the foot and lost consciousness. At this moment Hanna Reitsch 'leant over the inert General's shoulder and managed to reach the throttle and stick with enough control to reach the Brandenburg Gate and land in the road nearby, where they were picked up by a military lorry and driven to the bunker.'[33] It was a miraculous landing. The Storch's fuselage was ripped to pieces and its wings holed by artillery shells.[34] Hitler's secretary recalls her wearing her iron cross on her polo-neck jumper.[35] It is impossible not to be in awe of Reitsch's flying skills and fearlessness, which place her on a par with the very best male pilot. Remarkably until that flight she had 'no experience of flying under fire.'[36] The British air historian, Christopher Shepherd, ranks her flight with the rescue of Mussolini in 1943. In both exploits the Fi 156 'used its flying abilities to their maximum.'[37] Reitsch demonstrated the capability of the Storch to negotiate its way through intense enemy artillery fire at close quarters, whilst in the Gran Sasso raid the pilot took advantage of the Storch's remarkable high-lift slow speed characteristics.

The third event associated with the Storch at the very end of the Second World War took place two weeks before Speer's fateful flight to Berlin. In April 1945 an unarmed Storch encountered an American Piper Cub spotter plane, which was also unarmed. A website described the event, quoting the words of the US pilot, Duane Francies. The author writes that the incident was 'one of the most unusual aerial actions of the war.' But it was in fact rather more than that.

On 11 April Francies was taking part in an observation mission some 100 miles west of the capital city. It was his 142nd operational flight of the war. He noticed a German motorcycle, with the customary sidecar, speeding along a road near some of the 5th Armored tanks. When he and his observer William Martin went in to take a closer look at the motorcycle, they also noticed a German Fieseler Fi-156 Storch artillery spotter plane about 700 feet above the trees.

Francies later wrote:

The German Storch, with an inverted 8 Argus engine … spotted us and we radioed, 'We are about to give combat.' But we had the advantage of altitude and dove, blasting away with our Colt .45s, trying to force the German plane into the fire of waiting tanks of the 5th. Instead, the German began circling. Firing out the side doors with their Colts, the American crewmen emptied their guns into the enemy's windshield, fuel tanks and right wing. Francies had to hold the stick between his knees while reloading. He later recalled, 'The two planes were so close I could see the Germans' eyeballs, as big as eggs, as we peppered them.'

After the Storch pilot made a low turn, the plane's right wing hit the ground, and the plane cartwheeled and came to rest in a pasture. Setting down nearby, the Americans ran to the downed plane. The German pilot dived behind a huge pile of sugar beets to hide from them, but the

32   E. Brown, *Wings on my Sleeve*, p.114.
33   Ibid, p.120.
34   C. Mulley, *The Women Who Flew for Hitler: The True Story of Hitler's Valkyries*. See plate 37, opposite page 281, showing the wreckage of Storch.
35   T. Junge, *Bis zur letzten Stunde: Hitlers Sekretärin erzählt ihr Leben*, p.192.
36   Mulley, op. cit., p.279.
37   C. Shepherd, *German Aircraft of World War II*, p.19.

observer, who had been hit in the foot, fell to the ground. When Francies removed the observer's boot, a .45 slug fell out. Then Martin fired warning shots that brought the pilot to his feet, hands raised. Francies confiscated the pilot's wings and Luftwaffe shoulder insignia, as well as a Nazi battle flag.[38]

This disabling of the Storch is believed to be the only occasion in the entire war when an aircraft was brought down by a hand-gun. More significantly perhaps the episode is generally considered to be the very last dog-fight at the end of the Second World War in Europe. Although it was badly hit, the Storch did not plummet out of the sky. A skilful pilot brought it down, saving his own life and that of his companion. It is a curious fact that the very last air crew to be engaged in aerial combat in the entire conflict survived the last ordeal of its kind. The two German airmen can perhaps thank Gerhard Fieseler's company for designing such a remarkably versatile aircraft, into which he poured his own experience both as a fighter pilot and master of aerobatics. The days for the Storch's career in the Luftwaffe were all but over, but unlike almost all other German military aircraft its operational life did not come to an abrupt end.

Scorched earth

Four days after the mass murder at Kassel's main station battle and after a four-day battle with a dispirited German army and some house-to-house fighting in the city itself, American troops entered Kassel and proceeded to occupy it on 4 April 1945. The people of Kassel could now see for themselves how much Propaganda Minister Goebbels' denigration of Americans as ' plutocratic-decadent, morally at the bottom of the heap (*moralisch tiefstehend*), and underperforming' was actually true.[39] In the days that followed the American arrival, says Fieseler, Kassel was ruled by 'a weird atmosphere' and 'everyone went into hiding as best they could.' Fieseler describes the early, very tense days just before and after the American occupation, as a period 'about which the less said the better (*da schweigt des Sängers Höflichkeit*).'[40]

Two days before the Americans had arrived, a Nazi demolition squad (*Vernichtungskommando*) razed three hangars to the ground at Kassel-Waldau airport. These zealots were responding the Führer's order of 19 March entitled 'Demolitions on Reich Territory,' which decreed that 'All military transport, communication facilities, industrial establishments, and supply depots, as well anything else of value within Reich territory that could in any way be used by the enemy immediately or within the foreseeable future for the continuation of war, be destroyed.' This degree was otherwise known as Hitler's Nero order.

Fortunately this mad-cap order was not seriously implemented not least because Armaments Minister Albert Speer openly defied Hitler, whilst other Nazi officials carried out the instruction 'only sparingly according to their level of fanaticism.'[41] Fieseler mentions with some pride that some of his workers, presumably German ones, 'stood by their posts' to help keep the company's property intact (it is not clear if they tried to prevent the demolition). But, adds Fieseler gloomily, such loyal workers were 'laudable exceptions.'[42] Then he was beset with another frustrating problem.

The population in Kassel was virtually without work, so unemployment soared. The Reichsmark was losing purchasing power. Unless you had ration cards, food cost a fortune. A black market developed with people, ever more selfish for themselves and their families, buying and selling

38 Francies's story is available at: http://www.5ad.org/units/Duane%20Francies.htm
39 Henke, op. cit., p.87.
40 Ibid, p.285.
41 A. Roberts, *The Storm of War: A New History of the Second World War*, p.547.
42 Fieseler, op. cit., p.284.

anything they could. There was even a demand for items such as construction materials, tools and all manner of machinery. One place where such items were available was on the sites of factories. So, 'what was easier than to think of one's own place of work, where one know the lay-out?' notes Fieseler disdainfully.[43]

Word of the resulting larcenies got around and before long people with nothing to do with any particular company (*Betriebsfremde*) got in on the act. They had no moral scruples about it. Many factories in Kassel like Fieseler's were in effect state enterprises connected with armaments. As the Nazi state had all but collapsed, people could claim that their larcenies could not legally be breaking the law. Once that idea took hold, there was no holding them back. The novelist Heinrich Böll noted that people clung to 'whatever fell into their hands: coal, wood, books, building materials', and 'everyone justifiably could have accused everyone else of theft.'[44]

It must be the case that before the Americans arrived, Fieseler and his colleagues had destroyed files of documents, but he does not actually state this. But he does mention that many of his German staff absconded, notably Dr Thalau, who made a rapid disappearance only to turn up nearly two years later in Argentina with 14 other scientists.[45] Fieseler cites various examples of once close colleagues who in the panic of those days revealed a greedy, selfish side to their characters, but he reserves most contempt for Dr Göbel, his former commercial director. For as long as he had known him, Göbel had been 'a radical opponent of Hitler' and had never joined the Nazi party. For years Fieseler had had his time cut out steering Göbel out of harm's way. After the war his former colleague had gone on to found a host of small companies, having the gall to make use of property of the old Fieseler company. In 1947 his once loyal colleague was even brazen enough to say to Fieseler: 'If we hadn't got it first, others would have taken it.'[46] Worse, he had not offered Fieseler a single pfennig in compensation.

His German biographer Wiederhold is not impressed with this account, pointing out that Göbel had himself been appointed as a defence economy leader in April 1940. This title would not have been bestowed without a background check on his political reliability; any trace of an anti-Nazi disposition would have scuppered such an elevation.[47] What is more likely to be truth is that Göbel made some indiscreet remarks to Fieseler, out of which he (Fieseler) could conveniently concoct a story about how he saved Göbel from the wrath of the Nazis.

All the while in Kassel forced workers with their new-found freedom, 'looted and terrorised the almost women-only population.'[48] A major gathering point for those wretched souls all over Germany were the railways stations – 'the most dangerous places to be' – which became major hives of black-market activity, as they waited for trains to take them home.[49] There were no fewer than 8 million such displaced people seeking repatriation. It was now the Germans' turn to be abandoned to their fate, for the master race was on the point of being mastered itself. Waves of vengeance were about to be unleashed on Germany, and there would not be much mercy for people of the country which had blindly, naively or innocently followed Adolf Hitler.

But not all released foreign workers, it seems, were hell-bent on plunder and revenge. Fieseler records – records very proudly in fact – how 'troops' of his former foreign workers made their way to his house in Wilhelmshöhe and asked for autographed photographs of himself. If that is the case, then one is inclined to conclude that there cannot have been many instances of former forced

---

43   Ibid, p.284.
44   Cited in I. Buruma, *Year Zero: A History of 1945*, p.70.
45   AAP report 15 Germans smuggled to Argentina, Available at: http://trove.nla.gov.au/ndp/del/article/69070248
46   Fieseler, op. cit., p.285.
47   T. Wiederhold, *Gerhard Fieseler – eine Karriere: Ein Wirtschaftsführer im Dienste des Nationalsozialismus*, p.276.
48   Fieseler, op. cit., p.282-283.
49   Buruma, op. cit., p.157.

workers wanting such a personal memento of their bitter experience of Germany. Not one of that Dutch contingent of former GFW workers who visited Kassel in 1986 refers to any such event. But let us pause to reflect on this extraordinary situation as described by Fieseler. If he did indeed see 'troops' of his former workers approaching his house or hear their rapping on his front door, Fieseler may well have been struck with terror. Were they coming to get revenge after years of bullying and brutality, to butcher him?

And where was Frau Fieseler when the uninvited deputation – or deputations – arrived? Quite possibly she was cowering in the cellar, terrified like all German women that hordes of foreign men on the loose would ransack her home and rape her. But no, the crowd is seemingly good-humoured, has merely arrived to show gratitude to a man has who stood up to the Nazis for their sake and tried to relieve their servitude. It is but a grateful throng begging a souvenir. Whatever the truth of this extraordinary encounter, it is as if Fieseler was in Hollywood, depicting himself for posterity as some benign, if fallen pharaoh, greeting his erstwhile liberated slaves and granting them a trinket to cherish as a token of his benevolence.

For his part Fieseler had not absconded as such, but he certainly made himself scarce for a time. His biographer Wiederhold has unearthed some information about his doings, which Fieseler himself does not mention, after the Americans arrived. The archives of the Land of Hessen record that Fieseler quit his home to stay with a friend in Grebenstein not far from Kassel. Presumably his wife was with him. Previous to that, in anticipation of hard times to come, he had stashed away at his own home food, cigarettes, 100,000 Reichsmarks, not mention the tyres of his car, 'otherwise the Americans would had made off with them.'[50]

With the assistance of his the GFW garage manager he later hid his car – presumably without its tyres – in a barn some 30 kilometres outside Kassel.[51] It was a magnificent and no doubt well cherished 8 cylinder Horch, which possibly Fieseler never drove again. However, before he headed for Grebenstein, he had to undergo no fewer than five house searches by American soldiers.[52] The house searches suggest that Fieseler was an individual already identified by the American military as a person of interest; which was indeed the case. At this very tense and highly uncertain time he fared better than his counterpart Messerschmitt, whose house was taken over by US occupation troops, forcing him to live with his sister and her children in a cottage, where they slept on straw beds.[53]

On 30 April Hitler committed suicide. Other leading Nazis, including propaganda chief Joseph Goebbels, chose to share the same fate as their Führer; others fled, many using carefully prepared escape routes, Latin America being a favoured destination. After Germany's defeat in the First World War the vengeful Kaiser, who had no small part in bringing about that terrible conflict, had described the Germans as guilty of 'betrayal, downright felony, cowardice.'[54] In 1945 it was Hitler's turn to excoriate the Germans, who in his perverted mind had shown themselves incapable of fulfilling the great mission he had entrusted to them. In his bitterness he now condemned them for proving completely unworthy of *him*. He discarded them: 'if the Germans were not strong enough to be victors, they deserved to be vanquished, annihilated.'[55]

With the death of Hitler, 'national socialism as an institution and totalitarian ideology vanished almost overnight.'[56] Three days later, on 2 May, Fieseler was awarded 'on paper' his last and

---

50   Fieseler cited in: Wiederhold, op. cit., p.257.
51   Nagel und Bauer, op. cit., p.224.
52   Wiederhold, op. cit., p.257.
53   M. Pabst, *Willy Messerschmitt: Zwölf Jahre Flugzeugbau in Führerstaat*, p.85.
54   J. C. G. Röhl, *Kaiser Wilhelm II*, p.186.
55   M. Fulbrook, *History of Germany 1918-2000: The Divided Nation*, p.103.
56   M. Zeidler, Der Zusammenbruch des NS-Staates. In: A. Krüger, (ed.) *Kriegsende in Deutschland*. Hamburg: Ellert und Richter Verlag.

totally nugatory Nazi honour, namely the Knights Cross of the War Merit Cross (*Ritterkreuz des Kriegsverdienstkreuzes.*)[57] That, of course, was no compensation for unpaid GFW invoices totalling 'more than 85m Reichsmarks for delivered aircraft, parts and services.'[58] As for the German people at large, their 'sense of rage at having been abandoned by their leaders grew; so did the feeling that having lived under a dictatorship absolved one of personal responsibility for all that had happened.'[59] Gerhard Fieseler – former member of the Nazi Party, former honorary colonel in the National Socialist Flying Corps and former defence economy leader – was one who would identify with that latter sentiment until his dying day.

Brief reflections on a Nazi entrepreneur

As the war in Europe reached its climactic conclusion, the business which Gerhard Fieseler had built up since 1930 was utterly wrecked. In his memoir he is very keen to convey the impression that he was throughout the entire Third Reich an entrepreneur who simply had a job to do: build aircraft for his customer, which just happened to be the Nazi state. He saw nothing special or even reprehensible in that, because just about every other adult German who remained in Germany throughout that time was directly or indirectly serving the purposes of the regime. Let us then, before we discover what fate the post-war years have in mind for him, put his life as an entrepreneur in that most perturbing of times in context.

From an early age Fieseler was obsessed with aircraft and flying. He was a First World War air ace, who had used his talents in aerobatics to make money throughout the precarious years of the Weimar Republic. In 1930 he had accumulated enough money to buy a glider company as his entry into aircraft design and manufacture. His quest for perfection as an aerobatics pilot drove him to neglect his family. His wife and children were his sacrificial lambs. In 1933, after Hitler's assumption of the German chancellorship and the immediate prioritisation of the rapid expansion of the air industry, the new Reich Aviation Ministry was there with what every entrepreneur dreams of: huge financial resources and a ready market. Fieseler was exactly the kind of entrepreneur that the Nazi state needed: one of that new breed of technocratic managers who were, as we noted before, 'unhesitatingly enthusiastic' about the Nazi cause and bought into its heady rhetoric.[60]

He had panache as a former aerobatics world champion, a track-record in innovative design and, not to be overlooked, he was an outstanding industrial manager. In this latter capacity, and entirely self-taught in whatever he did, he demonstrated a rare talent for attracting and collaborating with highly productively with bright and ambitious young engineers and designers. However, the battles with his designers suggest that he was regarded by some as an interfering nuisance. At the same time he was a master networker. His network ran like veins not only throughout entire aero industry, but also within the Reich Aviation Ministry, where he enjoyed an especially close connection with Ernst Udet until his death in 1941 and as an armaments industry leader appointed by Göring he had the ear of the state secretary, Erhard Milch.

The Nazi regime backed opportunistic men like Fieseler with the full machinery of the state in terms of incentives, management know-how, coercive legislation, and a chance for personal glory through devotion to the Führer. Duly motivated, he built up a significant enterprise and ran it as a social-political entity designed to deliver technologically sophisticated products and to *perfect* a workforce that was not only obedient to the company management, but also subservient to the uncompromising guiding ideals of the Nazi state. The fact that the Gerhard Fieseler Works won

---

57   Nagel und Bauer, op. cit., p.224.
58   Ibid, p.432.
59   Stargardt, op. cit., p.546.
60   Henke, op. cit., p.479.

the highly competitive award as exemplary Nazi enterprise four years running suggests that it is was one of the most fit-for-purpose enterprises in the entire Reich. It is only too clear from today's perspective – but not then until it was too late – that Fieseler was on a slippery slope to catastrophe. But from today's perspective it is almost unimaginable that Fieseler could create a corporate culture that worked in precisely this way *and* produced perhaps the most sophisticated aircraft in its class at that time. But he did.

However, when as of 1940 his company was compelled to employ forced labour, he was drawn into an inhuman system of industrial management, for which he could have had not the slightest prior notion, but in which though he became knowingly complicit. According to his own account Fieseler did what he could for the well-being of those wretched workers in the last months of the war. But *why* he did whatever he did, we shall never know. His words convey no compassion for their plight; they are tinged with an unmistakable amoral veneer.

We are forced to conclude with a German commentator that 'we will never find out the whole truth.' This commentator adds that 'as research as shown time and again' many Germans in the Nazi period did anything to avoid endangering their families or to be classed as "unreliable", exonerating people like Fieseler on the grounds that he had no choice.'[61] Such a judgment, as we shall see, does not satisfy everyone in Germany today, but that is to get ahead of the story. With the war over, Fieseler might have thought that, once the members of his forced labour force had all returned to their countries, he could put the whole ghastly experience behind him rather as they would have to. But fate was not going to let him have the luxury of not confronting his past.

Stunde Null

On 8 May 1945 Nazi Germany capitulated, and 'all of a sudden' no-one, and that includes Gerhard Fieseler, was a Nazi.[62] An 'eerie silence' descended upon the entire country.[63] It is only possible to estimate approximately how many millions of people died in the Second World War, 'the greatest man-made disaster history.'[64] Noting that it lasted for 2,174 days, cost $1.5 trillion, the British historian Andrew Roberts writes that the war 'claimed the lives of over 50 million people', which 'represents 23,000 lives lost every day, or more than six people killed every minute, for six long years.'[65] Of those 50 or so million people, around 40 million perished in Europe 'on the field of battle, in the rain of bombs on cities, in the concentration camps.'[66] The war claimed the lives of more than 5.2 German servicemen and more than 2.4 million German citizens.[67] Of the latter some 400,000 Germans lost their lives and 800,000 were injured as a consequence of the Allied bombing campaign, whilst 7.5 million found themselves homeless.[68] But, if the clearing the cities of rubble, all 400 million cubic metres of it,[69] was 'a gigantic task', that was nothing compared to removing the rubbish from people's heads.'[70]

The Germans called the uncertain time after defeat *Stunde Null* – zero hour, a time for a fresh beginning, for the turning over of a new leaf. But it was never to be that and in any case there was

61 http://regiowiki.hna.de/Gerhard-Fieseler-Werke_GmbH.
62 Stargardt, op. cit., p.543.
63 Buruma, op. cit., p.60.
64 A. Beevor, *The Second World War,* op. cit., p.781.
65 Roberts, op. cit., p.579.
66 I. Langelüddecke und F. Otto. Das Ende des Weltenbrandes, in: *GEO Epoche Panorama: Trümmerzeit und Wiederaufbau*, p.6-9.
67 N. Ferguson, *Kissinger 1923-1968: The Idealist*, p.169.
68 C. Hartmann, Der Zweite Weltkrieg: Ursachen und Verlauf. In: V. Dahm, A. Feiber, H. Mehringer, und H. Möller, *Die tödliche Utopie; Bilder, Texte, Daten zum Dritten Reich.*, p.583
69 K. Diederichs und B. Weiss, Im Staub der Großstädte, in: GEO, op. cit., p.15.
70 H. Jaenecke, Die Stunde Null, in: *GEO Epoche. Deutschland nach dem Krieg 1945-1955*, p.29-30.

no question of their being left to their devices and rebuilding lives in their time. There was no chance for 'the slate [to be] wiped clean, and history to be allowed to start again.'[71] For Germans it was 'the lowest imaginable moment of their lives.'[72] Their country did not even belong to them; it was divided into four zones of occupation: American, British, French and Soviet. The Germans 'faced total defeat, unconditional surrender and occupation by foreign armies ... their country [was] all but destroyed physically and, in the eyes of the rest of the world, morally.'[73]

Before them loomed starvation, fuel shortages, black marketeering, vengeance and then, in 1949, the formal sundering of their territory into the Western-backed German Federal Republic and the Soviet-sponsored German Democratic Republic. On the matter of vengeance, it was women who bore the brunt in a sickening and degrading way. They were cases of rape by Western Allies, but on nothing like the scale perpetrated by the Soviet Army.[74] Military historian Anthony Beevor estimates that 'at least 2 million German women are thought to have been raped' by the Red Army, and 'a substantial minority, if not a majority, appear to have suffered multiple rape.'[75]

One Polish woman, who worked on a farm near Peenemüde, spoke for all women, when she said: 'In the flush of victory man becomes a wild beast.' (*Der Mensch wird in seinem Siegestaumel zur Bestie*).[76] Another of the countless victims, a journalist, kept a diary of her experiences of 'rape and sexual collaboration for survival' in Berlin when the Soviet Army came to town, and published her memoir anonymously first in English translation in 2004.[77] A German edition was published five years later. Here is a sample:

And now I am sitting here at our kitchen table. I've just refilled my pen with ink and am writing, writing, writing all this confusion out of my head and heart. Where will this end? What will become of us? I feel so dirty, I don't want to touch anything, least all my own skin. What I'd give for a bath or at least some decent soap and plenty of water.[78]

After the capitulation on 8 May 1945 the occupying powers – the USA, the British, the Russians and to a much smaller extent, the French – faced immediate monumental challenges: 'taking care of and repatriating displaced persons ... arresting of hundreds of thousands of German prisoners of war, confining tens of thousands of Nazi functionaries and war criminals, the liberation and care of many thousands of political prisoners or to some extent the emergency support of the civil population'[79] As for former Nazis – some six million Party members – they all 'feared for their future, their employment and their professional prospects.'[80] But they would not be allowed to melt into the background, for the victors decreed that there had to be accountability for the wrongs and crimes committed in the name of the Third Reich. One Party member was, of course, Gerhard Fieseler, who remained in or at least near Kassel.

Kassel found itself under the American occupation, and the Americans quickly began to denazify their zone with 'righteous retribution.'[81] Their avowed aim was to cleanse Germany of its poisonous

---

71 K. Lowe, *Savage Continent: Europe in the Aftermath of World War II*, p.xiv.
72 A. Beevor. *Berlin: The Downfall 1945*, p.419.
73 Sebestyen, op. cit., 37-38.
74 M. Jones, *After Hitler: The Last Days of the Second World War in Europe*. London: John Murray, p.52.
75 Beevor, op. cit., *1945*, p.410.
76 Middlebrook, p.228.
77 Anonymous, *A Woman in Berlin: Diary 20 April to 22 June 1945*, p.3.
78 Ibid, p.80.
79 Henke, op. cit., p.926.
80 A. Surminski, Der nicht enden wollende Krieg, in: Krüger, op. cit., p.10.
81 Ferguson, op. cit., p.184.

legacy and rebuild it as a democracy that would never go to war again.⁸² This was no knee-jerk response. Since April 1944 – in other words, since some weeks before D-Day – the Americans with the assistance of German emigrants – Jews and others who left Germany in the 1930s – 'had been compiling the so-called black and grey lists which were supposed to make it easier to track down 'dangerous and potentially unreliable Germans' upon the cessation of hostilities.⁸³ As soon as their occupation begun, a specially trained agency charged with their detection, apprehension and interrogation began making arrests without delay.

This agency was the American Counterintelligence Corps, whose remit of was 'to protect US forces from espionage, sabotage and subversion, to combat and disband German secret services and all secret police and paramilitary organisations, apprehend groups of people of interest (*bestimmte Personengruppen*) and assist in the disbanding of the Nazi Party'⁸⁴ Furthermore its agents were empowered to imprison members of the German general staff and thoroughly interrogate them at especially established interrogation centres.⁸⁵ It was a complex task. Even so, in the jitteriness of those times, one CIC unit was diverted from weightier concerns by keeping an eye on a US security guard who contrary to regulations about fraternisation was said to be 'flirting with a German girl.'⁸⁶

The most famous CIC agent, and a very well regarded one by his superiors and colleagues, was Henry Kissinger, who had left Germany in 1938 for a new life in the USA. Another agent of later prominence was J. D. Salinger, author of *The Catcher in the Rye*. In 1947 Kissinger was transferred to Oberammergau in southern Bavaria, where he became an instructor at the newly established European Theater Intelligence School, which was 'to give training to intelligence personnel who had not been adequately trained to meet the problems of occupation.'⁸⁷ Kissinger, who from his earliest days as a CIC agent had recognised the importance of the psychological aspects of his work, was invited to give various lectures. One of them was devoted to 'German mentality.' He devised a perceptive schemata of four German characteristics: selfishness, lack of inner assurance, submissiveness and lack of sense of proportion.⁸⁸

As the CIC agents went about their business, persons of interest taken into custody were divided into two groups. The first group consisted of those suspected of direct involvement in major war crimes, notably concentration camp personnel, members of the Nazi regime's security police as well as witnesses of Nazi crimes who were not prepared to report what they knew. The second group, much bigger, covered a very wide body of people who were considered to pose a threat to the safety and institutions of American troops: from SS personnel and senior political figures such as Gauleiters and other officials with responsibility for discharging the Nazi remit to all other Nazis who held important positions in the economy. Every member of this six million strong group could be said to have helped or served Hitler. Fieseler, of course, fell into this bigger catchment.

All potential culprits fell into a general category called 'Automatic Arrests.' In 1945 and 1946 the American interned around 120,000 suspects or, as the Americans grandiloquently called them 'counterintelligence personalities.' The task of tracking down, detaining and interrogating them was enormous and in next to no time the number of arresting and investigating officers and agents rose from 300 officers and 1,100 agents at the time of Germany's capitulation to 508 officers and 1,526 agents and other investigators by the end of 1945.⁸⁹ The Americans might well have a carte

82 Buruma, op. cit., p.173.
83 Ibid, p.258.
84 Henke, op. cit., p.255.
85 Ibid, p.253.
86 Buruma, op. cit., p.42.
87 Ferguson, op. cit., p.197.
88 Ibid, p.198.
89 Henke, op. cit., p.254.

blanche, but equally they were confronted by the most urgent of challenges if they were to crush the hydra of Nazism.

On 31 May Gerhard Fieseler was summoned to register with the American occupation authorities in Kassel. He was arrested on the spot without any kind of explanation. It was not a random arrest. His name already appeared on a list of 'Automatic Arrests', and, as already noted, his home had already been searched on five separate occasions for unspecified evidence.[90] He was seemingly not permitted to return home. In fact he would not be returning home for an entire year. No experience since he was so humiliated and bullied by his father nearly forty years previously was to sear itself so powerfully on his memory. From the beginning he saw himself as a victim of a vindictive process.

The Americans were not just interested in bringing to justice the most reprehensible of the Nazis, they were also keen to search out the Nazi regime's leading scientists and engineers to find out what had been going on in the various research establishments, to acquire valuable knowledge and, if expedient, offer employment opportunities in America. This initiative was called Operation Paperclip. The Americans were especially interested in those 'fields of science and military technology where the Germans were to some extent in the lead … rocket science, aircraft design, weapon design and special-purpose optical and electrical instrumentation.'[91]

As it happens, the very first highly valuable German scientist to be picked up by the Americans had been working for the Henschel company in Kassel. This took place on 1 May. His name was Herbert Wagner, and he was 'at the absolute top of the Americans' list of priorities' for his work on guided missiles. Wagner's know-how about these weapons had been identified as being 'of great potential' for the US war with Japan in the Pacific.[92] Their quarry, to the relief of his captors, 'proved to be truly amenable' and 'did not hesitate to make the fruits of his labour available.'[93] It seems more than likely that Fieseler as the builder of the V-1 flying bomb was acquainted with Wagner. At all events, by the time the Americans arrested Fieseler, Wagner was already in the USA serving his new masters.

Infamous treatment by the Americans

Fieseler was locked up with 16 other prisoners in a one-man cell in the only remaining part of police headquarters (*Polizeipräsidium*) in Kassel. Around 2.00am they were visited by two American guards, both stinking of alcohol and both bare-chested. They wanted to know which one of the prisoners was the greatest criminal. When a doctor retorted that none of them was a criminal, his face was smashed by a fist. That question of the guards staggering around their drunkenness was, says Fieseler, 'typical of the conviction of the victors at the time: that 'every German had the served or helped Hitler.' And, he adds, 'in line with this motto we were dealt with accordingly.'[94]

Unfortunately, Fieseler was slightly missing the point. At the time of his arrest the true scale of Nazi atrocities was only beginning to emerge. It was no longer a question of the concentration and extermination camps in Poland – the Auschwitzes of this world, so to speak – but the concentration camps in Germany itself. By now pictures of the abominable camps in Germany: Buchenwald, Bergen-Belsen, Dora-Mittelbau – among scores of others – appeared in army newspapers, then in the world press and then in news films so that the rest of the world – and Germans themselves – would be in no doubt about the unspeakable nature of Hitler's Germany.

90   Nagel und Bauer, op. cit., p.431.
91   Henke, op.cit., p.744.
92   Ibid, op. cit, p.748.
93   Ibid, p.749.
94   Fieseler, op. cit., p.285.

The next day Fieseler and some 60 others were driven in two US army trucks in an easterly direction. Two armed guards were assigned to each truck. Their destination turned out to be Ohrdruf, a sub-camp of the notorious Buchenwald camp. In the three months before the Americans arrived on 4 April, four thousand inmates had died or been murdered there; their emaciated bodies left the Americans numb with horror and revulsion.[95] The American General Patton was so shocked on his visit to the Ohrdruf and Buchenwald camps that 'he had a certain measure of understanding for the rough justice on the part of his soldiers.'[96] In short, scores of other officers of the victorious nations turned a blind eye to their soldiers' roughing up – sometimes killing – of anyone assumed to be a Nazi or Nazi sympathiser. Fieseler and his fellow prisoners were no doubt victims of two such GIs. However unjust it was, every one of them was seen by their American guards as capable of the barbarities which those GIs had read about and seen in newsreels. The signs – and smells – of that bestiality and savagery at Ohrdruf would not have vanished when Fieseler and his fellow prisoners lingered outside its gates at the end of May 1945.

It was not only Patton among senior American officers who had visited the Ohrdruf camp. Another was the commander in chief himself, General Dwight Eisenhower, who was so shocked that he telephoned Churchill to let him know the unbelievable things he had seen. He also wrote to his wife that he could not imagine how 'such cruelty, bestiality and savagery could exist in this world.'[97] Fieseler and the rest were told to wait outside the entrance to the Ohrdruf camp. It was a blazing hot day. They hung around for two hours, when they were told to get back into the trucks. They were returning to Kassel. Urgent telephoning among American control centres established that this part of Germany was about to be given to the Soviets as the agreed part of their occupation zone. The Americans did not want these particular prisoners to fall into Russian hands.

It may not have crossed Fieseler's mind, but he had two strokes of luck on that day. First, he never saw inside the camp, an experience which would have shaken him to the core. Second, the prompt American action had spared him from capture by the Soviet Army, from which two possible unpalatable consequences could be expected: that he would spend the rest of the days in Soviet-controlled part of Germany, which in 1949 would become the German Democratic Republic, or that as a military aviation specialist he would be taken to some god-forsaken location in the Soviet Union where he would help design aircraft for an unspecified number of years. Both possibilities would of course have been dependent on Fieseler not being executed.

Fieseler recalls that journey to and from Ohrdruf as something like a ride on a switch-back. The Americans drivers were going hell for leather as if it was 'the race of their lives.'[98] They were mightily amused that their hair-raising driving was causing their German prisoners to be jostled all over the place in the back, where they ended up flat on the floor. Perhaps even surviving that journey apart from a few knocks and bruises was his third stroke of luck that day. In the event Fieseler and the others were not taken back to the police cells of the previous night, but to the gaol in Wehlheiden, a district on the south-west side of Kassel. The original gaolers had been dismissed for having belonged to the Nazi Party. Among the new ones, who made 'an impression of ineptness' on Fieseler, were former members of site security at GFW in Kassel. When they saw their old boss, they looked sheepish and turned away.[99]

Five days later Fieseler was on the move again. He and some 100 others were bundled on to three trucks and driven to Bad Wildungen, which was the regional headquarters of the American

---

95   M. Gilbert, *The Holocaust: The Jewish Tragedy*, p.790.
96   Henke, op. cit., p.926.
97   Cited in Buruma, op. cit., p.226.
98   Fieseler, op. cit., p.286.
99   Ibid, p.286.

Counterintelligence Corps. As the trucks drew up, six or eight brutal and reckless-looking specimens of the military police appeared with cudgels and battens. They picked ten men at random from the German prisoners, who in front of the rest 'were beaten, kicked and maltreated in all manner of ways.'[100]

But the Germans were not yet at their final destination and were directed to some other trucks, which they had to reach on the double. As the last one attempting to board a high-sided vehicle, Fieseler was helped up by an American guard perhaps twenty years old, using his rifle-butt in the process. En route two of the German prisoners disappeared; no-one knew how. Fieseler, now in his fiftieth year, and some of his companions were physically exhausted and at the end of their tether, when they came to their journey's end, an army camp in Schwarzenborn in the Knüllgebirge. The CIC officers who met them made them know in no uncertain terms that they were being regarded as criminals. In a somewhat bizarre twist of fate some 400 Syrian refugees who sought asylum in Germany in 2015 were accommodated in a 'tent camp' in Schwarzenborn; perhaps on the very spot where Fieseler and his fellow prisoners were held. On 7 September the Syrians, after the death of one of their number, protested at the conditions they were being forced to live in; a protest in 1945 by Fieseler or one of the others may well have been met with a beating.[101]

In Schwarzenborn Fieseler found himself confined in the outbuildings of the farm near the camp. In all some 3,000 Germans were confined there in five sectionalised zones separated from each other by barbed wire. The camp was surrounded by an electrified fence and numerous watchtowers. The internees, as the Americans called them, were crammed twenty at a time in huts (*Buden*) about 14 metres square. Any furniture had been removed so that the internees had to sleep on the floor. Fieseler's batch was put into a hay-filled barn. Someone found a tin can in a ditch and that served as an implement for drinking watered down soup the next day. A few days later they were broken into two groups and moved into stables. The lucky ones, including Fieseler, made a bee-line for the commodious animal feed boxes which were well above the filthy floor.

The feed boxes provided not exactly comfortable sleeping space for three men. Fieseler's night-time companions were a former Gestapo informer and a man of 34, who had been trained as Catholic priest, but became disenchanted with his calling and joined the Nazi Party. His name was Hermann Abele and he would prove to have information about another former Nazi, which Fieseler would one day make use of in dramatic circumstances. The feed boxes brought together some unlikely social pairings: 'a factory worker next to a general manager, a collier next to a professor, a labourer next to a city mayor.'[102]

In the camp there was also a special barrack, cordoned off with barbed wire, where prominent members of the Nazi Party and the Gestapo as well various other people especially condemned for the Nazi past were kept in crammed conditions under extra surveillance. This was the dreaded barrack 27. Fieseler's 'Gestapo comrade' was moved there. With him out of the way, Fieseler had rather more space. But he was not to enjoy the new luxury for long. He 'went downhill', lay paralysed with fever and, only thanks to the intervention of a fellow inmate who was a doctor, was transferred to a hospital in Treysa, where he was diagnosed with tuberculosis. He did not stay in the hospital, but was given a bigger cell with a camp bed.[103]

At around the end of 1945 the German prisoners were allowed visits by priests from whom they picked up snippets of news about what was happening outside. Then they were told that they

---

100   Ibid, p.286.
101   Nach Tod eines Flüchtings in Schwarzenborn: Ein Blick ins Camp. http://www.hna.de/lokales/schwalmstadt/schwarzenborn-ort101492/nach-eines-fluechtlings-schwarzenborn-blick-lager-5503109.html
102   Fieseler, p.287.
103   Ibid, p.288.

could send and receive letters once a month, but these were heavily censored in both directions. In February Fieseler was beginning to feel at peace with himself, when without notice one night he and some 50 others were taken to a railway station and piled into cattle trucks. The sliding doors were slammed shut. The train moved, but no-one had any idea where to. Then it would stop for hours at a time. There was no straw on the floor nor was there a bucket to serve as a toilet. The destination turned out to be Darmstadt, where Fieseler and the others were disgorged at the station and marched to an enormous tented enclosure surrounded by barbed wire and watch towers.

Camp 91

This was Civil Internment Enclosure 91, otherwise known as Camp 91, where since June 1945 the Americans had confined some 25,000 detainees who were Nazis of various kinds: high-ranking officials, members of the Gestapo, SA and SS, as well as school teachers and university lecturers, and men like Fieseler, industrials who were seen as abettors (*Mitläufer*). This was where Messerschmitt, his fellow defence economy leader and *Standartenführer*, was also languishing. The internees, who were 'cooped up' twelve to a tent, were being held pending formal denazification and possible arraignment before war crimes trials.[104] As two-thirds of the inmates lived under canvas, the camp was indeed a veritable tent city. There was a separate section for women detainees. Camp 91 was said to be worse of the American detention camps; the tents were for the most part in poor repair and let the rain in.[105] Of the 25,000 inmates, some 179 would eventually be tried as Category 1 major war criminals. It was into this category that Gerhard Fieseler was destined to fall.[106]

The camp was to a large extent self-governing: the prisoners established a so-called 'municipal council' (*Gemeinderat*), where in true German deference to hierarchy there was not just a mayor, but even a senior mayor (*Oberbürgermeister*).[107] Inmates between the ages of 16 and 60, unless they were 'suffering from war injuries or were in the building trade', were required to take part in clean-up operations once a month. To ensure compliance and general good behaviour there was 'an order enforcement brigade' (*Ordnungsdienst*), its members sporting conspicuous white armbands emblazoned with the letters OD.[108] All those responsible for the smooth daily running of the camp and maintaining order about the place were said to carry out their duties 'with all due seriousness.'[109]

The camp, which was disbanded in the autumn of 1948, even had its own newspaper. Inmates received better food than was available to the general population. In that respect they were indeed very lucky. The 1945-46 winter was especially harsh, and there was mass-starvation throughout Germany. Camp life was not full of tedium, as there were activities to engage the minds and bodies of internees. Sporting activities were organised; there was even a 'university.'[110] Nevertheless, Fieseler's recollections are of a grim place, where time seemed to have stopped.

When he first arrived there, the nights were bitterly cold and the inmates only had a blanket to keep warm with. Fieseler once again went under both physically and mentally. He lay for three days without eating and was taken to the camp sick-bay, where he began to recover. What Fieseler calls his 'infamous treatment' by the Americans so distressed him that his 'only wish was to drop dead.' But, as his wish was 'to my surprise' not fulfilled, he felt 'a new spiritual force' within himself, he was suddenly detached from everything that was happening about him. But 'at almost

---

104   Fieseler, op. cit., p.289.
105   Wiederhold, op. cit., p.275.
106   https://darmundestat.wordpress.com/2014/04/12/das-lager-am-kavalleriesand/
107   The German word *Oberbürgermeister* is often translated as 'lord mayor' in English, which hardly fits in this case.
108   https://darmundestat.wordpress.com/2014/04/12/das-lager-am-kavalleriesand/
109   https://darmundestat.wordpress.com/2014/04/12/das-lager-am-kavalleriesand/
110   http://www.fr-online.de/zeitgeschichte/internierungslager-mit-eigener-zeitung-und-universitaet,1477344,2802516.html

the same time' a feeling of contempt and hatred' of his American captors festered within him.[111] Only with the fullness of time – indeed only at the very end of life – would his deep loathing for the Americans mellow.

Whilst in Camp 91, he was incarcerated with several old acquaintances, but he mentions none by name. As noted, one was his contemporary fellow defence economy leader and aircraft builder, Willy Messerschmitt, who in 1945, having been picked up by the Americans and handed over to the British for interrogation in London, ended up in various American detention camps, including the one at Heilbronn, where 'things were as bad as could be.'[112] Before his odyssey through internment camps Messerschmitt, confident of his value to the US military, had been developing the concept of an aircraft that would travel at supersonic speed between Europe and America.[113] He and other internees spent days and nights in the open air, rain or shine. Poor food and depression brought Messerschmitt to death's door. He was then transferred to the major US detention camp at Darmstadt, where he was put on suicide watch.[114] Another inmate of Camp 91, certainly known to Fieseler by name, was Otto Skorzeny, who had masterminded the Gran Sasso rescue of Mussolini, in which a Storch playing its vital role. He spent two years in detention at Darmstadt.[115] It is impossible to know whether Fieseler had any kind of direct encounter with either Messerschmitt or the man once dubbed 'the most dangerous man in Europe.'

The internees picked up information from the outside in various ways. Before long they heard that the relations between the Western allies and the Soviets had become hostile. This would have been music to the ears all those Nazis who believed that the true enemy in the Second World War had been the Soviet Union, whose barbaric hordes now threatened Western civilisation. At last Washington, London and Paris would realise that they really did have common cause with all the Germans held in their captivity. But this was wishful thinking, supporting Gitta Sereny's conviction that for the Germans 'the free acceptance of co-responsibility for their own country has simply been beyond their capacity.'[116] If that judgment makes unpleasant reading for some, its sentiment also fits in with a telling observation of the German author Alfred Döblin, who returning to Germany in 1945 after exile in America during the war, wrote of his fellow countrymen: 'I see their misery and see that they have not yet experienced what they have experienced.'[117] It could be said that Gerhard Fieseler was one to whom that pronouncement applied unambiguously for the rest of his life.

But Fieseler was right about two things concerning the emerging antagonisms between the Western Allies and the Soviets. First, the Soviet annexation of considerable amounts of Germany territory *did* concentrate Western minds on the ominous activities being orchestrated in the Kremlin. Second, the noticeable relaxation of harsh treatment by the Americans was a direct consequence of the stand-off. As he put it, 'there was an unclenching of the fist of the victors', for which 'irony of fate' one had to thank 'the sinister man who sat in the Kremlin,'[118] alias Joseph Stalin, who in a not necessarily outdated judgement may still remain 'the world's most accomplished totalitarian ruler of modern times.'[119]

---

111 Fieseler, op. cit., p.287.
112 H. Ebert, J, Kaiser und K. Peters, (eds). *Willy Messerschmitt – Pionier der Luftfahrt und des Leichtbaues,* , pp.320-321.
113 Pabst, op. cit., p.85.
114 Ibid, p.86.
115 C. Whiting, *Skorzeny: The Most Dangerous Man in Europe*, p.99.
116 G. Sereny, *The German Trauma,* p.60,
117 A. Döblin, A. Abschied und Wiederkehr (1946). In: A. Döblin: *Das Lesebuch – herausgegeben von Günter Grass*, p.493.
118 Fieseler, op. cit., p.290.
119 S. V. Utechin, *Everyman's Concise Encyclopedia of Russia,* p.512.

Not all items of news infiltrated the camp in necessarily surreptitious ways. Once the war trials got under way, the detainees 'had to listen over the tannoys to the Nuremberg judgments.' Fieseler described these trials as 'having so little to do with law as our imprisonment.'[120] This is no doubt what he felt at that time of incarceration, but it is surprising that he held and expressed that view when he wrote it as a very old man. One possible interpretation is that in his eyes Nazis great and small were being made victims of gloating victors, who were seeking vengeance and overrode legally just options in the process. An alternative interpretation is that the one person who should be on trial – Adolf Hitler – was not, and that those who faced the judgement of the victors – and by extension himself – were simply scapegoats. Furthermore, Fieseler implies that he and many others were being unfairly treated and should not be removed from their families and society at large. On the basis of his own choice of words then, Fieseler appears to be perilously close to saying that the major Nazi war criminals indicted at Nuremberg were as innocent as he saw himself.

Lastly, some might even deduce from his statement that Fieseler had emerged from the Second World War as an unreconstructed Nazi. Nor is that such a fanciful observation. During and after his time in American captivity – from November 1945 to December 1946 – the Americans 'conducted eleven polls, finding that on average 47 percent endorsed the proposition that National Socialism had been "a good idea carried out badly"; in August 1947, 55 percent of those polled endorsed this view.'[121] In Hessen, where Fieseler had lived since 1926, and in Berlin the figures reached 60-68 percent. It is hard to imagine that Fieseler held the minority view.

A friendly young man in an almost luxurious office
For Fieseler the first substantive change in his circumstances occurred in May 1946, as he approached the end of his first year in captivity. In March the American military authorities had passed their law on 'liberation from nationalism and militarism,' which paved the way for political purges and denazification. He was summoned to a meeting with a CIC agent, but he was apprehensive as he was being escorted to the interrogation room accompanied by a guard. He 'knew more than enough about the interrogation methods.'[122] Presumably he expected to be roughed up. Fieseler's breath was taken away when he found himself face to face with 'a friendly young man who occupied an almost luxurious office.' The officer's German was word-perfect, so Fieseler deduced, almost certainly correctly, that his interrogator was a Jew who had been brought up in Germany and had moved with his family to the USA in the 1930s. For all his skills the young officer found no way to engage Fieseler in conversation, who remained virtually taciturn in the encounter, merely mumbling confused yeses and nos.

Indeed Fieseler claims to have been so disoriented that he forgot to ask the CIC agent the reasons for his detention. At one point in the conversation the American let drop that he *knew* Fieseler and Kassel. But Fieseler appears not to have queried how this could conceivably be. At the end of the encounter he was fairly certain that the CIC man 'sensed my repudiation, even my contempt.' By contrast the attitude of Messerschmitt, who had experienced almost identical harsh treatment whilst in American hands, was judged by his captors in November 1946 to be 'cooperative during interrogation and apparently honest.'[123] Almost certainly Messerschmitt saw himself as someone of special value to the Americans. It made sense for him to make a good impression on them, just in case they would like to invite him to design his plane for supersonic travel between Europe and the USA.

120 Fieseler, op. cit, p.290.
121 Stargardt, op. cit., p.564.
122 Fieseler, op. cit., p.290.
123 Pabst, op. cit., p.88.

Fieseler's recollection of his interrogation, the most important event in his life since the war ended, is surely seriously deficient. Clearly his American interrogator knew exactly who Fieseler was and his status in the Nazi war machine; information which would have surely disarmed Fieseler. It seems very likely that he was asked about his contacts with senior Nazis like Göring, and Milch, about his involvement with the V-1 programme, and the employment conditions of forced labour at his factories. Fieseler was a combative man. It is therefore hard to imagine him remaining unprovoked by his interrogator. It is indeed odd that he does not mention any of the questions he was asked. It also seems unlikely that his answers were limited to yes or no. The fact is surely that Fieseler was far more forthcoming with his American captors than he would like us to believe. After all it was within the power of the CIC agent, subject to Fieseler's cooperativeness, to recommend his release or his further detention. All in all his recollection of his interrogation is more to do with the projection of bravado than providing a truthful account.

At the end of May he was indeed released with some forty others from American detention. His release papers revealed to him for the first time the reason for his internment. He had been found to be a member of the Nazi Flying Corps holding the rank of *Standartenführer* (not his actual rank of *Oberführer*). This was derisory as far as he was concerned. 'For that "honour"', he recorded bitterly, 'I had to endure humiliation, ill-treatment, mental anguish and desperation.'[124] Equally decisive in the arrest of Messerschmitt, who was released on 7 June, was the discovery at his home of his Flying Corps uniform. It seems then that the American occupiers attached considerable significance to the possession of a Nazi uniform reflecting senior officer rank, regardless of the wearer's 'mere' honorary status. To them it signalled a very close identification with the goals and methods of the Hitler regime. However, what the Americans may not have appreciated was that the Nazis 'wanted to get almost everyone into uniform, not least the children.'[125] Given that it was a regime in which it was almost unusual for anyone not to have one, Fieseler probably regarded his uniform as far less symbolic than his captors; hence his trivialisation of the nominal grounds for his arrest.

Once outside the camp, the other detainees 'rejoiced like children, as they jumped and danced on the way to the station.' Fieseler appeared not to take part in these high jinks. For his part he was sitting down on the kerb and yelping, so powerless, violated and insulted (*ohnmächtig, entehrt und beleidigt*) did he feel. According to one account, the tuberculosis he had contracted whilst in American detention and he left prison 'with diminished physical and mental health.'[126] Even so he was to live into his early 90s. However, after his release it never seems to have occurred to him that as a prisoner of the Americans he had received a taste of the kind of harsh treatment that all others who had been the victims of Nazi Germany had experienced: people like those from the Netherlands, Belgium, Poland and Russia, who had been press-ganged to build GFW aircraft in heartless conditions.

Those CIC agents with a very good – indeed native – command of German had techniques for disarming their quarries. One method was to say to a German of special interest, 'we know you're not important, you're just a small fry,'[127] appealing to the general German default position of 'I was just carrying out my orders.' The American tactic gave Germans a false sense of security and they would open up. We do not know whether Fieseler's interrogator actually used this gambit with him. At all events, Fieseler left American custody with the impression that he had been unjustly held in captivity for a year. No doubt he regarded, as did many others, the CIC as 'the Gestapo of the

---

124 Fieseler, op. cit., p.291.
125 A. Beevor, *The Second World War*, p.4.
126 http://ww2gravestone.com/people/fieseler-gerhard/
127 W. Isaacson, *Kissinger: A Biography*, p.49.

Americans.'[128] He returned to his wife and bomb-damaged home in Kassel, where under the terms of his release he was not permitted to engage in any gainful activity. This was because he was not yet a free man.

He would now need to face a denazification tribunal (*Spruchkammer*). The tribunals, run by Germans not Americans, were intended to deal with the cases of those who were not deemed to have been the very worst of the Nazis. They had stood trial at Nuremberg and there would be no repeat. His entire assets were duly confiscated, whilst his old Number Two and Number Three Works technically still belonged to the German Reich. He received a monthly local government allowance of 300 Reichsmarks, but that was reduced to 120 Reichsmarks on the grounds that he was still living in his own home. To add to his hardship as 'a person of interest' (*Betroffener*), he had to hang around for hours in the queue to personally collect ration cards for himself and his family. 'The greater your standing', he recalled bitterly, 'the greater the fall.'[129]

One task that befell him shortly after his release was the completion of a 131-point questionnaire, which the American occupation authorities sent to some 23 million Germans. The questionnaire elicited information from respondents as to their affiliations and sympathies during the Third Reich.[130] The idea was that through the questionnaire Germans could 'rank themselves on a precisely calibrated scale of malfeasance: major offenders, offenders, lesser offenders, followers and fellow travellers.'[131] But by the end 1945 the American military authorities had begun to realise that their idealistic approach to denazification was now becoming counterproductive.

In essence, the Americans were in a dilemma: 'You couldn't really gut the German elites, however distasteful they may have been, and hope to rebuild the country.'[132] Nor could they indefinitely detain thousands let alone millions of Germans who in their view should face some kind of trial. So it was that their 'zeal went out of fashion,' especially as the project was beyond the capacity of the Americans to administer. For a start they did not have enough collective German-language capability to assess the returned forms, though by no means were all of them ever submitted. Ironically, it was CIC agent Henry Kissinger who had identified as cardinal German trait a lack of sense of proportion. This is exactly what the Americans themselves displayed when it came to administering and analysing the 'the notorious *Fragebogen* (questionnaire).'[133]

Gerhard Fieseler filled in the questionnaire on 4 June 1946. If he had failed to do so, he might not have been able to obtain ration cards or could even face imprisonment. His questionnaire, along with millions of others, was despatched to Paris, where the answers were fed into an IBM index machine at the headquarters of the Central Registry of War Criminals and Security Suspects (CROWCASS): 'a bulky piece of machinery, rather like a cross between a motor car engine and a printer's linotype equipment.'[134] The system was habitually overloaded, and it was estimated that it would take more than two years to process the responses.[135] In the event Fieseler did not have to wait that long. On 5 March 1947, on the very day incidentally that his wife gave birth to his son Götz, he was notified that he had been classified as a major offender (*Hauptverbrecher*).[136] Thus classified, he would now have to face a denazification tribunal, which would decide his fate. But at least his case would be handled by his fellow Germans, and not by vindictive American prosecutors.

128   Ferguson, op. cit., p.186.
129   Fieseler, op. cit., p.293.
130   Ferguson, op. cit., p.183.
131   Ibid, p.184.
132   Buruma, op. cit., p.181.
133   Ibid, p.177.
134   Sebestyen, op. cit., p.227.
135   Ibid, p.232.
136   Nagel und Bauer, op. cit., p. 431.

All being well then he would find himself before a tribunal, whose members would condoningly understand that he was just one among millions who had helped Hitler one way or the other without necessarily supporting the Nazi programme of genocide and mass-murder. They might therefore come to the verdict that he was no major offender, just someone who worked reluctantly for the Nazi cause. As long as he appeared not to have gained unduly from his association with the Nazi state, then he could be seen a less culpable person: someone, who like countless unfortunate others, was, as the jargon had it, 'a beneficiary against one's will' (*Nutznießer wider Willen*). However, there was a small risk that he might be confronted by an unsympathetic tribunal, whose members might see in him a person to be made an example of. In the event things did not quite unfold in the one way or the other.

12

What was granted to him

The vast majority of Germans preferred to brush the troubling questions of the past under the carpet and channel their thoughts and energies into the happier task of building up the Wirtschaftswunder – itself a kind of atonement.

John Ardagh[1]

Memoirs must be treated with scepticism.

Simon Sebag Montefiore[2]

Who is this General Harras supposed to be?
One day after Fieseler learned that he was to be indicted by the denazification tribunal in Kassel for being a major offender, there was an expected knock on the front door of his wrecked home. In stepped two civilians accompanied by an armed American soldier. They searched every nook and cranny for evidence to hand over to the tribunal. Three years later he received his property back: '40 kilos worth of photographs, albums, epaulettes and military decorations and so forth.[3]' Whilst he awaited his trial, he contemplated the future. He was much exercised about the plan of Henry Morgenthau, Roosevelt's treasury secretary, for the so-called pastoralisation of Germany, whereby the country, once industrially castrated, could never wage war again. With that in mind, so Fieseler thought, Americans had already compiled lists of firms that had worked for the Wehrmacht and that would presumably be dismantled under the Morgenthau scheme.

And which firms had *not* been involved in the war effort, Fieseler wanted to know. As he saw things, the plan was now being implemented. Had not his own company already been requisitioned as part of some reparation scheme? In the event the Morgenthau plan was never put into operation. Even so he feared for the fate of his company, when he learnt that it was to be wound up in accordance with directives issued by the newly formed *Land* of Hesse. The writing was on the wall when Fieseler learnt that an official trustee (*Treuhänder*) had been appointed to oversee its transfer to the regional authorities.

The trustee in question had been a mere filing clerk (*Karteiführer*) in a local company until the end of the war. The man was not in good health and had seemingly received psychiatric treatment on three occasions. Now this former filing clerk held the title of 'general trustee' and had responsibility for winding down the former Fieseler works (Fieseler uses the word 'former'). What is more, this unsatisfactory man had the use of a large motor car and chauffeur for official business. In next to no time he disposed of and even auctioned off all the company's assets except those which were not clinched and riveted. On specious grounds he drew up various official contracts,

---

1 J. Ardagh, *Germany and the Germans*, p.500.
2 S. Sebag Montefiore, *The Romanovs 1613 – 1918*, p.xxx.
3 G. Fieseler, *Meine Bahn am Himmel*, p.293.

which Fieseler could not contest, to expedite these transactions. Worse, the trustee's actions did hundreds of thousands of Reichmarks damage to the company. As Fieseler was not permitted to enter the premises of his former company, the trustee would visit him at home accompanied by his commercial manager. It was a matter of some relief to Fieseler when the trustee was replaced by another. But there was by then virtually nothing left for his successor to sell off.[4]

With all this unpleasantness happening to him, Fieseler had to wait for his denazification tribunal to take place. It was, he said, an awful wait, especially as he seemed to expect 'the spirit of the Morgenthau plan' to finish Germany off. Following a summons the case opened in Kassel in February 1948. During this anxious time for him, and indeed for Germany at large, with the hunger and rampant black market for food, he started to receive luxury in the form of care-packages from the USA. These, it seems, were sent by 'two of my former Jewish purveyors who had emigrated there in 1934.'[5] But why exactly these people prioritised Fieseler over their fellow Jews is a mystery.

Shortly after Fieseler's release from Camp 91, though it is not clear exactly when, the figure of Ernst Udet, his great friend who had committed suicide in November 1941, came into his life in a literally dramatic way. We have already mentioned that the dramatist Carl Zuckmayer whilst in exile in the USA during war had written a play, *Des Teufels General*, seemingly about the last very stressed days of a high-ranking Nazi official. His protagonist was called Harras, and it was generally agreed that this suave, rakish character was based on Ernst Udet. Zuckmayer, however, denied this. According to Fieseler, 'every city was at pains to put on the drama on improvised stages as quickly as possible after the war.' In Kassel a discussion group calling itself 'the peace society' (*Friedensgesellschaft*) attracted some 25 people for a public discussion of the play. The people, including Fieseler, got together in a bombed-out house. The contributors made a wretched impression on Fieseler, as they mouthed things that they would not have dared say during Nazi times. And now here they were 'prattling on about events, of which they could know nothing, and getting the wrong end of the stick.'[6] Next they were identifying Udet with Harras as if it were the most obvious thing in the world.

Fieseler had heard enough. He took issue on behalf of Udet, pointing out that Zuckmayer's treatment was pure phantasy; things simply did not work that way under Hitler. He came to the point: 'the figure of General Harras is no portrayal of General Udet. The events as represented in his play had nothing to do with the real events in the Third Reich.' It seems that Fieseler was not alone in his condemnation: 'In other cities the play was savaged (*leidenschaftlich angegriffen*) by former front-line soldiers to the extent that Zuckmayer, who had returned to Germany after emigration, had to repeatedly make clear that the action in his play was made up.' Fieseler was withering in his condemnation of the playwright: 'He – an emigrant – had no objective conception of daily life as it was in Germany.'[7] Unfortunately Fieseler does not record the impact of his intervention on the rest of the audience nor does he reveal whether or not that he knew Udet extremely well and indeed was with him just two days before his death. In 1955 a film version of the drama came out. If Fieseler saw it, he did not say so.

Fieseler in the meantime had to do something with his time until he faced the denazification tribunal. Seemingly out of the blue he hit upon the idea of creating a small private hotel in his spacious, bomb-damaged home. For this purpose he obtained a loan from his bank, with which he had transacted substantial volumes of business until the end of the war. The bank evidently

---

4   Ibid, p.292.
5   Ibid, p.293.
6   Ibid, p.242.
7   Ibid, p.243.

Virtuoso of slow flight

Unlike his contemporary Messerschmitt, Fieseler does not appear to have dreamt of creating some kind of innovative aircraft. He may perhaps have heard that his Storch was being built in small numbers in Czechoslovakia after the war, but he would not have known that his cherished creation would receive a most unusual endorsement from an improbable source. It so happens that Britain's most accomplished test pilot during the war and post-war era, Eric 'Winkle' Brown, had flown the Storch along with no fewer than 487 aircraft types, which included practically every type that had taken part in the Second World War. Brown, who happened to be a German speaker, had met Udet and Hanna Reitsch before the war and after the war interviewed Göring in Luxemburg in June 1945 on the day before the Nazi potentate was transferred to Nuremberg to stand trial. Brown had flown a Storch, which he memorably characterised 'as a virtuoso of slow flight.'

More impressive is that the fact that he included the Storch in his personal list of top twenty 'greats,' covering aircraft from the mid-1930s to the 1970s, a period which Brown describes as 'my golden age of aviation.' His list was 'based on wide handling experience of aircraft of that era and judged by the sheer joy of knowing one was flying a real crackerjack.' The aircraft are listed alphabetically. Perhaps not surprisingly his entries include the Avro Lancaster bomber and the iconic Spitfire. In addition to the Storch he lists four other German aircraft: the Bücker Jungmeister ('an aerobatic gem'), the Focke-Wulf 190D-9 ('German fighter technology at its best'), the Junkers 88 ('efficient in all its multi-roles, and a delight to fly'), and the Messerschmitt 262 ('a quantum jump in fighter performance').[8]

It will be recalled that Fieseler was furious that Hitler failed to grasp the significance of the Messerschmitt 262. Fieseler's company, as we know, built Fw 190s under licence. Thus he may be the only person in Brown's list who is directly linked to two of his greats. Brown also compiled a list of key personalities to be interviewed by him, including Wernher von Braun, Ernst Heinkel, Willy Messerschmitt, Kurt Tank (the Focke-Wulf designer), Hanna Reitsch and the Horten Brothers (the leading glider designers). Fieseler almost certainly knew Heinkel, Messerschmitt and Tank, as they were all defence industry leaders and would have been present at Göring's tirade in Carinhall in 1938. It is possible that he met von Braun at Peenemünde. He definitely knew Hanna Reitsch from the 1930s. Brown goes on to record two notable flying experiences with the Storch, which Fieseler presumably never heard about. The first takes place in 1946, when he has the opportunity 'to baptise thoroughly … that remarkable slow-flying plane:'

> I took it to sea and landed it aboard the carrier *Triumph*. They put the barrier up for us, as the Storch had no arrester hook, but it was not needed. To the astonishment of the goofers[9] the little plane landed and came to a stop right on the after lift …We paid our way while we were on board by using the Storch's incredible gift for hovering to photograph the approach path to the carrier, something which had not been properly done before, and were also useful in investigating rundown turbulence, the violent swirl of air which is set up round the after end of the flight deck of a carrier.'[10]

---

8   E. Brown, *Wings on my Sleeve*. p.228-229.
9   An intrepid flighter pilot (WWII army airforces). Source: http://dictionary.reference.com/browse/goofer
10 Brown, op. cit., p.159.

In Brown's autobiography there is a photograph showing his Storch landing on HMS *Triumph*. This was almost certainly the first time that a Storch had landed on an aircraft carrier.

Brown's next innovative experience with the Storch took place at Farnborough. Two captured Storchs were used in 'a research programme, which was now urgent.' The challenge was to investigate 'helicopter rotor flow, which really tested the ingenuity of boffins and the nerves of the pilots. The experiment involved forcing coloured smoke along a long metal tube inside the aircraft. The idea was to get the smoke to drift over the rotor blades and photograph the pattern of the airflow. This could not be done without endangering the pilot and the helicopter. The solution was to get one Storch to dangle three canisters emitting coloured smoke for the helicopter to fly through, whilst the other one photographed it as it flew through the smoke trail.[11]

This was presumably the first time that the Storch with its helicopter characteristics was used to engage in a research programme about helicopters. So it was that the pilots and boffins of Fieseler's arch-enemy in the Second World War found two novel uses for the Storch. For certain, Fieseler would have given his back teeth to land a Storch on an aircraft carrier. Nor was that the only Storch in the immediate post-war years to be deployed in unexpected circumstances. One of the machines made by the Czech manufacturer Beneš-Mráz had been sold to Swissair who used it as an air-taxi, for mountain rescue and glacier flights.[12] Another had been delivered to Swissair in 1939 and remained in operation until 1963.[13]

Finally, there is a long-standing French connection with the Storch. It will be recalled that some Storch production was switched to Morane-Saulnier in 1942. Then:

In 1944, immediately after the Liberation, production was resumed at the direction of the newly-reconstituted French Air Force. Over the next twenty years almost one thousand aircraft were built in various modified forms, many of which were employed operationally in Indochina. Popularly known as Le Criquet, or cricket, the Fieseler proved sufficiently versatile to serve as both as an observation platform and as a means of evacuating casualties from makeshift landing strips beside outposts in even the remotest and most inhospitable of areas. Following the conclusion of hostilities in Indochine, Le Criquet continued in military service in Algeria, and was not finally withdrawn from the Air Force frontline inventory until the 1970s.[14]

Thus concluded the operational career of a truly remarkable military aircraft.

Armour-clad in self-denial

When his trial opened in February 1948, Fieseler was accused of building aircraft for the Hitler regime. The charge documentation gathered by the prosecutors ran to 300 lines over five pages. He was charged with being a major offender on the basis of alleged support for the Nazi regime as the managing director of an aircraft building company in his capacity of defence economy leader, as a person affiliated to the Nazi party, as honorary officer in the Nazi Flying Corps, and as an employer of forced labour. The president of the Kassel denazification tribunal was a certain Theodor Hüpeden. Fieseler was 'a big fish' for him, and the trial could expect to take place with full public galleries and attract wide press coverage.[15]

11 Ibid, p.165.
12 R. Nagel und T. Bauer, *Kassel und die Luftfahrtindustrie seit 1923: Geschichte(n), Menschen, Technik*, p.442.
13 Deutsches Museum, *Aviation: A Guide to the Aeronautics Collection*, p.63.
14 Personal communication with RAF Squadron Leader Steve MacFarland.
15 Fieseler, op. cit., p.294.

In preparing his own defence Fieseler had spent 'countless hours' gathering more than a hundred sworn statements which attested him as 'a reputable man who had not violated existing laws or had wronged other people.'[16] Such endorsements came from former GFW employees, including Kessler, the *Betriebsobmann* (who must have been a party stalwart!) and even one of his former Dutch forced labourers. His former wife Helene wrote that until 1933 Fieseler was a 'total pacifist … who despite joining the NSPAD had never concerned himself with party affairs.' There was also a statement by Wilhelm David, the Jewish shop owner from Grebenstein. David, as we shall see, even appeared at the trial in support of Fieseler's defence team. All such exonerating statements were jocularly called 'Persil certificates' (*Persilscheine*), an allusion to the soap powder: duly cleansed, defendants could emerge 'whiter than white.' In fact there was a black market for the Persil certificates, whereby 'well-known Nazis bought letters establishing their "innocence" from opponents of the old regime, which were enough to get them cleared by a *Spruchkammer*.'[17] There is no evidence that Fieseler resorted to this tactic.

The description of Fieseler's appearance before the denazification tribunal, as presented here, is based on his own account. It must be treated with extreme caution. Fieseler was being, as the saying goes, economical with the truth. His main purpose was to present himself as a reluctant supporter of the Third Reich, indeed as one who in various ways opposed it. He was, then, another of those Germans, who by unfortunate accident had found themselves inadvertently serving what turned out to be a morally corrupt regime. Fieseler's defence lawyers countered the indictment against him, arguing that their client had shown his aversion (*Abneigung*) towards the NSDAP, had in the earshot of others labelled Hitler and Göring as criminals, had concerned himself with the accommodation and food for his forced labourers, had not displayed at his home a swastika or photograph of a party personality and had subscribed to the *Kurhessische Landeszeitung* (i.e. the main regional newspaper, not a Nazi one). Particularly stressed was 'his concern for his workers' welfare.'[18]

Herr Wilhelm David to the rescue

As noted, one of the character witnesses was Herr Wilhelm David, who thanks to Fieseler's courageous intervention in 1936, had survived the war against inconceivable odds and had resumed life in nearby Grebenstein. David had been summoned to attend the hearing, but did not turn up. According to Fieseler, the day before he was due to appear, Hüpeden, in the connivance with a Jewish widow whose husband had perished in the war, had seemingly put pressure on David not to give evidence on Fieseler's behalf. When Fieseler got wind of this chicanery, he 'repeatedly reminded David of his moral obligation.'[19] It happened that there were 'cases of Jewish survivors being paid to testify that [defendants] had hidden their families or somehow helped them to survive.'[20]

But there is no evidence to suggest that Fieseler offered such an inducement to David. More to the point perhaps: it seems never to have crossed his mind that David's appearance before serried ranks of Germans might have been emotionally traumatising for the Jewish shopkeeper after his terrible experiences. In the end he duly appeared at the hearing and publicly declared: 'Herr Fieseler risked his life for me. He saved my life with a concocted letter.' This brought a sarcastic response from Hüpeden: 'Someone like Fieseler would do that, wouldn't he?' After five days the proceedings were postponed for six months.[21]

16 Ibid, p.294.
17 V. Sebestyen, *1946: The Making of the Modern World*, p.239.
18 T. Wiederhold, *Gerhard Fieseler – eine Karriere: Ein Wirtschaftsführer im Dienste des Nationalsozialismus*, p.277.
19 Fieseler, op. cit., p.294.
20 Sebestyen, op. cit., p.239.
21 Fieseler, op. cit., pp.294-295.

In his memoir Fieseler gives the impression that, thanks to that all-important letter he had concocted to protect him from Nazi persecution, David and his family had survived the war. But it is not so straightforward. According to Wiederhold, the family lived in the concentration camp near the Bohemian town of Theresienstadt.[22] However, this was not a 'normal' concentration camp, having the character of a holding camp and transit facility. It served, among other things, as a Nazi propaganda tool, being shown off to bodies like the Red Cross as a show-case place of resettlement for retired Jews. Although the conditions at Theresienstadt were a good deal less brutal than at other concentration camps, David and his family would have been compelled to perform forced labour.[23]

At the beginning of April 1945, as Soviet forces got nearer to Vienna, some 1300 survivors of Theresienstadt and Birkenau were evacuated by their Nazi captors and found themselves on a death march to Gusen, a satellite of the notorious concentration camp at Mauthausen.[24] Only 700 survived the horrors of that, including presumably the David family. However, as far as Fieseler himself was concerned, it was his letter of 1936 that spared the David family the grim fate which befell six million other Jews in the concentration camps. In January 1952 the David family migrated to Los Angeles.[25]

Whilst he waited for the resumption of the hearing, Fieseler presumably continued to supervise the building work in his home. Back in court, Hüpeden continued with what Fieseler called 'aspersions and bare-faced lies.'[26] Exactly what these alleged defamatory remarks referred to is not mentioned. It is of course possible that Hüpeden, with his own Nazi past in Kassel, got uncomfortably close to some unwelcome truths, as far as Fieseler was concerned. Fieseler states that all this calumny spread over nine days in court. In the end he was so choked with anger that he requested a special meeting with his lawyer on the following day. He told the lawyer that he happened by coincidence to have a damning information about Herr Hüpeden based on his personal file with his previous employer. This exposed his close links with the Nazi Party, and Fieseler wished to acquaint the tribunal with this shocking information at his disposal.

But how was it that he could make such a startling claim about the president of the tribunal? The story begins when he was being held captive at the internment facility in Schwarzenborn, where he had shared accommodation in the form of the large animal feed box with Hermann Abele, the agreeable young manager of a major insurance company. In conversations with Abele Fieseler had learnt that his predecessor was the self-same Theodor Hüpeden, who was now presiding over the Kassel denazification tribunal. Hüpeden, it seems, had been accused by the Nazis of high treason and was imprisoned in Kassel until he was freed by the Americans in 1945. Abele had told Fieseler what he knew about all this, which was based on Hüpeden's file in the personnel department of the insurance company. In essence Hüpeden had been pensioned off from his post there 'owing to political unreliability.'[27] He had though tried to get his job back, approaching senior party figures with evidence of his loyalty and protestations about how there was no incompatibility between his views and those of the Hitler regime. But he was not to be spared prison.

Upon his release the CIC, seeing in Hüpeden a man without an incriminating past, had appointed him to be president for the denazification tribunal for Kassel and the region. In this role Hüpeden had taken it upon himself, so the rumour mill had it, to take it out on every former Nazi party member in revenge for his incarceration. The reaction of Fieseler's lawyer was one of extreme

22   T. Wiederhold, *Gerhard Fieseler – eine Karriere: Ein Wirtschaftsführer im Dienste des Nationalsozialismus*, p.242.
23   http://www.ushmm.org/wlc/en/article.php?ModuleId=10005424 (website of the United States Holocaust Memorial Museum)
24   M. Gilbert, *The Holocaust: The Jewish Tragedy*, p.789.
25   Wiederhold, op. cit., p.242.
26   Fieseler, op. cit., p.295.
27   Ibid, p.288.

caution, advising his client not to put this information before the tribunal under any circumstances, adding that 'you could damage your own chances.' The conversation continued, but Fieseler found nothing to convince him to deter him from his intention. In the end the lawyer gave way, but told him under no circumstances to reveal that he (the lawyer) had prior knowledge of his intentions. Fieseler promised to comply.

'No sooner said than done', Fieseler rejoices, 'The next day the bombshell was dropped.' Hüpeden turned pale, Fieseler's lawyer feigned astonishment, whilst the public showed undisguised *Schadenfreude*. Hüpeden called an adjournment 'for consultations.' Half an hour later two young police officers took up stations behind Fieseler. This laughable show of power by Hüpeden fooled no-one. The consultations took three hours, after which a senior official took over to make one announcement: 'Today's proceedings are at an end. A new date will be announced.'[28]

Among other curious features of this extraordinary day was that Fieseler appeared to make his allegations about Hüpeden without producing the actual file containing the damning evidence. At all events there was a six-month delay, and in the end there was not to be another day in court. Instead Fieseler received a letter of release, informing him that the state would cover all the costs. Hüpeden did a disappearing act. However, Fieseler was not yet out of the woods. He could still make no claim for the restoration of his assets. Finally in January 1950, he received the all-important letter confirming that the denazification tribunal dropped all charges against him. Fieseler, after four and a half years of various forms of detention and litigation, was finally a free man. 'I could work again', he declared in triumph, adding rather testily 'so began the so-called economic miracle (*Wirtschaftswunder*), but it wasn't a miracle.'[29]

The letter in question, reproduced in Wiederhold's book, is a masterpiece of legal duplicity, being not just excessive in its justifications, but downright unbelievable.[30] The defendant was found to be 'a plaything' (*Spielball*) of the Reich Aviation Ministry. Although he had joined the NSDAP voluntarily, he was only a member in name (*nur ein formelles Mitglied*), who acted in 'a humane and entirely irreproachable manner' towards those who were persecuted on grounds of dissent and race. Not only did the case of David Wilhelm endorse that finding, but also his alleged actions aimed at providing work for Jewish people. For any German, if he or she could produce a Jew who spoke or wrote in his favour before a denazification tribunal, this was to sprinkle his defence with gold dust. Another notable 'apolitical' Nazi with a deficient memory – 'I have never belonged to any organisation or party' – the famed Luftwaffe aviatrix Hanna Reitsch was another notable 'apolitical' Nazi to make advantageous use of favourable Jewish testimony.[31]

The letter of exoneration also notes that Fieseler's personal stresses 'considerably aggravated an existing heart condition.' It records too that Fieseler had been heard to declare 'in a fairly wide circle of people' such things as 'Hitler is a criminal' Against that, it will be no doubt recalled that in the first issue in 1938 of the company newspaper he had referred to the Führer's cause as 'serving an incomparably higher purpose.' But, advises the letter, he had written such things 'under duress and with regard to the existing conditions.' But especially breath-taking is the argument that Fieseler could not be judged to be a beneficiary of the Nazi regime because his income after 1933 was 'only immaterially higher than in the years before 1933.'[32] No wonder then that by general agreement the post-war denazification tribunals were roundly seen as 'a farce',[33] and that the exoneration-

---

28 Ibid, p.296.
29 Fieseler, op. cit., p.296.
30 Wiederhold, op. cit., p.244.
31 C. Mulley, *The Women Who Flew for Hitler: The True Story of Hitler's Valkyries*, pp.342-343.
32 Wiederhold, op. cit., pp.306-307.
33 G. Sereny *The German Trauma:, Experiences and Reflections* 1938-2001, p.60.

geared rigmarole was known 'the fellow-traveller factory' (*Mitläuferfabrik*). One in ten Germans was said to have been a member of the Nazi party, but in the end only 150,000 former Nazis were convicted, the majority being classed as 'lesser offenders' (*Minderbelastete*), who received fines.

The tribunals may well have been set up with the best of intentions, but the results were unsatisfactory, as the historian Keith Lowe explains: 'Some zones of Germany pursued Nazis more vigorously than others; some categories of prisoners were treated more harshly than others; and many prominent Nazis got off scot free while their "fellow travellers" were punished.'[34] A further complication was that it was very difficult to find qualified people to work for the tribunals, seeing that such a high proportion of the new judiciary had themselves a Nazi past themselves. Furthermore, 'in many parts of the country Germans ostracised those who worked for the tribunals or the de-Nazification process in any way.'[35] As for the case of Fieseler, his was a good example of how 'denazification began as righteous retribution', but 'ended in local politics.'[36] Furthermore, Fieseler, having so effectively turned the tables during his trial, was another who got off scot-free. As far as he was concerned, he had been punished enough for crimes, which in any case had not been proved.

All in all the verdict of the tribunal was based on the conviction that Fieseler had acted under duress and had to his credit, and at risk to his own health, tried to help the oppressed in whatever way possible. By extension then Fieseler had himself been a victim of the Nazi regime. This is not to make a cynical interpretation of the verdict, which must be understood in its context. By the end of the 1940s the Germans wanted to put the whole ghastly experience of the Hitler state behind them. In March 1945 a report by the SD on the morale of German people facing defeat recorded this pronounced sentiment: 'We did not deserve to be led into such a catastrophe,' Germans therefore 'excused themselves of any guilt for the course that the war had taken.'[37] After the war 'a sense of German victimhood came to overshadow any sense of shared responsibility for the sufferings of Germany's victims.'[38] So it was that entrepreneurs like Fieseler who 'actively participated at all levels of the compulsory labor program' and did so 'with apparently little mind to the moral implications of their brutal actions,' were never held properly to account.[39]

The case of Fieseler is also a clear instance of the lack of public appetite for the search for perpetrators among the countless small-fry and indeed for more inquisitions, now that the Nuremberg trials had done their work. Enough was enough. As for Fieseler himself, who had spent a gruelling year in American incarceration without charge and endured nearly four years of uncertainty as a defendant in a denazification process, the verdict did not only allow him to see himself as a victim in the sense described, but it also meant that he was, in a manner of speaking, *an officially certified victim.* In case that sounds outlandish, here then is the verdict of his German biographer, Thorsten Wiederhold: 'neither in the proceedings of his denazification tribunal nor in his autobiography which appeared thirty years later did Gerhard Fieseler take the opportunity to create distance between himself and the Nazi era and to come to terms with (*aufarbeiten*) role in the Nazi system in a serious and credible way.'[40]

The point is that, once he had been released from American detention and found himself in the more accommodating environment of a tribunal presided over by his fellow countrymen, he could hide behind the premise that he cited in his memoirs that 'every German served or helped

---

34   K. Lowe, *Savage Continent: Europe in the Aftermath of World War II*, p.160.
35   Sebestyen, op. cit., p.239.
36   N. Ferguson, *Kissinger 1923-1968: The Idealist,* p.184.
37   N. Stargardt, *The German War: A Nation Under Arms, 1939-1945,* p.546.
38   Ibid, p.548.
39   S. J. Wiesen, *West German Industry 1945-1955 and the Challenge of the Nazi Past,* p.16.
40   Wiederhold, op. cit., p.290.

that criminal Hitler.'⁴¹ As Wiederhold points out, this form of evasion was perfectly 'commonplace (*gängig*) at the time.'⁴² It was certainly enough to make him armour-clad in self-denial about his own involvement *as a direct beneficiary* in the Nazi war machine. Every German relativized the Nazi crimes against humanity in his or her own particular way.

During the period of his denazification, Fieseler went through the anguish of losing his much-loved daughter Katharina in October 1948. When his son Manfred was killed in 1944, he was hit very hard by his death. But at least he knew that Manfred as a Luftwaffe fighter pilot faced death on daily basis. With Katharina, who was 24, it was a kind of death linked to the war, but in bizarre, unimaginable circumstances. In the company of her husband she had met a friend who had been held in captivity in the Soviet Union. This former soldier had returned to Germany with an infection, which he passed on to Katharina.⁴³ Fieseler records the event dispassionately, saying that she had been infected with 'the Asian jaundice' and that she died within a week of contracting it. Katharina left behind a husband and one-year old daughter.⁴⁴

When he received his letter of exoneration in January 1950, Gerhard Fieseler could at last feel that, as far as he was concerned, the Second World War was well and truly over. He had been cleared of any wrong-doing by the Americans and his own countrymen in consistency with regulations and legal structure in force at the time; there were no skeletons in the cupboard; he could begin to plan his life for the next few years. He would now look back on the Nazi years with amoral unit. But before we press on with his life, let us reflect on Germany's immediate post-war years.

The German Question in a new twist
At the Potsdam Conference of 1945, 'the three victors had decided that Berlin would be governed by the four occupying powers – the United States, Great Britain, France, and the Soviet Union – which would jointly administer Germany as well. As it turned out, the four-power administration of Germany lasted little more than a year.'⁴⁵ It was not long before all the former wartime Allies saw economic recovery as a more important aim than restoring a sense of justice, albeit for different reasons. At the same time the Soviets wanted to rebuild their "antifascist" Germany as a buffer against capitalist imperialism; the United States, Britain and their allies needed "their" Germany as a democratic bastion against communism.'⁴⁶ This ideological stand-off created the Cold War and led to the division of Germany in 1949.

At the end of the war some 18-20 million Germans were homeless: they lived 'in ruins, cellars, holes in the ground.'⁴⁷ Orphans roamed the big cities; larceny was everywhere, as was hunger; essential services such as water, gas and electricity were wanting; there was a huge black market; a pound of butter cost the equivalent of six week's wages; cigarettes were the ersatz currency. It was scarcely better in most other European countries that had been occupied and desolated by the Nazis. In 1947 Churchill had described Post-war Europe as 'a rubble heap, a charnel house, a breeding-ground of pestilence and hate.'⁴⁸ And yet in Germany 'many an economic-miracle career' began behind all those piles of ruins.⁴⁹ But apart from the physical ruins, there was the devastation

41   Fieseler, op. cit., p.282.
42   Wiederhold, op. cit., p.290.
43   Nagel und Bauer, op. cit., p.432.
44   Fieseler, op. cit., p.297.
45   H. Kissinger, *Diplomacy*, p.568.
46   Buruma, op. cit., p.181.
47   Lowe, op. cit., p.8.
48   Cited in: A. Deighton, The Remaking of Europe. In: M. Howard, and W. Louis, *The Oxford History of the Twentieth Century*, p.190.
49   H. Jaenecke. Die Stunde Null, in: *GEO Epoche – Deutschland nach dem Krieg 1945-1955*, pp.28-30.

of German lives: so many families were grieving for a husband, a father, a son, a brother. Then there were the thousands who were languishing in that abomination, the Soviet gulag. When would they come back? Would they ever come back?

True to their beliefs in the widest social good that derives from economic prosperity, in 1948 the Americans launched their European Recovery Programme (Marshall Aid). Importantly, Germany could benefit from it on an equal footing with its former enemies; a third of the funds went into reconstruction. But another measure in 1948 was equally crucial for the Germany: the currency reform, which abandoned the worthless Reichsmark and introduced the Deutschmark, one immediate consequence of which was the disappearance 'overnight' of the black market.[50] Every adult German was issued with 40 Deutschmarks; the per capita allocation was kept deliberately low to reduce inflation, of which Germans had a chronic fear. In the following year the Federal Republic (West Germany) and the German Democratic Republic were established. Germany would remain sundered until 1989. Fieseler has not a word to say about these momentous developments; presumably in the immediate post-war years his sole preoccupation was getting himself cleared of war crimes.

The new states found themselves – until 1989 – in awkward divided German space. With the one an ally of the West and the other paying homage to Moscow, the much discussed German question was turned on its head, whereby 'instead of a single Germany at the centre of Europe two Germanies had both moved to the edge of the global power system and were accordingly favoured by their respective hegemonic power.'[51] In the early part of the 19th century the so-called German Question revolved around the issue of whether the various states making up the entity of Germany should be unified in a political structure that included or did not include Austria. It was seen, among other things, that one structure or the other, given Germany's geographical location, would have implications for the unified country's relations with its neighbours. After two world wars in which Germany had invaded France, it was evident that the German Question had morphed into 'the dilemma of Germany's geographical position and belligerence.'[52] The division of Germany in 1949 thus recast the question in a hitherto unimaginable way because neither Germany was a product of German volition. Furthermore, their respective relationships with their neighbours were less important than its relationship with their respective super-powerful sponsors, namely the USA and the USSR, who behaved 'like two scorpions in a bottle.'[53] The result was 'the special vulnerability of West Berlin,' which had become 'the ultimate Cold War flashpoint.'[54]

By the time of the cleavage the West German economy was already responding to new conditions. The country was helped by the fact that the economic infrastructure had not suffered so badly from wartime destruction', whilst the post-war economy quickly became integrated into the US-dominated world economy.'[55] By the end of the 1940s Germany was experiencing an economic boom. Henry Kissinger, who visited the country in 1950 was astounded by the Germany that now confronted him: 'Whatever you may think of Germany, their recovery has been remarkable.'[56]

Germany's first post-war Chancellor was Konrad Adenauer, who was memorably described by Henry Kissinger in this masterpiece of verbal portrayal: 'Possessed of the granite like features of a Roman emperor, Adenauer also had the high cheekbones and slightly slanted eyes which suggested the hint of some Hun conqueror who might have trekked across the Rhineland in the previous

50   H. Schulze, *Kleine deutsche Geschichte*, p.198.
51   Ibid, p.201.
52   T. Marshall, *Prisoners of Geography*, p.101.
53   Ibid, p.233.
54   Ferguson, op. cit., p.428.
55   Interview with Professor G. in *GEO Epoche – Deutschland nach dem Krieg*, pp.122-129.
56   Cited in: Ferguson, op. cit., p.271.

millennium. Adenauer's courtly behaviour, acquired in his pre-World War I youth, reflected a serenity which was startling in the leader of an occupied country, few of whose adult citizens were able to recall a political past in which they could take pride ... By the time he had become Chancellor at the age of seventy-three, it seemed as if his entire life had been a preparation for the responsibility of restoring self-respect to his occupied, demoralised, and divided society.'[57]

When Gerhard Fieseler had completely regained his freedom and peace of mind in 1950 after his exoneration, Germany's post-war economic miracle – its famous *Wirtschaftswunder* – was already under way. Perhaps the most important factor behind the economic transformation of Germany was 'a simple human one, hard to prove or quantify. This is the fact that Germans at all levels, from the shop-floor workers to managers, just happen to be very disciplined, thorough and realistic.'[58]

Despite the influence of American business methods with the big emphasis on marketing, German business had a very pronounced orientation to social welfare, and before long the country would become – in contrast to Britain – 'a paradise of labour harmony,' whilst the Volkswagen Beetle would be recognised as the iconic symbol of post-war German economic recovery.[59] It was the time for entrepreneurs in companies great and small who 'in various guises: as the venture capitalist, the family manufacturer, the genius inventor would help put the country back together, and the benevolent company manager' would help put the country back on its feet.[60] They did it with astounding speed. Gerhard Fieseler was such an entrepreneur in waiting.

The renowned Wilhelm Furtwängler comes to stay

Fieseler found himself only too consciously a citizen in the fourth Germany of his lifetime. He been born in the Imperial Germany of the erratic Kaiser Wilhelm II, endured the Germany of the unloved Weimar Republic, and outlived the monstrous Third Reich. Now he was living the anxious Federal Republic in a divided country. Dying in 1986, he would fall short of living in the reunited Germany of today by three years. He described himself at around 1950 as one who 'closely observed the behaviour of the victors, the reaction of the German people and the creation and development of our new republic', adding that he beheld everything 'with the eyes of an experienced, critical and an as ever patriotically minded man', who was though 'strictly politically neutral.'[61] Later in his life he would reveal very his views on the new Federal Republic, and it was not in all respects to his liking. On the other hand, he never had the slightest inclination to cross into the GDR – the border was a stone's throw from Kassel – and live there.

At the end of the 1940s Fieseler plainly thought that he would have nothing more to do with the world of aviation, so his only option was one again to set up a business from scratch. Fortunately he was buoyed up with 'entrepreneurial spirit.'[62] His first business venture was his hotel, an idea that had taken his fancy in the midst of his tribunal hearings. The hotel opened its doors at the end of 1949 with accommodation for six guests, who shared three bathrooms. The venture became very successful at least for a time. By1951 the hotel could cater for 18 guests. If Fieseler had the idea for the hotel, it was his wife Ruth who ran it 'more or less alone', her husband having other preoccupations.[63] The rooms were well furnished, guests found the environment relaxing and Ruth was seemingly in her element skilfully attending to the guests, who remarkably included some of the foremost cultural figures of their day.

57   Kissinger, op. cit., p.502.
58   Ardagh, p.105.
59   Ardagh, op. cit., p.125.
60   Wiesen, op. cit., p.236.
61   Fieseler, op. cit., p.299.
62   Nagel und Bauer, op. cit., p.433.
63   Ibid, p.433.

Among their number were distinguished orchestral conductors, Wilhelm Furtwängler and Hans Schmidt-Isserstedt, the pianist Elly Ney, the French politician André François-Poncet, the actress Paula Wesseley, the operetta singer Marika Rökk as well as the actor Ernst Deutsch who played in the post-war classic *The Third Man*. Fieseler recalls one especially musical occasion when the renowned Spanish cellist Gaspar Cassadó was practising for a concert in his room, 'The whole house sounded like a cello. Nobody moved.'[64] It remains a complete mystery how such eminent people, mainly from the world of music, cinema and theatre and even from other European countries, became his guests. Evidently the Fieseler hotel had acquired a very good reputation. It is possible that one attraction was the very location of the hotel near the spectacular Wilhelmshöhe Park, as lovely an expanse of greensward that Germany has to offer.

It would of course be fascinating to know the contents of his conversations with these guests about the Nazi period. Furtwängler was principal conductor of the Berlin Philharmonic and had met Hitler on several occasions, whilst Rökk had appeared in one of Germany's most famous war time films and had been fawned over by Propaganda Minister Goebbels. Paula Wessely had starred with another Fieseler guest, Attila Hörbiger, in the 1941 anti-Polish propaganda film *Heimkehr*. Fieseler in turn might tell them about his encounters with Hitler, Göring and other top Nazis. The hotel only survived until 1951, when it closed. It has been suggested the Fieseler establishment could not compete with the newly opened Schlosshotel near the Wilhelmshöhe Park.[65] However, we can surmise that the whole venture was simply too much for Ruth to cope with single-handedly. So what then was her husband Gerhard up to?

For whatever reason Fieseler had tired of being a hotelier. For the greater part of his business career he had taken decisions and told people what to do. In the hotel trade he perhaps found that it did not suit him to be in a state of service to others and have to be continually nice. At all events he had been toying with the idea of doing something on the premises of his old Number One Works. He secured capital for refurbishment, which involved not only clearing up what was left of usable space and rebuilding nearby access roads. His plan was to manufacture light fittings and metal parts, such as slightly ornate legs for furniture, and also draft-free, heat-retaining window frames.

Around the same time his contemporary Willy Messerschmitt was designing prefabricated houses to replace the hundreds of thousands of German homes destroyed in the air raids.[66] Fieseler, for his part, was soon employing a hundred workers, many of whom who had worked for him before and during the war. Both he and Messerschmitt were aware of the huge demand for housing and decorative items for the home, as Germany recovered from post-war austerity. Messerschmitt would once again become a well-known name in and indeed beyond Germany for his iconic bubble car produced in the mid-1950s.

Unfortunately for Fieseler his new product line did not take off as expected with the result that he concentrated on manufacturing windows. But there was much competition for these as well, so he decided to try to develop windows that had something that his rivals did not have: certification by an approved body for their quality and performance. For this he needed the help of a specialist. As usual with Fieseler in such cases he tapped into his network and located Dr Hermann Winter, with whom nearly twenty years earlier he had collaborated on the design of the Storch. These days Winter was a member of faculty at the Braunschweig Technical University, where he was professor of mechanical engineering and lightweight construction.

---

64   Fieseler, op. cit., p.297.
65   Ibid, p.298.
66   L. Day and I. McNeill, *Biographical Dictionary of the History of Technology*, p.841.

A very awkward invitation

In 1953 Fieseler was taken aback to receive an astounding letter which contained a pretentious-looking invitation card. To his amazement the invitation came from America. It came at a time, he admits, when 'I could not forget so rapidly my encounters with the Americans at the end of the war.'[67] The pleasure of his company was being requested by an American aeronautical body to attend celebrations to mark the fiftieth anniversary of the Wright Brothers' famous flight in 1903. He learnt that invitations were sent to the best known pilots of several countries. He had been selected to attend the event with Wolfgang von Gronau, who in 1930 was the first person to fly across the Atlantic east to west, and Willy Messerschmitt as representatives of Germany. All the guests would receive a large medal engraved with their name and an honorary diploma to mark their respective ground-breaking contributions to aviation. Fieseler declined the invitation.

The ceremonies received wide coverage in the American press and through that publicity Jewish friends – unnamed – had tried to contact him when they heard that his name was on the list of invitees. It is just possible that the Jewish friends in question are the David family, which had emigrated to Los Angeles in 1952.[68] Learning no doubt to their surprise that Fieseler had not come to America, the friends asked why he had turned down the invitation 'I took the path of least resistance', writes Fieseler, 'citing illness as the reason for my absence.' He goes on, adding cryptically: 'They would not have understood the truth, I must confess: it would have been against my principles (*meinem Charakter fehlt es an Wendigkeit.*)'

His rejection of the invitation was surely due to his extreme reluctance to go to the USA, for which there can only be one explanation. In an interview when he was in his eighties he does not deny his interviewer's observation that he had a life-long loathing of the Americans after what he had endured at their hands in 1945-46. Why in all probability he could not be open with his Jewish friends was perhaps because he knew that his suffering was insignificant to theirs in Nazi-occupied Europe. Fieseler seems to have been so bitter about his experiences that he did not even seem to think that the invitation was actually a magnanimous gesture on the part of the Americans. By contrast Willy Messerschmitt, who was comparably badly treated by the Americans at the end of the war, had no such qualms. As a member of the German delegation, he was received by President Dwight D. Eisenhower.[69]

As noted earlier, nearly 500 German scientists and engineers had been picked by the Americans in 1945, one of them being the Fieseler protégé Willy Fiedler, who had been involved with the V-1 programme at Peenemünde. In 1948 he and his family emigrated to the USA. In 1956 he joined Lockheed and became chief scientist, working on the Polaris and Poseidon missiles.[70] It is from Fiedler, who could hardly have been a better informed source, that Fieseler learnt that the Fi 103 was indeed the forerunner of today's cruise missile. Fieseler does not indicate when he received this information, but it may not have been before 1959, the year in which the first attested usage of the term cruise was recorded in the US magazine, *Aviation Week*.[71] Fieseler is proud to recall that 'but for the Fi 103, the cruise missile might have not have existed.'[72] Another of Fieseler's colleagues who was 'acquired' by the Americans was Robert Lusser, the technical brains behind the V-1. In the US he worked for the Navy, the Jet Propulsion Laboratory and joined von Braun's rocketry team at Huntsville Alabama. There can be little doubt that Lusser and von Braun had met at Peenemünde.

---

67 Fieseler, op. cit., p.298.
68 Wiederhold, op. cit.,p. 242.
69 M. Pabst, *Willy Messerschmitt: Zwölf Jahre Flugzeugbau in Führerstaat*, p.9.
70 https://ritstaalman.files.wordpress.com/2014/09/willy-fiedler.pdf. See also: Nagel und Bauer, op. cit., p.456.
71 J. Ayto, *Twentieth Century Words*, p.333.
72 Fieseler, op. cit., p.268.

They were of course rivals then, though in all probability with great respect for each other's talents. Lusser eventually returned to Germany and worked for Messerschmitt-Bölkow-Blohm. Whether he made a point of contacting or even meeting his war-time boss, Gerhard Fieseler, is not known.

Into obstreperousness
The windows business was also not doing very well. By the mid-fifties the number of his employees fell to 35. To revive things, Fieseler appointed a 19 year old fitter, Hans-Joachim Meister, who was keen to work for Fieseler's company to get the experience. He proved to be loyal to Fieseler and a hard worker, even designing and building equipment to make the windows. But, as Meister became more and more involved, so his boss rarely put in an appearance, merely wanting to be put in the picture. To all intents and purposes Meister's contact with Fieseler was virtually non-existent. Fieseler's behaviour is a complete contrast to how he was in the GFW days: always hands-on, constructively critical, motivating.

Not only that: when he arranged for his men to install some windows at his home, Fieseler insisted on 'particular working times' so that 'there was no disruption to his rhythm of life.'[73] It was hard not to draw the conclusion that as he approached his sixtieth birthday, he was becoming a difficult, if not pernickety old man. He closed down the business in 1957 and with that his days as an entrepreneur came to a rather pathetic end. But, if, as they say, one doors shuts and another one opens, then that is exactly what happened on 27 April, when a Dornier 27, a single-engine STOL utility aircraft landed at Kassel-Waldau airport. It was being flown by Hans Schäfer, who worked for Dornier, but who more to the point had had joined GFW as a test pilot in 1936. Indeed he had transferred his experiences with the Storch into the design and performance of the Dornier machine.[74]

Fieseler made a point of going to Kassel-Waldau, greeting his old colleague and giving "the successor to the Storch," a very thorough look-over.[75] He sat in the cockpit and that was enough for him to take up flying again. He refound his own skills and bought himself a Cessna 182, an American four-seater, single-engine light plane. Plainly he was not short of money, but more to the point he was not prejudiced about buying an American-built aircraft. Once he was in the air again, he was invited by the German Aero Club to be a judge in aerobatics contests. Notably in 1960 he was chairman of the jury for the first post-war national aerobatics competition in Münster. Curiously, in his memoir he writes absolutely nothing about his renewed acquaintance with aviation and his involvement in it for the next few years. The source for what follows derives from the work of the German aviation historians, Nagel and Bauer.

In the following year he was on the panel to adjudicate in the German championships in Saarbrücken. The criteria for assessment were the very ones which Fieseler had himself helped to formulate for the Aero Club more than thirty years earlier. One of the pilots was Walter Wolfrum, a World War II fighter ace with 100 aerial victories to his name. He was competing in his Czech-built Zlin 126. As the event proceeded, Fieseler inexplicably decided to alter his preliminary score, whereby Wolfrum lost his lead and indeed by a fractional amount the competition. Air historians Nagel and Bauer, the source of this sorry episode, surmise that Fieseler was biased against aircraft from the Eastern Bloc and that in any case a German champion should be flying a German plane.[76] There is curiously a direct parallel between Fieseler's unfair treatment of Wolfrum and the way he

---

73 Nagel und Bauer, op. cit., p.435.
74 Ibid, p.435-436; p.121.
75 Ibid, p.436.
76 Ibid, p.438.

himself was cheated out of winning the aerobatics competition in Zürich in 1927. We shall never know if that connection of events ever crossed his mind.

Around the same time Fieseler, presumably in his capacity as an Aero Club adjudicator, opposed a new symbolic notation system for describing aerobatic figures. As Nagel and Bauer point out: 'For all the experience and know-how that he had given to aerobatics, Fieseler was stuck in the 1930s. Wolfrum, who in 2009 published a book on his life as a fighter and aerobics pilot, wrote this of Fieseler: 'self-righteous, downright high-handed and wedded to a purist idea of aerobatics, he rejected any innovation, whether it was about materials or regulations. That was a problem for us, because we began to become isolated internationally and put ourselves out of the running.'[77] In the 1930s Fieseler had been a daring aerobatics pilot, an innovative aircraft builder and outstanding industrial manager. But his decline in the 1960s into sheer cussedness is both pathetic to witness and hard to explain unless, of course, it was connected with possible mental damage he which occurred whilst he was in American detention in 1945 and 1946.

A further example of his increasingly pugnacious behaviour occurred in 1964 during documenta III (always with a small 'd'), the leading exhibition of modern and contemporary art, held every five years in Kassel since 1955. It turned that the distinguished British sculptor Henry Moore was an exhibitor (as was the painter Francis Bacon). Moore was the guest of Arnold Bode, the painter and university professor who had pioneered the documenta concept, and who happened to rent accommodation from Fieseler (who evidently had a side-line in the property business.)[78] One day, when he was in the bathroom, Moore turned on the gas water heater, and it exploded. Slightly burned and apparently concerned that someone had tried to assassinate him, he rushed into the street. Later Bode telephoned Fieseler complaining of the shoddy heater. Fieseler came round straightaway and got into a slanging match with Bode, which Moore who presumably witnessed. If Moore spoke German, he would have heard Fieseler call Bode 'an artistic dabbler,' and the offended painter accuse his landlord of being 'a crash-prone pilot.'[79] Fieseler's no doubt volcanic response to that slur is not recorded.

In 1964 Fieseler was invited to Bilbao, where he adjudicated at the 3rd world aerobatics championships. In that same year Fieseler and his wife moved to Königstein in the Taunus. Two years later he was a jury member at the German aerobatics championships in Coburg. Three pilots, one of them Wolfrum, were in the closest contention. Everything depended on the judges. The pilots were beginning to wait an inordinately long time for the decision. It happened that Fieseler took all the completed mark-sheets to his hotel room, where he proceeded to make changes to them, whereby Wolfrum dropped from first to second place. So for a second time Fieseler had done the dirty on him. The incident spelt the end of Fieseler's career with the Aero Club. Wolfrum was probably not the only person to be glad to see the back of him.

In 1967 Fieseler found himself in a different kind of controversy. The story begins in 1949, when Fieseler's erstwhile colleague, Professor Hermann Winter published a book in which he described his involvement with the creation of the Storch. This was picked up by some newspapers who wrote that Winter was its designer. In 1959, by when Winter had presumably ceased to be assisting Fieseler with his aluminium window frames, Fieseler's lawyers sought clarification from him, pointing out that the creator of the Storch was not Winter, but Reinhold Mewes. It appears that Winter accepted that. Accordingly Fieseler assumed that the matter was ended. But in 1966 the leading newspaper *Die Welt* wrote an article, in which Winter was credited with the design and

---

77 Cited in: Nagel und Bauer, op. cit., p.438.
78 Arnold Bode is not to be confused with August Bode, whose Kassel-based company built tanks during the Second World War.
79 Nagel und Bauer, p.438.

early development of the Storch. Again Fieseler's lawyers contacted Winter, but on this occasion he rebutted them.

This triggered threats of legal action. Then two professors of Braunschweig Technical University, evidently colleagues of Winter, got involved and even went to meet Fieseler, who after the discussion considered that they had accepted his version of events. But, no: one of the professors pressed Fieseler for approval of joint ownership of the design between Winter and himself. This was unacceptable to Fieseler who pointed out that such an arrangement would be tantamount to 'intellectual theft' and he threatened to take Winter to court. At this point Winter backed down.[80]

However, if that dispute took him back to the 1930s, another was looming that had its roots in the 1920s. It appears that there was some kind of mud-slinging between Fieseler and Hertha, the first wife of Antonius Raab who had fired Fieseler from his company in 1927. The defamation began with Hertha and soon started to involve Raab himself who accused Fieseler of calumny. Legal action ensued, but the case was thrown out of court. Before long, however, Fieseler and Raab would be crossing swords again. In the meantime Fieseler found himself taken to court. In 1968 he contravened a temporary ban on using Kassel-Waldau airport during renovation work. In court he argued that he had always used the runways for test flights of the Me 109 fighter, which GFW built before and during the war. This plea was, of course, pointless, and Fieseler was fined 300 DM.[81]

The years passed by. In 1970 he bought a house as a second home on the Swiss side of Lake Maggiore, and in the following year celebrated his 75th birthday with friends. In 1976 he had to undergo an operation for the removal of his larynx, which meant that for the rest of his days speaking was not straightforward. It was during his convalescence that he first thought of the idea of writing down his life's story.[82] In July 1973 his thirty-five year marriage to Ruth collapsed, and they divorced. He was seventy-seven. One consequence of this was that he started to drink heavily. At what point or how he controlled that, is not clear.

At all events in September of the following year he married for a third time: this time to a certain Ursula, whom Nagel and Bauer describe rather cryptically as 'his life's companion', presumably a long adored – and adoring – woman friend. They lived in the small town of Zierenberg some 20 kilometres west of Kassel. A click on her name leads to an obituary notice in the *Volksstimme*, a newspaper published in Magdeburg, which reveals that Ursula Fieseler, née Müller, died 'suddenly and unexpectedly' on 3 August 2015, thus outliving her husband by some 18 years. She evidently had children from an earlier marriage. The obituary notice reveals that she was born in 1925 and was therefore nearly thirty years younger than Gerhard Fieseler.[83]

Eight syllables of anguish

By the end of the 1960s the physical infrastructure of Germany – that is to say West Germany – had been largely rebuilt. But the repair of German hearts and souls was not yet complete; indeed the process is not yet over. The cities already looked much as they do today; it was impossible to imagine how they had been a quarter of a century earlier, when Allied bombing had reduced them to rubble. The German economy had become a powerhouse. Although the big corporations like Volkswagen, Mercedes-Benz, Siemens and Merck were well established as international names, it was Germany's SME sector – the *Mittelstand*, which a well-known German business professor would one day call 'German's hidden champions' which powered the *Wirtschaftswunder*. Such firms,

---

80 Ibid, pp.488-439.
81 Ibid, p.439.
82 Ibid, p.440.
83 http://anzeigenmarkt.volksstimme.de/q/id3099424/Trauer/Todesanzeige-Ursula-Fieseler-Traueranzeigen-Zeitung.html

he claimed, were 'authoritarian, centralised and dictatorial wherever the company's principles and values are concerned,' and had a tendency to 'relish their obscurity.'[84] Against all the new-found economic dynamism and prosperity, there was a shift in attitude towards the Third Reich and the terrible things carried out in its name.

After the war Germans who survived it all simply wanted to put the whole ghastly experience behind them: there was an 'uneasy taboo of silence.'[85] In 1951 there was a significant statement of official German policy, as described by the historian, Nicholas Stargardt: 'Chancellor Adenauer responded to the American pressure to rearm by asserting in the Federal Parliament that "there has been no breach in the honour of the former German Wehrmacht." Members of Parliament welcomed the opportunity to proclaim that the age of collective guilt is at an end.'[86] But this was not to be. The new generation in the 1950s and more vociferous 1960s 'grew up with the realisation that its own parents were the guilty ones or at least might be.'[87] If the older generation preferred to sweep such troublesome issues under the carpet, that was a forlorn hope. In time the issue of guilt, both actual, suspected and existential, had been morphed into eight syllables of anguish: *Vergangenheitsbewältigung*, 'the psychological acceptance and management of the Hitler past.'[88] Its literal translation in English 'coping with the past' does not begin to convey the anguish, perplexity and soul-wrenching that the Nazi past triggered among Germans.

Fieseler has not a word to say on this painful issue: he does not use the operative word once. The reason was, we may be sure, because he saw himself as a victim of Nazi times: indeed as a victim exonerated by American interrogators and by judicial decision following his protracted denazification process. But, as we shall presently see in two interviews he gave later in life, he made it crystal-clear that in the final analysis there was only one perpetrator responsible for the egregious misdeeds of the Nazis: Adolf Hitler. If by any chance he had been confronted by young people in the 1960s seeking to know his role in the Third Reich, it is more than likely that his stock answer, as evidenced in one of those interviewed, would be: 'You did not live through those times. You would not understand.'

In his own mind Fieseler was, as he struck one acquaintance, 'a patriot', meaning the kind of German who loves his country for its music and literature, its giants of science and philosophy, its mighty rivers and dark, romantic forests.[89] Such a patriotic German, who lived through the Third Reich, can therefore rise above that contaminated perversion of Germany created by Hitler and his accomplices. I recall speaking about Fieseler to friends of mine, a young professor from Munich University and his wife, describing him as a patriot in this sense. They emitted cackles of derision.

A battle-cruiser in the family
The memoirs of Fieseler, which are central to this biography, were in fact his second attempt. His first draft was turned down with a discouraging verdict by the publisher: no-one would take his 'critical reflections' seriously. These reflections covered Fieseler's opinion about the German economy in the 1970s, public debt, co-determination in German industry, new laws including legislation on the conduct of strikes not to mention 'the sharp increases of wages and the ever higher increases of the income and profits of entrepreneurs.'[90]

84   H. Simon. Cited in: N. J. Holden, German: a Language of Management Designed for *Klarheit*. In: S. Tietze (ed.). *International Management and Language,* p.102-113.
85   Ardagh, op. cit., p.498.
86   Stargardt, op. cit., p.586.
87   Ardagh, op. cit., p.499.
88   G. Sereny, *The German Trauma: Experiences and Reflections 1938-2001*, p.148.
89   Nagel und Bauer, op. cit., p.443.
90   Fieseler, op. cit., p.300.

It is hard not to come to the conclusion that Fieseler expressed powerfully held opinions about these issues in his by now characteristically blunt way. Six months later he read through the draft again and consigned it to the waste paper bin. Possibly the publisher advised him to concentrate on the story of his life, which might have more appeal to readers. He took up the challenge, admitting not entirely truthfully that he had no 'good old days' to write about. On the other hand, his life had overlapped with the 'stormy history of aviation', and he considered it his luck, ordained by fate, to have a part in its development and unfold his talents.[91] In that sense he thought that his was a life worth telling; which is true.

He began the serious writing after he felt sufficiently recovered from his operation in 1976 or 1977, when he was around 80 years old. After he had completed the first four chapters, which covered his early life, he sent them for comment and stylistic advice to an acquaintance who was a journalist who wrote on military matters. The response was encouraging, 'and by the way', said the acquaintance, 'I can solve the matter concerning your unknown grandfather.' Fieseler was astounded. How could he do that? 'I have my connections,' came the reply. Three weeks later, when Fieseler had all but forgotten about that discussion, the journalist telephoned him, saying 'regarding that matter concerning your grandfather, I've got an answer. He can only be the well-known general and army commander von Goeben.' Fieseler laughed incredulously. 'That's impossible', he replied.

But it wasn't impossible because of who his grandfather turned out to be, but because the name Goeben was already something of a known quantity to Fieseler. It so happened that *Goeben* was the name of a battlecruiser that in the First World War had operated in Turkish territorial waters and had played its part in the Salonika campaign, on the very front where he, his grandson, had been patrolling the skies as a fighter pilot. Fieseler embarked on 'thorough research.' He quickly established that dates and other information he had learnt as a boy fitted the picture. Then he got hold of photographs of August Goeben and his father, who had of course the same Christian name, and compared them: the likeness was beyond doubt. He next consulted history books and deduced that certain character traits – which he failed to mention – were shared between them.

August Goeben had indeed been a renowned army commander in the second half of the 19th century and won several battles. Upon retirement Kaiser Wilhelm II had granted him a stipend of 200,000 Talers, around 6 million marks in 1979. After his death in 1880 the Kaiser had unveiled a statue to him to Koblenz. His son Kaiser Wilhelm II named one of his new battle-cruisers *Goeben*. On 4 August 1914 the *Goeben* became famous for a daring action in the Mediterranean. On that day the *Goeben* and its light cruiser escort the *Breslau* passed at full speed within 8,000 yards of a British squadron, whose task it was to close off the Mediterranean to enemy shipping. The German boats were 'sitting ducks',[92] but the British commander, Sir Archibald Berkeley Milne, could not open fire, 'as Britain's ultimatum to Germany over Belgium had until midnight (German time) to expire.'[93] By the time he could open fire, the German ships had escaped and on 11 August safely put into Constantinople, which was their base for the rest of the war.

Duly impressed, the Ottomans were strongly inclined to ally themselves – at first secretly – with the Germans. In London the episode was seen as 'epic fumbling by the Royal Navy which enraged Winston Churchill', at the time First Lord of the Admiralty.[94] The German action ranks in glamour and daring with the much better known case of the German battle cruisers, *Scharnhorst* and *Gneisenau* and their bold dash through the English Channel in February 1942: a 'grievous

---

91 Ibid, p.10.
92 J. Hughes-Wilson, *A History of the First World War in 100 Objects*, p.92.
93 Ibid., p.92.
94 M. Hastings, *Catastrophe: Europe Goes to War,* p.110.

humiliation.'[95] Fieseler would have definitely known about this famous episode involving the *Goeben*. But in 1916, when he went to the Balkans, he was not aware that a hitherto mysterious family connection linked him in a curiously personal way to the famous battle cruiser. Fieseler does not mention another interesting fact about the *Goeben*: that in November 1938 under its Turkish name *Yavûz* it bore the remains of Kemal Atatürk, the founder of modern Turkey, from Istanbul to İzmit, from where it was transferred to Ankara for the state funeral.

A memorial to the pioneers of the air
In 1977 three friends, who had been gliding enthusiasts in the 1920s, happened to meet in Schweinfurt and reminisce about the good old times of those days. In their company was a journalist from the local daily paper, who wished to interview them. One of the old boys was a certain Edgar Dittmar, who had performed a tow-flight with the Gottlob Espenlaub, the very man who Fieseler had involved in his attempt to make the first such flight in history in 1927. On 25 June an article appeared in the newspaper, stating that the first-ever tow flight had been carried out by Dittmar and Espenlaub in that year. Somehow, Antonius Raab got hold of a copy of the article, who wrote to the newspaper stating that he and Katzenstein had carried out the first tow-flight on 3rd March 1927, adding the absolutely preposterous assertion that any claims to the contrary 'are false and based on Hitler's anti-Semitic and anti-socialist programme.'[96]

Then Fieseler got wind of all this. It so happened that he and Espenlaub had clashed over the issue of the first tow-flight in the 1940s. The dispute ended up in court, but, was thrown out on grounds of 'wartime unimportance.'[97] Neither man resumed legal action after the war and, when Espenlaub died in 1972, Fieseler must have thought with some relief that that would be end of the matter. Now it was flaring again and this time involved his old adversary Raab.

For once, Fieseler did not turn on Dittmar or Raab with all guns blazing. Rather he approached the arbitration committee of the German Aero Club to settle the issue between him and Dittmar. The committee made very thorough investigations and came to the verdict that it was Fieseler to whom the first glider tow-flight should be ascribed. However, this was not enough for Fieseler, who wanted the reference to the Dittmar-Espenlaub flight to be removed from the official verdict. Needless to say, Dittmar was not happy with that suggestion. In July 1981, and after further consideration, the arbitration committee accepted Dittmar's stand. But Dittmar did not want the official report to published in case that might provoke Raab. It seems that to his and no doubt Fieseler's great relief Raab was unaware of the verdict or, if he was (which was by no means unlikely), he decided to not to wade in again. But three years later he did.

In the meantime, in 1979, Fieseler had established in Kassel a foundation in his own name (Gerhard-Fieseler-Stiftung), whose purpose was to support charitable causes, concerning the welfare of the elderly, sports development and cultural activities. Its logo is the famous tilted F, which had first emblazoned Fieseler's aerobatics planes as of the late 1920s. By 2015 the foundation had denoted some 3.2 million euros to support more than 700 good causes.[98] However much this was an act of charity, it was also surely a gesture on Fieseler's part to re-establish his reputation as a respectable citizen of the new Federal Germany and to wipe the slate clean about his Nazi past. But, as we shall see, it was never going to be that straightforward. It so happens that in 1969 Willy Messerschmitt had also set up a foundation in his name with similar aims. Both he and Fieseler had

---

95   A. Roberts, *Masters and Commanders: How Roosevelt, Churchill, Marshall and Alanbrooke Won the War in the West*, p.118.
96   Nagel und Bauer, op. cit., p.440.
97   Ibid, p.440.
98   Ibid, p.446.

chosen to set up their foundations while they were still living. This was yet another odd coincidence between the lives of the two men.

In April 1984, a Dutchman made enquiries in Kassel about Herr Gerhard Fieseler. It turned out that he had been employed as a conscripted worker at the Fieseler plants during the Second World War. Was Fieseler still alive, he wanted to know, and, if so, where did he live? He learnt that Herr Fieseler was indeed still alive and was given his address. He went to his 'villa', but was told – presumably by a neighbour – that Fieseler was away in either Switzerland or Austria. If Fieseler had been at home, the Dutchman 'would have done something' (what is not clear). It was not a question of money, he just wanted 'some kind of gesture.'[99] It is impossible to know how Fieseler would have reacted to this spectre from his repressed past.

In the following year there came a more public reminder of this past. Professor Krause-Vilmar of the University of Kassel had been investigating the plight of conscripted foreign workers in Hesse during the Second World War. By chance one such Dutchman, Adrianus van Deutekom, alias 'ex-conscript worker, Fieseler No. 61030' had come across the work of Krause-Vilmar and offered to supply him information about his grim existence in war-time Kassel. Van Deutekom had been deported from his home in Rotterdam to Kassel in 1943. He worked first as a welder and then as an office worker at the Fieseler aircraft works.[100]

On a visit to Kassel in 1985 on a visit to Kassel Krause-Vilmar showed the 62-year-old van Deutekom what remained of his former places of work and his old 'home', the former concentration camp at nearby Breitenau. In a newspaper photograph the Dutchman is shown standing outside a factory building where he had worked and which had belonged to the Gerhard Fieseler Foundation. It was no doubt to the relief of its readers – and no doubt to that the foundation – that ex-conscript worker Fieseler No. 61030 said he had no hatred of the Germans; he only hated Hitler.[101] As a result of this contact Krause-Vilmar received 'more than 100 letters' from former Dutch unfortunates.

Then in April 1986 there took place in the Dutch town of Westmaas 'an extraordinary event.'[102] A group of some 120 of the Dutch ex-Fieseler workers, accompanied by their wives, held a reunion. In May of the following year they held their reunion in Kassel, where there was a reception for them hosted by the city's mayor. The party also visited Breitenau, a small concentration camp by Nazi standards, where some 53 of the ex-Fieseler workers endured daily humiliation and frequent beatings.[103] This would prove to be the first of such cathartic visits. A later one took place in 1999. On this occasion members of the group had requested financial assistance from the Gerhard Fieseler Foundation to help with their travel expenses. The foundation, very sensitive about their founder's role as a defence economy leader in the Nazi regime, declined to respond to this request. One of the Dutch visitors told that the local newspaper that he could 'not conceal his disappointment.'[104]

In 1981 Fieseler paid for the erection a memorial to the pioneers of the air in Kassel's main cemetery. The pioneers were those intrepid flyers of yesteryear starting with his boyhood hero Lilienthal, the glider king, who had sacrificed or had been willing to sacrifice their lives for the sake of advancing aviation as a supreme social good. Around the same he agreed to be featured in a magazine and to fill in a questionnaire, which would reproduce his answers to look as if they were

99   Cited in: Wiederhold, op. cit., p.199.
100 *Hessische Niedersächsische Allgemeine*, 17 May 1986. Segeltuch als Schuh-Ersatz. Cited in: G. Richter (2001). Niederländische Zwangsarbeiter während des 2. Weltkrieges in Kassel. Guxhagen: Gedenkstätte Breitenau. Available at: http://www.gedenkstaette-breitenau.de/publikat-Dateien/zwangsarbeiter.pdf
101 Ibid.
102 Ibid.
103 *Melsunger Allgemeine*, Schläge von morgens bis abends. 30 May 1987.
104 *Hessische Niedersächsische Allgemeine* 20 April 1999. Besuch soll Erinnerung wachhalten. Available at: http://www.gedenkstaette-breitenau.de/publikat-Dateien/zwangsarbeiter.pdf

yielded in an interview. The idea was that Fieseler would answer some 'amusing and also delicate questions,' which were supposed to elicit 'witty and humorous' responses. Doing humour had never been Fieseler's style, so it is slightly mysterious why he cooperated. More to the point: he must have expected questions about his family life, about which he was always studiously unforthcoming.

The first question asked what the greatest misfortune of his life had been. He replied: 'One's last misfortune is always the biggest one. In my case it was the surgical removal of my larynx.' There was another question in this vein. What would be the worse misfortune to befall him? His answer: to go completely to the dogs. Some questions invited him to comment on himself as a person. His answer to a question about his main characteristics produced the answer: 'reliable, precise, aggressive, economical and constructive thinking.' His dislikes? 'Hordes of drunken people out of control.' And what did he admire most in women? His answer is stiff and awkward: 'Womanly adaptability and the capacity in every situation to do the right thing for the marital hearth.'[105]

In April 1981, in celebration of his 85th birthday friends arranged a special event for Fieseler. Karl Kössler, a former test pilot and aviation historian, flew one the few remaining Storchs from Braunschweig to Kassel-Calden airport. Fieseler declined the offer to fly in his legendary creation. But his wife did go for a ride in it and 'could herself experience for once the aircraft, to which her husband had a special emotional attachment.'[106] In 1983 something grander was organised in his honour by the German Aero Club in Kassel. On 15/16 June there took place an international aerobatics contest, the top prize being the recently inaugurated Gerhard Fieseler Trophy.

The self-same Storch from Braunschweig put on a special display. Among other guests was the 76-years-old Vera von Bissing, his former associate from his aerobatics days in the 1929s and 30s. She had never had further active involvement with aviation after the war, though since 1979 she had been a member of the Old Eagles Association. Founded in 1927, this body brought together Germany's most famous aviators by invitation. Fieseler was himself a member. It is likely that he and Bissing had met up from time to time in the post-war years because she lived in Eschwege, which is only 40 kms from Kassel.

An autobiography like an American thriller?

In 1982 Fieseler's autobiography was published under the title *Meine Bahn am Himmel* (My path in the sky). It covered 314 pages, excluding the index, in small paperbook format. The final pages regale the reader with various philosophical ramblings, and there is a curious appendix in the form of an interview. He had apparently sent a draft of his book to various friends and acquaintances to help him ensure that his final text would suit 'the wishes of my readers.'[107] We can anticipate that these friends made various suggestions for improvement. But it is not certain how much he heeded these, as he probably did not want to do any significant rewriting.

However, being aware of various gaps and topics that might benefit from more explanation, Fieseler decided to ask one of the friends to formulate 'some fundamental questions', which he could answer. It is these questions and answers between 'reader' and 'author' which form the so-called interview, which, it must be said, has a singularly unauthentic quality. It seems to be a matter of vetted questions and unspontaneous answers, many of which seem to be the product of some ongoing philosophical and psychological cogitation.

He begins with reminiscences about his father, who was a Catholic of strong faith. Fieseler recalled how in a philosophical or religious discussion between them his father in older age would accept his son's views as correct, but then suddenly retreat into the security of his own fixed beliefs.

---

105 Nagel und Bauer, op. cit., 443.
106 Ibid., op. cit., p.441.
107 Fieseler, op. cit., p.305.

For Fieseler this is 'a contradiction.' His struggles with this question left him no peace, he says. Then, one day, he found the answer or rather an answer. He deduced that his father could only believe in that which was 'important for his inner equilibrium.' This fits into with Fieseler's conviction that free will is an illusion. Actions are driven by an inexplicable compulsion that we cannot control. It is this compulsion that 'governs (*diktiert*) one's being – whether one calls that soul, character, conscience or mood.'[108] He says that his exploration of philosophy and psychology, have always intrigued him, and certainly since the First World War when one of his comrades in arms on the Macedonian Front first aroused his interest.

Despite being with Ursula 'his life-long companion', Fieseler evidently pondered these weighty matters with his boxer dog, Ero. The last lines of his autobiography (i.e. before the interview) are a hypothetical discussion with Ero, who likewise wrestles with the same vexatious questions. In the end he concludes that this compulsion – this 'spiritual force of a higher nature' is God, whose 'all-present existence can be perceived everywhere in nature and in the incomprehensible vastness of the universe.' This is the conviction, he says, with which he can and must live. If his life has been a search for truth, then this is where his cogitations have led him. It is open to question whether it is a question of a 'mere' satisfying philosophical insight or a revitalising religious revelation as balm for the soul.

The first question invites Fieseler to comment on his motives for writing his memoirs. He wanted, he says, to write them as one of the last eyewitnesses of the eras he had lived through. His recent operation for cancer was 'the decisive experience': it was now or never. For the sake of authenticity he decided not to use a ghost writer. He felt that he had as an old man important experiences to pass on; but he does not specify these. The next question concerns his pointed avoidance of discussion of women and his private life. His reply is confined to conservative generalities about woman of the human species and the characteristics, which 'all-mighty God has given her' to stand by her husband through thick and thin. His view on family life? As a boy he experienced 'order, cleanliness and punctuality.' In every family these values – evidently the best ones, as far as he is concerned – can only maintained through a role-model and, when necessary, a figure of authority.

Then comes a question about his attitude to money. He was not, he says, like 'most people.' He never pursued money, For him it was all about success based on 'hard work, ability, energy, thrift and luck.' Then he was asked about his competitive drive, which shone through in the First World War, in his time as an aerobatics pilot and then as an aircraft builder. He responds with the observation that 'concerning eternal competition, that never interested me or only in a peripheral way.' Everything depended on external conditions as well as his own instincts, experience 'and my inner voice.'[109] Of course, you always encountered people who blocked you, but he could always console himself with the thought that any 'adversary or enemy had no free will.'

This not entirely clear response leads to the question: 'Do you see yourself as a philosopher? No, is the reply, he is just interested in philosophy, which he greatly enjoys discussing. He concedes, though, that 'many philosophers of antiquity and in modern times' reflect his views (which is not quite the same thing as saying that he reflects their views). He allows Goethe in Faust to capture his deterministic outlook on life with some two famous lines:

The whirlpool strives to get above,
Thou art shoved thyself, imagining to shove.[110]

---

108 Ibid, p.303.
109 Ibid, p.308.
110 The two lines of Goethe are: 'Der ganze Strudel strebt nach oben/Du glaubst zu schieben, und du wirst geschoben' (*Faust I*).

The subject changes. Why did he only grasp 'when it was relatively late … the true nature of the Third Reich?' He begins by saying that he had no interest in politics; he concentrated on his 'tasks and goals.' When he realised that Hitler was a gambler and criminal, it was too late. No-one who did not live through those times could understand them and 'how it came to the crimes (*Untaten*) of a mass-murderer.' (One mass-murderer, note). For his part he was 'helpless', but even so in 'words and behaviour risked my neck.' Pressed about how 'such inhuman things' could happen, he again blames Hitler with his 'in-built criminal tendencies … diabolical powers of persuasion, intelligence and brutal nature.' However, there would have been no Hitler but for 'Versailles *Diktat* and the absurd policies of the victorious powers.'

With reference to his commitment to the welfare of his workers, the questioner asks Fieseler about his attitude to socialism. His answer is that in theory everyone under socialism can attain freedom and good fortune, but that, for reason he does not explain, does not happen in 'the Eastern Bloc.' This leads him to ponder that no political system can guarantee those things. It is up to the individual. So that question does not get a proper answer. Then there is a question in another direction. He is asked to explain his 'lifelong hatred of the Americans.' His answer is singularly evasive. He notes that love and hate are powerful emotions, and in time 'even justified hate (*motivierter Haß*)' goes away. With this statement Fieseler seems to be saying that he has forgiven the Americans for their brutal treatment of him at the end of the Second World War.

The last question concerns his overall attitude to life after all its vicissitudes. The First World War made him into a fighter pilot and prepared to the way for him to become an entrepreneur in the Nazi period. The Second World War destroyed his factories and took away his children. How is one to hold everything together in the light of such a fate? His answer is forthright: 'Every person must cope with his fate. One person tries to resist and tussle with his lot, whilst the other reconciles himself to it.' He, Gerhard Fieseler, holds to the latter path. Overall his replies reveal Fieseler to be – at least at the end of his life – to be a somewhat pedantic, heavy-footed speaker.

Perhaps the most striking revelation in these answers is the degree to which Fieseler has been shaped by his childhood experiences and even retains social attitudes that reflect his parents' generation. Overall, the questions proved easy for him to deal with, and he escaped awkward questioning on his role in the Third Reich and his attitudes to the use slave labour during the war years. His other answers suggest that he would blame everything on Hitler, on Hitler only. His true views on those two questions, so painful and awkward to his generation with vivid, anguished memories, he took to the grave.

It cannot be accidental that Fieseler used his autobiography to show his readers that, as we have seen, he did what he could – what he dared – to alleviate the lot of Jews of his acquaintance and to improve the living conditions for the compulsory labour working for his company in the last two years of the war. He also makes a big point of demonstrating his willingness to defy and on occasion shout down Nazis with an exaggerated sense of their own importance. These self-exonerations were of course designed to not just to blur his role in the Nazi regime, but play it down. It is of course difficult to reconcile these pieties with what he wrote in his company newspaper about 'serving an incomparably higher purpose' and so forth. If though it is true that Germans are polarised between the necessity of 'sedulously' keeping the terrible memories alive and a sense that 'the past should not be raked up again any more,'[111] then Fieseler, once he set about writing his autobiography, knew where he was going to strike the balance.

In point of fact Fieseler's autobiography may be seen as a continuation of the self-exonerating writings of former Nazi industrialists to relativize their role in the Nazi regime. One German

---

111 Ardagh, op. cit, p.507.

historian, noting that these writings developed as of the 1950s, are 'a self-serving ... literary effort' which constitute 'a public relations offensive on behalf of German industry ... a *revamping* of the German industrial image to reach out to German and international public opinion' (original emphasis).[112] It is hard to believe that Fieseler saw himself as part of such a PR offensive. On the other hand, it cannot be denied that his aim like that of other industrialists of his ilk was to position himself as 'an unpolitical manager and technocrat (*Ökonom und Techniker*) and often even as a victim of the coercive policies of the Nazis.'[113] After all, as he would no doubt point out, his denazification tribunal not only cleared him of any wrong-doing but also commended his anti-Nazi steadfastness. From that it surely followed that he must have been a victim of the Nazi regime. QED.

The publisher's blurb on the back cover Fieseler's memoir invites readers to read about 'the thrilling life of a passionate aviator and aircraft builder', adding – absurdly – that 'the record of his life reads like an American thriller.' Fieseler's life is an utterly German one with contexts that cannot be mapped onto American society. For some people it can be cathartic to write about traumatic experiences of the past. For Fieseler there was no catharsis, no self-cleansing in his autobiography. But the incontestable fact remains that he, for all his qualms and reservations about the Third Reich as the war unfolded, supported the Nazi war effort to the end.

After the war Fieseler knew, like almost every other adult German, that he stood before the world as 'having served or helped Hitler'.[114] But in his case he was both a former member of the Nazi Party and of a Nazi paramilitary organisation as well as a builder of aircraft for the war effort in hock to the Reich Aviation Ministry since 1936. It stands to reason that his autobiography, written when the Nazi regime had been universally discredited, plays down the significance of these links.

What was granted to him
When his autobiography was published, Fieseler was 85 or 86 years old. He still had some five more years to live. But they were not to be peaceful ones. For a start in spring 1983 there was yet a further twist in the saga about the first tow-flight, when Dittmar, in denial of the verdict of the German Aero Club, published an article, in which he declared himself to be the first person to carry out the manoeuvre. Fieseler was understandably annoyed with this and in July he requested the Old Eagles Association to intervene. The point is that Dittmar was also a member. Fieseler specifically asked the President of the association to remove Dittmar from its membership for 'scurrilous behaviour'.[115]

The President could find no grounds to take disciplinary action against Dittmar. This prompted Fieseler to resign from the Old Eagles. Karl Kössler, an aviator friend, attempted to dissuade Fieseler from this action. Besides, as the story was bound to get round flying circles, he was worried that Raab would go on the attack again. Kössler was right to be worried. In July 1984 an aero magazine printed a story about that the 1927 tow-flight, stating that German Aero Club had declared that Fieseler and Espenlaub had performed the first such flight on 12 May 1927. Raab read the article and the issue once again came to a court case. But in March 1986 Antonius Raab died. He was a year younger than Fieseler, who himself was about to turn ninety. His death brought to end a dispute, which had first started sixty years earlier, between two very old and very stubborn men.

On 9 November 1989 East Germans breached the Berlin Wall. This was the death-knell of the German Democratic Republic, which formally became part of the Federal Republic on 3 October

---

112 K. C. Priemel, Gekaufte Geschichte. Der 'Freundeskreis Albert Vögler', Gert von Klass und die Entwicklung der historischen Unternehmerforschung nach 1945. *Zeitschrift für unternehmensgeschichte,* pp.177-202.
113 Ibid.
114 Fieseler, op. cit., p.282.
115 Nagel und Bauer, op. cit., p.444.

1990. Gerhard Fieseler did not quite live long enough to witness these momentous events. He died on 1 September 1987 aged 91. Two days later his death was announced in the regional newspaper (*Hessische Niedersächsiche Allgemeine/HNA*), describing his life as 'combative (*kämpferisch*) and successful.'[116] But he was not, as it happened, the oldest survivor of the air war over Macedonia. A British pilot, Hubert Williams, who like Fieseler joined up in 1915, died in 2002 aged 106. 'I am no hero', he said, 'I just consider myself lucky to have survived.'[117] Williams was shot down in his Sopwith Camel in 1918 and badly injured.[118]

Fieseler's funeral took place exactly a week after his death on the morning of 8 September in the main cemetery of Kassel. This was by no means a purely private event. It was attended by various dignitaries, representatives of the German aerospace industry, the Bundeswehr, the board of the Fieseler Foundation as well as former employees of the Gerhard Fieseler Works. He was buried with full military honours. Friends from the world of aviation organised a special tribute: a formation of three sports planes and a Storch did a fly-past over his grave. But his death provoked an altogether different kind of memorial from, of all people, one of the Dutchmen who had worked as compulsory labour at the Gerhard Fieseler Works during the Second World War.

In a book of poems, published in 1990 in Dutch and German, Wim de Vries wrote some lines on Fieseler's death. Here in free translation are the opening lines:

> His death has so shaken me
> That I must ask why it is
> That he lived more than forty years,
> While so many of his compulsory workers
> Suffered and died so young … [119]

De Vries then wonders if Fieseler is doing hard labour in the after-life. 'Could I be his boss?' the Dutchman ponders darkly and if so, would he do anything different in the oppressor-slave relationship? Wim de Vries had been ruminating for more than forty years on his own bleak experiences as an all too unwilling Fieseler employee. Fieseler himself philosophised over that very same question about his unusually long life-span, when others were destined to perish in their younger years. It would have been little consolation to de Vries to know that.

Fieseler's final resting place was, in accordance with his instructions, at the feet of the memorial to pioneers of the air, which he had had erected in 1981. Thus their memorial also became, exactly as he planned it of course, an epitaph to himself. He always saw himself as one of them and now, after a long, at times tumultuous and ever restless life, he had joined them. Obituaries of Fieseler in newspapers referred to him as a First World War pilot, who had won the Pour le Mérite, as an aerobatics champion, flight pioneer and aircraft builder. The regional newspaper for Hesse, which could be relied on for something more uplifting, proclaimed in extraordinary hagiographical vein that 'he still lives on in creative output and achievement.'[120] In this and other obituaries his direct involvement with the Nazi regime was 'repressed.'[121] The aviation writers Rolf Nagel and Thorsten Bauer have a different perspective, noting that 'through the Gerhard Fieseler Foundation, which he founded towards to the end of his life, he will remain in people's memory, especially in Kassel where

---

116 HNA, 3 September 1987.
117 Ferguson, op. cit., p.25.
118 For more details on Williams see http://www.theaerodrome.com/forum/showthread.php?t=830.
119 Vries, W. de, *Terug naar Kassel. De ballade van de waanzin /Zurück nach Kassel. Die Ballade vom Wahnsinn*, p.67.
120 Wiederhold, op. cit., 291.
121 Wiederhold, op. cit., p.291.

he lived from 1926 until his death in 1987.' Furthermore they claim that 'the Fieseler Storch has brought the worldwide renown to the city of Kassel among all those with a great interest in aviation and engineering.'[122]

But it is not quite so straightforward. The fact is that Fieseler, for all the undeniably good work of the Gerhard Fieseler Foundation and his own enduring reputation as one of the greatest aerobatics pilots in the early years of aviation, is still seen today 'by a small fraction of Kassel's population' first and foremost as a former member of the Nazi Party and defence economy leader.[123] One adherent to that view, writing in a publication of the students' union of Kassel University, makes an explicit reference to Fieseler, his 'repugnant V weapon' and 'the inconvenient aspects of the Storch,' at the same time criticising the city of Kassel's 'politics of memory (*Geschichtspolitik*),' – that is to say, with specific reference to the Nazi past – calling it 'questionable' (*bedenklich*).[124]

In the magazine interview published in or around 1983, Fieseler was asked what his motto was. He responded with the words: 'always believe in oneself and one's fate.'[125] Talented, passionate and self-believing, he had fulfilled his boyhood dreams about aviation beyond all imagination, becoming a decorated fighter pilot, a world champion aerobatics pilot and influential aircraft builder. Fate was generous to him in other ways too. He survived two world wars and lived through all manner of mortal danger as an aerobatics pilot and a test pilot. But not only that: once let off the hook by the Americans and exonerated by his own countrymen after the Second World War, Fieseler was spared facing up to the consequences of his actions in the Nazi years, not least those concerning his wartime record as the employer of a 6,000 strong force of slave labour. He had the freedom – the luxury even – to look back that period of his life without fear of retribution and, as his autobiography makes absolutely plain, with complete amoral disinterest. When he referred to himself as 'politically neutral' in the Third Reich, what Fieseler was surely saying was that he regarded himself *morally* neutral.

It is timely to reflect on another of Fieseler's revealing comments, in fact the one which appeared in the introduction to his memoirs and which was cited at the very beginning of this biography: 'What is granted to only a few people was fulfilled in me.'[126] But what exactly was granted to him? We see its manifestation in many ways: not only in the permanent admiration of the Storch on the part of aircraft enthusiasts and aviation historians worldwide and his lasting reputation as one of the greats of aerobatics, but also in the founding of the Fieseler Foundation, the commissioning of a memorial to the pioneers of the air, at whose feet he lies, and the publication of his memoirs. Taken together with the passing of the years, these epitaphs – mnemonic, physical, institutional – have served to transcend – but never quite erase – his energetic and committed participation in the building up of the Nazi war machine and any blemishes that attached themselves to him as a result of that.

What was granted to him, we may conclude, was to make a remarkable, distinctive but also perturbing contribution to German air-mindedness in peace and war: as a decorated aerial gladiator, an internationally acclaimed aerobatics pilot and a fearless test pilot; as a favoured builder of aircraft for the Nazis and, until he was required to take on forced labour, as an outstanding industrial manager; and as the begetter of a range of truly innovative aircraft – the F3, F5, the Storch and the V-1. The F3 was one of the very first delta-wing aircraft ever to fly, whilst the F5 was a truly

---

122 Nagel und Bauer, op. cit., pp.445-446.
123 Private communication with a Kassel acquaintance, October 2016.
124 M. Schulze von Glaser. Fieselers fieße V-Waffe, Medium: Zeitschrift der Studierendenschaft der Universität Kassel, p.23 Available at: http://michi.blogsport.de/images/mediumnr2Versionweb2.pdf
125 Nagel und Bauer, op. cit., p.43
126 Fieseler, op. cit., p.10.

magnificent sports aircraft. The aeronautically iconic Storch, his most celebrated creation, was a triumph of slow speed and one of the finest military aircraft of its type ever built. The V-1 was by strange contrast one of the fastest – and lethal – aerial devices in its era. But it is not just that his passion for aircraft and flying runs through these achievements. Even more striking than that is the singular fact that, whether as a pilot, aircraft builder and manager, he was entirely self-taught. Without that, in a manner of speaking, nothing would have been granted to him.

Appendix A

Fieseler Storch Thematic Chart

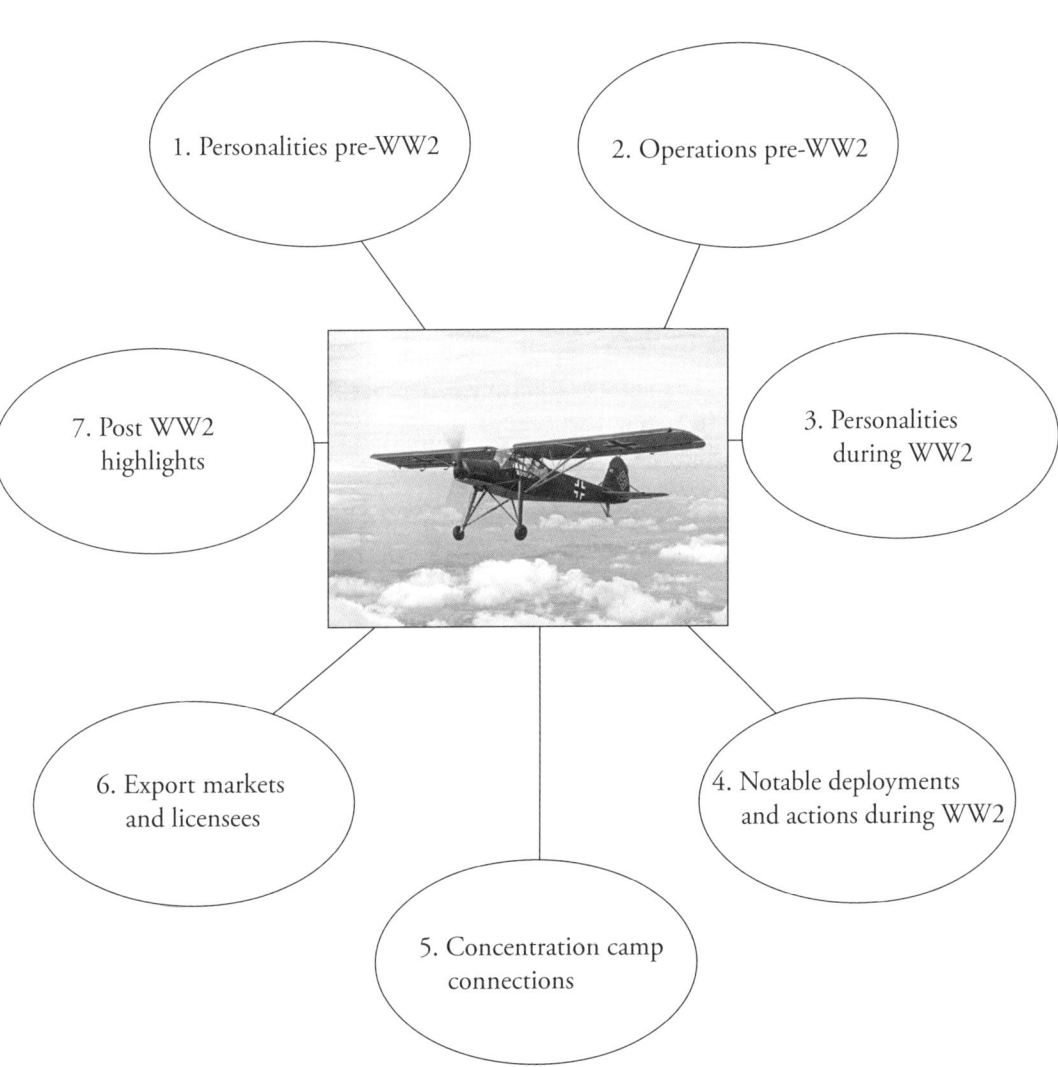

Key to Points 1–7

1. Personalities pre-WW2

- Ernst Udet, Head of the Technical Office at the Reich Aviation Ministry, gives the first public demonstration of the Storch at the Zürich Air Show
- Hitler gives a Storch as diplomatic gifts to Mussolini and to Stalin
- Stalin instructs his top aircraft designer, Oleg Antonov, to make a copy
- Goering presents Italo Balbo, heir apparent to Mussolini, with a Storch

2. Operations pre-WW2

- Spanish Civil War
- First Luftwaffe plane to land at Prague Airport after invasion of Czechoslovakia

3. Personalities during WW2

- Rommel praises the Storch in the Fieseler company newspaper
- Friedrich Paulus's last flight in Stalingrad
- Hanna Reitsch, Germany's most famous aviatrix, spends three weeks morale-boosting on the the Eastern Front
- Hanna Reitsch flies to the Führer's bunker
- Albert Speer also flies in one for his last meeting with Hitler
- Churchill hops in a captured Storch between generals for breakfast meetings after D-Day
- Eisenhower also uses a captured Storch after D-Day

4. Notable deployments and actions during WW2

- Invasion of Poland
- Invasion of the Low Countries
- Defeat of France (Place de la Concorde landing)
- Operation Barbarossa and the Battle of Stalingrad
- Skorzeny rescues Mussolini at Gran Sasso
- North Africa campaign
- Gerhard Fieseler flies from Kassel to Peenemünde to inspect V-1 test flights
- Last dog-fight of WW2, and perhaps only aircraft in WW2 to be brought down with a pistol

5. Concentration camp connections

- Inspector of Concentration Camps, Theodor Eicke, is killed in a crash near Kharkov
- Odilo Globocnik, complicit in the murder of 1.5m Jews, flies to Treblinka in a Storch
- Women inmates at the Flossenbürg concentration refer to a female guard as 'the Fieseler Storch' on account of her spindly legs
- Melitta von Stauffenberg, Luftwaffe test pilot, flies to Buchenwald and Sachsenhausen on humanitarian missions

6. (a) export markets, 1938–1944

- Bulgaria, Croatia, Finland, Hungary, Italy, Japan, Romania, Slovakia, Spain, Sweden, Switzerland

(b) licensee countries, 1942–1945

- Czechoslovakia, France, Romania

7. Post-WW2 highlights

- Eric 'Winkle' Brown, UK's leading test pilot, describes the Storch as 'a virtuoso of slow flight'
- Brown also lands a Storch on an aircraft carrier for the first time
- Storch is used in experiments on helicoptor design at RAE Farnborough
- Swissair employs Czech-made Storch aircraft for mountain rescue
- Fly-past by two Storch aircraft at the funeral of Gerhard Fieseler in 1987
- Deployment by the French Airforce in Indo-China and Algeria

Appendix B

Gerhard Fieseler's aerial victories in Macedonia from August 1917 to September 1918

Date	Type of aircraft	Location
20 August 1917	Nieuport 17	Pripel
9 September 1917	Nieuport Scout	Pogradets
30 September 1917	Nieuport 17	Mogila
5 April 1918	Nieuport 24	Chanishite
20 June 1918	SPAD	Makovo
5 July 1918	Nieuport 24	Pripel
24 July 1918	Nieuport Scout	Dobro Pole
25 July 1918	Nieuport Scout	Gradeshnitsa
28 July 1918	Bréguet 14	Kanatlartsi
4 August 1918	Nieuport Scout	Votilishte
5 August 1918	Nieuport Scout	Gradeshnitsa
11 August 1918	Nieuport Scout	Voden
16 August 1918	AR2	Negorchani
23 August 1918	SPAD 2	Votilishte
4 September 1918	Bréguet or SPAD 2	Budimirtsi
9 September 1918	Nieuport	Orhid
13 September 1918	Nieuport	Votilishte
15 September 1918	Nieuport	Dedebaltsi
18 September 1918	SPAD	Zavoi na Tsrna
19 September 1918	Nieuport	Vitola
20 September 1918	Bréguet or Nieuport	Troyatsi

Source: http://www.oldprilep.com/vojna-mir/neboto-nad-prilep.html

Note: This Macedonian source credits Fieseler with 21 aerial victories. He is usually credited with 19 confirmed victories.

Bibliography

All Internet references, which are cited as footnotes, were accessed from March 2013 to February 2017.

P. Addison, P. and J. A. Crang, *Firestorm: The Bombing of Dresden 1945,* London, Pimlico, 2006.
C. Ailsby, *A Collector's Guide to German Nazi Party Awards,* Hersham, Ian Allan, 2010.
S. Anderson, *Lawrence in Arabia: War, Deceit, Imperial Folly and the Making of the Modern Middle East,* London, Atlantic Books, 2013.
Anonymous, *A Woman in Berlin: Diary 20 April to 22 June 1945*, London, Virago, 2004.
J. Ardagh, *Germany and the Germans,* London, Penguin Books, 1995.
J. Ayto, *Twentieth Century Words,* Oxford, Oxford University Press, 1999.

R. Bassett, *For God and Kaiser: The Imperial Austrian Army,* New Haven, Conn., Yale University Press, 2015.
A. Beevor, *Berlin: The Downfall 1945,* London, Viking, 2002.
A. Beevor, *The Second World War*, New York, Back Bay Books, 2013.
C. Bielenberg, *The Past is Myself: An Englishwoman's Life in Berlin under the Nazis,* London, Corgi Books, 1970.
M. Bourne, *The Second World War in the Air: The Story of Air Combat in every Theatre of World War Two,* Kibworth Beauchamp, UK, Matador, 2013.
V. Brittain, *Testament of Youth*, London, Virago Press, 1978.
F. Brodbeck, M. Frese and M. Javidan, Leadership made in Germany: Low on compassion, high on performance, *Academy of Management Executive,* Vol. 16, No. 1, pp.16-29, 2002.
E. Brown, *Wings on my Sleeve,* London, Phoenix, 2007.
A. Bruce, *An Illustrated Companion to the First World War,* London, Michael Joseph, 1989.
G. Brütting, *Fliegen ist unser Sport: Geschichte des Deutschen Aero Clubs e.V.,* Wiesbaden, Wirtschaftsverlag, 1987.
B. Bryson, *One Summer: America 1927,* London, Black Swan, 2014.
L. Budrass, *Flugzeugindustrie und Luftrüstung in Deutschland 1918-1945,* Düsseldorf, Droste Verlag, 1998.
S. Burgdorff und K. Wiegrefe (Hrsg), *Spiegel Special über die Folgen: Die Katastrophe des 20. Jahrhunderts*, 2004.
O. Bürger, *Die Königlich-Bayerische Fliegertruppe in Schleißheim und ihre Spuren in die Gegenwart.* Schleißheim, Freunde von Schleißheim e.V., 2008.
M. Burleigh, *The Third Reich: A New History,* London, Pan Books, 2000.
A. Burney (ed), *Famous Fighters of World War 1,* Stamford, UK, Key Publishing, 2014.
I. Buruma, *Year Zero: A History of 1945*, London, Penguin Books, 2014.

E. Carter (with A. Loveless), *Force Benedict: Churchill's Secret Mission to Save Stalin,* London, Hodder and Stoughton, 2014.
L. Cartwright, *If Winter Comes,* Bloomington, IN Xlibris, 2009.

D. Cesarani (ed), *The Final Solution: Origins and Implementation,* London, Routledge, 2016.
C. Clark, *Kaiser Wilhelm II: A life in Power,* London, Penguin Books, 2009.
C. Clark, *The Sleepwalkers: How Europe Went to War in 1914,* London, Penguin Books, 2013.
J. S. Corum, 'World War I Aviation' in: M. Strohn (ed), *World War 1 Companion,* Oxford, Osprey Publishing, pp.61-76, 2013.
S. Corvaja, *Hitler and Mussolini: The Secret Meetings,* New York, Enigma Books, 2008.
P. Cziborra, *Frauen im KZ: Möglichkeiten und Grenzen der historischen Forschung am Beispiel des KZ Flossenbürg und seiner Außenlager,* Bielefeld, Lorbeer Verlag, 2010.
V. Dahm, A. Feiber, H. Mehringer und H. Möller, *Die tödliche Utopie: Bilder, Texte, Dokumente, Daten zum Dritten Reich,* München, AZ Druck und Datentechnik, 2010.
T. Darnstädt, Stunde der Abrechnung. In: Grossbongardt et al., op. cit., pp.252-265.
N. Davies, *Europe: A History,* Oxford, Oxford University Press, 1996.
L. Day and I. McNeill, *Biographical Dictionary of the History of Technology,* London, Routledge, 1998.
I.C.B. Dear and M. R. D Foot, *Oxford Companion to the Second World War*, Oxford, Oxford University Press, 1995.
W. Dettmar, *Die Zerstörung Kassels im Oktober 1943: Eine Dokumentation,* Fuldabrück, Druckerei Hesse GmbH, 1983.
Deutsche Kampfflugzeuge des Zweiten Weltkriegs, Eggolsheim, Dörfler Verlag, 2002.
Deutsches Historisches Museum, *Der Erste Weltkrieg in 100 Objekten,* Darmstadt, Wissenschaftliche Buchgesellschaft, 2014.
Deutsches Museum, *Aviation: A Guide to the Aeronautics Collection.* Deutsches Museum, Munich, 2010.
A. Döblin, Abschied und Wiederkehr (1946). In: *Alfred Döblin: Das Lesebuch – herausgegeben von Günter Grass,* Frankfurt am Main, Fischer Taschenbuch Verlag, 2012.

H. Ebert, J, Kaiser und K. Peters (Hrsg), *Willy Messerschmitt – Pionier der Luftfahrt und des Leichtbaues,* Bonn, Bernard & Graefe, 2008.
P. Ede. (ed.), *The Encyclopedia of Aircraft of WWII,* London, Amber Books, 2008.
D. Edgerton, *England and the Aeroplane: Militarism, Modernity and Machines,* London, Penguin, 2013.
M. Eppler, *The Wright Way: Seven Problems Solving Principles from the Wright Brothers that can make your business soar*, New York, AMACON Books, 2004.
F. Esposito, *Fascism, Aviation and Mythical Modernity,* London, Palgrave Macmillan, 2015.
R. Evans, *The Coming of the Third Reich,* London, Allen Lane, 2003.
R. Evans, *The Third Reich in Power,* London, Penguin Books, 2006.
R. Evans, *The Third Reich at War: How the Nazis led Germany from conquest to defeat,* London, Penguin Books, 2008.

N. Ferguson, *First World War in the Air,* Stroud, UK, The History Press, 2014.
N. Ferguson, *Kissinger 1923-1968: The Idealist,* London, Allen Lane, 2015.
G. Fieseler, *Meine Bahn am Himmel*, München, Wilhelm Heyne Verlag, 1982.
H. G.Fokker. *Der Fliegende Holländer: Die Memoiren des A. H. G. Fokker,* Frankfurt am Main, Wunderkammer Verlag, 2010.
R. Forczyk, *Rescuing Mussolini – Gran Sasso 1943.* Oxford, Osprey Publishing, 2010.
J. Friedrich, *Der Brand: Deutschland im Bombenkrieg 1940-1945,* München, Propyläen Verlag, 2003.
P. Fritzsche, 'Machine dreams: Airmindedness and the reinvention of Germany', *American Historical Review,* Vol. 89, No. 3, pp.685-709, 1993.

M. Fulbrook, *History of Germany 1918-2000: The Divided Nation,* Oxford, Blackwell Publishing, 2002.

J. Gardiner, *Wartime Britain 1939-1945,* London, Headline Book Publishing, 2004.
S. Garfield, *Private Battles: How the War almost defeated us,* London, Ebury Press, 2006.
M. Geppert, D. Matten, and K. Williams, *Challenges for European management in a global context: Experiences from Britain and Germany,* London, Palgrave Macmillan, 2002.
The German Army Handbook of 1918. (First edition published in April 1918 by the German General Staff), Barnsley, Frontline Books, 2008.
M. Gilbert, *The Holocaust: The Jewish Tragedy,* London, Fontana Books, 1986.
M. Gilbert, *A History of the Twentieth Century,* London, HarperCollins, 1997.
M. Glenny, *The Balkans: Nationalism, War and the Great Powers*, London, Granta Books, 2000.
A. Goodrum, *Balloons, Blériots and Barnstormers: 200 Years of Flying for Fun,* Stroud, UK, The History Press, 2009.
R. Gross, *November 1938: Die Katastrophe vor der Katastrophe,* München: C.H. Beck, 2013.
A. Grossbongardt, U. Klussmann und J. Mohr (Hrsg), *Der Erste Weltkrieg: Die Geschichte einer Katastrophe,* München, Deutsche Verlags-Anstalt, 2014.

C. Habbe, Wettlauf der Ingenieure. In: *Spiegel Serie über den Ersten Weltkrieg: Die Ur-Katastrophe des 20. Jahrhunderts,* 2004, pp.52-54.
S. Haffner, *Germany: Jekyll & Hyde – 1939 von innen betrachtet*, München, Droemersche Verlagsanstalt Th. Knaur, 2001.
S. Haffner, *Geschichte eines Deutschen: Die Erinnerungen 1914-1933,* München, Deutsche Taschenbuch Verlag, 2002.
P. Haining, *The Flying Bomb: Contemporary Accounts of the VI and V2 raids on Britain 1942-45*, London, Robson Books, 2002.
M. Hastings, *Catastrophe: Europe goes to War,* London, William Collins, 2013.
M. Hastings, *The secret war: Spies, Codes and Guerrillas 1939-1945,* London, William Collins, 2016.
R. Hattersley, *The Edwardians,* London, Abacus, 2004.
K-D. Henke, *Die amerikanische Besetzung Deutschlands,* München R. Oldenbourg Verlag, 1996.
H. Herlin, *Udet: A Man's Life,* London, Macdonald, 1960.
Hessische Niedersächsische Allgemeine (HNA), Kassel und die "Machtübernahme": Verfolgung von Andersdenkenden/Schwarz-Weiß-Rot neben dem Hakenkreuz, 1983, 29 January.
Hessische Niedersächsische Allgemeine (HNA), Reichskriegertag Kassel: Stimmungsmache für das neue Völkermorden, 13 April 1997.
N. J. Holden, German: a Language of Management Designed for *Klarheit.* In: S. Tietze (ed.). *International Management and Language,* London, Routledge, 2008.
N. J. Holden, 'From First World War Air Ace to Nazi Industrial Mini-Führer: A Commentary on the Life and Times of Gerhard Fieseler', *European Journal of International Management,* Vol. 8, No. 2, 2014, pp, 226-239.
H. D. Hölsken, *Die V-Waffen: Entstehung – Propaganda – Kriegseinsatz,* München, Deutsche Verlags-Anstalt, 1984.
E. L. Homze, *Arming the Luftwaffe: The Reich Air Ministry and the German Aircraft Industry 1919-1939,* Lincoln, NE: University of Nebraska, 1976.
M. Howard, and W. Louis, *The Oxford History of the Twentieth Century,* Oxford, Oxford University Press, 1998.
J. Hughes-Wilson, *A History of the First World War in 100 Objects*, London, Cassell/Imperial War

Museum, 2014.

J. D. Hunter, *The Blue Max,* London: Cassell, 2004.

D. Irving, *The Rise and Fall of the Luftwaffe: the Life of Luftwaffe Marshal Erhard Milch*, London, Weidenfeld and Nicolson, 1973.

R. Italiaander, *Drei deutsche Fliegerinnen – Elly Beinhorn, Thea Rasch, Hanna Reitsch – Drei Lebensbilder,* Berlin, Gustav Weise Verlag, 1942.

H. James, *A German Identity 1770 to the present day,* London, Phoenix Press, 2000.

Jane's Fighting Aircraft of World War II, Twickenham, UK, Tiger Books International, 1989.

W. E. Johns, *Biggles learns to fly,* London, Red Fox, 1992.

P. Johnson, *Reuter reporter in divided Germany 1955-58,* Olsztyn, Poland, Studio Poligrafii Komputerowej "SQL"/Nottingham, Adler Publications, 1998.

H. Jones, J. O'Brien and C.Schmidt-Supprian (eds.), *Untold war: New Perpectives in First World War Studies,* Leiden, Koninklijke Brill, 2008.

M. Jones, *After Hitler: The Last Days of the Second World War in Europe,* London, John Murray, 2015.

R. V. Jones, *Most secret war: British Scientific Intelligence 1939-1945,* London, Penguin Books, 2009.

T. Junge, *Bis zur letzten Stunde: Hitlers Sekretärin erzählt ihr Leben,* München, Claassen Verlag, 2002.

P. Kaplan, *Fighter Aces of the Luftwaffe in WWI,* Barnsley, UK, Pen & Sword Books, 2007.

J. Keegan, *The First World War,* London, Hutchinson, 1998.

L. Kennett, *The First Air War 1914-1918,* New York, Free Press, 1991.

I. Kershaw, *Hitler 1889-1936 Hubris,* London, Allen Lane, 1998.

I. Kershaw, *Making friends with Hitler: Lord Londonderry and Britain's path to War,* London, Allen Lane, 2004.

P. Kilduff, *The Red Baron: Beyond the Legend,* London, Cassell. 1994.

H. Kissinger, *Diplomacy,* New York, Touchstone, 1994.

M. Kitchen, *The Cambridge Illustrated History of Germany*, Cambridge, Cambridge University Press, 2000.

V. Klemperer, *I shall bear witness: The Diaries of Victor Klemperer,* London, Weidenfeld & Nicholson, 1998.

G. Knopp, *Hitlers Manager,* München, Wilhelm Goldmann Verlag, 2007.

D. Krause-Vilmar. Die nationalsozialistische Machtergreifung 1933 in der Stadt Kassel. Text of public lecture at Kassel University on 27 October 1999.

G. Krumeich, *Die wichtigsten 100 Fragen: Der Erste Weltkrieg,* München, Verlag C. H. Beck, 2014.

J-D Lepage, *Aircraft of the Luftwaffe, 1935-1945: An Illustrated Guide,* Jefferson, North Carolina, McFarland & Co, 2009.

B. H. Liddel Hart, *History of the First World War,* London, Book Club Associates, 1973.

O. Lilienthal, *Der Vogelflug als Grundlage der Fliegekunst*, 1889.

W. R. Louis, The European colonial powers. In: M. Howard, and W. R. Louis (eds.), *The Oxford History of the Twentieth Century,* Oxford, Oxford University Press, 1998, pp.91-102.

K. Lowe, *Savage Continent: Europe in the Aftermath of World War II*, London, Penguin Books, 2012.

N. MacGregor, *Germany: Memories of a Nation,* London, British Museum/Allen Lane, 2014.

R. MacLean, *Berlin: Imagine a City,* London, Weidenfeld & Nicolson, 2014.

S. McMeekin, *July 1914: Countdown to War,* London, Icon Books, 2013.

G. Mai, *Die Weimarer Republik,* München, Verlag C. H. Beck, 2013.

G. Mann, *Deutsche Geschichte des 19. Und 20. Jahrhunderts,* Frankfurt am Main, Fischer Taschenbuch Verlag, 2003.

Mantelli-Brown-Kittel-Graf, *The V1, the V2, the V3.* Rimini, Edizioni R.E.I., 2016.

T. Marshall, *Prisoners of Geography: Ten Maps that tell you all you need to know about Global Politics,* London, Elliott and Thompson, 2015.

L. Mayerhofer, Making Friends and Foes: Occupiers and Occupied in First World War Romania, 1916-1918. In Jones et al., op. cit., pp.119-149.

R. Meredith, *Phoenix: A Complete History of the Luftwaffe 1918-1945. Vol. 1 – The Phoenix is Reborn,* Solihull, UK, Helion & Company, 2016.

C. Messenger, *World War I in Colour,* London, Ebury Press, 2003.

M. Middlebrook, *The Peenemünde Raid 17/18 August 1943,* London, Penguin Books, 1988.

R. Miracco, *Futurist Skies.* Italian Cultural Institute, Italy. 2005.

R. Mitter, *China's War with Japan 1937-1945: The Struggle for Survival*, London, Penguin Books, 2014.

W. Mühlbauer, Die Fliegertruppe entsteht. *Flugzeug Special 12 Classic,* 2014.

H. M. Müller, *Schlaglichter der deutschen Geschichte.* Mannheim, Bibliographisches Institut & F. A. Brockhaus AG, 1996.

C. Mulley, *The Woman Who Flew for Hitler: The True Story of Hitler's Valkyries*, London, Macmillan, 2017.

R. Nagel und T. Bauer, *Kassel und die Luftfahrtindustrie seit 1923: Geschichte(n), Menschen, Technik,* Melsungen, Bernecker Verlag, 2015.

P. G. Neumann, *The German Air Force in the Great War,* Uckfield, UK, Naval & Military Press, 2014.

I. Nonaka and H. Takeuchi, *The Knowledge-creating Company: How Japanese Companies create the Dynamics of Innovation*, New York, Oxford University Press. 1995.

A. Norden, *Das Herz muss dabei sein: Der Flieger Gerhard Fieseler und sein Werk,* Kurhessenland Druck and Verlag GmbH, Kassel, 1941.

M. Pabst, *Willy Messerschmitt: Zwölf Jahre Flugzeugbau im Führerstaat,* Oberhaching, Aviatic Verlag, 2007.

A. Palmer, *The Gardeners of Salonika*, London, Andre Deutsch, 1965.

J. Piekalkiewicz, *The Air War 1939-1945*, Poole, UK, Blandford Press, 1985.

J. Piekalkiewicz, *Der Fieseler Fi 156 Storch im Zweiten Weltkrieg*, Stuttgart, Motorbuch Verlag, 1999.

O. A. Popa, *Bibliophiles and Bibliothieves: The Search for the Hildebrandslied and the Willehalm Codex (Schriften zum Kulturguterschutz) (Schriften Zum Kulturgüterschutz/Cultural Property Studies,* Berlin, De Gruyter, 2003.

K. C. Priemel, Gekaufte Geschichte. Der 'Freundeskreis Albert Vögler', Gert von Klass und die Entwicklung der historischen Unternehmensforschung nach 1945. *Zeitschrift für Unternehmungsgeschichte.* Vol. 52, pp.177-202, 2007.

A. Raab, *Raab fliegt: Erinnerungen eines Flugpioniers,* Hamburg, Konkret Literatur Verlag, 1984.

D. Richards, *RAF Bomber Command in the Second World War: The Hardest Victory,* London, Penguin Books, 2001.

M. von Richthofen, *Der rote Kampfflieger*, Hamburg, Publisher, 1990.

E. Rickenbacker, *Fighting the Flying Circus,* Memphis, USA, General Books LLC, 2012.

B. Rieger, *Technology and the Culture of Modernity in Britain and Germany 1980-1945,* Cambridge,

Cambridge University Press, p.1, 2008.

H. Ringlstetter, 'Erste alliierte Fliegerasse'. In: *Mühlbauer,* op. cit., pp.86-87.

H. Ringlstetter, 'Kampfeinsitzer der ersten Jahre.' In: *Mühlbauer,* op. cit., pp.54-59.

A. Roberts, *Masters and Commanders: How Roosevelt, Churchill, Marshall and Alanbrooke won the War in the West*, London: Allen Lane, 2008.

A. Roberts, *The Storm of War: A New History of the Second World War,* London, Allen Lane, (2009).

J. C. G. Röhl, *Kaiser Wilhelm II,* Cambridge, Cambridge University Press, 2014.

S. Rosenboom, *Im Einsatz über der 'vergessenen Front': Der Luftkrieg an der Ostfront im Ersten Weltkrieg,* Potsdam, Militärgeschichtliches Forschungsamt, 2013.

E. Sauer, *Absturz im Kinzigtal: Die Luftfahrt im hessischen Kinzigtal von 1895 zu 1950,* Heidelberg, I.H. Sauer Verlag, 2013.

U. Schneider, K. Boehm, P. Grünewald, U. Krause-Schmidt, R. Neuhaus und R. Winkler. (Hrsg.). *Hessen vor 50 Jahren – 1933,* Frankfurt am Main, Röderberg Verlag, 1983.

B. Schrep, 'Gebrochen an Leib und Seele'. In: *Die Spiegel-Serie über den 1. Weltkrieg und die Folgen: Die Ur-Katastrophe des 20. Jahrhunderts,* 2004, pp.58-60.

H. Schulze, *Kleine deutsche Geschichte,* München, Deutscher Taschenbuch Verlag, 2013.

W. Schwipps, *Kleine Geschichte der deutschen Luftfahrt,* Berlin, Haude & Spenersche Verlagsbuchhandlung, 1968.

S. Seabridge, *Blackpool's Aerodromes 1928-1936: Politics and Local Media,* MA dissertation: University of Central Lancashire, 2006.

S. Sebag Montefiore, *The Romanovs 1613 – 1918,* London, Weidenfeld & Nicolson, 2016.

V. Sebestyen, *1946, The Making of the Modern World,* London, Pan Books, 2014.

G. Sereny, *Albert Speer: His Battle for Truth,* London, Macmillan,1995.

G. Sereny, *The German Trauma: Experiences and Reflections 1938-2001,* London, Penguin Books, 2001.

C. Shepherd, *German Aircraft of World War II,* London, Book Club Associates, 1976.

W. Shirer, *The Rise and Fall of the Third Reich,* London, Book Club Associates, 1968.

O. Skorzeny, *Skorzeny's Special Missions: Memoirs of Hitler's Most Daring Commando*, Minneapolis, MN, MBI Publishing, 2011.

D. Sloggett, *A Century of Air Power: The Changing Face of Warfare 1912-2012,* Barnsley, UK, Pen & Sword, 2013.

T. Snyder, *Bloodlands: Europe between Hitler and Stalin,* London, Vintage Books, 2011.

Der Spiegel, Flugzeuge: Lustiges Ding, 11/1978, pp.148-151.

N. Stargardt, *The German War: A Nation under Arms, 1939-1945,* London, The Bodley Head, 2015.

R. Stark, *Wings of War: An Airman's Diary of the Last Year of World War 1,* London, Military Book Society, 1973.

M. Steber and G. Gotto (eds.), *Visions of Community in Nazi Germany: Social Engineering and Private Lives.* Oxford, Oxford University Press, 2014.

A. Steinweis. *Kristallnacht 1938.* Cambridge, MA., Harvard University Press, 2009.

J. Stephenson, *Women in Nazi Germany,* London, Routledge, 2001.

D. Stone, *The Kaiser's Army: The German Army in World War One,* London, Bloomsbury Publishing, 2015.

H. Strachen, *The First World War,* London, Simon & Schuster, 2014.

H. Strachen, Strategic Bombing and that Question of Civilian Casualties up to 1945. In: P. Addison and J. A. Crang, *Firestorm: The Bombing of Dresden, 1945.* London, Pimlico, pp.1-17.

M. Strohn (ed), *World War 1 Companion,* Oxford, Osprey Publishing, 2013.

M. Stürmer, *The German Empire 1871-1914,* London, Phoenix Press, 2001.

A. Surminski (Hrsg), *Kriegsende in Deutschland,* Hamburg, Ellert & Richter Verlag, 2015.

J. Sweetman, *The Dambusters Raid,* London, Cassell, 1999.

H-C. Täubrich, H-C. *Fascination and terror.* Nuremberg, Documentationszentrum Reichsparteitagsgelände, 2015.

A. J. P. Taylor, *The First World War: An Illustrated History,* Harmondsworth, UK, Penguin Book, 1987.

F. Taylor, *Dresden Tuesday 13 February 1945,* London, Bloomsbury, 2004.

F. Taylor, *The Berlin Wall 13 August 1961 – 9 November 1989,* London, Bloomsbury, 2006.

S. J. Taylor, *The Great Outsiders,* London, Weidenfeld & Nicholson. Cited in: Hattersley, op. cit.

The Times, 19 January 1915. Item on WWI reproduced in *The Times* on 19 January 2015.

A. Tooze, *The Wages of Destruction: The Making and Breaking of the Nazi Economy,* London, Allen Lane, 2006.

T. Treadwell, *Knights of the Black Cross,* Bristol, Cerberus, 2004.

H. Trevor-Roper, *The Last Days of Hitler,* London, Pan Books, 1995.

E. Udet, *Ein Fliegerleben,* Stuttgart, Motorbuch Verlag, 1981.

E. Udet, *The Ace of the Black Cross: The Memoirs of Ernst Udet,* Barnsley, UK, Pen & Sword Books, 2013.

S. V. Utechin, *Everyman's Concise Encyclopedia of Russia,* London, J. M. Dent & Sons, 1961.

F. Vann, *Willy Messerschmitt: First Full Biography of an Aeronautical Genius,* Haynes Publishing, Sparkford, UK, 1993.

J. Verhey, *The Spirit of 1914: Militarism, Myth and Mobilization in Germany,* Cambridge, Cambridge University Press, 2000.

W. de Vries, *Terug naar Kassel. De ballade van de waanzin = Zurück nach Kassel. Die Ballade vom Wahnsinn.* Robbemond, 's-Gravendeel, 1990.

P. Watson, *German Genius: Europe's Third Renaissance, the Second Scientific Revolution and the Twentieth Century,* London, Simon & Schuster, 2010.

A. Weir, *The Last Flight of the Luftwaffe: The Suicide Raid on the Eight Air Force, 7 April 1945,* London, Cassel, 1997.

C. Whiting, *Skorzeny: The Most Dangerous Man in Europe,* Barnsley, UK, Pen and Sword Books, 2010.

T. Wiederhold, *Gerhard Fieseler – eine Karriere: Ein Wirtschaftsführer im Dienste des Nationalsozialismus,* Kassel, Verlag Winfried Jenior, 2003.

K. Wiegrefe, Der Unfriede von Versailles, *Spiegel Special: Die Ur-Katastrophe des 20. Jahrhunderts,* 2004.

S. J. Wiesen, *West German Industry 1945-1955 and the Challenge of the Nazi Past,* Chapel Hill, University of North Carolina Press, 2001.

D. Winter, *The First of the Few: Fighter Pilots of the First World War,* Harmondsworth, Penguin Books, 1983.

S. J. Zaloga, *V-1 Flying Bomb 1941-1945: Hitler's Infamous "Doodlebug",* Oxford, Osprey Publishing, 2005.

E. Zegenhagen, *Schneidige deutsche Mädel: Fliegerinnen zwischen 1918 und 1945,* Göttingen, Wallstein Verlag, 2007.

Index

Index of Places

Africa 100, 126, 130, 147, 152, 201, 203–204, 225
Austria 35, 36, 55-56, 85, 186, 214, 273, 283

Balbo 138–139, 167
Bavaria 54, 66, 114, 254
Belgium 36, 112, 204, 235, 261, 281
Belgrade 35, 55
Bergheim 18, 21
Berlin 29, 32, 37–38, 40, 42, 47, 52, 56, 75, 97, 110, 116, 119–120, 123, 125–126, 141, 146–147, 150, 152–153, 160, 165–166, 168, 178, 181, 183, 190–191, 194, 198–201, 203, 207–208, 211, 224–226, 232, 246–247, 253, 260, 272–273, 275, 287
Bettenhausen (Kassel) 108, 146, 189, 209, 220, 224
Bonn 18–19, 21, 24, 26–27, 30, 32, 37, 47, 59, 75, 91, 96, 100–102, 136
Breslau 170, 214, 281
Britain vii–viii, 12, 24, 26, 36, 41, 43, 54–55, 85, 88, 91, 96, 124, 127, 145, 187, 192, 194, 198–199, 202, 206, 210, 214, 217, 220–221, 232, 235–236, 266, 272, 274, 281
Bucharest 55–56, 64, 137–138, 202
Buchenwald 146, 187, 214, 255–256
Bulgaria 55, 59, 164, 203

Carinhall 183–186, 199–200, 266
Caucasus 55–56, 205
Cologne viii, 17–19, 32, 41, 81, 152–153, 224
Colombo 138–139, 148, 150
Constantinople 55–56, 281
Croatia 203
Czechoslovakia 147, 169, 186, 202–203, 235, 266

Dachau 143, 146, 213
Darmstadt 38, 40, 258–259
Dresden viii, 133, 224, 241

England ii, 85, 107, 120, 123, 126–127, 130, 134, 193–194, 234
Eschweiler 101–102, 108–109

Finland 192, 205
Flanders 37, 79
Flossenbürg 214, 292
France 19, 26, 31, 36, 38–39, 51, 55, 79, 85, 88–89, 98–99, 118–119, 126–127, 136, 139, 148, 150, 152, 169, 187, 192, 194, 201–202, 204, 221, 232, 234–235, 242, 246, 272–273

Frankfurt 17, 19–20, 152–153, 222, 224

Glesch 18, 20–21, 38
Göttingen vii, 163, 224
Gran Sasso 215–216, 247, 259
Grebenstein 169–170, 250, 268

Hamburg 114, 219, 224–225, 241, 246
Harz mountains 186, 236
Hungary 36, 56, 85, 203, 206, 235

India 56, 130
Italy 126, 138, 152, 169, 206, 215, 225, 235

Japan 203–204, 255
Johannisthal 29, 32, 40–42
Jüterbog 52–53, 58

Kanatlarci 65, 72, 80–81, 87, 91
Kassel viii, 11–13, 108–111, 114, 116, 118–119, 123–126, 128–131, 133, 135–136, 138–143, 145–146, 150–153, 162–163, 168, 174, 177–178, 181, 185–187, 191, 196–197, 200–202, 206–207, 209, 218, 220–225, 227, 230–231, 236, 244–246, 248–250, 253, 255–256, 260, 262, 264–265, 267, 269, 274, 277–279, 282–284, 288–289

London 14, 22, 120–121, 141, 194, 211, 218, 220–221, 233–236, 259, 281

Macedonia 65, 70, 75–76, 80–81, 84, 88, 90, 99, 101, 218, 288, 294
Magdeburg 52, 227, 279
Mediterranean 55–56, 138, 152, 281
Moscow 104–105, 205, 273
Munich 14, 91, 95, 104, 107, 186, 280

Netherlands 91, 112, 196, 204, 244, 261
North Africa 147, 152, 201, 203–204, 225
Nuremberg 260, 262, 266, 271

Ottoman Empire 36, 55–56

Paris 37, 106, 115, 139, 146, 148–149, 152, 166, 187, 201–202, 204, 259, 262
Peenemünde 206, 209–211, 216, 218–221, 266, 276
Poland 147, 169, 191–192, 203, 210, 235, 255, 261
Potsdam 39, 272
Prilep 65, 67–68, 75, 88, 294

Rechlin 178, 204, 231, 246

Rhine, River 18, 21–22, 24, 242
Rhineland 18, 34, 98, 201, 273
Romania 55–56, 58–59, 202–203, 206
Russia 36, 84, 99, 105, 115, 200, 205, 217, 225, 235, 242, 261

Saarbrücken 78, 277
Salonika 58, 65, 76, 88, 281
Sarajevo 35, 37
Serbia 35, 40, 55
Soviet Union 169, 191–192, 204–205, 256, 259, 272
Spain 165–166, 206
Stalingrad 205–206, 217, 219
Sudetenland 186, 214
Sweden 104, 169, 206
Switzerland 117, 120, 126, 283

Treblinka 206, 213
Turkey 169, 282

United States of America (USA) 11, 14, 20, 22, 24–25, 34, 36–40, 44, 51, 56, 62, 67, 85, 91, 95, 97, 101–102, 107, 115, 124, 126, 130–131, 136, 150, 155, 169-170–172, 178, 181, 184–185, 189, 192–193, 200, 204–205, 214, 223, 233, 242–244, 247, 250–251, 253–256, 259-261, 266, 272–273, 276, 278

Vienna 35, 104, 216, 269
Vincennes 148–149, 151–153

Waldau 109, 118–119, 123, 136, 146, 151, 168, 197, 202, 248, 277, 279
Warsaw 152, 211
Weimar 11, 95, 97, 103–104, 139, 141–143, 145, 148, 172, 242, 251, 274
Wilhelmshöhe 162, 224, 245, 249, 275
Wolfsburg 224, 230–231

Zürich 115, 117–119, 127, 166, 222, 278

Index of People

Adenauer, Konrad 273–274, 280
Antonov, Oleg 192, 292
Arnolt, Emil 130–132, 137, 147, 160, 198, 208

Bachem, Erich 146–147, 151, 153, 207
Balbo, Italo 138, 139, 292
Bauer, Thorsten 12–13, 47, 90, 125–126, 128, 130, 136, 161–162, 196, 277–279, 288
Bäumer, Paul 50, 107–109, 114–115, 117
Beethoven, Ludwig van 21, 25, 32
Bender, Lieutenant 78–79, 81–82, 84
Bissing, Vera von 130, 133, 135, 149, 182, 188, 284
Braun, Wernher von 12, 210–211, 216, 218, 220, 236, 266, 276
Brown, Eric 'Winkle' 190, 218, 266–267, 293
Burckhardt, Lieutenant 66–67, 69, 78, 88

Cejka, Alois 155, 176, 189–190, 198
Churchill, Winston viii, 194, 210, 215–216, 246, 256, 272, 281, 292

David, Wilhelm 169–170, 268
Denk, Captain 61–62, 65
Détroyat, Michel 131, 133, 136, 148–151
Dornier, Claude 25, 30, 104, 159–160, 166, 179, 277

Eicke, Theodor 213
Eisenhower, Dwight 215, 256, 292
Espenlaub, Gottfried 110–111, 282, 287

Farman, Henri 23, 27, 29
Fiedler, Willy 178, 182, 208, 210–211, 218, 231, 276
Fieseler, Frau Katharina 76, 97, 250
Fieseler, Helene née Oidtmann 102, 108, 118, 186, 268
Fieseler, Katharina, née Marx 18, 20–22, 33, 102, 186, 272
Fieseler, Manfred 241, 272
Fokker, Anthony 29, 32, 37, 48, 64, 70, 73, 75, 81–82, 88–89, 91, 98, 109–110

Globocnik, Odilo 213-214, 292
Göbel, Tobias 160, 162, 168, 190, 249
Goebbels, Joseph 143, 178, 201, 211, 232, 236, 248, 250, 275
Goethe, Johann Wolfgang von 97, 285
Göring, Hermann 74, 126, 142, 144–145, 153, 159, 165, 167, 178–179, 183–187, 192, 194, 198–200, 202, 208, 217, 227, 232, 261, 266, 268, 275, 292
Greim, Ritter von 96, 123, 246

Haffner, Sebastian 113, 124, 159
Hastings, Max 221, 232, 235
Heinkel, Ernest 25, 104, 154–155, 159, 166, 168, 178–179, 186, 207, 216, 231, 266
Hess, Rudolf 170, 181
Himmler, Heinrich 191, 213–214, 244
Hitler, Adolf vii, 11, 13, 74, 91, 96, 103, 113, 115, 123–126, 129, 133, 140–145, 151, 154, 159, 166–167, 170–174, 177, 180–187, 189–194, 198–200, 202–206, 208–209, 213–219, 225, 227–228, 230–233, 235, 242, 244, 246–251, 254–255, 260–261, 263, 265–272, 275, 280, 282–283, 286–287, 292
Homze, Edward 99, 106, 140, 161

Jones, Reginald 220–221, 236
Junkers, Hugo 25, 47, 104–105, 117, 120, 123, 125, 155, 159–160, 166, 188, 222, 266

Katzenstein, Kurt 108, 110–111, 113, 122, 128, 282
Keitel, Wilhelm 191, 216
Kissinger, Henry 141, 254, 262, 273

Lilienthal, Otto 17, 27, 34, 105, 164, 283
Lippisch, Alexander 134–135, 198
Lusser, Robert 12, 207–211, 216, 220, 224, 230, 276–277